Darrin Wolter
2A Sys Des
85072640

D X4640 L6

MANAGERIAL ECONOMICS

2nd edition

Theory, Practice, and Problems

EVAN J. DOUGLAS

Concordia University

PRENTICE-HALL, INC., Englewood Cliffs, New Jersey 07632

Library of Congress Cataloging in Publication Data

Douglas, Evan J.
    Managerial economics.

    Includes bibliographies and indexes.
    1. Managerial economics.   I. Title.
HD30.22.D68   1983   658.4'03   82-21558
ISBN   0-13-550210-1

Editorial/production supervision and interior design by Margaret Rizzi
Cover design: Marvin Warshaw
Manufacturing buyer: Ed O'Dougherty

Printed in the United States of America

10   9   8   7   6

ISBN 0-13-550210-1

Prentice-Hall International, Inc., *London*
Prentice-Hall of Australia Pty. Limited, *Sydney*
Editora Prentice-Hall do Brasil, Ltda., *Rio de Janeiro*
Prentice-Hall Canada Inc., *Toronto*
Prentice-Hall of India Private Limited, *New Delhi*
Prentice-Hall of Japan, Inc., *Tokyo*
Prentice-Hall of Southeast Asia Pte. Ltd., *Singapore*
Whitehall Books Limited, *Wellington, New Zealand*

To my family

Contents

2
Decision Making Under Risk and Uncertainty, 39

part 2 DEMAND THEORY, ANALYSIS, and ESTIMATION

Contents

part
3 PRODUCTION and COST ANALYSIS

6
Production Functions and Cost Curves,   221

7
Cost Concepts for Decision Making,   259

Contents

Contents

12
Competitive Bids and Price Quotes, 446

Appendix A:
A Review of Analytic Geometry and Calculus: Functions, Graphs, and Derivatives, 531

Appendix B:
Present Value Tables, 550

Contents

Preface

Managerial Economics is concerned with the application of economic principles and methodologies to the decision-making process of the firm operating under conditions of uncertainty. The subtitle to this book, *Theory*, *Practice*, *and Problems*, is intended to convey three major features of the approach taken here. First, it is my belief that economic theory establishes important principles for business practice under conditions of uncertainty. Second, business practice must be recognized and incorporated into the discipline of managerial economics. For example, if firms choose to use markup-pricing policies rather than take the marginalist approach, then the task of the managerial economist is to assist the decision maker in finding the optimal level of the markup, rather than to harangue for marginalism. Third, the concepts and issues involved in managerial economics must be put into the context of real-world business decision problems in order to demonstrate methods of identifying problems and finding solutions. Thus each chapter incorporates business examples and is followed by provocative discussion questions and case-study problems.

Objectives of This Book

This book is designed for a one-semester course in managerial economics at the undergraduate or MBA level. The level of treatment presupposes a basic economics course, although this is not necessary for MBA students, since each concept is developed from basics on the presumption that most students need refreshing on their micro principles in any case. The approach is intended to present the material in a more cohesive way to improve comprehension and retention. It should "bring it all together" for the student who has taken the prerequisite course, without offering any disadvantage to the new student of economics. Similarly, students may feel more comfortable with this textbook if they have had basic calculus and statistics, but the required mathematical or statistical principles are explained at the point of first usage, and more detailed exposition of these principles is provided in Appendix A at the end of the text. Rather than have extensive mathematical and econometric review chapters at the beginning of the text, it was considered preferable to explain or review much of the mathematical and statistical material at the point at which it can be used by the student in solving a decision problem. This philosophy allows the students to get into the managerial economics material more quickly at the start of the term, avoids their having to understand concepts that they do not yet know how to use, and offers the advantages of "learning by doing."

Features of This Book

The two chapters in Part 1 of the book lay the groundwork necessary for decision making under certainty. Chapter 1 introduces the student to the field of managerial economics and the use of models and other analytical concepts and tools in the decision-making process. Present Value Analysis, Expected Value Analysis of uncertain outcomes, the firm's time horizon, and the appropriate objective functions of the firm are introduced here. In Chapter 2, risk analysis is incorporated into the decision-making process, and several more decision criteria are introduced which allow adjustment for risk. The notions of search costs and the value of information, which play a strategic role in managerial economics, are discussed in detail here.

Parts 2 and 3 examine the demand and cost conditions facing the firm. Each of these parts is introduced by a chapter on the theoretical underpinnings, with the treatment confined to those segments of the micro theory that are important to an understanding of the concepts that are used for decision making, and avoiding the more esoteric frills. The second chapter in each part is concerned with using this understanding to make better decisions. The third chapter in each part deals with estimation and forecasting of cost and demand conditions, in order to provide the information necessary for decision making.

Part 4 brings together the analyses of the earlier parts with two chapters on models of pricing behavior and two chapters on pricing decisions in practice. Markup pricing and competitive bidding are given particular emphasis. Part 5, the final part of the book, examines advertising and promotion, and capital budgeting, from a managerial economics perspective. In many commerce or business programs these topics will be covered in marketing and finance courses and hence may be excluded or covered more quickly if the instructor so desires. Most of the sections within most of the chapters are self-contained, and may be treated similarly if the students' preparation so warrants.

The major differences between this text and others available may be summarized as follows:

1. It contains more microeconomics than most, without this getting in the way of the managerial economics. Only the essential elements of microeconomics are covered, and this is done in order to build the foundation for effective economic decision making.

2. It includes a chapter on consumer behavior in which Lancaster's attribute (or characteristics) approach to consumer demand is incorporated in a simple manner, making it easily comprehensible. These principles are later recalled to clarify product differentiation, and as a basis for price strategies in oligopolistic markets.

3. It has four chapters dedicated to the implementation of price theory in practice. Chapters 5 and 8 on Demand Estimation and Cost Estimation, respectively, present methods for ascertaining the shape and location of the firm's revenue and cost curves, in order that the firm may select the price which appears to best serve its objectives. In cases where the firm expects the information search cost to exceed the value of information, Chapters 11 and 12 present methods of pricing to pursue the firm's objectives under conditions of uncertainty.

4. It caters to the renewed interest in pricing as a business strategy, with four separate chapters on the theory and practice of pricing. Chapters 9 and 10 present a variety of pricing models to be implemented if search costs permit, while Chapters 11 and 12 present methods of pricing to pursue the firm's objectives under conditions of uncertainty.

5. Particular emphasis is given to markup pricing and its suitability for firms facing high information search costs. Markup pricing is shown (in a not too technical way) to be both statically and dynamically optimal under a range of conditions.

6. It has a full chapter on competitive bidding markets, including a decision model for the satisficing firm. Markets in which buyers receive bids or price quotes are more common than usually realized, and this chapter allows a wide range of pricing (and purchasing) problems to be addressed. It also represents the culmination of the analysis of the preceding chapters of the book, resulting in a pre-exam review of the major elements of the course.

7. It has a full chapter on the firm's advertising and promotion decision, looking at the implications of advertising as a separate or joint (with pricing) business strategy.

8. It has a series of realistic business problems and case studies at the end of each chapter which will test students' comprehension of the material, help build their analytical power, and demonstrate the relevance of the material in the real world of business decision making.

Changes Since the First Edition

This has been a major review, not so much in the structure of the text but more in the specific content of each chapter. Chapters 1 and 2 are totally different from the first edition—Chapter 1 introduces the concept of the expected present value of profits, which is appropriate for decision making under risk and uncertainty with time horizons extending beyond the present period. The firm's objective functions under the various scenarios of certainty, uncertainty, present period, and future period are established at this point. Chapter 2 incorporates risk analysis into the decision-making process, establishes the concepts of risk aversion, neutrality, and preference, and introduces other decision criteria which are appropriate for the risk-averse decision maker. Search costs are considered in detail here and the concept recurs at many points in the text to explain the behavior of firms in the real world.

The two chapters on estimation and forecasting, Chapters 5 (demand) and 8 (cost) have been strengthened considerably with the addition of more expositional and empirical material. Students should find this material much more digestable in this edition. The learning curve phenomenon is considered in detail in Chapter 8 and is used again in Chapter 11 to explain pricing strategies observed in practice. Chapters 6 and 7, on production and cost theory and analysis, have been substantially revised for improved clarity and readability. Chapters 9 and 10 have undergone significant changes to improve the flow from basic pricing models (Chapter 9), to more realistic pricing models using modified behavioral assumptions and longer time horizons (Chapter 10), to pricing in practice (Chapters 11 and 12).

Both Chapters 11 and 12 contain new material in this edition: The markup pricing section is extended to show that with positive search costs the markup can be significantly "wrong" but still preferable to the alternative of spending search costs. A range of acceptable markups is seen to exist and the same markup rate is shown to remain effective despite substantial shifts in the firm's cost and demand functions. Competitive bidding is extended to the case of the satisficing firm pursuing capacity utilization and profitability targets.

Appendices to several chapters have been added, in most cases being based on material that was formerly incorporated within the chapter. Isolating this material at the end of the chapter reflects the advice of many reviewers and facilitates the student's progress through the chapter itself. The appendices are typically special topics that may be by-passed in shorter courses without loss of continuity.

The chapter on linear programming has been deleted, since this topic is now rarely included in Managerial Economics courses, being taught instead in Quantitative Methods courses in most undergraduate business and MBA programs.

Throughout the book, efforts have been made to improve the readability of the material. Three years of feedback from my students and other students and instructors provided a wealth of advice, most of which was followed. Some more esoteric sections have been relegated to footnotes or dropped completely and new material has been added at an appropriate level to facilitate student comprehension. I am confident that students will find this edition much more approachable than they did the first.

Pedagogical Aids

This text incorporates several pedagogical and learning aids not commonly found. Margin cues have been added in this edition to draw attention to Definitions, Examples, Notes (cautionary statements regarding the material under discussion), and Rules (normative rules for decision making). New concepts are defined when first introduced and are typically exemplified immediately or within a few paragraphs. By reference to the index, the student can always refresh his or her memory of a concept by going back to where it was first introduced and defined.

This text uses approximately 200 graphs and tables to support the exposition of the material and to facilitate the learning process. Tables lay out the data underlying examples used in the text, summarize material covered in preceding pages, and indicate decision trees and decision sequences for particular problems. Figures are used to show graphically the concepts and relationships being introduced and applied. More complex figures are developed in stages. As a by-product of this course, I believe students develop greater analytical ability as a result of working with graphical analysis of decision problems.

At the end of each chapter, there are ten discussion questions and between six and ten problems and short cases. The discussion questions typically require only verbal responses and are designed for the student's self-review of the material in the chapter. The problems and case studies are to be attempted once it is clear from the review of the discussion questions that all basic concepts and inter-relationships have been understood. The problems and cases typically require analysis, deduction, numerical calculations, and qualitative reasoning, and serve also to acquaint students with scenarios in the real world in which the textual material is applicable. Short answers to the odd-numbered problems are provided in Appendix C at the end of the book. Answers to all questions, problems and cases, plus other material, are provided in the Instructors' Manual available to adopters.

Acknowledgments

For their constructive comments and reviews of the first edition, my thanks are due to the following professors and students: R. M. Addudel; Roger Betts; Gary A. Bolla; Malcom C. Brown; Stuart Cochrane; Thomas Coyne; Masako N. Darrough; John Davis; J. Ronnie Davis; Richard A. Defusco;

Jonathan C. Deming; George Garman; Delbert C. Hastings; John P. Herzog; Duncan Holthausen; Harold Hotelling, Jr.; Robert Johnson; Thomas McCarthy; D. Needham; Michael Pickford; W. Duncan Reekie; Kenneth D. Riener; Abderrahman Robana; Stephen P. Robbins; Frank Slesnick; and P. Sprinagesh.

Many other students in my classes at Concordia University and also at the University of San Diego, where I was Visiting Associate Professor in 1981, deserve my sincere thanks for their input in classes and with regard to material in, or not in, the text. I am happy to say that I am still going to school to learn things, and that my students, particularly those with substantial business experience, have been very good teachers.

For typing, copying, and taking care of business, I must thank Laura Smith, Joanne Coté, and Kathleen Van Tassell of San Diego and Caroline Walwyn of Montreal, in particular. Others have also been very helpful in bringing this task to fruition and I thank you all for whatever part you played. My former teachers, Cliff Lloyd, Peter Kennedy, and Brian Johns deserve my continuing gratitude for their earlier efforts to edify me. My colleagues, past and present, Steve Robbins, Joe Kelly, Gary Johns, Ken Riener, and others, have helped me with concepts and ideas concerning the educational process.

At Prentice-Hall, David Hildebrand has continued to be a first-rate editor, and I like to think we make a good team. Behind him, of course, just as behind me, there are a legion of assistants and helpers to which we are both very grateful. The production editor, Margaret Rizzi, deserves my sincere thanks and admiration for her efforts in transforming the manuscript into this textbook as you see it.

Evan J. Douglas

INTRODUCTION

Introduction to Managerial Economics

1.1 INTRODUCTION

The purpose of this chapter is to introduce the reader to the field of managerial economics and to build the foundation necessary for decision making under uncertainty. In the next section we examine the *definition and scope* of managerial economics in order to establish the nature and direction of the discipline you are about to study. This leads us to a discussion of the use of *models* in managerial economics. We will see that models depicting the behavior of consumers and business firms can be of substantial assistance in decision analysis.

In the third section we consider the multiperiod nature of decision making, whereby decisions made now typically have cost and revenue implications not only for the present period but also for future periods. This necessitates the use of *present-value analysis*, also known as discounted cash flow analysis, to allow the proper weighting of future profits against present profits for effective decision making.

In the fourth section we consider the state of information available to the decision maker, and we conclude that full information, or certainty, is rarely available in the real world. Rather, the firm operates under conditions of uncertainty, facing a probability distribution of outcomes associated with each potential solution to the problem under review. We introduce *expected-*

value analysis to allow an appropriate evaluation of each potential solution, so that the optimal decision can be made.

Which decision is optimal depends on the firm's *objective*. In the fifth section of this chapter we consider the appropriate objective function for the firm and the *decision criterion* indicated under each of the four different scenarios. These scenarios are provided by the combinations of present period and multiperiod analysis and of certainty and uncertainty. Finally, we provide a brief summary of the chapter.

1.2 DEFINITION AND SCOPE OF MANAGERIAL ECONOMICS

DEFINITION: *Managerial economics* is concerned with the application of economic principles and methodologies to the decision-making process within the firm or organization. It seeks to establish rules and principles to facilitate the attainment of the desired economic goals of management. These economic goals relate to costs, revenues, and profits and are important within the business and the nonbusiness institution. Profit-oriented business firms certainly must strive to make optimal decisions about costs and revenues, but so too must nonbusiness organizations, such as hospitals and universities, seek to spend available funds to maximum effect. The decision problems in the business and nonbusiness institutions are essentially similar in many areas. The decision-making principles to be discussed in this textbook, although primarily introduced in the context of a business firm, are thus applicable to a great variety of economic decision problems in the nonbusiness institution as well.

Certainty vs. Uncertainty

The economic principles and methodologies of managerial economics are derived largely from microeconomics, which is that part of the economics discipline concerned with the behavior of individual economic units such as the consumers, the producers, and the suppliers of labor, capital, and organizational services. Unlike neoclassical microeconomics, however, in which optimal decisions are made in an environment of full information, or certainty, managerial economics has evolved to provide guidance for decision making in an environment of *uncertainty*. The existence of uncertainty requires the use of analytical tools, concepts, and notions from other disciplines, such as mathematics, statistics, operations research, finance, accounting, and marketing, in order to allow the managerial economist to choose the optimal solution to particular decision problems. Managerial economics is, therefore, something of an interdisciplinary course and operates as an integrative course in the business school curriculum, bringing together the tools and concepts from various disciplines within the general framework of economic decision making.

In the following chapters we discuss the principles of microeconomics, and the elements of the other disciplines mentioned, on the basis of the assumption that while you may have taken an introductory course in microeconomics and may have had some exposure to basic mathematical and statistical concepts, you are likely to be somewhat rusty on these principles and, therefore, will benefit from a review of this material. Thus, we develop each concept from the basic principles so that it should present little difficulty to those students who have not had a previous course in microeconomics, and it should provide a review for those who have. A review of basic calculus and analytical geometry is provided in Appendix A at the end of this book. You may wish to review this appendix at the start of your course or simply refer to it as needed to better understand issues which arise as you proceed through the course.

Positive vs. Normative Economics

Within the discipline of economics, the distinction is made between those areas that are "positive" and those areas that are "normative." Positive economics is descriptive: it describes how economic agents or economic systems *do operate* within the economy or society. Normative economics, on the other hand, is prescriptive: it prescribes how economic agents or systems *should operate* in order to attain desired objectives. In microeconomics, for example, it is assumed that the consumer wishes to maximize utility, and certain principles prescribe the behavior by which this objective may be attained. Similarly, macroeconomics prescribes certain measures for the attainment of objectives such as full employment and price stability.

Managerial economics is primarily normative, since it seeks to establish rules and principles to be applied in decision making to attain the desired objectives. But managerial economists must always be mindful of the actual practices in the business or institutional environment. For example, if firms choose their price level by applying a markup to their direct costs rather than by equating marginal revenue and marginal costs as implied by microeconomic principles, managerial economics should be concerned with determining the *optimal level* of the markup rather than attempting to persuade decision makers to use the marginalist principles. The approach taken in this textbook is to integrate business practice with economic principles. Thus, business practices, even if divergent from the strictures of normative microeconomics, are discussed in terms of the microeconomic principles. By reference to the microeconomic principles, the business practice can be evaluated in terms of its efficiency in attaining the desired objectives.

The Use of Models in Managerial Economics

DEFINITION: A *model* is defined as a simplified representation of reality. Models abstract from reality by ignoring the finer details which are not essential to the purpose at hand. They therefore concentrate on the major features and interrelationships existing among those features without obscuring the picture with less important details.

Types of Models.   There are three main types of models.[1] *Scale models* are typically miniaturized versions of the thing they represent and are used frequently by the builders of automobiles, airplanes, ships, buildings, and shopping complexes. These models abstract from the interior details yet give an idea how the object would look and perform in its full-size form. *Analogue models* have a different physical form from the object they represent, but have other important features in common. Maps representing geography, animals representing humans for medical testing, and wind tunnels representing motion, are analogue models. Although quite different in form, they are expected to provide the same information or react in a similar fashion as the thing they represent. *Symbolic models* use words and other symbols to represent reality, and they include descriptive speech, diagrams, and mathematical expressions. *Descriptive speech* usually simplifies or abstracts from reality, such as in the statement "A horse is a four-legged animal with a long brushy tail." Such a statement is a symbolic model of the members of the equine family, giving the general idea of what a horse is without mentioning the complexities involved in the physical or psychological makeup of a horse or the differences between a Thoroughbred and a Percheron. *Diagrams* similarly represent a situation of reality by means of lines, shading, and other features, and they abstract from the finer details. *Mathematical models* are usually further removed from reality and are used because reality is very difficult to depict visually or verbally or because it involves interrelationships that are extremely complex.

In this book we shall use mostly verbal and diagrammatic models to explain concepts and to analyze decision problems, although some mathematical models will be used, mainly in footnotes where these are appropriate. Diagrams (and mathematical expressions) are a very *efficient* means of representing reality; they are quicker to make and comprehend (once you understand them), and there is less ambiguity in such models, as compared to descriptive speech. Consider the following allusion to a chair: What has four legs, a broad seat, and a straight back? This verbal model is sufficiently ambiguous that one would be forgiven if one thought of an old racehorse! A picture of the object in question would quickly remove this ambiguity. A diagram (or mathematical expression) states precisely and concisely the

---

[1] Much of the following relies on the excellent discussion in I. M. Grossack and D. D. Martin, *Managerial Economics* (Boston: Little, Brown & Company, 1973), pp. 5-10.

relationships assumed to exist among facts, observations, or variables. If these assumed relationships are inaccurate, the inaccuracies will be exposed by later testing the model against reality; and our model may be modified to reflect the feedback received from this testing.

Why Use Models? The value of models in managerial economics and other disciplines may be summarized as follows. First, models have a *pedagogical* function: they are a useful device for teaching individuals about the operation of complex systems. Second, they are an *explanatory* device, since they are a vehicle for relating separate objects and events in a logical fashion. Third, models are valuable for *predictive* purposes, to the extent that past relationships between objects and events can be expected to hold true for future events. Let us discuss each of these three characteristics in some detail.

Models are used for *pedagogical* purposes, since they allow the abstraction from the complexity of reality to a framework or structure of manageable proportions. By excluding from consideration the minor details that do not affect the basic features or relationships that are at issue, the model allows us to deal with the central issues of the problem without the added complexity of relatively minor influences.

EXAMPLE: A student may learn about the interrelationships of an economic system in a basic economics course by using a simple model of four or five equations. Despite its being an extremely simplified version of reality, this model imparts an understanding of the most important variables and relationships which interact to determine the level of economic activity. Yet the major banks and certain federal departments use models of the economy encompassing as many as six hundred equations in order to derive a more accurate representation of the economic system for purposes of predicting price, unemployment, and aggregate economic activity levels. The purpose of the simple model, however, is not to predict but to educate the student about the basic relationships in an economic system. Once the student achieves an understanding of the basic relationships and interactions, the model may be extended by the use of more complex relationships and by the introduction of new variables and relationships, so that the student's knowledge is increased further.

The use of models as an *explanatory* device allows us to relate observation of objects and subsequent events in a logical fashion. The assumed link between the objects and the events may be tested for its authenticity by reference to real-world situations. If an observation that contradicts the link is made, then this link is refuted, while the link is supported (although not proved) by the repeated observation of supporting evidence. Models may aid the researcher in discovering relationships that exist between and among variables. If a high correlation is found to exist between two variables, the researcher may then attempt to discover the reasons for this relationship, construct a model incorporating the assumed relationship, and test for this relationship with future observations. Similarly, a model may be used for explanatory purposes when actual testing in the real environment is impossible or too expensive or too dangerous.

EXAMPLE: Examples of such experimentation to find the actual relationships include the testing of aircraft design in wind tunnels and the use of animals for medical and research purposes. The results of these tests are then generalized to apply to the situation they represent. Such models have explanatory value, since they show the probable reaction of the real situation to a particular stimulus or environment on the basis of the reaction of the model to that stimulus or environment.

The *predictive* value of a model is usually based upon the ability of that model to explain the past behavior of a system, and it uses this past relationship to predict the future behavior.

EXAMPLE: Suppose we have found that two events are causally related, such as low winter temperatures and high consumption of heating oil; we may predict increased consumption of heating oil the next time we observe temperatures falling. The model should specify the extent to which heating oil consumption is related to the temperature so that we may predict with some degree of accuracy the consumption of heating oil during a particular cold spell. This model will remain a good predictor as long as the relationships it represents stay constant. For example, if many households were to change to electric heating, the model would no longer represent reality as well as it did, and its predictions would be less accurate than before. A new or revised model would then be called for.

Must Models Be Realistic?   A model need not be realistic or be based upon reasonable, testable, or logical assumptions to be a good model for predictive purposes. Friedman has argued that it is not necessary for predictive purposes that the assumptions underlying a model be valid and testable.[2]

EXAMPLE: A model which predicts accurately yet which is based on demonstrably false assumptions involves the observation that a sunflower faces the east at sunrise and follows the path of the sun during the day until it is facing the west at sunset. During the night it slowly returns to its eastward-facing position awaiting the rise of the sun on the next morning. A simple model which would accurately predict this phenomenon for any newly-discovered sunflower is that the sunflower swivels at the base in response to a heat sensor located in the petals. This model, although simplistic, would nevertheless allow us to use the direction which the sunflower is facing to predict the location of the sun on a partly cloudy day.

For predictive purposes such a model could be quite useful, although for pedagogical and explanatory purposes such a model has no virtue. Even for predictive purposes, however, we may be somewhat cautious and skep-

---

[2] Milton Friedman, "The Methodology of Positive Economics," in his *Essays in Positive Economics* (Chicago: The University of Chicago Press, 1953). See also Lawrence A. Boland, "A Critique of Friedman's Critics," *Journal of Economic Literature,* 17 (June 1979), pp. 503-22.

tical about the model's ability to predict accurately on its *next* test. Since the relationship postulated is obviously false and the real determinants are apparently unknown, the latter could change without our noticing it and our prediction would turn out to be wrong. For example, the correct explanation of this phenomenon relates to the plant's need for heat and light. The installation of a bright light nearby might cause the sunflower to look at the light all day and to wrongly predict the location of the sun. Thus, we need to be more cautious in using such a model to predict, since it may fail as a predictor at any time if the underlying true relationship changes without our knowledge or observation.

How Do We Evaluate Models?   It should be clear from the above discussion that a model must be evaluated with an eye to its purpose. If a model is intended for pedagogic purposes, then it must be evaluated on this basis. Simple models of oligopoly, for example, do little to explain or predict the actual behavior of real firms in the real world, yet they do introduce the students to the problems of mutual interdependence in business situations. Criticisms of such models as being too simplistic or unrealistic are thus unwarranted to the extent that such models best introduce these concepts to the student. If an alternate model could allow the student to obtain a better understanding of the complex system being represented, for a similar input of time and mental effort, then we would have to judge that alternate model as being an improved model, since it best achieves the objective set for that model.

Models designed for explanatory purposes must be evaluated on the basis of how well they explain reality. If an observation is generated that is at variance with the model, then that model is refuted as an explanatory device. If there are two or more separate models that purport to explain a sequence of events, the best model is the one that most accurately depicts the important variables and relationships between and among these variables.

Models designed for predictive purposes must be judged by the accuracy of their predictions in subsequent tests. A predictive model is superior to an alternate predictive model if its predictions are more accurate more of the time. As the situation being depicted changes or evolves, we would expect existing models to become less accurate, since they must be modified to represent the evolving or changed situation.

NOTE: In all cases when evaluating models, it is important to keep in mind the distinction between the model and the situation of reality. The model is a simplified representation of reality and is thus intended to represent the general features of reality rather than the specific features of a particular instance in reality. Due to this abstraction from some of the finer points and details, the predictive or explanatory power of the model will generally not be exact for any particular instance, due to variables and relationships that have been excluded from the model for the sake of simplicity or expedience. For example, a model may predict that firms will increase the size of their inventories of raw materials when the price of those raw-material components is seasonally reduced. If such a model abstracts from the cash-flow situation of the firm, it may imperfectly predict the behavior of certain firms that are facing a liquidity problem at that particular time.

In the following chapters you will notice the considerable use of graphs to explain and analyze economic phenomena. Understanding graphs requires a basic knowledge of analytical geometry and calculus, and specifically, an understanding of such concepts as slopes, intercepts, linear functions, curvilinear functions, convexity, concavity, maximums, and minimums, among others. If your analytical geometry and basic calculus is rusty, I'd suggest you take half an hour or so to read about functions, graphs, and derivatives in Appendix A. Doing so may save many hours later, since graphs are an efficient tool for both understanding and expressing managerial economics. Someone once said "a picture is worth a thousand words." A graph is worth at least as much.

Jargon: The Use of Verbal Models for Efficient Communication. You will have noticed that the study of managerial economics involves a lot of specialized words, or *jargon*. Since the start of this book, you have been bombarded with "new" words, in the sense that these words convey a special meaning or connotation. Even words like *costs*, *revenues*, *profits*, *labor*, *capital*, and *risk* have special, more precise, meanings in the jargon of economics. Each of these jargon words and many others are formally defined at appropriate points in this book. We use a lot of jargon in managerial economics (as do all other disciplines of inquiry) to facilitate our discussion of complex phenomena.

Jargon words are really only verbal models of things or phenomena. They allow us to communicate with each other more efficiently, since they offer a concise and precise means of conveying the information we wish to convey. For example, "utility" is substantially quicker to say than is "the psychic satisfaction which a consumer expects to derive from the consumption of a product or service." And since jargon words are definitional terms, there should be no ambiguity about the precise meaning of these words. Thus, communication between economists, between managers, or between you and me through the medium of these printed pages, is facilitated and greatly enhanced by the use of jargon.

1.3 PRESENT-VALUE ANALYSIS AND THE FIRM'S TIME HORIZON

Many decisions involve a flow of revenues extending beyond the present period. In choosing between or among various alternatives, it is important to distinguish between revenues that are received immediately and those that are received at some later date. A dollar received today is worth more than a dollar received next year, which in turn is worth more than a dollar received the following year. The reason for this is that a dollar held today may be deposited in a bank or other interest-earning security, and at the end of one year it will be worth the original dollar plus the interest earned on that dollar. Hence, if the interest rate is, say, 10 percent, a dollar today will be worth $1.10 one year from today. Looking at this from the reverse aspect, a dollar earned one year from today is worth less than a dollar that is held today. Thus, the future earnings must be discounted by the interest rate they could have earned had they been held today.

In this section we introduce and examine the concept of the present value of cash flows that occur beyond the present period. Both revenues to be received and costs to be incurred in the future must be reduced to present-value terms for proper evaluation of decision alternatives. Net present value is found by subtracting the present value of costs from the present value of revenues and can be expressed alternatively as the present value of profits. The major convention used for discounting future cash flows to their present value is to treat all flows as if they arrive, or are incurred, at the end of year one, year two, and so on. We look also at other cash flow patterns, such as the receipt of funds sometime during the year, continuous cash flow over the year, and the treatment of annuities. Finally, we clarify the notion of the "present period" for the purposes of decision-making analysis.

Present Value and Future Value

DEFINITION: The *future value* in one year of $1.00 presently held is equal to $1.00 plus the annual rate of interest times $1.00. That is,

$$FV = PV\,(1 + r)$$

where FV denotes future value, PV denotes present value, and r is the rate of interest available.

EXAMPLE: If the interest rate is 10 percent, $r = 0.1$, the future value of $1.00 is

$$FV = \$1\,(1 + 0.1)$$
$$= \$1.10$$

Now suppose we could leave this money in the bank for a second year, also at 10 percent interest. The future value would be

$$FV = \$1.10\,(1 + 0.1)$$
$$= \$1.21$$

If a third year was possible, we would find

$$FV = \$1.21\,(1 + 0.1)$$
$$= \$1.331$$

and so on for future years. Note that the principle sum each year was simply multiplied by $(1 + r)$. In effect, the dollar was multiplied by $(1 + r)$ initially, then the resulting product was multiplied by $(1 + r)$, and then the product of that was multiplied by $(1 + r)$ again.

That is, for the three year deposit

$$FV = PV (1 + r) (1 + r) (1 + r)$$

which simplifies to

$$FV = PV (1 + r)^3$$

Generalizing for any number of periods into the future, we have

$$FV = PV (1 + r)^t \qquad (1\text{-}1)$$

where t represents the number of years into the future that the principle sum plus interest will be returned.

EXAMPLE: Suppose we lend $2,500 for a period of five years at 8.5 percent interest. What is the future value of the presently held $2,500?

$$FV = \$2,500 (1 + 0.085)^5$$
$$= 2,500 (1.085)^5$$
$$= 2,500 (1.50366)$$
$$= \$3,759.15$$

Thus $2,500 saved at 8.5 percent for five years will return the saver $3,759.15 at the end of the five-year period.

NOTE: The above process is known as *compounding* the principle sum plus annual interest over the period of the loan. It tells us that $2,500 held today is worth $3,759.15 in five years if we can obtain 8.5 percent interest compounded annually. The *compound factor* which we used to multiply the $2,500 to obtain $3,759.15 was 1.50366. This compound factor effectively says that $1.00 today is worth $1.50366 in five years, if the interest rate is 8.5 percent.

Now let's do it in the reverse direction. The *present* value of a *future* value can be found by manipulating Equation (1-1). Dividing both sides by $(1 + r)^t$ we find

$$PV = \frac{FV}{(1 + r)^t} \qquad (1\text{-}2)$$

EXAMPLE: Although we already know the answer, let's find the present value of $3,759.15 available in five years during which the available interest rate is 8.5 percent.

$$PV = \frac{\$3,759.15}{(1 + 0.085)^5}$$

$$= \frac{3,759.15}{1.50366}$$

$$= \$2,500.00$$

What we have just done is to *discount* $3,759.15 (future value) back to present value terms and demonstrate that the discounting process is simply the inverse of the compounding process. Whereas future value equals present value multiplied by the compound factor, present value equals future value divided by the compound factor. Alternatively, let us call the reciprocal of the compound factor the *discount factor* and say equivalently that present value is equal to future value multiplied by the discount factor. The reciprocal of 1.50366 is 0.66504, which is the discount factor when the interest rate is 8.5 percent. (Note that $3,759.15 multiplied by 0.66504 equals $2,500.00.)

DEFINITION: The *present value* of a sum of money to be received or disbursed in the future is the value of that future sum when discounted at the appropriate discount rate. Alternatively, it is the sum which would grow to that future sum when compounded at the appropriate interest rate.

The decision maker must choose the rate of discount quite carefully, since use of the "wrong" discount factor could cause a poor decision to be made in cases where the time profiles of future profit streams associated with alternative decisions differ markedly. The appropriate discount rate is the "opportunity" discount rate.

The Opportunity Discount Rate

DEFINITION: The *opportunity discount rate* is the rate of interest or return the decision maker could earn in his or her best alternative use of the funds at the same level of risk. Note that we require that the alternative use of the funds must involve the same level of risk or uncertainty, since many other alternative uses of the funds will be more or less risky or uncertain and are, thus, not strictly comparable with the present proposal.

EXAMPLE: Suppose that a firm intends to invest $10,000 in an expansion of its facilities but might otherwise invest the funds in a bond issue, which is considered to have similar risk and which would pay 12 percent interest compounded annually. The opportunity discount rate to be used when evaluating the future returns from the project under consideration is, therefore, 12 percent.

How do we ascertain whether the alternative investment or savings opportunities have similar risk? This issue is discussed in detail in Chapter 2. It is enough to say here that the risk in any decision lies in the dispersion of

TABLE 1-1. **Discount Factors for Several Different Opportunity Interest Rates and Time Periods**

Time Period (years hence)	OPPORTUNITY INTEREST RATE (%)			
	5	10	15	20
0	1.0000	1.0000	1.0000	1.0000
1	0.9524	0.9091	0.8696	0.8333
2	0.9070	0.8264	0.7561	0.6944
3	0.8638	0.7513	0.6575	0.5787
4	0.8227	0.6830	0.5718	0.4823
5	0.7835	0.6209	0.4972	0.4019
10	0.6139	0.3855	0.2472	0.1615
15	0.4810	0.2394	0.1229	0.0649
20	0.3769	0.1486	0.0611	0.0261
25	0.2953	0.0923	0.0304	0.0105

possible outcomes. Finding the equal-risk, best-alternative use of the funds, therefore, involves finding the alternative savings and investment opportunities which have the same or very similar dispersions of possible outcomes, and noting the highest rate of interest or rate of return on investment available within this subset. That rate is the opportunity discount rate to be used when discounting future cash flows associated with the decision under consideration.

It is important to see that the higher is the opportunity rate of interest (or opportunity discount rate), and the longer the time period, the lower is the discount factor. In Table 1-1 we show the discount factors associated with several different opportunity interest rates and several different periods of time. Each discount factor is calculated using the expression $1/(1 + r)^t$, and you can calculate the discount factor appropriate to any other opportunity interest rate and time period using the same expression. Note that the discount factor is inversely related both to the length of the time period and the opportunity interest rate. Discount factors effectively tell you the value of $1.00 at the end of a given period for any opportunity interest rate. Thus, at 10 percent opportunity interest rate, $1.00 is worth $0.9091 if received after one year; $0.6209 if received after five years; and $0.0923 if received after twenty-five years. Similarly, with a 20 percent opportunity interest rate, $1.00 is worth only $0.4019 if received after five years; $0.0649 after fifteen years; and only a fraction over one cent if received after twenty-five years!

EXAMPLE: Which would you prefer, $5,000 now, $20,000 in ten years, or $100,000 in 25 years? If the opportunity discount rate is 10 percent, the present values of these alternatives are $5,000, $7,710, and $9,230, respectively. Thus, you would prefer to take $100,000 in 25 years over the other opportunities. But note that if the opportunity discount rate is 15 percent, the present values become $5,000, $4,944, and $3,040, respectively. In the latter case it is preferable to take the $5,000 now. This demonstrates the powerful effect that higher opportunity discount rates have upon future cash flows and that the selection of the appropriate discount rate is critical for the effective evaluation of decision alternatives.

Table 1-1 is excerpted from Table B-1 in Appendix B of this book. The table in the appendix shows the discount factors for all opportunity interest rates from 1 percent to 40 percent over periods from one year to 25 years. This table is provided for your convenience, although with the aid of a calculator you can find the discount factor for any opportunity interest rate over any period of time using the formula supplied by Equation (1-2). For discount rates involving fractions, such as 16.5 percent, you will have to use your calculator, although an approximation can be obtained by a simple interpolation between the discount factors given in the appendix.[3]

Present Value of a Revenue Stream. Suppose we expect to receive a revenue stream over the next five years, as shown in the second column of Table 1-2. What is the present value of this revenue stream? First, we must decide on the opportunity discount rate. For the purposes of this example, let us assume the revenue stream is guaranteed by contract and will be received with certainty at the end of each year, as indicated in the table. Since there is no uncertainty involved, the appropriate discount rate will be the risk-free rate of interest one could obtain on the best use of the present value of funds if this sum was presently held and could be invested or deposited in an interest-bearing security. For risk-free interest rates we could look to Treasury bills or guaranteed bank deposits, for example. Suppose the best interest rate available given no risk of loss of the capital is 13 percent. Referring to Table B-1 in Appendix B, we find the appropriate discount factors, which are shown in the third column of Table 1-2.

The final column of Table 1-2 is the product of the second and third columns and shows the present value of each of the future sums to be

TABLE 1-2.   Present Value of a Revenue Stream

Year	Future Value $	Discount Factors (@ 13%)	Present Value $
1	20,000	.8850	$ 17,700.00
2	45,000	.7831	35,239.50
3	60,000	.6931	41,586.00
4	30,000	.6133	18,399.00
5	10,000	.5428	5,428.00
		Total Present Value	$118,352.50

---

[3] Interpolation is the imputing of values between two points in a data set. We stress that this interpolation is approximate because it is a linear approximation of a curvilinear relationship. Considerations of accuracy aside, for more complex interpolations (such as for 16.335 percent), you would most likely use a calculator and would find it more simple to compute the exact discount factor using Equation (1-2).

received. The total present value of the revenue stream, when discounted at 13 percent, is $118,352.50.

Note that we have assumed that the cash flows each occur at the end of year one, year two, and so on. Later in this chapter we examine alternative cash flow conventions which will be more appropriate in different circumstances.

Present Value of a Cost Stream.   Now let us consider a stream of costs. Suppose our firm plans to purchase and install a new air-conditioning plant. Two bids are received: One requires a single payment of $130,000 payable immediately, and it offers a complete no-cost guarantee on repair parts, labor, and maintenance costs. The second bid requires $115,000 at the end of the first year and an annual service contract of $10,000 for each year for the next four years. Supposing the opportunity discount rate to be 13 percent, we can use the same discount figures again, as shown in Table 1-3.

It may surprise you to find that the second bid, with a total nominal cost of $155,000, has the smaller present value of its cost, as compared with the $130,000 bid. This demonstrates the importance of using present-value analysis in choosing among decision alternatives.

Net-Present-Value Analysis

When a decision involves both revenues and costs in future periods, we could treat these separately, as in the above examples, but it is more simple to net the costs of each year against the revenues of each year and to simply find the present value of the net revenues, or net costs. Since profits are the excess of revenues over costs, and losses are the excess of costs over revenues, this amounts to finding the present value of the profits (or losses) associated with the decision in future years.

EXAMPLE: Suppose we are considering the installation of equipment to manufacture a novelty gift item, and we anticipate the cost and revenue streams shown in Table 1-4. The cost stream includes the initial capital cost and the annual operating costs of the equipment and associated labor and material costs. The revenue stream shows the revenue expected from sales of the

TABLE 1-3.   **Present Value of a Cost Stream**

Year	Future Value $	Discount Factors (@ 13%)	Present Value $
1	115,000	.8850	$101,775.00
2	10,000	.7831	7,831.00
3	10,000	.6931	6,931.00
4	10,000	.6133	6,133.00
5	10,000	.5428	5,428.00
		Total Present Value	$128,098.00

TABLE 1-4. Net Present Value of a Proposed Decision

Year	Revenue Stream ($'000)	Cost Stream ($'000)	Profit (Loss) Stream ($'000)	Discount Factor (@ 18%)	Present Value ($'000)
0	—	744.85	(744.85)	1.0000	−744.85
1	400.00	224.62	175.38	.8475	148.63
2	1,085.00	648.22	436.78	.7182	313.70
3	872.50	456.98	415.52	.6086	252.89
4	220.00	131.43	88.57	.5158	45.68
5	380.00	58.35	321.65	.4371	140.59
				Net Present Value	156.64

product and includes the salvage value of the equipment in the last year, when we assume the market will become saturated and production will cease. Since there is some uncertainty about the future revenue and cost streams, the risk-free interest rate will not provide the appropriate discount factors. Suppose we investigate this issue and conclude that the opportunity discount rate is 18 percent. We can then calculate the present value of the profits from the project as shown in Table 1-4.

Note that this example includes year zero, or the present period, in the calculations, since the capital expenditure on the equipment ($744,850) must be made in the present period. Thus, the appropriate discount factor is one, since this sum is *already* in present value terms. For each year in which there are both revenues and costs, the net revenues (profits) are discounted by the appropriate discount factor to find the present value of each year's profits from the proposed decision. Adding up the present values of each year's profits or losses results in a net present value of the decision of $156,640. If this is the best alternative open to the firm, we would certainly advise them to go ahead with it.

Other Cash-Flow Conventions

In the foregoing we have used the most common discounting convention, namely, that cash flows are treated as if they are received or disbursed at the *end* of the year in which they occur. In many instances this assumption is clearly inappropriate. How should we treat cash flows which occur semi-annually, quarterly, monthly, daily, or continuously? In this section we shall introduce a technique to deal with cash flows that occur anywhere in a future period. We then consider the treatment of continuous cash flows, such as the revenue from a grocery store which is open twenty-four hours daily, all year long. Finally, we shall discuss annuities, which are repetitive cash flows of the same value each year.

Cash Flows Occurring Within a Year.   For a cash flow of $1,000 expected in six months, for example, we know that its present value would be less than its future value of $1,000, because a lesser sum could grow to $1,000 in six months in a savings account or in some other interest-bearing security. We can find the present values of a cash flow occurring anytime within the present year with a simple modification to Equation (1-2). We simply divide the annual interest rate, r, by the number of times the year is divisible by the discount period. Thus,

$$PV = \frac{FV}{(1 + r/n)} \tag{1-3}$$

where n is the number of times the year is divisible by the period over which the cash flow will be discounted. For example, a cash flow expected in six months should be discounted by $(1 + r/2)$ to find its present value.

EXAMPLE: Suppose you expect to receive $2,000 in nine month's time. What is its present value if the opportunity discount rate is 15 percent?

$$PV = \frac{\$2,000}{(1 + .15/1.333)}$$

$$= \frac{\$2,000}{1.1125}$$

$$= \$1,797.75$$

You may confirm this by finding 15 percent of $1,797.75 to be $269.66. Three quarters (9/12) of this annual interest earned is $202.25, which, added to $1,797.75, makes $2,000.00 in total.

This technique can be adapted for any irregular date of receipt in the future. Suppose you expect to receive $1,000 in two years and two months. Using Equation (1-3), we can find the value of $1,000 for *two years hence* and then discount *that* sum back to present value. Note that two months is one-sixth of a year and proceed as follows:

$$PV = \frac{\$1,000}{(1 + .15/6)}$$

$$= \frac{\$1,000}{1.025}$$

$$= \$975.61$$

This is the future value of $1,000 in two years and two months (26 months), discounted back to the future value of that sum in two years (24 months). Now, using Equation (1-2) to find the present value of $975.61 received two years into the future, we have

$$PV = \frac{\$975.61}{(1 + .15)^2}$$

$$= \frac{\$975.61}{1.3225}$$

$$= \$737.70$$

Thus, $737.70 is the present value of $1,000 to be received 26 months in the future when the opportunity discount rate is 15 percent.

Continuous Discounting. The above process can be used to find the present value of a series of cash flows arriving every month, by dividing the interest rate by the appropriate number (12 for the first month, 6 for the second month, then 4, 3, 2.4, 2, 1.714, 1.5, 1.33, 1.2, 1.091, and 1.0 for the twelfth month), by calculating the present value of each cash flow, and by adding up these numbers to find the present value of the stream of monthly payments. This process is not too onerous for a stream of payments received monthly, but is considerably more wearisome for a stream of payments received weekly, and it becomes downright loathsome for a stream of payments received daily.

Many business situations do involve the daily, weekly, or monthly receipt of revenues and a similar pattern of expense payments. To be treated properly for decision-making purposes, these cash flows should be viewed in present-value terms. We can avoid the heavy burden of computation implied above by adopting the *continuous-cash-flow convention*. By treating the cash flows as if they arrive and are disbursed on a continuous basis, we can use a simplified calculation without great loss of accuracy. Table B-2 in Appendix B shows the discount factors appropriate for continuous cash flows.[4]

EXAMPLE: Let us return to the example we discussed earlier in Table 1-4, in which the firm was considering the purchase of equipment to manufacture a novelty gift item. Now, let us assume that the revenue and cost streams occur continuously over the five years of the project's life. In Table 1-5, we reproduce the annual net cost and revenue figures from Table 1-4 and discount these by the 18 percent discount factors found in Table B-2 in Appendix B.

Note that the net present value, using the continuous-cash-flow convention, is $235,530 and is substantially greater than the $156,640 found by

---

[4] For the theory underlying (and the formulas for calculating) the discount factors for continuous cash flows, see G.E. Clayton and C.B. Spivey, *The Time Value of Money* (Philadelphia: W.B. Saunders Company, 1978) or S.J. Khoury and T.D. Parsons, *Mathematical Methods in Finance and Economics* (New York: Elsevier North-Holland, Inc., 1981).

TABLE 1-5. Net Present Value Assuming Continuous
Cash Flows

Year	Future Profits (Losses) ($'000)	Discount Factor (@ 18%)	Present Value ($'000)
0	(744.85)	1.0000	−744.85
1	175.38	.9216	161.63
2	436.78	.7810	341.13
3	415.52	.6619	275.03
4	88.57	.5609	49.68
5	321.65	.4754	152.91
		Net Present Value	235.53

treating all cash flows as if they occurred at the end of each year.[5] You should understand that a particular profit stream will have greater present value if received continuously, because these funds can be deposited to earn interest *during* the remainder of the year in which they are received.

Note that both the end-of-year-cash-flow convention and the continuous-cash-flow convention represent extreme assumptions. Neither is exactly correct for cash flows which arrive monthly, for example. The end-of-year discount factors would discount these cash flows too heavily, while the continuous-discount factors would discount too lightly. Nevertheless, the continuous-cash-flow convention would seem to be the more appropriate convention to use in this case, recognizing that it will result in a slight overstatement of the present value. The degree of overstatement is diminished as the actual cash-flow pattern approaches a continuous flow. For example, the present value of a daily cash flow amounting to $10,000 annually would be only slightly overstated using continuous-discount factors, whereas it would be significantly understated using the end-of-the-year discount factors. It is up to the decision makers to exercise judgment about the appropriate discounting convention to apply. For example, a firm which does 80 percent of its business in the Christmas-New Year period and spreads the remaining 20 percent over the rest of the year would find the end-of-the-year convention more appropriate.

Annuities. A further simplification can be applied if the cash flow is regular and uniform for a number of periods. Such a uniform cash flow over several consecutive time periods is known as an annuity. You are probably

---

[5] Strictly speaking, the salvage value of the equipment should have been separated from the sales revenues of year five, since the revenue from salvage is doubtless received in lump sum at the end of year five. It should, therefore, be discounted using the end-of-year discount factors, while the sales revenue received during year five is more appropriately discounted using the continuous cash flow convention. Our purpose here was simply to demonstrate that the difference in the cash flow conventions can make a substantial difference in the present-value calculation.

aware of the concept of annuities. Retirement savings can be used to purchase an annuity which pays the owner a certain sum of money every year or every month for a prescribed number of years. Any regular and uniform stream of payments can be treated like an annuity. For example, a firm expecting to earn $50,000 each year for five years as the result of a particular decision, is, in effect, expecting an annuity.

DEFINITION: An *annuity* is a series of cash flows of uniform amount occurring regularly in each of a number of consecutive time periods.

It can be shown[6] that the present value of an annuity of $1.00 for t periods with opportunity interest rate r may be calculated as the *sum* of the discount factors for periods 1, 2, 3, and so on, up to period t.

EXAMPLE: A firm expects to receive $50,000 at the end of each year for five years as a result of a decision it is about to implement. What is the present value of this annuity if the firm's opportunity discount rate is 16 percent? In Table 1-6 we find the present value of the revenue stream of $50,000 each year for five years, given 16 percent discount factors. The sum of the present values of the annual payments is $163,720. Now, notice that the sum of the discount factors is 3.2744 and that this figure multiplied by $50,000 equals $163,720. The sum of the discount factors is known as the *present-value factor* for an annuity over that period of time.

Table B-3 in Appendix B shows the present-value factors for annuities up to periods of 25 years and for opportunity interest rates of 1 percent through 40 percent. It is certainly much quicker to find the present value of an annuity in a single calculation rather than to find the present value of each annual cash flow and then add these to find the present value of the revenue stream. Referring to Table B-3, we find the present-value factors for a 16 percent discount rate over five years to be 3.2743. (This is the more accurate figure, since the sum of the discount factors used above includes a discrepancy caused by rounding off at the fourth decimal place.) Thus, the

TABLE 1-6.   Present Value of an Annuity

Year	Revenue Stream $	Discount Factor (@ 16%)	Present Value $
1	50,000	.8621	43,105
2	50,000	.7432	37,160
3	50,000	.6407	32,035
4	50,000	.5523	27,615
5	50,000	.4761	23,805
	Totals	3.2744	$163,720

---

[6] See Clayton and Spivey, *The Time Value of Money*, p. 87; or Khoury and Parsons, *Mathematical Methods in Finance and Economics*, p. 26.

present value of the annuity is 3.2743 times the periodic payment of $50,000, or $163,715.[7]

The Firm's Planning Period and Time Horizon

DEFINITION: The firm's *planning period* is the period of time over which the firm takes into account the cost and revenue implications of its decisions.

EXAMPLE: Suppose a firm is considering investing in a new building and calculates the present value of the initial cost and future maintenance costs for the next fifteen years and sets against these costs the present value of the revenues it expects to receive from the building over the same fifteen-year period. This firm's planning period is, thus, fifteen years, since it has taken into account the cost and revenue implications of its decision to buy the new building only up to the fifteenth year into the future. The sixteenth and subsequent years' costs and revenues are ignored. The firm, in effect, considers them to occur so far into the future that they are insignificant to the decision.

DEFINITION: The firm's *time horizon* is the point in the future at which the firm no longer considers the cost and revenue implications of its decisions. The time horizon is, therefore, the end of the firm's planning period.

A firm's time horizon, and, thus, the length of its planning period, is likely to vary among firms for various reasons. Firms involved in intense competition for their day-to-day survival are less likely to worry about the longer-term cost and revenue implications of their decisions. Immediate or short-term costs and revenues may be given full weight in their decision making, to the complete exclusion of the longer-term profit implications of their actions. Conversely, a firm that is well established and secure in its market, without the constant pressure of day-to-day price competition, can afford the luxury of taking into consideration the future profit implications of its current decisions.

Another reason for differing planning periods among firms is the motivation of the manager. A manager who expects to retire in six months, or who is actively seeking a promotion within the year, may be expected to prefer actions which have greater short-term profit implications over those that promise greater longer-term profits. Conversely, managers who wish to make a career out of their position, or who prefer longer-term stability of employment and salary income, may be expected to take the longer view, preferring to take actions which promise greater profits over an extended planning period.

Finally, the firm's planning period may be inversely related to the

---

[7] If the annuity payments are received continuously throughout the year or approximately so, such as monthly or daily payments, the present value factor can be found by adding up the appropriate discount factors shown in Table B-2 in Appendix B.

general level of interest rates, because the present value of future profits declines as the opportunity discount rate increases. This presumes that the decision maker decides to suspend the search for information (concerning future costs and revenues associated with a particular decision) when the present value of $1.00 earned at the time horizon falls below a predetermined level.

EXAMPLE: A firm that places its time horizon at 15 years when the opportunity discount rate is 10 percent may shorten its planning period to 10 years when the opportunity discount rate is 15 percent, since the present value of $1.00 falls below $0.25 at the time horizon in each case. (You may confirm this in Table 1-1.)

The reason a firm may adopt a cutoff rule like this is related to the cost of obtaining information, or *search costs*, which we examine in Chapter 2. It will suffice to say here that if the firm expects to pay $0.25 now to find out that it will earn $1.00 in 10 years, it is profit maximizing to suspend search activity at that point if the present value of the $1.00 is less than $0.25.

The Length of the Present Period. We can dichotomize the firm's time horizon as occurring either at the end of the present period or at some point in the future. If it occurs at the end of the present period, we can treat all cash flows at face value, since they will already be in present-value terms. If the firm's time horizon lies beyond the present period, we must discount future cash flows back to present-value terms in order to compare them properly with present-period costs and revenues.

DEFINITION: For the purposes of this analysis we shall define the *present period* to be the period of time from the present moment to the point of time in the future when the decision maker decides it is preferable to calculate the present values of the cash flows to be received or disbursed.

Note that the present value of $1.00 to be received at some point in the future begins to decline as time ticks away from the present moment. For example, $1.00 to be received next week is worth fractionally less than $1.00 in present-value terms, because a sum less than $1.00 could grow to $1.00 (in a daily-interest savings account, for example) by the end of the week.

We assume that the decision maker recognizes the continuing decline in the present value of $1.00 (the further away that $1.00 is to be received) but does not begin using present-value analysis until it is *worthwhile* to do so. The point at which it will be worthwhile to begin discounting future cash flows depends upon the opportunity rate of interest and the search costs involved in translating the cost and the revenue data into present-value terms. It will cost the decision maker time and money to use present-value analysis; these search costs will be avoided until the point where the cost of using inaccurate data begins to exceed the search costs. Notice that nominal dollars overstate present-value dollars progressively more at higher interest rates. For example, if the opportunity interest rate is 10 percent, the present value of $1.00 to be received in six months is about $0.95. But, if the opportunity interest rate is 20 percent, $1.00 to be received in six months has a present value of about $0.90. Treating both cases in nominal dollars overstates the present value to a substantially greater degree when interest rates are higher.

Thus, the present period ends at the point where the decision maker decides to begin discounting future cash flows. This decision is made when it is determined that the search costs of generating present-value data are less than the costs involved (in terms of profits lost, for example) in using inaccurate data. We should expect decision makers to tolerate the inaccuracies involved in not discounting next week's, next month's, or next quarter's cash flows as a tradeoff against the search costs avoided. The present period for decision-making purposes will be inversely related to the opportunity discount rate and positively related to the search costs of transforming nominal cash flow data into present value data.

For our purposes we shall usually leave the length of the present period up to the judgment of the decision maker and simply speak of attempting to maximize profits during the present period. For much of this book we shall use the *present period* and the *short run* as interchangeable terms, although the latter is defined in somewhat different terms. For most decision-making purposes, it is a sufficient approximation to consider these terms as equivalent.[8]

1.4   EXPECTED-VALUE ANALYSIS OF UNCERTAIN OUTCOMES

In this section we establish a means for evaluating decisions *prior* to their execution, while there is still uncertainty about the actual outcome of the decision. We first clarify what is meant by certainty, risk, and uncertainty, and we discuss the probability distribution of outcomes surrounding a decision under each scenario. Expected-value analysis is then introduced as a means of summarizing each probability distribution of outcomes in a single value, which allows alternative decisions to be compared and the optimal decision to be made.

Certainty, Risk, and Uncertainty

The state of information under which a decision is made has important implications for the predictability of the outcome of that decision. If there is

---

[8] The short run is defined as the period of time during which at least some factors of production are in fixed supply, and, thus, total output of the firm's products is constrained to an upper limit. Given the time necessary to purchase and install new plant and equipment, it appears reasonable to say that the short run will be *at least as long* as the present period for most businesses. Thus, for example, short-run profit maximization will have the same implications for decision making as present-period profit maximization.

full information, the outcome of a decision will be foreseen clearly and unambiguously. In this situation (of certainty) the firm can accurately predict the outcome of each of its decisions. When there is less than full information, however, the decision maker may foresee several potential outcomes to a decision and, therefore, will be unable to predict consistently which outcome will actually occur. In this case we say that the individual or firm is operating under conditions of risk and uncertainty.

DEFINITION: *Certainty* exists if the outcome of a decision, or a contest of any sort, is known in advance without a shadow of a doubt. One speaks of acts or decisions that lead to events, or outcomes. Under conditions of certainty, an act leads to a single possible event, which is foreseen. *Risk and uncertainty* are situations in which an act leads to one of several alternative possible outcomes, but the exact outcome is not known in advance. Some people prefer to make a distinction between risk and uncertainty on the following basis: Under risk the *probabilities* of each of the possible outcomes can be assigned objectively, whereas under uncertainty these probabilities must be assigned on a subjective basis.[9] Let us look into this further.

The Probability Distributions of Possible Outcomes

Risk is involved when one flips a coin, throws dice, or plays a hand of poker. The probability of flipping a coin and having it land "heads" is $1/2$, since there are only two possible outcomes (ruling out the coin landing on its edge), and each is equally likely to occur, given an unbiased coin. Similarly, when one throws two dice, the probability that they will turn up "snake eyes," or any other pair of numbers, is $1/6 \times 1/6 = 1/36$. The probability of drawing a "royal flush" in poker, or any other combination of cards, can likewise be calculated.

In each of the illustrations above the probability of each outcome is known *a priori*. That is, on the basis of known mathematical and physical principles, we can deduce—prior to the act—the proportion of the total number of outcomes that should be attained by each particular outcome. We can confirm this calculation by undertaking a number of trials. Although "heads" might appear three or even four times out of the first four tosses of a coin, given a sufficiently large number of trials, the proportions will converge upon $1/2$ for each of the two possible outcomes.

A second class of risk situations is that in which probabilities are assigned *a posteriori*, or on the basis of past experience under similar circumstances. The business of insurance is based upon this type of risk situation. The possible outcomes are known: the life insured will or will not expire; alternatively, the building insured will or will not be destroyed by fire.

---

[9] Frank H. Knight, *Risk, Uncertainty and Profit* (Boston: Houghton-Mifflin, 1921).

Insurance companies keep extensive data on previous policies and claims and other pertinent data; from these they compile actuarial tables, which show the relative incidence of the various outcomes in past situations or trials. On the presumption that a particular life or a building is similar in all important respects to those of the data base, they are able to form an expectation (or assign a probability) of the chances of that particular life expiring or that building burning.

DEFINITION: A situation of *uncertainty*, as distinct from risk, is defined as one in which one of two or more events will follow an act, but the precise nature of these events may not be known and the probabilities of their occurring cannot be objectively assigned. That is, not all outcomes may be accurately foreseen, and the probabilities cannot be deduced or based on previous empirical data. Instead, the decision maker must use intuition, judgment, experience, and whatever information is available to assign the probabilities to the outcomes considered possible in such a situation. Thus, the assignment of probabilities in situations of uncertainty proceeds on a *subjective* basis, rather than on the objective basis of risk situations.

NOTE: It is clear that perhaps the great majority of business decisions are taken in an environment of uncertainty, as distinct from risk. The decision maker is usually required to estimate, rather than simply calculate, the probabilities of each event's occurring. Having made the traditional distinction between risk and uncertainty, we shall, for the most part, in the following use the terms interchangeably: the fine distinction concerning the objective or subjective assignment of the probabilities should be kept in mind, but in common usage the terms refer simply to situations in which more than one possible outcome follows an act.

The Expected Value of a Decision

Under conditions of risk and uncertainty the decision maker looks at each of the potential solutions to a problem and, for each of these possible decisions, foresees a probability distribution of outcomes. That is, several different levels of profit (or loss) are perceived as possible, and each of these is assigned a probability of occurring. How does the decision maker summarize all this data so that it can be compared with other potential solutions to the same problem?

DEFINITION: The *expected value* of an event is the value of that event multiplied by the probability of that event occurring. Since several events are possible under risk and uncertainty, the expected value of a decision is the sum of the expected values of all the possible events that may follow the decision.[10] The expected value of a decision thus allows the probability distribution of possible outcomes to be characterized by a single number, which can then be compared with the expected values of other potential solutions to the problem.

EXAMPLE: In Table 1-7 we show a hypothetical probability distribution of profit levels that are expected to be possible outcomes of a decision to invest in a particular investment project. The first column shows the possible profit levels, ranging from a loss of $50,000 to a profit of $250,000. The second column shows the probability of each profit (or loss) level, as assigned by the decision maker. Thus there is considered to be a 5 percent chance of losing $50,000, a 10 percent chance of only breaking even, a 15 percent chance of making $50,000 in profits, and so on. Note that the probabilities must total 1.00, since all possible outcomes are included and these outcomes are mutually exclusive.

The third column in the table is the product of columns one and two. The expected value of each possible outcome is equal to the possible profit (or loss) associated with each outcome, multiplied by the probability of that outcome's occurring. The sum of the expected values of all the possible outcomes is $117,500. This is the expected value of the decision to invest in this particular investment opportunity. Note that the *actual* outcome will

TABLE 1-7.   The Expected Value of a Decision

Possible Profit Levels ($)	Probability of Each Occurring (P)	Expected Value of Each Profit Level ($)
−50,000	.05	−2,500
0	.10	0
50,000	.15	7,500
100,000	.20	20,000
150,000	.25	37,500
200,000	.15	30,000
250,000	.10	25,000
Totals	1.00	117,500

[10] Formally, we define the expected value of a decision as

$$EV = \sum_{i=1}^{n} R_i P_i$$

where Σ connotes "the sum of"; R_i is the return of the ith outcome; $i = 1, 2, 3, \ldots, n$ identifies each separate possible outcome; n is the total number of possible outcomes; and P_i the probability of the ith outcome occurring.

not be known until after the investment is made and all returns are in. The expected value is an *a priori* measure of the decision that allows the probability distribution of outcomes to be summarized as a single number. This expected value is actually a weighted average of the possible profit levels, with each possible outcome weighted by the probability that it will occur.

Note that the possible profit levels are a finite set of points on a continuum. The actual outcome might be, for example, $67,964.45, which does not appear as a possible outcome in Table 1-7. Obviously we must restrict the *a priori* outcomes to a limited number, so that the calculation of the expected value is made relatively simple. Otherwise the table would be infinitely long with infinitesimally small prior probabilities for each outcome. For example, the probability that the outcome will be exactly $67,964.45 might be somewhere in the vicinity of 0.0000001. Clearly it is more simple, and with insignificant loss of accuracy, to select points on the continuum of possible outcomes and to regard these as the midpoint of a range of possible outcomes, each of which is equally likely to occur. Thus the possible outcome of $50,000 shown in Table 1-7 represents all outcomes from $25,000.01 to $75,000.00, the average of which is $50,000. Similarly, the $100,000 possible profit is the midpoint of the range of outcomes from $75,000.01 to $125,000.00, and so on.[11]

Thus, if a firm is faced with a decision problem, the decision maker(s) should investigate all potential solutions to that problem and evaluate the probability distribution of each potential solution in terms of its expected value. The firm should choose that alternative which promises the highest expected value, subject to considerations of risk, which we shall examine in Chapter 2. Note that decision problems are situations in which more than one alternative action is possible and these problems don't necessarily involve a crisis or the need for remedial action.

EXAMPLE: Suppose your firm has a large and stable market share and has enjoyed strong profitability over the past several years. A decision problem involving positive action will arise if your firm considers expansion. Should it diversify into related product lines, or into totally different product markets, or into new geographical areas, or simply build more productive capacity for its traditional product line? Each of these decisions, and permutations and combinations, can be evaluated using expected-value analysis. Alternatively, suppose your firm's sales have fallen substantially below projections for the past two quarters. This is a decision problem requiring remedial action. You

---

[11] To be completely accurate, and for situations in which the selected point is not the midpoint of the range in which it sits, each selected profit outcome may be regarded as the weighted average of all possible profit outcomes over the range it represents, where each possible profit outcome (for example, $67,964.45) is weighted by the probability of its occurring. Thus the possible loss of $50,000.00 might accurately represent the weighted average of losses ranging from minus infinity dollars to minus $25,000.00, when the probabilities of each loss figure in that range vary from zero for an infinite loss to some positive but very small value at minus $25,000.00. These probabilities total 0.05 for all the possible loss outcomes within the range, of course.

may consider several alternative solutions, including increased advertising, price reductions, new packaging, product improvements, and so on, and choose among these using expected-value analysis.

1.5 THE OBJECTIVES OF THE FIRM

Any decision problem should be approached with the firm's objectives clearly in mind, so that the actual decision taken will best serve the firm's objectives. What are the objectives of the business firm? Is it profit maximization or would the firm sacrifice some current profitability for an enlarged market share? Does the firm wish to maximize its rate of growth or is management content to attain profit, market share, and growth targets, while maximizing their own benefits and the quality of their lives?

At this point we shall confine ourselves to the assumption, which is well supported in the literature and the related disciplines of finance and accounting, that the decision maker's objective is to maximize the net worth of the firm over its time horizon, subject to considerations of risk and uncertainty. The other objectives mentioned above will be incorporated into the analysis and reconciled with this objective in later chapters.[12]

DEFINITION: *Net worth*, also known as *owner's equity*, is measured as the excess of the firm's assets (cash, securities, land, buildings, plant and equipment, and so on) over its liabilities (amounts owed to creditors, short-term and long-term loans, and so on). There are three main groups of items on the firm's balance sheet, namely, assets, liabilities, and owner's equity. Assets are equal to the sum of the other two. Thus, maximization of the net worth of the firm requires maximizing the difference between assets and liabilities, or, what amounts to the same thing, maximizing the owner's equity.

The above simple statement of the firm's objective function implies slightly different decision criteria for each of the different scenarios in which a firm may find itself. In the foregoing we have established two separate dichotomies, one referring to the time horizon (the present period versus future periods) and the second referring to the state of information (certainty versus uncertainty). There are four combinations of these circumstances, and we now proceed to specify the decision criterion which will allow the maximization of net worth under each scenario.

The Present Period with Certainty

The most simple scenario is that in which the firm's time horizon falls inside the present period, and the firm enjoys full information, or certainty, about

---

[12] We shall see in Chapter 10 that sales, or market share maximization, growth maximization, managerial utility maximization, and even "satisficing", can be regarded as real-world approximations for the maximization of the expected present value of profits.

the outcome of all decisions. Thus, there is no need for either present-value analysis or expected-value analysis. Rather, the firm may maximize its net worth by the pursuit of short-run profit maximization. Profits are calculated as the excess of total revenues over total costs. Total revenues add to asset accounts, such as cash and debtors, while total costs represent outflows of funds for materials, labor, and other services, and, if these costs remain unpaid, there will be an increase in the liabilities accounts for various creditors. When profits are made, assets increase more than liabilities, to the extent of the profits made. Owner's equity, or net worth, therefore, rises by the same amount. Maximization of profits thus ensures the maximization of the firm's net worth.

RULE: For the firm operating in an environment of *certainty* and with its time horizon falling within the *present period*, short-run profit maximization is the appropriate decision criterion to maximize the firm's net worth.

Future Periods with Certainty

If the firm has full information concerning revenues and costs but its time horizon falls in a future period, the firm must use present-value analysis in order to properly evaluate its decision alternatives. A decision which causes immediate profits and no future profits can be compared with another decision promising a stream of future profits only if both are expressed in present-value terms. The firm wishing to maximize its net worth in present-value terms, or its *net present worth*, should always choose the decision alternative which promises the greater net present value, or equivalently, which promises the greater present value of profits.

RULE: For the firm operating in an environment of *certainty*, and with its time horizon falling in a *future period*, maximization of the present value of (present and future) profits is the appropriate decision criterion to maximize the firm's net (present) worth.

The Present Period with Uncertainty

Uncertainty means that decisions have more than one possible outcome that is foreseen, and that decisions must be made on the basis of the prior probability distribution of outcomes. Expected-value analysis is, therefore, required to summarize the probability distributions of the various decision alternatives and to allow the selection of that decision which will maximize the expected value of the firm's profits. If the firm always chooses the alternative which offers the greatest expected value of profits, it will sometimes receive less than the expected value and sometimes more, but after many decisions the firm will find its actual total profits to be greater than they would have been by following any other strategy. If the probability distributions are accurately estimated, the law of averages will ensure that after many decisions the probability distributions will be validated by the actual outcomes.

RULE: For the firm operating in an environment of *uncertainty*, and with its time horizon falling within the *present period*, maximization of the expected value of (short-run) profits is the appropriate decision criterion to maximize the firm's net (expected) worth.

Future Periods with Uncertainty

The final scenario is that of the firm whose time horizon falls in a future period and the firm does not have full information about costs and revenues. It is clear that this is the predominant situation in the real world, where firms certainly consider the cost and revenue implications of their decisions that occur beyond the present period and where each decision alternative has a prior probability of outcomes. Thus, these firms must use *both* present-value analysis and expected-value analysis in order to select the optimal decision alternative.

How is this done? In the next chapter we shall proceed through several examples with the aid of "decision trees." There are two main steps to the procedure. First, all future cash flows are discounted to present-value terms at the appropriate opportunity discount rate. Then, the present value of each of the possible outcomes is weighted by the probability of its occurring, and the sum of these is the *expected present value* (EPV) of the decision. The decision maker then selects the decision alternative which has the highest EPV of profits.

RULE: For the firm operating in an environment of *uncertainty* and with its time horizon falling in a *future period*, maximization of the expected present value of profits is the appropriate decision criterion to maximize the firm's net (expected present) worth.

Thus, we have seen that the decision criterion for pursuit of the maximization of the firm's net worth is modified as the firm's time horizon moves from the present period to a future period and as the state of information changes from certainty to uncertainty. These criteria are summarized in Table 1-8, where the four scenarios are provided by the intersection of the conditions shown by the rows and the columns of the table. The decision criterion for maximization of the firm's net worth is shown in the interior of the table for each of the four scenarios.

You will notice that these decision criteria take no account of the *degree* of risk and uncertainty involved in each decision. They are, therefore, appropriate for a decision maker who has a neutral attitude towards risk; that is, one who neither likes nor dislikes risk. In Chapter 2 we continue to build the framework for business decision making by considering the con-

TABLE 1-8.   The Decision Criteria for Maximization of The
Firm's Net Worth under Four Scenarios

THE STATE OF INFORMATION	THE FIRM'S TIME HORIZON FALLS WITHIN THE	
	Present Period	*Future Period*
Certainty	Maximize short-run profits	Maximize present value of profits
Uncertainty	Maximize expected value of profits	Maximize expected present value of profits

cepts of risk aversion and risk preference. Risk aversion is more common, and risk-averse decision makers will wish to modify the basic decision criteria shown above by adjusting for the degree of risk involved in each decision alternative.

1.6   SUMMARY

In this chapter we have introduced the subject of managerial economics and proceeded to build a framework for business decision making. Managerial economics was defined as the application of economic principles and methodologies to the decision-making process within the firm or organization. It is a normative discipline, seeking to provide rules which allow the firm to best pursue its objective function. We stated that the firm's objective function is the maximization of its net worth, and we noted that the decision criterion for pursuit of this objective is modified as the scenario changes from a short planning period to a longer planning period and from certainty to uncertainty.

If the firm's planning period is sufficiently short that its time horizon falls within the present period, the firm should maximize its profits within the present period (if it has full information) or maximize the expected value of its profits (if it operates under uncertainty). If the firm's planning period is longer, so that its time horizon falls in a future period, the firm should maximize the present value of its profit stream (under certainty) or the expected present value of its profit stream (under uncertainty).

Present-value analysis and expected-value analysis were introduced and examined in detail. The former involves the discounting of future cash flows so that they may be properly compared with present cash flows for decision-making purposes. The appropriate rate of discount is the opportunity interest rate, defined as the best rate of return available elsewhere at similar risk. The length of the present period was seen to depend on the opportunity rate of interest and on the search costs of obtaining present-value data, as perceived by the decision maker. Different discounting conventions were examined, and three main conventions (end-of-year cash flows, continuous cash flows, and annuities) were advocated as simplifications, one of which will be more appropriate than the others for any particular pattern of cash flows.

Expected-value analysis allows the summary of a probability distribution of outcomes (associated with each decision alternative in an environment of uncertainty) in a single number, which may then be compared with the expected values of other decision alternatives. The expected value of a decision is defined as the weighted mean of the possible outcomes, where the weight for each outcome is the prior probability of its occurring. Expected present-value analysis requires the expected value of future profits to be discounted back to present-value terms before aggregation to find the expected present value of each decision alternative.

The use of models in managerial economics was examined, primarily to establish an understanding of the purposes of models in analytical processes such as decision making. It is important to understand that models may have a pedagogical purpose, an explanatory purpose, and/or a predictive purpose. Further, models should be judged on the basis of how well they achieve their purpose. Up to this point in the text we have used many verbal models (jargon) but no graphical models and few algebraic models. In later chapters our usage of graphs, in particular, will increase dramatically, and it is important to appreciate both the benefits and the limitations of such models in managerial economics and in decision analysis.

DISCUSSION QUESTIONS

1-1. Why would you expect managerial economics to be a normative discipline?

1-2. Under what circumstances is it appropriate that a model be based on assumptions that are extremely simplistic? Could it, nevertheless, be a good model? Could a model be based on false assumptions and yet serve a purpose? Discuss.

1-3. What advantages are there in the graphical or algebraic representation of a model, as compared with a verbal representation of the same phenomena?

1-4. How do search costs affect both the length of the firm's planning period and the length of the firm's present period?

1-5. What determines the opportunity discount rate to be used when evaluating the present value of a multiperiod profit stream?

1-6. Which discounting, or cash flow, convention should be used to most accurately calculate the present value of a stream of payments received each week throughout the year? Will this lead to an understatement or to an overstatement of the true present value of the revenue stream? Explain.

1-7. What is a decision problem? Is it necessarily a situation in which there is a crisis or in which remedial action is necessary? What has the firm's objective function to do with the existence (or nonexistence) of a decision problem?

1-8. Explain the notion of uncertainty in terms of the probability distribution of outcomes associated with each decision alternative.

1-9. The assignment of probabilities to each of the possible outcomes of a decision alternative may proceed on the basis of *a priori* principles, *a posteriori* data, or subjective considerations. Explain.

1-10. Summarize the modifications necessary to the firm's objective function as the firm's time horizon shifts from the present to a future period and as we relax the assumption of full information.

PROBLEMS AND SHORT CASES[13]

1-1.   A large internationally-recognized manufacturer of soft drink products has announced it will establish a foundation to provide scholarships to business students at your university. The company acknowledges a slight cash flow problem at the present moment and gives your university's President two choices: Either take a once-and-for-all grant of $10 million immediately or take $2.5 million immediately, $4 million more next year, and $5 million more in two years. Of course the President is euphoric and announces to the faculty that he intends to accept what he calls the "$11.5 million alternative." As an interested party, you are concerned that a complete analysis has not been made.

    (a)   Assuming that the opportunity discount rate is 14 percent, what is the present value of the second alternative?

    (b)   Explain to the President, in a memo of 200 words or less, what this revised estimate means and which alternative should be accepted.

    (c)   Would your decision change if the opportunity interest rate were 12 percent, or 16 percent, instead of the assumed 14 percent? Explain.

1-2.   The Words-Are-Cheap Publishing Company is considering extending a contract offer to an author who has written a book entitled *How to Deal With High Interest Rates in the Mid-1980s.* This project would involve reviewing, editing, artwork, and composition costs of $80,000, payable in full at the end of year one, before a single book has been printed. The publisher expects to sell 20,000 copies in year two, 17,500 in year three, 12,500 in year four, and 2,500 in year five. It plans to sell the rights to another publisher at the end of year five for $10,000. Its production, distribution, and royalty costs will be constant at $1.50 per copy, and it will receive $3.50 per copy for every copy sold.

The finance vice-president advises that the funds involved could alternatively be invested in a corporate bond issue, considered no more or less risky than this book project, at an interest rate of 18 percent, the best rate available.

    (a)   Calculate the net present value of the book project, assuming that all cash flows are received or disbursed at the end of the year in which they occur.

    (b)   Advise the publisher whether or not to extend the contract offer to the author.

1-3.   Your firm has called for bids for the fabrication and installation of a pollution-control system tailored specifically to meet the legal requirements applicable to your manufacturing process. The lowest bid is for $370,000, with delivery and installation in 32 months. Your firm plans to sign a contract with the supplier on the above terms, including a clause stating that the contract price of $370,000 is absolutely fixed (regardless of any cost overruns or production difficulties the supplier may encounter) and will be paid in full in 32 month's time, following the installation of the system. Between now and then your firm plans to invest its funds in the best available, guaranteed, interest-bearing securities, which pay interest of 12 percent per annum.

    (a)   What is the present value of the cost of the pollution-control system to your firm?

    (b)   Why is 12 percent the appropriate discount rate?

1-4.   Doreen Delights has invented a device which allows drinking drivers to self-test for excessive alcohol in their system. Rather than get into that business itself, the firm plans to license this device to the highest bidder. Company A has bid $40,000, payable $10,000 immediately, $15,000 after one year, $10,000 after two years, and $5,000 after three years. Company B has bid $42,500, payable $5,000 immediately, $10,000 after one year, $12,500 after two years, and $15,000 after three years.

The management of Doreen Delights considers that their opportunity discount rate is

---

[13] Short answers to the odd-numbered problems are provided in Appendix C at the back of this book.

9 percent. You are concerned that this is a little low, in view of recent upward movements in interest rates and foreseeable trends, and you feel that 11 percent is the appropriate discount rate.

(a) Calculate the present value of each proposal, using management's opportunity discount rate of 9 percent.

(b) Would the decision be different if the 11 percent discount rate was applied?

(c) Explain to management which option you feel should be chosen and the impact of the time profile of the cash flows on the relative present values.

1-5. The owner of a restaurant approaches you and offers you the following deal. You would manage his restaurant for two years while he goes back to his country to do his compulsory military service. He shows you all his records and you see that the restaurant has sales revenue of $100,000 spread more-or-less evenly over each year and operating costs of $80,000 similarly spread over each year. You expect the revenue and cost situations to remain stable for each of the next two years. The restaurant owner wants to sell you this opportunity on the following basis: You pay $30,000 initially to the owner but keep all the profits you make over the two years. You know that you could, alternatively, invest your $30,000 in corporate bonds for a 20 percent rate of return, and you consider that alternative no more or less risky than the restaurant venture.

(a) What is the present value of the opportunity to invest in the restaurant venture?

(b) Which alternative should you choose, presuming these are the best opportunities available? Are there any other issues involved?

1-6. You are reading the "Businesses for Sale" advertisements and notice a corner-store business offered for sale. Its assets comprise inventory of $50,000, equipment and plant of $80,000, and land and buildings of $120,000 (all assets are current market value). There are no debtors or creditors. The store's profit stream is $30,000 per year, received more-or-less continuously. Your time horizon is five years; your opportunity discount rate is 16 percent per annum; and you will re-sell the assets after five years for the same *real* value (you expect inflation to average 8 percent over the five years).

(a) What is the net present cost of the assets of the business?

(b) What is the present value of the profit stream over the five years?

(c) What is the net present value of the decision to buy the corner store?

(d) What is the maximum you would offer for the business? If the present owner were asking $400,000, how would you explain your lower offer?

1-7. The Swiss Crest Embroidery Company is considering the installation of a computerized loom, which would be substantially more efficient than their existing equipment. They have two options. Machine A costs $100,000 initially; would earn net profits of $60,000, $80,000, $40,000, and $20,000 on a more-or-less continuous basis throughout years one to four, respectively; and would have salvage (resale) value of $20,000 at the end of the fourth year. Machine B costs $120,000, but payment for this machine can be deferred for twelve months. Machine B promises to earn net profits of $70,000, $60,000, $50,000, and $30,000 throughout the first, second, third, and fourth years, respectively, and it would have resale value of $30,000 at the end of the fourth year.

The firm is considering alternate areas for expansion and the best of these other opportunities, which has the same degree of risk as the computerized loom project, promises to return 16 percent on the funds (which might otherwise be) invested.

(a) Evaluate the two machines in terms of the net present value of their cash flow streams.

(b) Advise the management about which machine they should select.

1-8. Your firm is considering diversification into a new product line. After extensive investigation the two most promising possibilities have been isolated. Product A is a line of personalized stationery, while Product B is a line of paper party decorations. Annual production and marketing costs for A will be $90,000 and those for B will be $115,000; in both cases these costs are incurred on a weekly basis throughout the year. Annual sales for A will be $100,000, received on a weekly basis, while those for B will be $125,000 and will be seasonally biased, being heavily concentrated in December of each year.

For each product, the market research team has predicted a five-year stream of costs and revenues, constant at the above levels. Rather than embark on this diversification, the firm's next best alternative, at equal risk, is to invest the funds in an expansion of the market share for its existing products, which is expected to yield an 18 percent return on investment.

(a) What are the present values of the decision alternatives A and B over the five-year planning period?

(b) Which alternative should the firm choose?

(c) How would you rank the alternatives open to the firm? Explain.

1-9. In September 1981 the Anglo-American Corporation of South Africa, the world's largest producer of gold, released the following forecast of gold prices in 1987, in the form of a table showing the percentage chance that the price will fall within each of several ranges, as follows:

Price Per Ounce (Range)	Chance (%)
Less than $876	1
$ 876 - $ 925	8
$ 926 - $ 975	8.5
$ 976 - $1,025	18.5
$1,026 - $1,075	24
$1,076 - $1,125	22.5
$1,126 - $1,175	12.5
More than $1,175	5

The analysts who provided these figures assumed an inflation rate of 9 percent over the six-year period. The prices shown are in 1987 dollars. When the forecast was released, the price of gold was about $450 per ounce.

(a) Form the data provided into a probability distribution. Defend your choice of the point estimate in each of the ranges shown above.

(b) Calculate the expected value of the gold price in 1987.

(c) Assuming 9 percent annual inflation, what is the real value of the expected 1987 price in 1981 dollars?

(d) What opportunity interest rate would be required to induce you to invest elsewhere, rather than in gold, on the basis of the above data and assumptions?

1-10. The manager of the Fearless Ambition Racing Team is faced with the following decision problem. There is one race left in the series and his driver could win the championship with a win or a second placing in the final race. He is concerned that the engine of the race car may be a little "tired" and is considering either a complete rebuilding of the engine or the purchase of a new engine. There is uncertainty involved in both alternatives. In a complete rebuilding of the engine the cost will vary, depending upon the mechanical components that must be replaced after inspection shows them to be worn beyond acceptable tolerances. Similarly, a new engine will be partially dismantled, examined, and subject to mechanical work and replacement of parts which are unlikely to withstand the rigors imposed by race conditions. Either option (to rebuild or to buy new) will result in an engine of the same power and durability. Based on past experience, the following probability distribution of costs associated with each option has been established.

REBUILD		BUY NEW	
Cost ($)	Probability	Cost ($)	Probability
25,000	.05	35,000	.05
30,000	.15	36,000	.10
35,000	.40	37,000	.30
40,000	.25	38,000	.35
41,000	.10	39,000	.15
50,000	.05	40,000	.05

If the team manager decides to rebuild the existing engine, the parts and labor expenses will be spread out over the next year, since he will be able to keep suppliers waiting for their money for various lengths of time, up to a maximum of twelve months. If he purchases the new engine, the supplier will give the team a special deal in lieu of direct sponsorship: payment for the engine itself ($35,000) can be deferred twelve months. The other expenses can be spread out over twelve months, as in the rebuild option. The opportunity interest rate is 14 percent per annum.

(a) What is the expected value of the costs for each option?

(b) What is the expected present value of the costs for each option?

(c) Which option should be selected? Explain.

SUGGESTED REFERENCES AND FURTHER READING

Baumol, W. J. "What Can Economic Theory Contribute to Managerial Economics?" *American Economic Review*, 51 (May 1961), pp. 142-46. Reprinted in Coyne, T.J., *Readings in Managerial Economics* (3rd ed.), chap. 1. Plano, Tx.: Business Publications, 1981.

Clayton, G.E., and C.B. Spivey. *The Time Value of Money*. Philadelphia: W.B. Saunders Company, 1978.

Fama, E.F. "Agency Problems and the Theory of the Firm," *Journal of Political Economy*, 88 (April 1980), pp. 272-84.

Gordon, G., and I. Pressman. *Quantitative Decision Making for Business*, chaps. 1, 2. Englewood Cliffs, N.J.: Prentice-Hall, Inc., 1978.

Grossack, I.M., and D.D. Martin. *Managerial Economics*, chap. 1. Boston: Little, Brown & Company, 1973.

Huber, G.P. *Managerial Decision Making*, chaps. 1, 2, 3. Glenview, Ill.: Scott, Foresman & Company, 1980.

Jensen, M.C., and W.H. Meckling. "Theory of the Firm: Managerial Behavior, Agency Costs, and Ownership Structure," *Journal of Financial Economics*, 3 (Oct. 1976), pp. 305-360.

Khoury, S.J., and T.D. Parsons. *Mathematical Methods in Finance and Economics*, chap. 2. New York: Elsevier North-Holland, Inc., 1981.

Papps, I., and W. Henderson. *Models and Economic Theory*. Philadelphia: W.B. Saunders Company, 1977.

Radford, K.J. *Modern Managerial Decision Making*, chaps. 1, 4. Reston, Va.: Reston Publishing Company, Inc., 1981.

Simon, H.A. "Theories of Decision Making in Economics and Behavior Science," *American Economic Review*, 49 (June 1959), pp. 253-80. Reprinted in Coyne, T.J., *Readings in Managerial Economics* (3rd ed.), chap. 2. Plano, Tx.: Business Publications, 1981.

Williamson, O.E. "The Modern Corporation: Origins, Evolution, Attributes," *Journal of Economic Literature*, 19 (Dec. 1981), pp. 1537-68.

2

Decision Making under Risk and Uncertainty

2.1   INTRODUCTION

In the preceding chapter we considered two processes that must be employed when decisions are made under risk and uncertainty and where these decisions have cost and revenue implications for future periods as well as for the present period. These processes, expected-value analysis and present-value analysis, must be applied to ensure that the information we do have is treated properly, so that the best decision can be selected from a set of decision alternatives.

In this chapter we proceed to incorporate risk analysis into the decision-making process. Many people, and perhaps most business decision makers, are risk *averse*, that is, they do not like bearing risk for its own sake. They will bear risk, however, if adequately compensated for doing so. Thus, we see a tradeoff between risk and return—more risk will be borne only if it is accompanied by a sufficiently greater return. This has implications for the decision criteria introduced in the first chapter; risk averters will wish to consider the risk of each alternative in conjunction with that alternative's profits, expected profits, or expected present value of profits.

In the following section we consider the measurement of the risk involved in decision alternatives. This section includes calculation of the standard deviation of the probability distribution of outcomes associated with each decision alternative and the introduction of "decision trees" to facilitate the analysis. The concepts of risk aversion, risk neutrality, and risk preference are then formally defined in terms of the psychic satisfaction (or dissatisfaction) risk brings to the individual.

In section three we introduce several decision criteria which allow for the incorporation of risk into the decision process. These criteria include a modification to the EPV criterion; the coefficient of variation criterion; the certainty equivalent criterion; and the maximin criterion. We also consider some noneconomic factors which may enter the decision-making process.

Section four considers the issue of search costs and the value of information. The absence of full information under conditions of risk and uncertainty can be at least partially rectified by the process of information search. The costs of this search process should be incurred, however, only if the decision maker has the prior expectation that the *value* of the information generated will exceed the (search) costs of that information. Search costs can be undertaken to reduce the risk and uncertainty faced by the firm, but in some cases the information costs more than it is worth and the firm should proceed without the information.

Finally, we look at the evaluation of the decision actually made by the decision maker. What is a good decision? Is a decision necessarily a bad decision if it results in a bad outcome? We shall see that decisions should be evaluated on the basis of whether sufficient search activity was undertaken, whether the information was fully and properly utilized, and whether the appropriate decision criterion was applied. The sensitivity of the final decision to the validity of the assumptions on which it is based is also discussed in this context.

2.2 RISK ANALYSIS OF DECISION ALTERNATIVES

In Chapter 1 we defined risk and uncertainty as situations of less than full information, in which a decision has two or more possible outcomes. Probabilities can be attached, or assigned, to each possible outcome so that a probability distribution of potential outcomes is associated with each decision alternative. We use expected-value analysis to reduce the probability distribution to a single number in order to compare the different decision alternatives.

We now consider the *degree* of risk and uncertainty and the appropriate measure of risk which allows us to quantify and compare the risk of competing decision alternatives.

The Degree of Risk and Uncertainty

DEFINITION: The *degree of risk* associated with a particular decision is defined as the dispersion of the prior probability distribution of possible outcomes around the expected value of those outcomes.

Dispersion of outcomes means the spread or range of outcomes within which the actual outcome may fall after the decision is made. Before the decision is made, some decision alternatives will exhibit greater dispersion of possible outcomes than will other decision alternatives, and we say that these have a greater degree of risk involved, or that they are more risky.

EXAMPLE: Suppose one of the domestic automobile manufacturers is in the process of choosing between decision A, to give a $500 rebate on all cars sold within the next month; and decision B, to maintain the basic price structure but include as standard equipment several items which are presently extra-cost options, also for a one-month period only. Imagine that the firm's market research department has constructed the probability distributions of possible outcomes, as shown in Table 2-1. Note that the columns headed X_i refer to the ith outcome for each decision, where $i = 1, 2, 3, \ldots, n$ possible outcomes. ($n = 6$ in this example.) Similarly, P_i represents the probability of the ith outcome, and EV_i is the expected value of the ith outcome. The sum of the EV_i is the expected value of the decision. Notice that the expected value of decision A is $340,000, whereas it is only $320,000 for decision B.

The dispersion of outcomes under decision A is substantially greater, however. The possible outcomes range from $100,000 to $600,000 (a range of $500,000) as compared with decision B's range of outcomes from $200,000 to $450,000 (or a range of only $250,000). If the firm is risk averse, it is not clear that A is the best decision. Although A has the higher expected value, it also exhibits the greater dispersion, or degree of risk. We shall see in the next main section how the risk-averse firm might make its decision between these two decision alternatives.

The range of outcomes is a rather crude measure of the dispersion of a probability distribution, primarily because it ignores the relative probabilities. The extreme points on the probability distribution may be only remotely possible—for example, have probabilities of only 0.0001—yet the range will stay the same. A superior measure of dispersion around the expected value is the standard deviation of the probability distribution.

TABLE 2-1. Relative Dispersions of Probability Distributions

DECISION A			DECISION B		
X_i ($000)	P_i	EV_i ($000)	X_i ($000)	P_i	EV_i ($000)
100	.05	5	200	.05	10
200	.15	30	250	.15	37.5
300	.40	120	300	.40	120
400	.20	80	350	.20	70
500	.15	75	400	.15	60
600	.05	30	450	.05	22.5
Expected Value		340	Expected Value		320

The Standard Deviation of a Probability Distribution

DEFINITION: The *standard deviation* of a probability distribution shows the average absolute deviation of all possible outcomes from the expected value of that probability distribution. The deviation of each possible outcome from the expected value is weighted by the probability of each outcome occurring to find the weighted-average deviation. We seek the absolute deviations (that is, without regard to whether they are positive deviations (above the expected value) or negative deviations (below the expected value)), because we don't want the negative deviations to offset the positive deviations. We get rid of the minus signs on the negative deviations by first squaring the deviations and later taking the square root of the sum of weighted deviations. Symbolically,

$$\sigma = \sqrt{\sum_{i=1}^{n} (X_i - \text{EV})^2 P_i} \tag{2-1}$$

where σ (lower case *sigma*) is the conventional symbol used to denote standard deviation; Σ (upper case *sigma*) connotes the sum of the series of squared and weighted deviations from $i = 1, 2, 3, \ldots, n$; X_i represents the ith possible outcome; P_i the probability of that outcome; and EV is the expected value of the probability distribution.

EXAMPLE: Let us calculate the standard deviation for each of the probability distributions in the automobile manufacturer's decision problem introduced above. We show in Table 2-2 the full calculations. Column 1 lists the X_i possible outcomes and column 2 shows the expected value for each probability distribution, as calculated in Table 2-1. Column 3 shows the deviation of each possible outcome from the expected value, and column 4 is the square of each of these deviations. Column 5 repeats the probability information from Table 2-1, and column 6 is the product of columns 4 and 5 to find the weighted squared deviations of each possible outcome from the expected value.

The next step, as evident in Equation (2-1), is to find the sum of these weighted squared deviations, known as the *variance* of the probability distribution. The final step is to calculate the square root of the variance to find the standard deviation of the probability distribution. Notice that the standard deviation of decision A is 120, exactly twice the standard deviation of decision B, just as the range of outcomes for A was twice that for B. But, recall that the probability distributions were of the same shape; for example, 0.5 probability for the smallest possible outcome, 0.15 for the next, and so on. Different-shaped probability distributions would have caused the standard deviation of decision A to be more or less than twice the size of

TABLE 2-2. Calculation of the Standard Deviation for a Probability Distribution

			DECISION A		
X_i ($000) (1)	EV ($000) (2)	$X_i - EV$ ($000) (3)	$(X_i - EV)^2$ ($000) (4)	P_i (5)	$(X_i - EV)^2 P_i$ ($000) (6)
100	340	−240	57,600	.05	2,880
200	340	−140	19,600	.15	2,940
300	340	− 40	1,600	.40	640
400	340	60	3,600	.20	720
500	340	160	25,600	.15	3,840
600	340	260	67,600	.05	3,380
				Variance	14,400

Standard Deviation $= \sqrt{\text{Variance}} = 120.0$

			DECISION B		
X_i ($000) (1)	EV ($000) (2)	$X_i - EV$ ($000) (3)	$(X_i - EV)^2$ ($000) (4)	P_i (5)	$(X_i - EV)^2 P_i$ ($000) (6)
200	320	−120	14,400	.05	720
250	320	− 70	4,900	.15	735
300	320	− 20	400	.40	160
350	320	30	900	.20	180
400	320	80	6,400	.15	960
450	320	130	16,900	.05	845
				Variance	3,600

Standard Deviation $= \sqrt{\text{Variance}} = 60.0$

B's standard deviation, even though A's range of outcomes is exactly twice B's range of outcomes.[1]

Decision Trees and Joint Probabilities

When decisions made under conditions of uncertainty have cost and revenue implications in future periods, as well as in the present period, there will be probability distributions of outcomes in each period. Outcomes in later

---

[1] For example, if A's probability distribution was 0.025, 0.10, 0.45, 0.30, 0.10, and 0.025 for the six possible outcomes, respectively, its standard deviation would be *less* than twice B's standard deviation, since the extreme values have lower probabilities than before. Conversely, if the central outcomes had lower probabilities and the extreme outcomes had higher probabilities, the standard deviation of decision A would be *more* than twice that of decision B.

periods will, in some cases, be contingent upon the outcome of an earlier period, and the probability of a later outcome will depend in part on the probability of the earlier outcome. A useful tool for the analysis of more complex decision problems is the *decision tree*, so called because it illustrates the various consequences that follow from decisions in a chart resembling the branches of a tree. A decision tree is shown in Table 2-3 for the decision problem faced by a firm considering the installation of either a large capacity machine or a smaller capacity machine to produce metal stampings.

The branches of the decision tree show the outcomes which are expected in the first and second year after the decision is made. Three demand situations are thought possible; these are characterized as "heavy," "medium," or "light" demand. The profits associated with each demand situation, in nominal dollars, are shown in the table. With the large machine the expected outcomes for year one are profits of either $10,000 or $4,000, or a loss of $1,000. In the second year demand may change as compared with the first year. For example, the demand may be light the first year, yet be either

TABLE 2-3.   The Decision Tree for the Metal Stamping Machine Decision

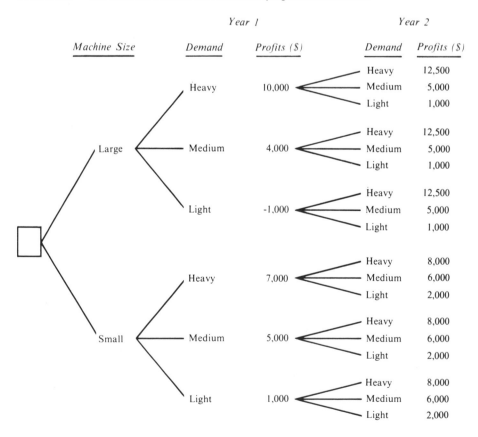

heavy, medium, or remain light in the second year. In this case we say that the second year's outcomes are *independent* of the first year's outcomes. Profits under each of the possible demand situations in the second year, for each decision alternative, are shown in the table. The level of profits that is expected to occur in each of the possible outcome situations apparently reflects the different cost situations of the large and small machines and the different prices that may be obtained under differing demand conditions. For the purposes of this simple example we shall assume that the product has a market life of only two years; that the large machine costs $2,000 initially, as compared with an initial cost of $1,700 for the small machine; that neither machine has any scrap value after two years; and that depreciation expense is not tax deductible.[2]

To decide which machine the firm should install we must evaluate the expected present value (EPV) of the profits promised by each alternative. First, we need to assign probabilities to the possible situations of heavy, medium, and light demand in each of the two years, and then we must choose the appropriate discount rate. Let us suppose that the results of market research into the demand for this particular product indicate that in the first year there is a 20-percent chance that demand will be heavy, a 30-percent chance that it will be medium, and a 50-percent chance that it will be light. The same research, however, indicates that in the second year there is a 40-percent chance that demand will be heavy, a 40-percent chance that it will be medium, and a 20-percent chance that it will be only light. On the issue of the appropriate discount rate we shall suppose that the firm could have earned 10 percent per annum by investing the necessary financial out lay in other assets of comparable risk. Therefore, we shall use a 10-percent opportunity discount rate (ODR) in evaluating the future profits from the enterprise. For the purposes of the discounted cash-flow analysis let us suppose that the first year's profits are received in lump sum at the end of year one and that the second year's profits are received at the end of year two.

The calculation of the expected present value from each of the two machines is shown in Tables 2-4 and 2-5. In each table, column 1 indicates the size and initial cost of the alternatives. Column 2 details the demand possibilities and the probabilities that these demand situations will occur, and column 3 shows the profits expected under each of the demand and plant combinations. Column 4 shows the present value of these profit levels, given a discount rate of 10 percent, which implies a discount factor of 0.909. The demand situations in year two and the profits derived from them are listed in columns 5 and 6. Column 7 shows the present value of the profits in column 6 using a discount factor of 0.826, since this is the present value

---

[2] The significance of the latter simplifying assumptions, if not known to you now, will become clear in Chapter 14 where the issue of capital budgeting is treated in more detail.

TABLE 2-4. Calculation of Expected Present Value for the Large Machine

Machine (cost) [1]	YEAR 1			YEAR 2			CALCULATION OF EPV		
	Demand (prob.) [2]	Profits [3]	PV (DF=.909) [4]	Demand (prob.) [5]	Profits [6]	PV (DF=.826) [7]	Total PV [8]	Joint Prob. [9]	Weighted PVs [10]
Large ($2,000)	Heavy (P = 0.2)	$10,000	$9,090	Heavy (P = 0.4)	$12,500	$10,325	$17,415	0.08	$1,393.20
				Medium (P = 0.4)	5,000	4,130	11,220	0.08	897.60
				Light (P = 0.2)	1,000	826	7,916	0.04	316.64
	Medium (P = 0.3)	4,000	3,636	Heavy (P = 0.4)	12,500	10,325	11,961	0.12	1,435.32
				Medium (P = 0.4)	5,000	4,130	5,766	0.12	691.92
				Light (P = 0.2)	1,000	826	2,462	0.06	147.72
	Light (P = 0.5)	−1,000	−909	Heavy (P = 0.4)	12,500	10,325	7,416	0.20	1,483.20
				Medium (P = 0.4)	5,000	4,130	1,221	0.20	244.20
				Light (P = 0.2)	1,000	826	−2,083	0.10	−208.30
							Expected present value		$6,401.50

TABLE 2-5. Calculation of Expected Present Value for the Small Machine

Machine (cost) [1]	YEAR 1			YEAR 2			CALCULATION OF EPV		
	Demand (prob.) [2]	Profits [3]	PV (DF=.909) [4]	Demand (prob.) [5]	Profits [6]	PV (DF=.826) [7]	Total PV [8]	Joint Prob. [9]	Weighted PVs [10]
	Heavy (P=0.2)	$7,000	$6,363	Heavy (P=0.4)	$8,000	$6,608	$11,271	0.08	$ 901.68
				Medium (P=0.4)	6,000	4,956	9,619	0.08	769.52
				Light (P=0.2)	2,000	1,652	6,315	0.04	252.60
Small ($1,700)	Medium (P=0.3)	5,000	4,545	Heavy (P=0.4)	8,000	6,608	9,453	0.12	1,134.36
				Medium (P=0.4)	6,000	4,956	7,801	0.12	936.12
				Light (P=0.2)	2,000	1,652	4,497	0.06	269.82
	Light (P=0.5)	1,000	909	Heavy (P=0.4)	8,000	6,608	5,817	0.20	1,163.40
				Medium (P=0.4)	6,000	4,956	4,165	0.20	833.00
				Light (P=0.2)	2,000	1,652	861	0.10	86.10
							Expected present value		$6,346.60

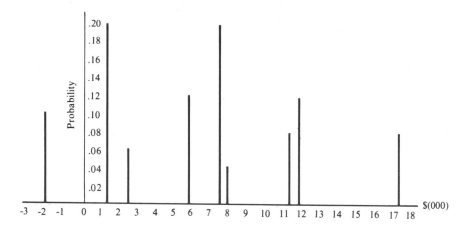

FIGURE 2-1.   Probability Distribution of the Outcomes Associated with the Large Machine

of $1.00 received two years hence, given the 10-percent ODR. Column 8 shows the aggregate present value of the profits of years one and two, minus the initial cost of the machine (which is already in present-value terms). Column 9 shows the probability that each of these total present values will be achieved. Note that these probabilities are *joint* probabilities, since being at each particular branch of the tree depends upon the preceding year's activity. The appropriate probability, then, is the product of the probability that demand will be heavy in the first year and, for example, also heavy in the second year. Thus the joint probability of the uppermost branch is 0.08, which is the product of 0.2 times 0.4. In column 10 the expected present value of the alternatives is calculated by summing the weighted present values. It can be seen that the large machine has an expected present value of $6,401.50, as compared with the small machine's $6,346.60. The

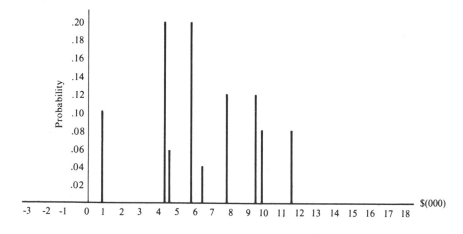

FIGURE 2-2.   Probability Distribution of the Outcomes Associated with the Small Machine

INTRODUCTION

expected-value criterion would therefore suggest the implementation of the large machine.

As we have noted, however, the expected-value criterion does not take into account the risk of the possible outcomes. It can be seen from column 8 of the two tables that the outcomes for the large machine vary over a wider range than do the outcomes for the small machine. These outcomes are plotted in Figures 2-1 and 2-2 as a probability distribution. It is apparent that the degree of risk associated with the large machine is greater than for the small machine, since the actual outcome may lie quite distant from the expected value; moreover, these distant outcomes have relatively large probabilities of occurring.

TABLE 2-6. Calculation of the Standard Deviation for the Large and Small Machine Decision

Large Machine

X_i $000	EV $000	$X_i - EV$ $000	$(X_i - EV)^2$ $000	P_i	$(X_i - EV)^2 P_i$ $000
17.415	6.4015	11.0135	121.297	0.08	9.7038
11.220	6.4015	4.8185	23.218	0.08	1.8574
7.916	6.4015	1.5145	2.294	0.04	0.0917
11.961	6.4015	5.5595	30.908	0.12	3.7090
5.766	6.4015	−0.6355	0.404	0.12	0.0485
2.462	6.4015	−3.9395	15.520	0.06	0.9312
7.416	6.4015	1.0145	1.029	0.20	0.2058
1.221	6.4015	−5.1805	26.838	0.20	5.3675
−2.083	6.4015	−8.4845	71.987	0.10	7.1987
				Variance	29.1136

Standard Deviation = $\sqrt{\text{Variance}}$ = 5.3957 or $5,395.70

Small Machine

X_i $000	EV $000	$X_i - EV$ $000	$(X_i - EV)^2$ $000	P_i	$(X_i - EV)^2 P_i$ $000
11.271	6.3466	4.9244	24.250	0.08	1.9400
9.619	6.3466	3.2724	10.709	0.08	0.8567
6.315	6.3466	−0.0316	0.001	0.04	0.0000
9.453	6.3466	3.1064	9.650	0.12	1.1580
7.801	6.3466	1.4544	2.115	0.12	0.2538
4.497	6.3466	−1.8496	3.421	0.06	0.2053
5.817	6.3466	−0.5296	0.281	0.20	0.0561
4.165	6.3466	−2.1816	4.759	0.20	0.9519
0.861	6.3466	−5.4856	30.092	0.10	3.0092
				Variance	8.4309

Standard Deviation = $\sqrt{\text{Variance}}$ = 2.9036 or $2,903.60

In order to quantify the degree of risk associated with each of the decision alternatives, we will calculate the standard deviation of the probability distributions represented by columns 8 and 9 in Tables 2-4 and 2-5. Note that column 8 in each table represents the nine possible outcomes after two years, and column 9 represents the (joint) probability of achieving each of the possible outcomes. You will note that the joint probabilities add up to 1.0 in each case, as they must if all possible outcomes are included, and these outcomes are mutually exclusive. The calculations for the standard deviation for each probability distribution are shown in Table 2-6. The standard deviation for the large machine decision alternative is $5,395.70, and it is $2,903.60 for the small machine. Thus, the degree of risk associated with the large machine is substantially greater, as was evident from the dispersion of outcomes in Table 2-4.

In this section we have defined the degree of risk as the dispersion of possible outcomes around the expected value of those outcomes, and we have introduced the standard deviation as the appropriate measure of the degree of risk. Later in this chapter we shall utilize the standard deviation to adjust for risk in decision making, but first let us clarify what is meant by *risk aversion*, *risk preference*, and *risk neutrality*.

Risk Aversion, Risk Preference, and Risk Neutrality

DEFINITION: *Risk aversion* is defined as the feeling of disutility caused by uncertainty. That is, the dispersion of possible outcomes of an act causes the risk averter to experience psychic dissatisfaction, or disutility. In general, we expect business decision makers to be risk averse: That is, they do not like risk *per se* and are only prepared to undertake risky situations if adequately compensated for bearing the risk involved. Risk averters regard risk as a "bad"—an item which gives them disutility—as compared with a "good"—one which gives them utility. Risk averters accept risk only if they at the same time expect to gain sufficient utility from the return (or profits) associated with the proposed investment project. The greater the risk perceived, the greater the return the investor requires to offset that risk. Conversely, risk averters are willing to accept lower expected returns if these are associated with lower degrees of risk. This risk-return trade-off is the characteristic of a risk averter: he or she is prepared to take risks, but only if there is sufficient compensation expected.

We can depict a risk averter's preference structure between risk and return in terms of indifference-curve analysis, which we shall examine in detail in the following chapter. It will suffice to say here that indifference curves are lines joining combinations of variables which give the consumer, or decision maker in this case, the same amount of utility. Thus, the decision maker will be indifferent as to which combination is chosen. We shall show in Chapter 3 that higher indifference curves are preferred to lower indifference curves, that indifference curves do not meet or intersect, and that they are convex to the origin. Indifference curves showing combinations of goods from which the consumer derives utility will be negatively sloping throughout, since more of one good must be combined with less of the other good in order for the consumer to remain indifferent between the combinations. But, since a risk averter gains utility from returns (or profits) and disutility from risk, the indifference curves are not like the negatively sloped ones of consumer-behavior analysis. Rather, they are *positively* sloping to reflect the fact that risk is a "bad" and that it generates disutility rather than utility.

In Figure 2-3 we show risk—measured by the standard deviation of possible profit levels—on the horizontal axis, and we show returns—measured by the expected value of the possible profit levels—on the vertical axis. Three arbitrarily chosen indifference curves are shown as I_1 to I_3. The direction of preference is upward and to the left—that is, I_1 is preferred to I_2, and I_2 is preferred to I_3. Notice that the indifference curves are convex from below, just as in the regular case, reflecting diminishing marginal utility of expected profits and increasing marginal disutility of risk.

EXAMPLE: Suppose the decision maker is considering four different solutions to a particular decision problem, which we shall identify as decision alternatives A, B, C, and D. Point A in Figure 2-3 represents decision A, which has expected present value E_2 and standard deviation σ_2. The decision maker is indifferent between this project and the zero-risk, zero-return situation represented by the origin. You can see that the decision maker requires E_2 dollars of expected return to compensate for bearing σ_2 dollars of standard deviation, or risk. Note that decision A is preferred to decision B, which has the same expected value but higher risk, σ_3. Similarly, decision C is preferred to both A and B, since it has the same expected value but lower risk, σ_1. Finally, decision D is regarded as equally desirable to decision B, but it is inferior to both A and C. Decision D has the same risk as A but less ex-

FIGURE 2-3. Indifference Curves for a Risk Averter in Risk-Return Space

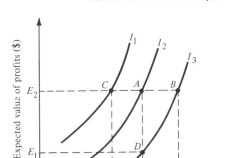

pected profits, and has both more risk and less return, as compared with decision C.

NOTE: The slope of the indifference curves between risk and return indicate the individual's degree of risk aversion. The slope of an indifference curve represents the individual's *marginal rate of substitution* (MRS) between the two variables under consideration. In the present case, one is a "good" and the other is a "bad," but the slope of the indifference curve still shows the rate at which the individual is just willing (without losing or gaining utility) to substitute one variable for the other. In Figure 2-3, the individual regards decisions D and B as equally desirable, and his MRS of return for risk over the intervening range is equal to the ratio AD/AB. Given point D as a starting place, the decision maker is indifferent toward decision B, which has both extra risk $(\sigma_3 - \sigma_2)$ and extra profit $(E_2 - E_1)$. To be more precise, the decision maker's MRS is the amount of expected return he or she requires before accepting an extra unit of risk. You can see that the individual's MRS between risk and return is positive and increases as the level of risk and return increase, due to the diminishing marginal utility of expected profits and the increasing marginal disutility of risk.

Differing Degrees of Risk Aversion. Different people have different degrees of risk aversion. Graphically this is reflected in steeper or flatter indifference curves in risk-return space. In Figure 2-4, we show a person with a relatively high degree of risk aversion contrasted with a person whose preferences indicate a relatively low degree of risk aversion. Points A and D are the same on both graphs. Project D is inferior to project A, since for the same expected return, E_0, it has the larger risk, σ_1. In both cases the person would accept the risk level σ_1 only if this is accompanied by an expected profit larger than that of project A. How much additional expected profit would it take to

FIGURE 2-4. Different Degrees of Risk Aversion

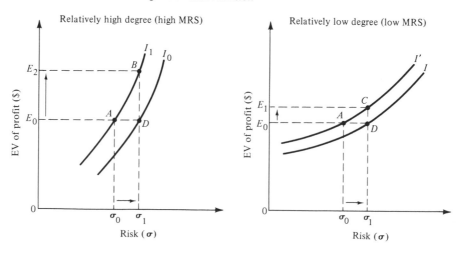

FIGURE 2-5. Risk Preference and Risk Neutrality

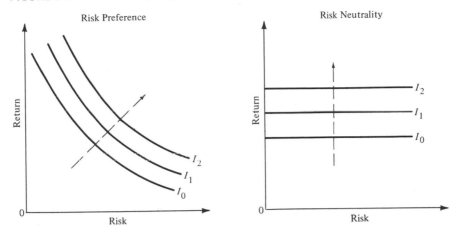

make each person indifferent between project A and a project containing σ_1 units of risk? The more risk-averse person in the left-hand graph requires DB dollars in order to remain at the same level of utility and thus has a relatively high MRS of return for risk, measured by the ratio BD/AD. The less risk-averse person on the right-hand side requires only the considerably smaller amount of extra expected profit, DC dollars, for the extra risk, $\sigma_1 - \sigma_0$, and thus exhibits a relatively low MRS of return for risk measured by the ratio CD/AD.

Risk Preference and Risk Neutrality.   Risk preference and risk neutrality are not common among business decision makers. Consumers, on the other hand, may show risk preference or neutrality in such situations as gambling, sporting, and recreational activities. Risk preference means that risk is viewed as a utility-producing good, and so the individual's indifference curves are negatively sloping as in the left-hand graph of Figure 2-5. Such an individual is prepared to give up expected profits for a larger amount of risk. For example, a gambler might prefer a game in which the risk is greater (odds are poorer) and the expected value of gains is lower, over a safer bet on another game in which the expected value is somewhat higher.

Risk neutrality means that the individual is completely indifferent to risk, receiving neither utility nor disutility from risk regardless of the amount of risk involved. Such an individual's indifference curves would be horizontal, as in the right-hand graph of Figure 2-5. The arrow shows the direction of preference—more expected profit is preferred to less, regardless of the risk. Consider an athlete who desperately wants to win the final game of the season. This individual will do whatever is necessary to help his team score or to prevent the opposition from scoring. Thus, hockey players block shots on goal with their faces and bodies, football players make suicidal plays that could easily result in broken bones, and racing drivers attempt that final pass on the last turn before the checkered flag.

2.3   ADJUSTMENT FOR RISK IN DECISION MAKING

In this section we examine several methods by which the risk-averse decision maker can compare decision alternatives on a *risk-adjusted* basis and select the alternative that best serves the firm's objective function, subject to the decision maker's degree of risk aversion. The first two methods, the coefficient-of-variation criterion and the expected-value criterion using different discount rates, are relatively crude measures conceptually, but at least they can be calculated and compared with little difficulty, thus saving search costs. The third method, the certainty-equivalent criterion, is conceptually elegant but its application presents certain problems. The fourth method, the maximin criterion, although appropriate in only a limited range of situations, allows the decision maker to avoid the worst outcomes.

Coefficient-of-Variation Criterion

DEFINITION: The *coefficient of variation* is defined as the ratio of the standard deviation to the expected value. The coefficient of variation for a probability distribution thus indicates the amount of standard deviation, or risk, per dollar of expected value, or return.

EXAMPLE: In the large machine-small machine example discussed earlier we calculated both the expected value and the standard deviation for each decision alternative. For the large machine the standard deviation was $5,395.70 and the expected value was $6,401.50. The ratio of these figures, or the coefficient of variation, is 0.8429. For the small machine the standard deviation was $2,903.60 and the expected value was $6,346.60. The coefficient of variation for the small machine is, thus, only 0.4575. In effect, these figures say that the large plant promises a little over $0.84 average absolute deviation from the expected value, per $1.00 of expected value. The small machine, on the other hand, offers a little less than $0.46 average absolute deviation from the expected value, per $1.00 of expected value.

RULE: The coefficient-of-variation decision criterion involves choosing the decision alternative with the lowest coefficient of variation. It thus selects the alternative with the least risk per $1.00 of return, or the least return-adjusted risk. The reciprocal of the coefficient of variation, namely the ratio of expected value to standard deviation is, conversely, a measure of risk-adjusted return. Choosing the alternative with the smaller coefficient of variation, thus, amounts to choosing the alternative with the larger risk-adjusted return.

It is important to note that the coefficient of variation may lead to a wrong decision in some instances, because it does not account for differing degrees of risk aversion. We shall return to this issue after discussing the certainty-equivalent criterion, later in this section.

The Expected-Value Criterion Using Different Discount Rates

An alternative method of adjusting the expected-value criterion for risk is to use higher discount rates for the more risky decision alternatives. Recall that the opportunity discount rate (ODR) is the best rate of interest that could be earned elsewhere at the same degree of risk. Thus, if one decision alternative has a dispersion of outcomes (and resulting standard deviation value) similar to a corporate bond issue yielding 10 percent and another decision alternative has a dispersion of outcomes similar to a 12-percent corporate bond issue, the appropriate ODRs are 10 percent and 12 percent, respectively.

EXAMPLE: Looking back at the large-machine—small-machine decision, we note that the dispersions (and the standard deviations) of the two alternatives are significantly different. Suppose 10 percent is the correct ODR for the small machine, but that the risk of the large machine's expected outcomes is similar to that of a 12-percent bond issue. In Table 2-7 we show the calculation of the EPV of the large-machine decision using the 12-percent discount factors shown. As you can see, discounting the expected cash flows by the higher rate reduces the EPV to $6,150.67. This is now substantially less than the small machine's $6,346.60. Thus, the expected-value criterion, using different ODRs, now favors the decision to purchase the small machine, just as the coefficient-of-variation criterion did.

RULE: The expected-value decision criterion, adjusted for differing risks of decision alternatives, involves selecting the alternative with the greatest expected value (or EPV), after each alternative has been discounted using the appropriate opportunity discount rate.

NOTE: You may be wondering why we didn't discount the large machine-small machine alternatives at different discount rates in the first instance. Essentially, there are two different ways to adjust the EPV criterion for risk. One is to discount both (or all) decision alternatives at the same discount rate and then use the coefficient of variation as the risk-adjusted expected value criterion. The second method is to foresee the different degrees of risk involved in the different decision alternatives and to discount each alternative at its appropriate ODR. One method or the other may be used but not a combination of the two. For example, if you discount two alternatives at different ODRs and then calculate the coefficient of variation, you will have doubly adjusted for risk and may choose the wrong alternative.

These two methods are basically similar and would normally rank decision alternatives in the same order. But which one is superior? In terms of data required to use the criterion, the coefficient-of-variation criterion can be used with much lower search costs, as compared to the proper implementation of the "different ODR" criterion. The latter requires that a study be made of the dispersion of possible outcomes of a broad range of alterna-

TABLE 2-7. Expected Present Value of the Large-Machine Decision Using 12% ODR

Initial Cost ($) (1)	YEAR 1 Demand (prob.) (2)	YEAR 1 Profits ($) (3)	YEAR 1 PV DF=.8929 (4)	YEAR 2 Demand (prob.) (5)	YEAR 2 Profits ($) (6)	YEAR 2 PV DF=.7972 (7)	CALCULATION OF EPV Total PV ($) (8)	Joint prob. (9)	Weighted PV (10)
-2,000									
	Heavy (P=0.2)	10,000	8,929	Heavy (P=0.4)	12,500	9,965	16,894	0.08	1,351.52
				Medium (P=0.4)	5,000	3,986	10,915	0.08	873.20
				Light (P=0.2)	1,000	797	7,726	0.04	309.05
	Medium (P=0.3)	4,000	3,572	Heavy (P=0.4)	12,500	9,965	11,537	0.12	1,384.39
				Medium (P=0.4)	5,000	3,986	5,558	0.12	666.90
				Light (P=0.2)	1,000	797	2,369	0.06	142.13
	Light (P=0.5)	-1,000	-893	Heavy (P=0.4)	12,500	9,965	7,072	0.20	1,414.42
				Medium (P=0.4)	5,000	3,986	1,093	0.20	218.62
				Light (P=0.2)	1,000	797	-2,096	0.10	-209.57
							Expected Present Value		$6,150.67

tive investments, so that the correct ODR may be ascertained for each decision alternative. The coefficient-of-variation criterion is usually implemented using the firm's *cost of capital* as the discount rate. Since the firm knows its cost of capital (the rate of interest which the firm pays to borrow funds), the firm does not need an extensive search procedure each time it makes a decision.[3]

The Certainty Equivalent Criterion

DEFINITION: The *certainty equivalent* of a gamble (or decision alternative with more than one possible outcome) is the sum of money, available with certainty, that would cause the decision maker to be indifferent between taking the gamble and accepting the certain sum of money.

EXAMPLE: Suppose that I offer to give you either $0.50 or "toss you" for double or nothing. If you accept the $0.50, that means you prefer the certain sum ($0.50) to the gamble which has two possible outcomes ($1.00 or nothing). To find your point of indifference I would now offer you the choice of $0.30 with certainty or the toss for $1.00 or nothing. Suppose you now prefer to take the gamble. Somewhere between $0.30 and $0.50 is your certainty equivalent of the gamble. Suppose that after several more offers I find that you are indifferent between accepting $0.42 with certainty and taking the gamble. Thus, your certainty equivalent (CE) for that gamble is $0.42. In effect, the CE is the sum of money that will almost bribe you to give up the gamble.

The notion of an individual's certainty equivalent involves the concept of utility and indifference, and it incorporates the decision maker's degree of risk aversion (or risk preference). The more risk-averse decision maker would exhibit a lower CE than a less risk-averse (or a risk-preferring) decision maker for the same gamble. Moreover, it can incorporate other considerations as well. If the gamble is to be repeated many times, we would expect the CE to be equal to the expected value (in this case $0.50). If the gamble is to be taken just once or a few times, we expect a risk averter's CE to be less than the EV. In effect, the risk averter is trading off expected return for

---

[3]See Eugene F. Brigham, *Financial Management Theory and Practice*, 2nd ed. (Hinsdale, Ill.: The Dryden Press, 1979), pp. 555-593.

Note that the firm's cost-of-capital (CC) may or may not be equal to the firm's opportunity discount rate. The rate at which the firm borrows will most likely be one or two percentage points above the rate at which it could lend money (because of the interest rate differential from which banks make their money) and, thus, the cost of capital may understate the ODR. Using the CC as the ODR in these circumstances tends to *overdiscount* and, thus, understate the EPV of the decision alternative. Business people are often relatively conservative, however, and prefer to err on the low side just in case their predictions of demand and profits turn out to be too optimistic. But note also that the firm's CC reflects the lender's view of the risk of the firm, rather than the firm's view of the risk of the decision alternative. Thus, the CC may be above, below, or equal to the ODR, depending on the circumstances.

removal of the risk. Conversely, a risk preferrer's CE is expected to exceed the EV, since this person gets utility from risk and will require more than the gamble's EV to be bribed into giving it up. Finally, suppose a person is desperate for a given sum of money. For example, a student needs $0.75 to wire home and ask for more money: That individual's CE is likely to be $0.75. Any lesser sum doesn't solve the problem, and the student will be prepared to gamble for the best payoff until assured of the $0.75 with certainty. This person, whatever his or her usual attitude towards risk, would be acting like a risk preferrer in this instance.

Expressed in terms of indifference-curve analysis, the certainty equivalent of a gamble (or a decision alternative) can be shown as the point on the vertical axis joined by an indifference curve to the gamble under consideration.

EXAMPLE: In Figure 2-6 we show the two decision alternatives introduced as the large machine-small machine decision problem earlier. Note that we have shown the small machine as the preferred alternative, since it lies on the higher indifference curve. The point CE_S on the expected-value axis is the certainty equivalent of the combination of expected value and risk represented by point S. It is the certainty equivalent because *risk*, on the horizontal axis, has been reduced to zero and, thus, the decision maker is indifferent between $$CE_S$ with certainty and $6,346.60 with risk (standard deviation of $2,903.60). Similarly, the certainty equivalent of the large machine, point L, is $$CE_L$.

RULE: The certainty-equivalent criterion involves selecting the decision alternative which has the highest certainty equivalent. Note that since indifference

FIGURE 2-6.   **Certainty Equivalents of the Large Machine-Small Machine Decision**

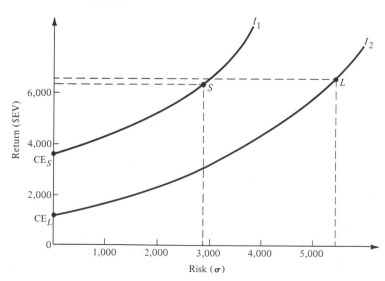

INTRODUCTION

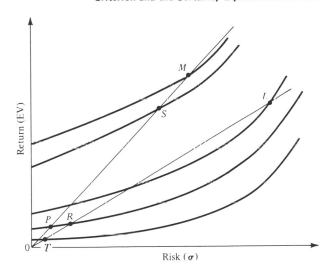

curves neither meet nor intersect and since higher curves are preferred to
lower curves, the certainty-equivalent criterion is entirely consistent with the
utility theory of rational consumer (or decision-making) behavior.

Unfortunately, we are now in a position to see that the earlier methods
of adjusting for risk, namely, the coefficient-of-variation and the EV criterion using different discount rates, are not entirely consistent with utility
theory and may sometimes indicate the choice of a decision alternative
which would not be optimal in terms of the decision maker's utility. Consider Figure 2-7 in which the points S and L, for the small and large machine
alternatives are shown on rays emanating from the origin. The slopes of these
rays reflect the ratio of expected value to standard deviation or what we
have earlier called risk-adjusted return. The slope of each ray is equal to the
reciprocal of the coefficient of variation. Thus, as we saw earlier, the small
machine, point S, is preferred to the large machine, point L, on the basis of
both the coefficient-of-variation and the certainty-equivalent criteria.

But consider points M and P which have the same value for their coefficient of variation as point S, yet are ranked differently in terms of their certainty equivalents: M is preferred to S, which in turn is preferred to P. The
coefficient-of-variation criterion is unable to distinguish between M, S, and
P and ranks them as equals. In effect, it says that the ray from the origin
$0PSM$ is an indifference curve, with all points on it giving equal utility (or
certainty equivalent) to the decision maker. Similarly, it effectively says
that the ray $0TRL$ is a *lower* indifference curve, with all points on that ray
regarded as equal, but inferior to any point on the higher ray $0PSM$. The
curvilinear indifference curves shown in Figure 2-7 indicate that this is
untrue for the case presented: L is preferred to R, which in turn is preferred

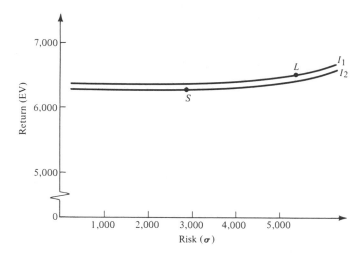

FIGURE 2-8. Coefficient-of-Variation Criterion Refuted for a
Slightly Risk-Averse Decision Maker

to T, and, moreover, L is preferred to P, and R is equivalent to P, despite P's lower coefficient of variation (or higher risk-adjusted return).

Thus, although the coefficient-of-variation criterion correctly ranked points S and L, it incorrectly ranked most of the other points shown! In fact, the coefficient-of-variation criterion may incorrectly rank S and L for a particular decision maker. In Figure 2-8 we show a decision maker who is only slightly risk averse (with very low marginal rate of substitution of expected return for risk) who *prefers* point L over point S. Point L lies on a higher indifference curve for this individual and, accordingly, has a higher certainty equivalent. Note that the expected-value criterion with different discount rates also incorrectly ranked the small versus large machine alternatives for this particular decision maker and would similarly make mistakes between other pairs of decision alternatives.

Why does this problem arise? Essentially, the coefficient-of-variation criterion, and the EV criterion using different ODRs, assume a linear and constant tradeoff between risk and return. In fact, most risk averters exhibit a nonlinear risk-return tradeoff. In economic terms we explain this as diminishing marginal utility of wealth and increasing marginal disutility of risk. The more wealth (expected return) one is offered, the less utility one receives from the marginal dollar, and the more risk one is offered, the greater the disutility one receives from the marginal unit of risk.

Should we throw away the coefficient-of-variation and the EV criterion using different ODRs and simply use the certainty equivalent? Without doubt the latter gives the better answers for maximizing the decision maker's utility function. This might be quite different from maximizing the firm's objective function, however. For the firm with a single owner-manager, maximizing net worth and maximizing the decision maker's utility may well amount to the same thing, but for a widely-held firm with a variety of decision makers within the management team, it is not at all clear that maximizing managerial utility will lead to the maximization of net worth. One could argue that the firm *does* have a constant tradeoff between risk and return. More importantly, perhaps, the coefficient-of-variation criterion, and the EV using different ODRs to a lesser extent, can be calculated and subjected to scrutiny, whereas certainty equivalents and utility are more cerebral and intuitive notions that are more difficult to defend quantitatively.

RULE: The solution to this apparent impasse is to use all three methods with caution and with reservations. For example, one would say that the small machine appears to be preferable on a risk-adjusted basis, unless the firm is only very slightly risk averse, to the extent that the firm would be willing to accept an additional \$2,492.10 standard deviation (that is \$5,395.70 − \$2,903.60) for an additional \$54.90 expected return (that is, \$6,401.50 − \$6,346.60). The caveat attached to this recommendation can be settled by management consensus (or by the boss's opinion). If the consensus is that the extra risk should be undertaken for the extra expected return, the simple risk-adjustment criterion is overturned. Alternatively, if the consensus (or the owner's opinion) is not to accept the extra risk for the extra return, the simple risk-adjustment criterion is supported.

NOTE: In many cases there will be no doubt which decision alternatives dominate others for the risk-averse decision maker or firm. Consider Figure 2-9 in which we show one of several possible outcomes, labeled point A. Relative to point A, we show quadrants I, II, III, and IV. Any point in quadrant IV is unambiguously superior to point A (for a risk averter) since it has either more return for the same or less risk, or less risk for the same return. Simi-

FIGURE 2-9.   Superior and Inferior Quadrants with respect to a Particular Decision Alternative

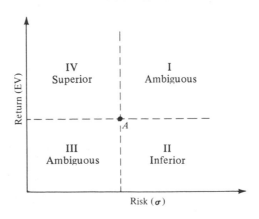

larly, any point in quadrant *II* is unambiguously inferior to point *A*, having either less return for the same or more risk, or more risk for the same return. Quadrants *I* and *III*, relative to point *A*, on the other hand, do represent potential areas of conflict between the coefficient-of-variation and the EV criteria using different ODRs, on the one hand, and the certainty-equivalent criterion on the other. Points in quadrant *I* have both more risk and more return, and in quadrant *III* there is both less risk and less return. When decision alternatives fall in quadrants *I* and *III* with respect to each other, one must use the "caution and reservation" rule suggested above.

The Maximin Decision Criterion

DEFINITION: The *maximin* is the term given to the largest (the maximum) of the smallest outcomes (the minimums) associated with each decision alternative.

EXAMPLE: Using the large machine-small machine decision outlined earlier, there are nine possible outcomes after two years for each alternative, depending upon whether demand was heavy-heavy, heavy-medium, heavy-light, and so forth. The nine possible outcomes were shown in column 8 in Table 2-4 for the large machine and in Table 2-5 for the small machine. The minimum outcomes are expected to be −$2,083 for the large machine and $861 for the small machine. The maximin outcome is, thus, $861, the larger of the smallest outcomes.

RULE: The maximin decision criterion is to select the alternative containing the maximin outcome. Thus, the maximin criteria also selects the small machine in preference to the large machine.

In effect, the maximin criterion rules out every decision alternative except the one with the best of the worst outcomes. This is a risk averter's decision criterion in the sense that it avoids alternatives which contain worse "downside" outcomes. But note that it also ignores the probability distribution and would have chosen the small machine even if its worst outcome probability was high and the large plant's worst outcome probability was very low. Note also that the maximin criterion ignores all other outcomes. The large machine shows several relatively high outcomes, yet these don't enter into consideration at all.

When is the maximin criteria appropriate? For repeated decisions it is clearly too pessimistic, always expecting the worst to happen, when, in fact, the law of averages should cause the EV to be attained (on average) over many trials. For a one-shot deal, however, where the firm simply cannot afford to suffer the worst outcomes associated with some of the decision alternatives, the maximin criterion may be appropriate.

EXAMPLE: In the large-machine—small-machine decision, suppose that any loss over $1,000 would cause the firm to go bankrupt and be liquidated by its creditors. The decision maker might then be unwilling to take the risk of the $2,083 loss associated with the large machine and choose the small machine to avoid the possibility of a loss exceeding $1,000.

Similarly, a decision maker looking for a promotion in the near future may reason that a loss resulting from one of his or her decisions will most likely prevent that promotion, and may decide to apply the maximin criterion. Thus, in particular situations, usually involving relatively short time horizons in which the law of averages cannot be relied on and in which the firm or the decision maker cannot afford the outcomes associated with some of the decision alternatives, the maximin criterion may be appropriate.

Which Criterion Should Be Applied?

The choice among the various decision criteria available depends upon three major factors. First, one must consider the frequency with which one is confronted by the particular decision. Second, one must consider the magnitude of the gamble. Third, the decision maker's attitude toward risk and uncertainty is important. To illustrate each of these factors we shall consider another example, that of insurance.

EXAMPLE: Suppose a firm has two major insurance contracts: one for collision damage to its fleet of automobiles and the other for fire damage to its plant and buildings. The firm is considering whether it should renew these contracts or carry the risk itself. The risk is known to the firm from insurance company data. The odds are 5 in 100 that each of the company's vehicles will be damaged to a mean value of $5,000. Hence, the expected value of the damage is $250 per vehicle. The insurance company, however, charges a premium of $275 per vehicle, since it wishes to contribute to its overhead expenses and profits. The odds are 1 in 1,000 that the company's plant will burn down. The value of the plant is $10 million, and thus the expected value of the possible loss is $10,000. The insurance company's premium for this policy is $11,000. Will the firm carry its own insurance? Let us consider the three factors mentioned above.

First, regarding the frequency with which the company takes the particular gamble, we must remember that risk involves the law of averages. If one runs the risk a large number of times, one might reasonably expect to win and lose in the same proportions as the general population. On the other hand, if one runs the risk only once, then one might be fortunate enough to avoid the unhappy event of an accident or a fire; but, on the other hand, one might suffer all the bad luck all at once. In the case of the firm deciding to carry its own insurance, the automobiles represent a high frequency of taking the gamble. The company has, say, 100 vehicles, and this is a sufficiently large number that it might expect the probability of any one being damaged to be similar to the population of vehicles at large. On the other hand, the firm has only one plant and the frequency of this gamble is only once. It does not have one hundred plants; it does not take this gamble at a large number of locations; and, therefore, it should not expect the average vulnerability to fire damage.

Concerning the second factor, the magnitude of the gamble, the important point to consider here is whether or not the decision maker can afford

TABLE 2-8.   Auto Fleet Insurance Problem

	INSURE			NOT INSURE		
	Cost	Prob.	EV	Cost	Prob.	EV
Accidents	$−27,500	0.05	$− 1,375	$−500,000	0.05	$−25,000
No accidents	−27,500	0.95	−26,125	0	0.95	0
Expected value			$−27,500			$−25,000
Standard deviation			0			119,895.75
Coefficient of variation			0			4.80

the worst possible outcomes. That is, can it afford the loss it would sustain if things turned out very badly? In the case of our company considering its insurance, it is possible that it could withstand the (unlikely) loss of all its vehicles for a total loss of $500,000. On the other hand, the loss of the plant and buildings to the tune of $10 million would probably represent a significant setback to that company. Thus, the second factor would militate in favor of the company renewing its insurance policy for fire damage to the plant and buildings, but not for the automobile fleet.

The third factor, the decision maker's attitude toward risk and uncertainty, involves the individual's degree of risk preference or aversion. The crucial factor is the willingness of the decision maker to accept risk *and its consequences.* Thus, even though the first two factors above indicate that the firm should perhaps bear the risk on its motor vehicles, the attitude of the decision maker might be such that the policy will be renewed. Alternatively, even though the first two factors above indicate that the firm should probably renew its insurance for fire damage for that plant, a risk-preferring decision maker might decide to cancel that policy.

Tables 2-8 and 2-9 show the payoffs, expected values, standard deviations, and coefficients of variation for each of the two problems confronting the firm. From these data we can choose the appropriate decision using each of several criteria discussed above. Using the expected-value criterion, the decision maker would insure neither the fleet of automobiles nor the plant and buildings. Under the maximin and coefficient-of-variation criteria, the decision maker would insure both the fleet and the plant buildings. Under

TABLE 2-9.   Plant and Buildings Insurance Problem

	INSURE			NOT INSURE		
	Cost	Prob.	EV	Cost	Prob.	EV
Fire	$−11,000	0.001	$ −11	$−10,000,000	0.001	$−10,000
No fire	−11,000	0.999	−10,989	0	0.999	0
Expected value			$−11,000			$−10,000
Standard deviation			0			316,701.75
Coefficient of variation			0			31.67

TABLE 2-10. Comparing Decision Criteria

Criterion	Auto Fleet	Plant and Buildings
Expected value	Not insure	Not insure
Maximin	Insure	Insure
Coefficient of variation	Insure	Insure
Certainty equivalent	(Not insure?)	(Insure?)

the certainty-equivalent criterion, we are unable to say, since this depends upon the decision maker's individual attitude toward bearing risk and uncertainty. On the basis of the three factors considered above, however, we may hazard a guess that under this criterion a risk-averse decision maker would choose to renew the insurance policy on the plant and buildings, and possibly to allow the collision policy on its fleet of cars to lapse. This information is summarized in Table 2-10.

Noneconomic Factors in Decision Making

Modern business firms are typically complex organizations in which decisions are made at several levels by a variety of decision makers. In such a system it would be surprising if the firm's objectives were completely served by every decision made. Instead, we should expect the presence of certain noneconomic factors, such as instances of self-serving behavior by decision makers, misplaced efforts fostered by inappropriate reward systems, and a preference for nonmonetary objectives in place of some degree of profitability. Let us discuss each of these in turn.

Robbins has defined *organizational politics* as including any behavior by an organizational member that is self-serving.[4] Political behavior by the decision maker may be "functional" in that it operates to enhance the objectives of the organization, or it may be "dysfunctional" in that it hinders the attainment of the firm's objectives. Since in many cases the objectives of the decision maker and the firm may differ and since the decision maker has the power to make the decision, we should not expect the decision to necessarily reflect the single-minded pursuit of the organization's objectives. The personal gains to the decision maker include a wide variety of tangible and intangible benefits, such as power, prestige, comfort, insulation from a competitive environment, job security, promotion, and perhaps even bribes and/or goods and services received in appreciation of a particular decision. These political gains accrue not to the firm but to the decision maker personally. Hence, we may see a decision taken that appears irrational, in the

---

[4]Stephen P. Robbins, *The Administrative Process* (Englewood Cliffs, N.J.: Prentice-Hall, Inc., 1977), p. 64.

sense that company objectives are not being pursued to the limit, but which is rational from the viewpoint of the decision maker.

Reward systems internal to the firm may cause behavior at variance with the firm's objectives. If an executive's salary, annual bonus, power, prestige, or other reward is dependent upon criteria such as maintaining market share or matching actual costs with budgeted costs, these criteria may become *de facto* objectives and may cause the firm's overall profits or net worth to fall short of what it might have been.[5] On the other hand, rewards for spectacular increases in profitability may induce decisions that although potentially highly profitable are also very risky, with the result that the firm's objectives would have been better served by an alternative project with a lower expected value and a lower risk attached. Similarly, if rewards are primarily associated with short-term profit performance, we may expect to see decisions made that cause immediate cash flow but which are inferior to alternative projects in terms of the total present values of the alternative projects.

The objectives of the firm itself and/or of the decision makers within the firm may include certain nonmonetary goals, such as an aesthetic business environment and a lack of anxiety from competitive pressures within and outside the firm. The gratification received from these factors may be expected to have a monetary equivalent that the firm and/or the decision maker is prepared to forego in order to attain these nonmonetary goals. Accordingly, we may expect that in practice some decisions will be taken that appear inferior in terms of the strictly economic criteria but which serve other noneconomic criteria to the overall satisfaction of the firm and/or the decision maker.

2.4 SEARCH COSTS AND THE VALUE OF INFORMATION

Search Costs

In an environment of uncertainty the firm lacks full information about the actual outcomes of its decision. If it chooses, it may engage in search activity to improve its information. Information can be improved by various means, starting with simple surveys of potential customers and progressing all the way to complex computer modelling and simulation. Advice and information can be purchased from consultants or the firm can engage its own personnel in search procedures. The information which decision makers often need will not simply be the raw data but will usually require adjustment in some way, such as finding the expected values and/or present values of the raw data. In addition, raw data will often need to be seasonally ad-

---

[5]See A. R. Cohen, H. Gadon, and G. Miaoulis, "Decision Making in Firms: The Impact of Non-Economic Factors," *Journal of Economic Issues*, 10, No. 2 (June 1976), pp. 242-58.

justed or deflated by a price index, in order to be in the form most useful to the decision maker. Naturally, this search process costs money, and the costs of obtaining information are usually inversely related to the speed with which the information must be generated.

DEFINITION: *Search costs* are defined as the costs of obtaining information in the form needed by the decision maker and within the time constraints required by the decision maker.

The Value of Information

DEFINITION: The *value of information* is defined as the difference between what you can earn with the information already held and what you could earn if you were to know with certainty the outcome prior to making the decision. In cases where the search costs are expected to be greater than the value of the information, the decision maker should proceed on the basis of the information already held and should not undertake the cost of obtaining any extra information, since its cost outweighs the benefits derived.

EXAMPLE: Recall once more the decision problem of the firm considering the installation of either the large metal-stamping machine or the small machine. Now, suppose that a market research firm offers to undertake some intensive studies in order to tell the firm what the state of demand will be over the two-year period, before the firm has to make its decision. The market research firm advises that its fee will be $1,000, including all expenses. Should the firm incur these search cost or not?

If the firm did know in advance the exact state of demand over the next two years (for example, that it would be medium in year one and heavy in year two), it would simply choose the alternative which offers the greatest net present value under those circumstances. Similarly, for any other state of demand—once this is known in advance—it becomes a simple decision that can be made under conditions of certainty, since a single outcome follows each decision.

In Table 2-11 we repeat the outcomes for each decision alternative under each of the nine jointly-possible states of demand. Given the prior information concerning the actual state of demand, the firm would select the machine with the highest PV of profits under that state of demand. The machine that should be chosen under each possible state of demand is indicated in column 4 of Table 2-11, with the resultant profits in column 5.

What is the probability that the market researchers will advise the firm that the actual state of demand will be heavy-heavy, for example? Prior to receiving the additional information the firm still has only its joint probability distribution shown in column 6. The firm's decision maker would weight each of the payoffs in column 5 by its prior probability of occurring, and add these weighted payoffs to find the expected present value of the decision under conditions of certainty. As we can see, this sum is $7,651.00.

TABLE 2-11.   Expected Value of Choosing the Best Alternative Given Full Prior Information

State of Demand $ (1)	PRESENT VALUE OF PROFITS IF Large Machine $ (2)	PRESENT VALUE OF PROFITS IF Small Machine $ (3)	Choice with Certainty (machine) (4)	Present Value of Profits (5)	Joint Probability (6)	Weighted PV's $ (7)
Heavy-heavy	17,415	11,271	Large	17,415	0.08	1,393.20
Heavy-medium	11,220	9,619	Large	11,220	0.08	897.60
Heavy-light	7,916	6,315	Large	7,916	0.04	316.64
Medium-heavy	11,961	9,453	Large	11,961	0.12	1,435.32
Medium-medium	5,766	7,801	Small	7,801	0.12	936.12
Medium-light	2,462	4,497	Small	4,497	0.06	269.82
Light-heavy	7,416	5,817	Large	7,416	0.20	1,483.20
Light-medium	1,221	4,165	Small	4,165	0.20	833.00
Light-light	−2,083	861	Small	861	0.10	86.10
				Expected Present Value		$7,651.00

NOTE: The value of information is the difference between this sum, $7,651.00, and the expected value of the best alternative with the information already held. The large machine had the higher EPV of profits, namely $6,401.50, and the difference is, therefore, $7,651.00 − $6,401.50 = $1,249.50. Thus, the value of information is $1,249.50, and the cost of that information is $1,000. The firm should hire the market researchers, since it expects to be $249.50 ahead by doing so.[6]

2.5   EVALUATION OF THE DECISION MADE

How do we evaluate decisions? What is a good decision? Is a decision a bad one if the actual outcome is bad? For example, if the firm chooses the large machine and the actual outcome is −$2,083 (the worst possible outcome foreseen), should the decision maker be castigated for the quality of his or her decision? The answer is "not necessarily." The quality of the decision depends on three main issues.

Three Basic Considerations

First, was the information search undertaken to the point where it would not be marginally profitable to continue the search procedure? Second, was the information obtained used in the appropriate form—for example, expected-

---

[6]We are assuming that the researchers' findings will be borne out by the firm's experience. Typically, the firm would require a substantial margin for error in case the "full information" turns out to be wrong.

present-value terms? Third, was the appropriate decision criterion used? If the answer is yes to all three questions, it *was* a good decision regardless of the actual outcome.

NOTE: The quality of decisions must be judged *a priori*, before the actual outcomes. Decision making under risk and uncertainty necessarily involves unsatisfactory outcomes from time to time. You win some and you lose some, but consistent application of the appropriate decision criterion, using as much good information as it seemed profitable to purchase, should ensure maximization of the firm's net worth, subject to risk considerations, over a series of decisions made. A bad decision will be made if the decision maker doesn't seek information when its cost is expected to be less than its value, if the decision maker ignores or discards information, or if an inappropriate decision criterion is used to make the decision. If such a decision turns out to be very profitable, the decision maker was just lucky and should not expect this luck to hold forever.

The Timing of the Decision

Since information tends to grow with the passage of time, decisions should not be made irrevocably before they *must* be made. A commitment made too early cannot (easily) be altered if new information comes along a little later. For example, if bids are solicited for a contract and the deadline for the submission of bids is at noon on the last day of the month, the firm should work through all the analysis and make a tentative decision (on the price of its bid), but it should delay submitting the bid until just before the deadline in case new information, such as a substantial increase in a major cost item or the bankruptcy of a major competitor, should come to light and cause the firm to want to change its commitment.

RULE: Whether or not there is a specific deadline, the timing rule is to defer the decision until the expected value of deferring the decision further is equal to the expected profits foregone by not making the decision. This does not mean procrastination, but rather that the decision maker should consider and attempt to quantify the advantages of waiting and actually make the decision when it is apparent that more is lost than gained by further waiting.

What if important additional information does arrive after the decision is made? This happens all the time. At that point a new decision problem occurs: Should the decision maker stick with the decision just made or make another decision, modifying the earlier decision or even completely rescinding the earlier decision despite the costs that this will involve. This new decision should be evaluated on the basis of the EPVs of each alternative, their relative risks, and so on. It may well be that the new decision is to stick with the *status quo*, or alternatively, to modify it in some way. Even if the new decision is to change the earlier decision, this does not make the earlier decision a bad one. If it was made on the basis of all information available at the time (after search had been carried to the optimal point), by the application of the appropriate decision criterion, and at a time when it appeared optimal to actually make the decision, then it was a good decision.

Sensitivity Analysis

Finally, the decision maker should consider the *sensitivity* of the decision to the assumptions on which it is based. All decisions are based on some assumptions—for example, that the data is accurate, that probability distributions will be validated by future events, that the discount rate used is appropriate, that fixed cost categories do not, in fact, vary with output levels, and so on.

DEFINITION: *Sensitivity Analysis* is defined as the examination of a decision to find the degree of inaccuracy in the underlying assumptions which can be tolerated without causing that decision to be inappropriate.

EXAMPLE: The expected present value of the large machine is $6,401.50, as compared with $6,346.60 for the small machine, a difference of only $54.90. If the costs of the large machine were underestimated by any figure over $54.90 (and the small plant's costs were accurately estimated), the decision should shift to the small machine. This figure, $54.90, represents less than 1 percent of the EPV of the large machine. Thus, we would say that the decision to install the large machine (on the basis of its higher EPV) is highly sensitive to the assumptions on which it is based. Such sensitivity should be considered explicitly, since it may induce further search activity to confirm or to revise the cost estimates, or alternatively it may convince the decision maker to select an alternative with less risk of cost variability. In effect, the decision maker may decide to trade off some expected profit against the reduced risk of cost variability. In every case the decision maker should be aware of the sensitivity of the decision to the validity of its underlying assumptions.

2.6 SUMMARY

In this chapter we have continued our examination of the basic foundations of economic decision making. The expected-present-value analysis of Chapter 1 was extended to incorporate risk analysis. Most business decision makers appear to be risk-averse; that is, they derive disutility from risk and uncertainty. The degree of risk can be measured by the standard deviation of the probability distribution of outcomes, and the degree of risk aversion can be measured by the rate at which the decision maker is willing to trade off expected value (or profits) for reduced risk. For complex decision alternatives with probability distributions of outcomes in each year there will be a joint probability distribution of outcomes at the end of the planning period. Such decision problems are best handled by the use of decision trees, which array the possible outcomes and joint probabilities in a manner which facilitates the understanding and the solution of the problem.

Four more decision criteria were introduced, each incorporating some method of adjustment for risk. The coefficient-of-variation criterion effectively makes the decision on the basis of the least risk per dollar of expected value. The expected-value criterion can be adjusted for risk by the use of differing discount rates for alternatives with differing degrees of risk. The certainty-equivalent criterion is more comprehensive than the above two, and adjusts for risk by choosing the decision alternative with the combination of risk and return which gives the decision maker the highest level of utility. Finally, the maximin decision criterion adjusts for risk in a crude way by avoiding the decision alternatives which have inferior "downside" outcomes. The appropriate criterion for any particular decision depends on the firm's and/or the decision maker's objectives, the frequency and magnitude of the decision, and the firm's and/or the decision maker's attitude towards risk. We noted that political and aesthetic considerations and inappropriate reward systems within the firm may result in a decision that does not completely serve the objective of the firm.

Search costs should be incurred up to the point where the value of additional information falls to equal the costs of obtaining that information.

Decisions should be evaluated on an *ex ante* basis, rather than on an *ex post* basis. Good decisions are those that are (1) based on properly adjusted information; (2) obtained from a search procedure taken to the optimal point; (3) found by applying the appropriate decision criterion; (4) made at the optimal point of time; and (5) suitably qualified by a statement of the sensitivity of the decision to the assumptions on which it is based.

DISCUSSION QUESTIONS

2-1.   Define risk and uncertainty. How can we measure risk and uncertainty? Can you think of any other, more appropriate, measure of risk and uncertainty?

2-2.   Define risk aversion. Does a risk averter refuse to take risks? Will a risk averter ever select the more risky alternative? Explain.

2-3.   Explain why a risk preferrer might prefer a high-risk, low-stakes gamble to a low-risk, high-stakes gamble. Are you a risk averter, a risk preferrer, or are you risk indifferent? How do you know?

2-4.   Demonstrate that the investor's *degree* of risk aversion (or preference) is an important element in determining his or her choice among investment alternatives.

2-5.   Go through the thought process of determining your own certainty equivalent for a fifty-cent lottery ticket that is one of 100,000 sold for a $10,000 prize.

    (a)   What is the expected value of the ticket?

    (b)   Would you buy such a ticket? Why?

    (c)   How much more or less expensive would the ticket need to be to *just* induce you to buy it?

    (d)   Is that price your certainty equivalent for the gamble? Explain.

2-6. The product manager of a large company has had a series of disastrous new-product offerings. He fears that another failure will cost him his job. He is currently trying to make up his mind between two rather different new products for his next new-product launching. Product A has the greater expected value and has both a smaller minimum outcome and a larger maximum outcome as compared with Product B. Which product do you think the product manager will choose, and why?

2-7. In some cases the coefficient-of-variation criterion ranks decision alternatives in a different order, as compared to their ranking by the certainty-equivalent criterion. Explain.

2-8. Explain how the value of additional information is calculated.

2-9. Discuss the factors you would consider when evaluating a decision made by somebody else. Is it possible that you might conclude that it was a "good" decision even if the actual outcome was a disaster? Explain.

2-10. What is sensitivity analysis? How would you incorporate this into your recommendation to management concerning the choice between several decision alternatives?

PROBLEMS AND SHORT CASES

2-1. Sounds True, Inc., a small company producing stereo amplifiers, has found that its leading model has suffered substantial market-share losses because of the competition from other producers' newer models. The company is considering two alternatives for the coming year: either to give the existing product a minor facelift or to introduce a totally new model. The success or failure of these strategies will depend ultimately upon the state of the economy, as is evident from the payoff matrix:

		DECISION ALTERNATIVES	
		Minor Facelift	*New Model*
States of	Downturn	10	−20
the	Constant	30	20
Economy	Upturn	80	150

The payoffs shown represent thousands of dollars net profit. The company considers that the probabilities of a downturn, a constant economy, and of an upturn, are 30 percent 50 percent, and 20 percent, respectively.

(a) Calculate the expected value, standard deviation, and coefficient of variation for each decision alternative.

(b) Apply the expected-value, coefficient-of-variation, and the maximin decision criteria to find which alternative is indicated under each criterion.

(c) Which alternative will have the greater certainty equivalent? Explain.

2-2. The Mark U. Cosmetic Company is considering whether or not to develop and market a new men's cologne. Development costs are estimated to be $125,000, and there is a 70-percent probability that development will succeed, based on the company's previous experience. If it does succeed, the product will be marketed at $4 per bottle. Cost of production is expected to be constant at $1.50 per bottle regardless of volume. If the product is "highly" successful (estimated probability 35 percent), it will sell an estimated 95,000 bottles over the year. If it is only "moderately" successful (45 percent probability), it will sell an estimated 33,000 bottles. If it is "marginally" successful (20 percent probability), it will sell only the initial production run of 10,000 bottles.

Should development not be undertaken, the plant capacity could be utilized for an outside contract to produce 20,000 units of a chain-store cologne, which will sell to the retailer for $1.25 profit per bottle.

(a) Construct the decision tree that reflects the above decision problem.

(b) Should Mark U. go ahead with the product development or simply take the contract with the chain store? (Assume all costs and revenues are incurred and received within the present period so that discounting is not required.)

2-3. Your firm is considering the introduction of a new product, and you are required to set the price. You are considering three price strategies: high ($6), medium ($4), and low ($2.50). Your market research team has indicated that the probability distribution of sales at these prices is as follows:

	HIGH PRICE		MEDIUM PRICE		LOW PRICE	
	Sales	Prob.	Sales	Prob.	Sales	Prob.
First year	3,500	0.1	5,000	0.2	10,000	0.4
	2,500	0.3	4,000	0.5	7,500	0.3
	1,500	0.6	3,000	0.3	5,000	0.3
Second year	5,000	0.2	8,000	0.3	12,000	0.3
	4,000	0.3	6,500	0.4	9,000	0.5
	3,000	0.5	5,000	0.3	7,500	0.2

The initial investment will be $22,000, and per-unit variable costs will be constant at $1 regardless of volume. You are advised by the finance department that the $22,000 could otherwise be invested (at comparable risk) in a forthcoming bond issue at 12.5 percent per annum.

(a) Using decision-tree analysis, find which pricing strategy promises the greatest net present value over the two-year period.

(b) Should the investment funds be used to buy the bonds instead? Why?

(c) Rank the strategies in order of their risk. Explain the basis for your ranking.

(d) Rank the strategies in order of their risk-adjusted expected value.

(e) Is the coefficient-of-variation criterion contradicted by the certainty-equivalent criterion in this case? Explain.

2-4. To help pay your way through college you plan to operate either a hot-dog stand or an ice-cream stand at every home game of your local baseball team. The actual outcomes associated with each decision alternative depend to a large degree on the weather, since hot dogs will be in greater demand on cloudy and rainy days, whereas ice cream will be in greater demand on sunny days. The following payoff matrix shows the expected value of profits for each baseball game and for each decision alternative, under the three different states of nature considered possible. Your research at the local meteorological office indicates that over the past ten baseball seasons it was raining for 15 percent of the home games, cloudy for 55 percent of the games, and sunny for 30 percent of the games. You must decide which product to choose for the entire season, either hot dogs or ice cream.

		DECISION ALTERNATIVES	
		Hot Dogs	Ice Cream
States	Rain	$300	$ 75
of	Cloud	250	150
Nature	Sun	100	400

(a) Calculate the expected value and coefficient of variation for each decision alternative. Which alternative would you choose? Explain, including a statement about your certainty equivalent for each of the two alternatives.

(b) Suppose that you could purchase, for $50 per game, the right to choose between hot dogs and ice cream on the day of each game, so that you could always have the appropriate product for the state of nature encountered each time. (Someone else would take the other product on each occasion.) (1) What is the value of the information to be gained (about the weather) by delaying your decision until the day of the game? (2) Assuming you must, before the season starts, decide among option A (to sell hot dogs), or option B (to sell ice cream), or option C (to buy the right to sell either hot dogs or ice cream, depending on the weather for each game), which option would you choose? Explain.

2-5. A small clothing firm has invested $10,000 in a machine to produce neckties. It is considering the joint decision of the price and quality of the single type of necktie it will market. Three possibilities are considered feasible: (A) lower-quality materials and workmanship, resulting in a per-unit direct cost of $5 and priced at $8 per unit; (B) better-quality materials and workmanship, with direct cost of $6 per unit and priced at $11; and (C) top-quality materials and workmanship, with direct cost of $7 per unit and priced at $14. The firm has a planning horizon of two years, after which time the machine will be worthless. The firm considers its opportunity discount rate to be 10 percent.

To help in the decision, the firm employed the Astigmatic Research Company to generate estimates of probable sales for each of the above-mentioned price/quality modes. A.R.C. has produced the following carefully estimated projections of sales volumes for the next two years.

	SALES VOLUME	PROBABILITIES	
	Each Year	Year 1	Year 2
Necktie A	2,000	0.10	0.05
	4,000	0.25	0.20
	6,000	0.40	0.35
	8,000	0.20	0.30
	10,000	0.05	0.10
Necktie B	2,000	0.15	0.10
	4,000	0.30	0.25
	6,000	0.25	0.30
	8,000	0.20	0.25
	10,000	0.10	0.10
Necktie C	2,000	0.20	0.25
	4,000	0.35	0.40
	6,000	0.25	0.25
	8,000	0.15	0.10
	10,000	0.05	0.00

(a) Apply the expected-value, maximin, and coefficient-of-variation criteria to these alternatives to find which alternative is indicated under each criterion.

(b) Which price/quality mode should the firm choose, in your judgment?

2-6. Safeguard Stores is a relatively small chain operation in the retail supermarket industry. The area manager for Montreal, Nick Wolkowski, is considering opening a new store in a rapidly expanding suburb. Two sizes of store have been suggested: the regular size of 27,000 square feet and the superstore size of 40,000 square feet. The initial costs, expected-demand situation, profits, and probabilities are as follows:

Store Size	Initial Cost	Demand Situation	YEAR 1 Profits	YEAR 1 Prob.	YEAR 2 Profits	YEAR 2 Prob.
	$ 000		$ 000		$ 000	
Regular	850	Low	300	0.2	500	0.2
		Medium	500	0.5	800	0.4
		High	800	0.3	1,000	0.4
Super	1,000	Low	300	0.6	600	0.4
		Medium	600	0.3	900	0.3
		High	1,000	0.1	1,200	0.3

Mr. Wolkowski is considering only a two-year horizon, since he hopes to be regional manager by then. He feels that the appropriate discount rate is 10 percent. (Treat the profits as though they are received in lump sum at the end of year one and year two. The costs are incurred immediately.)

(a) Which store size promises the larger expected net present value?

(b) Which decision criterion do you think Mr. Wolkowski should apply, given his desire to impress his superiors sufficiently to obtain his promotion?

2-7. The Express Delivery Company operates a courier and parcel delivery service between the major cities in southern California. Management is considering whether to lease or buy an additional truck it needs in order to extend its services. Careful analysis of costs and the potential demand situation has led to the following estimates of net cash flows (NCF) for each of the first two years.

Lease Option:

YEAR 1 NCF	YEAR 1 Probability	YEAR 2 NCF	YEAR 2 Probability
−5,000	.25	5,000	.30
5,000	.40	10,000	.50
15,000	.35	15,000	.20

Buy Option:

YEAR 1 NCF	YEAR 1 Probability	YEAR 2 NCF	YEAR 2 Probability
−5,000	.10	10,000	.15
0	.20	15,000	.35
5,000	.50	20,000	.40
10,000	.20	25,000	.10

The management considers that a two-year time horizon is appropriate, since it would replace this truck with a new one in two years whether it was leased or purchased. If purchased, the truck will have a salvage value of $5,000 at the end of the second year, and this value is included in the above NCF figures. The lease agreement is for two years with no possibility of cancellation once signed. Management could alternatively invest the funds involved in corporate bonds, considered to be of similar risk to the strategy of expanding its services, and these bonds would yield 15 percent at current prices. Assume that all cash flows are spent or received at the end of each year in a single lump sum and ignore any tax considerations.

Decision Making under Risk and Uncertainty

(a) Using decision-tree analysis, find the expected net present value of each alternative.

(b) Calculate a measure of risk for each alternative.

(c) Apply several decision criteria and make your recommendation to management.

(d) State any qualifications and/or reservations you would wish to add to your recommendation.

2-8. The Walwyn Widgets Company operates a thriving mail-order business and has achieved considerable success using television advertisements to promote new products, novelty items, record and tape collections of current music, and so forth. The Director of New-Product Development, Charles van Winkle, has presented to the Executive Committee three new product suggestions, one of which will be the next product produced and sold. Due to limited availability of television time, sales personnel, and production facilities, only one of these projects can be implemented now. The other two will be set aside and will compete with any new possibilties that arise in the future.

Product A is a device containing a battery-powered clock and an aerosol can of room freshener which is attached to a wall and which periodically sprays a fine mist of deodorizer into the selected room. Market research indicates that the product life cycle for this product will be quite short, with sales being minimal after the second year. Product B is a phonograph record containing a collection of "reggae" music. This product is expected to encounter very stiff competition after the first two years. Product C is an antitheft alarm system for automobiles which is also expected to have only a two-year life because of rapid technological advances. Mr. van Winkle has obtained the following estimates of profits and probability distributions associated with each product.

	YEAR 1		YEAR 2	
Product	Profits	Proba-bility	Profits	Proba-bility
A	$ 10,000	0.10	$ 20,000	0.15
	50,000	0.50	40,000	0.50
	80,000	0.30	60,000	0.25
	100,000	0.10	80,000	0.10
B	−$100,000	0.05	0	0.05
	100,000	0.25	100,000	0.30
	300,000	0.50	250,000	0.40
	500,000	0.20	400,000	0.25
C	−$ 50,000	0.10	10,000	0.15
	0	0.10	25,000	0.15
	50,000	0.40	50,000	0.40
	100,000	0.40	75,000	0.30

Assume that these profits are received at the end of the year and that Walwyn Widgets could otherwise invest the funds at 14 percent in a mutual fund, judged by Mr. van Winkle to be roughly equal in risk to the three proposals presented.

(a) Using decision-tree analysis, find the expected net present value of each proposal and calculate a measure of risk for each proposal.

(b) Apply several decision criteria to the choice problem and advise Mr. van Winkle which product he should choose.

(c) State any qualifications and/or reservations you would wish to add to your decision.

2-9. Novo Products Ltd. buys inventions and markets them as new products. Management has studied the inventions that are currently available to it and has decided on the products code-named S, B, and F. It plans to introduce S in the current year and F next year, but it can't decide whether to introduce B this year or next. Management has established the following probability distributions of profits associated with each strategy:

Strategy 1 (S first year, B and F second year)

YEAR 1		YEAR 2	
Profits ($ millions)	Probabilities	Profits ($ millions)	Probabilities
4	.3	8	.00
3	.5	7	.15
1	.2	6	.25
0	.0	5	.30
		4	.15
		3	.10
		2	.05
		1	.00

Strategy 2 (S and B first year, F second year)

YEAR 1		YEAR 2	
Profits ($ millions)	Probabilities	Profits ($ millions)	Probabilities
8	.00	4	.4
7	.05	3	.5
6	.10	1	.1
5	.15	0	.0
4	.25		
3	.20		
2	.15		
1	.10		

Rather than invest in these new products, Novo could alternatively lend the money for household mortgages at 16.75 percent per annum.

(a) Calculate the expected net present value of each strategy.

(b) Calculate a measure of risk for each strategy.

(c) Apply several decision criteria and make your recommendation to management.

(d) State explicitly any qualifications or assumptions which underlie your analysis.

2-10. Your firm has suffered a declining market share over the past year and management has considered various means of reversing the trend. Extensive analysis has narrowed the options to two.

Plan A is to conduct a point-of-purchase promotion campaign involving the manufacture of special samples and the disbursement of these in shopping centers and on city streets. This plan would take a year to set up and would cost $100,000 during the first year. The increase in the firm's profits in year two is expected to be either $40,000, $60,000, or $80,000 (with probabilities of 0.2, 0.5, and 0.3, respectively), depending upon whether the promotion is fairly, moderately, or highly successful, respectively. If fairly successful in year two, year-three profits will be increased by either $50,000, $100,000, or $150,000, with probabilities of 0.4, 0.3, and 0.3. If moderately successful in year two, year-three profits will be increased by either $80,000, $120,000, or $160,000 with probabilities of 0.3, 0.4, or 0.3. If highly successful in year two, year-three profits will be increased by either $100,000, $150,000, or $200,000, with probabilities of 0.2, 0.5, and 0.3. All cash flows under plan A will occur more-or-less continuously throughout each year.

Plan B is to contract out to an advertising agency that would prepare a series of campaigns for use predominately in the print media. This would cost $150,000 in the first year, and increased profits of $50,000, $100,000, and $150,000 are expected in the second year, with probabilities of 0.1, 0.5, and 0.4, depending upon whether the campaign is fairly successful, moderately successful, or highly successful. If year two is fairly successful, increased profits in year three will be $50,000, $100,000 and $150,000, with probabilities of 0.2, 0.4, and 0.4. If year two is moderately successful, year three's increased profits will be $100,000, $150,000, and $200,000, with probabilities of 0.2, 0.5, and 0.3. If year two is highly successful, profits in year three will be increased by $150,000, $200,000, or $250,000, with probabilities of 0.1, 0.5, and 0.4. Due to the financial arrangements associated with plan B, all cash flows will occur at the end of each year. The firm's opportunity discount rate for both projects is 18 percent.

(a) Construct the decision tree for each decision alternative and calculate the expected present value of profits for each plan.

(b) Calculate the standard deviation of the outcome for each plan.

(c) Apply the expected-value, maximin, and coefficient-of-variation criteria to find the plan favored by each criterion.

(d) Discuss the application of the certainty-equivalent criterion to this problem, on the presumption that management is risk-averse.

SUGGESTED REFERENCES AND FURTHER READING

Arrow, K.J. "Risk Perception in Psychology and Economics," *Economic Inquiry*, 20 (Jan. 1982), pp. 1-19.

Baumol, W. J. *Economic Theory and Operations Analysis* (4th ed.), chaps. 18, 19, 25. Englewood Cliffs, N.J.: Prentice-Hall, Inc., 1977.

Brigham, E. F. *Financial Management Theory and Practice* (2nd ed.), chaps. 5, 12, 15. Hinsdale, Ill.: The Dryden Press, 1979.

Dean, G., and A. Halter. *Decisions Under Uncertainty*. Cincinnati, Ohio: South-Western Publishing, 1971.

Friedman, D. "Why There Are No Risk Preferers," *Journal of Political Economy*, 89 (June 1981), p. 600.

Friedman, M., and L. J. Savage. "The Utility Analysis of Choices Involving Risk," *Journal of Political Economy*, 56 (Aug. 1948), 279-304.

Gordon, G., and I. Pressman. *Quantitative Decision Making for Business*, chaps. 3, 4, 5. Englewood Cliffs, N.J.: Prentice-Hall Inc., 1978.

Hirshleifer, J. "Investment Decisions Under Uncertainty: Choice-Theoretic Approaches," *Quarterly Journal of Economics*, 79 (Nov. 1965), 509-36.

Horowitz, I. *Decision Making and the Theory of the Firm*. New York: Holt, Rinehart & Winston, 1970.

Huber, G. P. *Managerial Decision Making*. Glenview, Ill.: Scott, Foresman & Company, 1980.

Radford, K. J. *Modern Managerial Decision Making*. Reston, Va.: Reston Publishing Company, Inc., 1981.

Raiffa, H. *Decision Analysis: Introductory Lectures on Choices under Uncertainty*. Reading, Mass.: Addison-Wesley Publishing Co., Inc., 1970.

DEMAND THEORY, ANALYSIS, and ESTIMATION

3

Utility
Analysis
of
Consumer
Behavior

3.1 INTRODUCTION

Since the first step toward business profits is the demand expressed by consumers, an understanding of the principles underlying and explaining consumer demand is indispensable to the modern business decision maker. We cannot simply assume that demand will always be there, since it is sensitive, among other things, to changes in prices, changes in consumer incomes, and changes in the prices and availability of substitute products. In this chapter we address ourselves to the consumer's reactions to these economic variables, so that better decisions may be made, especially in the pricing area.[1]

The next two sections of this chapter review the traditional approach to economic consumer behavior, that is, indifference-curve analysis of consumer choice between and among products. This review is at the level of

---

[1] This chapter may be bypassed without serious loss of continuity if, for example, the instructor deems this necessary because of limited course length or appropriate because the students already have a strong background in the underlying principles of demand theory. Chapter 4 looks at *aggregate* consumer demand and is written so that it can stand alone without the necessity of understanding all the underlying principles of *individual* consumer demand. Alternatively, the main sections of Chapter 3 can be treated as separate units. Only section 3.2 might be studied, for example, or only sections 3.2 and 3.4, depending on the course design, the time available, and so on.

an intermediate microeconomics course. If your previous exposure to microeconomics has been at the intermediate level, you may wish to skim over these sections or to bypass them completely (if your memory is perfect!). If your background in microeconomics is restricted to an introductory course, however, I suggest you read these sections carefully, since they introduce the terms and concepts necessary for the following sections.

The fourth section of this chapter examines an alternative and relatively new approach to consumer behavior: the *attribute* approach to consumer choice. Whereas the traditional approach assumes that consumers derive utility from the consumption of products, the attribute approach assumes that consumers derive utility not from the products *per se* but from the attributes (or characteristics) embodied in or attached to the products. Using the example of an automobile, the traditional view is that the consumer derives utility from the automobile itself, while the attribute approach is that utility is obtained from the benefits derived from the automobile, such as transportation, comfort, prestige, power, economy, and other features perceived and appreciated by the consumer.

The attribute approach has important implications for managerial economics, especially in the pricing area. Since attributes have utility value to consumers, prices of products should be chosen with regard to the presence, absence, or degree of desirable attributes associated with the product. In fact, the attribute approach provides the bridge between the theory of economic consumer behavior and the pricing practices of marketing managers, as we shall see in Chapters 11 and 12.

NOTE: In the first two chapters we established the basis for decision making under conditions of risk and uncertainty. In those chapters we spoke generally of costs, revenues, and profits, and we utilized those concepts to find the decision alternative which best served the firm's objectives. Now, we go back to basics to examine the principles underlying consumer demand and, hence, the firm's revenues. Our objective is to examine the behavior of consumers to determine their most likely response to changes in variables that the firm can control, such as prices, product design, and promotional expenditures, as well as to examine the probable response of consumers to changes in variables that the firm cannot control, such as consumer incomes and the prices (and other competitive strategies) of other sellers. With a strong understanding of the principles underlying consumer behavior, we are then in a better position to explain and predict the impact on the firm's revenues as a result of changes in the factors that operate to determine the level of those revenues.

3.2 INDIFFERENCE-CURVE ANALYSIS OF CONSUMER BEHAVIOR

DEFINITION: An *indifference curve* is defined as the locus of combinations of two products, or of other variables, among which combinations the consumer is indifferent. That is, each point (each combination of the two variables) on an indifference curve is equally desirable, giving the consumer the same level of utility.

DEFINITION: *Utility* is defined as the psychic satisfaction which the consumer obtains from the consumption of goods and services. We postulate that consumers are basically hedonists and wish to maximize their utility. Thus, they choose products for consumption on the basis of the utility they expect to receive from each product. But since most goods and services cost money and since the income, or wealth, of most consumers is limited, consumers must allocate their available funds among the goods and services, taking account of the differing prices and differing utility expected from different products so that their utility is maximized, given the income constraint. A consumer who is pursuing the maximization of utility is said to be acting "rationally."

Preference and Indifference

DEFINITION: A consumer is *indifferent* among combinations of goods and services that give the same amount of utility. A consumer wishing to maximize utility from a limited income will *prefer* any combination of goods and services that gives a higher level of utility. For each combination that gives a higher level of utility there will be other combinations that also give this (higher) level of utility. Thus, the consumer's preference structure may be depicted as a series of indifference curves in product space. This "indifference map" will show which combinations are preferred, which combinations are equal, and which are inferior in relation to any particular combination. For simplicity of exposition and feasibility of graphical treatment we shall use the simple case of only two products being considered by the consumer. Using algebraic techniques we could extend this analysis to larger numbers of products, but the following two-dimensional model is sufficient to explain and demonstrate the principles involved. By extension, these principles also apply to the n-dimensional-real-world consumer choice situation.

EXAMPLE: Let us consider a particular consumer's demand for two particular products. Suppose a college student buys hamburgers and/or milkshakes for lunch and we wish to know what weekly combination of hamburgers and milkshakes would maximize her utility from those two products. Figure 3-1 shows hamburgers on the vertical axis, measured in physical units, and milkshakes on the horizontal axis, also measured in physical units. The lines I_1 and I_2 are two of the student's indifference curves. The combinations of hamburgers and milkshakes represented by indifference curve I_1, such as five burgers/one shake and three burgers/two shakes, gives her the *same* level of expected utility. Combinations that lie to the right and above indifference curve I_1 promise a *higher* level of utility and combinations that lie to the left and below that curve promise a *lower level* of utility.

For each point in the product space represented by Figure 3-1 there will be a series of other points among which the student is indifferent.

FIGURE 3-1.   Indifference Curves between Products

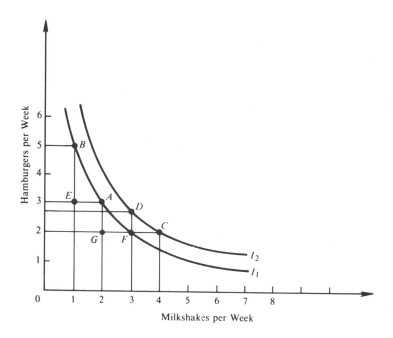

Consider point C on indifference curve I_2, which represents two burgers/ four shakes. Starting from this point we could find the other points on indifference curve I_2 by a process of questioning the student about her preference or indifference between other combinations of burgers and shakes.

Suppose we ask the student which would she prefer: two burgers and four shakes (point C) or three burgers and three shakes? If she prefers the latter combination, it is evident that the extra burger in the latter combination more than compensates her in terms of utility for the shake that was taken away. If we then offer this consumer the choice of the initial combination C, or of two and one-half burgers and three shakes, and she expresses preference for the initial combination, we know that the extra half burger does not compensate her for the loss of the one shake. Continuing this iterative process of questioning, we could find a new combination of burgers and shakes for which the consumer is indifferent when faced with a choice of this combination or with the combination represented by point C. Suppose this occurs at point D, which is two and three-quarters burgers and three shakes. When confronted with this choice the student says that she has no preference between the two combinations, that either one is as good as the other. Hence points D and C are on the same indifference curve. By the same process we could generate a multitude of combinations that this consumer feels are identical (in terms of utility derived) to points D and C and which, therefore, also lie on indifference curve I_2.

Since we could start this process from any combination of hamburgers and milkshakes, it follows that there is an indifference curve passing through every point in the figure. We have shown simply two of the infinite number of indifference curves that represent this particular consumer's taste and preference pattern between the two products. To the right of those curves shown there will be curves that depict progressively higher levels of utility; and to the left and below indifference curve I_1 there will be curves that depict progressively lower levels of utility.[2]

Assumptions Underlying the Analysis

We require four simple assumptions to facilitate our analysis of consumer behavior. First, we assume that the consumer is able to *rank* preferences in the order of utility derived. Notice that we simply require an ordinal ranking and do not expect the consumer to place a value on the amount of utility derived. We simply ask which of two combinations is preferred, but we do not need to know by how much one is preferred to the other.

Second, we require that the consumer's preferences be *transitive*. Transitivity of preference implies, for example, that if C is preferred to A, and A is indifferent to B, then C is preferred to B. This assumption simply requires that the consumer be consistent in the preferences and indifferences expressed.

Third, we assume that the consumer always prefers more of a commodity to less of that commodity. This assumption of *nonsatiation* is reasonable in the real world, in view of the wide variety of products from which a consumer must choose and the consequent improbability of a rational consumer's consuming any one of those products to the point where the additional utility derived would become zero or negative.

Fourth, we assume that the consumer experiences *diminishing marginal utility* for all commodities. That is, as the consumer purchases progressively more of any commodity within a particular time period, the additional utility derived from each consecutive unit will diminish. Thus, marginal utility monotonically declines from the first unit, approaching but never reaching the value of zero because of the assumption of nonsatiation.

DEFINITION: *Marginal utility* (MU) is defined as the change in total utility resulting from a one-unit change in the rate of consumption of a particular product. The assumption of diminishing MU is well supported by empirical evidence that consumers derive progressively declining MU as they increase their consumption of a particular product during any given period of time.

---

[2] It is unlikely that it would ever be feasible for a firm to try to discover the indifference curves of its customers. Such an exercise would be extremely time consuming and expensive. The purpose of the model being employed here is to explain the utility-maximizing responses of consumers to changes in their economic environment. The model has pedagogical, explanatory, and predictive value without necessarily being economically feasible in the real world.

NOTE: Products for which it is said one must "acquire a taste," such as caviar, frog's legs, and truffles, are often suggested as contradictions to the principle of diminishing marginal utility, since, as you eat more and more caviar, for example, you may enjoy it more and more. But the principle of diminishing marginal utility is only contradicted if, at any one meal, you enjoy subsequent spoonfuls of caviar more than you enjoyed preceding spoonfuls. Trying caviar again a week later and enjoying it more this time is not the same as having a second serving on the first occasion. The principle of diminishing marginal utility refers to the decline of marginal utility during a particular period of time when more than one unit of the product is consumed. Thus we expect marginal utility to decline as the consumer increases the *rate* of consumption during a given time period. Even if you like caviar more the second time you try it (for example, a week later), your MU is expected to decrease as you increase your rate of consumption.

The Properties of Indifference Curves

These assumptions allow us to state the following four properties of indifference curves:

1. Points on higher indifference curves are preferred to points on lower curves.
2. Indifference curves are negatively sloped throughout.[3]
3. Indifference curves neither meet nor intersect.
4. Indifference curves are convex from below.

Let us examine each property in turn and relate it to the underlying assumptions. Points on higher indifference curves are preferred to points on lower curves because of the assumptions of nonsatiation and transitivity. Consider three combinations, A, B, and C, of products X and Y. Combination A is $4X$ and $2Y$; combination B is $5X$ and $4Y$; and combination C is $3X$ and $6Y$. Suppose that combinations B and C are on the same indifference curve. Combination B must be preferred to A since it has more of both X and Y (due to the nonsatiation assumption). Combination C must also be preferred to A, despite its having less X and more Y, since it is on the same indifference curve as B. Since B is preferred to A, C is also preferred to A (because of the transitivity assumption).

Indifference curves are negatively sloped because of the assumption of nonsatiation. Nonsatiation means that the consumer will always derive positive marginal utility by consuming more of any product and, conversely, that a consumer's total utility will decrease if that person consumes less of

---

[3] Indifference curves in product space will be negatively sloped as long as both products are regarded as utility-generating "goods." We saw in Chapter 2 that when a disutility-generating "bad," such as risk, is placed on one axis, the indifference curves will be positively sloping. Note that the other three properties hold true for the risk-return indifference curve discussed in Chapter 2.

any product. Thus, for two combinations of X and Y to be on the same indifference curve (that is, to give the same total utility) one combination must have more X and less Y than the other combination and, thus, a line joining these points must be negatively sloped. This is illustrated by points D and C in Figure 3-1. In moving from point D to C the consumer gains utility from the additional milkshake but loses the same amount of utility by giving up about three-quarters of a hamburger.

Indifference curves cannot intersect or run tangent to each other due to the assumptions of transitivity and nonsatiation. If two indifference curves *did* cross (or run tangent), there would be a combination of goods which was simultaneously on both indifference curves. Transitivity would then imply that all points on both curves are equivalent, notwithstanding that some combinations must include more of both products, as compared to the intersection point. The latter is ruled out by the assumption of nonsatiation. Given these two assumptions, therefore, indifference curves neither cross nor run tangent to each other.

Finally, indifference curves are convex to the origin due to the assumption of diminishing marginal utility for all products. To explain this let us introduce the concept of the marginal rate of substitution.

The Marginal Rate of Substitution

DEFINITION: The *marginal rate of substitution* (MRS) is defined as the amount of one product that the consumer will be willing to give up for an additional unit of another product, in order to remain at the same level of utility. The proviso that the consumer remains at the same level of utility makes it clear that the MRS refers to a movement along a particular indifference curve. By convention we define the MRS between two products for a movement *down* a particular indifference curve. Thus, the MRS is the ratio of the amount given up of the product on the vertical axis, to the one-unit increment of the product on the horizontal axis.

The MRS is thus equal to the *slope* of an indifference curve at any point on that curve, since it is defined in terms of the vertical rise (or fall) over the horizontal run. Symbolically, and in terms of our example,

$$\text{MRS} = \frac{\Delta H}{\Delta M} \qquad (3\text{-}1)$$

where ΔH is the decrement to hamburger consumption necessary to maintain utility at the same level given the one-unit increase in milkshake consumption, ΔM. (The Greek letter Δ, uppercase *delta*, is the conventional symbol for denoting a change in a variable.)

Since convexity of an indifference curve means that the slope will decrease progressively as we move from left to right along the indifference curve, convexity also means that the MRS will diminish progressively as we move down each indifference curve. In terms of Figure 3-1 the MRS between points B and A on indifference curve I_1 is the ratio BE/EA = 2. The MRS for the next (third) milkshake per week is equal to the ratio AG/GF = 1. Observing Figure 3-1 you can see that the MRS for the fourth milkshake is approximately 0.5 and that the MRS continues to diminish as the consumer exchanges more hamburgers for milkshakes along indifference curve I_1.

NOTE: The MRS declines because it is equal to the ratio of the marginal utility of the product on the horizontal axis divided by the marginal utility of the product on the vertical axis. That is,

$$\text{MRS} = \frac{MU_m}{MU_h} \tag{3-2}$$

To appreciate this, note that the movement from point B to point A along indifference curve I_1 in Figure 3-1 left the consumer at the same level of utility after substituting one milkshake for two hamburgers. The marginal utility attached to the milkshake received must have been equal to the marginal utility given up by sacrificing *two* hamburgers. Thus, the ratio of the marginal utility of milkshakes to the marginal utility of hamburgers is equal to two. Similarly, from point A to point F, total utility stays constant as the consumer gives up one more hamburger for one more milkshake. Thus, the marginal utilities attached to the two products must be equal, and their ratio is equal to one. Since the MRS is equal to the ratio of the MU of the product being acquired to the MU of the product given up, and since we have assumed diminishing marginal utility for all products, it is clear that MRS must diminish, since MRS is the ratio of a numerator that is falling and a denominator that is rising, as we move down along any given indifference curve. Thus, the assumption of diminishing marginal utilities causes indifference curves to be convex to the origin.[4]

The Consumer's Income Constraint

Since the consumer prefers higher indifference curves to lower indifference curves, it is evident that to maximize utility the consumer would proceed to the highest indifference curve possible. The limits of possibility are defined

---

[4] In the case of indifference curves in risk-return space the marginal utility of return (a "good") is assumed to diminish, while the marginal *disutility* of risk (a "bad") is assumed to *increase* as the risk averter accepts more and more units of risk. The slope of an indifference curve in risk-return space is MD-risk/MU-return = MRS. As the risk averter accepts more risk in conjunction with more expected return, MD-risk rises and MU-return falls. Thus, the MRS ratio rises and the indifference curve becomes progressively more steep as we move along it to the right. Consequently the indifference curve is convex from below, as in the regular case of negatively sloped indifference curves between combinations of goods.

DEMAND THEORY, ANALYSIS, AND ESTIMATION

by the consumer's ability to afford the combinations desired. Were it not for a constraint upon income, wealth, and other financial resources, the consumer might proceed upward and to the right to a state of infinite euphoria! The income constraint, however, keeps our consumer's feet on the ground, since certain combinations of the two products are simply not affordable.

DEFINITION: The *income constraint* is defined as the total income or wealth the consumer is able to spend on goods and services per period. Symbolically,

$$B \geqslant \sum_{i=1}^{n} P_i \ Q_i \qquad (3\text{-}3)$$

where B represents the total budget available; Σ connotes "the sum of"; P_i represents the price of the ith product; Q_i represents the quantity purchased of the ith product; and $i = 1, 2, 3, \ldots, n$, where n is the number of products available. Thus, the sum of the expenditures on each of the available products must not exceed the total budget available. The assumption of nonsatiation allows us to express the income constraint as an equality rather than an inequality (Equation 3-3), since the consumer will derive additional utility from every last cent of the available budget and therefore will spend it all in search of maximum utility.[5]

In the simple two-commodity situation discussed above we can rewrite the budget constraint as

$$B = P_h \cdot H + P_m \cdot M \qquad (3\text{-}4)$$

where B is the total dollar budget available to the consumer; P_h and P_m are the prices per physical unit of hamburgers and milkshakes; and H and M are the number of physical units of hamburgers and milkshakes purchased by the consumer.

In this equation three symbols represent parameters that will be known to the consumer, namely, the budget available, the price of hamburgers, and the price of milkshakes. The remaining symbols are variables that will take on the values necessary to maximize the consumer's utility. Equation (3-4) is actually a linear equation in those two variables. This will be more obvious if we rearrange terms and express the equation in terms of one of the variables. Subtracting B and $P_h \cdot H$ from both sides, we have

$$-P_h \cdot H = -B + P_m \cdot M$$

---

[5] Savings are like any other product in the sense that the consumer expects to derive utility by allocating part of available income to that end. Thus the model does not preclude savings; the consumer is free to "spend" money on savings if this contributes to utility maximization.

Dividing both sides by $-P_h$ gives us

$$H = \frac{B}{P_h} - \frac{P_m}{P_h} \cdot M \qquad (3\text{-}5)$$

In this form H is a linear function of the variable M and three parameters, where B/P_h is the intercept term, and the coefficient to M (namely, $-P_m / P_h$) is the slope term.

EXAMPLE: Suppose the parameters take the values B = $5.00, P_h = $1.00, and P_m = $0.50. To solve for the intercept we set M = zero and find B/P_h = 5. Thus, if the consumer spends her entire budget on hamburgers, she will be able to purchase 5 units weekly. Alternatively, if she spends her total available income on milkshakes, she can purchase 10 units weekly. In Figure 3-2 we show Equation (3-5) plotted in product space. Note that it intercepts the vertical axis at 5 units and the horizontal axis at 10 units. Starting from the vertical intercept, if milkshake consumption is increased from zero to 1, we note from Equation (3-5) that the value of H is drawn down in the ratio $-P_m/P_h$. This ratio of prices is of course the slope of the line and is constant throughout the length of the line, since the price ratio is constant.

All combinations of hamburgers and milkshakes that occur on that line cost exactly $5, as may be verified from Figure 3-2. All combinations that lie above and to the right of the income constraint line are unattainable combinations, since they cost more than $5, and all combinations lying below the line cost less than $5.

FIGURE 3-2.   The Budget Constraint between Products

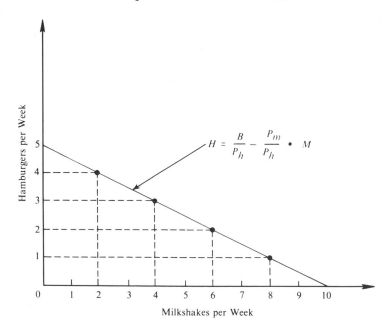

DEMAND THEORY, ANALYSIS, AND ESTIMATION

FIGURE 3-3. Maximization of Utility from Products

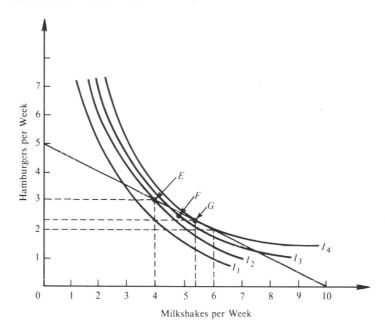

Utility Maximization

Let us now superimpose the indifference curves of Figure 3-1 upon the income constraint line of Figure 3-2. This is shown in Figure 3-3. Suppose the consumer is at point E, spending all her available income on three hamburgers and four milkshakes and enjoying a utility level denoted by indifference curve I_2. If the consumer shifted to combination F, this would allow greater utility but would not use all available income. This shift, while preferable to point E, is not yet the utility-maximizing combination. It can be seen that point G is superior to both of the previous two points and, moreover, that it allows the consumer to attain the highest possible indifference curve. Any higher indifference curve does not touch any of the attainable combinations and therefore is not affordable. The combination of hamburgers and milkshakes that appears to maximize our consumer's utility is thus approximately two and one-third hamburgers and five and one-third milkshakes.[6] By a quick calculation we can confirm that this combination does not break the consumer's income constraint. The two and one-third hamburgers will cost approximately $2.33, and the five and one-

---

[6] These fractional units should not bother us, since we can eliminate them by extending the time period. For example, every three weeks the consumer should purchase seven hamburgers and sixteen milkshakes.

third milkshakes will cost approximately $2.67, making a total expenditure of $5.00.

RULE: Utility maximization therefore requires that the consumer choose the combination on the budget constraint line where this line is tangent to an indifference curve. Tangency between the budget line and an indifference curve requires that their slopes be equal. Recalling that the slope of an indifference curve is the marginal rate of substitution and that the slope of the budget line is the price ratio, we can express the condition for utility maximization as

$$MRS \ = \ \frac{P_m}{P_h} \qquad (3\text{-}6)$$

given that all available income is spent. We have previously seen that

$$MRS \ = \ \frac{MU_m}{MU_h} \qquad (3\text{-}2)$$

so we may alternatively express the maximizing condition as

$$\frac{MU_m}{MU_h} \ = \ \frac{P_m}{P_h} \qquad (3\text{-}7)$$

Rearranging terms, we have

$$\frac{MU_m}{P_m} \ = \ \frac{MU_h}{P_h} \qquad (3\text{-}8)$$

Thus the condition for maximizing utility is to spend the available income such that the ratio of marginal utility to price is the same for all products purchased. In the hamburger/milkshake example it is clear that the consumer must expect to derive twice as much utility from the marginal hamburger, as compared with the marginal milkshake, since its price is twice as great.

Generalizing to n products, the condition for utility maximization is

$$\frac{MU_1}{P_1} \ = \frac{MU_2}{P_2} \ = \frac{MU_3}{P_3} \ = \cdot \ \cdot \ \cdot \ = \frac{MU_n}{P_n} \qquad (3\text{-}9)$$

given the equality of

$$B \ = \ \sum_{i=1}^{n} P_i \, Q_i \qquad (3\text{-}10)$$

where the subscripts $i = 1, 2, 3, \ldots, n$ represent the identity of the n products available.

The above analysis is concerned with the consumer's utility maximization given a set of available products, their prices, and the consumer's income. We turn now to an analysis of the consumer's utility-maximizing *response* to *changes* in his or her economic environment.

3.3 PRICE, INCOME, AND SUBSTITUTION EFFECTS

We are concerned with the behavior of the consumer in response to a change in a variable that influences the consumer's choice between and among products. The variables we will consider are changing prices, changing income levels, and changing taste and preference patterns.

The Price Effect

DEFINITION: The *price effect* is defined as the change in the quantity demanded of a particular product due to a change in the price of that product, *ceteris paribus*.[7] Let us investigate the reaction of a particular consumer to changes in the price level of a particular product.

EXAMPLE: In Figure 3-4 we show the indifference curves of an individual consumer between self-service and full-service gasoline.[8] Suppose the initial prices of self-service gas (SSG) and full-service gas (FSG) and the consumer's income level are such that the appropriate budget line is $N_1 M_1$. Thus, the consumer maximizes utility at point A, at which he purchases X_3 units of FSG and the indicated amount of SSG.

Let us now suppose that the price of FSG is reduced. This causes the budget line to swing around to that shown as $N_1 M_2$ since its vertical intercept is unchanged while the slope coefficient falls. The consumer responds by moving to point B with a higher level of utility. Notice that after the price reduction for FSG, the consumer's consumption of this product was raised from X_3 to X_4. Let us now suppose that the price of FSG is *raised*

---

[7] If you have forgotten, *ceteris paribus* means "all other things remaining the same," which means in this case that the consumer's monetary income and the price of all other available products must remain the same. The price effect requires a constant *monetary* income, while the substitution effect, explained on page 98, requires a constant *real* income.

[8] We can legitimately regard these as separate products since they are composed of different attributes. Full-service gas comes complete with smiling attendant eager to check your oil, fan belt, filters, radiator water and hoses, and tire pressures and to wash your windows, headlights and taillights. (This is clearly a *textbook* example.) Self-service gas comes without the above but with a significant saving per tankful and no anxiety about lost filler caps. Many consumers will demand both types of gas since they desire the attributes of each at different times.

FIGURE 3-4. The Price Consumption Curve

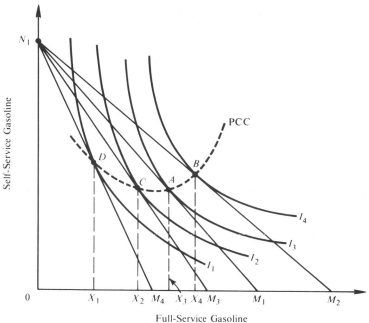

such that the appropriate budget line is $N_1 M_3$. The consumer will now maximize utility by attaining the point C, where consumption of FSG has fallen to X_2 units. If the price of this product were raised still further, such that the appropriate budget line was $N_1 M_4$, the consumer would select point D on that budget line and would maximize utility by consuming X_1 units of FSG and the indicated amount of SSG. If we join the points A, B, C, and D, we obtain what is known as the "price consumption curve."

DEFINITION: The *price consumption curve* (PCC) is the locus of the points of tangency between the appropriate budget constraint line and the highest attainable indifference curve at various price levels of the product on the horizontal axis. It shows how the consumption of one product (and implicitly of the other as well) changes as the price of that product varies. It is apparent that the relationship between the price of a product and the quantity demanded of that product is an inverse one.

The Law of Demand and the Demand Curve

DEFINITION: The *law of demand* states that as the price is raised the consumer demands progressively less of the product and, oppositely, as the price is reduced the consumer demands progressively more of the product. It is an empirical law, meaning that it is commonly observed in practice. The law of

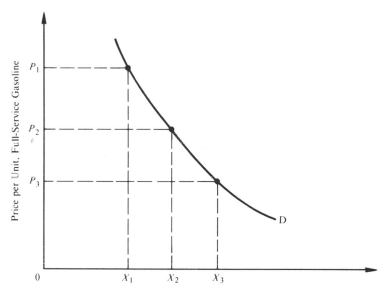

FIGURE 3-5.   Demand Curve for an Individual Consumer

Price per Unit, Full-Service Gasoline

P_1
P_2
P_3

0   X_1 X_2 X_3

D

Quantity Demanded, Full-Service Gasoline (per unit of time)

demand is expressed graphically as a negatively sloping line relating price to units of quantity demanded; this line is the *demand curve*. The consumer's demand curve for full-service gasoline is shown in Figure 3-5.

Notice that the actual data that underlie the demand curve depend upon the individual's reaction to changes in the price. This consumer's demand curve is not likely to be exactly the same as the demand curves of other consumers, who have their own taste and preference patterns and hence their own reactions to changes in the price of the product. These differences in reaction may be traced back to different marginal rates of substitution in their taste and preference patterns, as reflected in their indifference curves which have greater or lesser degrees of curvature. The above analysis, however, serves to demonstrate that although other consumers may not react to the *same degree* as our present example, they will react in the *same direction* in response to a change in price if they are attempting to maximize their utility from a limited income source. Since consumers typically attempt to get the most out of their money, we expect the law of demand to hold for consumers in general, although some consumers may react to price increases or decreases to a greater or lesser degree than others.

The Income Effect

DEFINITION: The *income effect* is defined as the change in the quantity demanded of a particular product when there is a change in the consumer's income, but when all other factors, such as the prices of the products and the consumer's

FIGURE 3-6.   Income Consumption Curve for Normal Goods

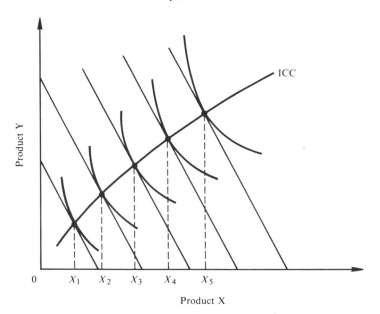

tastes, remain unchanged. Whereas the price effect was always negative, the income effect may be either positive or negative. A positive income effect means that the consumer's income level and consumption of Product X move in the same direction. We call products that exhibit a positive income effect "normal," or "superior," goods. Products for which the income effect is negative—that is, for which consumption of the product falls as the income rises, or rises as the income falls—are known as "inferior" goods.

EXAMPLE: For most people, perhaps, products such as housing, automobiles, and travel by air exhibit a positive income effect and hence are known as normal or superior goods. On the other hand, for many people products such as bologna, ground beef, and travel by train exhibit a negative income effect. For these people, therefore, these products are regarded as inferior goods.

In Figure 3-6 we show the income effect for a pair of normal goods. A particular consumer's pattern of tastes and preferences is represented by the indifference curves shown in the figure. The income constraint line is moved outward and to the right by successive increments, to indicate a progressively increased income for that particular consumer. For each increase in the income constraint, the consumer is able to find an equilibrium (tangency) point on a higher indifference curve and thus enjoy an increased level of utility. The locus of these points of tangency is known as the "income consumption curve."

DEFINITION: The *income consumption curve* (ICC) is the locus of points of tangency between the consumer's income constraint, at various levels of

DEMAND THEORY, ANALYSIS, AND ESTIMATION

income, and the highest attainable indifference curve for each level of income. It demonstrates how the consumer will change his or her consumption of the two products in response to successive increases in income. Both products X and Y are normal goods, since for successive increases in income the demand for each product is successively increased.

In Figure 3-7 we show the income consumption curve where Product X is an inferior good. Note that beyond a certain point, shown as point *A*, the income consumption curve takes a negative slope, indicating that for successive increments of income the consumer chooses to demand successively smaller quantities of Product X.

EXAMPLE: Suppose that Product X is ground beef and that Product Y is steak. The income consumption curve indicates that at low income levels both steak and ground beef exhibit positive income effects, but beyond point *A* ground beef becomes regarded as an inferior good, and the consumer apparently substitutes in favor of steak and away from ground beef as that consumer's income level rises. It is completely feasible that at still higher levels of income this particular consumer might come to regard ground beef as a normal good again. Suppose this consumer is the proud owner of a purebred Harlequin Great Dane. Being reluctant to feed such an impressive beast ordinary dog food, this consumer may begin to purchase progressively more ground beef (for the dog) as his or her income continues to rise. Hence ground beef exhibits a positive income effect once more.

For any particular product at any particular point of time, it is apparent that some consumers may regard that product as a superior good while others may regard it as an inferior good. This difference in attitude toward a particular product stems from either a difference in income levels or a

FIGURE 3-7.   Income Consumption Curve where X is an Inferior Good

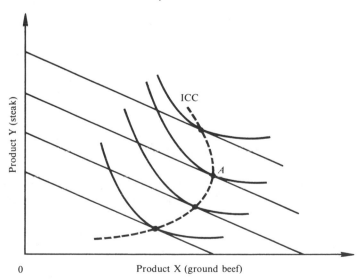

different pattern of tastes and preferences. Just as the price effect varies between and among consumers, the income effect should also be expected to vary between and among consumers, being high and positive for some, perhaps, while being low, or even negative, for others.

The Substitution Effect

DEFINITION: The *substitution effect* is defined as the change in the quantity demanded of product X, given a change in its price, and *ceteris paribus*. To find the substitution effect the consumer's *real* income must be held constant, unlike the price effect, for which only the consumer's *monetary* income is held constant.

NOTE: It is important to make the distinction between a consumer's monetary, or *nominal*, income and his *real* income. Nominal income is the amount of money the consumer has to spend. Given a set of product prices, the consumer can buy certain amounts of various products. Suppose the price of one product is now reduced. The consumer is thus able to buy the same combination of goods and services as before but now spends a *smaller* amount of nominal income. The consumer thus has some money left over to purchase more of the commodity whose price has decreased or any other product. This increase in purchasing power, which follows the reduction of any product price, represents an increase in the consumer's *real* income. Real income, or the purchasing power of nominal income, may be expressed as the ratio of nominal income to a price index that represents the prices of all commodities. Hence, if the price index is reduced because of the lowering of any particular price, the consumer's real income is increased. Conversely, if the price of any product is raised, the consumer's real income is reduced.

Since the substitution effect requires constant real income, we need to adjust the consumer's nominal income to compensate for the change in real income that follows a price change. In Figure 3-8 we illustrate the isolation of the substitution effect. Suppose that the consumer's initial point of equilibrium is point A on the indifference curve I_1 and budget line MN. At this point the consumer chooses to purchase X_1 units of product X. Suppose now that the price of X is reduced, such that the income constraint line swings around to the new line MN', allowing the consumer to attain point B on indifference curve I_2. The consumer now chooses to purchase X_2 units of product X, and the total effect of the price change is to increase his consumption of product X by the distance $X_2 - X_1$. It can be seen that this total effect of the price change is what we have called the price effect, since a line joining points A and B would be part of the consumer's price consumption curve. We are now aware, however, that some part of this price effect is caused by an increase in the consumer's real income, which we

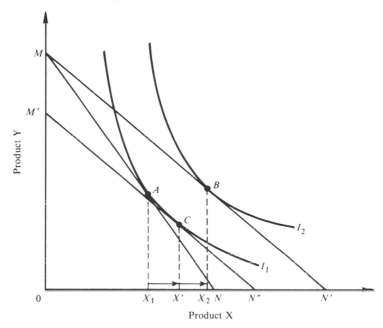

have called the income effect.[9] Thus, the price effect is comprised of the income effect and the substitution effect.

Separating the Income and the Substitution Effects of a Price Change. If we can account for and eliminate the income effect, we will be able to identify the remainder of the price effect as the substitution effect. We can account for the income effect by adjusting the consumer's monetary income until it allows the same level of real income as it did before the price change. To eliminate the increase in the real income, we must reduce the consumer to his previous level of real income. A method of comparing levels of real income is to compare the utility that may be derived from particular levels of nominal income. Hence if we were to reduce this consumer to the initial level of utility by a reduction in his nominal income, we would, in effect, have reduced the consumer to the initial level of real income. Thus, we wish to move the consumer from the level of utility at point B in Figure 3-8 down to a level of utility which is equivalent to point A and therefore lies on the indifference curve I_1.

By hypothetically reducing the consumer's nominal income, we begin

---

[9] In our earlier discussion of the income effect we did not make the distinction between real and monetary changes in the consumer's income level, since with unchanged prices, an increase in monetary income would mean an equal increase in real income.

to move the MN' budget constraint line downward and to the left, such that it remains parallel to MN'. When this hypothetical budget line is tangent to indifference curve I_1, the consumer's level of utility is reduced to a level of real income equivalent to that previously derived from point A. This occurs with budget line $M'N''$ at the tangency point C. At the hypothetical point C the consumer would choose to purchase X' units of product X. The movement from point C to point B, or from X' units to X_2 units, is the income effect, since a line joining points C and B would, in fact, be part of this consumer's income consumption curve. The remaining part of the total effect of the price change, from X_1 to X', is the substitution effect. The change in consumption of X from X_1 to X' is simply the result of the differing price ratio, exhibited by the slope of budget line $M'N''$ as compared to the initial line MN, since all other factors, including consumer's real income, remain unchanged.

To reinforce your understanding of the process of separating the income and substitution effects of a price change, let us repeat the process, this time using an inferior product on the X-axis.

Inferior Goods. In Figure 3-9 we show the income and substitution effects of a price change for an inferior good.[10] Again the initial point is a tangency between budget line MN and indifference curve I_1 at point A. The price of Product X is reduced such that the budget line swings around to MN', allowing the consumer a new higher level of utility at point B on indifference curve I_2. The total effect of the price change, or the price effect, is the movement from A to B, which in terms of Product X is a change in consumption from X_1 to X_2. To isolate the income effect we hypothetically reduce the consumer's income until a budget line with the same slope (that is, with the same price ratio) as budget line MN' is just tangent to the original indifference curve. This occurs at point C. The income effect is thus the movement from C to B, or in terms of Product X from X' to X_2.

In this case the income effect is negative, since the increase in real income caused by the price reduction was accompanied by a decrease in the quantity demanded of Product X. A line drawn between the points C and B, which is part of the consumer's income consumption curve, would have a negative slope, confirming that Product X is regarded by this consumer as an inferior good. The substitution effect is once again the movement along the initial indifference curve from point A to point C. This fulfills our

---

[10] The indifference curve map must reflect the inferiority of Product X in order for our graphs to "work out" correctly. When Product X is regarded as inferior, the indifference curves will not be parallel but will be closer together at the top end than they are at the bottom end, as shown in Figure 3-9. While indifference curves are everywhere dense (meaning that one passes through every point on the graph), they are also infinitely narrow, so that the multitude of indifference curves that exist between the lower parts of curves I_1 and I_2 have no problem squeezing through the more narrow space at the top end of those curves.

FIGURE 3-9.   Income and Substitution Effects of a Price Change
for an Inferior Good

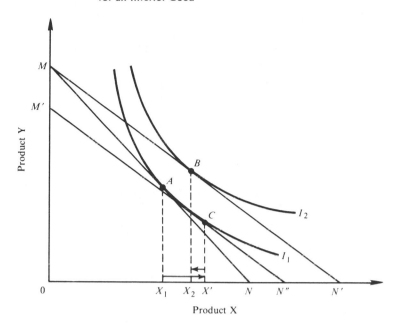

definition of the substitution effect, since it is the change in quantity demanded of Product X when the price of Product X changes, with all other
factors—including the consumer's real income—held constant. The substitution effect of a price reduction for Product X is thus an increase in the
quantity demanded of Product X from level X_1 to X'. This is partly offset
by a negative income effect from X' to X_2, such that the total effect (or
the price effect) is from X_1 to X_2.

NOTE: Notice that in both the normal goods case and the inferior goods case the
substitution effect was negative. Given the general validity of the assumptions that underlie the construction of a consumer's indifference curve, the
substitution effect is *always* negative; that is, for price reductions corrected
for the income effect the consumer will always purchase more of the product, while for price increases corrected for the income effect the consumer
will always purchase less of the product. The income effect, however, may
be either positive or negative, and, if negative, it offsets part of the substitution effect.

It is theoretically possible that a large negative income effect could
more than offset the substitution effect, in which case a price reduction
would be followed by a decline in the quantity demanded, or a price increase would be followed by an increase in the quantity demanded. A
product that behaved in this way would exhibit a positive price effect and
would therefore run counter to the empirical law of demand. Such a product

is known as a *Giffen good*.[11] A modern day example of a Giffen good is difficult to find, keeping in mind that we require *ceteris paribus* to hold when the price of the product in question is changed. A situation that may seem to indicate a Giffen good is one in which a product sells for a while at one price and later sells more units at a higher price. If and only if *ceteris paribus* prevailed over the entire period of the observations would the product be a Giffen good. More likely, however, one or more of the underlying factors has changed during the period (such as consumer tastes, incomes, and the prices and availability of other products). If so, the two observations are not on the same demand curve but are on separate demand curves, because of a shift of the demand curve caused in turn by a change in an underlying determinant.

EXAMPLE: Suppose a merchant offers hand towels for sale at $0.59 each and demand for these towels is somewhat less than enthusiastic. If the merchant now raises the price to $0.99 and customers eagerly purchase the towels, does this mean that those hand towels are a Giffen good? The answer is probably no. Consumers tend to make price-quality associations when they are unable to judge quality on any other basis. At the lower price the hand towels were perceived as "low-quality" hand towels, whereas at the higher price they were perceived as "better-quality" hand towels. The consumers' taste and preference patterns between low-quality and high-quality hand towels are probably the same as they were when they were first confronted by the hand towels. The error in calling hand towels a Giffen good rests upon failing to distinguish that consumers regard the higher-priced hand towels as a different product from the lower-priced hand towels. Our analysis of the income and substitution effects of a price change for a particular good depends upon successive units of that product being identical with the preceding and following units.

In the above example the two observations are most likely part of two separate negatively sloping demand curves, rather than of a single positively sloping demand curve. "Shifts" versus "movements along" demand curves are discussed in detail in Chapter 4, and the "identification problem," which causes confusion between shifts and movements along demand curves in practice, is discussed in Chapter 5.

To summarize, the price effect is composed of an income effect and a

---

[11] The existence of such perverse price effects was noted in the case of potatoes during the Irish famine of 1846 to 1849. Although the price of potatoes had increased as a result of a blight affecting the crops and reducing supplies, many families were consuming more potatoes than they were at earlier prices. The Irish peasant was typically so poor that potatoes formed the major part of the family diet, supplemented by meat and other foodstuffs. When the price of potatoes was increased, the demand for potatoes actually increased, since the money left over for meat and other foodstuffs (after buying the same quantity of potatoes) was insufficient to buy enough of these less-bulky items to satisfy the family appetite. Thus, demand for the more-filling potato was increased despite its higher price. See G.J. Stigler, "Notes on the History of the Giffen Paradox," *Journal of Political Economy*, 55 (April 1947), pp. 152-56.

substitution effect. The income effect is the change in quantity demanded because of the change in real income which accompanies a price change, given *ceteris paribus*. The substitution effect is the change in quantity demanded because of a change in the relative prices of two products, given *ceteris paribus*. To isolate the income effect we move the new budget line into tangency with the initial indifference curve to return the consumer to the initial level of real income. The change in quantity demanded that this would cause is the income effect and the remainder of the price effect is the substitution effect.

NOTE: For a price *increase*, the analysis is the same, only the direction is different. A price increase would cause the budget line to swing downward and the consumer to adjust to a lower indifference curve. The reduction in the quantity demanded of X is caused by an income effect and a substitution effect. Moving the new budget line up until it is tangent to the initial indifference curve will indicate that part of the reduction in demand for X which was caused by reduced real income, and the remainder of the price effect will be the substitution effect, since product X is now relatively more expensive than it was before.

Changes in Consumer Tastes and Preferences

In the above analysis consumer tastes and preferences were assumed to remain constant while changes took place in price and income levels. We must recognize, however, that consumer tastes and preferences may change from time to time, either in line with the latest fashions or trends, or as the result of the advertising and promotion expenditures of business firms. However induced, changes in consumer tastes and preferences have profound implications for the quantity demanded of particular products. In the following we shall analyze the implications of changes in consumer tastes and preferences for the demand for a product.

EXAMPLE: Suppose the sellers of Product X institute an advertising campaign to promote the demand for Product X. In the absence of simultaneous new campaigns from the sellers of other products, we would expect this campaign to influence at least some buyers in the direction of Product X. Referring to Figure 3-10, suppose the initial situation is represented by the tangency at point A on indifference curve I_1. An advertising campaign that causes Product X to be regarded more favorably than previously would cause that particular level of utility represented by indifference curve I_1 to be attained by the consumption of fewer units of Product X, since X is now regarded more highly. Suppose that, whereas consumers previously required X_1 units of Product X to attain the utility level depicted by indifference curve I_1, it now takes only X_1' units of Product X to attain the *same level* of utility, in conjunction with Y_1 units of Product Y. In effect, then, indifference curve I_1 has swung downward and to the left, since the same level of utility can be

FIGURE 3-10.   A Change in Tastes and Preferences in Favor of Product X

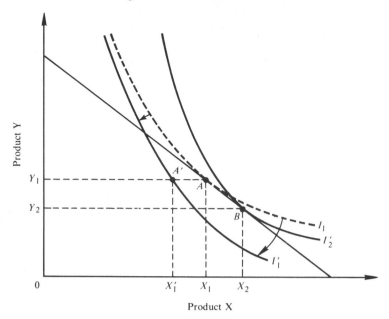

obtained with lesser combinations of X and Y due to the new appreciation the consumer has for Product X. Under the new taste and preference conditions, indifference curve I_1 is irrelevant, since it refers to a previous pattern of tastes and preferences.

Thus the consumer *could* derive the same level of utility by shifting back from point A to point A'. Instead the consumer will wish to reallocate his or her budget such that utility is maximized under the new circumstances. Indifference curve I_2' is the highest attainable indifference curve given the budget constraint, and hence the consumer reallocates his or her income between Products X and Y such that he or she is located at point B. Notice that the change of tastes and preferences in favor of Product X has led to an increase in the consumption of Product X, from X_1 to X_2, and to a reduction in the consumption of Product Y (the only other alternative product available), from Y_1 and Y_2. In this simple two-commodity model the gain of Product X necessarily came at the expense of Product Y, whereas in a multicommodity system the shift of tastes and preferences in favor of Product X would be at the expense of some, but not necessarily all, of the other products.

It is unlikely that all consumers will be influenced by a particular advertising campaign or by a trend or fashion that is sweeping society, and therefore some consumers will not change their consumption of Product X because neither their taste and preference pattern nor their perception of the product has changed. Moreover, some consumers will be affected more than other consumers, and hence their demand for Product X will be increased to a larger degree.

Real Price Changes vs. Nominal Price Changes

Throughout the above discussion we have been speaking of price changes by a particular nominal amount, with the implied assumption that the real value of the monetary unit remains constant. In the real world, however, we have become accustomed to "inflation," or the depreciation of the monetary unit over time. We should not expect governments to completely eliminate inflation, since an inflation rate of a few percentage points annually is said to be beneficial for business confidence, business investment, employment, and also, one might argue, for the reelection of the government. Thus, we must deal with nominal price changes in a currency unit that is typically slowly depreciating.

To the extent that the price of a particular product increases over a period of time at a rate equal to the rate of inflation, the price increases may be regarded as adjustments to the depreciating value of the currency unit and therefore prices remain relatively constant in real, or purchasing-power, terms. When the nominal price increases by *more* than the rate of inflation, this amounts to an increase in the real price level. When the nominal price increases by less than the rate of inflation, does not change, or is actually reduced, this amounts to a decrease in the real price level.

For most business firms, prices cannot be changed continuously according to the rate of inflation and therefore must take upward "steps" over time while the general price level continues more smoothly upward. Thus, real prices tend to fall progressively, then rise abruptly as nominal prices are adjusted, then fall progressively, and so on. Increasing productivity in the use of resources, expanding markets that permit economies of larger-scale operation, and other factors frequently mean that a firm can allow its prices to increase at a rate slower than that of inflation without suffering a squeeze on profits. On the contrary, the consequent reduction in real prices may allow the firm to make significant gains in sales and in market share.

NOTE: It is important to remember that the entire analysis of consumer behavior presupposes a constant value of the monetary unit. In real-world situations where nominal price changes are observed, we must be careful to evaluate the price change in real terms before concluding that the law of demand is inoperative or that one of the other predictions of consumer behavior theory is inaccurate.

3.4 THE ATTRIBUTE APPROACH TO CONSUMER CHOICE

Although it is useful for pedagogical and limited explanatory purposes, the traditional model of consumer behavior suffers from several shortcomings that have prevented its widespread use as an explanatory, or predictive, model. For practical purposes, such as the marketing of a firm's products, it would be desirable if we could apply the model to explain, for example, why some consumers in a particular market prefer brand A, whereas others prefer brand B. Alternatively, we might wish to predict the increase in market share following an improvement of our product or to foresee the vulnerability of our sales to the emergence of a new product.

The traditional, or neoclassical, model does not examine *why* particular consumers buy one particular product rather than a competing brand. This model has typically adopted the approach that the underlying reasons are the territory of the psychologist and sociologist and that an economist takes the consumer's taste and preference pattern as given. Using the notion of *revealed preference*, the economist took the view that the consumer's preference is revealed by that consumer's purchases of goods and services. Why does the consumer buy two beers and one hamburger? Because the consumer expected to maximize utility by so doing. Why the consumer purchases Budweiser beer rather than Schlitz, Coors, or Molson is subsumed under the presumption that this particular consumer prefers Budweiser to the other brands of beer. It is, therefore, Budweiser beer that is being compared with hamburgers to find the utility-maximizing combination. Similarly, why a hamburger and not a hot dog, a taco, or some fried chicken? These issues are of immense interest to the marketer in the practical application of consumer behavior theory. Traditional economic theory, however, cannot easily provide adequate answers.

Kelvin Lancaster introduced the *attribute analysis* of consumer behavior in 1966 and expanded this substantially in 1971.[12] This new theory of demand, while continuing to use utility and indifference curve analysis, departed from the traditional approach by asserting that consumers derive utility not from the products themselves but from the characteristics or attributes provided by the products.

EXAMPLE: An automobile is desired not for its "automobileness"—its physical composition of nuts, bolts, steel, and plastic—but for the services it provides —transportation, comfort, convenience, prestige, security, and privacy. Consumer demand for an automobile (or any other product) is thus a *derived* demand, in the sense that it is derived from the demand for various services or attributes; the automobile simply provides those attributes. Similarly, a meal in a fancy restaurant is not purchased simply to fill one's stomach but rather to enjoy the attributes of pleasant surroundings, courteous service, exotic food, good company, and no mess to clean up. Sky diving is undertaken not by those wishing to fall out of an airplane but by those in search of danger, exhilaration, solitude, exclusiveness, an outlet for their courage, or a conversation opener.

If it is the attributes that are desired, rather than the products in which they are found, it is instructive to examine the consumer's demand for the attributes *directly*, rather than *indirectly* as in the products approach. This

---

[12] K. Lancaster, "A New Approach to Consumer Theory," *Journal of Political Economy*, 74 (April 1966), pp. 132-57; and *Consumer Demand: A New Approach*, (New York: Columbia University Press, 1971).

is especially useful when a particular attribute—excitement, for example—is available in a wide variety of products, such as automobiles, sky diving, roller coasters, and skate-boarding on freeways. In such a case the consumer derives an "excitement quota" from some but not necessarily from all of the available sources of supply. The attribute approach allows us to explain this behavior. Unlike the product approach, which takes the consumer's preferences between and among products as an imponderable fact, the attribute approach looks behind these preferences to explain them in terms of the attributes of those products. The product approach is unable to explain in simple terms why a particular consumer would, for example, never buy a particular type of automobile or never visit some nearby restaurants. The attribute approach greatly facilitates the explanation of consumer choice within such groups of substitutes and readily allows us to incorporate new products into the analysis.

Depicting Products in Attribute Space

The consumer derives utility from the consumption of attributes but must buy products in order to obtain the desired attributes. The products are simply the means by which the attributes are supplied to the consumption process. Each product will supply one or more attributes in a particular ratio.

EXAMPLE: To demonstrate how a consumer might choose among products in order to maximize utility derived from the attributes, consider the case of an aspiring gourmet, Mr. Magnus Corpus, who dines out frequently and has a choice of six nearby restaurants. Mr. Corpus chooses among six products (the meal and its associated attributes at each of six restaurants), so that his utility is maximized. In order to treat the problem graphically, let us suppose that he seeks only two attributes: exotic atmosphere and haute cuisine. The six restaurants provide these attributes in differing proportions and at different prices. Let us suppose that after visiting all six restaurants Mr. Corpus rates each one on a scale of 100 for both exotic atmosphere and haute cuisine, as shown in Table 3-1.

In Figure 3-11 the six products are depicted in attribute space as rays from the origin. The slope of each ray is determined by the ratio of exotic

TABLE 3-1. Attributes and Prices of Meals at Six Restaurants

Restaurant	Price of Meal ($)	ATTRIBUTE RATING		Ratio of Atmosphere to Cuisine	Meals per $100
		Atmosphere	Cuisine		
A	22.22	89	22	4.05	4.50
B	25.00	94	50	1.88	4.00
C	27.30	76	86	0.88	3.66
D	26.47	57	90	0.63	3.78
E	18.95	18	72	0.25	5.28
F	19.74	10	77	0.13	5.07

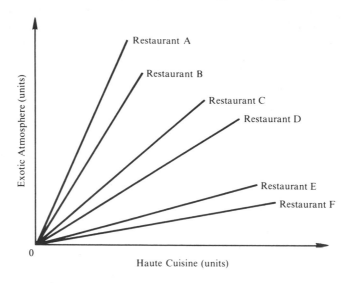

FIGURE 3-11.   Depicting Products in the Attribute Approach

atmosphere to haute cuisine, as listed in Table 3-1. If Mr. Corpus has a meal at restaurant A, he "travels out" along the steepest ray, absorbing the two attributes in the ratio of 4.05:1—4.05 units of exotic atmosphere to each unit of haute cuisine. The other restaurants (products) are indicated by the lower rays. These offer atmosphere and cuisine at a lower ratio. Notice that a product for which one of the attributes was completely absent, such as home cooking, would be represented by one of the axes. (*You* decide which axis!)

The Budget Constraint and the Efficiency Frontier

How far along each ray would the gourmet go? That is, how much of Product A, or any other product, is it possible to purchase? The answer of course is up to the limit of his budget constraint. Suppose Mr. Corpus examines his finances and decides to allocate $100 monthly to eating in one or more of the six restaurants. The prices at the restaurants for a given meal are not identical, as shown in Table 3-1. If Mr. Corpus spends his entire $100 in restaurant A, he could have 4.5 meals at the price of $22.22 per meal (including taxes and tip) before exhausting his budget. Now 4.5 meals at restaurant A produce 4.5 × 89 = 400.5 units of the attribute exotic atmosphere and 4.5 × 22 = 99 units of the attribute haute cuisine. This point in attribute space is marked as point A in Figure 3-12. It shows the maximum intake of the two attributes that can be obtained by consuming product A, given the budget constraint of $100. Repeating this procedure for each of the other five restaurants, we find the limiting points B, C, D, E, and F on each product ray, which represent the entire budget (hypo-

FIGURE 3-12.   The Efficiency Frontier in the Attribute Approach

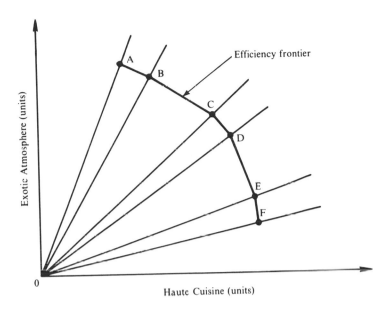

thetically) spent at each of the restaurants. Joining the points *ABCDEF* we have what is known as the efficiency frontier in attribute space.

DEFINITION: The *efficiency frontier* is the outer boundary of the attainable combinations of the two attributes, given the budget constraint. We shall presently see that any point on the frontier is attainable by consuming combinations of the two adjacent products; it is called *efficient* because a rational consumer will prefer a combination of attributes on the frontier rather than any combination inside the frontier.

Maximizing Utility from Attributes

Just as consumers were able to express preference or indifference between combinations of products, they will be able to express preference or indifference between combinations of attributes. At any given combination of exotic atmosphere and haute cuisine, our gourmet will be able to express a marginal rate of substitution between the two attributes: an extra unit of haute cuisine will be worth giving up some amount of exotic atmosphere in this consumer's mind. Thus, Mr. Corpus will have an indifference map in attribute space expressing his tastes and preferences between the two attributes at all levels of those attributes. We show the gourmet's indifference map in Figure 3-13. As before, higher curves are preferred to lower curves, the curves have negative slopes throughout, they neither meet nor intersect, and they are convex to the origin.

FIGURE 3-13.   **Indifference Curves between Attributes**

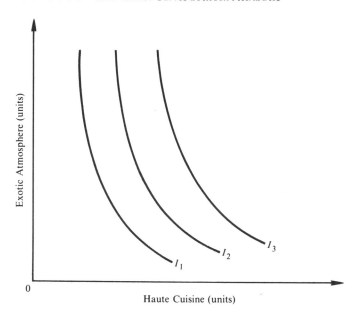

Since both the indifference map and the efficiency frontier are in attribute space, we can superimpose one upon the other to find the combination of attributes that allows the consumer to reach the highest attainable indifference curve. In Figure 3-14 we show indifference curve $I*$ as tangent

FIGURE 3-14.   **Maximization of Utility from Attributes**

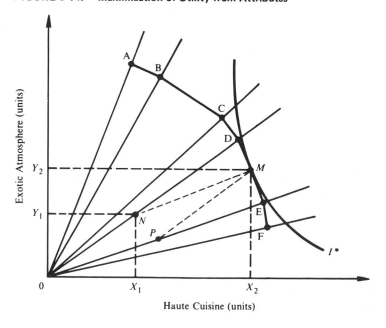

DEMAND THEORY, ANALYSIS, AND ESTIMATION

to the efficiency frontier at point M. Thus, the combination of attributes Y_2 of exotic atmosphere and X_2 of haute cuisine allows Mr. Corpus to maximize his utility.

The Mixability of Products. Notice that combination M lies *between* the rays representing Restaurant D and Restaurant E. There is no restaurant available that provides the attributes in exactly the ratio represented by point M. The gourmet can attain combination M, however, by mixing Product D and Product E. That is, by visiting Restaurant D and Restaurant E a number of times each, Mr. Corpus can absorb—by aggregating the attributes absorbed at each restaurant over his total number of visits during the month—exactly the combination of attributes represented by point M. If Mr. Corpus visits Restaurant D until he reaches point N on that ray, he will accumulate Y_1 units of exotic atmosphere and X_1 units of haute cuisine. At point N he should then switch to Restaurant E in order to accumulate the attributes in the ratio necessary to achieve point M. The line NM in Figure 3-14 has the same slope as the ray representing Restaurant E. By spending the remainder of the $100 in Restaurant E, the gourmet derives an extra $Y_2 - Y_1$ units of exotic atmosphere and $X_2 - X_1$ units of haute cuisine, bringing his total to Y_2 units of the former and X_2 units of the latter, thereby maximizing his utility.

Alternatively, the gourmet could attain point M by visiting Restaurant E until he had in effect reached point P on the ray representing Restaurant E, and he could then switch to Restaurant D to accumulate the remaining units of the two attributes in the ratio necessary to reach point M. The two paths to maximum utility are thus $0NM$ or $0PM$ in Figure 3-14. Since $0NMP$ is a parallelogram, however, the path $0PM$ is equivalent to $0NM$, because $0N = PM$ and $0P = NM$. Mr. Corpus may visit either restaurant first or in whatever sequence suits his whims, as long as the attributes accumulate to the combination M without exceeding the $100 budget constraint.[13]

NOTE: You may think it strange that the consumer patronizes only two of the six restaurants. This is a function of our two-attribute model. The more attributes the consumer desires, the more products one would expect to be necessary to supply the optimum combination of those attributes. In the two-attribute case, the optimum combination of attributes could have been supplied by just one of the available products, if the highest attainable indifference curve had touched one of the corners of the efficiency frontier.

---

[13] The consumer could arrive at point M by combining nonadjacent products, for example, D and F. This is inefficient, however, since it would cost more than $100. One hundred dollars spent on some combination of D and F brings the consumer to a point on a straight line joining points D and F, since it is a linear combination of those points. The straight line joining D and F must necessarily lie below the section of the frontier DEF, and therefore does not include point M. To reach point M by combining nonadjacent products, therefore, costs more than $100. See Lancaster, "A New Approach to Consumer Theory," pp. 132-57.

(In Figure 3-14 these corners are the points A, B, C, D, E, and F.) Where the highest attainable indifference curve is tangent to a flat section of the efficiency frontier, a combination of two goods is necessary, as in the above case. If, for example, the consumer desires n attributes, as many as n products (restaurants) might be required to provide the optimal combination of attributes.[14]

Indivisibility of Products.   Where products cost a large amount of money in relation to the consumer's income or are otherwise available only in discrete units, the consumer may have to settle for a suboptimal combination of attributes. With a very large and indivisible purchase, such as an automobile, the consumer must choose one product or another and is therefore constrained to one of the corners on the efficiency frontier. Consider Figure 3-15, in which we show three automobiles in economy-comfort attribute space. Brand A automobile offers a relatively high ratio of economy to comfort, followed by brands B and C. If these products were mixable, the efficiency frontier would be the kinked line ABC, and the consumer would maximize utility by mixing brands A and B at point W to attain indifference curve I^*.

But if the consumer cannot mix brands A and B (by renting both cars or by agreeing with another person to buy the other car and then share), the consumer must be content to attain either point A, point B, or point C. Of these options, point A allows the attainment of the highest indifference

FIGURE 3-15.   **Indivisibility of Products Necessitating a Suboptimal Combination of Attributes**

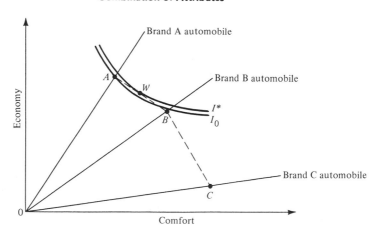

DEMAND THEORY, ANALYSIS, AND ESTIMATION

curve, shown as I_0. The indivisibility of the products thus prevents the consumer from reaching indifference curve I^*, and the consumer must be satisfied with the suboptimal point A on indifference curve I_0. Given the constraint imposed by the indivisibility of the product, the consumer chooses the best available option.

The Price Effect

Suppose the price of one of the products embodying the desired attributes is changed. What effect will this have on the demand for this product? What effect will it have on the demand for the other (substitute) products which the consumer also considers purchasing in order to obtain the desired attributes?

EXAMPLE: Consider the case of an audiophile who has a cassette tape deck and frequently purchases new tapes. She desires two major attributes in these tapes, namely, "clarity of sound reproduction" and "reliability of tape operation." There are five brands available, and we show the efficiency frontier and two of the audiophile's indifference curves in Figure 3-16.

Initially, the prices of the five brands are such that the efficiency frontier is $ABCDE$, and the consumer is able to maximize utility at point C, where indifference curve I_1 just touches the frontier. Now suppose that the price of Brand B is reduced, such that the efficiency frontier moves out

FIGURE 3-16.   The Price Effect Shown by the Attribute Approach: Audiophile 1

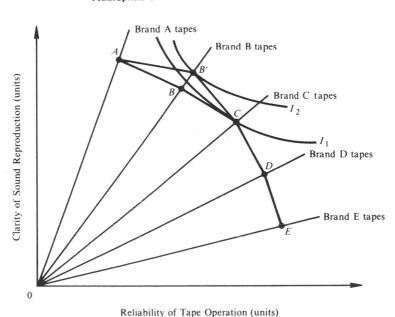

Reliability of Tape Operation (units)

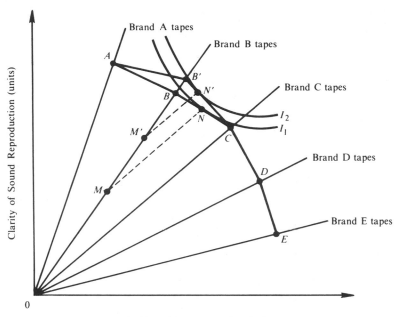

Reliability of Tape Operation (units)

along the Brand-B ray to point B' and is now represented by $AB'CDE$. The audiophile can now attain a higher indifference curve (I_2) by switching to Brand B tapes. Product B offers the attributes in a different ratio to the previously preferred Product C, but the consumer exhibits a marginal rate of substitution between the attributes and is willing to trade off some "reliability" for more "clarity" at the lower price in order to increase her total utility derived.

In Figure 3-17 we show a different case in which a different consumer is initially mixing two products in order to obtain the desired combination of attributes. Our second consumer has a different taste and preference pattern between the two attributes, as compared with the consumer depicted in Figure 3-16. The second audiophile's indifference map is such that his highest-attainable indifference curve, given the initial efficiency frontier $ABCDE$, is tangent to the frontier at point N. This consumer prefers to purchase both Brand B and Brand C tapes, presumably using the Brand B tapes for applications where "clarity" is relatively more important. Let us suppose his path to the frontier is $0MN$.

Again we reduce the price of Brand B tapes, and the new efficiency frontier becomes $AB'CDE$. Our second audiophile is able to increase utility by moving to point N' on indifference curve I_2. He still purchases both Brand B and Brand C tapes, but he now will purchase more Brand B tapes and fewer Brand C tapes. Whereas his previous path to the frontier was

$0MN$, it is now $0M'N'$. The segment $0M'$ exceeds $0M$, indicating the consumer's greater absorption of the attributes from Product B and hence greater purchases of Product B. The segment $M'N'$ is shorter than MN, indicating the consumer's reduced purchases of Product C. Thus the law of demand is demonstrated by the behavior of both audiophiles: each one responded to the reduced price of Brand B tapes by buying more of that brand and less of a substitute brand.

Pricing a Product out of the Market.   Given a consumer's perception of the attributes embodied in a particular product, there is a maximum price that the consumer will pay for that product even if it exactly mirrors his taste and preference pattern. In Figure 3-18 we show a simple case where three products offer the two desired attributes X and Y. The initial price situation generates the efficiency frontier ABC, and the consumer maximizes utility on indifference curve I_2 by purchasing only Product B. Suppose the price of Product B is now increased such that the efficiency frontier becomes $AB'C$. The consumer is now unable to reach indifference curve I_2 and must be content with the lower curve I_1 at point B', still purchasing only Product B but necessarily purchasing fewer units of Product B because of its higher price and the consumer's unchanged budget.

If the price of Product B is raised still further, such that the consumer's entire budget spent on Product B would purchase only the combination of attributes shown by point B'' for example, this consumer will no longer buy any units of Product B. The efficiency frontier remains at $AB'C$ and Product

FIGURE 3-18.   Pricing a Product "Out of the Market"

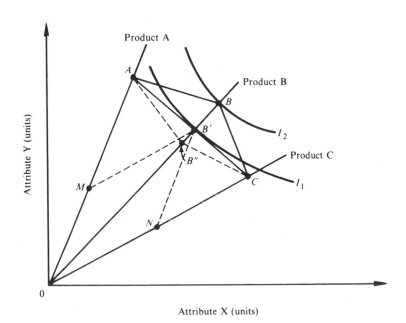

B has fallen inside the frontier. Purchase of Product B would now be an inefficient use of the consumer's budget, since the other products provide the desired attributes more inexpensively. The consumer is still able to attain point B' on the efficiency frontier and on indifference curve I_1, but will now travel via the path $0MB'$ or $0NB'$ rather than along the ray representing Product B. That is, the consumer will now prefer to combine Products A and C in order to maximize utility from a given budget rather than purchase any of Product B. Thus Product B has been priced out of reach for this consumer, even though it provides the attributes in exactly the preferred ratio. (I feel the same way about Ferraris.)

Other consumers may continue to purchase Product B if they perceive more units of the attributes in each unit of Product B as compared with the perception of the consumer discussed above. Alternatively, some consumers may purchase Product B for a different attribute that is provided by the product but was unimportant to the above consumer. In both cases Product B may remain on the efficiency frontier and be purchased by those consumers who need it to maximize their utility despite its increased price.

Thus we see that the price effect, or the law of demand, still applies to products even though they are purchased as a means of acquiring desired attributes. As price falls, consumers already purchasing the product in question will purchase more units, and other consumers will begin to buy their first units of that product. Alternatively, as price is increased, consumers will buy fewer units or will drop out of the market for that product completely. Substitute products will tend to sell more units when the price of a product on an adjacent ray increases and will tend to sell fewer units when the price of that product is reduced.

Changes in Consumer Perceptions and Tastes

The attribute content of a product depends critically upon the consumer's perception of those attributes. In the production process a product may be endowed with great strength and durability, but if a consumer thinks it looks "flimsy," then this strength and durability is not perceived. Advertising and promotional activity by sellers of particular products, as well as information from other sources (word of mouth or published reports by consumer testing agencies), may change the consumer's perception of the quantity of particular attributes embodied in each unit of a particular product. We now examine the impact this might have on the demand for the product.

NOTE: The first thing we must do is to make the distinction between changes in perceptions and changes in tastes. A consumer's perceptions relate to the amount of each attribute perceived to exist in each unit of the product. A consumer's tastes refer to the amount of utility expected from each unit of the product. Attribute analysis allows us to separate these quite neatly: a change in perceptions shifts one or more of the product rays and may shift the efficiency frontier, whereas a change in tastes shifts the indifference curves (via changes in marginal utilities that are involved in the marginal rate of substitution and hence the slope of indifference curves).

EXAMPLE: Consider a situation in which a consumer perceives three products A, B, and C in attribute XY space, as in Figure 3-19. Suppose the efficiency frontier is initially ABC. The consumer attains the highest possible indifference curve at point C and therefore purchases Product C. Suppose now that Product B benefits from an advertising campaign, so that our consumer now perceives a larger quantity of both attributes Y and X in Product B for the same price level. If the consumer perceives the attributes to have increased in the same ratio, the efficiency frontier moves out along the Product B ray from point B to point B'. This allows the consumer to attain a higher indifference curve, I_2, by choosing Product B.

Hence this particular consumer is motivated to purchase Product B as a direct result of the advertising campaign. Similarly, other consumers who were previously purchasing either no units of Product B or some units of Product B in combination with adjacent products are now motivated to purchase more units of Product B, since this allows each of these consumers to attain higher indifference curves. For some consumers, of course, the changed perception of Product B is not sufficiently great to cause those consumers to buy any—or any more of—Product B.

FIGURE 3-19. Attribute Analysis of a Change in Consumer Perception of a Product

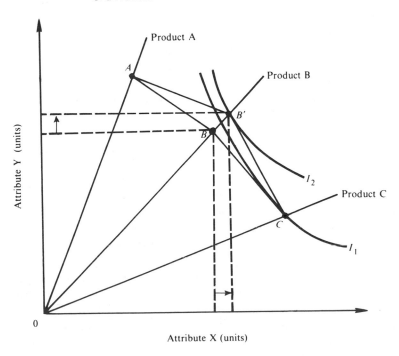

If the advertising campaign or new information received by the consumer causes the consumer to believe that the attribute content of a product has changed in different proportions, the product ray changes its slope in attribute space. Refer to Figure 3-20 in which we depict three economy cars in the comfort-economy attribute space. Suppose that initially the efficiency frontier is ABC and the consumer chooses Product C, attaining indifference curve I_0. Now suppose that Volkswagen begins to advertise their diesel-engine Rabbit using the theme that economy means more than just fuel economy. Operating economy includes the savings on electrical parts and tune-ups one expects with a diesel engine. Diesel engines have no carburetor, no spark plugs, no points, no condenser, no distributor (and no power, too!). The absence of these parts saves money since they don't have to be recalibrated and replaced.

Let us assume the consumer is convinced by this reasoning and now perceives the Rabbit to contain the same amount of comfort as before, but more economy. In terms of Figure 3-20 the consumer perceives an extra $X_1 - X_0$ units of economy in the Rabbit. This causes the Rabbit's product ray to shift from $0B$ to $0B'$, and the efficiency frontier to move from ABC to $AB'C$. In the case depicted the consumer can now attain a higher indifference curve by switching to the Rabbit from Product C. Thus a changed perception of the attribute content of one or more products may change the shape or location of the efficiency frontier, without affecting the consumer's indifference curves.[15]

It is completely possible that consumers' tastes for attributes could change at the same time or in response to different stimuli. Suppose a consumer suddenly becomes more aware of the energy shortage and wants to be more socially responsible by using less fuel. This is reflected by a steepening of the consumer's indifference curves in comfort-economy space. The consumer's MRS between comfort and economy would increase as a result of this change in taste for the attributes. A change in the indifference map is likely to cause a new point of tangency, of course, and the consumer may rearrange his or her purchases as a result.

NOTE: It is important to see that this change in tastes is independent from any change in perceptions of the attribute content of the products. The attribute approach allows us to make this distinction, whereas the product approach simply says consumers (for whatever reasons) have changed their tastes between or among products, without being able to distinguish whether this was caused by changes in perceptions of the products, changes in tastes for the attributes, or some combination of the two.

---

[15] If a product is an inefficient supplier of the desired attributes, changed perceptions of this product do not change the efficiency frontier, unless these changes are sufficient to cause the product to be viewed as an efficient supplier of the attributes. Oppositely, of course, new information or experience with a product may cause a consumer to view a product as inefficient for the first time. A distasteful or boring advertising campaign could change a consumer's perceptions of attribute content downward.

DEMAND THEORY, ANALYSIS, AND ESTIMATION

FIGURE 3-20. Changed Consumer Perception of a Product:
the Volkswagen Rabbit Diesel Example

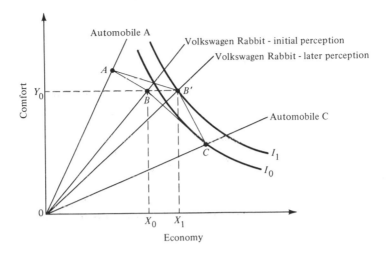

New Products

The advent of new products prevents no difficulty for the attribute approach; a new product can be represented on an existing graph as a new ray. If the ratio of attributes offered by the new product is the same as for an existing product, it will occupy the same ray as that existing product. If, however, the new product offers more of this combination of attributes per dollar, as compared with the existing product, the new product will push the efficiency frontier outward and will eclipse the existing product in the eyes of rational consumers. Since the new product offers more utility per dollar than the old, no rational consumer would buy the older product. In the case of market entry by a new product that is not identical in its offering of product attributes when compared with existing products, there will be a new ray in the figure. If the highest affordable point on that ray (where total income is spent entirely on the new product) occurs outside the existing frontier, the new product will serve to push the frontier outward at a point where it was previously flat. In both the above cases, where the new product extends the frontier, some consumers will change their consumption in favor of the new product, since the new frontier will now poke through their previously attained indifference curves and allow them to reach a new higher curve.

EXAMPLE: In Figure 3-21 we show an initial situation of only three products—A, B, and C. The initial efficiency frontier perceived by the consumer is thus ABC, and he or she attains indifference curve I_1 by purchasing Product B. We now suppose a new product is launched, which competes with Products A, B, and C in the sense that it also offers attributes X and Y. The new product offers these attributes in a different ratio, however, between those

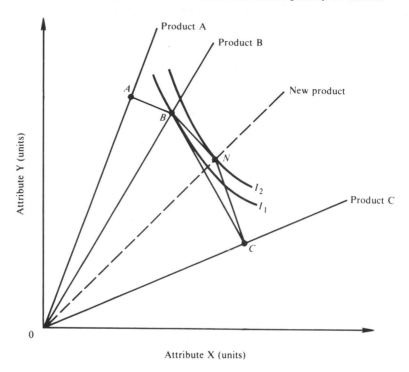

of Products B and C. The new product is priced so that the efficiency frontier is extended to *ABNC*. The consumer is now able to reach indifference curve I_2 by switching to the new product. Notice that the new product steals sales from both B and C, but does not affect A unless there are more than two attributes desired by consumers. In the real world, of course, consumers do demand more than two attributes simultaneously, and we should expect the advent of a new product (or new model of an existing product) to affect the sales of a range of other products.

Market Segments

DEFINITION: *Market segments* are groups of consumers who have similar taste and preference patterns and who therefore tend to buy similar products. Groups of consumers with similar marginal rates of substitution, at a particular combination of attributes, will tend to find their highest-attainable indifference curve tangent to the efficiency frontier at similar points. Consumers with relatively *low* MRS between the attributes will tend to buy products with relatively *high* attribute ratio rays, and vice versa.

EXAMPLE: In the case of the cassette tapes discussed earlier, we may characterize the "music clarity" segment as consisting of those who will have low marginal rates of substitution (relatively flat indifference curves) between clarity and reliability and who therefore tend to purchase Brands A and B. On the other hand, consumers with relatively high marginal rates of substitution (relatively steep indifference curves) will tend to buy Brands D and E and may be characterized as the "reliability" segment. Similarly, consumers with a low MRS between exotic atmosphere and haute cuisine tend to eat at restaurants A, B, and C and might be characterized as the "exotic" segment of the market, whereas the patrons of restaurants D, E, and F might be called the "gourmet" segment.

Knowledge of the tastes of consumers for the various attributes allows firms to design their products to incorporate the attributes in the ratios desired by a particular group of consumers. This group of consumers becomes the firm's *target market*. Similarly, consumers in a particular market segment seek out firms that supply products providing the attributes in the desired ratios.

Problems of Identifying and Measuring Attributes

Some attributes are readily identifiable and measurable, such as the "power" and "economy" associated with an automobile. Objective measurement of "power" might proceed on the basis of engine horsepower, horsepower divided by vehicle weight, or some similar cardinal measure. Economy likewise can be measured by a standard unit of measure, such as miles per gallon or liters per hundred kilometers. Problems arise, however, with attributes that are measurable only subjectively, such as "modern styling," "prestige," "status," "comfort," and "security." The consumer will typically have an intuitive evaluation of these attributes and will be able to make what appears to that consumer as an optimal decision in the light of the information held.

The identification and measurability problems really arise when we attempt to explain or predict consumer behavior in real-world situations. As you will appreciate, the implications of attribute analysis for the pricing, promotion, product, and distribution strategies of the business firm are profound. If the firm is able to identify *which* attributes consumers base their choices upon and on *what basis* they evaluate the attributes, it is in a better position to increase sales and profits by adjusting one or more of its marketing strategies.[16] We return to this issue in the context of pricing policy in Chapter 11.

---

[16] In marketing research the technique of *conjoint analysis* is being used to establish consumers' perceptions and tradeoffs between attributes embodied in competing products. See, for example, Paul E. Green and V. Srinivasan, "Conjoint Analysis in Consumer Research: Issues and Outlook," *The Journal of Consumer Research*, 5 (Sept. 1978), pp. 103-23. Also Albert Madansky, "On Conjoint Analysis and Quantal Choice Models," *Journal of Business*, 53 (July 1980), pp. S37-S44.

3.5 AGGREGATION OF INDIVIDUAL DEMAND CURVES

Independent Consumer Preferences

To find the market demand for a particular product we need to aggregate the demands of all the individual consumers who express demand for the product at each price level. In the simple case in which consumer demands are independent of each other, we simply add (horizontally) the demand curves of all consumers. For each price level there is thus a total market demand which is the simple sum of all individual demands at that price level. Since the individual demand curves are negatively sloping, the aggregate of these will also be negatively sloping. In fact, the law of demand is often more noticeable in aggregate than it is in individual cases. We have all seen instances in which individuals seem to respond to price increases by apparently not reducing consumption much, if at all. Increasing the price of gasoline, for example, does not seem to cause some people to drive their cars less. To explain this we must first be assured that a price increase was real and not simply nominal. Second, we must recognize that consumer tastes and preferences may differ substantially among consumers, causing the rational response of some to be an extremely slight adjustment in quantity demanded. Third, we must note that consumer adjustment often takes time to accomplish. Consumers are unlikely to change immediately to a more economical car on the strength of an increase in gas prices, but when the car is replaced it may well be by a more economical model.

In aggregate the response to changed price levels will be more noticeable and immediate, however, as the sum of many small changes accumulate to something quite noticeable in terms of a reduction (or increase when price is reduced) in the firm's total demand.

The Bandwagon Effect

Since individual demand curves are constructed on the basis of *ceteris paribus*, a simple horizontal summation is valid only where consumer demands are independent of each other. For many consumers, however, the quantity they demand of a particular product depends to some degree on the quantity that other people are simultaneously demanding. For example, in the clothing industry a new style becomes fashionable as more and more people adopt that style. An individual's demand for a particular style may depend upon the overall market acceptance of that style. In many cases the widespread market acceptance of a style will cause individuals to demand *more* than they would have demanded had it not been so popular.

The tendency to change one's taste and preference pattern in favor of a particular product (or attribute) in some positive relationship with total demand for that product (or attribute) has been called the "bandwagon" effect.[17] Consumers in effect jump onto the bandwagon so that they can be where the crowd is. They allow their own tastes to be influenced positively by the tastes of the populace, and they may be said to gain utility from the knowledge that their consumption behavior is similar to that of their peer groups or to other groups of consumers.

The bandwagon effect will cause the indifference curves to shift in favor of the product that is experiencing the bandwagon effect. Figure 3-10 is appropriate in this case. Rather than advertising, which changes the marginal rate of substitution in favor of Product X, it is an increase in the consumers' appreciation of the virtues of Product X, due to its wider social acceptance, that causes the movement of the indifference curves.

The Snob Effect

The opposite relationship of individual consumer demand to total market demand is known as the "snob" effect. In this case individual demands will be reduced by the knowledge that a product is gaining wide market acceptance. Whereas under the bandwagon effect it was the attribute of "social conformity" that made the product more desirable, under the snob effect it is the attribute of "exclusivity" that makes the product more desirable. As the product loses this attribute due to widespread market adoption, some consumers will find the product less desirable and will buy fewer units than they would have bought if market demand had been smaller.

Thus, if the bandwagon effect applies, the individual's demand curve will shift outward at all price levels as market demand in total is increased. On the other hand, if the snob effect applies to an individual, his or her demand curve will shift back at all price levels as more and more consumers purchase the product. Thus total market demand will exceed the simple sum of independent individual demands if the bandwagon effect prevails, and it will fall short of the simple sum of individual demands if the snob effect prevails.

If simultaneous purchases by other consumers *are* taken into account when constructing the demand curves of individuals, the market demand curve is again the simple summation of all individual demands at each price level. Each consumer would be asked how much of Product X he or she would buy when market demand is at various levels, in order to determine the presence or absence of either the bandwagon or the snob effect. Some consumers may exhibit bandwagon effects at the same time that others demonstrate snob effects. Market demand is the sum of all individual demands and hence is greater or smaller than the sum of "independent" demands, to the extent that a *net* bandwagon effect or a *net* snob effect prevails.

---

[17]H. Leibenstein, "Bandwagon, Snob and Veblen Effects in the Theory of Consumer Demand," *Quarterly Journal of Economics*, (May 1950), pp. 183-207.

3.6 SUMMARY

In this chapter we have demonstrated how the rational consumer will adjust to changes in certain economic variables. The price effect gives rise to the individual's demand curve for individual products. In general, these demand curves show an inverse relationship between the price of the product and the quantity demanded by a particular consumer. This price effect can be divided into two component parts: the income effect and the substitution effect. The income effect may be either positive or negative, depending upon the taste and preference pattern of the consumer in question and the level of income of each consumer. The substitution effect is always negative; that is, the relationship between price and quantity demanded, with real income constant, is an inverse one. The sum of the income effect and the substitution effect—that is, the price effect—is typically negative, since the Giffen good seems to be a historical relic. We caution that in the real world the price effect may sometimes be obscured by the effects of inflation or by the simultaneous movement of another variable that influences demand.

The attribute approach to consumer behavior was examined for its implications for consumer choice between and among products. This approach gives several valuable insights into consumer choice which are not so readily apparent using the product approach. The attribute approach allows the entire range of substitutes available to the consumer to be depicted on the same graph. It is thus able to explain quite clearly why a consumer buys one brand of a product in preference to the other brands available: the preferred brand offers the consumer the greatest amount of the preferred attribute mix per dollar. Moreover, the analysis easily explains why a consumer will purchase combinations of substitute products: this allows the consumer to obtain the desired attribute ratio even when there is no product that offers the attributes in this ratio. New products are easily handled by the attribute approach, since they are simply added to the existing analysis. The implications for pricing, promotion, product, and distribution policy are more obvious under the attributes approach: the price level determines the degree to which the product extends the efficiency frontier, and the other three policies determine the combination of attributes and hence the product's placement on the frontier.

If tastes and preferences change in favor of a particular product, a larger amount of that product will be demanded by consumers. Tastes and preferences may change due to social phenomena or as a result of advertising or promotional activities conducted by business firms. Market demand for a product is, in a simple sense, the sum of all individual demand curves. When individual demands are dependent upon what other individuals are demanding, the aggregate market demand can be either greater than (if the bandwagon effect prevails) or smaller than (if the snob effect prevails) the simple summation of individual demands.

Studying individual consumer behavior is important, for it explains why consumer responses to changes in economic variables are basically predictable, in *direction* if not always in *magnitude*. To the extent that consumers do wish to allocate their available income rationally (i.e., such that they derive the greatest psychic satisfaction from their income), we can expect price reductions to be followed by increases in quantity demanded, and we can expect price increases to be followed by reductions in quantity demanded. It is therefore myopic to expect that price changes will go "more or less unnoticed" by consumers or that the price level is not as important as some of the other instruments available to the decision maker to increase profitability. When price changes are regarded in the real, or purchasing power, sense and when the impact of other variables can be accounted for, we must expect a negative price effect to prevail. The ramifications of this for revenues, profits, and general business decision making are explored in subsequent chapters.

DISCUSSION QUESTIONS

3-1. Why does the assumption of transitivity of preferences mean that indifference curves do not cross each other? (Hint: Show that a situation of crossed indifference curves violates transitivity of preferences.)

3-2. Explain how the MRS, at a particular combination of the two products, would differ between two consumers—one who "likes" hamburgers and "loves" milkshakes and another who "loves" hamburgers and merely "likes" milkshakes.

3-3. How does the availability of credit affect the consumer's budget constraint in the short term and over a longer period?

3-4. In the self-service versus full-service gasoline example used in the text, how would the indifference map of a person who is knowledgeable about preventive maintenance, economy-minded, and not lazy, compare with that of another person who is the opposite in these respects?

3-5. For a given price change, will the substitution effect be larger or smaller for a consumer whose indifference curves are relatively steep as compared with one whose indifference curves are relatively flat? Why?

3-6. How would the indifference map between X and Y look different for a consumer who regards X as a normal good (or attribute) as compared with another who regards X as an inferior product (or attribute)?

3-7. What attributes do you think are being sought by a consumer who chooses to fly somewhere for a holiday as compared with another consumer who would drive the same distance for the same holiday?

3-8. Why would a consumer not be acting "rationally" in purchasing a product that fell short of the efficiency frontier in attribute space?

3-9. Distinguish between a change in consumer perceptions and a change in consumer tastes.

3-10. How would new-product policy benefit from an analysis of the attributes demanded by consumers in the overall market for several substitute products?

PROBLEMS AND SHORT CASES

3-1. In the text the income and substitution effects are explained for price reductions only. To indicate that you understand the procedure, separate the income and substitution effects for a price *increase*. (Don't look at any other text!) If that is too easy, separate the income and substitution effects for a price increase of the product on the *vertical* axis.

3-2. Products X and Y are fairly close substitutes. A price increase is contemplated for Product X, but the people at Company X are worried that sales will fall quite steeply as a result of this price increase. The managerial economist suggests that prior to increasing price, a campaign should be undertaken to increase consumer awareness of the special features of Product X and to, therefore, lessen the reduction in sales that will follow the price increase.

Explain the managerial economist's reasoning, using indifference curve analysis of the consumer's choice between Products X and Y. Pay special attention to the substitution effect of the price change.

3-3. Company A sells a Product X which has several close substitutes. At its present price, however, it is not making a sufficient contribution to the firm's profitability. A price rise is contemplated. The marketing manager is adamant that an advertising campaign must be undertaken before the price is raised. The finance department says that this expenditure is unnecessary. Explain the marketing manager's reasoning in terms of the attribute approach to consumer behavior.

3-4. Imagine two consumers—Mr. A, who simply appreciates classical music and Ms. B, who is wildly enthusiastic about it. Suppose that in a simple two-product situation both buy classical music records in conjunction with some other Product Y.

(a) Using the indifference maps you think are appropriate for each consumer, derive each of their demand curves from their price consumption curves. (Assume that they have the same income and face the same prices.)

(b) Aggregate their individual demands to find their total demand for the records at each price.

3-5. In the automobile market, various segments of the market are catered to by the manufacturers. Show graphically how three different consumers might choose three different automobiles in the simple case where they desire only two attributes, "power" and "economy."

3-6. In a western region two brands of beer are sold which between them share almost all the market. Through careful research it has been found that their main differences are perceived to be in the attributes "lightness" and "thirst-quenching." Brand A is perceived to contain 10 "units" of thirst-quench and 5 "units" of lightness and costs $0.80 per bottle. Brand B is perceived to contain 5 "units" of thirst-quench and 10 "units" of lightness and costs $0.67 per bottle.

Research has also indicated that a significant share of the market would become available if a third beer were introduced, as long as its price was not too high. The Norbert Brewing Company has a new "premium" beer that incorporates 10 "units" of each attribute in each bottle.

For a consumer who has $10 monthly to spend on beer and who perceives the attributes in the ratios implied above,

(a) what is the maximum price that may be charged for Norbert's beer such that $10 will buy a combination of the attributes that lies on the efficiency frontier? (An approximate answer derived from your graph will suffice.)

(b) Supposing that Norbert prices the new beer at $0.72 per bottle, will the above consumer necessarily switch to Norbert's beer or stay with one or the other of the initial brands? Why?

3-7. Richard Poirier has recently graduated from college, and upon receipt of his first pay check he began planning to buy a sports car. He is considering four major attributes: prestige, performance, reliability, and resistance to rust. The value he attaches to these attributes varies depending upon whether he will drive the car all year round or in the summer only. The latter decision depends upon whether he is to be transferred 1,500 miles north by his employer. If he moves north he will use the car in the summer only.

If he is to drive the car only in the summer, Richard considers performance to be twice as important as reliability, prestige to be three times as important as reliability, and rust resistance to be only half as important as reliability. For year-round driving, he considers rust resistance to be three times as important as reliability, performance half as important as reliability, and prestige twice as important as reliability.

Richard has found three sports cars for sale; each one is secondhand and costs $5,000. All are in good condition, and he decides to buy one of the three. After considering the problem and talking with some experts, he has rated each car on a scale of 10 for each of the four attributes, as follows:

	Car A	Car B	Car C
Prestige	8	9	6
Performance	8	8	9
Reliability	7	6	9
Rust resistance	8	7	6

(a) Please advise Richard about which sports car he should buy to maximize his expected utility if he is in fact transferred 1,500 miles north.

(b) Which car should he buy if he is sure that he will not be transferred?

(c) Which car should he buy if the probability of his being transferred north can be reliably estimated at 0.7? (Explain your reasoning in each case.)

3-8. The demand for telephone installation is peaked around the first day of each month, since many subscribers request service on that day because they are moving to a new house or apartment. The Tanguay Telephone Company (T.T.C.) is examining a means to reduce this monthly demand peak, which accounts for 40 percent of all installations. The problem has been aggravated in recent years by the increasing hourly cost of labor, the reluctance of unionized employees to work overtime, the increased "no access" problems caused by the greater number of working households, and the decline of profitable auxiliary sales to the subscriber (colored telephones, extension phones, etc.) due to access being given by a third party (landlord, neighbor, etc.).

T.T.C. is considering opening several "Phoneshops" in its area, so that customers may obtain their telephones and install them in their own homes. The company would prewire all homes in its territory, installing one or two phone jacks in each room; the installation by the customer would simply involve plugging in the sets where desired. The company would continue to offer home installation for those unable or unwilling to visit the Phoneshops. Two types of Phoneshop are being considered: more conveniently located stores which would offer a moderate saving as compared with the traditional home installation and less conveniently located stores which would offer a more substantial saving due to the lower overhead costs in the less convenient locations.

A market survey has found that telephone subscribers want two major attributes in their purchase of a new installation—"convenience" and "economy." A "typical" customer has been found who rates the three options on a scale of 100 for "convenience" as follows: Home Installation 100; More Convenient Store 75; and Less Convenient Store 25. The "economy" of the second and third options will be measured by the savings from the $20 it will continue to cost to have home installation. Thus "economy" will be determined by prices that T.T.C. decides to charge for the latter two options.

(a) Supposing initially that T.T.C. prices the More Convenient (MC) Phoneshop service at $16 and the Less Convenient (LC) Phoneshop service at $12, show the consumer's options in attribute space, with "convenience" on the vertical axis and "dollars saved" on the horizontal axis. (Since the consumer wants *one* unit only of *one* of the three services, these options will be represented by points in attribute space, not rays.)

(b) For a consumer who has an MRS = 10 at the point represented by the MC Phoneshop (i.e., who is prepared to give up 10 units of convenience for $1 saved), which of the three options should be selected?

(c) For a person who has an MRS = 15 at the point represented by the MC Phoneshop, which of the three options should be selected?

SUGGESTED REFERENCES AND FURTHER READING

Auld, Douglas. "Imperfect Knowledge and the New Theory of Demand," *Journal of Political Economy*, 80 (Nov., Dec. 1972), 1287-94.

Baumol, W.J. *Economic Theory and Operations Analysis* (4th ed.), chap. 9. Englewood Cliffs, N.J.: Prentice-Hall, Inc., 1977.

Cornell, B. "Relative vs. Absolute Price Changes: An Empirical Study," *Economic Inquiry*, 19 (July 1981), pp. 506-14.

Green, P.E. and V. Srinivasan. "Conjoint Analysis in Consumer Research: Issues and Outlook," *The Journal of Consumer Research*, 5 (Sept. 1978), 103-23.

Hendler, R. "Lancaster's New Approach to Consumer Demand and Its Limitations," *American Economic Review*, 65 (March 1975), 194-9.

Hirshleifer, J. *Price Theory and Applications* (2nd ed.), chaps. 3 and 4. Englewood Cliffs, N.J.: Prentice-Hall, Inc., 1980.

Lancaster, K. "A New Approach to Consumer Theory," *Journal of Political Economy*, 84 (April 1966), 132-57.

———. *Consumer Demand: A New Approach.* New York: Columbia University Press, 1971.

Leibenstein, H. "Bandwagon, Snob and Veblen Effects in the Theory of Consumer Demand," *Quarterly Journal of Economics*, (May 1950), 183-207.

Ratchford, Brian T. "The New Economic Theory of Consumer Behavior: An Interpretive Essay," *Journal of Consumer Research*, 2 (Sept. 1975), 65-75.

——————. "Operationalizing Economic Models of Demand for Product Characteristics," *Journal of Consumer Research*, 6 (June 1979), pp. 76-84.

Rosen, Sherwin. "Hedonic Prices and Implicit Markets: Product Differentiation in Pure Competition," *Journal of Political Economy*, 82 (Jan., Feb. 1974), 34-45.

Roth, Timothy P. "On the Predictive Power of the New Approach to Consumer Theory," *Atlantic Economic Journal*, 7 (July 1979), 16-25.

Schoemaker, P.J.H. "The Expected Utility Model: Its Variants, Purposes, Evidence and Limitations," *Journal of Economic Literature*, 20 (June 1982), pp. 529-563.

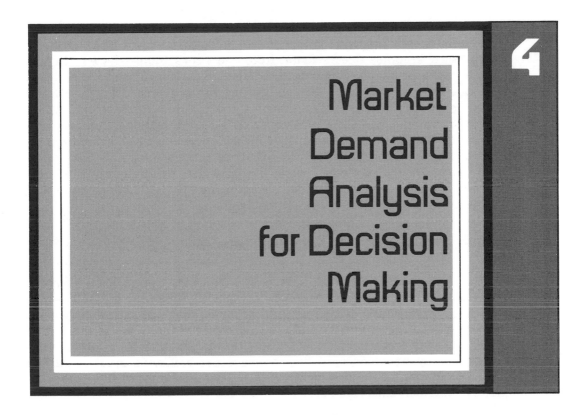

4.1 INTRODUCTION

In Chapter 3 we examined the behavior of individual consumers who make utility-maximizing decisions to purchase goods and services.[1] They make these decisions on the basis of their own incomes and on the basis of the price and availability of various products. Although individual consumers exhibit price, income, and substitution effects and may change their tastes and preference patterns, we do not expect the actions and reactions of any individual consumer to change the environment for subsequent behavior by that consumer. Consumers in aggregate, on the other hand, can and do influence the prices and availability of goods and services. Their collective actions constitute the demand side of the product markets, and as such they are responsible, in conjunction with the supply side of each market, for the determination of the price and output levels in each of the product markets.

Aggregate demand in any particular product market, or market demand, as it is commonly called, is an important force in our economic sys-

---

[1]Chapter 3 is not a necessary prerequisite to this chapter, although it does allow a more thorough understanding of individual consumer behavior. In Chapter 4 the consumers' reactions to change in their economic environment are restated briefly, and this will allow a sufficient understanding of market demand analysis.

tem because it enters the product markets supported by the income that consumers expect to spend in order to maximize their utility. This consumer expenditure becomes sales revenue from the firm's point of view. In this chapter we consider the major factors likely to influence the total demand and sales revenue for a product as well as the probable direction of the influence in each case. We then examine the interrelationships among the important revenue concepts, namely total revenue, marginal revenue, and average revenue (or price per unit). A means of measuring and summarizing the direction and magnitude of the influence that each variable has on the total demand for a particular product is provided by the concept of elasticity of demand, and we consider several different elasticity measures and their application to decision-making problems.

4.2 THE DEMAND FUNCTION AND THE DEMAND CURVE

NOTE: Let us immediately make the following distinction. The demand *function* refers to the relationship that exists between the quantity demanded of a particular product and *all factors* that influence that demand. The demand *curve* refers to the relationship that exists between the quantity demanded of a particular product and the *price* of that product, with all other influencing factors held constant. The demand curve is thus a subset of the demand function in the case where *ceteris paribus* applies to all of the independent variables except price.

The Independent Variables in the Demand Function

The demand function is a specification of the relationship existing between the quantity demanded of product X and the variables influencing the demand for that product. The quantity demanded of X, or Q_x, is known as the dependent variable in the demand function, since its value depends on the values of the influencing variables, which are known as the independent variables. What are the independent variables that influence Q_x? Let us discuss them one by one.

Price. We have seen in the preceding chapter that quantity demanded typically varies inversely with the price of the product, given *ceteris paribus*. The price of product X is the number of currency units paid for each unit of X. If a discount from list price is given or if consumers habitually bargain, bringing the price down from list price, the appropriate price is the actual price paid rather than the price initially asked. For increases in the price of X we expect the quantity demanded to fall, and for decreases in the price of X we expect the quantity demanded to rise.

Prices of Related Products. The price of *substitute* products enters the demand function for product X because of the willingness of consumers to purchase products that are substitutes for product X, given changes in the relative prices of this group of products. If the price of one or more of the substitute products increases, we expect the demand for product X to increase, since individual consumers tend to switch from the substitute products to product X. We expect the converse for reductions in the prices of substitute products.

The prices of *complementary* goods, on the other hand, are expected to have a negative relationship to the quantity demanded of product X. Complementary goods are products that are typically consumed in conjunction with the consumption of product X. For example, coffee and cream, gasoline and tires, and beer and peanuts are pairs of complementary goods for many people. If the prices of complementary goods rise, we expect the quantity demanded of product X to decrease, since the consumption of product X and its complementary products is now more expensive. Conversely, if the prices of complements decrease, the quantity demanded of X should increase, since the "package price" for X and its complements is now reduced.

Advertising and Promotional Efforts. Advertising and other promotional efforts by the sellers of product X can be expected to influence the quantity demanded of that product, since these efforts are designed to influence the taste and preference patterns of consumers. Advertising related to product X is expected to be followed by an increase in the quantity demanded of product X. On the other hand, advertising of rival products is expected to have a negative influence on the quantity demanded of X, since it should be expected to induce consumers to switch their consumption from product X toward one of the substitute products. Advertising of complementary goods is expected to have a positive influence on the quantity demanded of product X, since it makes the complementary good more attractive to consumers who, in turn, tend to buy more units of product X, since they purchase product X and that complementary good in some proportionate way.

Product Quality and Design. Consumers typically appreciate quality and good design and may be expected to purchase more of a product when they perceive it to be of higher quality or of a more functional or fashionable design. Oppositely, if the quality is judged inferior to other products or represents a reduction in quality, as compared to the firm's earlier production, consumers are expected to reduce their aggregate demand for the product. Similarly, nonfunctional, dangerous, or just plain ugly designs are likely to reduce consumer demand for the product. The firm can influence product quality and design, of course, by undertaking research and development expenditures, including market research, to ascertain what people want prior to production of the product. It may also be argued that firms may also influence consumers' *perceptions* of the products' quality and design after it has reached the market by the use of advertising and promotional efforts.

Distribution Outlets and Place of Sale. Total demand for the firm's product is directly influenced by the number of sales or distribution outlets and by the location of these outlets. Having a larger number of outlets allows the firm to reach consumers who may not otherwise be exposed to the product, to make it more convenient for consumers to purchase the product, and to offer ancillary services (such as technical advice, repairs, and warranty service) which help to augment total sales. The location of sales outlets is an important consideration, of course. A retail store in a busy shopping center may have triple the sales volume of a similar store on a low-traffic side street. Thus, firms choose the locations of their wholesale and retail outlets with an eye to the potential sales volume (and hence sales revenue) that is expected to result from each location.[2]

Consumer Incomes. The relationship between consumer income and quantity demanded of product X can be expected to be either positive or negative, depending on the product in question and the level of consumer income. We saw in Chapter 3 that for some consumers at some income levels a particular commodity could have a negative income effect, whereas for other consumers at other income levels the income effect might be positive. We are interested here in the *aggregate* income effect. Thus, if to most purchasers the product is an inferior good, its demand will decrease when income levels rise or increase when income levels fall. On the other hand, if it is a normal or superior product for most purchasers, quantity demanded and income levels move in the same direction.

Consumer Tastes and Preferences. The tastes and preferences of consumers may be expected to be in a continual state of flux, with some people shifting their purchases toward a particular product and others shifting away. In explaining aggregate demand we are interested in the net effect of changing tastes and in the general trend of tastes and preferences toward or away from the product in question. A measure, or index, of aggregate tastes and preferences is the market share held by product X. A net gain in market share has a positive impact on quantity demanded, as long as the total market is constant or growing, of course. Thus we expect the index of tastes and preferences to be positively related to Q_x except for secularly declining markets where it may be either positive or negative.

Consumer Expectations. Consumer expectations about the future price, availability, and substitutability of product X influence their present demand for product X. For example, if you expect gasoline to be significantly more expensive or less readily available in the near future, you may be motivated

---

[2] Distribution strategy is covered in detail in marketing courses. See Philip Kotler, *Principles of Marketing* (Englewood Cliffs, N.J.: Prentice-Hall Inc., 1980), chapters 14 and 15. Marketers speak of the four P's—price, promotion, product design, and place of sale— as the firm's controllable variables among those that influence consumer demand. Other influencing variables, such as actions by competitors, consumer incomes, and population are uncontrollable, and others, such as tastes and preferences and expectations, may be regarded as partially controllable by the firm through its product design and promotional strategies.

to increase your current demand for gasoline, by keeping your tank full most of the time or even by filling extra containers with gasoline. Similarly, if you expect a new model of product X to be released in the near future and if you expect this new model to be a significant improvement, you may reduce your purchases of X now and wait for the new model. Thus, consumer expectations have a positive impact on current demand for product X if the expectations are pessimistic with respect to future prices, availability, or quality of product X. Conversely, consumer expectations have a negative impact on current demand if the expectations are optimistic.

Other Factors. Such variables as weather conditions, demographic factors, and cultural beliefs may enter the demand function for particular products. For example, the amount of rainfall appears to be a determinant of the demand for umbrellas (and for taxicabs). In any particular area a rainy autumn causes more umbrellas and taxi rides to be sold than if the season is relatively dry. Next, the population of potential consumers of product X is expected to be positively related to the demand for product X. If the population rises, for example, because of net immigration or rising fertility rates, we expect this to have a positive impact on the quantity demanded for product X. When the market for the product is regional rather than national, we must take into account population shifts between regions that increase or decrease the potential market for the product in question. Other factors include the cultural milieu and such demographic variables as the composition of the work force, median age levels, and average retirement age.

Symbolically, we can express the demand function for product X in terms of its major determinants as follows:

$$Q_x = f(P_x, P_s, P_c, A_x, A_s, A_c, K_x, O_x, Y, T, E, N, \ldots) \qquad (4\text{-}1)$$

where

Q_x is total quantity demanded in physical units of product X.
P_x is the price of product X.
P_s is the average price of other products that are substitutes for product X.
P_c is the average price of other products that are complementary to product X.
A_x is the advertising and promotional effort devoted to product X.
A_s is an index of the advertising effort devoted to the substitutes for product X.
A_c is an index of the advertising effort devoted to the complementary products.
K_x is the quality and design of product X.
O_x is the number and location of distribution outlets for product X.
Y is an index of consumers' disposable income levels.
T is an index of consumer taste and preference patterns.
E is an index of consumers' expectations regarding future prices, availability, and the nature of product X.
N is the total market population.

Other variables such as weather conditions, demographic factors, and cultural beliefs may enter the demand function for particular products.

Equation (4-1) expresses in general form the dependence of Q_x on the independent variables indicated. *The specific* form of the demand function for a particular product is an empirical question. That is, collection and analysis of data may reveal Q_x to be a linear function of its determinants or, alternatively, a multiplicative function of several independent variables. The linear form of the demand function is exemplified by the following:

$$Q_x = \alpha + \beta_1 P_x + \beta_2 P_s + \beta_3 P_c + \beta_4 A_x + \beta_5 A_s + \beta_6 A_c$$
$$+ \beta_7 Y + \beta_8 T + \beta_9 E + \beta_{10} N \qquad (4\text{-}2)$$

where

α (the Greek letter *alpha*) is that part of quantity demanded determined exogenously or by other variables not explicitly mentioned in the demand function.

$\beta_1, \beta_2, \ldots \beta_{10}$ (β is the Greek letter *beta*) are the coefficients of the demand function indicating the marginal impact of each independent variable upon the quantity demanded.

Alternatively, two or more variables may be found to have a multiplicative impact on Q_x, as follows:

$$Q_x = \alpha P_x{}^{\beta_1} N^{\beta_2} O_x{}^{\beta_3} \qquad (4\text{-}3)$$

In this case, quantity demanded for product X is the product of the variables for the price of X, total market population, and number of outlets for product X.

The coefficients in the demand function (namely α, β_1, β_2, β_3, and so on) may be estimated using regression analysis and other techniques, as we shall see in Chapter 5. Equations (4-2) and (4-3) are, in effect, symbolic models of the demand function for product X. Each one is an explanatory model used to explain the demand for X in terms of the levels of each of the independent variables. Such models explain changes in the value of Q_x as the result of a change in one or more of the independent variables. A model of the demand function can also be used for predictive purposes, given estimates of all the β coefficients and the residual term α.

EXAMPLE: Suppose the demand function for product X has been estimated using regression analysis to be as follows:

$$Q_x = 5{,}030 - 3{,}806.2 P_x + 1{,}458.5 P_s + 256.6 A_x - 32.3 A_s + 0.18 Y$$
$$(4\text{-}4)$$

where the symbols for the independent variables are the same as introduced previously, and the coefficients are replaced by their numerical equivalents. Note that the positive or negative sign preceding each independent variable indicates the direction of the influence that variable has on Q_x. Given this specification of the demand function, we can predict the sales level for product X, given the values of the independent variables. Suppose $P_x = \$8$; $P_s = \$6$; $A_x = \$168$ (in thousands); $A_s = \$182$ (in thousands); and $Y = \$12,875$. Substituting for these variables in Equation (4-4), we find:

$$Q_x = 5,030 - 30,449.6 + 8,751.0 + 43,108.8 - 5,878.6 + 2,317.5$$

$$= 22,879.1$$

Thus, we predict that at the present values of the independent variables, quantity demanded of product X should be 22,879.1 units, given *ceteris paribus*.

The Demand Curve Derived from the Demand Function

The demand curve is a special subcase of the demand function in which *ceteris paribus* applies to all independent variables except the price of the product in question. Since none of the other independent variables or the residual term α vary when *ceteris paribus* is in force, we can compress them all into a single term A and express the demand function as follows:

$$Q_x = A + \beta_1 P_x \qquad (4\text{-}5)$$

where the parameter A includes the influence of all the other independent variables and the residual term α on Q_x, and is, therefore, equal to $\alpha + \beta_2 P_s + \beta_3 P_c + \ldots$ and so forth, from Equation (4-2).

NOTE: The demand curve expresses the relationship between Q_x and P_x with all other things remaining the same, and Equation (4-5) is, therefore, an expression of the demand curve. But economists, following the convention set by a nonmathematical classical economist, traditionally place the independent variable (price) on the vertical axis for their graphical analysis. Given this convention, it is important for efficient communication that we also observe this practice, keeping in mind that Q_x is the dependent variable and P_x is the independent variable. Economists typically state the demand curve in the form:

$$P_x = a + bQ_x \qquad (4\text{-}6)$$

Equation (4-6) is easily obtained from Equation (4-5) by a couple of manipulations and substitutions. Working on Equation (4-5), subtract A from both sides and divide both sides by β_1 to find

$$P_x = -\frac{A}{\beta_1} + \frac{1}{\beta_1} Q_x \qquad (4\text{-}7)$$

Letting $a = -A/\beta_1$ and $b = 1/\beta_1$, we have

$$P_x = a + bQ_x \qquad (4\text{-}6)$$

Note that the numerical value of β_1 is expected to have a negative sign because of the law of demand. Thus the parameter a will be a positive number and b will be a negative number.

EXAMPLE: From the numerical example introduced earlier, we can find:

$$Q_x = 53,328.7 - 3,806.2P_x \qquad (4\text{-}8)$$

The number 53,328.7 is the sum of the α term (5,030) and the influence of all other independent variables except P_x. It is usually more convenient when dealing with large numbers to express them in larger units, such as thousands or millions, in order to simplify calculations. Expressing Q_x in thousands of units, we have:

$$Q_x = 53.3287 - 3.8062P_x \qquad (4\text{-}9)$$

To invert this expression to the form $P_x = a + bQ_x$ we add $3.8062P_x$ to both sides, subtract Q_x from both sides, and divide both sides by 3.8062, as follows:

$$3.8062P_x = 53.3287 - Q_x$$

$$P_x = \frac{53.3287}{3.8062} - \frac{1}{3.8062}Q_x$$

$$P_x = 14.011 - 0.26273Q_x \qquad (4\text{-}10)$$

Thus, we have derived an expression for the demand curve from the estimate of the demand function. Note that we have price expressed as a linear function of quantity demanded, *ceteris paribus*, where a is the intercept term on the vertical (price) axis and b is the slope term. In Figure 4-1 we show the aggregate demand curve for product X. Note that the curve intercepts the price axis at the value a, and slopes downward at the rate b, or $1/\beta_1$. The intercept on the horizontal axis is, of course, the value A, since this is the value of Q_x, where P_x is zero.[3] Note that when $P_x = \$8$, $Q_x = 22,879.1$, as calculated earlier.

---

[3]We should be cautious about extending the analysis to extreme values of P_x and Q_x. It is sufficient to say that the intercept terms a (on the vertical axis) and A (on the horizontal axis) simply *locate* the demand curve at its appropriate height. We expect the demand curve to depict the relationship between P_x and Q_x adequately only within the relevant range of observations, which is in the vicinity of the current price and demand levels. For the same reason it is a sufficient approximation to show the demand curve as linear through the relevant range, although for extreme values of P_x and Q_x the demand curve is likely to become curvilinear.

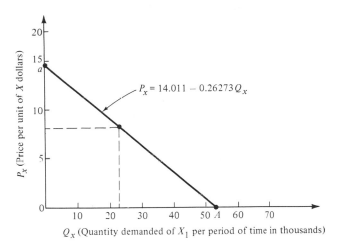

FIGURE 4-1.   The Market Demand Curve for Product X

P_x (Price per unit of X dollars)

a

$P_x = 14.011 - 0.26273 Q_x$

Q_x (Quantity demanded of X_1 per period of time in thousands)

Movements Along vs. Shifts of the Demand Curve

A *movement along* the demand curve will occur when there is a change in price (and consequently quantity demanded) while all other variables (reflected in the intercept term a) remain constant. In Figure 4-2 the price change from P_1 to P_2 leads to a movement along the demand curve from point A to point B with the associated change in quantity demanded being from Q_1 to Q_2, given *ceteris paribus*. Note that this could be calculated from Equation (4-10), given the values of P_1 and P_2.

A *shift* of the demand curve will occur when *ceteris paribus* does not apply, and thus the value of the intercept term changes. In Figure 4-3 we show shifts of the demand curve which are the result of changes in one or more of the other factors while price is held constant. Suppose that the initial demand curve is that shown as D, such that at price P_1, quantity demanded is Q_1. If, for example, consumer incomes increased (or there was an increase in some other variable that has a positive coefficient in Equation (4-4) or a decrease in a variable that has a negative coefficient), the demand curve would *shift* to the right, as shown by the movement to demand curve D'. For the same price level P_1 the quantity demanded is now Q'; the additional quantity demanded is caused by a change in one or more of the other variables. On the other hand, had there been a reduction in consumer incomes (or a shift in consumer tastes away from Product X or any of a number of other changes in the determining factors), the demand curve would shift to the left, to a position such as that shown by demand curve D''.

NOTE: Thus changes in price will, *ceteris paribus*, lead to a *movement* along an existing demand curve, whereas changes in any of the other variables will cause a *shift* of the demand curve. Given the new set of the other variables,

FIGURE 4-2. **A Movement along the Demand Curve for Product X, with** *Ceteris Paribus*

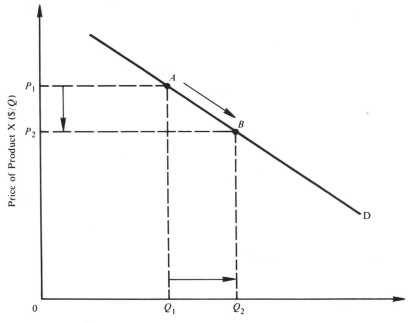

Quantity (Q) Demanded of Product X (per unit of time)

FIGURE 4-3. **Shifts of the Demand Curve for Product X**

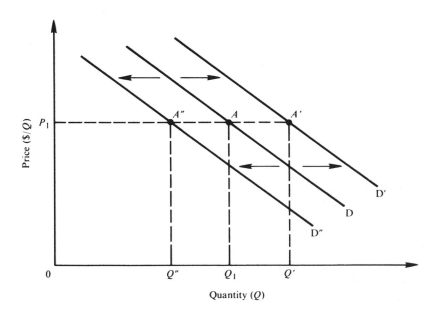

Quantity (Q)

DEMAND THEORY, ANALYSIS, AND ESTIMATION

there will be a new demand curve that is appropriate, and the initial demand curve will now be inappropriate. Given this new set of the other variables, we may now speak of movements along the new demand curve in response to changes in the price level, *ceteris paribus*. When analyzing the effect on quantity demanded of a change in the price level, it is therefore extremely important to ascertain whether or not any of the other factors have changed before concluding that there has been a movement along the envisaged demand curve.

EXAMPLE: To illustrate the combined impact of movements along demand curves and shifts of demand curves, consider the substantial price increase of coffee during 1977, caused by the price increase of imported coffee beans by exporting countries (who had earlier seen the oil-producing countries do the same thing). The left-hand part of Figure 4-4 shows the price and quantity demanded of coffee in supermarkets before and after the increase in coffee bean prices (P_1, Q_1 and P_2, Q_2, respectively). A superficial analysis of this situation might lead to the conclusion that the supply curve for coffee had shifted from S_1 to S_2, causing a movement along the aggregate demand curve from point A to point B. This would indicate that consumers' demand for coffee was not very sensitive to price increases and may lead to consideration of further price increases.

Closer analysis reveals that the substantial change in the price level was the result of both a movement along *and* a shift of the demand curve. The right-hand part of the figure shows the supply curve having shifted from S_1 to S_2 as a result of the increase in coffee bean prices. This alone would cause supply and demand to be equal at price P', considerably below the actual price that eventuated (P_2). The actual price was higher because there had been a *shift* of the demand curve as well: fearing that coffee might not be available in the near future, many consumers bought more than they normally would in order to build personal stockpiles. This reaction manifested itself as a shift of the demand curve from D_1 to D_2, due to a change in consumers' expectations concerning future prices and availability of the

FIGURE 4-4.   Shifts distinguished from Movements along Demand Curves

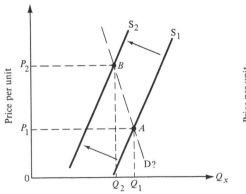 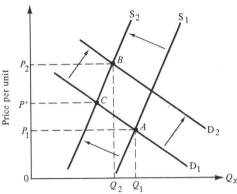

product. Thus the price change was the result of two separate influences: from P_1 to P' as the result of a movement along the initial demand curve and from P' to P_2 as a result of the shift of the demand curve from D_1 to D_2. Consumer demand is, therefore, more responsive to price increases than might at first be supposed. The movement along demand curve D_1 from A to C is offset to some degree by a simultaneous shift in the demand curve. Further price increases would probably find consumers much more responsive, since by then they would have built up adequate inventories of coffee at home and would no longer cause a continuing outward shift of the demand curve.

Interrelationships among Price, Total Revenue, and Marginal Revenue

Why are we interested in the variation between price and quantity of a particular commodity? Our concern is to see what happens to total sales revenue when prices and quantities are varied. Whatever the decision maker's objective function, total revenue is likely to play a major role in the optimization of that objective function. In Table 4-1 we demonstrate the variation of total revenue for the demand curve specified by $P_x = 11 - 0.001\,Q_x$.

EXAMPLE: Suppose this represents the demand curve for a carton of twelve cans of dog food at a discount supermarket during a particular month. For this simple demand curve the intercept on the price axis is thus $11, and the slope is -0.001. Thus, for every price reduction of $1.00, quantity demanded will increase by 1,000 cartons. Substituting different values of price into this equation, we are able to determine the quantity that will be demanded at all prices, as shown in the second column of Table 4-1. Total revenue at each price is derived by multiplying the price by the quantity demanded at that price, to find the total revenue associated with each price (or quantity) level. It can be seen that total revenue increases progressively as price is lowered from $10 to $6; that the price reduction to $5 leaves the

TABLE 4-1.   Revenue Implications of the Law of Demand

Price ($/unit)	Quantity Demanded (units)	Total Revenue ($)	Marginal Revenue ($/unit)
10	1,000	10,000	—
9	2,000	18,000	8
8	3,000	24,000	6
7	4,000	28,000	4
6	5,000	30,000	2
5	6,000	30,000	0
4	7,000	28,000	−2
3	8,000	24,000	−4
2	9,000	18,000	−6
1	10,000	10,000	−8

DEMAND THEORY, ANALYSIS, AND ESTIMATION

total revenue unchanged; and that further price reductions cause total revenue to decline.

Note that high prices are not necessarily the best prices. By progressively lowering the price, we were able to increase total revenue up to a point. Similarly, neither is a very low price necessarily a good strategy; although it does expand the quantity demanded, it causes a smaller total revenue, as compared with that which may be earned at a higher price level. In Table 4-1 the fourth column shows the marginal revenue associated with each price level.

DEFINITION: *Marginal revenue* is defined as the change in total revenue that results from a one-unit increase in quantity demand. Since quantity demanded increases by blocks of 1,000 units in Table 4-1, marginal revenue is calculated here as the row-to-row difference in the total revenue column divided by the change in quantity demanded. It can be seen that marginal revenue falls progressively to zero and becomes negative as price is reduced.

In Figure 4-5 we plot the values for the demand curve (given by the price/quantity combinations) and the total revenue and marginal revenue curves to illustrate the relationships that exist between and among these curves. These relationships hold for any demand curve that is negatively sloped. Total revenue increases at first as prices are lowered, reaches its maximum, and thereafter declines as prices are reduced further. Marginal revenue will always be less than price at each output level; will fall to zero at the point where total revenue reaches its maximum; and will take negative values if price is reduced any further, since this causes an absolute reduction in total revenue.[4]

Price and Marginal Revenue. The relationship between the demand curve and the marginal revenue curve bears further observation. Since both may be derived from the total revenue curve, it is clear that there must be a relationship between them. To find this relationship we begin by expressing the total revenue as the product of price and quantity:

$$\text{TR}_x = P_x \cdot Q_x \tag{4-11}$$

Equation (4-6) gave us the following expression for P_x:

$$P_x = a + bQ_x \tag{4-6}$$

---

[4]The price reductions shown in Table 4-1 were made by discrete $1.00 units, and hence the changes in quantity-demanded observations were in blocks of 1,000 units. Marginal revenue calculated from these data is strictly the *average* change in total revenue per one-unit change in quantity demanded for each of the 1,000-unit blocks. If we had shown smaller price reductions, we would have found that the price generating the highest revenue would be $5.50. At this price level, 5,500 units would be demanded and total revenue would be $30,250. Strictly, then, marginal revenue is zero at these price and quantity levels, as shown in Figure 4-5, rather than the more crude approximations shown in Table 4-1.

FIGURE 4-5.   Relationships between Demand, Marginal Revenue, and
Total Revenue

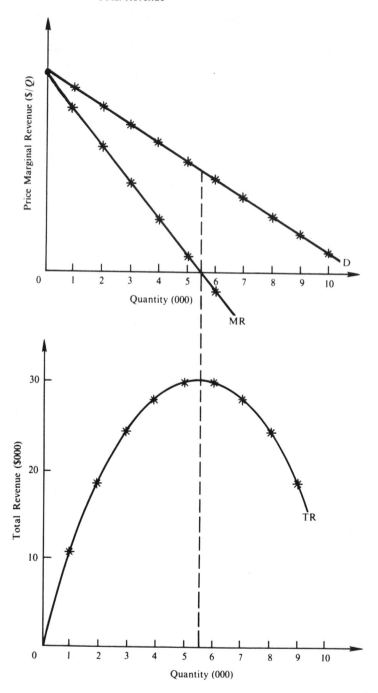

DEMAND THEORY, ANALYSIS, AND ESTIMATION

Substituting for P_x in Equation (4-11), we obtain

$$\text{TR}_x = aQ_x + bQ_x^2 \qquad (4\text{-}12)$$

Since *marginal revenue* is defined as the change in total revenue for a one-unit change in quantity demanded, it can be expressed as the first derivative of Equation (4-12) with respect to Q_x. Thus,[5]

$$\text{MR}_x = a + 2bQ_x \qquad (4\text{-}13)$$

Now compare the expression for the demand curve, Equation (4-6), with the expression for the marginal revenue curve, Equation (4-13). The intercept term of each is a, indicating that both curves must emanate from the same point on the vertical axis of the graph, and the slope term in the marginal revenue expression is exactly twice the slope term in the price or demand curve expression.

NOTE: Thus the marginal revenue curve does have a fixed relationship with the demand curve from which it is derived. It begins at the same point on the price axis and its slope is twice that of the demand curve.[6]

EXAMPLE: From the estimated demand function provided earlier, we had derived the following expression for the demand curve:

$$P_x = 14.011 - 0.26273Q_x \qquad (4\text{-}10)$$

The marginal revenue curve associated with this demand curve will have the same intercept term on the price axis and twice the slope and can, therefore, be expressed as:

$$\text{MR}_x = 14.011 - 0.52546Q_x$$

The above relationships between price, quantity demanded, total revenue, and marginal revenue can be summarized in a single number known as the "price elasticity" of demand. The concept of elasticity is used widely in

---

[5]The derivative of Equation (4-12) with respect to Q_x was obtained using the *power rule*. If this is unfamiliar to you it is explained in Appendix A.

[6]In the above, we have confined our discussion to *linear* demand curves. It is nevertheless also true that the marginal revenue curve for a *curvilinear* demand curve will have the same intercept and twice the slope of the demand curve at any given output level. That is, a tangent to the (curvilinear) marginal revenue curve will have twice the slope of a tangent to the curvilinear demand curve at any given output level. Horizontal demand curves, such as in pure competition, are coextensive with the marginal revenue curve and, thus, have the same intercept and the same slope. But since the slope of a horizontal line is zero and since twice zero is still zero, the general rule (that MR has the same intercept and twice the slope of the demand curve) is not violated.

economics and expresses the responsiveness of one variable to a change in another variable. Stated a little more rigorously, an *elasticity* is the percentage change in the dependent variable occasioned by a one-percent change in an independent variable. It thus shows the proportionate response of one variable to a change in one of the variables that influence that variable. In the following sections the dependent variable is the quantity demanded, and the independent variables are a selection of the independent variables shown in Equation (4-1).

4.3 PRICE ELASTICITY OF DEMAND

DEFINITION: *Price elasticity of demand* is defined as the percentage change in quantity demanded divided by the percentage change in price which caused the change in quantity demanded. That is,

$$\epsilon = \frac{\% \text{ change in } Q_x}{\% \text{ change in } P_x} \tag{4-14}$$

where ϵ (the Greek letter *epsilon*) is the conventional symbol for price elasticity of demand. Expanding Equation (4-14) we have

$$\epsilon = \frac{\dfrac{\Delta Q_x}{Q_x} \cdot \dfrac{100}{1}}{\dfrac{\Delta P_x}{P_x} \cdot \dfrac{100}{1}} \tag{4-15}$$

where Δ (the Greek letter *delta*) connotes a change. Rearranging terms and cancelling the 100/1 terms, we have

$$\epsilon = \frac{\Delta Q_x}{Q_x} \cdot \frac{P_x}{\Delta P_x}$$

or

$$\epsilon = \frac{\Delta Q_x}{\Delta P_x} \cdot \frac{P_x}{Q_x} \tag{4-16}$$

Note that $\Delta Q_x / \Delta P_x$ is equal to the reciprocal of b, the slope term in the demand curve. Hence price elasticity is equal to the reciprocal of the slope multiplied by the ratio of price to quantity demanded, P_x/Q_x. On a linear demand curve the slope term is constant, and therefore the term $\Delta Q_x / \Delta P_x$ is constant in Equation (4-16). Note, however, that the P_x/Q_x term in the elasticity expression is not constant, but varies throughout the length of the demand curve. At points high on the demand curve, the ratio of P_x to Q_x is relatively large, whereas for points low on the demand curve, the ratio of P_x to Q_x is relatively low. In fact this ratio approaches infinity as we move toward the intercept on the price axis. It approaches zero as we move toward the intercept on the quantity axis. Since elasticity is the product of a constant and a number that varies from infinity to zero, it is apparent that the value for price elasticity must vary from infinity to zero as we move from the price intercept down a linear demand curve to the quantity intercept.

NOTE: Strictly, the value of price elasticity varies from *minus* infinity to approach zero from the *negative* side, because $\Delta Q_x/\Delta P_x$ has a negative sign. Either ΔQ_x or ΔP_x is negative, depending on whether we move up or down the demand curve. By convention, however, we speak of price elasticity in *absolute* terms, saying for example that $\epsilon = -5$ is greater than $\epsilon = -3$.

Now, since elasticity varies from minus infinity to zero as we move down the demand curve, it must at some point be equal to -1. Let us assert and then prove that $\epsilon = -1$ at the midpoint of the demand curve. Take a specific demand curve, such as $P_x = 5 - 0.625Q_x$. You can visualize this demand curve as having a vertical intercept of $5, since $P_x = 5$ when $Q_x = 0$ and as having a horizontal intercept of 8 units, since $Q_x = 8$ when $P_x = 0$. The slope of the demand curve is $\Delta P_x/\Delta Q_x = -0.625$, which is of course, equal to $-5/8$, the vertical intercept value over the horizontal intercept value. The reciprocal of the slope, $\Delta Q_x/\Delta P_x$, which enters the elasticity calculation, is therefore $-8/5$, or -1.6. This demand curve is shown in Figure 4-6.

For the value of price elasticity to be equal to -1, and given $\Delta Q_x/\Delta P_x = -8/5$, the other half of the elasticity formula—the price-quantity ratio—must equal $5/8$. The *only* pair of price-quantity observations on the demand curve $P_x = 5 - 0.625Q_x$ having the ratio $5/8$ is $P_x = 2.50$ and $Q_x = 4$. Thus elasticity is equal to -1 at price $2.50 and quantity demanded of 4 units. Now notice that these are the midpoint values between the origin and the

FIGURE 4-6.   **Price Elasticity Equals 1 at the Midpoint of the Demand Curve**

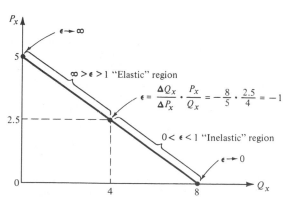

intercept on each axis. It follows (by proof for congruent triangles) that the coordinates $P_x = 2.50$ and $Q_x = 4$ are the midpoint of the demand curve.[7]

NOTE: Thus elasticity ranges from -1 to infinity above the midpoint and from -1 to zero below the midpoint. By convention, we say demand is *elastic* when ϵ is greater than 1 and it is *inelastic* when ϵ is less than 1 (in absolute terms). At the midpoint there is *unitary* elasticity. The knowledge that the midpoint divides the demand curve into these two ranges of elasticity is quite useful, since we can, by inspection of any point on a demand curve, immediately conclude whether its elasticity exceeds, is equal to, or is less than 1. Let us demonstrate the significance of elasticity being greater than, equal to, or less than 1.

Price Elasticity, Marginal Revenue, and Total Revenue

We now examine the relationship that exists between price elasticity and marginal revenue. Since the marginal revenue curve begins at the same intercept on the price axis as the demand curve but has twice the slope of the demand curve, it must intersect the quantity axis in half the horizontal distance from the origin to the point where the demand curve intersects the quantity axis. Thus, in terms of Figure 4-6 the marginal revenue curve must pass through the point where $Q_x = 4$. It is therefore apparent that the marginal revenue is negative when elasticity is less than unity.[8]

Let us now look at the relationship between price elasticity of demand

---

[7]Prove that $AB = BC$. Proof: $AD = BE$
$DB = EC$
Angle ADB = Angle BEC
$\therefore$ Congruent triangles
$\therefore AB = BC$

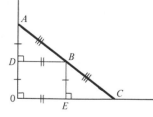

[8]The specific relationship existing between marginal revenue and elasticity may be derived as follows. Recall that total revenue is price times quantity, as expressed in Equation (4-5). Marginal revenue is the first derivative of Equation (4-5); it can be found to be

$MR_x = P_x + Q_x \dfrac{dP_x}{dQ_x}$ using the function of a function rule (since P_x is a function of Q_x).

By multiplying the last term by P_x/P_x and factoring out P_x, we obtain

$$MR_x = P_x \left(1 + \frac{Q_x}{P_x} \cdot \frac{dP_x}{dQ_x} \right)$$

Note that the term in parentheses is equal to 1 plus the reciprocal of the expression for price elasticity we found in Equation (4-16). Thus $MR_x = P_x(1 + 1/\epsilon)$ expresses the relationship between MR, P, and ϵ. Use this cautiously, however, since P and ϵ vary together. It can only be used to find MR, given P and its matching ϵ.

DEMAND THEORY, ANALYSIS, AND ESTIMATION

TABLE 4-2.   Relationship between Price Elasticity and Total Revenue

Elasticity Value	Price Increases	Price Decreases
$\infty > \epsilon > 1$	TR falls	TR rises
$\epsilon = 1$	TR constant	TR constant
$0 < \epsilon < 1$	TR rises	TR falls

and *total* revenue. Referring back to Figure 4-5, recall that when marginal revenue is positive (that is, when elasticity exceeds unity), total revenue increases for successive increases in quantity, and when marginal revenue is negative (that is, when elasticity is less than unity), total revenue decreases for successive increases in quantities. In Table 4-2 we summarize what happens to total revenue when price is either increased or decreased and when elasticity is greater than 1, equal to 1, and less than 1.

The relationship between price changes and price elasticity and the change in total revenue should be intuitively obvious when one recalls our initial definition of price elasticity. We defined it as the percentage change in quantity demanded divided by the percentage change in the price. Elasticity exceeds unity when the percentage change in quantity exceeds the percentage change in price. Hence it should be obvious that if, for example, a price is raised by 10 percent and the quantity demanded falls by 15 percent, that total revenue must fall, since the reduction in quantity demanded is proportionately greater than the increase in the price level. The extra revenue per unit from the quantity actually sold is outweighed by the loss of the revenue from the units that were previously being sold, but that are not now being sold.

Point vs. Arc Elasticity

We distinguish between *point* elasticity of demand and *arc* elasticity of demand on the basis of the size of the change in price and quantity represented by Δ in the preceding elaboration of the elasticity concept. We use point elasticity when the changes in price and quantity are infinitesimally small, since such a small price change represents a virtual point on the demand curve. For more substantial price changes we speak of arc elasticity, since we are considering a discrete movement along, or an arc of, the demand curve.

For point price elasticity, the formula is modified to read

$$\epsilon = \frac{dQ_x}{dP_x} \cdot \frac{P_x}{Q_x} \qquad (4\text{-}17)$$

where the letter d is substituted for Δ to reflect the infinitesimally small change in the variables P_x and Q_x.

Point price elasticity is the appropriate concept for finding the elasticity value at a particular price level if the demand curve is *known*. That is, if you know the slope of the demand curve, you simply weight the reciprocal of that slope by the price-quantity ratio to find the elasticity.

EXAMPLE: In the example introduced earlier we have an estimate of the firm's demand curve, namely:

$$P_x = 14.011 - 0.26273Q_x \qquad (4\text{-}10)$$

We have earlier found that when $P_x = \$8.00$, $Q_x = 22{,}879.1$. What is the price elasticity of demand at this price-quantity combination on the demand curve? Using the formula for point price elasticity, Equation (4-17), we insert the known values for P_x and Q_x and recall that dQ_x/dP_x is the reciprocal of b, which is shown as -0.26273 in Equation (4-10). Thus:

$$\epsilon = \frac{1}{-0.26273} \cdot \frac{8}{22{,}879.1}$$

$$= -1.33$$

Alternatively, we could have multiplied the dQ_x/dP_x term, which was given in the initial estimate of the demand function as $-3{,}806.2$, by the price-quantity ratio to arrive at the same value for point price elasticity. Thus, demand is "elastic" at the price of $8.00—total revenue would increase if price were reduced or would decrease if price were raised.

In the real world, however, a firm may not know how its demand curve slopes through its present price-quantity coordinate. To find out, they must change the price and see what happens to the quantity demanded. But infinitesimally small price changes are not likely to attract the attention of consumers in the marketplace: *discrete* price changes, or significant and noticeable movements of the price level, are necessary to overcome consumer thresholds of price awareness. Thus we are unable, in many real-market situations, to generate the data required to calculate point price elasticity. In order to use the data we can generate, we must modify the formula to reflect the fact that $\Delta Q_x/\Delta P_x$ is relatively large, as compared with the infinitesimally small dQ_x/dP_x used in the point elasticity formula.

DEFINITION: *Arc price elasticity*, therefore, is defined as the relative responsiveness of quantity demanded to a *discrete* change in price, whereas point price elasticity is defined as the relative responsiveness of quantity demanded to an *infinitesimal* change in price.

EXAMPLE: Let us illustrate the arc price elasticity of demand with reference to the following example. Suppose a small store has been selling hanging flowerpots over the last few months at a price of $8 per unit and sales appear to be stabilized at about 32 units per week. The store now reduces the price of those flowerpots to $7 per unit and after a couple of weeks finds that sales have stabilized at a new level of 44 units per week. If all other factors entering the demand function have remained constant, we expect that the two price-quantity combinations above are points on the demand curve for those flowerpots. The small store is, therefore, able to estimate the $\Delta Q_x / \Delta P_x$ term required for its elasticity calculation as follows:

$$\frac{\Delta Q_x}{\Delta P_x} = \frac{Q_1 - Q_2}{P_1 - P_2} \tag{4-18}$$

where the subscripts refer to the sequence of the observations. Substituting for the two price and quantity observations, we have:

$$\frac{\Delta Q_x}{\Delta P_x} = \frac{32 - 44}{8 - 7}$$

$$= \frac{-12}{1}$$

$$= -12$$

Given this estimate of the $\Delta Q_x / \Delta P_x$ value, we can conclude that point price elasticity at the price of $8.00 is:

$$\epsilon = \frac{-12}{1} \cdot \frac{8}{32} = -3.00$$

and that point price elasticity at price $7.00 is:

$$\epsilon = \frac{-12}{1} \cdot \frac{7}{44} = -1.9091$$

As we should expect, the point price elasticity is lower for the lower price, as this represents a point further down the demand curve.

Thus, point elasticity has provided us with *two* figures for the responsiveness of quantity demanded to changes in the price level. Arc elasticity, on the other hand, provides a *summary measure* of price elasticity over the range of prices between $7.00 and $8.00 per unit. For the arc elasticity calculation, we weight the $\Delta Q_x / \Delta P_x$ term by the *average* price and *average* quantity demanded.[9] That is,

---

[9] We choose the average price and quantities as the weights to calculate arc elasticity because these represent the midpoint of the arc. The midpoint values of price and quantity minimize the variance from all other price and quantity points on the arc, as compared to any other point on the arc. Other formulas have been suggested for arc elasticity, such as using the new price and the old quantity or the old price and the new quantity. These formulations are inferior, since they base the elasticity calculation on a combination of P and Q which does not lie on the demand curve.

$$\epsilon_{arc} = \frac{\Delta Q_x}{\Delta P_x} \cdot \frac{\dfrac{P_1 + P_2}{2}}{\dfrac{Q_1 + Q_2}{2}}$$

Substituting for ΔQ_x and ΔP_x and allowing the 2's to cancel out, we have:

$$\epsilon_{arc} = \frac{Q_1 - Q_2}{P_1 - P_2} \cdot \frac{P_1 + P_2}{Q_1 + Q_2} \tag{4-19}$$

Inserting the values for P_1, P_2, Q_1, and Q_2 into Equation (4-19), we find:

$$\epsilon_{arc} = \frac{32 - 44}{8 - 7} \cdot \frac{8 + 7}{32 + 44}$$

$$= \frac{-12}{1} \cdot \frac{15}{76}$$

$$= -2.368$$

It can be seen that the value of the arc price elasticity of demand lies between the two values of the point elasticities calculated above. We should expect this, of course, since the arc elasticity is actually the point elasticity at the midpoint of the arc. It is, however, a better *summary measure* of the elasticity over the arc than are the point elasticity values at either extreme on that arc. The arc elasticity value becomes progressively less accurate as we move toward the end of the arc, but the degree of inaccuracy is much less than the value given by the point elasticity at the *other* end of the arc.

Implications for Optimal Prices

Having obtained an estimate of the slope of its demand curve, what can the flowerpot seller do with this information? The seller can derive an expression for its demand curve and check to see if the present price level is optimal, given its objectives. Let us assume that the firm wishes to maximize profits and knows that its marginal costs are constant at $5.00 per unit regardless of output levels. Is the price of $7.00 profit maximizing? That is, is marginal cost equal to marginal revenue at that price level? To find out we must derive an expression for the demand curve and then for the marginal revenue curve.

We know from Equation (4-6) that the firm's demand curve is of the form $P_x = a + bQ_x$, and that P_x is currently $7.00, Q_x is forty-four units, and $b = \Delta P_x / \Delta Q_x = 1/-12 = -0.08333$. Substituting these into Equation (4-6), we have:

DEMAND THEORY, ANALYSIS, AND ESTIMATION

$$7 = a - 0.08333(44)$$

Hence, $a = 10.6667$, and the expression for the firm's demand curve is:

$$P_x = 10.6667 - 0.08333Q_x$$

The marginal revenue expression (with the same intercept and twice the slope) is, therefore:

$$MR = 10.6667 - 0.16667Q_x$$

Setting $MR = MC = \$5.00$ and solving for Q_x, we have:

$$5 = 10.6667 - 0.16667Q_x$$
$$Q_x = 34$$

This is the profit-maximizing output level where $MC = MR$. To find the profit-maximizing price, we substitute for $Q_x = 34$ in the demand curve expression:

$$P_x = 10.6667 - 0.08333(34)$$
$$= 10.6667 - 2.8333$$
$$= 7.8333$$

Thus, the profit-maximizing price is $\$7.83$ rather than the current price of $\$7.00$ per unit.

Suppose instead that the firm wishes to maximize total revenue from the sale of the flowerpots. What price level would serve this objective? To maximize total revenue we know that marginal revenue must fall to zero. (See Figure 4-5.) Setting the expression for MR (obtained above) equal to zero and solving for Q_x, we find:

$$0 = 10.6667 - 0.16667Q_x$$
$$\therefore Q_x = \frac{10.6667}{0.16667}$$
$$= 64.00$$

Substituting for $Q_x = 64$ in the demand curve expression, we find:

$$P_x = 10.6667 - 0.08333(64)$$
$$= 10.6667 - 5.3333$$
$$= 5.333$$

Thus, the total revenue-maximizing price is $5.33, at which 64 units of the flowerpot are expected to be sold. We can verify this by observing that this price-quantity combination represents the midpoint of the demand curve. The price, $5.33, is halfway to the intercept on the price axis, and the quantity, 64 units, is halfway to the intercept on the horizontal axis ($Q_x = 128.00$ when $P_x = 0$).

A Priori Guestimation of Price Elasticity

What factors would lead us to expect the price elasticity for one product to be greater or smaller than for another product? The theory of consumer behavior points to the following two major factors as determinants of the value of price elasticity:

1. The substitutability of the product.
2. The relative expense of the product.

We saw in the preceding chapter that the substitution effect of a price change is always negative; that is, a price change in one direction will lead to a quantity-demanded response in the opposite direction. This substitution effect is the result of consumers' seeking alternative means of satisfying a particular desire by switching to an available substitute product. Thus, the greater the number of substitute products and the more closely substitutable those products are, the more we would expect consumers to switch away from a particular product when its price rose or toward that product when its price fell. Thus, the more substitutes and the more closely these substitutes resemble the product in question, the greater we expect the price elasticity of demand for that product to be.

A feature of products that is related to this substitutability is their versatility, or the number of uses to which they may be put. A product is more versatile if it can serve two or more purposes rather than only one purpose. A *more versatile* product is likely to be *less substitutable*, since it may require two or more other products to serve the purposes of the more versatile product. Hence, the more versatile the product, the less sensitive is its demand likely to be to price changes, and vice versa.

NOTE: Regarding the availability of substitutes, we need to distinguish between substitutability of products from within the same group of products and substitutability from other groups of products. For example, coffee is a group of products in the larger family of beverages; but within the product group of coffee there are many different brands and types. If we are concerned with the price elasticity of a particular brand of coffee, such as Maxwell House, and the prices of all other coffees and other beverages remain unchanged, we should expect the price elasticity for Maxwell House coffee to be relatively high. On the other hand, if all coffee prices were likely to rise in unison (due to an increase in the price of the imported coffee beans, for example), there would be little or no substitutability between or among coffee brands, but there may be substitutability away from coffee as a class toward other groups of beverages. Therefore, in the case where all close substitutes are expected to follow a similar price strategy, we expect the price elasticity to be somewhat lower, since the substitutability will be toward only the more distant substitutes.

The relative expense of the product as a determinant of price elasticity is related to the income effect of a price change. You will recall from the preceding chapter that for any product, when price is increased for example, the consumer suffers a loss in real income. The consumer is thus able to buy less of all products, including the product for which the price has risen. The larger the fraction of the consumer's budget that the purchase of this product represents, the larger the influence on the consumer's real income level that we would expect from a given percentage change in price in that product. It is clear that a 10 percent change in the price of an automobile, for example, would cause the consumer's real income to be changed considerably, whereas a 10 percent change in the price of bread would have a minimal impact. Alternatively, one might argue that for a given percentage change in a low-priced product as compared with a high-priced product, consumers are less sensitive to the smaller absolute change, and hence price elasticity will tend to be lower when the absolute cost of the item is lower and/or when the cost, relative to their income level, is lower.

EXAMPLE: In view of the above factors influencing elasticity, would you expect the price elasticity of demand for kitchen salt to be high or low? With regard to substitutability it would seem that salt has few close substitutes for its kitchen uses. The relative expense, or proportion of the consumer's income spent on that commodity, is always very low. Thus, both the substitutability and the relative expense factors militate in favor of salt having a relatively low price elasticity of demand. On the other hand, consider the demand for a particular automobile, such as a Chevrolet Caprice. There are numerous substitute automobiles, many of them quite close substitutes while others are more distant substitutes. The proportion of the consumer's income that is involved in the purchase of an automobile is typically high. Hence, both determinants militate in favor of the price elasticity for a particular automobile being quite high. If the price of all automobiles rises simultaneously, such as at the start of a new model year, the elasticity of demand faced by the Chevrolet Caprice will be somewhat lower, since the substitutability toward other products is limited to the more distant substitutes such as mass transit, bicycles, and walking.

In some cases the substitutability of a product will indicate high price elasticity, while the relative expense will indicate low price elasticity, or vice versa. Guestimation of the value of price elasticity must then proceed on the basis of judgment about which factor will be stronger if a decision must be taken immediately. If the decision can be delayed, research into the nature of the demand function and its elasticities should be undertaken. This, however, is the subject matter of the following chapter. We now turn to some other important elasticity measures.

4.4 INCOME ELASTICITY OF DEMAND

DEFINITION: The *income elasticity* of demand may be defined as the percentage change in quantity demanded divided by the percentage change in consumer income, *ceteris paribus*. That is,

$$\Theta = \frac{\%\Delta Q_x}{\%\Delta B} \tag{4-20}$$

where Θ (the Greek letter *theta*) is the conventional symbol for income elasticity and B is the consumer's budget, or income constraint. Eliminating the percentage signs and expressing it in terms of the proportionate changes, we have

$$\Theta = \frac{\dfrac{\Delta Q_x}{Q_x}}{\dfrac{\Delta B}{B}}$$

or

$$\Theta = \frac{\Delta Q_x}{\Delta B} \cdot \frac{B}{Q_x} \tag{4-21}$$

Notice that the size of $\Delta Q_x / \Delta B$ is undefined as yet. If we know the relationship between income and quantity demanded of X, we could find point income elasticity as follows:

$$\Theta = \frac{dQ_x}{dB} \cdot \frac{B}{Q_x} \tag{4-22}$$

If, on the other hand, we need to observe a significant income change to ascertain the effect on Q_x, we would find the arc income elasticity as follows:

$$\Theta = \frac{Q_1 - Q_2}{B_1 - B_2} \cdot \frac{B_1 + B_2}{Q_1 + Q_2} \tag{4-23}$$

where the subscripts reflect the sequence of the observations of the two quantity and income levels.

EXAMPLE: Recall the numerical example introduced early in the chapter. The demand function had been estimated as:

$$Q_x = 5{,}030 - 3{,}806.2P_x + 1{,}458.5P_s + 256.6A_x - 32.3A_s + 0.18Y \tag{4-4}$$

where the variable Y represents the average disposable income of consumers or some other measure of spending power, such as gross national product (GNP) per capita.

From the demand function we can calculate the *point* income elasticity of demand, given our knowledge of the current value of Y, which we said was \$12,875, and the current value of Q_x, which we calculated to be 22,879.1.

$$\Theta = \frac{dQ_x}{dY} \cdot \frac{Y}{Q_x}$$

$$= 0.18 \cdot \frac{12,875}{22,879.1}$$

$$= 0.101$$

Note that the coefficient to the income term in the demand function represents the dQ_x/dY term we need to calculate the income elasticity. (Strictly, the coefficient to Y is the *partial* derivative, $\partial Q_x/\partial Y$, but this is equivalent for our purposes.)

As an example of *arc* elasticity, suppose that in a different situation per capita disposable income is \$15,650 and that the quantity demanded of stereo receiver-amplifiers is 36,000 per month. Now, suppose that (real) per capita disposable income rises to \$17,215, because of cuts in personal income taxes and a reduction in the rate of inflation. As a result of this (with *ceteris paribus*) we observe an increase in the quantity demanded of stereo receiver-amplifiers to 40,320 units per month.

Using Equation (4-23) for the arc income elasticity calculation, we find:

$$\Theta = \frac{36,000 - 40,320}{15,650 - 17,215} \cdot \frac{15,650 + 17,215}{36,000 + 40,320}$$

$$= \frac{-4,320}{-1,565} \cdot \frac{32,865}{76,320}$$

$$= 1.189$$

Now, what do these numbers mean? Calculating the income elasticity of demand allows us to classify products as either necessities, luxuries, or inferior goods, and gives insights into the shift of the demand curve that will follow changes in consumer incomes.

Necessities, Luxuries, and Inferior Goods

DEFINITION: *Necessities* are defined as products which have an income elasticity of demand which is positive but less than one. The first example calculated above is, therefore, classified as a necessity good, since its income elasticity is

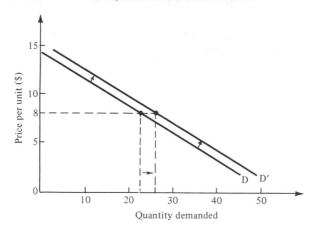

FIGURE 4-7. A Shift of the Demand Curve for a Necessity Good, Given an Increase in Income

0.101. This means that the quantity demanded increases as income increases but that the change in Q_x is less than proportionate to the change in income. In this example, if income changed by 10 percent, we would expect Q_x to change by only 1.01 percent. Examples of necessities are some foodstuffs and items of apparel.

Graphically, the impact of a change in consumer incomes is reflected by a *shift* of the demand curve for product X. Recall that the quantity demanded of product X that is caused by the income variable becomes part of the intercept term of the demand curve. If *ceteris paribus* does not hold, for example, consumer incomes change, the intercept term of the demand curve changes, and we must have a shift of the demand curve. In Figure 4-7 we show that the demand curve for the necessity good has shifted from D to D' as a result of an assumed increase in consumer incomes.

DEFINITION: *Luxuries* are defined as products for which the proportionate change in quantity demanded is greater than the proportionate change in consumer income levels; income elasticity is, therefore, positive and greater than unity. The arc elasticity calculation above indicates, therefore, that stereo-receiver amplifiers are luxury goods, since $\Theta = 1.189$. Other examples of luxury goods are items such as fur coats, travel by air, and the use of hotel accommodations. Note that *luxury good* is now a definitional term, a piece of our jargon. In common usage you might refer to something as a "luxury," but here the connotation is that it is a product whose quantity demanded responds more than proportionately to changes in consumer incomes.

Graphically, the impact of a change in income upon the quantity demanded of a luxury good is shown in Figure 4-8. Note that the shift of the demand curve in response to a change in incomes is more substantial for a luxury good than for a necessity good.

FIGURE 4-8. A Shift of the Demand Curve for a Luxury Good, Given an Increase in Income

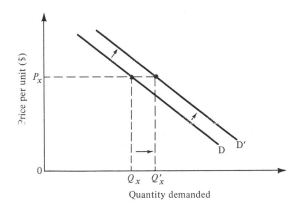

DEFINITION: *Inferior goods* are defined as commodities which exhibit an income elasticity which is negative. These products experience a decline in quantity demanded as income levels rise. Oppositely, if income levels (in real terms) decline, the quantity demanded of an inferior good will increase. Examples of inferior goods may be items such as potatoes, baked beans, ground beef, bologna, low-quality clothing, and travel by train. As incomes rise, people tend to switch away from these items to more desirable substitutes. As incomes fall, people (reluctantly) switch back to these cheaper alternatives and away from the more desirable but typically more expensive substitutes.

NOTE: The shift of the demand curve for an inferior good will be in the opposite direction to the change in incomes. In Figure 4-9 we show the demand

FIGURE 4-9. A Shift of the Demand Curve for an Inferior Good, Given an Increase in Income

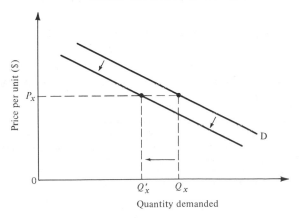

curve shifting back to the left, following an increase in consumer incomes. Consumers now buy *less* of this product than they did before, as a result of the increase in their incomes. The extent of the shift depends, of course, on the value of income elasticity—small negative values mean small shifts to the left while relatively large negative income elasticities mean relatively large shifts to the left, in both cases in response to an increase in real incomes.

In all the cases mentioned above the demand curve will shift in the *other* direction for a reduction in the real income of consumers.

Business Implications of Income Elasticity

The implications of income elasticity of demand to the business decision maker are considerable. If the income elasticity for your product exceeds unity, the demand for your product will grow more rapidly than does total consumer income or it will fall more rapidly than does total consumer income when income levels are generally falling. Hence, while income elasticity greater than one in a growing economy indicates a "growth industry," it also indicates a greater susceptibility to fluctuations in the level of aggregate economic activity. On the other hand, if the income elasticity of demand for your product is positive but less than one, the demand for your product will grow more slowly than the gross national product or consumer income, but it will be relatively "recession proof" in the sense that the demand will not react in the volatile fashion of luxury goods. Third, if your product is regarded by the market as a whole as an inferior good, you must expect the quantity demanded of your product to decline as the gross national product rises, yet exhibit an anticyclical pattern when the economy is subject to fluctuations in the level of aggregate activity. Good corporate and product planning would therefore indicate the desirability of having all three types of products in your product mix.

4.5 CROSS ELASTICITIES AND OTHER ELASTICITIES

We now consider the responsiveness of quantity demanded of product X to changes in the prices of related products. *Related* products are either substitutes or complements, and cross elasticity of demand provides a measure of the *degree* of substitutability, or complementarity, between product X and some other product.[10]

---

[10]Cross elasticity is the abbreviated name for cross-price elasticity, since we are concerned with the impact of a change in P_y on Q_x. Given that product Y is a substitute, we should also expect a cross-*advertising* elasticity, for example, indicating the impact of a change in Y's advertising efforts on Q_x. By convention, cross elasticity means cross-price elasticity, unless specifically noted otherwise.

DEFINITION: *Cross elasticity of demand* is defined as the percentage, or proportionate, change in quantity demanded of product X, divided by the percentage, or proportionate, change in the price of some product Y. That is,

$$\eta = \frac{\%\Delta Q_x}{\%\Delta P_y} \qquad (4\text{-}24)$$

where η (the Greek letter *eta*) is the conventional symbol for cross elasticity.
Following our earlier analysis, we can restate this as a *point* cross elasticity
measure, as follows:

$$\eta = \frac{dQ_x}{dP_y} \cdot \frac{P_y}{Q_x} \qquad (4\text{-}25)$$

In practice it may be necessary to have a significant change in P_y before an
impact is noticed on Q_x; we, therefore, use the *arc* cross elasticity formula, as
follows:

$$\eta = \frac{Q_1 - Q_2}{P_1 - P_2} \cdot \frac{P_1 + P_2}{Q_1 + Q_2} \qquad (4\text{-}26)$$

Note that the Q symbols refer to Q_x; the P symbols refer to P_y; and that the
subscripts reflect the sequence of the data collection.

EXAMPLE: From the earlier example of the estimated demand function for product X (Equation (4-4)) we can calculate the point cross elasticity of demand
between products X and Y, because the term dQ_x/dP_y has already been estimated. It is, of course, the coefficient to the term P_s in the demand function
for Q_x and was seen to be 1,458.5. Using Equation (4-25) and substituting
for variables P_y and Q_x, we have:

$$\eta = 1,458.5 \cdot \frac{6}{22,879.1}$$

$$= 0.382$$

What does this number tell us? It says that for a 1-percent change in the
price of product Y the quantity demanded of product X will change by
0.382 percent. Note that the changes will be in the same direction since the
sign of the cross elasticity is positive. This indicates that there is a movement
of consumers from product Y, as its price rises, across to product X, given
ceteris paribus, and that, hence, products X and Y must be substitutes for
each other.

Substitutes

DEFINITION: *Substitutes* are defined as products among which the cross elasticity of demand is positive. Suppose that the price of a product Y is reduced from $10 to $9, and that this induces a change in the quantity demanded of a product X from 100 units to 85 units, as shown in Figure 4-10. Since these are discrete price changes the arc cross elasticity formula is appropriate. Inserting these values into Equation (4-26), we see that the cross elasticity between product X and product Y is:

$$\eta = \frac{100 - 85}{10 - 9} \cdot \frac{10 + 9}{100 + 85}$$

$$= \frac{15}{1} \cdot \frac{19}{185}$$

$$= 1.54$$

In terms of Figure 4-10 it is clear that Products X and Y must be substitutes for each other, since when the price of Product Y was reduced the quantity demanded of Product X was reduced from 100 units back to 85 units. Given that *ceteris paribus* prevails, it is clear that the gain of quantity demanded for Product Y came at the expense of the demand for Product X. Recall that the price of Product Y enters the demand function for Product X as a shift parameter; a reduction in the price of Product Y would cause the demand curve for Product X to shift to the left, such that at price P_x the quantity demanded for Product X would be somewhat less. Examples of a pair of substitute products include the product groups of tea and coffee or pairs of products within either of these groups, such as Maxwell House coffee and Yuban coffee.

FIGURE 4-10.　Cross Elasticity between Substitute Products

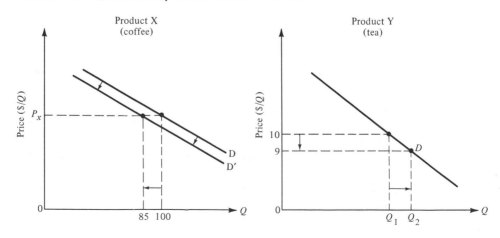

DEMAND THEORY, ANALYSIS, AND ESTIMATION

Complements

DEFINITION: *Complements* are defined as products among which the cross elasticity of demand is negative. Suppose that a 10-percent price reduction for product Y leads to a 20-percent increase in demand for product X. For example P_y is reduced from $1.00 to $0.90 and Q_x increases from 100 units to 120 units. The value of cross elasticity is

$$\eta = \frac{100 - 120}{1.0 - 0.9} \cdot \frac{1.0 + 0.9}{100 + 120}$$

$$= \frac{-20}{0.1} \cdot \frac{1.9}{220}$$

$$= -1.73$$

Such a situation is illustrated in Figure 4-11. In this case it is clear that the price reduction in Product Y, while accompanied by an increase in the demand for Product Y was also accompanied by an increase in the demand for Product X. Given *ceteris paribus*, it is clear that the increase in consumption of Product Y called forth an increase in the consumption of Product X, notwithstanding that the price of Product X did not change. Hence, Products X and Y are complementary goods in that they are apparently used jointly in consumption and in some predetermined ratio. Notice that in this case the cross elasticity of demand between Product X and Product Y must have a negative sign. Examples of products with negative cross elasticity are coffee and cream, beer and pretzels, and gasoline and tires.

Alternatively, a change in price of Product Y may have zero or minimal

FIGURE 4-11.   **Cross Elasticity between Complementary Products**

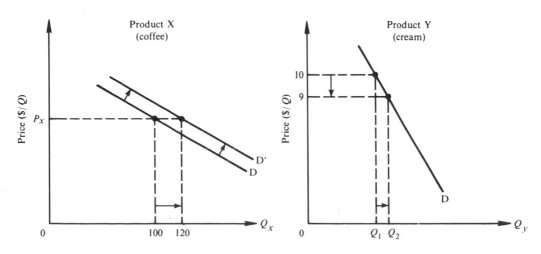

TABLE 4-3. Substitutes, Complements, and Cross Elasticity of Demand

Cross Elasticity	Relationship	Increase in P_Y	Decrease in P_Y
$\infty > \eta > 0$	Substitutes	Q_x rises	Q_x falls
$\eta \simeq 0$	Unrelated	Q_x unchanged	Q_x unchanged
$0 > \eta > -\infty$	Complements	Q_x falls	Q_x rises

impact upon the demand for Product X. In this case we must conclude that Products X and Y are unrelated in consumption. That is, Products X and Y are neither substitutes nor complements. Table 4-3 summarizes the relationships existing between the cross elasticity of demand and the relationship that apparently exists between the two products under examination. As we see in the table, cross elasticity may vary over the range from infinity to minus infinity, and hence the relationship of substitutability or complementarity varies from very strong substitutability or complementarity to quite weak substitutability or complementarity as cross elasticity approaches zero from either the positive or the negative side.

At what level do we define cross elasticity as indicating that we have a pair of "strong" substitutes as compared with "weak" substitutes? Alternatively, how large and negative must the cross-elasticity value be before we decide that the products are "strong" complements rather than simply "weak" complements? In fact, the answer is quite arbitrary. A cross elasticity value of 2 will mean that a competitor's price adjustment will have a significant impact upon your quantity demanded, but whether we would call this a strong or a weak relationship is essentially a matter of taste. Certainly if another product shared a cross elasticity of 5 with your product, for example, we would be able to say that the latter product is a *stronger* substitute for your product than is the former product.

Advertising and Cross-Advertising Elasticities

We know from the demand function that the quantity demanded of Product X will be responsive to both the advertising in support of Product X and the advertising in support of related products. The advertising elasticity of demand for Product X measures the responsiveness of the change in quantity demanded to a change in advertising budget expended for Product X. We expect a positive relationship between advertising and quantity demanded, but we also expect that the responsiveness of sales to advertising will decline as advertising expenditure continues to increase. Hence, advertising elasticity will decline as advertising expenditure increases. There will be a lower limit on the value of the advertising elasticity if advertising expenditure is not to be carried beyond an optimal level. We defer this issue until Chapter 13 where we will see that the critical value of advertising expenditure (and hence advertising elasticity) depends upon the profit contribution expected from each additional unit sold as a result of the advertising.

DEMAND THEORY, ANALYSIS, AND ESTIMATION

Cross-advertising elasticity measures the responsiveness of quantity demanded (sales) of Product X to a change in the advertising efforts directed at another product, Y. We expect cross-advertising elasticity to be negative between substitute products and positive between complementary products. For example, increased advertising efforts for a particular movie would be expected to reduce the quantity demanded (sales) of admission tickets to other movies and attractions but to increase the sales of the refreshment kiosk in the lobby of that particular movie theatre. In effect, the increased advertising would have shifted the demand curves to the left for all substitute attractions and would have shifted the demand curve to the right for the refreshment kiosk.

It is clear that we might calculate the elasticity of demand with respect to any of the independent variables in the demand function. For example, under some conditions, such as high levels of migration or high fertility rates, the population elasticity of demand may be of considerable value to the decision maker. Using the general concept of elasticities, we can construct the appropriate formula and measure population elasticity or any other elasticity useful for decision-making purposes.

The Value of Elasticities

Many would argue that the various elasticities of demand simply summarize information that is already known to the decision maker and that if one has the information necessary to calculate the elasticities of demand, the elasticity value is redundant. (In the case of price elasticity for example, if one knows the two price and quantity coordinates, one can quite simply calculate the change in total revenue that results when moving from one coordinate to the other.) So the question arises, Why calculate elasticities?

NOTE: Essentially the value of elasticities is twofold. First, they are useful as a summary measure which indicates at a glance the direction of change in total revenue given a price change or whether products are substitutes, complements, luxury, necessity, or inferior. The magnitude, and in some cases the sign, of the various elasticity measures says in the briefest way possible what there is to know about the relationship between the two variables. Second, by categorizing this relationship in the terms of a single number, we are able to reduce a variety of relationships between products to a common denominator, such that we may rank the values of elasticity for comparison purposes. Hence, if Product X is related to a number of other products, we might rank those other products in order of their cross elasticity with Product X. Those with the highest value of cross elasticity would be the stronger substitutes, and those with the largest negative values would be the stronger complements.

Moreover, we shall see in Chapter 11 that the calculation of price elasticity facilitates selection of the optimal markup to be applied to costs in order to determine the profit-maximizing prices of various products. In fact, the value of price elasticity provides the link between the pricing theory of economics and the pricing practice of the marketplace!

4.6 SUMMARY

In this chapter we examined the *demand function*, which expresses the dependence of the quantity demanded (or sales) of a particular product upon a variety of independent variables. We examined the impact we would expect changes in these variables to have upon the quantity demanded of a particular product. The *demand curve* was defined as part of the demand function when price is the only variable independent factor. That is to say, when all other factors remain constant and price changes *along* a particular demand curve. If any other factor does not remain constant we must expect a *shift* of the demand curve, which will cause a differing quantity to be demanded at the prevailing price level.

The relationship between price, quantity demanded, total revenue, and marginal revenue was examined, and it was determined that for any negatively sloping demand curve, total revenue would initially increase as a price is reduced but would later decline. Consequently, marginal revenue would initially be positive and later negative.

Several measures of the elasticity of quantity demanded were discussed. Price elasticity of demand is particularly useful for indicating the direction of change in total revenue when there is a particular directional change in price. Moreover, when a firm has several products, the relative price elasticities of these products will indicate which of these products can best sustain a price increase versus those for which a price increase would be a poor strategy. Income elasticity of demand is important for growth and stability considerations in the firm, since the demand for luxury products will tend to be relatively responsive to changes both up and down in the aggregate level of activity. Similarly, we argued that necessity goods are relatively recession proof and that inferior goods are expected to exhibit counter-cyclical demand patterns.

Cross elasticities of demand allow the summary and classification of the relationships existing between a particular product and all other products. The decision maker should be interested in knowing which of the other products on the market are substitutes for a particular product and which of these represent the more serious competition to that product. Alternatively, product-line considerations require knowledge of the complementarity of other products with a particular product, and negative values of cross elasticity indicate product complementarity and the relative strength of this complementarity.

The concepts and principles outlined in this chapter will be called upon in subsequent chapters. Pricing of the product requires a strong knowledge of the demand conditions existing in a particular market, and an understanding of the responsiveness of demand to the various factors that influence that demand is therefore of considerable importance.

DISCUSSION QUESTIONS

4-1. Which factors do you think should be held constant in a discussion about the demand curve for season tickets to the home games of a National Football League team?

4-2. What is the relationship between the coefficient of price in the demand function and the slope term in the demand curve? Explain.

4-3. Set up a matrix with $\epsilon > 1$, $\epsilon = 1$, $\epsilon < 1$ down the left-hand side and "TR increases" and "TR decreases" along the top. Fill in the six parts of the matrix to indicate whether the coordinates imply an increase or a decrease in the price level.

4-4. Summarize the methodological error and the resultant overestimate or underestimate that is involved when the point elasticity formula is used to calculate elasticity from observations of discrete price and quantity changes.

4-5. Explain how you could calculate the price elasticity at any particular price if you know the parameter values in the mathematical expression for a particular demand curve.

4-6. Classify the probable price elasticity value of the following products as either "relatively high" or "relatively low":
   (a) soft drinks
   (b) Coca-Cola
   (c) Diet Pepsi
   (d) compact automobiles
   (e) Levi jeans
   (Support each classification with your reasoning.)

4-7. Explain how you would derive the demand curve for a particular product X, given the information that $P_x = \$4.50$; $Q_x = 25$; and price elasticity of demand is -1.5.

4-8. Explain why you would expect the demand for luxury goods such as fur coats and jewelry to be more volatile in periods of fluctuating incomes as compared with items such as groceries and meat.

4-9. How would you explain a situation in which two products have both a positive cross-price elasticity of demand and a positive cross-advertising elasticity of demand?

4-10. Define the "rainfall elasticity" of demand for umbrellas, using your knowledge of the elasticity concept. What possible usefulness could such an elasticity have?

PROBLEMS AND SHORT CASES

4-1. The Silverstein Coffee Co. faces the following demand schedule in the relevant price range for one of its products.

Price (lb)	Quantity Demanded (lb/wk)
$5.00	970
4.95	1,000
4.90	1,026
4.85	1,049
4.80	1,071
4.75	1,085
4.70	1,095
4.65	1,105
4.60	1,114
4.55	1,122

(a) Plot the associated demand curve, marginal revenue curve, and total revenue curve on a graph.

(b) Calculate the price elasticity for each price change.

(c) Over what range is demand (1) elastic, (2) inelastic, (3) unitary elastic?

4-2. Billabong Boomerangs Inc. and Swahili Spears are direct competitors in the fast-growing segment of the hunters' equipment market. Because of the recent intense competition, both companies have redeveloped their main product, requiring the users' skills to be less developed than before and thus avoiding extensive field trips by company representatives for on-the-job training. This also reduced the need for costly instruction manuals. Stephen Pesner, president of Billabong Boomerangs, has decided to hire a local market research company to assist his company in planning its strategy. After extensive research using modern methods of data collection and statistical analysis, the researchers came up with Billabong's demand function:

$$Q_B = -1700P_B + 750Y_H + 350A_B - 250A_S + 1585P_S + 1.05Pop + 7.25W$$

where

Q_B is the quantity demanded of boomerangs.

P_B is the price of boomerangs.

Y_H is the average income of hunters (in thousands).

A_B is the advertising budget for Billabong Boomerangs (in thousands).

A_S is the advertising budget for Swahili Spears (in thousands).

P_S is the price of spears.

Pop is the total population (in millions).

W is the estimated population of wildlife (in hundreds).

The current values of the independent variables are P_B = 29.95; Y_H = 12.5; A_B = 680; A_S = 525; P_S = 32.25; Pop = 24.68; and W = 8.75.

(a) What is the current level of demand for Billabong boomerangs?

(b) Calculate the values of price elasticity, cross-price elasticity, and advertising elasticity.

(c) Is the price of boomerangs too high or too low in view of Mr. Pesner's desire to maximize profits? Explain.

4-3. The demand function for Fritz Reinhart premium beer has been estimated as

$$Q_x = 2{,}486.5 - 1{,}931.6P_x + 283.9P_y + 168.2A_x - 18.8A_y$$

where

Q_x = demand for the Reinhart beer (in cases).

P_x = price of the Reinhart beer (in dollars).

P_y = price of the main rival beer (in dollars).

A_x = advertising expenditure for Reinhart ($000).

A_y = advertising expenditure for the rival beer ($000).

The current values of the independent variables are P_x = 4.50; P_y = 4.39; A_x = 168; and A_y = 182.

(a) Calculate the price elasticity of demand for Reinhart beer.

(b) Calculate the advertising elasticity of demand for Reinhart beer.

(c) If the marginal cost of producing Reinhart beer is constant at $2.00 per case, should the firm change its price in order to maximize profits? Explain.

(d) Suppose instead that the Reinhart company wishes to maximize sales revenue from this beer. What price should it set?

4-4. The Gutowski Grocery Company markets a brand of a particular food item for which there are a number of reasonably similar substitutes. The company has been subject to a series of cost increases recently but feels that the present level of costs is expected to continue in the near future. These recent cost increases have caused the monthly profit to fall below the target of $15,000, and the management feels that this target could be attained if the price were reduced to $3.99 unit, presuming that rivals are unlikely to retaliate. Average variable costs are constant up to the maximum output level of 120,000 units. The following data refer to this month's operations.

Variable costs per unit	$2.74
All other costs per unit	1.57
Price per unit	4.45
Total profit for month	$11,431.28

(a) What is the price of elasticity of demand for the product in the vicinity of the present and contemplated price levels?

(b) Find the profit-maximizing price and the maximum profit level. (Show all calculations and defend your methodology.)

(c) What qualifications and assumptions underlie your analysis?

4-5. The Thompson Textile Company has asked you for advice about the optimality of its pricing policy with respect to one of its products, Product X. The following data are supplied:

Sales (units)	282,500
Price per unit	$2.00
Marginal cost per unit is constant at	$1.00
Price elasticity of demand	−3.25

(a) Is the present price level optimal if the firm wishes to maximize profits? If not, can you say what price it should charge?

(b) What is the sales revenue maximizing price for Product X?

(c) Explain to the management of Thompson Textile Company the assumptions underlying your analysis and the sensitivity of your price recommendations to these assumptions.

4-6. The Bustraen Company is one of five firms that manufacture washing machines. The five firms are all about the same size, have approximately equal market shares, and produce very similar products. Bustraen sells approximately 200,000 washing machines per annum. The company has engaged a market research consultant to provide estimates of the price elasticity and cross elasticity of demand for its product. These estimates have just been received and are as follows: price elasticity of demand for Bustraen's washing machine, −1.85; cross elasticity of demand for Bustraen's washing machine, 0.45, vis-a-vis any one of the other firm's machines; and price elasticity of demand for all washing machines (if all prices changed together), −0.55.

(a) Explain what Bustraen should expect to happen to its sales if it were to raise prices by 10 percent and no other firm changed its price.

(b) Explain what Bustraen should expect to happen to its sales if one of its rivals were to raise its price by 10 percent, with *ceteris paribus*.

(c) Explain what would happen if Bustraen raised its price 10 percent and all other firms did the same.

(d) What assumptions and qualifications underlie your analysis?

4-7. Paul McLaughlin recently purchased the M.F.F. Company, a large company that specializes in the manufacture of minifreezers. Mr. McLaughlin has a reputation for revitalizing companies and reselling them, and he has purchased this company with the intention of holding onto it for a period of two years, after which he would sell the entire operation. The management of the M.F.F. Company gave Mr. McLaughlin the following demand function for their product, which they said was based on a number of years of experience:

$$Q = 3000 - 800P + 0.05A + 2Y$$

where

Q = quantity demanded each quarter.
P = price.
A = advertising expenditures (dollars per quarter).
Y = personal disposable income per capita (dollars per annum).

As Mr. McLaughlin's special consultant, you are faced with the following problems:

(a) Mr. McLaughlin wishes to maximize sales revenue. He informs you that he is allocating $23.5 million each quarter for advertising expenditures and that the estimated personal disposable income per capita is $11,000. In order that he might maximize his sales revenue, what price should be charged for his product and how many minifreezers can he expect to sell at this price level? Illustrate this both mathematically and graphically.

(b) Alternatively, let us assume that Mr. McLaughlin had originally priced his product at $450 and had set his sales goal at 2 million minifreezers for the four quarters of the first year. Price ($450) and personal disposable income ($11,000) have remained constant throughout the first three quarters and are not expected to change during the fourth quarter. His advertising expenditures were as follows:

First quarter	$18,000,000
Second quarter	$15,000,000
Third quarter	$23,000,000

Given these figures, what should his advertising expenditures be for the fourth quarter so that he will be able to reach his goal of 2 million products sold?

4-8. The Alpha Beta Company produces and sells toaster ovens. Mr. Learmonth has just been appointed marketing vice-president and is determined to be the first VP to guide the company past the million-dollar sales mark. To do so, ABC must average $84,000 per month for the last nine months of the year.

Mr. Learmonth has been given a free hand to run the marketing side of ABC, subject to the following constraints:

1. Perceived social responsibilities dictate that ABC, as the town's largest employer, produce a minimum of 5,800 units per month to avoid layoffs. With overtime the plant can turn out a maximum of 8,100 units per month.

2. Budgetary considerations have limited increases in advertising to 15 percent above current monthly levels ($5,000). ABC has already contracted for a minimum of $5,000 per month with local media.

Mr. Learmonth's first move as VP was to have the Con-Sulting Company, a local marketing research firm, do some analytical work, and this company has developed the following normative model based on statistics supplied by Mr. Learmonth:

$$Q = 3000 + 0.3A + 0.4Y - 300P$$

where Q represents the number of ovens demanded; A represents the monthly advertising expenditure; Y represents the per capita income; and P represents the selling price of the ovens. Current selling price is $14, and current values of A and Y are $5,000 and $14,000, respectively. You have been given the assignment of recommending a strategy for the remainder of the year.

(a) What price level do you recommend?

(b) What do you recommend with regard to advertising?

(c) Calculate the income elasticity. What does this indicate about the nature of the product?

(Make any assumptions required for the solution of the problem, indicating why they were made. Show all calculations.)

SUGGESTED REFERENCES AND FURTHER READING

Ferguson, C. E., and S. C. Maurice. *Economic Analysis: Theory and Application* (3rd ed.), chap. 2. Homewood, Ill.: Richard D. Irwin, Inc., 1978.

Hirshleifer, J. *Price Theory and Applications* (2nd ed.), chap. 5. Englewood Cliffs, N.J.: Prentice-Hall, Inc. 1976.

Johnson, A. C., Jr., and P. Helmburger. "Price Elasticity of Demand as an Element of Market Structure," *American Economic Review*, (December 1967), 1218-21.

Leftwich, R. H. *The Price System and Resource Allocation* (7th ed.), chaps. 3, 5. Hinsdale, Ill.: The Dryden Press, 1979.

Mansfield, E. *Microeconomics* (3rd ed.), chap 5. New York: W. W. Norton & Co., Inc., 1979.

Martin, R. L. "Price Elasticity and a Shifting Demand Curve," *Economic Inquiry*, 17 (Jan. 1979), pp. 153-54.

Miller, R. L. *Intermediate Microeconomics*, chap. 5. New York: McGraw-Hill Book Company, 1978.

Nicholson, W. *Intermediate Microeconomics and Its Application* (2nd ed.), chaps. 4, 5. Hinsdale, Ill.: The Dryden Press, 1979.

Simon, H. "Dynamics of Price Elasticity and Brand Life Cycles: An Empirical Study," *Journal of Marketing Research*, 16 (Nov. 1979), pp. 439-52.

Thompson, A. A., Jr. *Economics of the Firm* (3rd ed.), chap. 5. Englewood Cliffs, N.J.: Prentice-Hall, Inc., 1981.

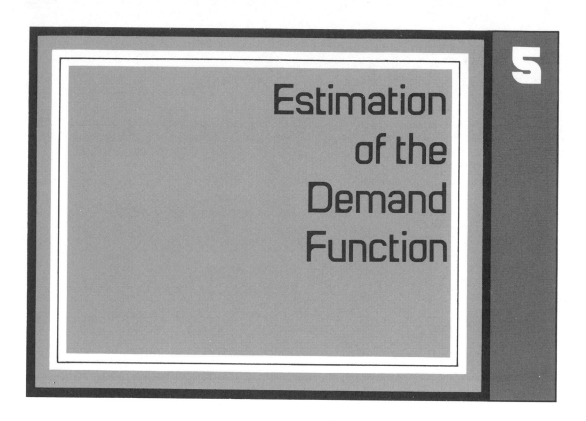

Estimation
of the
Demand
Function

5

5.1 INTRODUCTION

Much of the discussion in the foregoing chapters was based on the presumption that we could get reliable data concerning the demand situation. Specifically, we presumed to know the impact on the quantity demanded of changes in the price level, in consumers' incomes, in prices of related products, and so forth. It is obvious, however, that this information may not be readily available. Given the prior expectation that the value of the information will exceed the search costs of obtaining that information, the decision maker must generate the data, using a variety of techniques from market research and statistical analysis. This chapter examines the methods by which we may obtain the data for real-world decision problems.

NOTE: We distinguish between demand estimation and demand forecasting on the basis of the period for which demand data are sought. *Demand estimation* will be taken to mean the process of finding *current* values for the coefficients in the demand function for a particular product. *Demand forecasting* will be taken to mean the process of finding values for demand in *future* time periods. Current values are necessary to evaluate the optimality of current pricing and promotional policies and in order to make day-to-day decisions in these strategy areas. Future values are necessary for planning production, inventories, new-product development, investment, and other situations where the decision to be made has impacts over a prolonged period of time. This chapter is confined to the issue of demand estimation. Demand forecasting is treated in the appendix to the chapter. Although we shall treat estimation and forecasting separately, demand estimation often forms the basis for demand forecasting. We shall examine the major methods of both estimation and forecasting and indicate the major problems and pitfalls one may expect to encounter.

In the preceding chapter we considered the demand function in the form where demand (or sales) is expressed as a function of the variables price, advertising, consumer incomes, consumer tastes and preferences, and whatever other variables are thought to be important in determining the demand for a particular product.

$$Q = \alpha + \beta_1 P + \beta_2 A + \beta_3 Y + \beta_4 T + \dots + \beta_n N \qquad (5\text{-}1)$$

The β coefficients represent the amount by which sales will be increased (or decreased) following a one-unit change in the value of each of the variables. The present level of each of the variables is known or can be found with some investigation. It is the coefficients of these variables that are the mystery and that are important to us for decision making. That is, we wish to know what will happen to the sales level if we change a particular independent variable by a certain amount, holding all other variables constant. Stated alternatively, we wish to know whether or not a change in the value of any of these variables from their present levels would have a beneficial impact on the attainment of our objectives.

Of course, not all of these independent variables are controllable, in the sense that we have the ability to adjust their level. The *controllable* variables are price, promotional efforts, product design, and the place of sale, which are probably known to you as the "4 P's" of marketing. The *uncontrollable* variables in the demand function are those that change independently of the firm's efforts, and they include such variables as consumer incomes, taste and preference patterns, the actions of competitors, population, weather, and political, sporting, and social events or happenings. But even if the firm is unable to influence these variables, knowledge of the probable value of the coefficients is useful, since it reduces the uncertainty of the impact of changes in those variables. Given an expectation of the effect of increased consumer incomes, for example, the firm is able to plan more effectively its production, inventories, and new-product development, in view of expected changes in the affluence of consumers.

Direct vs. Indirect Methods of Demand Estimation

Methods of estimating the values of these beta coefficients may be classified as either direct or indirect. *Direct* methods are those that directly involve the consumer, and they include interviews and surveys, simulated market situations, and controlled market experiments. Thus, consumers are either asked what their reactions would be to a particular change in a determining variable, or they are observed when actually reacting to a particular change. *Indirect* demand estimation proceeds on the basis of data that have been collected and attempts to find statistical associations between the dependent and the independent variables. The techniques of simple correlation and multiple-regression analysis are employed to find these relationships. Direct methods of demand estimation are covered in detail in marketing research courses, while indirect methods are examined in quantitative methods courses. In this chapter we confine ourselves to the application of these methods to the problem of estimating the parameters of the demand function, and we refer the reader to the sources cited at the end of the chapter for more detailed treatments and other applications.

5.2 INTERVIEWS, SURVEYS, AND EXPERIMENTS

Interviews and Surveys

The most direct method of demand estimation is simply to ask buyers or potential buyers how much more or how much less they would purchase of a particular product if its price (or advertising, or one of the other independent variables) were varied by a certain amount. Although seemingly simple, this approach is fraught with difficulties. The first problem is that the individuals interviewed or surveyed must represent the market as a whole so that the results will not be biased. Thus, a sufficiently large sample, generated by random procedures, must be interviewed in order to form a reasonable estimate of the market's reaction to a proposed change. Apart from biased samples, however, the results may be unreliable because the buyer is being asked a hypothetical question and will doubtless give a hypothetical answer. The answer may not reflect the buyer's true intentions if the buyer feels that the interviewer wants to hear a different response. This problem (of interviewer bias) is also involved in situations where the true answer would suggest some socially deprecating character trait, such as gluttony or alcoholism and where the respondent provides a more socially acceptable answer to avoid embarrassment. Furthermore, even if the answer does reflect the buyer's true intentions, the buyer may change these intentions before actually making such a purchase decision. Finally, the consumer may be unable to answer the question for the simple reason that the answer is unknowable. For example, if asked how you would react to increased advertising by a particular company for its products, can you say that you would buy more or buy less and how much more or less you might buy? Not knowing the quality of the advertising or the actual impact that type of advertising may have upon you, how could you be expected to give an accurate response?

A great deal of research has gone into the problems of questionnaire formulation in order to derive reliable results from interviews and surveys. Rather than asking questions directly, the answers to a specific question may be derived from the respondent's answer to a number of other questions. Reliability of responses to specific questions may be checked by asking the same questions in a different form at a later point during the interview or on the questionnaire.[1] Thus the types of questions may include direct questions, indirect questions, and questions asked to verify the answers to preceding questions. The form of the question can influence the nature of the results: open-ended questions allow the consumer to express in his or her own words what the response may be, while structured questions, such as multiple-choice questions where the respondent must use one of four or five specific responses, suggest an answer to the consumer and may bias the results toward something the researcher expected to find. The choice of words is an important consideration, since nuances may be involved and some words have different meanings to different people. The questions must be sequenced in a way that creates and holds the subject's interest, provokes accurate responses, and does not create an emotional reaction that may influence subsequent answers or cause the respondent to refuse to continue.[2]

Thus the interview or survey approach cannot proceed on the basis of a few simple-minded questions if significant results are to be obtained. Considerable care and thought must be included in the construction of the questionnaire, and reasoned analysis must be involved in interpreting the results of the survey. In the case of products that have an established marketing history, these results may be compared with previously obtained results of interviews and with other methods of demand estimation in order to determine whether they corroborate or contradict earlier findings. With new products, however, interview results may be the only source of information obtainable, and decisions may need to be made without the support of alternate information sources.

EXAMPLE: The Sylvain Leather Products Company intends to introduce a new men's wallet and wishes to estimate the demand curve for the new wallet. Members of the market research department have conducted a questionnaire survey of one thousand people interviewed while shopping for goods of a similar nature. The interviewees were each asked to choose one of six responses as to whether they would actually purchase the new wallet at one of five price levels. The responses were (a) definitely no; (b) not likely; (c) perhaps, maybe; (d) quite likely; (e) very likely; and (f) definitely yes. The number of people responding in each category at each price level is shown in Table 5-1. The analysts have determined that the probabilities

---

[1]See, for example, P. E. Green and D. S. Tull, *Research for Marketing Decisions*, 3rd ed. (Englewood Cliffs, N.J.: Prentice-Hall, Inc., 1975), esp. chaps. 4 and 5; and D. J. Luck, H. G. Wales, and D. A. Taylor, *Marketing Research*, 4th ed. (Englewood Cliffs, N.J.: Prentice-Hall, Inc., 1974), esp. chaps. 9 and 10.

[2]See P. Kotler, *Marketing Management*, 3rd ed. (Englewood Cliffs, N.J.: Prentice-Hall, Inc., 1976), pp. 430-31.

Price ($)	NUMBER OF PEOPLE RESPONDING AS					
	(a)	(b)	(c)	(d)	(e)	(f)
9	500	300	125	50	25	0
8	300	225	175	150	100	50
7	100	150	250	250	150	100
6	50	100	100	300	250	200
5	0	25	50	225	300	400

of actually buying the product for each of the six responses are 0.0 for response (a); 0.2 for response (b); 0.4 for response (c); 0.6 for response (d); 0.8 for response (e); and 1.0 for response (f).

From this data, we can find the expected value of quantity demanded at each price level. At a price of $9, for example, the expected value of quantity demanded is the sum of the expected value of sales to each group of respondents. That is,

$$E(Q) = 500 \, (0.0) + 300 \, (0.2) + 125 \, (0.4) + 50 \, (0.6) +$$

$$25 \, (0.8) + 0 \, (1.0) = 160 \text{ units.}$$

Proceeding similarly, we can calculate that expected quantity demanded at prices of $8, $7, $6, and $5 is 335 units, 500 units, 640 units, and 800 units, respectively. Plotting these price-quantity coordinates on a graph, as in Figure 5-1, we see that they trace out a demand curve which intercepts the price axis at approximately $10.07 and which has a slope of approximately −0.0063 units. That is, dP/dQ, or the change in price for a one-unit

FIGURE 5-1.   Sylvain Leather Products Estimated Demand
                      and Marginal Revenue Curves

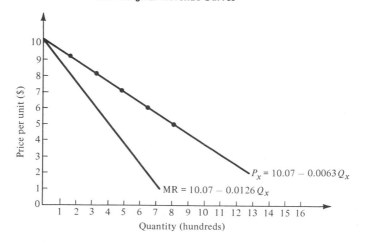

$$P_x = 10.07 - 0.0063 \, Q_x$$

$$MR = 10.07 - 0.0126 \, Q_x$$

change in quantity is approximately 0.63 cents or almost two-thirds of a cent. Put another way, for quantity demanded to increase by 100 units, price must be reduced by 63 cents.

Thus, the estimate of the demand curve is $P_x = 10.07 - 0.0063Q_x$; and from this the firm can easily find $MR_x = 10.07 - 0.0126Q_x$, since the marginal revenue curve has the same intercept and twice the slope as the demand curve.

NOTE: This estimate of the demand curve and the marginal revenue curve depends upon the sample of shoppers being a random sample which is representative of the people in the market for leather wallets. It also presumes that the responses were free from interviewer bias and that their intentions would actually culminate in purchases to the extent indicated by the probabilities. We also require *ceteris paribus* with regard to consumer incomes, tastes, perceptions, prices of rival products, and so forth. In particular, if any of these factors change between the time when the data were collected and analyzed and the time when the wallet is actually offered for sale, we should expect the above specification of the demand curve to be inaccurate because of a *shift* in the actual demand curve.

Simulated Market Situations

Another means of finding out what consumers would do in response to changes in price or promotion efforts is to construct an artificial market situation and observe the behavior of selected participants. These so-called consumer clinics often involve giving the participants a certain sum of money and asking them to spend this money in an artificial store environment. Different groups of participants may be faced with different price structures between and among competing products and/or differing promotional displays. If the participants are carefully selected to be representative of the market for these products, we may—after observing their reactions to price changes of different magnitudes and to variations in promotional efforts—conclude that the entire market would respond in the same way.

Results of such simulated-market test situations must be viewed carefully, however. Participants may spend someone else's money differently from the way they would spend their own money, a phenomenon amply demonstrated by business executives' use of expense accounts! Alternatively, participants may feel that they are expected to choose a particular product when its price is reduced in order to demonstrate that they are thrifty and responsible shoppers. Consumer clinics are likely to be an expensive method of obtaining data, however, since there is a considerable setup cost, participants must be provided with the products they select, and the process is relatively time consuming. Given these factors, it is likely that the samples involved will be quite small, and hence the results may not be representative of the entire market's reaction to the pricing and promotional changes.

TABLE 5-2.   Simulated Market Experiment for Brazilian Gold Coffee

Group	BRAZILIAN GOLD Price ($ per lb)	BRAZILIAN GOLD Quantity Demanded (lb)	BEST-SELLING BRAND Price ($ per lb)	BEST-SELLING BRAND Quantity Demanded (lb)
1	3.39	112	3.49	150
2	3.29	123	3.49	145
3	3.49	94	3.49	165
4	3.19	154	3.49	134
5	3.69	37	3.49	190
6	3.59	71	3.49	175

Nevertheless, such experiments may provide useful insight into the price awareness and consciousness of buyers and into their general reaction to changes in specific promotional variables.

EXAMPLE: The Brazilian Gold Coffee Company wished to ascertain the responsiveness of consumers to changes in the price of its coffee. Six groups of one hundred shoppers each were organized for a simulated market experiment. The membership of the groups was chosen such that the socioeconomic characteristics of the groups were roughly equal and similar to the market in total. Within one afternoon each group was allowed thirty minutes to shop in a simulated supermarket. Each participant was given $30 in "play money" to purchase any items on display in the simulated supermarket. Brazilian Gold coffee was displayed prominently alongside the best-selling brand of coffee. For each of the six groups, Brazilian Gold was priced at different levels while the price of the best-selling brand was held constant. The price levels and the resultant quantities demanded are shown in Table 5-2.

In Figure 5-2 we plot the price-quantity coordinates for Brazilian Gold coffee and sketch in the demand curve which seems to be indicated by these data points. Note that we have not simply joined the observations with a

FIGURE 5-2.   Estimated Demand Curve for Brazilian Gold Coffee

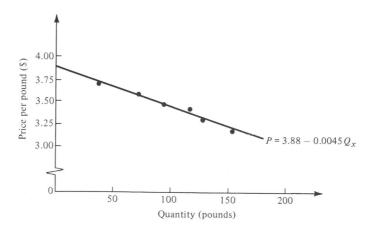

$P = 3.88 - 0.0045 Q_x$

DEMAND THEORY, ANALYSIS, AND ESTIMATION

jagged line but have, instead, superimposed a "line of best fit." In the next section we shall see how to calculate the exact line of best fit using regression analysis. In the present example, we have simply "eye-balled" the line of best fit across the data points. That is, we have sketched in the demand curve which seems visually appropriate to the points shown. We show it as a straight line for simplicity and because the data does not clearly indicate a nonlinear relationship between price and quantity demanded. The intercept of the line of best fit occurs at approximately $3.88 on the price axis, and the slope of the line is approximately 0.0045, which can be calculated by taking a particular vertical change (e.g., $3.88 to $3.38, or $0.50) and dividing this by the horizontal change indicated by the line of best fit (in this case, from zero to about 110 units). Thus, 0.50/110 = 0.0045.

Thus, the simulated market experiment has generated data which allow the demand curve for Brazilian Gold coffee to be estimated as $P_x = 3.88 - 0.0045Q_x$, *ceteris paribus*. The firm can then easily determine the expression for its marginal revenue curve or calculate the price elasticity of demand at any price level. Note that for the price-elasticity calculation one would use the reciprocal of the slope term, namely $1/-0.0045$, or -222.22, as the term dQ_x/dP_x and read the coordinates P_x and Q_x from the line of best fit. For example, the price elasticity at price $3.59 would be calculated as:

$$\epsilon = -222.22 \cdot \frac{3.59}{65}$$

$$= -12.27$$

Note that we have used the *estimated* quantity demanded (at a price of $3.59) of 65 units, read from the demand curve (line of best fit) rather than from the *observed* quantity (in the experiment) of 71 units. We do this because we recognize that all the observations probably contain random errors and we expect (from consumer behavior theory) that the demand curve will be a smooth line between price-quantity combinations. The next time we set price at $3.59 the random disturbances may cause demand to be, for example, only 58 units. Our *best estimate* of demand at price $3.59 is given by the line of best fit, and therefore our best estimate of price elasticity at that price should be based on the estimated demand curve rather than on the actual data observed.[3]

---

[3]Note that if we had only two pairs of price-quantity observations, such as those for the prices $3.69 and $3.59, we would calculate *arc* elasticity of demand and we would have to use the observed price-quantity points in that calculation. Given more observations, however, we are able to see that the slope of the line joining the two coordinates above is not our best estimate of the slope of the demand curve. Given more than two data points, we are able to estimate the line of best fit (demand curve) and use the information provided by this curve (rather than the raw data containing probable random disturbances) for our elasticity calculations.

Estimation of the Demand Function

FIGURE 5-3.   Relationship between the Price of Brazilian Gold
and the Quantity Demanded of the Other Brand
of Coffee

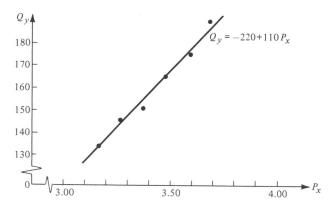

NOTE: Given the data in Table 5-2, we can also calculate the cross elasticity of demand between Brazilian Gold coffee and the best-selling brand. Note that we have the data for various prices of Brazilian Gold and for various quantities demanded of the best-selling brand. Thus, we can find the responsiveness of the best-selling brand's quantity demanded to changes in the price of Brazilian Gold.

   To calculate cross elasticity we need an expression for the term dQ_x / dP_y.[4] We obtain this in the same manner as the price-elasticity calculation above. Plotting the quantities of the best-selling brand against the prices of Brazilian Gold, as in Figure 5-3, we sketch in the line of best fit and from this estimate its slope. The slope of this line is easily calculated by taking the vertical rise over the horizontal run for a given interval. For example, between prices $3.19 and $3.69 (a horizontal run of $0.50) the line of best fit appears to have a vertical rise of approximately 55 units (from about 132 units to 187 units). Thus, we conclude that the term dQ_x /dP_y is equal to 55/0.5, or 110. The cross elasticity of demand at a particular price of Brazilian Gold, say $3.69, can, therefore, be estimated as:

---

[4]Note that we are obliged to find the relative responsiveness (cross elasticity) of the best-selling brand's quantity demanded to changes in the price of Brazilian Gold, since the data provided are for various prices of Brazilian Gold and for various quantities demanded of the best-selling brand. The resulting cross-elasticity figures may be quite different from the relative responsiveness in the *other* direction—that is, the impact on Brazilian Gold's quantity demanded because of changes in the price of the best-selling brand. If the products are very similar, the term dQ_x/dP_y may be similar in both directions, but the ratio P_y/Q_x will be quite different if the products have substantially different prices and/or substantially different market shares (or absolute quantities demanded).

$$\eta = \frac{dQ_x}{dP_y} \cdot \frac{P_y}{Q_x}$$

$$= 110 \cdot \frac{3.69}{187}$$

$$= 2.17$$

Thus, the cross-elasticity calculation confirms that the two coffees are substitutes, since the value is positive. Moreover, it indicates that they are relatively strong substitutes, since the value is quite high. It indicates, for example, that a 10 percent decrease in the price of Brazilian Gold would cause a decrease of approximately 22 percent in the quantity demanded of the best-selling brand.[5]

Direct Market Experiments

The procedures mentioned under the simulated market situations might be implemented in actual market situations with the use of past information or with information from a control market to compare buyers' reactions to changes in specific variables. In a regional market, for example, the firm might reduce the price of its product by 10 percent and compare the reaction of sales in that market over a particular period with previous sales in that market or with current sales in a similar but separate regional market. Alternatively, the firm may increase its advertising in a specific area or introduce a promotional gimmick or campaign in a particular market to judge the impact of that change before committing itself to the greater expense and risk of instituting this change on a nationwide basis.

EXAMPLE: Many firms in the United States launch new products and conduct experimental promotional campaigns in regional test markets. San Diego, California, was used by the Miller Brewing Company as a test market for its new "Special Reserve" beer during 1981, prior to the nationwide availability of that beer. Similarly, light (low calorie) wines were test marketed first in the San Diego area by Taylor California Cellars to test market acceptance of the product and to judge consumer reaction to the price level and promotional campaign. San Diego is used as a test market because it is demographically representative of southern California. Similarly, Denver,

---

[5]We say approximately because 10 percent represents an *arc* on the curve relating quantity of the best-selling brand to price of Brazilian Gold (as shown in Figure 5-3), but the elasticity calculation is for *point* cross elasticity at the price of $3.69. The actual percentage change in the quantity of the best-selling brand, for a 10-percent decrease in the price of Brazilian Gold, is easily estimated from the line of best fit in Figure 5-3.

Baltimore, Phoenix, and Providence were chosen as test markets by Miller for the new beer since they are representative of other areas of the United States in terms of demographics, income levels, lifestyles, and so forth.[6]

Direct marketing, in which the consumer responds to an advertisement placed by the seller in any of several media, including newspapers, magazines, radio, television, and direct mailings to consumers, is a form of dealing with consumers that facilitates market experiments. The mail and telephone orders which follow a firm's advertisement or direct mailing represent cash-up-front and are much more reliable indicators of market demand than are simple statements of consumer intentions. By placing different advertisements and price offers in different regions or by making different offers to different samples within the same region (using direct mailings to randomly selected samples of the target market), the impact of different prices and promotional strategies on the entire target market can be reliably estimated. As a bonus, the feedback is usually fairly quick—responses to TV advertisements requiring mail or telephone orders are concentrated within the next few days following the advertisement, while magazine advertisements and direct mailings generate the great majority of the total responses within six or eight weeks. Note, however, that direct marketing represents a different channel between the producer and the consumer and may appeal to a different type of consumer, such that the findings from experiments using direct marketing may not be generally applicable to other marketing channels, such as retailing through suburban and city stores.[7]

NOTE: With any change in price or other marketing strategy there is likely to be an initial or "impact" effect followed by a gradual settling of the market into the new longer-term relationship between price (or other controllable variable) and the sales level. Consumers will eagerly try a new product or respond to a price reduction or a promotional campaign, but having tried the product, many will go back to the rival product they were previously purchasing. Consumers may respond to a price reduction by purchasing several cartons of the product to build up their personal inventory of the product in the belief that the lower price is only temporary. The initial surge in consumer demand for a new product or for an established product at a lower price (or following a promotional campaign) may substantially overstate the sales gain the firm can expect in several weeks or months after consumers have finished making their adjustments in response to the change in prices, product availability, promotion, or in some other variable.

---

[6]Lanie Jones, "San Diego's Role as Test Market Toasted as Cap Comes off New Beer," *Los Angeles Times*, August 17, 1981, pt. 2, pp. 1, 10; Also Dan Berger, "Miller Introduces New Beer Here," *San Diego Union*, August 13, 1981.

[7]See Bob Stone, *Successful Direct Marketing Methods*, 2nd ed. (Chicago: Crain Books, 1979).

In order to observe more than the impact effects of a change, market experiments must be conducted over a reasonably prolonged period of time. During this period, however, one or more of the uncontrollable variables are likely to have changed, and thus the observed change in sales over the period will not be due simply to the change in the controllable variable. To separate the effects of changes in other variables the researcher may use a "control market," which should be chosen to exhibit a similar socioeconomic and cultural profile and be subject to the same climatic, political, and other uncontrollable events. The change in sales in the control market over the period of the experiment will be solely the result of the uncontrollable factors. On the assumption that the same change would have occurred in the test market, this magnitude is deducted from (if positive) or added to (if negative) the change in sales in the test market to find the net change in sales caused by the manipulation of the controllable variable(s).

To the extent that an uncontrollable variable changes in the test market but remains constant or changes to a different degree in the control market, the results of the market experiment will be less reliable. Even when the control market is nearby, the climatic influence may vary, local politics may intervene, or some other event may cause an impact on the sales level. Competitors may react to the change in the test market by lowering prices or increasing promotional efforts, for example, while maintaining the *status quo* in the undisturbed control market. Under such circumstances the market experiment could prove to be an expensive exercise in terms of the reliability of the data generated.

Aside from the setup costs of a market experiment and the risk that these costs will be incurred for unreliable results, there are other costs that may be associated with this form of estimating the parameters of the demand function. Customers lost during the experiment may not be regained after the experiment, since they may be satisfied with a newly-tried substitute product. An inelastic response to a price reduction may (depending on the cost situation) cause a loss of profits relative to the continuance of the status quo. And if the price is raised to its former level after the experiment, sales may fall below their former level due to the loss of allegiance of some customers who resent being manipulated or who are provoked otherwise at this point to try a substitute. Longer-term damage to sales in the test market may also be inflicted by a distasteful or insensitive promotional campaign.

Thus, direct market experiments must be implemented with caution; some luck must be forthcoming so that uncontrollable variables do not distort the results, which must be interpreted with care. If the pitfalls are largely anticipated and subsequently avoided, such experiments may provide information whose value (in terms of the present value of the additional future sales revenue) far exceeds its cost. We now turn to a means of estimating the demand coefficients from secondary data, in contrast to the above reliance on primary data.

5.3 REGRESSION ANALYSIS OF CONSUMER DEMAND

DEFINITION: *Regression analysis* is a statistical technique used to discover the apparent dependence of one variable upon one or more other variables. It is thus applicable to the problem of determining the coefficients of the demand function, since these express the influence of the independent variables upon the demand for a product. For regression analysis we require a number of sets of observations, each consisting of the value of the dependent variable Y plus the corresponding values of the independent X_i variables. Regression analysis allows conclusions to be drawn from the pattern that emerges in the relationships between these pairs or sets of observations, and can be applied to either time-series or cross-section data.

Time-Series vs. Cross-Section Analysis

DEFINITION: *Time-series analysis* uses the pairs or sets of observations that have been recorded *over time in a particular situation.* For example, monthly price and sales levels of a product in a particular firm may have been collected for the past six or twelve months. A problem with time-series analysis is that some of the uncontrollable factors that influence sales tend to change over time, and hence some of the differences in the sales observations will be the result of these influences rather than the result of any changes in the price level. If the changes in the uncontrollable variables are observable and measurable, we may include these variables as explanatory variables in the regression analysis. Actions of competitors and changing consumer income levels, for example, should be quantified (either directly or by use of a suitable proxy variable) and incorporated into the analysis.

Changing taste and preference patterns, on the other hand, are difficult to observe and measure, but they are likely to change over time. Using time as an explanatory variable in the regression analysis will pick up the influence of *all* factors (not otherwise included in the analysis) that tend to change over the period. The resulting trend factor may then be extrapolated into future periods as a proxy for changing consumer tastes and whatever other factors may be changing over time.

DEFINITION: *Cross-section analysis* uses the sets or pairs of observations from different firms in the same business environment at the *same point or period of time.* Hence cross-section analysis largely eliminates the problem of uncontrollable variables that change over time, but it introduces other factors that may differ between and among firms at a particular point of time. If factors such as the effectiveness of sales personnel, cash-flow position, level of promotional activity, and objectives of management differ among firms, they should be expected to have differing impacts on the sales level. Again, if these factors can be quantified and data obtained, they may be entered into the regression analysis to determine their impact upon the dependent variables.

Linearity of the Regression Equation

Having hypothesized that Y is a function of X or of several X variables and having collected data on the variables, we must then specify the form of the dependence of Y upon the X variables. Regression analysis requires that the dependence be expressed in the linear form

$$Y = \alpha + \beta_1 X_1 + \beta_2 X_2 + ... + \beta_n X_n + e \qquad (5\text{-}2)$$

where the e term is added to represent the error or residual value that will arise as the difference between the *actual* value of each Y that has been observed in association with each set of X values, and the *estimated* value of each Y that the above regression equation would associate with each X value. For individual observations we should expect either a positive or a negative residual term, because of the influence of random variations or unspecified influences on the variable Y.[8]

Although the regression equation must be of the linear form, the hypothesized relationship between the Y and X values need not be linear. Nonlinear forms such as quadratic, cubic, exponential, hyperbolic, and power functions may be used if these best fit the data, since these forms may be converted to linear form by mathematical transformation. The most commonly used nonlinear form is the power function, such as

$$Y = \alpha X_1^{\beta_1} X_2^{\beta_2} \qquad (5\text{-}3)$$

where the independent variables, X_1 and X_2 in this case, have a multiplicative (rather than additive) influence on the dependent variable Y. This curvilinear relationship can be expressed as a rectilinear relationship by logarithmic transformation. Taking logarithms of the values for Y, X_1, and X_2, we can express Equation (5-3) as:

$$\log Y = \log \alpha + \beta_1 \log X_1 + \beta_2 \log X_2 \qquad (5\text{-}4)$$

In this form, the equation is linear, and the coefficients β_1 and β_2 can be found directly using regression analysis. The coefficient α in Equation (5-3) can be found by reversing the transformation (that is, taking the

---

[8]For the accurate calculation of the coefficients in the regression equation, we require that the residuals occur randomly, be normally distributed, have constant variance, and have an expected value of zero. When the pattern of residuals does not conform to these restrictions, several problems arise, as we shall see later in this section.

antilog) of the log α value provided by the regression analysis. We shall work through an example of this in chapter 8, in the context of cost forecasting.

Alternatively, you may feel that the appropriate functional form between the dependent variable and the independent variables is quadratic, like the form for the total revenue curve. A quadratic function can be expressed linearly as follows:

$$Y = \alpha + \beta_1 X_1 + \beta_2 X_1{}^2 \qquad (5\text{-}5)$$

Note that the last variable in this expression is the same independent variable (X_1) squared. Similarly, if the appropriate functional form is thought to be cubic, as in the case of the production function or total cost function to be discussed in Chapter 6, we can postulate the relationship to be:

$$Y = \alpha + \beta_1 X_1 + \beta_2 X_1{}^2 + \beta_3 X_1{}^3 \qquad (5\text{-}6)$$

and use regression analysis to determine the values of the α, β_1, β_2, and β_3 parameters.

Estimating the Regression Parameters

The "method of least squares" is used to find the α and β parameters such that the regression equation best represents or summarizes the apparent relationship between the X_i values and the dependent variable Y. To illustrate this, we shall proceed using a simple example of only one independent variable. (This is usually referred to as "simple regression" analysis, or "correlation" analysis rather than "multiple regression" analysis, when we have two or more independent variables.)

EXAMPLE: Suppose that we have collected ten pairs of observations on the variables Y and X—that is, the Y value and its associated X value on each of ten different occasions in a single situation (time-series data) or from ten different situations during the same period of time (cross-section data). These data points are shown as the asterisks in Figure 5-4. Observing these data points, we hypothesize a relationship of the form $Y = \alpha + \beta X$ and use regression analysis to estimate the α and β parameters, which allow the line $Y = \alpha + \beta X$ to *best fit* (or represent most accurately) the apparent relationship between the variables Y and X.

The method of least squares, often called ordinary least squares (OLS), is a mathematical process which chooses the intercept and slope of the line of best fit such that the sum of the squares of the deviations (or errors) is minimized. These deviations are shown in Figure 5-4 as the vertical distance between the line of best fit, $Y = \alpha + \beta X$ and the actual value of Y observed for a particular value of X. For example, given X_1 in Figure 5-4, the estimated value of Y is $\hat{Y}_1$ (known as Y_1 *hat*, where the *hat* (circumflex) over the Y_1 indicates the estimated, or expected, value of Y_1, given X_1). The

FIGURE 5-4.   The Line of Best Fit

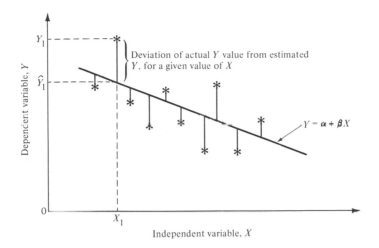

vertical difference between the observed Y_1 and the estimated $\hat{Y}_1$ is known as the deviation, or residual, or error term, and was connoted as e in equation (5-2).

The line of best fit is the line that minimizes the total vertical distance between the actual Y observations and the $\hat{Y}$ values that would be estimated (for each X) by the regression equation. To find the line of best fit, we square these residuals to avoid the positive deviations (those falling above the line) offsetting negative deviations of similar magnitude when these residuals are summed, and to weight more heavily the larger deviations.[9]

Since computer programs (and preprogrammed or programmable hand calculators) for obtaining correlation and regression equations are becoming more readily available and since the theory underlying regression analysis is typically covered in other courses, we shall not go too deeply into the theory or calculation of regression equations. It is instructive, however, to work through a simple two-variable case to demonstrate some of the issues and problems involved. Without proof, we state the following expressions for α and β:[10]

$$\alpha = \overline{Y} - \beta \overline{X} \qquad (5\text{-}7)$$

---

[9]See Richard I. Levin, *Statistics for Management*, 2nd ed., (Englewood Cliffs, N. J.: Prentice-Hall, Inc. 1981), pp. 463-65.

[10]See J. Johnston, *Econometric Methods* (New York: McGraw-Hill Book Company, 1963), pp. 9-19. Note that your calculator, if it has a regression-equation program, may be programmed for a simplified formula, and you may, as a consequence, arrive at a slightly different answer. The degree of inaccuracy is usually very small, however.

and

$$\beta = \frac{n\Sigma XY - \Sigma X \, \Sigma Y}{n\Sigma X^2 \; - \; (\Sigma X)^2} \qquad\qquad (5\text{-}8)$$

where

$\overline{Y}$ is the arithmetic mean of the Y values.

$\overline{X}$ is the arithmetic mean of the X values.

Σ (sigma) connotes the sum of the term indicated (for example, ΣXY is the sum of the products of X and Y for all pairs of X and Y observations).

n is the number of observations or data points.

Given a set of X and Y observations, we solve (preferably using a calculator) for the line of best fit for the relationship that appears to exist between those two variables. Let us introduce a hypothetical example.

EXAMPLE: Suppose a chain of department stores sells its own brand of frozen broccoli in each of its six stores. The chain is interested in knowing the price elasticity of demand for this product. Its six stores are in similar middle-income suburban neighborhoods, and all are currently selling the item at $0.79 per package. Monthly sales at the six stores average 4,625 units per store, with no store's sales being more than 150 units away from this level. Suppose the management decides to conduct an experiment: it will set the prices at different levels in each of the six stores to observe the reactions of sales to the different price levels. As a control it will maintain the price at $0.79 in the first store. The prices set for the other stores and the sales levels (in thousands) at each of the six stores over the one-month period of the experiment, are shown in Table 5-3.

TABLE 5-3.   Price/Sales Observations for Broccoli at Six Stores and the Calculations for Least-Squares Analysis

Store No.	Price X ($)	Sales Y (000)	XY	X²	Y²
1	0.79	4.650	3.6735	0.6241	21.6225
2	0.99	3.020	2.9898	0.9801	9.1204
3	1.25	2.150	2.6875	1.5625	4.6225
4	0.89	4.400	3.9160	0.7921	19.3600
5	0.59	6.380	3.7642	0.3481	40.7044
6	0.45	5.500	2.4750	0.2025	30.2500
	4.96 (ΣX)	26.100 (ΣY)	19.5060 (ΣXY)	4.5094 (ΣX^2)	125.6798 (ΣY^2)

$$\overline{Y} = \frac{\Sigma Y}{n} = \frac{26.1}{6} = 4.35$$

$$\overline{X} = \frac{\Sigma X}{n} = \frac{4.96}{6} = 0.8267$$

DEMAND THEORY, ANALYSIS, AND ESTIMATION

The table includes the calculations necessary for the solution of the α and β parameters. Using Equation (5-8), we have

$$\beta = \frac{6(19.506) - 4.96(26.1)}{6(4.5094) - (4.96)^2}$$

$$= \frac{-12.42}{2.4548}$$

$$= -5.0595$$

and from Equation (5-7), we have

$$\alpha = \overline{Y} - \beta\overline{X}$$

$$= 4.35 - (-5.059)(0.8267)$$

$$= 8.5327$$

Thus, $Y = 8.5327 - 5.0595X$ is the "line of best fit" to the data, when sales (Y) are measured in thousands of units. As shown in Figure 5-5, the intercept of this line is thus 8,532.7 units on the Y axis and the slope is $-5,059.5$ units of sales per dollar increase in price (which is to say 50.595 units for each cent the price is increased). The intercept value should not be interpreted as the sales level that would be expected at the price of zero, since the range of price observations is from \$0.45 to \$1.25, and the values of α and β are estimated only for that range. Outside this range a different

FIGURE 5-5. Graphical Plot of Price/Sales Observations

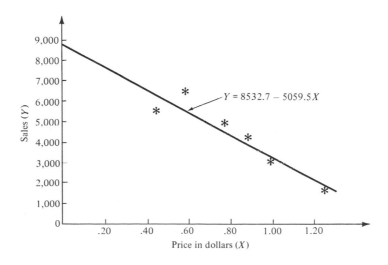

relationship may hold between X and Y. The intercept parameter serves only to locate the line of best fit such that it passes through the observations at the appropriate height. To interpret the intercept as the sales value when price is zero would be an example of the dangerous practice of extrapolation!

NOTE: The regression equation calculated above shows the dependence of quantity demanded on the price per unit. We can easily convert this into the form $P = a + bQ$ traditionally used to represent the demand curve. Substituting for Q and P in the regression equation, we have:

$$Q = 8.5327 - 5.0595P \qquad (5\text{-}9)$$

Subtracting Q from both sides, adding $5.0595P$ to both sides, and dividing both sides by 5.0595, we have:

$$5.0595P = 8.5327 - Q$$
$$P = 1.6865 - 0.19765Q \qquad (5\text{-}10)$$

The marginal revenue curve is obtained from this estimate of the demand curve, based on our knowledge that it has the same vertical intercept and twice the slope. Thus,

$$MR = 1.6865 - 0.3953Q \qquad (5\text{-}11)$$

Price elasticity of demand at any price level may be estimated using $dQ/dP = -5.0595$ from the regression Equation (5-9) and the estimated quantity demanded at that price level. For example, given $P = 0.85$, we find $\hat{Q}$ by substituting for P in Equation (5-9) as follows:

$$\hat{Q} = 8.5327 - 5.0595\,(0.85)$$
$$= 4.2321$$

Inserting these values into the point price elasticity expression, we find:

$$\epsilon = \frac{dQ}{dP} \cdot \frac{P}{Q}$$

$$= -5.0595 \cdot \frac{0.85}{4.2321}$$

$$= -1.0162$$

The price elasticity of demand at the price level of $0.85 is, therefore, fractionally above unity, indicating that total revenue would be virtually constant for either (very small) price increases or price reductions from the price of

$0.85. We should note, however, that the results of this hypothetical experiment may be simply the short-term reaction of consumers to the changes in the price levels. We have noted that the "impact" effects of a change in a marketing strategy may well differ from the longer-term effects, since buyers in aggregate take time to adjust to changes in their economic environment. If the experiment were conducted over a longer time period, with assurances that all other determining factors remained constant, we should expect to find the response of consumers to this price change somewhat more elastic than that indicated by the above results.

The Coefficient of Determination

DEFINITION: The *coefficient of determination*, conventionally expressed as R^2, is a number indicating the proportion of the variation in the dependent variable which is explained by the variation in the independent variable(s).

In effect, the R^2 value tells us *how well* the regression equation fits the data. An R^2 value of 0.98, for example, indicates that changes in the value(s) of the independent variable(s) account for 98 percent of the changes in the dependent variable. An R^2 value of 1.0 would indicate that *all* the variation in Y is explained by the variation in the X variable(s), and consequently, all data points would actually lie on the line of best fit. Oppositely, an R^2 value of, for example, 0.32, would indicate a broadly scattered set of data points with relatively large deviations from the line of best fit and a relatively weak relationship between the dependent and independent variables.

The coefficient of determination can be calculated using the following formula:[11]

$$R^2 = \left(\frac{n\,\Sigma XY - \Sigma X\,\Sigma Y}{\sqrt{[n\Sigma X^2 - (\Sigma X)^2]\,[n\Sigma Y^2 - (\Sigma Y)^2]}} \right)^2 \qquad (5\text{-}12)$$

EXAMPLE: Inserting the values as calculated in Table 5-1, we have

$$R^2 = \left(\frac{6(19.506) - 4.96(26.1)}{\sqrt{[6(4.5094) - (4.96)^2]\,[6(125.6798) - (26.1)^2]}} \right)^2$$

$$= \left(\frac{-12.42}{\sqrt{178.8783}} \right)^2$$

$$= \left(\frac{-12.42}{13.3745} \right)^2$$

$$= (-0.9286)^2$$

$$= 0.8624$$

---

[11]See Johnston, *Econometric Methods*, pp. 30-32.

Thus, we are able to say that slightly more than 86 percent of the variation in the sales observations was due to the influence of the differences in the price levels. The remaining unexplained variance is due to some other influence on sales. This remaining variability could be due to differences in promotional activity, consumer incomes, consumer tastes, or other factors that may differ between and among the six stores.

The Standard Error of Estimate

Most computer regression programs include as standard output several other statistics which allow the decision maker to evaluate the confidence that may be placed in certain predictions. The first of these is the standard error of estimate.

DEFINITION: The *standard error of estimate* is a measure of the dispersion of the data points from the line of best fit. Given the standard error of estimate (S_e), we can calculate the confidence interval (around the estimated value for the dependent variable) for different levels of confidence. The *confidence interval* is the range of values within which we expect the actual observation to fall a given percentage of the time. For example, we can be confident at the 95-percent level that the actual value of Y for a given X will fall within a certain range of outcomes above and below the estimated value (that is $\hat{Y}_i$) if we know that 95 percent of the time it *should* fall within this interval.

Assuming that the error terms (deviations or residuals) are normally distributed about the line of best fit, we can use the properties of a normal distribution to say that there is a 68-percent probability that actual observations of the dependent variable will lie within the range given by the estimated value plus or minus one standard error of the estimate. Furthermore, there is a 95-percent probability that the future observations will lie within plus or minus *two* standard errors of its predicted value and a 99-percent probability that the observed value will lie within plus or minus *three* standard errors of the estimated value.

By adding and subtracting the standard error to and from the estimated value of Y for each value of X, we establish a band within which we can expect the value of Y to fall for a particular value of X. A broader band is established when we add or subtract two standard errors of the estimate, and as noted above the probability is raised to 95 percent that the actual observation will lie within this band. The latter band is perhaps the most widely used in decision making, and it establishes what are known as the upper and lower 95-percent confidence limits. That is, we can be 95-percent confident that the actual observation will lie in the band and that the best and worst outcomes associated with the particular value of the independent variable will be no further than the limits of the band.

DEMAND THEORY, ANALYSIS, AND ESTIMATION

We can calculate the standard error of estimate using the following expression:[12]

$$S_e = \sqrt{\frac{\Sigma Y^2 - \alpha \Sigma Y - \beta \Sigma XY}{n-2}} \qquad (5\text{-}13)$$

EXAMPLE: For the broccoli example introduced earlier we can insert the values which were calculated in Table 5-3 and the α and β values subsequently derived to find the standard error of estimate associated with the line of best fit:

$$S_e = \sqrt{\frac{125.6798 - (8.5327)(26.1) - (-5.0595)(19.506)}{6-2}}$$

$$= \sqrt{\frac{1.66694}{4}}$$

$$= \sqrt{0.41673}$$

$$= 0.64555$$

Thus, the standard error of estimate is 0.64555, or 645.55 units, since the sales data were in thousands. To find the 95-percent confidence interval, we would simply add twice this figure to $\hat{Y}$ to find the upper confidence limit and subtract twice this figure to find the lower confidence limit. Selecting a price near $\bar{X}$, such as $0.85, we estimate sales to be:

$$\hat{Y} = 8.5327 - 5.0595 \ (0.85)$$

$$= 8.5327 - 4.3006$$

$$= 4.2321$$

Thus, when the price is $0.85, our best estimate of sales is 4,232.1 units. But we don't really expect the actual sales to fall at exactly that number because the estimate is derived from data that exhibited deviations from the line of best fit. The standard error of estimate uses the observed

---

[12] See Levin, *Statistics for Management*, pp. 471-77. Note that this value of S_e is only accurate at the mean values of X and Y and that it understates the confidence intervals by progressively more as we move away from $\bar{X}$ and $\bar{Y}$. The *exact* value of the standard error for each value of X_i can be calculated using:

$$S_p = \sqrt{S_e^2 \left(1 + \frac{1}{n} + \frac{(\bar{X} - X_i)^2}{\Sigma X^2 - n\bar{X}^2} \right)}$$

From this expression, you can see that S_p diverges from S_e as n becomes smaller and X_i is more distant from $\bar{X}$. Thus, the confidence intervals given by the rule of thumb (for example, plus or minus $2S_e$ around $\hat{Y}$ indicates the 95-percent confidence interval) are accurate at $\bar{X}$ and for reasonably large values of n, but *understate* the confidence intervals for X_i more distant from $\bar{X}$ and when n is relatively small. For greater accuracy when using small samples, the S_e should be multiplied by the appropriate *t-statistic* (rather than simply 2) to find the 95-percent confidence interval. See Levin, pp. 476-77.

Estimation of the Demand Function

deviations to establish confidence intervals on the presumption that later observations will similarly contain random disturbances and tend to scatter around the line of best fit. The upper bound of the 95-percent confidence interval is equal to:

$$\hat{Y} + 2S_e = 4.2321 + 2\,(0.64555)$$
$$= 5.5233$$

and the lower bound of the 95-percent confidence interval is equal to:

$$\hat{Y} - 2S_e = 4.2321 - 2\,(0.64555)$$
$$= 2.9409$$

Thus, we can be confident at the 95-percent level that when price is set at $0.85, sales will fall within the range 2,940.9 units to 5,523.3 units. Clearly, we would prefer to discover a smaller standard error of estimate, since the confidence interval would then be smaller, and we could be more confident of experiencing an actual outcome close to the expected outcome, $\hat{Y}$.

The Standard Error of the Coefficient

DEFINITION: The *standard error of the coefficient* is a measure of the dispersion of the marginal relationship between the dependent variable and an independent variable. It allows us to express confidence that the calculated value of β, the coefficient estimating the marginal relationship between Y and X, is the *true* value of the marginal relationship.

Assuming that the deviations are normally distributed, we can use the features of a normal distribution to say that there is a 68-percent probability that the true coefficient will lie in the interval of the estimated coefficient plus or minus one standard error of the coefficient; a 95-percent probability that the true coefficient will lie in the interval given by the estimated coefficient plus or minus two standard errors of the coefficient; and a 99-percent probability that the actual relationship will be within plus or minus three standard errors of the coefficient of the estimated marginal relationship. Clearly, the smaller the standard error of the coefficient, the greater the confidence we can have in the regression coefficients generated by the data as reliable indicators of the true marginal relationships between the X_i values and the Y value.

The standard error of the coefficient can be calculated using the formula:[13]

$$S_\beta = \frac{S_e}{\sqrt{\Sigma X^2 - n\overline{X}^2}} \tag{5-14}$$

---

[13]See Levin, *Statistics for Management*, pp. 491-93.

EXAMPLE: For the broccoli example, the estimated coefficient, $\hat{\beta}$, was -5.0595. What are the 95-percent confidence limits associated with this estimate? Inserting the data calculated earlier into Equation (5-14), we find:

$$S_\beta = \frac{0.6456}{\sqrt{4.5094 - 6(0.8267)^2}}$$

$$= \frac{0.6456}{0.4088}$$

$$= 1.5792$$

Thus, the 95-percent confidence limits for the estimated coefficient are $-5.0595 + 2\ (1.5792)$ and $-5.0595 - 2\ (1.5792)$, or -1.9009 and -8.2181.

A simple rule of thumb to test for confidence in the regression coefficient is to take twice the value of the standard error of the coefficient and compare this with the estimated regression coefficient. If the regression coefficient exceeds twice its standard error, we can be 95-percent confident that the estimated coefficient is significantly different from zero and that there is a statistically significant relationship between the variables. In the present example, $\beta = -5.0595$ and is substantially more than twice the size of S_β, so we *can* be confident at the 95-percent level that the price level is a statistically significant determinant of the quantity demanded of the broccoli.[14]

The foregoing discussion in the context of simple regression, or correlation, analysis applies *mutatis mutandis* to multivariate regression analysis. The formulas for calculating the regression parameters for multivariable situations are given below.[15] The calculations become increasingly more complex and time consuming as the number of variables is increased and are thus a problem ideally suited to computer solution. The wide availability of computer programs for regression analysis means that essentially we need to know only how to enter the data and to interpret the results rather than to know the mechanistic processes of obtaining the results.

---

[14] Alternatively, if the regression program generates *t-statistics* for each independent variable, we would require that the *t-value* exceed 2, since the *t-statistic* is calculated as the correlation (or regression) coefficient divided by its standard error adjusted for the degrees of freedom. See Levin, *Statistics for Management*, pp. 491-93.

[15] For the multivariate regression equation $Y = a + \beta_1 X_1 + \beta_2 X_2$, we can find α, β_1, and β_2 by simultaneous solution of the equations:

$$Y = n\alpha + \beta_1 \Sigma X_1 + \beta_2 \Sigma X_2 \qquad (1)$$
$$\Sigma X_1 Y = \alpha \Sigma X_1 + \beta_1 \Sigma X_1{}^2 + \beta_2 \Sigma X_1 X_2 \qquad (2)$$
$$\Sigma X_2 Y = \alpha \Sigma X_2 + \beta_1 \Sigma X_1 X_2 + \beta_2 \Sigma X_2{}^2 \qquad (3)$$

For more than two independent variables, the equations are commensurately more complex. Using computer programs, such as the STATPAK Multiple Regression Program, complex regression equations can be solved much more quickly and accurately. See Levin, *Statistics for Management*, pp. 511-16.

Understanding how to enter the data and how to interpret the results nevertheless requires a solid appreciation of the major problem areas likely to be encountered in regression analysis. If one or more of these problems do arise, the mechanistic regression analysis will still turn out regression parameters and statistics, but these results may well be spurious and therefore give misleading explanations and poor predictions. (Computers act in good faith, presuming that researchers know what they are doing.) We shall address the major problems in turn.

Specification Errors. The first place to create unreliability in the results is in the specification of the relationship that is hypothesized to exist between the dependent variable and the independent variable(s). Two main types of problems occur under this heading: first there is the misspecification of the functional form of the relationship and second there is the omission of important independent variables. We noted above that the regression equation must be calculated in linear form, but that this could be achieved for nonlinear relationships by logarithmic transformation of the function to linear form. The first specification error is to specify the relationship as linear when in fact it is nonlinear of some form, or vice versa. How do we know which functional form is the "true" relationship? We find which functional form "best fits" the data by comparing the coefficient of determination (R^2) for various functional forms. By running the data in both the linear form (Equation (5-2)) and, for example, the power form (Equation (5-3)), the R^2 statistics can be compared to determine which functional form best explains the variance in the dependent variable. For bivariate correlation analysis, of course, a simple plot of the Y values against the X values should allow a visual assurance that the relationship is either linear or nonlinear.

The second specification error involves the omission of an important explanatory variable. This leads to probable unreliability in the regression coefficients and the likely violation of the restrictions that we place upon the error terms. Essentially, since one or more of the explanatory variables are not included in the regression equation, the influence of these variables is attributed to the variables that *are* included, or it shows up as an unexplained residual.

EXAMPLE: To illustrate this problem recall the broccoli example discussed earlier, in which the variability in sales levels was regressed upon the variability of prices in the six stores. Suppose we now learn that *ceteris paribus* did not hold for the period of the experiment: the promotional activity of the six stores differed during the period because of differences in the availability of advertising space in the suburban weekly newspapers and differences in the circulation of these newspapers. Multiplying pages of advertising by circulation in each area, we obtain a proxy measure of advertising exposure for each store as shown in Table 5-4 with the original price and sales data.

TABLE 5-4. Price, Sales, and Advertising Exposure for Six Stores during the Experiment

Store No.	Sales Y (000)	Price X_1 ($)	Advertising X_2 (proxy units)
1	4.650	0.79	23,000
2	3.020	0.99	18,500
3	2.150	1.25	24,600
4	4.400	0.89	26,200
5	6.380	0.59	25,100
6	5.500	0.45	16,800

We now hypothesize that $Y = \alpha + \beta_1 X_1 + \beta_2 X_2$, and we call upon the services of a regression program to estimate the α and β parameters. The regression equation that "best fits" the data in Table 5-4 is

$$Y = 5718.02 - 5802.62X_1 + 0.153X_2$$

and we are provided with the following statistics:

Standard error of estimate:	238.38098
Standard error of the X_1 coefficient:	399.746
Standard error of the X_2 coefficient:	0.0298
Coefficient of determination (R^2):	0.986

Note that the magnitudes of these standard errors and the standard error of estimate indicate that the independent variables are reliable for predictive purposes, according to the rules of thumb mentioned earlier. The coefficient of determination indicates that the two variables, price and advertising exposure, jointly explain 98.6 percent of the variance of Y. Note also that the coefficient to X_1 has changed by the addition of the second explanatory variable, and that the R^2 value has increased, when compared with our earlier bivariate correlation analysis. Thus the omission of a significant determining factor in the earlier analysis led to a misleading coefficient for the price variable and to a subsequently misleading estimate of the price elasticity of demand.

A third specification problem arises when there are two closely correlated independent variables and the wrong one is included in the regression equation. Suppose that, in fact, Y depends on X, and that X and Z both depend on some other variable W and therefore tend to vary together. Suppose the researcher hypothesizes that $Y = f(Z)$ and tests for the explanatory power of Z upon the value of Y. Since X and Z tend to vary together, the regression analysis will indicate the existence of a statistical dependence of Y on Z. Statistical relationships need not indicate causal relationships, however, and the researcher must be satisfied with the logical causality between the independent and the dependent variable before using the results for explanatory purposes. As indicated in Chapter 1, however, the regression equation may be used (with caution) for prediction purposes as long as the underlying relationship does not change significantly.

Measurement Errors. Having decided which variables to include in the regression equation and the appropriate functional form of the relationship, the next pitfall to be avoided is the improper measurement of the variables. In the chain-store problem above, for example, does the proxy measure of advertising exposure *accurately* depict the determining variable we wish to measure? To the extent that some suburban weeklies may have a superior advertising format or to the extent that the newspaper tends to lie neglected on the porches (or under the Porsches!) of some suburbs, the simple measure of advertising exposure may not accurately depict the influence of advertising efforts on sales. If a more accurate measure of a particular variable can be generated, at a cost not exceeding the value of the additional information derived, this measure should be used in the regression calculations.

The price variable is notorious for its problems of measurement. The most readily available measure of price is usually the "list price" or "manufacturer's suggested price," but in many instances this may not accurately depict the actual price paid. Whenever bargaining, discounts, or trade-ins are involved, the actual money changing hands may be somewhat less than the list price. Researchers are likely to encounter difficulty in determining the actual price paid on each particular sale, since sellers will be reluctant to divulge this information (fearing it will jeopardize their bargaining position in subsequent price negotiations with customers), and the customers are typically so widely dispersed that a survey of them would be prohibitively expensive. Of course, for many products the price displayed on the item will be an accurate measure of the actual price paid if discounts, trade-ins, and customer bargaining are not customary in the purchase of those products. The purpose of the above discussion is largely to stress that if the data used do not accurately measure the level of the variables, the programmer's adage "garbage in, garbage out" is likely to be appropriate.

Simultaneous Equation Relationships. In many situations the single regression equation cannot adequately represent the true relationships existing between and among the variables. The regression analysis proceeds on the assumption that the influence of all other variables remains constant while we investigate for the influence of the specified independent variables. That is, we assume that a single equation explains the entire relationship. One problem with demand estimation arises because the price level is the result of the solution of the simultaneous equations for both demand and supply. Hence, if supply is shifting over the period for which the data were collected, some part of the variation in the observations may be due to the influence of this second unspecified relationship.

EXAMPLE: Suppose we have three price/quantity observations that have been collected over a period of time and are as shown in Figure 5-6. They seem to indicate a negative relationship between price and quantity and hence

FIGURE 5-6.   The Identification Problem

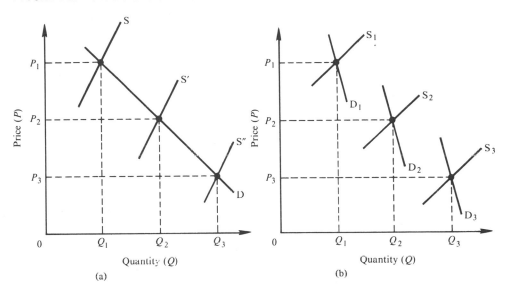

may be thought to trace out the demand curve shown in part (a) and be the result of a shifting supply curve that has moved to the right over time, causing progressively lower intersection points on the demand curve. Alternatively, the three observations may be a result of the scenario depicted in part (b) of the figure. The first price/quantity observation may be the result of the intersection of supply and demand curve S_1 and D_1, while the subsequent price/quantity observations are the result of shifting demand and supply curves as indicated. Regression analysis, however, would conclude that part (a) is the appropriate interpretation of the data, which, if erroneous, would give a misleading view of the slope and placement of the demand function.

The problem arises because there are insufficient data in the regression analysis to identify the existence of both relationships, and hence this is often called the *identification problem*. This problem arises particularly with time-series data in demand estimation, since we cannot expect the supply function to remain constant over time, because of changing technology and factor costs, and we cannot expect the demand function to remain stable for any extended period of time, because of changing influences such as consumer incomes and preference patterns. This problem may be avoided by the use of cross-section data, however, given an appropriate control for comparison with a previous time period (as in the chain-store example above).

Multicollinearity.   The problem of multicollinearity arises when the independent variables are not independent (of each other) at all. If two or more of the explanatory variables vary together because of their dependence on each other or on another variable, the coefficient assigned to each of the variables by the regression solution may have no relationship to the "true" marginal influence of these variables upon the dependent variable. The regression analysis is unable to detect the true relationships and will assign an arbitrary value to the coefficients. Besides reducing the explanatory and predictive power of the regression equation, the presence of multicollinearity is likely to cause the standard error of the coefficient (or *t-test*) to be an unreliable indicator of the statistical significance of the coefficients.

The presence of multicollinearity may be uncovered by checking the coefficients of determination between pairs of independent variables. Where variables are highly correlated we may remove all but one from the regression equation, taking care not to fall foul of the specification error of using an independent variable with no logical causal relationship to the dependent variable.[16]

NOTE: Multicollinearity can be tolerated in the regression equation if the purpose of that equation is simply *predictive*. Recall that we have acknowledged three purposes of models: namely, pedagogical, explanatory, and predictive. The demand function estimated by regression analysis is in effect an explanatory and predictive model—explaining and predicting the value of Q_x in terms of the independent variables. As an explanatory model, it is important that there is no multicollinearity in the data, since we ascribe importance and significance to the individual coefficients in the regression equation. For example, the β coefficient to price is used to calculate price elasticity and to find the slope of the demand curve. Consequently, it is important that this β coefficient be an accurate estimate of the marginal relationship between Q_x and P_x and that it is not distorted by the presence of multicollinearity. But when the estimate of the demand function is used to *predict* Q_x in a subsequent period, given the values of all the independent variables, we look at the impact of the independent variables as a *group* rather than individually. Thus, it does not matter if individual coefficients are inaccurate because of multicollinearity, since it is the total effect on Q_x which interests us. Remember from Chapter 1 that predictive models do not have to be realistic or based on accurate assumptions—the test of a predictive model is how well it predicts. Thus, if the presence of multicollinearity increases the R^2 and makes the regression equation a better predictor, it can be tolerated as long as the equation is used only for predictive purposes, with the independent variables viewed as a group rather than individually.

Heteroscedasticity. The regression analysis presumes homoscedasticity of the error terms; that is, that the residuals or deviations from the line of best fit occur randomly with respect to the magnitude of the independent variables.

---

[16]See Levin, *Statistics for Management*, pp. 201-6; or see A. S. Goldberger, *Topics in Regression Analysis* (London: Macmillan, Inc., 1968), pp. 79-83.

FIGURE 5-7.   Evidence of Heteroscedasticity in
Regression Analysis

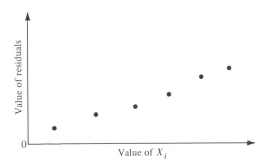

When the error terms do not occur randomly but exhibit a systematic relationship with the magnitude of one or more of the independent variables, we have the condition of heteroscedasticity. This violation of the requirement that observations have uniform variability about the line of best fit (implied by the restrictions placed on the error term) makes regression analysis an inappropriate procedure and thus produces results that are likely to be unreliable. The presence of heteroscedasticity is likely to cause the standard error of the coefficient to give misleading indications and cause the coefficient of determination to overstate the explanatory power of the regression equation.

A simple means to discover the presence of heteroscedasticity is to plot the values of the residuals against the values of the independent variable(s). Many regression programs will produce these graphs for visual inspection; any systematic relationship that appears will indicate the presence of heteroscedasticity. For example, in Figure 5-7 we show a situation in which the residuals exhibit a systematic positive relationship with the variable X_i. This problem may be removed by respecifying the independent variables, by changing the functional form of the relationship, by a transformation of the data, or by using a weighted least-squares regression technique.[17]

Autocorrelation.   Autocorrelation is another problem that arises when the error terms do not conform to the restrictions required for regression analysis. Autocorrelation (also known as serial correlation) is indicated by a sequential pattern in the residuals. If successive values of the error terms exhibit a particular trend or cyclical pattern, as shown in Figure 5-8, this indicates that some other variable is changing systematically and influencing the dependent variable. Autocorrelation may be removed by adding to the regression equation the variable thought to explain the systematic pattern. For example, if the residuals appear to follow a cyclical pattern over time,

---

[17]This takes us into the big league. These rectifications are discussed in advanced statistics texts, such as in N. R. Draper and H. Smith, *Applied Regression Analysis* (New York: John Wiley & Sons, Inc., 1966), pp. 77-81.

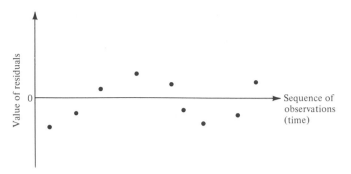

FIGURE 5-8. Evidence of Autocorrelation of Residuals in Regression Analysis

this may be found to correlate well with the levels of national income over the same period. Alternatively, a continuing upward or downward trend in the residuals could be eliminated by adding time as an explanatory variable.

Most regression programs include as output either a sequence plot of the residuals or the Durbin-Watson statistic, which is calculated to indicate the presence or absence of autocorrelation. A Durbin-Watson statistic around the value of two indicates the absence of autocorrelation, while values significantly greater or less than two indicate that the residuals do not occur randomly and, therefore, that the results are likely to be unreliable.[18]

Regression analysis is an extremely useful tool for estimating the coefficients of the demand function. But like fire, precautions must be taken with the use of this tool. Most regression programs will produce the various statistics mentioned above and will plot the residuals such that the experienced researcher can readily discover the presence of one or more of the major problems that may occur. Clearly, the greatest care must be taken in the initial steps of specifying the assumed relationship and collecting the data. Once the regression analysis has been conducted, the researcher must carefully interpret the results before concluding that these results are a sufficient basis for decision-making purposes.

5.4 SUMMARY

Demand estimation is concerned with finding the values of the parameters in the demand function that are currently appropriate. This information is important for current decision making and in evaluating whether decisions are optimal in terms of the current demand situation.

Buyers' reactions to changes in the independent variables in the demand function may be gauged by interviews and surveys, simulated market experi-

---

[18]See Johnston, *Econometric Methods*, chap. 7.

DEMAND THEORY, ANALYSIS, AND ESTIMATION

ments, or by direct market experiments. Care must be taken to ensure the selection of a random sample which properly reflects the target market, and the size of each sample should be large enough to allow confidence in the findings. Questionnaire design is critical to the accuracy of the predictions from interviews and surveys. A problem that is difficult to sidestep is that consumer intentions do not always accurately translate into actions at a later point. Interviewer bias and lack of consumer interest or information may also distort the estimates derived.

Simulated market experiments and direct market experiments allow the observation of the consumer during the consumption-decision process and conclusions may be drawn from the actual behavior of consumers. Care must be taken to isolate impact effects from longer-term effects and to ascertain whether the behavior of people in consumer clinics accurately reflects their usual behavior patterns. Direct marketing techniques provide an ideal opportunity to test the impact of different levels of price or other strategic variables, and regional test markets have proved useful for ascertaining the impact of different strategies at the retail level.

Regression analysis of data collected allows the calculation of the coefficients in the demand function, as well as the calculation of several statistics which indicate the confidence that can be attached to the estimates derived. Regression analysis is a powerful tool, when used correctly, for estimating the parameters of the demand function, on the basis of the statistical association that appears between and among variables in either time-series or cross-section data observations. The pitfalls that may invalidate this technique were outlined in some detail so that the researcher can better set up the problem for analysis and better interpret the results of that analysis.

DISCUSSION QUESTIONS

5-1. Why is it useful to the decision maker to have an estimate of the impact (on the quantity demanded) of variables that are not controllable by the decision maker?

5-2. List the problem areas that one must be cautious about when using interviews and surveys to derive estimates of the market demand function for a particular product.

5-3. List ten questions you would ask a sample of people in order to estimate their demand function for a specific brand of toothpaste.

5-4. Suppose you were to interview a large number of people, asking each person whether he or she would buy a particular product at a series of prices starting from a relatively low price and then raising the price until each person would *not* buy the product. How would you translate this information into an estimated demand curve?

5-5. Design a simulated market situation intended to ascertain customers' responses to changes in prices, packaging, and point-of-purchase promotion for a particular product.

5-6. What factors must be monitored while conducting a direct market experiment in order to allow confidence that the results obtained give reliable information about the demand function?

5-7. Suppose you had data on the annual quantity demanded of newsprint and the price per ton of newsprint over the past twenty years and that you had found the regression equation relating quantity demanded to price. Why would this be an unreliable estimate of the demand curve?

5-8. Explain the importance of the assumptions concerning the residuals, or error terms, to the accuracy of the estimate of the demand function derived using regression analysis.

5-9. Explain how you would satisfy yourself that your analysis did not contain any specification errors.

5-10. Summarize the issues you would need to check before concluding that the results of a regression analysis were a reliable basis for estimating the demand function.

PROBLEMS AND SHORT CASES

5-1. Jose Hermanos Liquors has conducted a simulated market experiment aimed at finding the price which would maximize total revenue from the sale of one item in its product line, namely Hermanos Gold Tequila. Six samples of 100 persons each were assembled at intervals one hour apart and allowed to select bottles of liquor up to a total value of $50 from a simulated liquor store display. The Hermanos tequila was displayed prominently between two major brands of tequila and its price was different for each sample of shoppers. All other prices and promotional variables remained the same over the six tests.

After the six groups of shoppers had finished the experiment, the following results were tabulated:

Group	HERMANOS TEQUILA Price $	HERMANOS TEQUILA Quantity Demanded	OTHER TWO BRANDS Quantity Demanded
1	9.55	17	30
2	7.85	24	26
3	8.25	21	27
4	10.75	10	32
5	6.45	32	23
6	6.95	28	25

(a) Sketch the line of best fit representing the demand curve for Hermanos Tequila for market size of 100 consumers. Estimate the intercept and slope terms of this demand curve.

(b) Generalize this demand curve to the total market in the region, estimated to be 1 million people. What changes does this cause in your demand curve expression?

(c) What price promises to maximize total revenue for Hermanos Tequila?

(d) What are the values of the price elasticity and cross elasticity of demand at that price? Explain what these values indicate.

5-2. The Direct Deal Marketing Company operates a mail and telephone order business, selling products directly to consumers who order DDMC's products after seeing advertisements in magazines or after receiving informational materials and samples through the mail. At the present time, DDMC is considering a mailing to 500,000 subscribers of *Road and Track* magazine, offering custom-fitted sheepskin seat covers to fit most automobiles sold in North America. Before incurring the major expense associated with this large mailing, however, DDMC has conducted a market experiment in order to ascertain consumer responsiveness to price. It has rented four separate lists of names of *Road and Track* subscribers, each list randomly generated by computer from the total subscription list and each containing 2,500 names and addresses. In its mailing to these four subsamples all other promotional and information material was the same, but each sample was offered a different price. After two months DDMC has received orders from each of the sub-samples, as shown below, and considers that all orders are in after waiting this long.

Subsample	Price	Pairs Ordered
A	$179.95	51
B	$199.95	38
C	$219.95	26
D	$239.95	14

(a) Estimate the intercept and slope term for DDMC's demand curve for the seat covers, given that the proposed mailing will reach 500,000 subscribers.

(b) What is the price elasticity of demand at each of the four price levels indicated?

(c) Suppose that the marginal cost to fulfill each order is $150 per pair, including postage and handling costs. What price should DDMC establish for the proposed mailing in order to maximize its profits from this particular product?

(d) State all assumptions which underlie your analysis and predictions.

5-3. The Leiberman Plastics Company wishes to predict sales for its plastic pails for the 1983 year. It has recorded data for its past ten years' demand and has obtained data on the number of households within its market area. This information is listed in the accompanying table.

Leiberman Plastics Company

Year	Sales of Pails (units)	Number of Households (000)
1973	7,000	350
1974	6,750	462
1975	7,150	548
1976	8,300	610
1977	8,000	694
1978	9,200	830
1979	9,050	985
1980	10,100	1,080
1981	10,300	1,210
1982	10,600	1,330

(a) Plot the annual sales data against the number of households in the market area and draw in the "line of best fit" that seems to be visually appropriate.

(b) Measuring the intercept and slope of the above line of best fit, state the approximate functional relationship between the two variables.

(c) Suppose the number of households is projected as increasing by 165,000 in 1983. Use the above functional relationship to forecast the demand for plastic pails during 1983.

(d) Comment upon the probable accuracy of your forecast.

5-4. The Karich Electronics Corporation manufactures stereo equipment and has recently developed a distinctly new-looking stereo receiver. As a result of surveying several thous-and people about their perceived quality and expected price level, the marketing de-partment of Karich has estimated the probabilities of sales at several levels for each of five price levels (see table).

Karich Electronics Corporation

Price ($)	Sales (units)	Probability of Sales
	7,500	0.20
	6,000	0.25
100	4,500	0.40
	3,000	0.10
	1,500	0.05
	6,000	0.10
	5,000	0.20
125	4,000	0.45
	2,500	0.20
	1,000	0.05
	4,500	0.10
	4,000	0.20
150	3,000	0.40
	2,000	0.20
	750	0.10
	3,500	0.05
	3,000	0.10
175	2,500	0.50
	1,000	0.20
	500	0.15
	3,000	0.05
	2,500	0.15
200	1,500	0.30
	1,000	0.25
	500	0.25

(a) Calculate the expected value of quantity demanded at each price level.

(b) Use these expected values to estimate the demand curve for the new product.

(c) If the marginal cost of the stereo receivers is $112.50 per unit, regardless of volume, what price would you recommend?

(d) What qualifications would you add to your recommendation?

5-5. Wido Heck, manager of the Red Baron Flying School, is wondering how many instructional hours will be demanded during the coming season. He needs to have an estimate of demand in order to hire instructors. He has just completed a survey by questionnaire among the students and has summarized the results, as shown in the table. He feels that any influx of new students will do no more than balance the attrition of existing students and that their demands for flying time will be similar to those of the students they replace.

Demand for Flying Instruction

Price per Flying Hour ($)	Hours per Day Demanded
10	64
15	53
17	43
20	37
27	29
30	23

(a) Plot prices against quantity demanded and establish an estimate of the demand curve by a freehand smoothing line.

(b) Using regression analysis, calculate and state the demand curve equation and calculate the coefficient of determination. (Show all workings)

(c) Using the regression equation calculated above, estimate the flying hours per day demanded at a price of $23/hr. Comment on the probable degree of accuracy of this estimate.

(d) If Mr. Heck is now charging $25/hr. and his marginal cost is constant at $10/hr., should he raise or lower his price? At what price is his profit maximized?

5-6. The Lifestyle Leisure Company produces and sells hot-tubs for the southern California market. It has recently been varying the price of its best-selling unit and observing the quantity sold at each price level. Based on this data the following regression equation has been calculated:

$$Q_x = 38,658.235 - 8.667 P_x$$

where Q_x is quantity sold and P_x is price per unit. The regression analysis also produced the following statistics: coefficient of determination, 0.723; standard error of estimate, 3,251.625; and standard error of the coefficient, 5.213.

Lifestyle Leisure's marginal cost of producing these hot-tubs is constant at $1,500 per unit for all forseeable output levels.

(a) What is the profit-maximizing price for the hot-tubs?

(b) What is the sales-revenue-maximizing price?

(c) Calculate the price elasticity of demand at the profit-maximization price and comment on the value obtained.

(d) At the profit-maximizing price, what is the 95-percent confidence interval for sales?

(e) What other qualifications and assumptions underlie your prediction?

5-7. Ambivalent Autronics has commissioned a study to quantify the determinants of the demand for its cruise-control device. This device is installed in an automobile to allow the vehicle to maintain a constant cruising speed, with subsequent fuel economy advantages.

Based on the data available to it from all sources, the Demand Data Research Company has calculated the following regression equation:

$$Q_x = 125,062.85 - 1,862.52P_x + 1,226.94P_s + 524.18A_x + 28,672.74Y + 0.035S$$

where

Q_x is quantity demanded of the cruise-control unit per month.

P_x is the price per unit set by Ambivalent Autronics (in dollars).

P_s is the average price (in dollars) of the three other cruise control units which are considered the closest substitutes for AA's unit.

A_x is AA's advertising budget per month (in thousands of dollars).

Y is the level of per capita disposable income per month (in thousands of dollars).

S is the level of sales of new automobiles per month.

The regression analysis also provided the following statistics:

Coefficient of determination (R^2):	0.8675 — Se
Standard error of estimate:	6,432.75
Standard errors of the coefficients:	for P_x, 725.6; for P_s, 482.8; for A_x, 106.2; for Y, 188.1; for S, 0.015.

AA's cost of production of the cruise-control units has stabilized and it can produce for all foreseeable demand situations at a constant marginal cost of $132.50 per unit. The current values of the independent variables are P_x = 189.95; P_s = 195.00; A_x = 12.65; Y = 1.53; and S = 895,645.

(a) Calculate the price elasticity, the cross elasticity, and the income elasticity of demand for the product and comment on the values obtained.

(b) Derive expressions for the firm's demand and marginal revenue curves for the product.

(c) Calculate the profit-maximizing price for the cruise-control unit.

(d) At that price, in what range of figures do you expect quantity demanded to fall at the 95-percent confidence level?

(e) What other qualifications underlie your analysis?

5-8. The demand function for product X has been established, using regression analysis, as follows:

$$Q_x = -5,154.605 - 35.83P_x + 82.97P_y + 78.67P_z - 64.03P_w$$

where P_x, P_y, P_z and P_w are the prices of products each identified by the subscript. The current price levels are as follows: P_x = \$188.50; P_y = \$103.75; P_z = \$119.25, and P_w = \$32.50.

The regression program also generated the following statistics: R^2 = 0.92; S.E.E. = 80.01; Standard errors of the coefficients: for P_x, 8.62; for P_y, 33.91; for P_z, 60.82; and for P_w, 35.82.

(a) What price would maximize sales revenue from the sale of product X?

(b) Suppose the marginal cost of producing X is constant at $100 per unit. What price would maximize profits from the sale of product X?

(c) Suppose the price of product Y is raised to $114.95. Does this have any impact on the profit-maximizing price for X? Explain.

(d) What qualifications and/or assumptions underlie your analysis?

SUGGESTED REFERENCES AND FURTHER READING

Baumol, W.J. *Economic Theory and Operations Analysis* (4th ed.), chap. 10, Englewood Cliffs, N.J.: Prentice-Hall, Inc., 1977.

Bennett, S., and J.B. Wilkinson. "Price-Quantity Relationships and Price Elasticity under In-Store Experimentation," *Journal of Business Research*, 2 (January 1974), 27-38.

Draper, N.R., and H. Smith. *Applied Regression Analysis.* New York: John Wiley & Sons, Inc., 1966.

Goldberger, A.S. *Topics in Regression Analysis.* London: Macmillan, Inc., 1968.

Green, P.E., and D.S. Tull. *Research for Marketing Decisions* (3rd ed.), esp. chaps. 3-5. Englewood Cliffs, N.J.: Prentice-Hall, Inc., 1975.

Johnston, J. *Econometric Methods*, chaps. 1, 2, 4, 7, and 8. New York: McGraw-Hill Book Company, 1963.

Kotler, P. *Marketing Management* (3rd ed.), chap. 19. Englewood Cliffs, N.J.: Prentice-Hall, Inc., 1976.

Levin, R.L. *Statistics for Management* (2nd ed.), chaps. 11, 12. Englewood Cliffs, N.J.: Prentice-Hall, Inc., 1981.

DEMAND THEORY, ANALYSIS, AND ESTIMATION

Luck, D.J., H.G. Wales, and D.A. Taylor. *Marketing Research* (4th ed.), esp. chaps. 9, 10, 12, and 14. Englewood Cliffs, N.J.: Prentice-Hall, Inc., 1974.

Pessemier, E.A. "An Experimental Method for Estimating Demand," *Journal of Business*, 33 (October 1960), 373-83.

Stone, B. *Successful Direct Marketing Methods* (2nd ed.), esp. chap. 15. Chicago, Ill., Crain Books, 1979.

APPENDIX 5A: DEMAND FORECASTING

The forecasting of sales in future periods has an additional dimension when compared with demand estimation in the current period. In demand estimation we knew or could ascertain the current value of the independent variables, and the problem was to find the level of the coefficients. In demand forecasting the problem is to forecast both the level of the independent variables and the level of the coefficients to those variables. Forecasting the future level of demand is an issue of concern not only to business firms but also to governments, banks, and other institutions. Consequently, there is a considerable amount of forecasting activity at the aggregate, sectoral, and industry levels. Decision makers in firms and institutions have access to the results of much of this forecasting activity and should utilize this material in forming their own forecasts. If the demand for their particular products is closely correlated with GNP or some other measure of aggregate activity, the published forecasts, such as those in the *Monthly Conditions Digest* issued by the U.S. Department of Commerce, will serve as an inexpensive source of data on future demand levels. On the other hand, individual components of the aggregate may move in different directions, and with lags or leads, and the decision maker must modify the forecast for aggregate, sectoral, or industrial activity to suit the specific circumstances of the individual firm.

A full discussion of the methods and techniques of demand forecasting constitutes a course in itself and would take us far beyond the space constraints of this appendix. We shall therefore confine ourselves to a brief discussion of the major methods of demand forecasting and refer the reader who requires more detail to the suggested readings listed at the end of this appendix. In the following section we shall outline the methods of demand forecasting under three broad headings: intention surveys, projection of known relationships, and barometric indicators.

Intention Surveys

Two main intention surveys are conducted periodically: the survey of consumer intentions and the survey of investor intentions. Both are used to judge the level of confidence the consumer or investor feels concerning the desirability of spending for consumption or investment in the future. If consumers are hesitant about continuing their purchases of consumer durables or semidurables in the near or not-too-distant future because of pessimistic expectations about the state of the economy (and indirectly the likelihood of their incomes remaining at high levels), we might forecast an attenuation of the demand for these products in future periods. For many purchases, especially nondurables such as food, the consumers' purchases may be expected to continue at a relatively constant level almost regardless of the level of aggregate economic activity. For durables and semidurables, however, the consumer may postpone such purchases if the immediate outlook is less promising. If consumer expectations take a general turn toward the pessimistic, we would expect demand for such products to fall in the ensuing period.

Investors' intentions are important not only as an indicator of the future level of aggregate economic activity but also for the implications these intentions have for the demand for a variety of products, such as construction materials, office supplies, and plant and equipment. Decision makers interested in the demand for these products must therefore remain aware of such intentions for the implications that these will have on the demand for their own products.

Investors' intentions are similarly highly dependent upon their expectations about the future levels of aggregate activity. Investors will feel more confident about investing if they expect aggregate activity to remain high or to increase from its present level, since this has implications for the degree of idle capacity in future periods. If the investors' expectations are relatively pessimistic, we might expect investment projects to be postponed or cancelled, with subsequent impacts upon the level of aggregate economic activity. The ironic feature about both consumers' and investors' expectations is that these expectations tend to become self-fulfilling prophecies. To counter this phenomenon, governments, banks, and business leaders often express great confidence in the future levels of aggregate economic activity at times when all other indications imply the opposite.

The problems with intention surveys as a forecasting device are similar to those that occur when surveys are used to estimate present levels of the demand parameters, except that some of these problems are increased by our asking the consumers or investors to predict their actions far into the future instead of our simply observing their current actions. A continuing survey of intentions does serve, however, as an ongoing "finger on the pulse" of the people who make the demand decisions. Any change in the expectations of these decision makers, and by association a change in expected future demand levels, should become immediately apparent. Thus, decision makers have an advance warning of likely changes and can plan their production, inventories, and other matters more effectively.

DEMAND THEORY, ANALYSIS, AND ESTIMATION

Projection of Established Relationships

In the second major category of forecasting, relationships that are assumed to be known are projected into the future. This involves the implicit assumption that the relationship that has held in the immediate past will be a reasonably good predictor of the relationship that will hold in the immediate future. Chisholm and Whitaker speak of "naïve" forecasts as including all simple extrapolations of apparent statistical relationships into the future.[1] In such forecasts no modification is made for any new information that has been received, such as the current state of consumer or investor intentions. Such forecasts are based solely on the presumption that the best indicator of the near future is the experience of the recent past.

Trend Line Projection. The trend-line-projection method consists of taking this year's sales level and multiplying it by the trend factor that has become apparent over the past few years, to find the projected level of sales for the next year or the following years. Suppose that from time-series data on sales we have found the correlation equation

$$S_t = \alpha + \beta T_{t-1974} \qquad (5A\text{-}1)$$

where S_t is the sales level; T is the number of time periods since 1974 (the year in which the observations started); t is the present year; and α and β are the parameters of the line of best fit to the time-series data. Suppose that the data used to construct the trend line refer to the ten-year period 1974-1983 and that the trend equation is $S = 4,585.87 + 175.8T$, where the parameters express thousands of units of sales. This indicates that the intercept of the trend line is 4.58587 million units and that sales increased by 175,800 units per year (on average) over that period. If we wish to estimate the sales level for 1984 and subsequent years, we simply insert into this expression values for T of 11, 12, and higher numbers, since this would be the 11th, 12th, and later period from the beginning of the time-series data. We would be very fortunate, however, if the actual sales levels of subsequent years fell right on the trend line, since a multitude of influences may cause actual sales to fall below or above the trend. For longer-term projections, when we can take the good with the bad over a number of periods, trend extrapolation may be a relatively useful method, but it is likely to be a relatively unreliable indicator of the actual year-to-year value of sales.

Constant Growth Rate Projection. The trend extrapolation model discussed above imputes a constant absolute increase to sales in successive

---

[1]R. K. Chisholm and G. R. Whitaker, Jr., *Forecasting Methods* (Homewood, Ill.: Richard D. Irwin, 1971), chap. 2.

periods. A common feature of the real world, however, is that series tend to grow at a constant rate of change rather than at a constant absolute change. Thus, if sales grew an average 5 percent each year over the preceding year for a certain period, we could express the sales function as

$$S_t = S_o \ (1 + k)^t \tag{5A-2}$$

where S_o is the initial year's sales; k is the average rate of growth of sales per annum; and t is the number of periods after the initial period. Thus, sales compound at the rate of k, and we may predict sales in a future period by inserting the appropriate values into the above expression. You will recall that power functions may be transformed to linear form by expressing the relationship in logarithms, and hence the parameters of Equation (5A-2) may be estimated using the least-squares regression technique. Given a series of sales levels for previous years, we may fit both the linear expression and the power function to these data and choose for prediction purposes the form that exhibits the higher coefficient of determination.

Difference Equations. A third method of using time-series data from past years to predict the sales level for future periods is that of difference equations, whereby the sales of the current period are found to be a function of the sales of previous periods in the general form

$$S_t = aS_{t-1} + bS_{t-2} + cS_{t-3} + ... \tag{5A-3}$$

where the subscripts refer to the time period of the sales observations. We should expect the values of the coefficients to decline as we take successively more distant sales observations to explain the current level of sales. One such system involves the use of exponentially declining weights, which in effect implies that by far the largest influence on the present level of sales is exerted by the immediate-past levels, with successively smaller influences exerted by more-distant-past sales observations. Like the above trend extrapolation and constant growth rate models, the difference equation approach also neglects any current influence on sales, and instead gives full weight to the historical pattern that has emerged over previous years. To predict sales in the next period (period $t + 1$), we would insert the weights indicated by the past relationship and express S_{t+1} as a function of S_t, S_{t-1}, and so forth.

Regression Analysis. The regression analysis of the preceding chapter can be used for forecasting purposes by assuming that the estimates of the coefficients will reliably indicate the future relationship between each of the independent variables and the dependent variable. The levels of the independent variables in the future periods must then be forecast in order to find the forecast level of demand in future periods. Forecasting the level of the independent variables may proceed on the basis of trend extrapolation, constant growth rate, or difference equations, as indicated above, especially for such factors as consumer incomes, tastes, and price levels. In all cases the naïve forecast should be modified by any information received which would indicate that the historic pattern of events would provide a poor indication of the most likely future pattern of events.

Econometric Methods. Where a single equation is inadequate to represent the factors that determine sales, we may need to develop a multiple-equation model that incorporates a system of equations to explain the interactions that underlie the demand level at any particular point of time. By plugging in the forecast values for the independent variables and by assuming that the coefficients discovered in earlier testing will be reliable indicators of the future relationship, we are able to solve the system of simultaneous equations for the forecast level of demand in future time periods. Suppose we have found that the level of sales has been estimated fairly accurately by the following system of equations:

$$S_t = a - bP_t + cY_t \qquad (5A\text{-}4)$$

$$P_t = d + e(Y_{t-1} - Y_{t-2}) \qquad (5A\text{-}5)$$

$$Y_t = Y_{t-1}(1+k) \qquad (5A\text{-}6)$$

In this system current sales are a function of current prices and income levels, but current prices and incomes are in turn a function of past income levels. Since income grows at a constant rate k, we are able to project future income levels and future price levels. Hence, given the estimates of the parameters a, b, c, d, e, and k, we are able to project the level of sales in future periods.

Barometric Indicators: Leading Indicators and Diffusion Indices

A *barometer* is a device that predicts changes in one variable (weather) by measuring the change in another variable (air pressure). Since falling air pressure foretells the arrival of relatively inclement weather and rising air pressure indicates that the weather will begin to improve, the barometer is able to predict tomorrow's weather on the basis of today's air pressure. Barometric indicators in forecasting are named for the same ability: Movements in the barometric indicator typically lead movements in the variable that we wish to predict. Thus, by observing the level of the barometric time series and its changes, we are able to predict changes in the variable of interest, based on the previous association between these two time series.

Leading Series Indicators. The first type of barometric indicator consists of a single leading series. In this case we find a particular time series that tends to consistently lead the performance of the demand for our products.

TABLE 5A-1. Steel Production as a Leading Indicator
for Coal Shipments (hypothetical)

Year	Quarter	Steel Production— % Changes (qtr. to qtr.)	Coal Shipments— % Changes (qtr. to qtr.)
1980	1	2.5	1.6
	2	3.1	3.2
	3	1.8	2.4
	4	−0.2	1.8
1981	1	−1.4	1.2
	2	−1.8	−0.4
	3	0.6	−3.8
	4	2.4	−4.1
1982	1	3.0	1.6
	2	−1.2	3.2
	3	−2.1	3.6
	4	0.8	−2.5

By "lead the performance" we mean that the barometric indicator will experience turning points (the changes in direction from growth to contraction or from contraction to growth) in advance of the turning points of demand for our products. In addition, a pattern may emerge between the rate of growth or decline of the barometric series and the rate of change of the demand. Examination of time-series data for various industries and sectors should unearth a time series that tends to act as a leading indicator for the sales of our products. We may find, for example, that the shipments of coal and the production of steel vary as indicated in Table 5A-1.

In Table 5A-1 it can be seen that reductions in steel production (the negative percentage changes) tend to precede the reductions in coal shipments by two quarters, just as the increases in steel production tend to precede the increases in coal shipments by two quarters. We can rationalize this as the time period it takes for the steel producers to become aware of the reduction in demand for their product and to organize a reduction in their orders for coal. Producers of coal thus have a six-month warning for turning points in the demand for their product, which should aid their production and inventory planning considerably. In this case, then, steel production acts as a barometric indicator of changes in the level of demand for coal.

Single-series leading indicators are unlikely to *consistently* lead the series they are intended to, and moreover they are unlikely to lead by a consistent *lead period*. A multitude of other factors influence the demand for steel in the above example or the barometric indicator in the general case. It is difficult in practice to find a leading indicator that leads even 90 percent of the time, since random factors intervene to cause the barometric indicator to sometimes indicate continued growth when in fact the dependent time series is already falling, or vice versa.

DEMAND THEORY, ANALYSIS, AND ESTIMATION

TABLE 5A-2. Selected Leading, Coincident, and Lagging Indicators

Leading Indicators

1. Average workweek, production workers, manufacturing
2. Nonagricultural placements, BES
3. Index of net business formation
4. New orders, durable goods industries
5. Contracts and orders, plant and equipment
6. New-building permits, private-housing units
7. Change in book value, manufacturing and trade inventories
8. Industrial materials prices
9. Stock prices, 500 common stocks
10. Corporate profits after taxes
11. Ratio, price to unit labor cost, manufacturing
12. Change in consumer debt

Roughly Coincident Indicators

1. Employees in nonagricultural establishments
2. Unemployment rate, total (inverted)
3. GNP in constant dollars, expenditure estimate
4. Industrial production
5. Personal income
6. Manufacturing and trade sales
7. Sales of retail stores

Lagging Indicators

1. Unemployment rate (unemployment > 15 weeks, inverted)
2. Business expenditure, new plant and equipment
3. Book value, manufacturing and trade inventories
4. Labor cost per unit of output, manufacturing
5. Commercial and industrial loans outstanding
6. Bank rates on short-term business loans

From Table 2 in J. Shiskin and L. H. Lempert, "Indicator Forecasting," in W. F. Butler et al., *Methods and Techniques of Business Forecasting* (Englewood Cliffs, N.J.: Prentice-Hall, Inc., 1974), pp. 48-9.

Composite Leading Indices. To avoid the problem of the unreliability of a single indicator, composite barometric indices have been established. Several leading indicators are aggregated to form an index, with the result that the random movements in any one series tend to be offset by opposite movements in one or more of the other series. The result is that the composite index provides a more reliable indication of actual turning points in the series we are attempting to predict. Table 5A-2 shows the major leading, coincident, and lagging indicators, as identified by the National Bureau of Economic Research and by other sources. The value of the latter two categories for forecasting is their ability to indicate when the peak or trough has in fact passed. Since the coincident indicators are expected to turn at about the same time as GNP or aggregate economic activity and since lagging indicators are expected to turn after the GNP has turned, we may be confi-

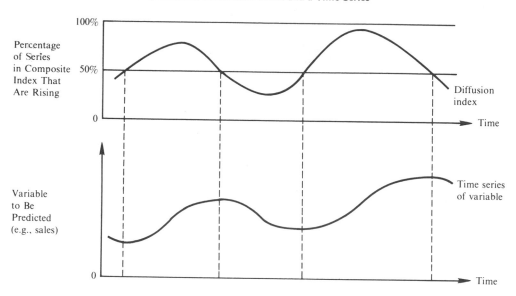

dent when we observe these series turning that GNP has in fact turned as indicated by the leading indicators, without having to wait for actual measurement of GNP to confirm that there has been a turning point.

The Diffusion Index.   A third category of barometric indicators involves the diffusion index, which· shows the proportion of the total number of series in a chosen collection that are rising at any point of time. For prediction of GNP, for example, when the diffusion index exceeds 50 percent we expect that GNP will be rising, and when it is less than 50 percent we expect that GNP will be falling. We can construct a diffusion index to predict the sales of any product by using past data to choose the series to be included in the index so that it will best predict turning points of the sales for that product. In Figure 5-4 we show the relationship between the diffusion index and the variable that we are hoping to predict by the use of the diffusion index. In the ideal situation where the series in the diffusion index are weighted by the exactly appropriate amounts, as the diffusion index rises to 50 percent and above the variable to be predicted reaches its lower turning point and continues to rise. When the diffusion index reaches a maximum the variable to be predicted should exhibit an inflection point, and as the diffusion index drops below 50 percent the variable to be predicted will attain a maximum and thereafter fall. There are likely to be random shocks to the diffusion index such that it will not appear smooth, as in Figure 5A-1. To better judge the direction of change of the diffusion index we may need to use a moving average of the past few weeks or months.

The major limitation of barometric indicators generally is that they predict turning points only and not the magnitudes of the change, so that we must use some other method to find the likely magnitude of the change in the variable to be predicted. Thus barometric indicators, like surveys, are more suited to short-run forecasting, since they require little lead time and indicate turning points rather than the general longer-term direction of sales. Projection techniques, on the other hand, require substantial preparation time in some cases, and in all cases they generate the general trend of the data and may incorrectly predict the immediate direction and magnitude of the change in the variable.

Summary

Demand forecasting is concerned with the future values of the parameters and independent variables of the demand function, and it is clearly vital for decision problems where expected sales in future periods must be estimated.

Forecasts of the future demand situation may be constructed with the aid of intention surveys, projections, and barometric indicators. Several of the techniques outlined would allow the researcher to estimate the future level of sales and the probable turning points of sales for the product(s) in question. Considerable forecasting activity is undertaken by governmental and other agencies, and the information generated should be used as input to the individual firm's or organization's forecasting deliberations. In many cases these public sources may serve as an adequate guide to future demand conditions, but in others it will be necessary to construct surveys, projection models, and barometric indicators for the specific situation to be predicted.

DISCUSSION QUESTIONS

5A-1. Outline the methods by which you would obtain a forecast of demand for a particular product group (such as automobiles).

5A-2. What problems exist with the use of surveys of consumer and investor intentions as a basis for forecasting demand?

5A-3. Discuss the different methods of obtaining a trend projection from past observations to make future estimates of quantity demanded.

5A-4. What do you think would be the main problems associated with using a regression equation for the demand function as a basis for projections about future quantity demanded.

5A-5. Outline the major types of barometric indicators and the uses of these to predict changes and turning points in the level of economic activity and/or the demand for a particular product or service.

PROBLEMS AND SHORT CASES

5A-1. The Johnston Raymond Corporation has established a "composite index of demand" which has been relatively accurate in predicting the annual quantity demanded of its cement products. A number of variables are included in the index, such as GNP in current dollars, the Index of Industrial Production, Personal Disposable Income, Manufacturing and Trade Sales, and Industrial Materials Prices. Also included is the average price of JRC's cement products and the prices of substitute products. By trial and error, JRC has adjusted the weights to each of these variables such that composite index has performed very well in predicting sales in the recent past. Historical data for the past twelve years are shown in the following table:

Johnston Raymond Corporation:
Historical Data

Year	Sales (units) (Y)	Demand Index (X)
1971	1,950	500
1972	2,570	658
1973	3,140	801
1974	3,280	843
1975	3,360	853
1976	3,570	917
1977	3,750	953
1978	3,980	995
1979	5,800	1,485
1980	6,170	1,567
1981	6,650	1,729
1982	7,130	1,854

(a) Calculate the regression equation showing the relationship between the quantity demanded and the value of the composite index.

(b) How reliable is the composite index as an explanatory variable?

(c) Form a projection of the value of the composite index over the next five years.

(d) Use this projection in the regression equation to forecast the quantity demanded in each of the next five years.

5A-2. A large cosmetics company markets its products directly to customers in eighteen separate campaigns annually. Sales brochures are prepared and printed for each campaign and are sold to the sales representatives, who are paid by commission only. In order to allow time for printing and distribution and to give the sales representatives sufficient time to utilize the brochures while making their normal rounds to clientele, it is necessary to forecast sales of the brochures three campaigns in advance. The quantity of brochures sold to representatives in a particular territory for each campaign during 1980, 1981, and the first six campaigns of 1982 are shown in the accompanying table, along with the scheduled print runs for campaigns 7, 8, and 9.

(a) Have you any comments on the levels of the printing runs for the seventh, eighth, and ninth campaigns?

(b) Forecast the sales of brochures for the tenth, eleventh, and twelfth campaigns of 1982, using trend projection.

Actual Brochure Sales

Campaign	1980 (000)	1981 (000)	1982 (000)
1	1,013	865	997
2	923	811	965
3	779	712	877
4	897	712	877
5	819	774	965
6	874	831	1,051
7	879	845	1,091*
8	885	878	1,122*
9	906	840	1,100*
10	869	824	
11	844	800	
12	823	803	
13	834	786	
14	789	847	
15	833	878	
16	986	1,011	
17	1,027	1,090	
18	1,024	1,141	

*Scheduled production based on sales forecasts.

SUGGESTED REFERENCES AND FURTHER READING

Butler, W.F., R.A. Kavesh, and R.B. Platt. *Methods and Techniques of Business Forecasting*, esp. pts. 1, 2, and 4. Englewood Cliffs, N.J.: Prentice-Hall, Inc., 1974.

Chisholm, R.K., and G.R. Whitaker, Jr. *Forecasting Methods.* Homewood, Ill.: Richard D. Irwin, Inc., 1971.

Granger, C.W.J. *Forecasting in Business and Economics*, New York, N.Y.: Academic Press, 1980.

Hanke, J.E. and A.G. Reitsch. *Business Forecasting.* Boston, Mass.: Allyn and Bacon, 1981.

Nelson, C.R. *Applied Time Series Analysis for Managerial Forecasting.* Holden Day, 1973.

U.S. Department of Commerce. *Survey of Current Business* and *Business Conditions Digest.* Springfield, Va.: National Technical Information Service, current issue.

PRODUCTION and COST ANALYSIS

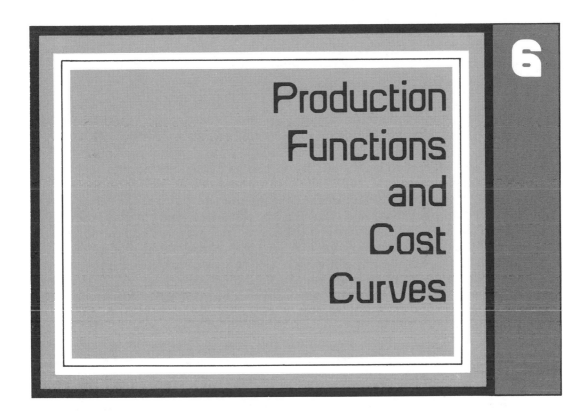

6.1 INTRODUCTION

DEFINITION: *Production* can be defined in broad economic terms as the transformation of resources into products, or the process whereby inputs are turned into outputs. In this chapter we introduce several new terms and concepts in order to better understand the relationships involved in the production process. We are concerned with the economic efficiency of production—that is, we wish to minimize the cost of producing any particular output level during a given period of time.

The efficiency of the production process depends upon the proportions in which the various inputs are employed, the absolute level of each input, and the productivity of each input at each input level and ratio. Since inputs are generally not free but have a cost attached, the degree of efficiency in production translates into a level of costs per unit of output. Production and costs are thus intimately related. In this chapter the theory of production and costs is presented in a way that both underscores this interrelationship and demonstrates the impact of changing efficiency in production upon the shape and placement of the cost curves. We examine the theory of production and costs in order to lay a sufficient conceptual foundation for the discussion of practical cost concepts and techniques of cost estimation in the two subsequent chapters.[1]

Short-Run vs. Long-Run Distinction

DEFINITION: In production and cost theory the distinction is made between the *short run*, in which the quantities of some inputs are variable while others are in fixed supply, and the *long run*, in which all factors may be varied. Consequently, it is useful to classify the inputs on the basis of whether or not they are variable in the short run. Since labor has traditionally been variable and capital is typically fixed in the short run, these headings are commonly used to denote, respectively, *all* variable and *all* fixed resources.[2] When using the terms *labor* and *capital* in this sense we should think of one unit of labor as including, say, one hour of a worker's time plus a "package" of all the necessary raw materials, fuel, and other variable inputs, and we should think of capital as including all the plant, equipment, land, buildings, managers' salaries, and other expenses that do not vary with the level of output.

NOTE: It is important to understand that "the long run" does not refer to a long period of time. It is a peculiarity of the economists' jargon that the term has no direct connection with time at all, and that the firm is likely to be in a long-run situation for relatively short periods of time. When intending to change its scale of production, the firm must continue to operate in a short-run situation until its most-fixed factor becomes variable. At this point of time the firm is in a long-run situation, since it can vary the input levels of all factors. As soon as the firm is committed to new levels of plant, buildings, and other fixed facilities, it is back in a short-run situation, since the input of these factors cannot be varied from their chosen level. Notice that the short run could be a few days for some very simple types of firms (such as a street vendor selling flowers from a wheelbarrow) or as much as five years for large manufacturing concerns (such as steel mills or automobile

---

[1] In this chapter we confine our attention to a production process that has a single output. This allows us to demonstrate all the concepts in a relatively simple manner. The technique of linear-programming analysis deals with the problem of choosing the optimal product mix in the multiple-output situation. This topic is typically covered in Operations Research or Quantitative Methods courses. See Baumol, W. J., *Economic Theory and Operations Analysis*, 4th ed., chaps. 5 and 6. Englewood Cliffs, N.J.: Prentice-Hall, Inc., 1977.

[2] Note that with the increasing membership of labor unions, labor is becoming more and more fixed in many production processes. In cases where reductions in the labor supply may be made only through attrition, labor tends to be varied by using overtime work for existing employees rather than hiring and firing of extra workers as volume fluctuates. Whenever labor is hired by contract over a period of time, this labor must be classified as a fixed expense in the sense that it is independent of output levels for the duration of the contract.

producers). Thus the phrase "in the long run" should be taken to mean "at the end of the short run" or "when factors that are currently in fixed supply can be increased or decreased." Since the long run may be either a short or a long time coming, we will use the alternate phrase "the long term" to refer to an extended period of time and reserve "the long run" for its specific connotation in the jargon of economics.

Our simple pedagogical model abstracts from some of the complexities of the real world. In most real production processes there is a *gestation period*, or a time lag, between the conception of the idea to change plant size and the birth of the new plant. This time lag means that the firm must make its long-run decision (choice between available plant sizes) during a short-run period and continue in that short-run situation until the new plant is fabricated and installed, at which time it shifts into the new short-run situation. Also, in the real world, firms with multiple outputs tend to be continually changing plant size for one of their multiple production processes.

EXAMPLE: Consider the production process for the assembly of an automobile. Which inputs are fixed and which are variable? Remember that the criterion is whether or not the inputs vary in order to cause changes in the output level. Certainly the land and building are fixed inputs and are not varied from day to day in order to cause changes in the output level. So too are the assembly lines, the computerized plant and equipment, and the various tools and machines used to assemble the cars. What about the assembly workers themselves? To the extent that management can increase or decrease the input of labor as production needs dictate, assembly labor is a variable input. But if these workers are strongly unionized and threaten to strike if some are laid off, management cannot reduce their input at short notice, and labor, in this case, is fixed, at least in the downward direction. Increases in labor input can usually be effected by paying overtime rates to workers who continue into the next shift or by hiring new workers on a strictly temporary basis. Other inputs, such as component parts, fuel, and power, are certainly fully variable inputs to the production process.

6.2 PRODUCTION IN THE SHORT RUN

The Production Function

DEFINITION: The *production function* is a technical specification of the relationship that exists between the inputs and the outputs in the production process. In general form it says simply that output is dependent upon the inputs in an unspecified way. That is, quantity produced is a function of the inputs of capital and labor, as follows:

$$Q = f(K,L) \tag{6-1}$$

where Q is the quantity of output; f represents the functional relationship existing between the inputs and the output; and K and L are the conventional symbols representing the input levels of capital and labor, respectively.

In specific form the functional relationship is stated explicitly, and the functional form of the equation is the one that best expresses the actual relationship between the inputs and the output. Output may be expressed, for example, as a linear additive function of the inputs or alternatively as a multiplicative power function of the inputs. The exact mathematical specification of the production function depends upon the productivity of the input factors at various levels of all inputs.

The State of Technology. The productivity of the factors of production depends on the state of technology. Labor can be more productive if it works with modern mechanical and computer-assisted equipment. Similarly, the plant or equipment can be more productive if it is being operated by highly skilled and well-trained workers. Thus the *state of technology* refers to the inherent ability of factors of production to produce output, given the simultaneous efforts of all other inputs to the production process. For example, three units of labor and two units of capital may combine to produce fourteen units of output. If technology improves, that is, if either or both labor and capital become more productive, the same combination of labor and capital may then be able to produce, say, eighteen units of output. Thus, the state of technology is incorporated into the specification of the production function and is reflected by the precise mathematical form taken by any particular production function.[3]

Given the specific form of the production function, we can insert values for labor and capital and find for every combination of labor and capital the output that would result. A tabular array of the output levels associated with various input levels of all factors for the hypothetical case of automobile assembly by a small company that produces sports cars is shown in Table 6-1. The output levels in the body of the table represent the number of vehicles assembled. The table reflects the substitutability of labor and capital: note that particular output levels can be produced using different combinations of capital and labor. For example, 23 vehicles can be assembled using either 4,000 machine-hours and 200 person-hours or 2,000 machine-hours and 500 person-hours. By interpolation between the figures in the table, we could find several combinations of labor and capital that would culminate in the assembly of 23 vehicles.

---

[3]A linear production function can be expressed as $Q = \alpha + \beta_1 K + \beta_2 L$, where the α and β parameters are estimated from observed input and output data using regression analysis. A power function such as $Q = AK^\alpha L^\beta$ enables us to compute the multiplicative effect of capital and labor, if it exists. Regression analysis using logarithmic transformation of the observed data can be used to estimate the parameters A, α, and β. This power function is often referred to as the Cobb-Douglas production function, named after the writers who developed this concept. See C. W. Cobb and P. H. Douglas, "A Theory of Production," *American Economic Review*, 16 (1928), pp. 139-65. Also Paul H. Douglas, "Are There Laws of Production?" *American Economic Review*, 38 (March 1948), pp. 1-41.

TABLE 6-1. **Motor Vehicle Assembly Production Function**

		LABOR UNITS (hundreds of person-hours)							
		1	*2*	*3*	*4*	*5*	*6*	*7*	*8*
Capital	1	1	3	7	10	12	13	13½	13
Units	2	3	8	14	19	23	26	28	29
(machine-	3	8	18	29	41	52	62	71	79
hours, 000)	4	11	23	36	50	65	78	90	101
	5	12	26	42	60	80	98	112	124

NOTE: Table 6-1 depicts both the short run and the long run. In the short run the level of capital input would be fixed at a particular level, and output is constrained to that shown in the *row* opposite that level of capital and can only be varied by adding or subtracting labor units. In the long run, that is, when all input quantities are variable, any point in the table may be achieved. Thus if only 3,000 machine-hours were available, output levels would vary as shown along the third row of Table 6-1 as we added or subtracted labor. Given the opportunity to change its plant size, the firm could move to any other row of the table to which it would be constrained for the duration of the following short-run period.

The actual values of output shown in the table reflect a number of important concepts in the theory of production which are more easily explained in terms of the "production surface."

The Output Hill and the Production Surface

Let us regard the values in the table as indicating the elevation of a surface above the base of the grid formed by the labor and capital axes. (As an analogy, think of a hill that has been surveyed for elevation above sea level.) The inputs of labor and capital can be regarded as giving rise to a hill of output, the upper surface of which represents the maximum output that can be attained from the particular combination of labor and capital. A three-dimensional output hill and its production surface is shown in Figure 6-1.

If the production surface is to be smooth, this implies that the input quantities of labor and capital are divisible into infinitesimal pieces. That is, the smooth transition between the figures in the table depends upon fractional units of labor and capital being added or subtracted. This assumption of infinite divisibility of inputs does not contradict a situation in which machines are only available in one size, however. Although it would be impossible to employ one-tenth of a machine, it is possible to employ one machine for one-tenth of the production period, by renting it, for example. Similarly, one could use overtime labor or employ part-time personnel in order to make up fractional labor units.

We can use the production surface to demonstrate a number of impor-

FIGURE 6-1.   The Output Hill and the Production Surface

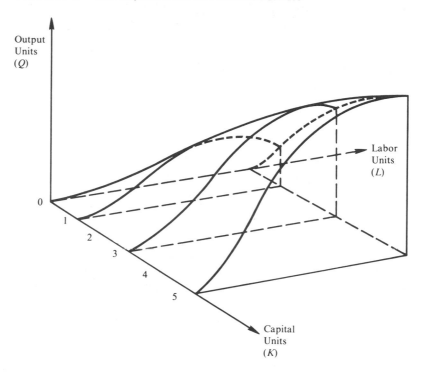

tant concepts in the theory of production. We do this by slicing the output hill through different planes and observing the shapes of the resultant line cut into the production surface.

The Law of Diminishing Returns

DEFINITION: The *law of diminishing returns* states that as additional units of the variable factor are added to the fixed factor base, after some point the increment to total product will decline progressively.

The *law of diminishing returns* is concerned with the relative productivity of the marginal units of the variable factor as we progressively add units of the variable factors to the fixed inputs. Prior to the point where diminishing returns set in, there may be *increasing* returns to the variable factors followed by *constant* returns to the variable factors. The law of diminishing returns can be stated more broadly as the "law of variable proportions," which states that as more and more of the variable factors are added to a given quantity of all other factors, the increment to output attributable to each of the additional units of the variable factor will increase at first, will later decrease, and will eventually become negative.

Notice that this phenomenon relates to the short run, since fixed inputs are involved, and can be witnessed in any row of Table 6-1, where the differ-

TABLE 6-2. The Law of Variable Proportions Exhibited by the Marginal Product of the Variable Factors

Units of the Variable Factor	Units of Output (for K = 3)	Increment to Output over Preceding Row	Returns to the Variable Factor (for K = 3)
0	0	—	—
1	8	8	Increasing
2	18	10	Increasing
3	29	11	Increasing
4	41	12	Increasing
5	52	11	Diminishing
6	62	10	Diminishing
7	71	9	Diminishing
8	79	8	Diminishing

ences between the adjacent numbers increase at first and later decrease as more labor is added to a particular level of capital. In Table 6-2 we show the increments to output as we move along the third row of the production function exhibited in Table 6-1. Notice that increasing returns prevail up to and including the fourth unit of labor when applied to three units of capital, after which point diminishing returns to the variable factor prevail.

Total Product and Marginal Product Curves

In terms of the output hill and its surface the law of variable proportions can be demonstrated by a vertical slice along a baseline representing a constant input of capital. Three such slices are shown in Figure 6-1 for capital inputs of one, three, and five units. The top line of each slice relates total output to the input of labor units, with the capital input constant, and is usually referred to as the "total product" curve. The law of variable proportions is evident from the shape of these total product curves. Each curve is convex from below at first, showing output increasing at an increasing rate as labor units are added. After the point of inflection the curve is concave from below, reflecting diminishing returns to the variable factor. Note that we are talking about the rate of change of total product as the variable factor input is changed. This change in total product, as the result of a one-unit change in input of the variable input, or the rate of change of total product in relation to that of labor, is defined as the "marginal product of labor." In Figure 6-2 we show one of the total product curves in two dimensions (since K is constant), along with the marginal product curve which can be derived from the total product curve.

DEFINITION: *Marginal product* is defined as the rate of change of total product as labor is increased, and it is equal in mathematical terms to the first derivative of the total product function with respect to labor. This is the same as saying that marginal product is given by the *slope* of the total product curve at

FIGURE 6-2.   The Total Product and Marginal Product Curves

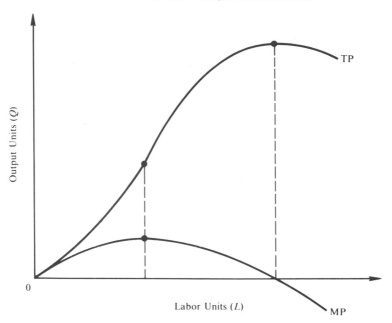

every level of labor input. Note that at the point of inflection, where the total product curve changes from being concave upward to concave downward, the total product curve is at its steepest, and marginal product attains its maximum value. Similarly, at the input level where total product reaches its maximum and later falls, marginal product falls to zero and becomes negative. The law of variable proportions can thus be expressed in terms of the behavior of the marginal product of the variable factor: there are increasing returns to the marginal unit of the variable factor while marginal product is rising, and there are decreasing returns thereafter as the marginal product falls.

The law of variable proportions is an "empirical" law, which is to say it has frequently been observed in actual production situations. This empirical law is not a judicial law, however, and hence there is no compulsion for every production function to exhibit the pattern described above. The range of increasing returns to the variable factors may be quite brief or indeed absent in many production processes. The point of inflection may be extended to exhibit a prolonged range of constant returns to the variable factor. Decreasing returns to the variable factor are a necessary feature of all short-run production situations, however. Sooner or later, as units of the variable factor are added to the fixed supply of capital resources, the marginal product of the variable factor must begin to decrease, because of simple overcrowding if for no other reason. Hence, this law is more commonly referred to as the law of diminishing returns. But note that the law of diminishing returns refers only to the section of the total product curve that is

PRODUCTION AND COST ANALYSIS

concave from below, or to the negatively sloped portion of the marginal product curve.

6.3 CHOICE OF PLANT SIZE IN THE LONG RUN

We noted earlier that the firm can change its plant size when it is in a long-run situation. In effect, it can shift from one row to another in Table 6-1. It will wish to adjust its plant size (that is, the input of capital) if its existing plant size is too small or too large in view of its current (and projected) demand situation, and if it appears *worthwhile* to do so. In a context of certainty, or full information, the firm will change to a new plant size in the long run if the new plant size (whether larger or smaller) promises a lower per unit cost of product at the firm's desired output level. Under conditions of uncertainty, the firm will find it worthwhile to change plant size if the firm's expected present value of profits from the new plant exceeds the expected present value of profits from the existing plant.

We can use "isoquant analysis" to demonstrate the circumstances under which a firm would choose to change its plant size.

Isoquant-Isocost Analysis

DEFINITION: An *isoquant* is a line joining combinations of inputs which generate the same level of output. The word *isoquant* comes from the Greek word *iso* meaning equal and the Latin word *quantus* meaning quantity. Note that we can find isoquant curves from the output hill by slicing the hill horizontally at any particular output level. Any horizontal slice in the output hill will result in a curved line being cut into the production surface. This line is an isoquant, since it shows the various combinations of labor and capital that can be used to produce a particular output level. Since the output level is constant for each isoquant curve, we can depict them in two dimensions as in Figure 6-3. Note that isoquant lines are, in effect, contour lines on the production surface, since all points on a particular line show equal elevation above the base of the output hill.[4]

Technical and Economic Efficiency.   A combination of capital and labor is *technically efficient* if none of either factor can be subtracted without reducing the output level, given *ceteris paribus*. All combinations on negatively sloped sections of the isoquant curves are technically efficient, since if one factor input is reduced while the other factor input is held constant, output will decline and the new input combination will lie on a lower

---

[4] To stay in accord with the traditional treatment of isoquant curves we put capital on the vertical axis and labor on the horizontal axis.

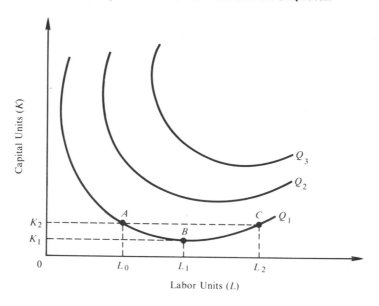

FIGURE 6-3. Isoquant Curves: Contour Lines on the Output Hill

isoquant curve. On the other hand, all combinations on positively sloped sections of isoquant curves are *technically inefficient*, since some of both factors may be subtracted without output's being reduced. In terms of Figure 6-3 output level Q_1 can be produced by different combinations of capital and labor at points A, B, and C. Combination C is technically inefficient, however, since the same output level could be produced at combination A by subtracting $L_2 - L_0$ units of labor or at combination B by subtracting both $L_2 - L_1$ units of labor and $K_2 - K_1$ units of capital. By the same process of reasoning, *all* points on positively sloped sections of the isoquants are technically inefficient combinations of the inputs.

The slope of an isoquant at any point is the ratio of the amount of capital that can be subtracted from the production process to the amount of labor that is added to the production process, such that output level remains constant. For a one-unit increment in the labor input, this ratio is known as the *marginal rate of technical substitution* of capital for labor.

DEFINITION: *The marginal rate of technical substitution*, (MRTS), is the rate at which labor can be substituted for capital in the production process, *such that output remains unchanged*. Note that it is equal to the amount of capital that can be subtracted from the production process for a one-unit increase in labor added to the production process. Thus,

$$\text{MRTS} = \frac{\Delta K}{\Delta L} \qquad (6\text{-}2)$$

where ΔK is the decrement to capital that will just allow output to remain unchanged given a one-unit increment, ΔL, to the labor input. Thus, the marginal rate of technical substitution reflects the slope of an isoquant curve, and the MRTS will be negative for all technically efficient combinations of the factors and positive for all technically inefficient combinations.

The combinations of capital and labor on the negatively sloped sections of the isoquants represent the range of possibilities open to the rational firm. The actual combination of capital and labor chosen to produce each output level (in the long-run situation where the firm is free to vary all inputs) will depend on the relative prices of the inputs. Only one of the technically efficient ways of producing each output level will be *economically* efficient; that is, only one will allow the lowest cost of producing that output level. To show this we need to introduce isocost lines, which are analogous to the budget lines of consumer behavior theory and which show combinations of capital and labor that cost the same amount.

DEFINITION: An *isocost* line is a locus of combinations of inputs that require the same total expenditure.

Let us express the firm's expenditure on inputs as

$$E = K \cdot P_K + L \cdot P_L \qquad\qquad (6\text{-}3)$$

where E is the total dollar expenditure; P_K and P_L are the unit prices of capital and labor, respectively; and K and L are the number of physical units of capital and labor that are to be employed in the production process. This can be rearranged to appear as

$$K = \frac{E}{P_K} - \frac{P_L}{P_K} \cdot L \qquad\qquad (6\text{-}4)$$

in which form it is perhaps more recognizable as a linear equation explaining K in terms of L and three known values. It can therefore be plotted in the same space as the isoquant curves. The intercept of the isocost line on the capital axis occurs when the labor input is zero, and this intercept is simply the total expenditure divided by the price of the capital units, resulting in a certain physical quantity of capital units. As we purchase units of labor it is evident that our purchase of capital units, for the same expenditure (isocost) level, is drawn down in the ratio of the price of labor to the price of capital.

For each output level there will be a minimum-cost combination of the factors necessary to produce that output level. In Figure 6-4 we show three isoquant curves representing 20, 40, and 60 units of output. The cost of producing 20 units is minimized at point A, since any other capital/labor combination producing 20 units, such as at A', will lie to the right of the isocost line MN and would thus require a larger total expenditure to purchase. Recall that the intercept on the capital axis is equal to E/P_K, where P_K is presumed to remain unchanged. Hence, larger total expenditures are represented by higher intercept points and higher isocost lines. Similarly,

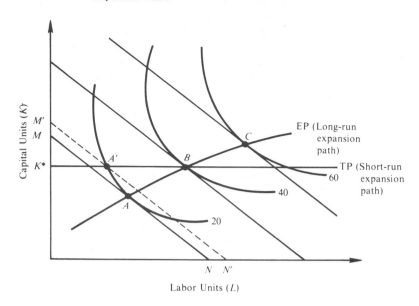

FIGURE 6-4. Isoquant-Isocost Analysis showing Short-Run and Long-Run Expansion Paths

the output level of 40 units is produced at the least cost by the input combination represented by point *B*, and 60 units are produced at the least cost by the input combination at point *C*.

The Expansion Path: Long Run and Short Run

DEFINITION: A locus of the tangency points between various isoquants and various isocosts is called the *expansion path*, since it shows the least-cost combinations of labor and capital a firm would choose as it expanded its output level, if it were free to vary both labor and capital and if it were given constant factor prices and a constant state of technology. This expansion path is shown as the line EP in Figure 6-4. Note that this must be the *long-run* expansion path, since all factors must be variable to allow the adjustment in both capital and labor involved in the movement along the line EP.

Suppose the firm wishes to produce 40 units of output and thus selects the combination of factors represented by point *B* on the long-run expansion path. The firm's capital input will now be fixed at *K** units, and the firm is in a short-run situation. If the firm wishes to vary its output level in the short run, it must simply add or subtract labor to or from the fixed capital input *K**. The *short-run expansion path* is therefore a horizontal line at the capital input level *K**, and we have shown it as the line TP in Figure 6-4. This short-run expansion path is in fact the total product curve viewed from above the output hill.

Notice that for every output level except the one where TP crosses EP, it costs more to produce the output in the short run than it does in the

PRODUCTION AND COST ANALYSIS

long run. Any isocost line that *intersects* an isoquant curve on the TP line must lie farther to the right when compared with the isocost line that is *tangent* to each isoquant curve. This is demonstrated in Figure 6-4 for the output level of 20 units. In the long-run situation the optimal input combination is at point A, and the lowest attainable isocost line is shown as MN. In the short-run situation with capital input of K^*, 20 units must be produced by the input combination represented by point A', since the firm is constrained to the "short-run expansion path," TP. The minimum cost of producing 20 units with combination A', is shown by the isocost line M'N', which lies to the right of the line MN. The short-run situation costs more than the long-run situation for all except one output level, because the firm is unable in the short run to change the input of capital and is thus forced to have an inappropriate factor combination for all except one output level. In the case shown, only at the output of 40 units does the level of capital (K^*) allow the tangency situation of economic efficiency to be attained.

Factor Substitution Due to Changed Factor Prices

Economic efficiency depends upon the relative factor prices. If the price of one factor changes, with *ceteris paribus*, the profit-maximizing firm will attempt to substitute away from the factor that has become relatively more expensive and in favor of the factor that has become relatively less expen-

FIGURE 6-5. Factor Substitution due to Changed Relative Factor Prices

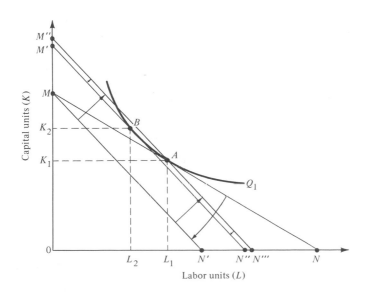

sive. Suppose the initial situation in Figure 6-5 is at point A. Output level Q_1 is being produced economically efficiently by the factor combination K_1 units of capital and L_1 units of labor, and factor prices are such that the lowest-attainable isocost line is MN.

Suppose now that labor prices rise, for example, because of a new agreement with a labor union or because of legislation requiring the firm's contribution to an employee health scheme or to similar benefits. Imagine that the increase in the cost of labor is such that the isocost line swings down from MN to MN'. If the firm wishes to maintain its output level at Q_1, in order to hold its market share, for example, it will need to spend more money on the inputs in order to produce Q_1.

In the short run, the firm is constrained to the plant size indicated by K_1 and must produce Q_1 units of output at point A. This necessitates the total expenditure indicated by the isocost line $M''N'''$. Given a long-run situation, the firm can adjust both capital and labor inputs and will increase its plant size to K_2 units of capital and reduce labor input to L_2 units in order to produce Q_1 units of output with economic efficiency at point B, given the new factor-price ratio. Thus the firm substitutes away from labor and in favor of capital when the price of labor increases relative to that of capital, given time to adjust the input of all factors. History has given us the opportunity to observe this phenomenon, of course: as the price of labor has increased relative to that of capital, we have observed that production processes have become relatively more capital-intensive with the introduction of labor-saving equipment such as mobile assembly lines by Henry Ford and the more recent use of computerized production technology.

EXAMPLE: In 1981 there were over 5,000 robots working in American industry. These computer-controlled machines, which in some cases have visual and tactile skills, have replaced human labor for two main reasons. First, they are cheaper. General Motors reports that where robots are used in automobile assembly, they cost only about $6 an hour, compared with the average $20 an hour paid to assembly labor. Second, robots are more productive than the humans they replace. Hour after hour they methodically and precisely repeat their tasks, never stopping for coffee breaks, chats, washroom visits, and the like. As for sick leave and reporting to work with a hangover, these mechanical marvels do not know such opportunities exist. Should they break down, they are quickly repaired, since they can indicate which part needs replacing. General Electric (GE) found that robots were 10 percent to 35 percent more productive than humans in coating dish racks with polyvinyl. Although their initial cost averages $50,000 each, GE found that their first robot paid for itself in ten months as a result of its greater productivity. Estimates are that there will be 120,000 robots at work by 1990, replacing as many as 1 million workers. This represents a rational business response to the changing relative costs (and productivities) of labor and capital.[5]

---

[5] See Joann S. Lublin, "Steel-Collar Jobs: As Robot Age Arrives, Labor Seeks Protection Against Loss of Work," *Wall Street Journal*, October 26, 1981, pp. 1, 17.

PRODUCTION AND COST ANALYSIS

Different Factor Price Ratios in Different Economies

If the relative costs of capital and labor differ between different countries or even between regions within the same country, we should expect to see differing capital-labor ratios being utilized in these different situations.

EXAMPLE: The cotton textile and apparel industry is remarkable in that it is found around the world with significantly differing degrees of capital and labor intensiveness. In North America, for example, this industry is relatively *capital-intensive*, using computer-controlled equipment and relatively few people per unit of output. In many less developed countries, on the other hand, production processes are relatively *labor-intensive*, with dozens of people using much more rudimentary equipment in order to produce a given output level. Does this mean that the industry is inefficient in these less developed countries? Quite the contrary, as we shall see.

In terms of isoquant-isocost analysis, firms in both situations are trying to attain tangency between their isocost line and the appropriate isoquant line. Suppose a firm in each group wishes to produce a particular output level, shown as Q^* in Figure 6-6. In the less-developed economy, labor is relatively cheap, whereas capital is relatively expensive, giving rise to an isocost line like M_2N_2. The economically efficient input combination for the firm in this situation is thus K_2, L_2, where the isocost curve is tangent to the isoquant at point B. In the more highly developed country, labor is relatively expensive, and capital is relatively cheap, giving rise to an isocost line like M_1N_1, which is tangent to the isoquant line at point A, indicating that K_1 and L_1 constitute the economically efficient input combination for the firm in the more developed economy.

FIGURE 6-6. Different Economically Efficient Combinations in Different Economic Situations

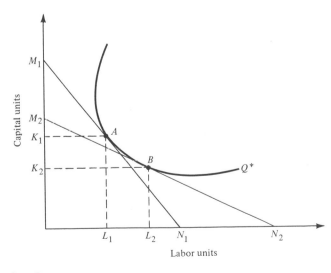

Thus both situations are probably both technically and economically efficient given the factor productivities and factor prices facing the firm in each situation. The crunch comes for the North Americans when their economically-efficient input combination for any given output level costs *more* than the economically-efficient input combination in less-developed economies. Hence the North American textile industry finds itself subject to the competition of imported textiles that are sold at a lower price in their market.

A similar example is found in the automobile industry. In 1981 automobile assembly workers in Japan were paid only about $12 per hour in wages and benefits, compared with the above-mentioned $20 per hour in the United States.[6] The cost of capital in these countries (and for large automobile companies) is more nearly equal, however, given the greater international mobility of capital and the international capital markets. Thus, we should expect the Japanese automobile industry to be somewhat more labor-intensive than the United States automobile industry. But, given their labor cost and other cost advantages, said to amount to $1,500 per car, the Japanese are able to compete very effectively in the American market and have enjoyed significant growth in their market share in recent years. Between 1978 and 1981, imported cars increased their share of the American market from 18 percent to 27 percent, and Japanese vehicles account for 80 percent of the imports.[7]

Isoquant-Isocost Analysis of Short-Run Production Problems

Isoquant-isocost analysis can be used to solve short-run production problems as well. Variable inputs are often substitutable for each other, and the firm faces a short-run decision concerning the combination of variable factors (in conjunction with fixed factors) which would minimize cost for a particular output level. A firm may have the choice of hiring either "generalist" labor (who can accomplish a sequence of tasks) or, alternatively, hiring "specialist" labor who can each do only one of the required tasks. Thus, these two different types of labor are substitutable in the short run, presuming each can be hired or fired at management's discretion.

Similarly, labor may be substitutable for raw materials in some production processes. For example, three workers and ten yards of cloth may combine (along with the fixed factors) to produce five shirts per hour. Alternatively, five workers and eight yards of cloth may combine to produce five shirts per hour. The extra labor allows more careful cutting of the cloth so that there is less waste of the material. A further example is the substitut-

---

[6] See Robert L. Simison, "Ford Asks for 50% Pay-Benefit Cut in Bid to Align Labor Costs with Japanese," *Wall Street Journal*, October 22, 1981.

[7] See *Business Week*, "Why Detroit Still Can't Get Going," November 9, 1981, pp. 106-10.

PRODUCTION AND COST ANALYSIS

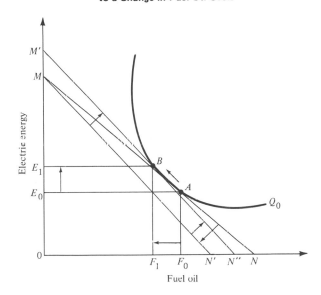

ability among different sources of energy. A firm can install electric heating to supplement or replace its oil heating system if the cost of oil rises relative to that of electricity.

EXAMPLE: The "energy crises" of 1974 and 1979 spurred the movement away from petroleum-derived energy and towards alternative energy sources. Oil prices shot up dramatically during 1979, following the turmoil in Iran, and after a short decline, continued their upward thrust when war broke out between Iran and Iraq in September 1980. Heating oil consumption in the winter of 1980-1981 was substantially below projections, however, indicating the shift from petroleum as an energy source to competing energy sources.[8]

In terms of Figure 6-7, where we show fuel oil on the horizontal axis and electrical energy on the vertical axis, suppose that the initial price ratio was such that the isocost line in early 1979 was MN. To produce output level Q_0, the firm would choose the combination of fuel oil and electrical energy represented by point A, or F_0 units of fuel oil and E_0 units of electrical energy. The rise in oil prices is indicated by the shift of the isocost curve to MN'. To maintain its output at level Q_0, the firm (and households which had the ability to do so) would prefer to substitute away from fuel oil and towards electric energy to point B on isoquant Q_0. Thus, after the adjustment process, the firm would purchase E_1 units of electrical energy

---

[8] See Mary Greenebaum, "The Sudden Popularity of Heating Oil Contracts," *Fortune*, February 23, 1981, pp. 127, 130.

and F_1 units of fuel oil. In fact, we observed a shift away from petroleum-derived energy and towards a variety of other energy sources, including solar and nuclear energy.

6.4 SHORT-RUN AND LONG-RUN COST CURVES

In the preceding sections we have examined the requirements for technical and economic efficiency in production in both the short-run and long-run situations. Since economic efficiency involves the costs per unit of each of the inputs, it is a simple matter to restate this in terms of the input cost per unit of output and to derive the cost curves for all levels of output in both the short run and the long run. Let us begin with the short-run cost curves.

The Total Variable Cost Curve

In the short run the firm is constrained to a fixed level of capital input and must increase or decrease output along the total product curve. The total variable cost (TVC) curve can be derived from the TP curve simply by multiplying the level of variable inputs by the cost per unit of those inputs and by plotting these cost data against the output level. Suppose that the variable factor units cost $10 each. Using the data from the total product curve, shown on the right-hand side of Figure 6-8, and multiplying each unit of the variable factor by $10, we can plot the cost of the variable input against the output, in the left-hand side of Figure 6-8.

For simplicity we have chosen the scale on the left-hand side of the horizontal axis to be ten times that on the right-hand side, so that the curve

FIGURE 6-8.   Relationship between the Total Product and Total Variable Cost Curves

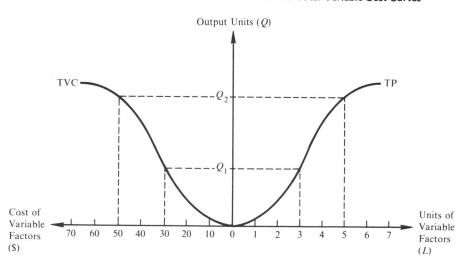

PRODUCTION AND COST ANALYSIS

which reflects the total cost of the variable factors for all levels of output is a mirror image of the total product curve. Note that three units of the variable factors, or \$30 spent on the variable factors (which amounts to the same thing), will produce Q_1 units of output. Similarly, five units, or \$50 spent on the variable factors, will produce Q_2 units of output. Thus, the shape of the total variable cost curve derives directly from the form of the production function and the number of units of capital employed, since these factors underlie the shape of the total product curve.

Average Variable and Marginal Costs

DEFINITION: *Average variable cost* is equal to TVC divided by output Q at every level of Q. That is,

$$AVC = \frac{TVC}{Q} \qquad (6\text{-}5)$$

In Figure 6-9 we show the TVC curve tipped on its side—rotated $180°$ to the right—with the associated average variable and marginal cost curves. The AVC for each output level is equal to the ratio of the *vertical distance* from the quantity axis to the TVC curve to the *horizontal distance* from the cost axis to the TVC curve. In terms of the graph, this amounts to the vertical rise over the horizontal run, or to the slope of a ray from the origin that joins the point on the TVC curve. Average variable cost at point A on the TVC curve is equal to the ratio $AR/0R$, or the value of the slope of the line $0A$, and is shown as point A' on the AVC vertically below.

It can be verified that the slopes of lines between the origin and points on the curve become progressively flatter as we begin to move up the TVC curve away from the origin. Thus the AVC, which is equal to the value of these slopes, must fall over this range. A point is reached, however, where the ray from the origin can become no flatter and still touch the TVC curve. Point C, where the ray is just tangent to the TVC curve in Figure 6-9, signifies the lowest value for AVC. Since the rays become steeper for points on the TVC to the right of the tangency point, AVC must rise after this output level, as shown in the figure.

DEFINITION: *Marginal cost* is the change in total costs caused by a one-unit change in output:

$$MC = \frac{\Delta TC}{\Delta Q} \qquad (6\text{-}6)$$

where $\Delta Q = 1$. Since output changes cause only variable costs to change, we can equivalently define marginal costs as the change in total variable costs for a one-unit change in output. Hence,

$$MC = \frac{\Delta TVC}{\Delta Q} \qquad (6\text{-}7)$$

where $\Delta Q = 1$. In this form you see that marginal cost is defined as the vertical rise over the horizontal run along the TVC curve for a one-unit change in output. *MC* is thus equal to the slope of the TVC curve at each output level.

If we were to put tangents against the TVC curve at every output level, we would see that the slopes of these tangents would fall at first, up to the point of inflection on the TVC curve, and would then rise. In Figure

FIGURE 6-9.   Derivation of Average Variable and Marginal Cost Curves from Total Variable Cost Curve

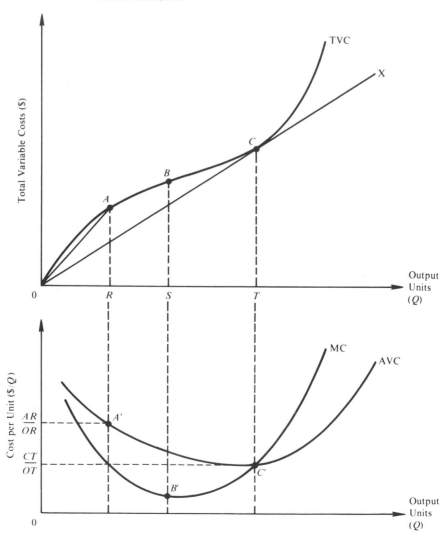

PRODUCTION AND COST ANALYSIS

6-9 the point of inflection occurs at point B, where the TVC curve changes from convexity from above to concavity from above. The slope of the TVC becomes progressively flatter until point B, and it becomes progressively steeper after point B as output is increased. This indicates that the marginal cost curve is U-shaped, falling to a minimum at the output level where the TVC exhibits its inflection point and rising thereafter.

NOTE: It is important to note that while the marginal cost curve lies below the average variable cost curve, the latter is falling. In effect, the lower marginal cost is pulling down the average. Conversely, when the MC curve lies above the AVC curve, the latter must be rising, being pulled up by the marginal costs. It follows that when the MC crosses the AVC, the AVC must be at its minimum value. This can be verified in Figure 6-9 at point C on the TVC curve. Marginal costs and average variable costs must be equal, since both are given by the slope of the tangent to the TVC curve at that point.

Marginal costs are the value counterpart of the marginal product of the variable factors. When marginal productivity of labor is falling, marginal cost of output is rising, and *vice versa*. If the efficiency of the marginal units of the variable factor is constant, output can be produced at a constant level of marginal cost.

These relationships can be confirmed by another look at Figure 6-8. Notice that when the TP curve is concave from above, exhibiting increasing marginal productivity of the variable factor(s), the TVC curve is indicating decreasing marginal costs per unit of output. Alternatively, when diminishing returns set in for the variable factor(s) after the inflection point, the TVC curve begins to increase at an increasing rate, and marginal costs are increasing over this range.

Short-Run Average Costs

DEFINITION: *Short-run average costs* (SAC) are defined as Total Costs (TC) per unit of output.

$$SAC = \frac{TC}{Q} \qquad (6\text{-}8)$$

Total costs are the sum of TVC and Total Fixed Costs (TFC). To complete the short-run cost picture, therefore, we need to add the costs of the fixed factors. Show TFC as a horizontal line when plotted against output, as shown in Figure 6-10, since these costs are constant whatever the level of output. To find the total of fixed and variable costs, we add vertically the TFC and TVC curves on the graph. This, in effect, causes the TVC curve to be moved upward a constant distance equal to the total fixed costs. Thus, the total cost (TC) curve and the TVC curve have the same shape, as is evident in Figure 6-10. As noted previously, the marginal cost curve can thus be derived from the TC curve instead of the TVC curve.

FIGURE 6-10.   Derivation of Short-Run Average Cost Curve

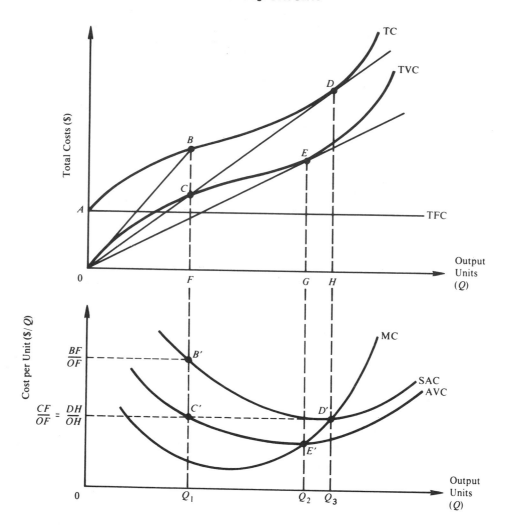

Average total costs, or short-run average costs (SAC), may be derived from the TC curve by the same technique as was used to derive the AVC curve. The slope of a ray from the origin to a point on the TC curve gives the value of SAC for each output level. Thus at point B in the upper part of Figure 6-10, SAC is equal to the ratio BF/OF, or the slope of the line OB. At the same output level, AVC $= CF/OF$, or the slope of the line OC. In the lower part of the figure these values are shown as points B' and C', respectively. Given the shape of the TC curve, SAC must fall at first, reach a minimum, and then rise. Note that at the minimum point, found where the ray from the origin is just tangent to the TC curve, the slope of the ray is equal to that of the TC curve, and hence SAC and MC are equal at that output level.[9]

Different Production Functions Cause Different Cost Curves

The total product curve is not necessarily a cubic function of the inputs of the variable factors, as indicated by the S-shaped curves in Figures 6-2 and 6-8. The shape of the TP curve is an empirical question—for some plants it may be cubic, for others quadratic or a power function, and it may even be sufficiently approximated by a linear function (over the relevant range) in other plants. Estimation procedures (to be considered in Chapter 8) will ascertain the shape of the TP curve in any particular production process. The cubic function we have been using is the most general case, since it allows for the entire range of returns to the variable factors: it shows increasing returns at first, then constant returns momentarily at the point of inflection, and finally diminishing returns after the point of inflection.

In some production processes we may expect diminishing returns to set in immediately—that is, for marginal product to decline from the outset. This may be true of very small plants which allow the variable inputs to be most efficient at low output levels. In Figure 6-11 we demonstrate that diminishing returns from the outset imply a quadratic TP curve (or other curve which increases at a decreasing rate, such as a power function). The TVC will take its shape from the TP curve and the resulting AVC and MC curves must be upward sloping throughout. Note that the SAC curve falls at first because of the influence of falling average fixed costs, but rises later as the rising AVC outweighs the falling average fixed costs.

Finally, there are cases in which it can be argued that constant returns to the variable factors prevail throughout, or at least over an extended range of output levels. This may occur in a production process in which the variable inputs interact primarily with each other and there is minimal impact with the fixed inputs. For example, the marginal product of the variable inputs in a basket-weaving production process may be constant over a wide range of outputs, since the variable inputs (labor and the straw) interact with each other virtually independently of the fixed factors (which provide shelter, marketing support, and so on). In Figure 6-12 we show a linear TP and MP curve and the resulting linear TVC curve. The per unit cost curves which are associated with the linear TVC curve are shown in the lower left-hand part of Figure 6-12. Note that MC is constant from the

---

[9] An alternative method of deriving the SAC curve is to find the average *fixed* cost (AFC) curve and add that to the AVC curve. The AFC curve must slope downward to the right as output is increased. Since TFC is constant, AFC will decline progressively as output increases, since the fixed costs are spread over progressively more units of output. Note that the SAC curve and the AVC curve converge on each other as output increases, as they differ by a decreasing margin—namely, the declining value of AFC.

FIGURE 6-11.   Diminishing Returns throughout the Production Process and the Resulting
                Cost Curves

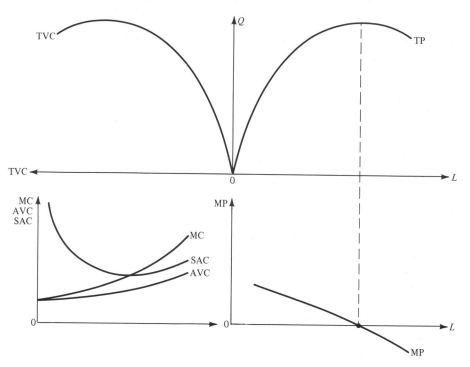

FIGURE 6-12.   Constant Returns throughout the Production Process and the Resulting
                Cost Curves

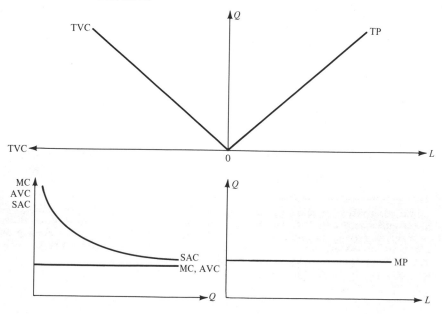

PRODUCTION AND COST ANALYSIS

outset and is, therefore, coextensive with the AVC curve. And note further that SAC falls to converge on AVC because of the influence of the falling average fixed costs.

Linear TVC Curves Due to Plant Divisibility

In many production processes the plant, or fixed factors, are indivisible in the sense that the firm must utilize all of the fixed factors or none at all. In a steel mill the blast furnace is either on or off, and it tends to be relatively inefficient at low output volumes. Similarly, the assembly line in an automobile plant is either moving or it is not moving. The TVC curve associated with such plants might reasonably be expected to be a cubic function of the variable inputs, reflecting falling marginal costs at first and rising marginal costs later.

In other production processes, however, the plant, or some parts of it at least, are divisible in the sense that the variable inputs are not obliged to work with the entire plant but may instead work with a more efficient subset of the plant. In these cases the firm may be able to avoid situations in which "too few" units of the variable factors are working with "too much" capital and may instead be able to maintain the capital-labor ratio at the most efficient level over a considerable range of output levels.

EXAMPLE: Consider the situation of a firm which manufactures stuffed satin toys. Its variable inputs are labor (cutting-machine and sewing-machine operators), satin material, filler, cotton thread, and electrical energy to power the machines. Its fixed inputs, or plant, include four cutting machines, eight sewing machines, the building, fixtures, and all related overhead costs, and the inputs of the managers, administrators, secretaries, clerks, and so on. Some part of the plant is divisible—namely, the cutting and sewing machines. At low levels of output, that is, low levels of the variable inputs, it is clear that some cutting and sewing machines would not be used at all. As demand for the product grows, the firm would hire more labor, order more materials, and expand output by starting up its idle machines.

In terms of Figure 6-13, suppose that L_1, L_2, L_3, and L_4 represent the first four "units" of the variable factors. For example, L_1 might represent 1 cutting-machine operator, 2 sewing-machine operators, 30 yards of satin cloth, 50 pounds of filler, 100 yards of cotton thread, and the electrical energy to run one cutting machine and two sewing machines. These variable inputs, if applied to all four cutting machines and eight sewing machines, might produce only Q' units of output on the curvilinear total product curve shown as TP. Doubling the inputs of the variable factors to L_2 would increase output to Q''; tripling inputs to L_3 would produce Q'''; and quadrupling inputs to L_4 is the level of variable inputs which maximizes the average product of the variable inputs (Q_4/L_4). The average product of the variable inputs is given by the slope of the ray from the origin to a

FIGURE 6-13.   Linear TP and TVC Curves Due to Divisibility of Plant

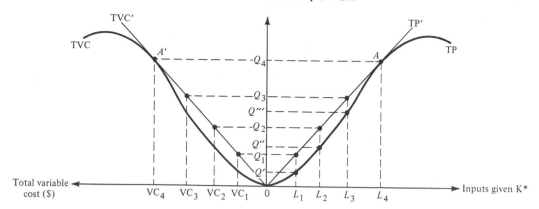

point on the total product curve and is maximized at the point where this ray is tangent to the curvilinear TP curve. From the total variable cost (TVC) curve on the left-hand side of the figure, we see that average variable cost (AVC) is also minimized at the output level Q_4 and the underlying input level L_4.

Note that at input level L_4 there are four cutting-machine operators operating four cutting machines and eight sewing-machine operators operating eight sewing machines. (The most efficient ratio of operators to machines is assumed to be one to one for both the cutting and the sewing machines.)

Now, suppose output had to be reduced because of a drop in demand. The firm would reduce its variable inputs back to L_3 units, but instead of asking the remaining workers to operate *all* the machines, it would close down one cutting machine and two sewing machines, maintaining the most efficient ratio of operators to machines. Thus, output would fall only to Q_3 rather than to Q'''. Thus, AVC stays at the minimum level. Similarly, if variable inputs were reduced to L_2 units, the firm could maintain AVC at its minimum level by shutting down another cutting machine and two more sewing machines.

Thus, if the firm can divide its fixed factors into units which may or may not be operated depending on the demand for its product, it may be able to maintain the most efficient ratio of its variable factors to those divisible fixed factors, such that it regards the straight lines TP' and TVC' as its total product and total variable cost curves, respectively. In this case the firm's marginal and average variable costs will not be U-shaped but will be linear, as shown in Figure 6-12. The SAC curve will approach AVC asymptotically as the fixed costs are spread over successively larger output levels up to Q_4.[10]

---

[10] Output could be increased beyond Q_4, either by adding more labor, materials, and energy to the existing plant (in which case, AVC would rise) or by also adding more cutting and sewing machines, in which case AFC (and SAC) would shift upwards. The latter option implies a long-run plant size adjustment.

The Short-Run Supply Decision

In the short run the firm must incur its fixed costs, since it cannot, by definition, change the input of these factors of production. The firm's variable costs, on the other hand, are *discretionary*, in the sense that the firm may decide whether or not to incur these costs, since the input of variable factors can be varied all the way back to zero. What induces a firm to incur costs? We argued briefly in Chapter 1 that the firm is profit-oriented and incurs costs when it expects to more than cover those costs with revenues. Thus, a firm will set up a plant and incur fixed and variable costs to produce a particular product, because it expects to more than cover these fixed and variable costs with revenues and thereby make a profit.

Once committed to its present size of plant, however, the firm is obliged to incur the fixed costs of that plant in the short run. Variable costs, on the other hand, will be incurred only if the firm expects revenues to exceed these variable costs. Suppose price exceeds average variable cost but is less than the average total cost, meaning that the firm makes a loss. If the firm ceases production, it incurs no variable costs, earns no revenues, and therefore makes a loss equal to its fixed costs, which must be paid whether or not the firm produces anything. If the firm continues production when P is greater than AVC but is less than SAC, there is, for each unit sold, some excess of revenue over variable costs that contributes toward the fixed costs. Therefore, the firm reduces its losses by producing the product when $SAC > P > AVC$, rather than by ceasing production.

RULE: Thus the firm decides to incur variable costs and hence supply the product to the market, whenever price exceeds the firm's average variable cost level. If price also exceeds the SAC level, the firm makes a profit. If price falls below SAC, the firm suffers a loss, but it can minimize those losses by staying in production as long as $P > AVC$. If price slips below AVC, the firm minimizes losses by ceasing production and waiting until either the price rises above AVC again or until it can liquidate its fixed factors and terminate the associated fixed costs. The latter option implies a long-run situation, of course.

In most business situations the rule governing the decision "to supply or not to supply" is more clearly stated in terms of total revenues and total variable costs, rather than in terms of (per unit) $P > AVC$. That is, if $TR > TVC$, the firm should supply its product(s), whereas if $TR < TVC$, it should not incur the variable costs and, consequently, not supply the product(s). This rule is equivalent to the $P > AVC$ rule, since totals divided by quantity demanded equal the per-unit values. But in the real world, quantity demanded tends to vary day by day and month by month because of seasonal factors, chance circumstances, weather conditions, and competing attractions. In effect, the demand curve shifts back and forth in response to these shift factors. Most firms cannot change their prices daily to reflect the differing states of demand that eventuate. Rather, they set prices on the basis of some notion of the average, or normal, demand situation and hold these prices steady as sales fluctuate daily, monthly, or seasonally around this conceptually normal volume. Hence price is constant while AVC varies substantially from day to day depending on the volume produced. In such a situation the firm may find it easier to decide whether or not to supply its product in the short run on the basis of whether or not it expects TR to exceed TVC.

EXAMPLE: During a severe snowstorm many stores close early or remain closed for the day, since the manager predicts that sales would be so small that it is not worth opening the store and incurring the associated variable costs. Or, for example, a coffee shop might stay open until 3 A.M. on Saturday night but close at midnight or earlier on weeknights, based on the manager's expectation that sales revenues would or would not cover the total variable costs involved. In these cases, fixed costs are being incurred and would be incurred regardless of whether the firm is open for business. The supply decision depends upon whether or not the total sales revenue is expected to exceed the discretionary total variable costs relevant to the time period under consideration.

The Long-Run Average Cost Curve

DEFINITION: The *long-run average cost* (LAC) curve shows the least cost of production for each output level when all inputs may be varied. It is a hypothetical construct, composed of pieces of many different SAC curves. It is the locus of points on the various SAC curves which allow each output level to be produced at lowest cost, given the ability to change plant size (or vary the input of capital).

To derive the long-run average cost curve we can proceed by finding the SAC curve that relates to every level of fixed factors. Each level of capital (fixed factor) input will give rise to a TP curve, from which we can derive a TVC curve and ultimately obtain the appropriate SAC curve as we did above. This procedure would give us a series of SAC curves, each with a slightly larger capital input level as we move from left to right. As shown in Figure 6-14, the long-run average cost (LAC) curve is the "envelope curve" of all these short-run curves. A corollary of this is that for any point on the LAC curve there is a SAC curve lying tangent at that point.

NOTE: The LAC curve may not be a smooth U-shaped line for every firm in the real world, since the smooth U-shape depends upon the availability of a large number of plant sizes, with the sizes of these plants varying by relatively small increments from the smallest available to the largest available. In many industries there are only a few alternative sizes of plant, each significantly different in size from the next largest and the next smallest.

EXAMPLE: Consider the case of a small private airline company that plans to initiate a feeder service from a remote area to a major city. In choosing the

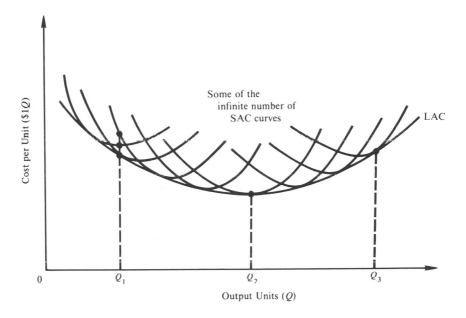

aircraft for this route the firm must, in effect, choose its size of plant, since
light aircraft are available in 4-, 6-, 8-, and 10-seat models. In this case, plant
sizes are available only in discretely increasing, rather than continuously
increasing, sizes, and the LAC curve will exhibit a series of kinks, or scallops,
rather than be a smooth line. In Figure 6-15 we show the LAC curve as the
heavy line encompassing only those sections of each SAC curve *which
allow output to be produced at lowest cost.*

FIGURE 6-15.   Long-Run Average Costs with Discrete Plant
                Size Differences

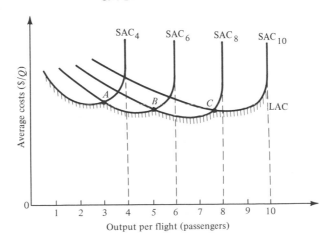

The four SAC curves represent the available plant sizes, with the subscripts indicating the maximum number of seats in each plant size. Note that each SAC becomes vertical at the point where it reaches its maximum output (passenger) level. The LAC curve is the envelope curve of these four SAC curves; it contains kinks at points A, B, and C, where it becomes less costly (per passenger) to choose the next largest plant size.

Note that if there were an aircraft available that seated 5 passengers (including the pilot), the SAC curve of that plant size would have nestled between SAC_4 and SAC_6, and it would have caused the kink in the LAC curve at point A to disappear. Similarly, if planes were also available with 7 and 9 seats, the other kinks might be removed or at least replaced by smaller kinks. With plant size continuously variable, the LAC curve would be a smooth line. In the real world, however, the LAC curve is most likely to exhibit kinks because plant size is not continuously variable.

The Long-Run Marginal Cost Curve

DEFINITION: The *long-run marginal cost* (LMC) curve shows the marginal cost of producing each additional unit of output when the firm is free to vary the inputs of all factors of production. As you should by now expect, the LMC lies below the LAC when the latter is falling, and it lies above the LAC when the latter is rising. In fact, LAC falls precisely because the LMC lies below it, pulling down the average cost. Similarly, LAC rises precisely because the marginal units cost more than the average to produce.

In Figure 6-16 we show the LMC associated with a particular LAC curve and three short-run cost situations. Notice that at output level Q_1, the short-run average cost is equal to the long-run average cost at Point A. It follows that short-run marginal cost must equal LMC at this output level, since the two averages have converged upon each other precisely because

FIGURE 6-16. Long-Run Marginal Costs and Their Relationship to Other Cost Curves

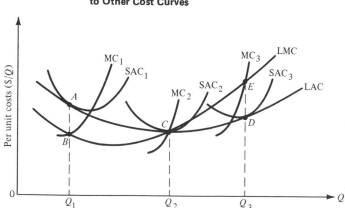

PRODUCTION AND COST ANALYSIS

the two marginals were converging on the same value (at point B). Similarly, at output level Q_2 we have SAC_2 = LAC = LMC = MC_2. We know that the LMC must pass through the minimum point of the LAC curve and that the short-run MC must pass through the minimum SAC point. Since SAC = LAC at the minimum points of both, we have the above four-way equality. Finally, at output level Q_3, average short-run and long-run costs are equal at point D, because marginal short-run and long-run costs are equal at point E.

Returns to Plant Size and Firm Size

DEFINITION: *Economies of plant size*, or increasing returns to plant size, are evident when the LAC curve slopes downward to the right, indicating that successively larger plant sizes have corresponding SAC curves lying lower and to the right. These economies arise because of such factors as an output level that is large enough to allow the firm to utilize more efficient capital-intensive methods, for instance, computer-controlled assembly lines, and that allows personnel to specialize in the areas of their greatest expertise. After some point, increasing inefficiencies in other areas, caused, perhaps, by the increasing bureaucracy of larger establishments, offset these cost advantages. The firm experiences *diseconomies of plant size* when successively larger plant sizes exhibit SAC curves that lie progressively higher and to the right.[11]

NOTE: The LAC curve is *not* the locus of the minimum points of each SAC curve. Since each SAC curve is tangent to the LAC curve, this is true only if the LAC curve is horizontal. If economies and diseconomies of plant size exist, the LAC curve will at first be negatively sloping and then positively sloping. Thus, tangencies with SAC curves must occur at first on negatively sloping parts of SAC curves and then on positively sloping parts. It follows that SAC curves are tangent to the left of their minimum points when there are economies of plant size and tangent to the right of their minimum points when there are diseconomies of plant size. Only for the SAC curve that is

---

[11]One can make the distinction between economies of *scale* and economies of *plant size*. Economies of scale are found when *all* factors are increased in the same proportion. This involves an expansion path in isoquant analysis that is a straight line from the origin, reflecting a constant capital-labor ratio. Economies of plant size derive from the least cost expansion path, which is not necessarily a straight line, although it does emanate from the origin. That is, firms are unlikely to want to expand all inputs in the same proportion (as they increase their output under long-run conditions), because a different capital-labor ratio is likely to be cost minimizing because of differing marginal productivities of the inputs at different input levels. If the production function is *homogeneous*, the least cost expansion path is a straight line from the origin and the same ratio of inputs is optimal at all output levels. In this case there are both economies of scale and economies of plant size, if proportional increases in all inputs lead to greater proportional increases in output or there are both diseconomies of scale and diseconomies of plant size, if output increases by proportionately less. See P. H. Douglas, "Are There Laws of Production?" *American Economic Review*, 38 (March 1948), 1-41.

tangent to the minimum point of the LAC curve, often called *the optimum size of plant*, will the minimum point of an SAC curve be a point on the LAC curve. This is evident in Figure 6-16.

Economies of Firm Size and Multiplant Operation. Certain other economies arise as a result of the absolute size of the firm. For example, larger firms are usually able to obtain discounts for bulk purchases of raw materials, which gives them a cost advantage over smaller firms. These cost advantages are often referred to as *pecuniary economies* of plant or firm size; they are clearly different from the economies of plant size that are dependent upon increasing efficiency in production. Many large firms derive further pecuniary economies as the result of operating more than one plant. These cost savings are likely to result from spreading certain under-utilized fixed costs, such as managerial talent, computer rental, and advertising expenditures, over more than one plant. The average cost curve for the first plant is, therefore, expected to sink downward to some degree as a result of opening a second and subsequent plants, since some part of the fixed costs previously charged to a single plant are now charged to one of the newer plants. This situation is illustrated in Figure 6-17.

EXAMPLE: McDonald's fast-food restaurant chain is a good example. In a couple of decades this chain has burgeoned from a single fast-food restaurant to a worldwide network of almost identical restaurants. Whether in North America, Europe, Asia, or Australia one can walk right up to that familiar counter and place an order for a Big Mac, large order of french fries, an apple turnover, and a milkshake. Most of the phenomenal growth of McDonald's can be attributed to franchising, whereby local entrepreneurs supply a substantial capital investment in return for part ownership in a new

FIGURE 6-17. **Pecuniary Economies causing Cost Curves to sink Downward**

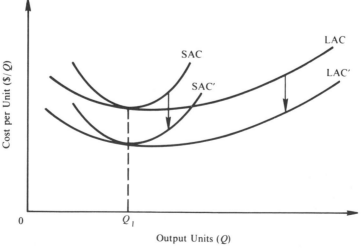

PRODUCTION AND COST ANALYSIS

outlet and several container loads of furniture, signboards, equipment, and fixtures that characterize a McDonald's restaurant. This familiar environment attracts customers who have tried McDonald's elsewhere and who know they can expect the same menu, the same quality, and the same prices. (This lack of uncertainty about prices and quality is very comforting to the wary consumer, who may have suffered disappointments and surprises at other fast-food restaurants.) In addition, McDonald's attracts new customers and reinforces preference patterns of regular customers by substantial expenditures on advertising and on other promotional efforts.

On the cost side there seems to be little indication that McDonald's benefits from economies of plant size, since all their restaurants seem to fall within a relatively small size range, although this is largely determined by the size of local markets for each outlet. On the other hand, there is little doubt that McDonald's benefits from economies of multiplant operation. Each additional plant (new outlet) probably allows McDonald's to reduce the per unit cost of its foodstuffs, since these are prepared in central locations and shipped to each franchised outlet. Advertising and promotion costs per outlet are reduced as the number of outlets sharing these costs is increased. Also the cost of replacing chairs, tables, and wall decorations is expected to decrease as the market (number of outlets) for these products increases. Thus, we expect the cost curves of any particular McDonald's outlet to drift downward (in constant-value dollars, or *real* terms) over time as more and more outlets are opened.

6.5 SUMMARY

The concepts involved in the theory of production and costs can be explained and demonstrated in terms of the output hill and the production surface. Relating all the concepts back to the production surface serves to emphasize the interdependence of these concepts. The shape of the long-run average cost curve depends upon the various short-run average cost curves. The shapes of the short-run cost curves in turn depend upon the total product curves. The shapes of the total product curves depend upon the production surface. This in turn depends on the specific or mathematical form of the production function. Thus the U-shaped short-run cost curves are the result of the law of variable proportions, and the shape of the long-run average cost curve is the result of the economies and diseconomies of plant size. All of this is involved in the underlying production surface. Whenever we draw a particular set of cost curves, we therefore implicitly presume the shape of the underlying production surface. Similarly, whenever a production function is specified, the shape and position of the cost curves is simultaneously implied.

It is important to emphasize that the long-run average cost curve does not refer to any long period of time, since factor costs and technologies will change over time, causing any particular LAC to become inappropriate.

Instead, it refers to the minimum costs for each output level at a point of time, when factor costs and technologies can reasonably be assumed to be constant. When a firm decides what output level to produce, it then chooses its level of capital input and hence the SAC that produces that output most efficiently. Thus the LAC shows the possibilities (the various plant sizes) that are available to the firm when the firm is free to vary both capital and labor (that is, at the end of the short run). Once the firm has chosen a particular size of plant, it is then constrained to that plant for the duration of the following short-run period, that is, until a sufficient period of time has elapsed, so that the firm can liquidate its existing plant, renew all its contracts, and employ more or less of the resources that are fixed in the short run.

This chapter provides the reader with a theoretical base for a critical examination of the use of various cost concepts in decision making, which is the subject matter of the following chapter. In decision making we must always be aware of the likelihood that per unit costs will change from their present levels because of changes in the output level. This cost change may be due to the presence of increasing or diminishing returns to the variable factors or the experience of economies or diseconomies of plant or firm size. Underlying the present cost structure for all output levels is the state of technology and the prices of the input factors. If these change, the entire set of cost curves will shift, requiring a reevaluation of the present output level for its suitability in the light of the firm's objectives.

DISCUSSION QUESTIONS

6-1. Explain how a tabular representation of a production function represents both the long-run and the short-run situations at the same time.

6-2. Suppose your production process has three inputs—machinery, highly skilled labor, and raw materials. If you wanted a new (larger or smaller) machine, it would take six months to be fabricated, delivered, and installed. Your present workers are all under contract for another eight months. New workers would take three months to acquire, because of the lengthy process of advertising, interviewing, and so forth. Raw-material supplies must be ordered four weeks in advance. How long is your short run? When can you make your long-run decision to expand or contract your plant size?

6-3. How does the law of variable proportions differ from the law of diminishing returns?

6-4. Why is the point of inflection on the total product curve the point where diminishing returns begin?

6-5. The smooth curve of an isoquant curve implies the ability to substitute continually small amounts of labor for capital. Given that fractions of labor and capital do not exist in a physical sense, how can we achieve the substitutions implied by a smooth isoquant curve?

6-6. Distinguish between technical efficiency and economic efficiency in the production process.

6-7. Why would you expect the textile industry of some countries to use hand looms (which take, say, two hours of labor per square meter of cloth) while in other countries highly mechanized processes (which take, say, thirty seconds of labor per square meter of cloth) are preferred?

6-8. Explain why the shape of the short-run average variable cost curve depends on the specific form of the production function.

6-9. Explain the construction of the long-run average cost curve and its relationship with the long-run marginal cost curve and the various short-run average cost curves.

6-10. Distinguish between economies of scale, economies of plant size, and economies of firm size. Under what conditions would a firm's expansion be an example of all three phenomena at once?

PROBLEMS AND SHORT CASES

6-1. Donald K. Brown and Company operates a pearl-diving operation in the North Pacific Ocean. Mr. Brown owns a large trawler with all the required equipment. He hires local divers from the nearby islands and pays each of them on the basis of the weight of oysters recovered. He sells the pearls and the oyster meat separately. Over the past month he has been out pearling eight times in the same general area, taking all the divers who showed up for each trip. The particulars are as follows:

Trip Number	Divers Employed	Oysters Recovered (kg)
1	6	38
2	17	76
3	9	56
4	5	32
5	12	74
6	3	15
7	14	80
8	16	78

(a) Over what ranges do there appear to be increasing, constant, and diminishing returns to the variable factor?

(b) What number of divers appears to be the most efficient in terms of output per diver?

(c) What number of divers appears to be most efficient in terms of the utilization of the trawler and other equipment?

6-2. Taras Panache is the owner-manager of Panache Shirts Enterprises, which manufactures shirts by using rented space and equipment in a large warehouse. Due to the technical aspects of shirt production and the available equipment, separate production centers are used, each consisting of one cutting machine, two sewing machines, and three operators. Six months ago Mr. Panache had only one such production center, but recently he doubled, then tripled, and finally quadrupled the number of production centers by renting more space and equipment and by hiring more operators. Throughout the expansion Mr. Panache has personally supervised all the operators and has handled all other aspects of the business. He kept a record of the average daily output from the entire plant for each of the four situations, as follows:

One production center	20.6 shirts/day
Two production centers	42.4 shirts/day
Three production centers	60.8 shirts/day
Four production centers	76.3 shirts/day

(a) Can the expansion of Panache Shirts be regarded as a case of an increase in the *scale* of operations or simply an increase in the *size* of operations? Why?

(b) Are there economies and/or diseconomies of scale/size evident? Explain.

(c) Indulge in some speculation about the probable cause of the economies and diseconomies, if any.

6-3. Given a production function of the form

$$Q = 38.6K + 3.2K^2 - 1.8K^3 + 16.3L + 2.8L^2 - 0.85L^3$$

where K represents units of the capital input (in $1,000 units) and L represents units of the labor input (in hundreds of labor hours), solve the following:

(a) Construct the total product and marginal product curves for the case of $K = 5$.

(b) At what level of labor input do diminishing returns become evident?

(c) If labor were available to you at no cost (students wishing to gain work experience and willing to work without wages), what input level would you choose? Why?

6-4. The Himam Foods Corporation is a relatively small firm producing grocery items. Recently its research department developed a new salad dressing. Production of this new dressing would involve the use of the firm's mixing machine, which combines, shakes, rotates, and warms the ingredients to a specified temperature before pouring the mixture into bottles which are then capped and labeled. Some of the above procedures can be done manually, however, and Himam wants to choose the optimal proportions of machine time and labor time. The production function has been estimated as shown below:

Himam Foods—Production Function
(output in thousands of units)

		LABOR-HOURS PER YEAR (000)					
		1	2	3	4	5	6
Machine Hours	1	25	80	110	120	125	115
per Year (000)	2	70	102	120	135	145	150
	3	86	117	140	160	175	182
	4	96	125	150	170	185	195
	5	95	130	155	175	192	205
	6	90	127	158	178	196	210

Machine-hours cost $25 per hour, and labor costs are $10 per hour. (Raw material costs are constant per bottle and are covered by a separate budget.) Due to the current difficult financial situation, Himam can allocate a budget of only $80,000 for the machine and labor costs of producing the new dressing.

(a) Using isoquant-isocost analysis, show graphically the technically efficient factor combinations as distinct from the technically inefficient factor combinations.

(b) Estimate from your graph the maximum output level which Himam can produce within its budget constraint and the factor combination that is required to achieve this level.

(c) Demonstrate what would happen if the cost of labor hours were to increase to $15 per hour. Estimate the new optimal factor combination and output level.

6-5. Gewurz Fabricators Limited manufactures and assembles small aluminum buildings suitable for garden toolsheds, garages, and children's playhouses. Stephen Gewurz, the owner, is considering opening a new plant to diversify into the production of luxury dog kennels for the expanding large dogs' market. He has carefully considered the labor and capital requirements and the substitutability between these inputs at various output levels and has summarized the production function as shown below:

Gewurz Fabricator—Production Function
(output in units per year)

		LABOR INPUTS (person-years)							
		1	*2*	*3*	*4*	*5*	*6*	*7*	*8*
Capital Inputs	1	30	52	80	110	130	145	155	162
(machine-years)	2	50	80	120	164	200	220	235	248
	3	80	124	175	226	260	274	282	287
	4	100	160	218	272	302	320	335	345

(a) Supposing that the cost of each unit of capital is $20,000 and the cost of each unit of labor is $10,000, derive the SAC curve for each of the four plant sizes indicated.

(b) What conclusions can you draw about the returns to increasing plant size in this example?

(c) Which of the four plants should be selected if demand is expected to be (1) 125 units? (2) 250 units? (3) somewhere within the range of 200-300 units? (Explain and defend your decision fully.)

6-6. The newly-formed Beaudry Automobile Corporation plans to produce an expensive sports car and has asked your consulting firm for advice on the size of plant to construct. Due to the union contract and technical features of automobile production, labor must be paid $12,000 per person per annum, and each incremental change in plant size involves $900,000 in annual expenses for depreciation, interest, and other fixed costs. The maximum the firm will have available for expenditure on capital and labor is $9 million per annum. BAC has supplied the following details of its production function, meticulously derived by its chief engineer. (The data in the body of the table represent automobiles produced, in units.) Labor can be varied virtually continuously; the table shows units of 50 persons for convenience. All other variable expenses are constant at $2,500 per vehicle produced.

Capital	LABOR (units of 50 persons)					
(units of $900,000)	*1*	*2*	*3*	*4*	*5*	*6*
1	20	40	70	90	100	108
2	30	50	100	130	140	147
3	40	90	140	170	180	185
4	60	120	180	220	230	236
5	100	170	230	250	260	268
6	170	200	240	270	280	289

BAC's market research indicates that the new vehicle should be sold at $35,000 per unit and that the expected demand situation is as follows:

Units Demanded (annually)	*Probability*
0	0.05
50	0.05
100	0.25
150	0.35
200	0.25
250	0.05

(a) Plot the SAC curves suggested by the production function and input cost figures.

(b) Comment upon the economies and diseconomies of plant size (if any) which are evident in your graph.

(c) Which plant do you suggest that BAC build, and why?

SUGGESTED REFERENCES AND FURTHER READING

Baumol, W. J. *Economic Theory and Operations Analysis* (4th ed.), chap. 11. Englewood Cliffs, N.J.: Prentice-Hall, Inc., 1977.

Chamberlin, E. H. "Proportionality, Divisibility and Economies of Scale," *Quarterly Journal of Economics*, 1948, pp. 229-57.

Cole, C. L. *Microeconomics: A Contemporary Approach*, chaps. 6 and 7. New York: Harcourt Brace Jovanovich, Inc., 1973.

Douglas, P. H. "Are There Laws of Production?" *American Economic Review*, March 1948, pp. 1-41.

Gold, B. "Changing Perspectives on Size, Scale, and Returns: An Interpretive Survey," *Journal of Economic Literature*, 19 (March 1981), pp. 5-33.

Leftwich, R. H. *The Price System and Resource Allocation* (7th ed.), chaps. 8 and 9. Hinsdale, Ill.: The Dryden Press, 1979.

Thompson, A. A., Jr. *Economics of the Firm* (3rd ed.), chaps. 6-8. Englewood Cliffs, N.J.: Prentice-Hall, Inc., 1981.

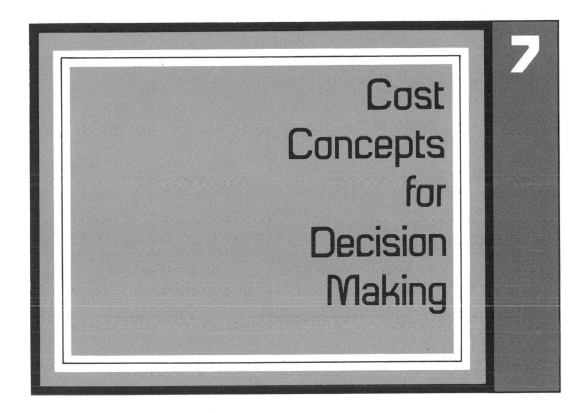

Cost
Concepts
for
Decision
Making

7

7.1 INTRODUCTION

The cost concepts introduced in this chapter are those that may be used in day-to-day decision making by the business executive. In some cases these are crude when compared with the theoretical nicety of the concepts discussed in the preceding chapter. Real-world business situations, however, seldom provide the data necessary for direct application of the theoretical concepts. Nevertheless, an understanding of the theoretical concepts is important to ensure the proper application of the concepts that will be discussed in this chapter. Decision makers sometimes tend to apply convenient rules of thumb to problems that confront them without first examining the applicability of those rules to the particular problem at hand. The danger of incorrectly applying these shortcuts is perhaps nowhere greater than in the area of costs, since poor decisions here operate directly to erode profitability.

In this chapter we shall first examine the differences between economic and accounting concepts of costs and profits. We shall see that some accounting costs, such as the depreciation of an asset purchased in an earlier period or the cost of an item taken from inventory purchased at an earlier, lower, price, must be evaluated in terms of the current or future cost for economic decision-making purposes. This leads to a discussion of the relevant costs for decision making—some costs are relevant and others are irrelevant to the decision problem at hand. The relevant costs are all "incremental" costs and the three main types of incremental costs are introduced and discussed. "Contribution analysis" is based on the incremental costs of a decision and the last section before the summary uses contribution analysis in the context of several examples of decision problems. The appendix to this chapter considers "breakeven analysis," with an examination of its applications and its limitations in the decision-making process.

7.2 ECONOMIC VS. ACCOUNTING CONCEPTS OF COSTS AND PROFITS

The data for decision making with respect to costs typically come not from economists but from accountants. In most cases these data are adequate and appropriate, but in some cases, since they were derived for different purposes, they are less suitable for direct insertion into economic decision-making procedures. We shall examine several different economic and accounting cost concepts and the relationships between them.

Direct and Indirect Costs

In the business firm some costs are incurred that can be directly attributed to the production of a particular unit of a given product. The use of raw materials, labor inputs, and machine time involved in the production of each unit can usually be determined. On the other hand, the cost of fuel for heating, electricity, office and administrative expenses, depreciation of plant and buildings, and other items cannot easily and accurately be separated and attributed to individual units of production (except on an arbitrary basis). Accountants speak of the *direct*, or *prime*, costs per unit when referring to the separable costs of the first category and of *indirect*, or *overhead*, costs when referring to the joint costs of the second category.[1]

Direct and indirect costs are not likely to coincide exactly with the economist's variable cost and fixed cost categories. The criterion used by the economist to divide cost into either fixed or variable is whether or not the cost varies with the level of output, while the criterion used by the accountant is whether or not the cost is separable with respect to the production of individual output units. To bring the accounting costs into line with the economic concepts we must find that part of the indirect or overhead costs that varies with the output level. Accounting statements often divide overhead expense into "variable overhead" and "fixed overhead" categories, in which case we would add the variable overhead expense per

---

[1]See, for example, C. T. Horngren, *Introduction to Management Accounting*, 5th ed. (Englewood Cliffs, N.J.: Prentice-Hall, Inc., 1981), chap. 3.

PRODUCTION AND COST ANALYSIS

TABLE 7-1.   Costs and Output of Metal Castings over Two Months

PRODUCTION PERIOD	JUNE		JULY	
OUTPUT LEVEL (TONS)	1,480		1,620	
	Total	Per Unit	Total	Per Unit
Costs of Production	$	$	$	$
Direct Materials	77,700	52.50	85,050	52.50
Direct Labor	36,260	24.50	42,000	25.93
Variable Overhead	4,930	3.33	5,600	3.45
Fixed Overhead	36,800	24.86	36,800	22.72
Totals	$155,690	$105.19	$169,450	$104.60

unit to the direct cost per unit to find what economists call *average variable cost.*

EXAMPLE: Suppose that production in a metal-casting plant varies from month to month and that we have the data shown in Table 7-1. From this data we can find total variable costs (TVC) and average variable costs (AVC) by adding up the first three cost categories for each output level. Thus, TVC were $118,890 for 1,480 units of output, and $132,650 for 1,620 units of output. Similarly, AVC were $80.33 per unit at 1,480 units and rose to $81.88 per unit at 1,620 units.

NOTE: Fixed overhead costs were constant at $36,800 per month in both June and July, showing no change as a result of the change in the output level. In some situations, fixed overheads will change from month to month as a result of external factors, such as an increase in city taxes, or the costs of office materials, or as the result of internal factors, such as salary increases to management, office employees, and so on. Fixed costs can change in the short run, but not as a result of changes in the output level.[2]

Explicit and Implicit Costs

The accounting process is predominantly concerned with explicit costs. These are costs that actually involve a transfer cf funds from the firm to another party that had previously supplied some materials or services. These are "out-of-pocket" expenses in the current time period, since they are an actual cash outflow in payment for resources. Other cost items, however, are implicit costs, in the sense that they do not involve an actual cash outflow in the current time period.

---

[2]Simply adding variable overhead to direct labor and materials to find total variable cost, and hence AVC, may still involve error if the assignment of costs to the variable or fixed overhead categories was made on any basis other than the variability of the cost with respect to changes in the output level. In Chapter 8 we examine the "gradient method" and other cost estimation techniques which allow a more precise estimate of average variable and marginal costs. At that time we will stress the importance of examining changes in all cost categories to see that the changes were output related and not simply due to changes in factor input prices or some other reason.

EXAMPLE: One such cost in the accounting framework is *depreciation*, which seeks to charge against each year's revenue some portion of the cost of acquiring the capital equipment necessary to generate that revenue. The accounting procedures involve taking the initial cost of the asset, subtracting from this the asset's estimated scrap or salvage value at the end of its useful life, and apportioning this net cost against revenues over the life of the asset. Straight-line depreciation procedures allocate the net cost evenly over the life of the asset, while other methods, such as the sum-of-the-digits methods and double-declining-balance method, allocate proportionately more of the net cost against revenues early in the asset's life.[3] Thus, the accountant charges an implicit cost against revenues each year in order to spread the explicit cost of the asset over the period during which the asset is being used in the production process.

Opportunity Costs and Historic Costs

Accountants are constrained by the tax laws and by the laws governing financial reporting to shareholders to express many costs in terms of the actual or historic costs paid for the resources used in the production process. For decision-making purposes, however, both accountants and economists agree that the appropriate cost concept is not the past cost at which the resource was purchased, but the current or future cost at the time in which it is involved in the decision to be made.

DEFINITION: *Opportunity costs*, or alternative costs as they are often called, refer to the value of a resource in its best alternative employment. For resources that are purchased outright or hired, such as raw materials and labor inputs, there is usually little difference between historic costs and opportunity costs. The market price at which they are purchased or hired should reflect their opportunity cost, since producers must bid for these goods in their respective markets. If producers are not willing to pay at least what the resources are worth in their best alternative usage, they will not be able to purchase the services of these resources.

A difference will almost certainly arise between historic cost and opportunity cost if the resources are purchased and held in inventory for some time before they are used in the production process. If the market value of those resources changes, the opportunity cost diverges from the historic cost. Given the continuing problem of inflation, input prices tend to move upwards on a more-or-less continuous basis, although in some cases rapid technological advances can cause the market value of resources held in inventory to decline. For decision-making purposes the current market value of the resource is its implicit cost to the firm, and this cost should be incorporated

---

[3]See C. T. Horngren, *Introduction to Management Accounting*, pp. 344-46.

into any decision process rather than the (either higher or lower) historic cost. Note that if the firm wanted to replenish its inventories it must pay the current market price for the resource, or alternatively, if it wanted to sell the resource to another firm, it could do so at the current market value, rather than at the historic cost of the resource.

Now let us reconsider depreciation, which is the implicit cost of assets such as land, buildings, and equipment purchased in the past, and which is charged against the current period's revenues. The accountant depreciates the cost of these assets by allocating a portion of the net cost of the asset against the current period's revenues. The economist determines the opportunity cost of these services on the basis of what the land and buildings might have earned in alternative employment or on the basis of the interest which the capital tied up in those assets could have earned in alternative investment, whichever is greater. The opportunity costs of the capital tied up in land, buildings, and equipment may be quite different from the depreciation charge made against revenues, since the latter is determined on an entirely different basis. For decision-making purposes, depreciation of assets involved in the production process must be treated as the opportunity cost of those assets. The opportunity cost is typically equal to the reduction in the asset's salvage (or resale) value over the production period, since this represents the funds given up by not selling the asset now and using it instead in the production process.

NOTE: In cases where an asset could be used in an alternative production process, the opportunity cost is the value of profits forgone (in that alternative use) by using the asset in its present employment.

EXAMPLE: A farmer might forego $10,000 per annum in camping fees by continuing to use the land for farming rather than to take in campers. This is the opportunity cost of the land, unless the market value of the land is so high that the interest earned on the proceeds of the farm's sale would earn more. Suppose the farm could be sold for $100,000, which the farmer (supposing he owns the farm free and clear) could deposit for 15 percent interest. Thus, the opportunity cost of continuing to farm the land is $15,000, this being the *best* alternative use of the resource.

The farmer's own labor must similarly be valued at its opportunity cost. If he could alternatively work for another farmer or take a job demonstrating and selling farm machinery, at say $20,000 per annum, this figure is his opportunity cost and should be included in the analysis for decision-making purposes.

Costs and Profits

The economist's concept of profit differs from that of the accountant. Both consider profit as the excess of revenues over costs, but they regard costs differently. The accountant subtracts from revenues only the costs that are actually incurred plus an allowance for depreciation of some of the previously incurred one-time expenditures, such as the cost of plant and machinery. Profits thus represent the net income to the owners of the firm; profits are their reward for having invested time and capital in the venture. The economist, on the other hand, is concerned with the wider notion of efficient allocation of resources and is thus concerned that all resources are employed where they will earn the maximum for their owners. A means of ensuring this is to consider the opportunity cost of each resource.

EXAMPLE: Let us illustrate with reference to the example of a small-store owner who has $50,000 invested as equity in the store and inventory. As shown in Table 7-2, the annual sales revenues were $200,000, from which must be deducted the cost of goods sold, salaries of hired labor, and depreciation of equipment and buildings. The accounting profit to the store is thus $55,000.

In Table 7-3 we show the economic statement of profit of the same store. Note that the sales revenues, cost of goods sold, salaries, and depreciation are the same as in the preceding table. (We suppose that we have checked and found that the market values of the equipment and buildings have in fact declined by $5,000 over the current year and that the depreciation charge, therefore, fairly reflects the opportunity costs of these resources.)

The economist, however, would add two other items relating to the implicit cost of resources that are owned by the manager. Suppose that the owner-manager could earn $15,000 as a departmental manager in a large store and that this is his best opportunity for salary. Then we would add a cost to the business of $15,000, the imputed salary of the owner-manager.[4] Similarly, the owner-manager has $50,000 equity in the store and inventory, a sum of money that could easily be employed elsewhere for financial gain. Suppose it could be banked or invested elsewhere at comparable risk and would receive 8 percent interest on the principal, or $4,000 per annum. By choosing to invest the $50,000 in the store rather than elsewhere, the owner-manager is therefore foregoing an income of $4,000 per annum, and the economist adds this as an implicit cost on the income statement. Thus, the

TABLE 7-2.   Accounting Income Statement
for the Small-Store Owner

Sales		$200,000
Cost of goods sold	$120,000	
Salaries	20,000	
Depreciation expense	5,000	145,000
Accounting profit		$ 55,000

---

[4]If the owner-manager were to make drawings from the business of cash or goods, these must be accounted for. Suppose he had drawn $10,000 from the business in cash and goods over the year. This, plus another $5,000 should be charged against sales revenues, in order that his opportunity cost is properly valued at $15,000.

TABLE 7-3.   Economic Statement of Profit to Small-Store Owner

Sales		$200,000
Cost of goods sold	$120,000	
Salaries	20,000	
Depreciation expense	5,000	
Imputed salary to owner-manager	15,000	
Imputed interest cost on equity	4,000	164,000
Economic profit		$ 36,000

total economic costs, or the opportunity costs of all resources used in the production process, are $164,000, and the economic profit of the store is $36,000.

Normal and Pure Profits

DEFINITION: *Normal profits* are earned when total revenues equal total costs, if total costs are calculated to reflect the opportunity costs of *all* services provided. If revenues just equal these costs, then all factors are earning the same in that particular employment as they could earn elsewhere. If revenues exceed these costs, we say that the firm is earning a *pure*, or economic, profit. Remembering that the owners of the firm are the effective suppliers of the services of the land and buildings mentioned, you will see that an economic profit means that the owners of the firm are earning more profit than they could by investing their capital elsewhere. The accounting profit must be adjusted for the opportunity cost of the owned resources—that is, for what the firm would pay for the services of those resources if they were purchased or hired—before the alternative investment possibilities can be assessed. Accounting profit will exceed economic profit if some implicit opportunity costs are not subtracted from revenues.

This is not to say that either the accountant's or economist's view of profit is incorrect; each is designed for a different purpose. The accountant's purpose is to find, once the capital has been invested in a particular pursuit, the return to the owners of that capital. The economist's purpose is to ensure that all resources are employed in their most efficient uses. The existence of economic profit confirms that this is so.

NOTE: A normal profit (when TR = TC) does not mean *no* profit. Since total costs in the economic sense include the opportunity cost of all resources used, the return on capital invested is included as a cost, rather than counted as a residual in the accounting sense. Normal profit means a *sufficient* return on the owner's investment in the firm, sufficient to prevent him or her from liquidating this investment and investing it in the next best alternative investment, since the return on the next best alternative investment opportunity is included as an economic cost of production. Normal profit, therefore, means as much profit as the owners could get elsewhere.

Normal Profits and Risk Considerations

Considering that investments are not equally risky, we need to qualify our concept of normal profits to take into account the different degrees of risk in investment opportunities. Investing money in government bonds is relatively risk free, for example, since there is virtually no risk of default in mature economies. Dividends are paid on schedule, and bonds are redeemed on the due date as long as the government exists. Investing money in the development of a new product, on the other hand, is relatively risky. Investors may not receive dividends on their investments and in many cases they may lose all the capital they put in. This is why government bonds pay a relatively low rate of interest (5 percent to 10 percent), whereas companies prospecting for oil and minerals, or introducing new products, and other high-risk businesses, must offer relatively high rates of interest (15 percent to 20 percent) in order to attract the required investment funds. Although investors are generally averse to risk, they are willing to take risks, but only if there is a promise of sufficiently higher returns to compensate for the risks they are taking. The extra return on high-risk investments necessary to compensate investors is known as the *risk premium*. The higher the risk involved, the larger the risk premium demanded by investors.[5]

Since alternative investment opportunities could earn more or less, depending on the degree of risk, we must confine our considerations to alternative investments of the same or similar degree of risk, for the sake of comparability. In effect, this is the familiar *ceteris paribus* requirement: the comparison of one investment with other investments of *equal* risk. The highest return on these alternative investments of equal risk is the opportunity cost of investing in the chosen area. It follows that the opportunity cost of investing in a low-risk business is lower than the opportunity cost of investing in a relatively high-risk business. This, in turn, means that the normal profit of a low-risk business is lower than the normal profit of a high-risk business. In accounting terms, a firm in a low-risk business may be content to earn an 8-percent return on investment after taxes, whereas a firm in a high-risk industry might require a 15-percent return on investment after taxes in order to keep them in that particular business.

We turn now to incremental costs, the most important cost concept for decision making.

7.3   INCREMENTAL COST ANALYSIS

DEFINITION: *Incremental costs* are those costs that will be incurred as the result of a decision. Incremental costs are measured by the change in total costs that results from a particular decision's being made. Incremental costs may

---

[5] These issues are discussed in more detail in Chapter 14, in the context of capital-budgeting decisions.

therefore be either fixed or variable, since a new decision may require purchase of additional capital facilities plus extra labor and materials. When compared with incremental revenues, that is, with the change in total revenues that occurs as a result of the decision, we can see whether a proposed decision is likely to be profitable or not. Clearly, if incremental revenues exceed incremental costs, the proposed decision will add to total profits (or will reduce losses if the total revenues generated do not cover the total costs incurred).

NOTE: Incremental costs are not identical with marginal costs. As defined in the preceding chapter, *marginal costs* are the change in total cost for a one-unit change in the output level. Incremental costs, on the other hand, are the aggregate change in costs that results from a decision. This decision may involve a change in the output level of twenty or of two thousand units, or it may not involve a change in the output level at all. For example, the decision may be whether or not to introduce a new technology of producing the same output level. Knowledge of marginal costs, however, may be very important for the calculation of the incremental costs.

The incremental costs must be accurately identified. Only those costs that actually change as a result of the decision may be included, but all costs that change as a result of the decision must be included. Factors that have been lying idle, with no alternative use, do not have an incremental cost and therefore may be regarded as being costless for the particular decision at hand. Similarly, costs that have been outlaid in the past for machinery or plant and buildings must be regarded as *sunk* costs and should not enter the decision-making procedure unless their opportunity cost is positive. That is, unless there is a competing and profitable use for an owned resource, the incremental cost of involving that resource in the present decision will be zero.

Relevant Costs and Irrelevant Costs

DEFINITION: The *relevant costs* for decision-making purposes are those costs that will be incurred as a result of the decision being considered. The relevant costs are, therefore, the incremental costs. Costs that have been incurred already and costs that will be incurred in the future regardless of the present decision, are *irrelevant* costs as far as the current decision problem is concerned.

EXAMPLE: The manager of a gift store thinks that he has found a miracle product that will sell rapidly and give him large profits. It is an "antenna hat" comprised of two brightly colored balls on the end of flexible springs affixed to a headband. When worn by a person, the balls swing around like the antennae of some giant insect. The manager is convinced these "hats" will sell and has purchased 5,000 of them. His cost was $1.00 each, payable $0.50 immediately and $0.50 within thirty days. He then spent $2,500 promoting these gimmicks, in newspaper advertisements and by hiring students to wear them around campus and at public events. He set the price at \$4.95 and waited for his fortune to come rolling in. Three weeks have passed and he still has 4,975 of these antenna hats. His assistant manager suggested that he cut the price to \$1.25 in order to get rid of what was obviously an ill-considered venture. The manager is adamant that he will never let the price fall that low since "his cost" was \$1.50 per unit and he doesn't want to take a loss on this item.

But is \$1.50 the relevant cost? The manager is about to make a pricing decision, and, as a result of that decision, costs may or may not be incurred and revenues may or may not be earned. The relevant costs are those that will be incurred as a result of the decision. The initial outlays of \$2,500 on the antenna hats and \$2,500 on promotion are irrelevant costs since they have already been incurred and cannot be retrieved. These are sunk costs. The second payment of \$2,500 for the hats is also an irrelevant cost since it must be paid whether or not the price is changed and whether or not any more of the hats are sold. The relevant costs are those, if any, that will be incurred following the pricing decision. Suppose that storage costs must be incurred if the hats are not sold within another week. These costs will be incremental to a decision to maintain price at \$4.95 but not incremental to a decision to cut price to \$1.25, presuming that the assistant manager's judgment is correct and all units would sell at the lower price. Note that the marketability of the item is declining; it is a novelty item and must be sold before the public tires of its novelty value. Thus, price should be set not with an eye on the irrelevant costs (sunk costs and committed costs) but with an eye on the incremental costs. To include the irrelevant costs in the present decision is to let an earlier bad decision cause another bad decision to be made. In business parlance, the gift-store manager should "cut his losses" and "avoid sending good money after bad."

Incremental Cost Categories

There are three main categories of relevant, or incremental, costs. These are the present-period explicit costs, the opportunity costs implicitly involved in the decision, and the future cost implications which flow from the decision. Let us examine these in turn.

Present-Period Explicit Costs. Direct labor and materials costs and changes in the variable overhead costs, such as electricity, are fairly easy to anticipate as a consequence of a decision, for example, to increase the output level. If this increase also requires the purchase of additional capital equipment, this capital cost is incremental to the decision and should be included in full rather than apportioned in any way, notwithstanding that the equipment may have a useful life remaining after the present decision has been carried out.[6]

---

[6]If future revenues may be expected from an item of equipment or from other capital investment, these will be incorporated into the analysis on the revenue side of contribution analysis, as we shall see in the next section.

Thus, the incremental costs of a decision will include all present-period explicit costs which will be incurred as a consequence of that decision. It will exclude any present-period explicit costs that will be incurred regardless of the present decision.

Opportunity Costs. Items taken from inventory may not have an explicit present-period cost if the firm does not choose to replace them in inventory by current purchases. Nevertheless, the relevant cost is the opportunity cost of that item—it could presumably be sold to another firm for its market value. If an item in inventory is worthless, having no market value (because it is outmoded by a new item, for example), its opportunity cost is zero, regardless of its historic cost. The historic cost of purchasing the item is an irrelevant, sunk, cost for the purposes of the present decision.

The most common application of the opportunity cost doctrine in decision making concerns the situation in which a particular resource has one or more uses at the same point of time. In this case, if the resource is used in the production of a particular output, it precludes the production of one or more other outputs.

EXAMPLE: Telarah Lite-Fab Industries produces steel gates, fences, balcony and porch railings, and similar items cut and welded from wrought iron. This firm does custom orders but also produces standard gates and railings, which are sold to retail hardware stores. The firm finds it can sell as much as it can produce of the standard gates and railings but prefers to do custom orders since the latter are invariably more profitable. At the present time the firm has no custom orders outstanding and is producing standard items at the rate of $10,000 per week sales value. Materials cost is $2,000 per week. Suppose now that a large custom order arrives that would take a week to manufacture and would cost $4,000 in materials. What is the opportunity cost of the firm's resources presently employed in the manufacture of the standard gates and railings? Note that with the standard items the firm is making $8,000 per week over and above materials cost. It must forego this $8,000 contribution to its other costs and profits if it takes the custom order. Thus, the firm must make at least $8,000 over and above materials cost on the custom order before it should even consider accepting the order. That is, the materials cost and the opportunity cost of the custom order add up to $12,000, and the firm must set its price at least that high or it would be better off sticking to the standard items.

Future Costs. Many decisions will have implications for future costs, both explicit and implicit. If the firm can form an expectation of a future cost which will be incurred or is likely to be incurred, as a consequence of the present decision, that cost must be included in the present analysis. Of course, it will be incorporated in present-value terms if known for certain or in expected-present-value terms if there is a probability distribution of the future cost's occurring.

EXAMPLE: A firm decides to produce a special order which it knows will cause severe wear and tear on its equipment, to the point where an overhaul will

TABLE 7-4.   Expected Present Value of Future Incremental Costs

Costs Expected $	Present Value	Probability	Expected Value $
0	0	0.10	0
50,000	32,875	0.20	6,575.00
100,000	65,750	0.30	19,725.00
150,000	98,625	0.25	24,656.25
200,000	131,500	0.10	13,150.00
250,000	164,375	0.05	8,218.75
	Expected Present Value		$72,325.00

be required within one year after the job is completed. Otherwise, the equipment would serve out its useful life without a major overhaul. This overhaul is expected to cost $2,000 and will be paid one year from now. Supposing an opportunity discount rate of 15 percent, the appropriate discount factor is 0.8696, and the present value of that cost is $2,000 × 0.8696 = $1,739.20. This figure should be included as an incremental cost of deciding to produce the special order.

EXAMPLE: Consider now a future cost which has a probability distribution of outcomes. Suppose a firm is considering copying another firm's design and knows that the other firm may sue for loss of business as a result. The possible legal costs and damages and the probabilities attached to each level of these costs are shown in Table 7-4. Given the congestion in the courts, it will take three years for the case to be resolved. We suppose that the firm's opportunity discount rate is 15 percent. Thus, the discount factor used to find the present value of the expected costs is 0.6575.

Thus, the EPV of the future legal costs are $72,325, a figure that should be included in the incremental costs of the decision to copy the other firm's design. Note that the firm should consider the possibility of such legal claims even when it does not willfully copy another firm's design. It may feel that its design is sufficiently different but that a court may nevertheless rule against it in the event of a lawsuit. In such cases the firm should calculate the EPV of the possible lawsuit and include this in its calculations.

Other future costs include labor problems; loss of future business; deterioration of supplier relations leading to higher input prices; cash flow problems necessitating borrowing costs; and so on. Any future cost, whether explicit or implicit, which can reasonably be expected to follow as a consequence of the current decision should be quantified in EPV terms and included in the incremental costs of the decision.

7.4   CONTRIBUTION ANALYSIS

We proceed now to use the concept of incremental costs in the contribution analysis of decision problems.

DEFINITION: The *contribution* of a decision is defined as the incremental revenues of that decision less the incremental costs of that decision. It should be interpreted as the "contribution made to overhead costs and profits" by the decision. Clearly, only those decisions that have a positive contribution should be undertaken; and where decisions are mutually exclusive, the one with the larger expected contribution is to be preferred. We shall illustrate contribution analysis with three common types of decision problems, but first let us clarify the notion of incremental revenues.

Incremental Revenues

DEFINITION: *Incremental revenues* are defined as the revenues which follow as a consequence of a particular decision. Like incremental costs, we should expect incremental revenues to have an explicit current-period component, a possible opportunity component, and a possible future component.

EXAMPLE: A firm bidding on a contract to supply electric light fixtures to a government office building tenders a very low bid for $265,000 and expects to avoid layoff costs of $100,000 if it wins the contract. It also expects to win future government contracts if it is the successful bidder on this contract, since this contract provides the firm with the opportunity to prove that it can supply a quality product and meet its production schedule.

The explicit current-period incremental revenues, if the firm wins the contract will be $265,000. But the contract is worth much more than $265,000 to the firm. If it doesn't win the contract, it will have to layoff workers and incur subsequent severance pay and future start-up costs associated with recruiting and training that amount to $100,000. If the firm does win the contract, this $100,000 is not spent and therefore stays in the bank. Avoidance of a cost as the result of a decision amounts to an opportunity revenue of the same amount.

DEFINITION: An *opportunity revenue* is a cost avoided as the result of a decision. Although there is no actual inflow of revenues, the outflow of revenues is avoided so that money that would otherwise be spent is still sitting in the bank, and the net effect is the same.

The *future* revenues associated with this pricing decision will be the expected present value of the contribution to overheads and profits associated with the future business generated as the result of winning the present contract.

EXAMPLE: Suppose the firm feels that if it wins the present job, it has a 50 percent chance of winning a similar contract next year. Suppose further that the next contract would be for $300,000 and would have an incremental cost of $250,000. The contribution from the next contract is, thus, $50,000 (if won). Given an opportunity discount rate of 15 percent, the present value of this is $50,000 $\times$ 0.8696 = $43,480. The expected present value is the present value times the probability of receiving it, or $43,480 $\times$ 0.50 = $21,740.

Thus, the EPV of the future revenue is $21,740, and this figure should be included in the incremental revenue calculation.

Thus, the firm's incremental revenue is the sum of the present-period explicit revenues, the opportunity revenues, and the EPV of future (consequential) revenues. Thus, the contract has total incremental revenues of $265,000 + $100,000 + $21,740, or $386,740 in total. This contract would, therefore, offer a positive EPV of contribution as long as incremental costs were less than $386,740.

NOTE: The EPV of the contribution to be received from future business resulting from the present decision can be regarded as the *goodwill* associated with the present decision. Goodwill is the EPV of contribution from future business, and if a decision involves an increment to goodwill, the amount of that contribution in EPV terms should be included as an incremental revenue. Oppositely, the present decision may cause the loss of future business. The EPV of the future contribution lost as the result of the present decision can be regarded as the *illwill* associated with this decision.

EXAMPLE: Consider the case of a construction firm that is considering bidding for a contract to move city garbage while the garbage workers are on strike. If this contract involves the possibility that the firm will lose future construction contracts due to the buyer's fear of retaliatory disruption by unionized construction workers, the EPV of the contribution expected to be lost on future jobs must be included as an incremental cost of taking the present contract to move the city's garbage.

Let us now demonstrate the application of contribution analysis in the context of three common types of decision problems.

Project A or Project B?

EXAMPLE: Suppose a firm is considering adopting either Project A or Project B but cannot adopt both, since they use the same set of machinery and labor. Project A, as shown in Table 7-5, promises sales of 10,000 units at $2 each, with materials, labor, variable overhead, and allocated overhead costs as shown, such that there is an apparent profit of $2,000. Project B promises sales revenues of $18,000, with materials, direct labor, and variable and allocated overhead as shown. The apparent profit from Project B is $4,000, and it

TABLE 7-5.   Income Statements for Projects A and B

Project A			Project B		
Revenues (10,000 @ $2)		$20,000	Revenues (6,000 @ $3)		$18,000
Costs			Costs		
Materials	$2,000		Materials	$5,000	
Direct labor	6,000		Direct labor	3,000	
Variable overhead	4,000		Variable overhead	3,000	
Allocated overhead	6,000	18,000	Allocated overhead	3,000	14,000
Profit		$ 2,000	Profit		$ 4,000

TABLE 7-6. Contribution Analysis for Projects A and B

Project A			Project B		
Incremental revenues		$20,000	Incremental revenues		$18,000
Incremental costs			Incremental costs		
Materials	$2,000		Materials	$5,000	
Direct labor	6,000		Direct labor	3,000	
Variable overhead	4,000	12,000	Variable overhead	3,000	11,000
Contribution		$ 8,000	Contribution		$ 7,000

would seem that Project B is preferable to Project A by virtue of its higher profitability.

When contribution analysis is applied to the above decision problem, however, the answer may be surprising. Consider Table 7-6, in which the incremental costs are subtracted from the incremental revenues to find the contribution of each project. Since the allocated overheads were not a cost incurred as a result of this particular decision, they are excluded from the contribution analysis, and it can be seen that Project A contributes more to overheads and profits than does Project B. The danger of including arbitrary allocations of fixed overheads is exemplified here. The overheads were allocated on the basis of a particular criterion, in this case as 100 percent of direct labor, but if they had been included in the decision process they would have caused an inferior decision to be made. Whatever method of overhead allocation is used, the danger is likely to persist. Hence we use contribution analysis, which allows an incisive look at the actual changes in costs and revenues that follow a particular decision.

Note that in this example we implicitly assumed the absence of all opportunity costs and revenues and that we proceeded as if there were neither future costs nor future revenues associated with either project. In practice, decision makers should not proceed so blithely but instead should assure themselves that *all* incremental costs and incremental revenues are included in the decision analysis. In the above example the difference between project A and B was only $1,000. Hence, our decision to choose project A was very sensitive to the assumption of zero opportunity and future costs and revenues. Our decision would have been reversed, however, if A had opportunity and future costs (in EPV terms) exceeding $1,000, for example. More generally, if the *net* opportunity and future revenues of project B had exceeded those of A by more than $1,000, the decison would have been reversed.[7]

---

[7]Recall our discussion of sensitivity analysis from Chapter 1. A decision is sensitive to the assumptions on which it is based to the extent that a change in those assumptions would cause a different decision to have been preferable. Thus, it is important to consider the dollar amount of cost variability or difference in contribution, which would cause the decision to be inappropriate. It is also useful to express this in terms of the totals, to see the *percentage* cost variability which would change the decision. In the present example, if the incremental costs of project A are understated by more than $1,000 or by more than $1,000/12,000 = 8.5 percent and the incremental costs of project B are accurate, the decision would be reversed.

TABLE 7-7. Wilson Tool Company: Bearing Department Costs

	Total	Per Unit
Direct materials	$ 38,640	$ 0.56
Direct labor	126,390	1.81
Allocated overhead	252,780	3.63
	$417,810	$ 6.00
Total bearing units produced:		69,635

Make or Buy?

EXAMPLE: The Wilson Tool Company manufactures high-quality power tools such as drills, jigsaws, and sanders. All these tools require the same roller-bearing unit, which the company manufactures in its own bearing department. Pertinent cost data for the past year of operations in that department are shown in Table 7-7.

Demand estimates indicate that the company should expand its production of some of the power tools and that an additional 7,500 bearing units will be required. The company could produce these in its bearing department but is considering having the additional units supplied by a specialist bearing firm. Wilson anticipates that it will require an increase of 15 percent in total direct labor costs and 12 percent in total materials costs to produce these additional units in-house. No additional capital expenditure will be necessary, since some machines currently have idle capacity. A specialist bearing producer who has been approached has studied the specifications and has offered to supply the 7,500 bearing units at a total cost of $30,000, or $4 per unit. Should Wilson make or buy the additional units?

We begin by comparing the incremental costs of the two alternatives facing Wilson. The incremental costs of buying them from the specialist come to $30,000, since this is the dollar amount that Wilson must outlay to obtain the additional units. To calculate the incremental costs of making the units in-house, we begin by calculating the increases in materials and direct labor costs that would be occasioned by the manufacture of those units. The 12-percent increase in the total material cost would imply an incremental material cost of $4,637, and a 15-percent increase in total direct labor costs would imply a $18,959 increase in that cost category. As shown in Table 7-8, the total of these two figures is $23,596, which is less than the incre-

TABLE 7-8. Incremental Costs of Making the Bearing Units

	Total	Per Unit
Direct materials	$ 4,637	$0.62
Direct labor	18,959	2.53
Allocated overhead	(?)	(?)
	$23,596	$3.15

mental cost of buying the units from outside. The decision to make, rather than buy, the additional units would thus appear to save the Wilson Tool Company a total of $6,404.[8]

Variability of Overheads.   The above analysis, however, does not consider the possibility that some part of overhead expenses may vary with the level of production of the bearing units. It is conceivable that some overhead cost components, such as electricity, office and administration expense, and cafeteria expense, might vary to some degree as a result of producing these units in-house. Rather than make arbitrary assumptions about the proportion of overheads that will vary, and since we do not have the information necessary to make a reasoned judgment, let us perform a sensitivity analysis on the decision that has been made. That is, we wish to know by how much the overhead expenses may vary before the decision to make the product would be the wrong decision. The answer is obviously that if overheads vary more than $6,404 as a result of this decision, the best decision would be to buy the product from the outside supplier. A $6,404 variation in overhead represents slightly more than a 2.5 percent variation in the allocated overhead. It is up to the decision maker to judge whether a variation of this percentage or dollar magnitude is likely to follow the decision to produce the product in-house.

Longer-Term Incremental Costs.   A number of other considerations should also enter into this decision. First, there is the issue of long-term supplier relations. Since Wilson may need a specialist producer some time in the future when it may be unable to produce the bearings in-house due to capacity limitations, it can perhaps establish itself as a customer of the supplier by giving this contract out at the present time, so that in future situations supply could be assured.

Second, there is the issue of the quality of the bearing units supplied by the outside firm as compared with those produced by Wilson. The decision maker would have to be assured that the units supplied from outside would be at least equal in quality to the standards desired. On the other hand, the specialist producer may be able to produce consistently higher quality bearing units, with subsequent impact upon the quality of Wilson Tools and on long-term buyer goodwill.

Third, the issue of labor relations must be considered. The decision to make the units involves an increase in the labor force, which may lead to crowded working conditions and overtaxed washroom and cafeteria facilities. The data indicate that labor efficiency is decreasing, since the incremental cost per unit to make the additional 7,500 units is $3.15 as compared with the total of $2.37 for direct materials and labor per unit shown in Table

---

[8]Since the incremental revenue is the same whether Wilson makes or buys the parts, we can do the contribution analysis on the basis of the incremental costs alone. Presuming that the incremental revenues exceed the incremental costs, the "make" alternative would seem to contribute more to overheads and profits than does the "buy" alternative.

7-7. It is conceivable that the hiring of additional labor units and the resultant increased congestion and reduced efficiency could cause a lowering of employee morale, with subsequent longer-term disadvantages to the profitability of the Wilson Tool Company.

In total, the decision maker must decide whether or not the expected present value of these eventualities, plus the possible variable components in overhead costs, is likely to exceed $6,404. If so, the decision should be to buy the product from outside.

Other Considerations. Certain additional doubts may be cast upon the above problem. First, the decision maker would need to be assured of the accuracy of the estimations that are involved in this decision. If, for example, demand for the tools does not increase as predicted and Wilson purchased the roller-bearing units from outside, this would be an irreversible commitment involving considerable expense, whereas the decision to make the units in-house could soon be suspended. The cost estimates are likewise subject to some doubt. These are presumably extrapolations on the estimated marginal costs of producing the units in-house. The decision maker would need to be assured that these extrapolations were based on the most reasonable assumptions concerning the efficiency of direct labor and material usage and that they are, consequently, the best estimates. To the extent that there is a distribution of both demand and cost estimates, a decision based on the most likely point estimate alone may result in an outcome that is quite different from the one expected.

Another question that arises in the above problem is whether or not the price quotation received is in fact the lowest-cost source of supply of these bearing units. We might assume that bids were solicited and that the lowest bid was being considered, but if this were not the case the decision maker should consult alternative sources of supply to confirm that the $30,000 price was in fact the best price at which the units may be bought from outside.

With these qualifications in mind, we turn now to the third category of decision problems in which contribution analysis is an appropriate solution procedure.

Take It or Leave It?

EXAMPLE: The Idaho Instruments Company produces a variety of pocket calculators and sells them through a distributing company. The purchasing agent for a large chain of department stores has recently approached Idaho Instruments with an offer to buy 20,000 units of its model X1-9 at the unit price of $8. Idaho's present production level of that model is 160,000 units annually, and it could supply the additional 20,000 units by foregoing production (and sale) of 5,000 of its more sophisticated X2-7 model. Pertinent data relating to these two models are shown in Table 7-9. Because of the highly mechanized production process, the per unit variable costs of each

TABLE 7-9. Idaho Instruments Company:
Per Unit Data on Calculators

	Model X1-9	Model X2-7
Materials	$ 1.65	$ 1.87
Direct labor	2.32	3.02
Variable overhead	1.03	1.11
Fixed overhead	5.00	6.00
Profits	2.00	2.40
Price to distributor	$12.00	$14.40

model are believed to be constant over a wide range of outputs. The sales manager for Idaho Instruments is reluctant to sell the X1-9 model for $8 when he normally receives $12 from the distributing company, and he has attempted to negotiate with the purchasing agent. The latter, however, insists that $8 is his only offer. Should Idaho Instruments take it or leave it?

Since the average variable cost for both models is expected to be constant over a wide range, we can calculate the incremental cost of this decision on the basis of the average variable cost. The average variable cost is the sum of the first three components in the table, and hence 20,000 additional units of the model X1-9 (with AVC = $5.00) will add $100,000 to the cost levels. This figure is not the total incremental cost, however, since there is an opportunity cost involved. The production of the additional 20,000 units will come partly from the idle capacity that is to be utilized and partly at the expense of 5,000 units of the model X2-7. The opportunity costs of using the resources that previously produced the X2-7 are the value of those resources in that alternate use. The net value to Idaho Instruments of employing the resources in the production of 5,000 units of the X2-7 is the contribution made by those 5,000 units. From Table 7-9 it can be found that the contribution per unit to overheads and profits is $8.40. Hence the opportunity costs are the total foregone contribution, or $42,000. In Table 7-10 we show the contribution analysis of this problem. The incremental revenues are $160,000, and the incremental costs add up to $142,000. Hence the contribution to overheads and profits that would follow from the

TABLE 7-10. Contribution Analysis of Calculator Decision Problem

Incremental revenues		
20,000 units of X1-9 @ $8.00		$160,000
Incremental costs		
Variable costs		
20,000 units of X1-9 @ $5.00	$100,000	
Opportunity costs (Contribution foregone)		
5,000 units of X2-7 @ $8.40	42,000	142,000
Contribution		$ 18,000

decision to take the department store's offer is $18,000. Thus profits would be $18,000 greater than they would be otherwise, or losses would be $18,000 less.

An alternate method of arriving at the same contribution would be to subtract from the incremental revenues the revenues forgone when the 5,000 units of X2-7 were not sold at $14.40 (that is, $72,000) and subtract from the incremental cost of producing the extra units of the model X1-9 the decremental costs of not producing 5,000 units of the model X2-7 (that is, $30,000). The net adjustment as the result of these manipulations is $72,000 — $30,000, or $42,000, which is exactly the opportunity cost figure we have entered in Table 7-10. The opportunity cost method achieves the same results with some economy of effort, but more importantly, perhaps, it draws the decision maker's attention to the possible alternate uses of resources.

There are some qualifications to the above decision, however. The first issue is that of substitutability between the units sold to the department store and those sold to the distributing company. The above analysis has proceeded upon the implicit assumption that the sale of 20,000 units to the department store will be *in addition to*, and nonsubstitutable with, the 160,000 units sold through the distributing company. To the extent that some customers now buy this product through the department store rather than through the distributing company, Idaho Instruments will be foregoing an amount of $4 per unit, or the difference in the price charged to the two wholesale buyers. If the department stores will tap a totally new market for the calculators, we can presume that total sales will increase by the entire 20,000 units and that there would indeed be a contribution of $18,000 following this decision. On the other hand, if the sale to the department store reduces normal sales, to what degree could this happen before the decision to take the offer becomes the wrong one? Since the difference in contribution per unit is $4, the number of units that it would take to erode that $18,000 total contribution down to zero is $18,000 ÷ 4 = 4,500. Thus, if in the judgment of the decision maker there are likely to be at least 4,500 units purchased from the department stores which would otherwise have been purchased from the normal distribution channels, the decision should be reversed.

An additional consideration here is that of retailer relations. Doubtless the firms in the normal distributing channels will become aware that the department stores were given a better deal, and these firms may in turn look elsewhere for their supplies. Thus any short-term gain by selling to the department store may be outweighed by longer-term losses from a deterioration of the relationship currently enjoyed with the distributing company and with other firms.[9]

A third area of concern relates to the image of Idaho Instruments' cal-

---

[9]In fact, if Idaho Instruments continues to favor the department store with a lower price, it may run afoul of legislation concerning price discrimination. Legal constraints on pricing are discussed briefly in Chapter 11.

PRODUCTION AND COST ANALYSIS

culators. Presumably the department stores, having purchased at a relatively low cost per unit, will price below the current market price for the model X1-9. This may have a detrimental impact upon the quality image currently held by that model. Since many consumers judge quality on the basis of price when they have no alternate means of discovering quality or durability, the lowering of the price of the X1-9 may reduce the consumer's perception of its quality. Alternatively, this contract with the department store may be the beginning of a long and successful relationship with that particular buyer and may add to rather than detract from the image of the calculators and the total sales.

In summary, then, the decision maker must consider all possible future ramifications of the decision and must calculate the expected present value or loss of each eventuality. The net expected present value or loss must be added to or subtracted from the immediate contribution before the final decision is made.

Multiperiod Contribution Analysis

Many decisions involve costs that will be incurred or revenues that will be received in future time periods. As discussed in Chapter 1 these costs and revenues must be converted to present-value terms in order to make them comparable with cost and revenues incurred or received in the present period. In Chapter 1 we spoke simply of "profits" in the first and subsequent periods which had to be discounted back to present value. We now know that it is the *contribution* in each future period that is important for decision making, and not profits in either the accounting or the economic sense.

Longer-term considerations enter the decision-making problem in multi-period analysis. First, some fixed expenses may become variable at a point in the future and may need to be replaced, increased, or reduced as a result of the decision that has been taken. Those fixed costs that are incurred as a result of the implementation of a current decision must be included as an incremental cost. Second, incremental revenues and incremental costs in future periods will be subject to some uncertainty, and the decision maker may be supplied with a distribution of possible future revenues and costs related to each decision. The decision maker must then calculate the expected value of incremental revenues and incremental costs for each alternative before attempting to calculate the present value of the contribution from the alternative decisions.

EXAMPLE: Suppose a metal-fabricating firm is considering entry into the metal windows market. The firm must produce either steel windows or aluminum windows. The initial investment in plant and equipment would be the same whichever market is entered, but the production of steel windows causes the plant and equipment to wear out every two years, whereas aluminum windows are less demanding in that they allow plant and equipment to be used

TABLE 7-11. Multiperiod Contribution Analysis: Steel Windows

| | YEAR OF OPERATION | | | |
	1	2	3	4
Incremental revenues	$60,000	$50,000	$40,000	$30,000
Incremental costs				
Materials	15,000	14,000	12,000	10,000
Direct labor	25,000	23,000	16,000	12,000
Indirect labor	1,000	—	1,000	—
Plant and equipment	6,000	—	5,000	—
Contribution	$13,000	$13,000	$ 6,000	$ 8,000
Discount factors (12%)	.9454	.8441	.7537	.6729
Present values	$12,290	$10,973	$ 4,522	$ 5,383

Total contribution (undiscounted) $40,000
Present value of total contribution $33,168

for a period of four years. Suppose that the firm's planning horizon is also four years and that the projected incremental revenues and costs are as shown in Tables 7-11 and 7-12.

The data in the tables reflect the following features of the production and marketing of the alternate products. Steel windows use cheaper materials but are more expensive in the use of labor and machines. The current market price is considerably higher for steel windows but is expected to decline progressively over the period of four years because of the growth of competition in this relatively profitable segment. Aluminum windows, on the other hand, are more expensive in the use of materials but require less labor and equipment cost per unit. The aluminum windows segment is considerably larger than that for steel windows but is characterized by a lower price level and a greater number of competitors. The firm expects, however,

TABLE 7-12. Multiperiod Contribution Analysis: Aluminum Windows

| | YEAR OF OPERATION | | | |
	1	2	3	4
Incremental revenues	$ 30,000	$35,000	$50,000	$70,000
Less incremental costs				
Materials	15,000	17,000	22,000	28,000
Direct labor	10,000	11,000	15,000	18,000
Indirect labor	1,000	—	—	—
Plant and equipment	6,000	—	—	—
Contribution	$−2,000	$ 7,000	$13,000	$24,000
Discount factors (12%)	.9454	.8441	.7537	.6729
Present values	$−1,891	$ 5,909	$ 9,798	$16,150

Total contribution (undiscounted) $42,000
Present value of total contribution $29,966

to increase its market share over the four-year period and to progressively raise its price by small increments as it becomes more firmly extablished in the market. Note that the incremental cost of indirect labor refers to the cost of installing the plant and equipment and that the purchase and installation of plant and equipment for the production of steel windows occurs again in year three.

The total contribution over the four-year period (undiscounted) is higher for the aluminum windows by a margin of $2,000. We must compare the *present values* of these expected returns, however. Suppose the firm's next best investment opportunity for the funds involved (at a similar level of risk) is to put the funds into bond issues with a return of 12 percent per annum. Thus the firm's opportunity discount rate is 12 percent. In this case we should expect costs and revenues to be incurred and received more or less *continuously* throughout the year, rather than as a lump sum at the end of each year. Table B-2 in Appendix B gives the appropriate discount factors for continuous cash flows.[10]

In the lower part of Tables 7-11 and 7-12 we calculate the present values of the contributions of each year for each option. Adding up these present values of the contributions of each year, we find that the total present value is $3,202 greater for the steel window project than for the aluminum window project, notwithstanding the fact that the total (undiscounted) contribution from the latter is expected to be $2,000 greater. This demonstrates the influence that the conformation of the stream of contributions has upon the present value of that stream. For steel windows the major part of the contribution is to be received in the first two years, whereas for aluminum windows it is expected to be received in the latter two years. Dollars received further into the future are discounted more heavily, and hence the present value of the steel window proposition is expected to be greater. Had the decision been made simply on the basis of total contribution (undiscounted), a suboptimal decision would have been made.

In the above decision-making problem we must assume that the decision maker has examined all alternative investment possibilities and is convinced that the two projects under consideration are the two best projects that the firm may become involved in. If the decision maker is not satisfied that this is so, he or she should undertake a review of all possible alternatives. Unforeseen opportunities that may arise during the second or subsequent year of production cannot be evaluated, however. The decision must be made *now* on the basis of information that is currently available. If a lucrative opportunity were to arise during one of the latter years, the decision maker would be faced with the decision problem of whether to continue the involvement in steel windows or to divert resources to the new opportunity. That decision would of course be made at the later point in time on the basis of the information available at that time.

---

[10]The appropriate cash flow conventions were discussed in Chapter 1 in detail, and you may wish to refresh your memory by referring back to pages 11-22.

7.5 SUMMARY

The cost concept of prime importance for decision making is that of incremental costs. *Incremental* costs are those that are incurred as a result of the decision under consideration. To calculate incremental costs, however, the decision maker must consider a variety of other cost concepts, such as direct and indirect, explicit and implicit, opportunity and historic, and relevant and sunk costs. Each of these cost concepts was illustrated with reference to a particular business example.

Contribution analysis seeks to ascertain the contribution to overheads and profits, or the excess of incremental revenues over incremental costs, which is expected to follow a particular decision. The decision-making criterion outlined in this chapter was that one should choose the alternative that promises the greatest positive contribution to overheads and profits. As shown in some of the examples, however, the relevant incremental costs and revenues included a host of future considerations, some of which are not easily quantifiable. The issues that must be investigated include the following: data accuracy, false leads in the data, opportunity costs, cash-flow considerations, competitor reactions, labor relations, supplier relations, customer relations, and whether or not the decision can be made in isolation from other decisions. The decision maker must attempt to quantify each of these issues and weigh these against the immediate contribution associated with each alternative.

Breakeven analysis is related to contribution analysis and is largely concerned with examining the feasibility of certain cost, price, and output levels. Breakeven analysis is examined in the appendix to this chapter. In Chapter 8 we shall examine cost estimation techniques that allow estimates of cost functions and the calculations for average variable costs, marginal costs, and incremental costs to be made.

DISCUSSION QUESTIONS

7-1. How might the accountant's calculation of indirect costs differ from the economist's calculation of fixed costs?

7-2. Explain how the economist would calculate the implicit cost of a fixed factor, such as plant and equipment, which is used in the production process.

7-3. When is the opportunity cost of an input to the production process equal to zero? If an input has several different alternative uses, how is the opportunity cost of that input determined?

7-4. Explain the economist's notions of normal and pure profits. Why wouldn't a firm wish to liquidate its investment and leave the industry if it was simply breaking even with $TR = TC$?

7-5. Define the *relevant costs* for decision making. When do the relevant costs include some elements of fixed costs?

7-6. Why does contribution analysis ignore the fixed overhead costs that might otherwise be included in the cost analysis of a decision?

7-7. How should future considerations be evaluated and included in contribution analysis?

7-8. In multiperiod contribution analysis, what determines the choice of the appropriate discount factors?

7-9. Explain how you would calculate the incremental cost of a decision which might lead to a future class-action lawsuit by consumers for damages caused by your product.

7-10. Explain and contrast the concepts of opportunity costs and opportunity revenues.

PROBLEMS AND SHORT CASES

7-1. The Muscle-Man Company manufactures forklift tractors, and it supplies some parts to other manufacturers of forklifts. It fabricates most of the component parts but buys the engines, hydraulic systems, wheels, and tires from suppliers. Demand estimates indicate that Muscle-Man should increase its production level from 60 forklift units monthly to 70 units monthly. Sufficient slack exists in most departments to allow this, except that production of 10 extra chassis assemblies could be attained only by reallocating labor and equipment from fork-assembly manufacture to chassis-assembly manufacture. The fork-assembly department currently produces 90 units monthly, and it supplies the 30 surplus units to other manufacturers at $188 each. With the expanded production level, 70 forks would be required, but the labor and equipment responsible for the remaining 20 units is thought to be just sufficient to produce the 10 extra chassis assemblies. Alternatively, the extra chassis assemblies could be purchased from a supplier, and the lowest quote is from Fenton Fabricators, for $305 per unit. The costs of the chassis and fork departments for a representative month were as follows:

| Costs | DEPARTMENT | |
	Chassis	Fork
Direct materials	$ 4,650	$ 2,070
Direct labor	6,300	4,050
Depreciation	750	500
Allocated burden of fuel, electricity, office, and other overheads (200% of direct labor)	12,600	8,100
Total	$24,300	$14,720
Production level	60	90

(a) Should Muscle-Man make or buy the ten extra chassis assemblies?

(b) What qualifications would you add to your decision?

7-2. The Crombie Castings Company produces two products, A and B, for which pertinent data are as follows for the past month:

	A	B
Sales (units)	840,000	220,000
Price per unit ($)	2.50	4.25
Materials cost ($)	386,400	105,600
Direct labor ($)	529,200	277,200
Overheads ($)	567,893	297,467

C.C.C.'s plant and labor are operating at absolute full capacity, but the company is unable to meet the demand for Product A, which is thought to be one million units per month. One way to meet the demand for A would be to reduce the output of Product B and to shift resources to the production of A. For each unit reduction in the output of B, the firm could produce two units of A with the labor that is released. Note that average variable costs are constant in both production processes. Alternatively, C.C.C. could contract out to have Product A manufactured by another firm in the same industry and sold as if this product were from the C.C.C. plant. Donald, Dodge, and Draper, a firm that holds a minor share of the same markets and has considerable excess capacity, was approached on this issue. D.D.D. is willing to sign a contract to supply the extra 160,000 units of A at a price of $2.25 per unit.

How should C.C.C. resolve this problem? Support your answer with discussion of the various issues involved.

7-3. Commodore Candies produces a three-pound box of chocolates which it sells at a price of $6.75 to various retail outlets. Commodore's output capacity for this product is 10,000 units per month with a one-shift operation, but it can produce more using overtime labor, which has a premium of 15 percent over regular labor cost. Variable overhead expenses would be 10 percent higher per unit of output for overtime production. Average variable costs are constant from 8,000 to 10,000 units and are then constant at the higher level. Costs of production for the current month's output of 8,000 units are as follows:

	Total Costs $
Raw materials	9,600
Direct labor	17,600
Variable overhead	9,200
Fixed overhead	14,500

Today Commodore is faced with a decision problem. A large retail chain has offered to purchase a bulk order of 4,000 units at $6 per unit, to be delivered within thirty days. Should Commodore take this order? Support your answer with discussion of the issues involved. Defend any assumptions that you make.

7-4. The XYZ Co. produces and sells a product directly to consumers at a price of $6 per unit. Sales have been increasing at 10 percent per month and this trend is expected to continue. Average variable costs are expected to remain constant at the current levels. The company's maximum output capacity is 200,000 with the present investment in plant and equipment.

Following is a summary record of the firm's January production and cost levels:

	January
Sales (units)	171,661
Materials ($)	211,143
Direct labor ($)	520,133
Indirect factory labor ($)	110,500
Office and administrative salaries ($)	64,000
Light and heat ($)	12,116
Other fixed expenses ($)	24,680

A national mail-order company has asked XYZ to consider the following deal: 10,000 units of the product, to be ready at the end of February, at the price of $5 per unit.

Should XYZ accept the order from the mail-order company? What strategy do you suggest? Support your answer with discussion of the various issues involved.

7-5. A large department store has called for bids for the following contract: A truck plus its driver must be available, given one day's notice, whenever the store's own trucks are fully utilized, to deliver goods to suburban households. The number of days for which a truck will be required is twenty, and the number of miles is expected to be 4,000 for the coming year.

You are the manager of the Clark Rent-a-Truck Co. and have a number of trucks that you rent out on a day-to-day basis. One truck is a little older than the others, and it is always the last to be rented out because it does less for public relations than the new trucks. In the absence of a contract with the department store, you expect this older truck to be rented out two-thirds of the three hundred "rental days" this coming year. Your normal rental charge is $25.00 per day plus $.35 per mile.

You estimate the costs of operating the older truck to be as follows, assuming 10,000 miles of rental over the coming year:

Depreciation	$ 800
Interest on investment in truck	360
License fees and taxes	125
Insurance	440
Parking fees (permanently rented space)	300
Gasoline	1,367
Oil, grease, and preventive maintenance	600
Repairs	1,450
Allocated overheads	1,650

You can hire a driver on one-day's notice for $50 per day. A one-time cost of $400 will be involved in fitting the truck with a special loading ramp required by the contract. This ramp will not interfere with the normal use of the truck.

On the basis of this information, and making whatever assumptions you feel are necessary and reasonable, calculate your incremental costs of undertaking this contract.

7-6. Corcoran Calculators Incorporated is one of the leading manufacturers in the electronic calculator industry. Management is now considering plans for the production of the company's latest development—the minicomputer. The company already manufactures most of the parts, but the design of the new fuse trays would require the additional expenditure of $23,000 for special auxiliary equipment, which has a useful life of only two years and has no scrap value. The marketing department has estimated that sales would require the production of 4,500 fuse trays the first year and 7,000 the following year.

The company has the option of either producing these trays in-house or having them supplied by an outside electronics specialist at a cost of $32.50 per tray. Corcoran would incur additional storage and carrying costs associated with this latter alternative of $26,000 over the first year and $40,000 over the following year.

The breakdown of the in-house manufacturing expenses for the 11,500 units is expected to be as follows:

		Unit Cost
Labor		$10.00
Raw materials and components		20.00
Variable overhead		4.00
Fixed cost		
Existing equipment	$3.50	
New equipment	2.00	5.50
		$39.50

The company's opportunity discount rate is 15 percent. The payments to the supplier would be made in a lump sum at the end of each of the two years. If produced in-house, there would be a continual outflow of funds as the units were produced, although the special equipment would have to be paid for immediately.

Assuming that the increased production will have a negligible effect on the present operation of the plant, what would your recommendation be on the question of making or buying the fuse trays? (Justify your answer with all supporting calculations and any qualifications you might wish to make.)

7-7. The Tico Taco Company has estimated the following total variable cost function from cost and output data pairs observed over the past ten weeks:

$$\text{TVC} = 435.85 - 1.835Q^2 + 3.658Q^3$$

where TVC represents thousands of dollars and Q represents thousands of boxes of tacos produced. TTC is currently producing 2,000 boxes weekly and is considering expanding its output to 2,200 boxes weekly. To do this, it will have to hire another taco machine operator ($400 per week) and lease another taco machine ($200 per week).

(a) Estimate the incremental costs of the extra 200 boxes weekly.

(b) State all the assumptions and qualifications which underlie your answer to part (a).

7-8. You are the manager of a ski resort. Based on industry projections of this season's demand, your competitive position, and your estimates of costs, you have set the lift ticket price at $8 per day. Due to the variability of demand between weekdays, weekends, and holidays, you hire labor on the basis of the expected demand for each particular day, based on past years' records and on current snow conditions. Extra labor is readily available on a day-to-day basis from the pool of local "ski-bums."

You employ one lift attendant for every 250 tickets sold, in addition to a basic staff of four lift attendants. Ski-patrol persons are required at the rate of one for every 400 tickets sold in addition to the two patrol persons who are required regardless of ticket sales volume. All other labor employees connected with the skiing operation are required regardless of sales volume. Lift attendants are hired at the rate of $25 per day plus a free lift ticket to be used subsequently. Ski-patrol persons receive $30 per day plus a free meal in your restaurant that evening.

Your restaurant serves only one standardized meal, an "all you can eat" buffet for $3 per person. Based on expected demand fluctuations, you have hired various people on a full-time and part-time basis for the season. The $3 price represents the average cost of materials and direct labor plus a 50-percent markup to contribute to restaurant overheads and profits. Unexpected fluctuations in demand can be handled, since you keep a large inventory of supplies and can hire temporary labor at short notice. There is, however, an additional $10-per-person cost for this temporary labor, since these people are handled through an employment agency and require transportation to the restaurant. To maintain your standard of meals and service, you hire kitchen staff at the rate of one person for every 45 meals expected to be sold and serving staff at the rate of one person for every 80 meals expected to be sold.

Today you received a phone call from the Students' Association of a nearby university which is asking around various ski resorts for the following deal: Ten busloads of students (500 in total) will come to your resort on Friday of next week if they can get a lift ticket *and* a meal for $4 per person. Your expected sales for that Friday, before this possibility arose, were 1,500 lift tickets and 900 meals.

Should you give the students the deal they are asking for? Explain your decision and state any possible qualifications to that decision.

PRODUCTION AND COST ANALYSIS

Davidson, S., J. S. Schindler, C. P. Stickney, and R. L. Weil. *Managerial Accounting— An Introduction to Concepts, Methods, and Uses*, chaps. 4, 5, 6. Hinsdale, Ill.: The Dryden Press, 1978.

Greer, H. C. "Anyone for Widgets?" *Journal of Accountancy*, April 1966. (Despite its title, this paper contains an excellent discussion of relevant and irrelevant costs.)

Haynes, W. W., and W. R. Henry. *Managerial Economics: Analysis and Cases* (3rd ed.), chaps. 2 and 5. Dallas, Tex.: Business Publications, 1974.

Horngren, C. T. *Cost Accounting: A Managerial Emphasis* (5th ed.), chaps. 2 and 3. Englewood Cliffs, N.J.: Prentice-Hall, Inc., 1982.

————. *Introduction to Management Accounting* (5th ed.), chaps. 2, 3, 4, 5. Englewood Cliffs, N.J.: Prentice-Hall, Inc., 1981.

Pappas, J. L., and E. F. Brigham. *Managerial Economics*, (3rd ed.), chap. 8. Hinsdale, Ill.: The Dryden Press, 1979.

Simon, J. L. *Applied Managerial Economics*, chaps. 8 and 9. Englewood Cliffs, N.J.: Prentice-Hall, Inc., 1975.

Webb, S. C. *Managerial Economics*, chap. 5. Boston: Houghton Mifflin, 1976.

APPENDIX 7A: BREAKEVEN ANALYSIS: APPLICATIONS AND LIMITATIONS

A graphical tool of some value in decision making is the breakeven chart. When applied correctly it allows the decision maker considerable insight into the decision problem and aids in the choice of the optimal price, cost, and output levels for each product.

DEFINITION: The *breakeven volume* is defined as that sales level for which total revenue equals total cost. Decision makers are concerned with the breakeven volume level, since it is beyond this level that revenues begin to exceed costs and the decision becomes profitable. To the extent that the breakeven point can be surpassed, the decision maker is likely to smile more broadly; the worrisome factor is usually whether or not sales volume will attain the breakeven level.

In Figure 7A-1 we show the breakeven charts under three different cost and revenue situations. In part (a) of the figure you will notice that total revenue and total cost are equal at two separate output levels. At point *A* total revenue has risen to equality with total costs, and at point *B* total revenue has fallen to equality with the rising total cost. In the interval between point *A* and point *B* the firm is experiencing profits, as shown by the profit curve on the same graph, and to the left of point *A* and to the right of point *B* the firm experiences losses. In part (b) of the figure we show a situation where the price level remains constant, while costs are similar to those in part (a). Again there are two breakeven points, and profits are positive in the

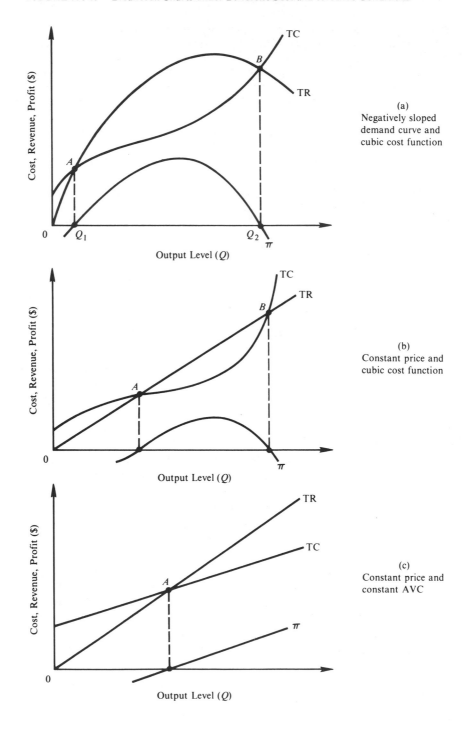

FIGURE 7A-1.   Breakeven Charts under Different Cost and Revenue Conditions

(a)
Negatively sloped
demand curve and
cubic cost function

(b)
Constant price and
cubic cost function

(c)
Constant price and
constant AVC

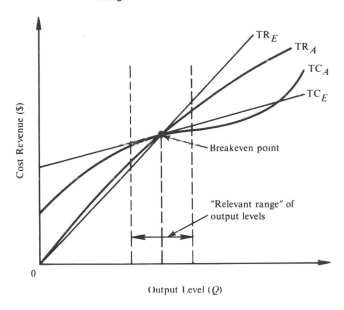

FIGURE 7A-2. Linear Revenue and Cost Functions in the Relevant Range

output range between these two breakeven points. In part (c) of the figure we show the most commonly used form of breakeven analysis, in which both price and average variable cost are constant. Notice that the profit function is therefore a straight line.

The use of linear total costs and total revenue functions, as in part (c) of Figure 7A-1, greatly facilitates breakeven analysis. Typically the decision maker will obtain an estimate of expected volume level and of the cost and price levels at that volume level. Linear extrapolation from those expected cost and price values around the expected volume level obviates the problem of ascertaining the actual variance in average variable costs, and it recognizes that prices are not likely to be variable by small amounts because of the price awareness thresholds of customers.

It is important to recognize, however, that linear revenue and cost functions are generally approximations of the actual form of the cost and revenue functions. The assumption of constant prices and average variable costs is likely to become progressively less accurate as we move away from expected volume levels. Most decision problems, however, will concern output levels within a fairly limited range of expected volume levels, and we call this limited range the *relevant range*. In Figure 7A-2 we show linear revenue and cost functions that are tolerably good approximations of the curvilinear revenue and cost functions over the range of output levels in which the decision maker is interested. Within this relevant range the linear functions are a sufficient approximation of the actual functions for most decision-making purposes.

Applications of Breakeven Analysis

Breakeven analysis can be of considerable value to the decision maker when decisions must be made about the price and quality levels of a proposed product. In Figure 7A-3 a comparison is shown of the breakeven points at two different price and variable cost levels. Suppose that initially the decision maker was considering the price and cost levels represented by the curves TR and TC. The indicated breakeven sales volume is shown as Q_4. Let us suppose that the decision maker feels that it is unlikely that the product will attain that sales volume and hence is likely to incur losses. The decision maker may rectify this situation in one way or in a combination of two ways: First, the price may be raised; and/or second, the average variable cost may be lowered. The latter adjustment has implications for the quality of the product, since lowering average variable costs presumably implies the use of lower-quality raw materials or the use of less labor input per unit of output. It can be seen that at the initial price a reduction in the average variable cost level reduces the breakeven volume to that shown as Q_3. Alternatively, an increase in the price level with costs per unit remaining unchanged would reduce the breakeven volume to output level Q_2. Finally, an increase in the price level and a reduction in the cost level would reduce the breakeven volume to Q_1. The decision maker must consider each of these breakeven volume points in conjunction with the estimates of sales volume at those price and quality levels.

FIGURE 7A-3.   Comparison of Breakeven Points at Different Price and Variable Cost Levels

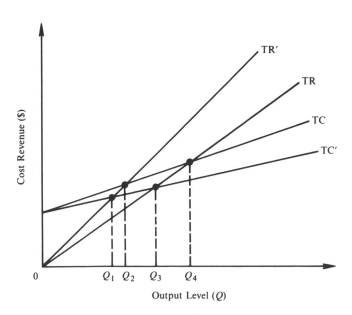

PRODUCTION AND COST ANALYSIS

Algebraic calculation of the breakeven point is likely to be less time consuming than the graphical procedure. To find the formula for the breakeven volume, recall that it occurs where total revenue equals total costs, which may be expressed as follows:

$$P(Q) = \text{AVC}(Q) + \text{FC}$$

$$\text{or} \quad Q(P - \text{AVC}) = \text{FC}$$

$$\text{or} \quad Q = \frac{\text{FC}}{P - \text{AVC}} \tag{7A-1}$$

Since $(P - \text{AVC})$ is equal to the contribution margin per unit, we may restate this as

$$Q = \frac{\text{FC}}{\text{CM}} \tag{7A-2}$$

Thus, the breakeven volume may be calculated simply by dividing the total fixed costs by the contribution margin per unit.[1]

In multiproduct firms, where each product must attain a particular profit target to maintain its place in the product mix and to withstand being replaced by another profitable product, breakeven analysis can be used to find the sales volume at which this profit target will be attained. Note that a profit target is a constant dollar value, just as fixed costs are a constant dollar value. Hence the profit target may be added to the fixed-cost figure to represent the total dollar amount that must be obtained via contributions from each unit, before fixed costs and the profit target are covered. Algebraically, this may be expressed as follows:

$$Q = \frac{\text{FC} + \pi}{\text{CM}} \tag{7A-3}$$

Having calculated the sales volume necessary to cover the fixed costs and to attain the desired target profit, the decision maker must then consider whether or not that target sales volume is likely to be achieved. If this appears quite unlikely, the decision maker may wish to revise the target profit, change either price or average variable costs, or delete this product from the product mix in favor of a more profitable product.

A third area in which the breakeven analysis may be useful is that where a particular product may be manufactured under two or more technologies of production. Suppose a firm is considering three alternate means of manufacturing a product for which the market price is established at

---

[1]Note that this form is applicable only for linear *TR* and *TC* functions. If either or both of these are not linear, the contribution margin will vary with the level of output, and Equation (7A-1) should be used to find the breakeven point.

FIGURE 7A-4. Breakeven Charts for Different Production Technologies

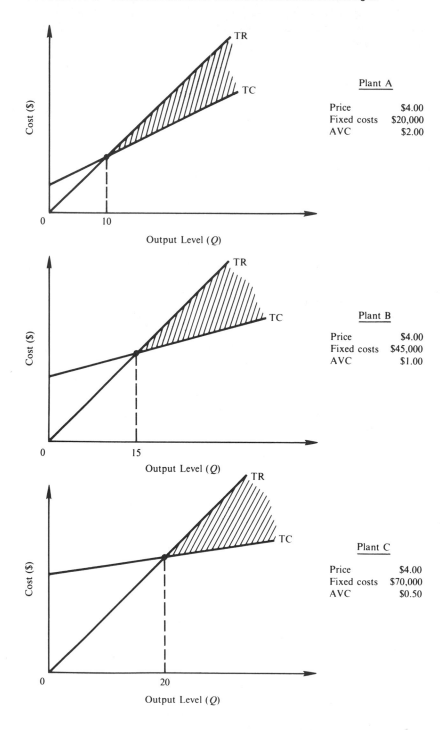

Plant A

Price	$4.00
Fixed costs	$20,000
AVC	$2.00

Plant B

Price	$4.00
Fixed costs	$45,000
AVC	$1.00

Plant C

Price	$4.00
Fixed costs	$70,000
AVC	$0.50

$4.00 per unit. In Figure 7A-4 we show the three technologies under which this product may be manufactured. The total revenue function in each graph is the same, indicating that the firm does not expect to be able to influence market price by its actions. Plant A is characterized by fixed costs of $20,000 and a constant average variable cost of $2.00 per unit of output. Plant B is characterized by fixed costs of $45,000 and a constant average variable cost of $1.00 per unit. Plant C involves the much higher fixed costs of $70,000 but a low and constant average variable cost of $0.50 per unit. Using this information and Equation (7A-2), one may verify that the breakeven points are 10,000, 15,000, and 20,000 units, respectively.

Suppose the decision maker's estimate of sales volume is distributed around a mean of 12,000 units. The breakeven charts of Figure 7A-4 indicate that Plant A would be the most suitable choice, since its breakeven point is at the low end of this distribution. And barring an eventuality at the extreme left-hand tail of the distribution, Plant A would be profitable at the likely sales levels.

In Table 7A-1 we show the profitability levels at various expected sales levels for each of the three technologies. Table 7A-1 summarizes the information given in Figure 7A-4. Plant A remains the most profitable up to the output level of almost 29,000 units, at which point it is overtaken by Plant B. Plant C does not become the most profitable technology until it has an output level greater than 50,000 units. The decision maker must use this information in conjunction with the probability distribution of expected sales levels, before deciding on the size of plant to implement.

Operating Leverage. The differences in the contribution per unit after the breakeven point are due to the extent to which fixed factors are substituted for variable factors in the production process. The greater this substitution, or the more capital intensive the technology, the greater the operating leverage of the production process. *Operating leverage* refers to the extent to which the incremental units sold contribute to overheads and profits. With linear cost and revenue functions, it is constant over the relevant range (equal to the contribution per unit); but with nonlinear total costs and/or total revenue functions, the operating leverage will vary as the slopes of the functions vary. Operating leverage shows the sensitivity of total contribution

TABLE 7A-1. Profitability at Various Output Levels with Differing Technologies

Expected Sales Level	Plant A	Plant B	Plant C
10,000	Breakeven	−15,000	−35,000
15,000	10,000	Breakeven	−22,500
20,000	20,000	15,000	Breakeven
30,000	40,000	45,000	35,000
40,000	60,000	75,000	70,000
50,000	80,000	105,000	105,000
60,000	100,000	135,000	140,000

to changes in volume. Since the difference between total contribution and total profits is a constant (that is, fixed costs), operating leverage also shows the sensitivity of total profits to changes in volume. When a product is subject to volatile swings in sales in response to fluctuations in general economic conditions, greater leverage involves greater risk of wide variations in profits.[2]

Limitations of Breakeven Analysis

At the beginning of our discussion of breakeven analysis, the cautious note was injected that breakeven analysis is a useful tool *when correctly applied*. It is essential that the form of the total revenue and total cost functions used in breakeven analysis accurately reflect, or at least be a tolerable approximation of, the actual cost and revenue conditions. As indicated, the assumption of linear cost and revenue conditions may be a tolerable approximation within a relatively limited range of outputs but becomes progressively less accurate at higher output levels, because of the likelihood of diminishing returns to the variable factors and/or the necessity of reducing price in order to actually sell those higher output levels.

Second, breakeven analysis must be used in the incremental sense. That is, the total cost function must represent those costs that are incurred as a result of a decision to produce this particular product, and it must not include costs that would be incurred regardless of this decision. In the case of a firm that produces only one product, the total cost function will represent all costs incurred by the firm. If implicit costs are included at their opportunity cost value, the breakeven point will be the point of zero economic profits. Similarly, within a multiproduct firm where each department produces a single product, the total overhead costs of a particular department may be included in the total cost function in breakeven analysis. Beyond the breakeven point, the profits earned by that department will represent a contribution to the overheads and profits of the entire firm. Otherwise, in multiproduct firms, only the incremental overheads should be included and then profits are the contribution to the joint overheads and profits of the entire firm. Care must be taken, therefore, that the vertical intercept of the total cost function relates to simply the incremental and/or separable fixed costs associated with that particular product.

Summary

Breakeven analysis, like the decision tree, is a graphical aid to decision making. It allows the decision maker to consider the sales volumes which would be required in order to break even, given certain prices and cost structures. By

---

[2]Operating leverage is in fact an elasticity measure. Since it measures the relative responsiveness of profits to a change in quantity demanded, it can be calculated as the percentage change in profits over the percentage change in quantity demanded. It is the "volume elasticity of profit," if you wish.

reference to the estimates of the demand curve for a product of a given quality, the decision maker can see whether or not the breakeven volume can be attained. If not, the quality of the product may be upgraded or downgraded, if the breakeven volume of the product (at the changed quality and cost level) is attainable.

A simple calculation, namely the division of the fixed costs and profit target by the contribution margin per unit, allows the breakeven volume to be readily found for any combination of price and average variable costs per unit, as long as these are both constant over the relevant range.

Operating leverage measures the responsiveness of profits (or contribution to overheads and profits) to changes in sales volume. In conjunction with the breakeven volume calculation, operating leverage indicates the extent to which profits will increase as sales surpass the breakeven point.

Care must be taken with breakeven analysis to ensure that the cost and revenue functions used are sufficient approximations of the actual incremental costs and revenues.

DISCUSSION QUESTIONS

7A-1. Discuss the applications of breakeven analysis to business decision making.

7A-2. Summarize the limitations involved in the use of breakeven analysis.

7A-3. Derive an expression for the operating leverage of a particular plant, expressed in terms of the percentage changes in the appropriate variables.

7A-4. Under what circumstances is it appropriate to show the TR and TC curves as linear functions of output for breakeven analysis purposes?

7A-5. Derive an algebraic expression for the breakeven volume for the case where TR is a quadratic function of output (and TC is linear).

PROBLEMS AND SHORT CASES

7A-1. For the total revenue curve $TR = 45Q$ and the total cost function $TC = 120 + 12.5Q$, where Q represents thousands of units, show graphically the breakeven volume. Confirm your answer algebraically. Suppose now that a demand study estimates the demand curve to be $P = 80 - 10Q$. What do you advise?

7A-2. The Franklin Razor Company is considering the introduction of a new product which will facilitate shaving in the shower. It is considering three alternative quality levels for the product. Produced in plastic without any detailing, the product would cost $0.125 per unit over a wide range of outputs. Produced in a more expensive clear plastic material which allows intricate design work, the product would cost $0.1875 per unit over a wide range of outputs. Produced in an aluminum alloy, the product would cost $0.2225 per unit over a wide range of outputs. Fixed and set-up costs would be $120,000, $180,000, and $250,000, respectively, for each of the three alternative quality treatments.

Market research has indicated that consumers would perceive the products to contain good value when priced at $1.25, $1.49, and $1.98, respectively.

(a) Calculate the breakeven volumes for each of the three quality treatments.

(b) What other information would you prefer to have before making your recommendation?

SUGGESTED REFERENCES AND FURTHER READING

Horngren, C. T. *Introduction to Management Accounting* (5th ed.), chap. 2. Englewood Cliffs, N. J.: Prentice-Hall, Inc., 1981.

Davidson, S., J. S. Schindler, C. P. Stickney, R. L. Weil. *Managerial Accounting—An Introduction to Concepts, Methods, and Uses*, chap. 6. Hinsdale, Ill.: The Dryden Press, 1978.

8

Cost
Estimation
and
Forecasting

8.1 INTRODUCTION

Cost estimation and forecasting for decision making are concerned with finding the shape and placement of the firm's cost curves. Both the short-run cost functions and the long-run cost functions must be estimated, since both sets of information will be required for some decisions. Knowledge of the short-run cost functions allows the decision maker to judge the optimality of present output levels and to solve decision problems using contribution analysis. We saw in the preceding chapter that the concept of incremental cost is fundamental to short-run decision making on cost issues. Incremental costs will include the variable costs, but they will also include any changes in those costs that are normally regarded as fixed costs. In any short-run situation we may experience increases in some of the fixed-cost items, since these particular facilities may meet their full capacity constraints and need to be increased. Incremental cost analysis is concerned with the variability of all cost components and therefore requires an appreciation of the degree of idle capacity in existing fixed-cost categories. When fixed-cost categories are expected to meet their full capacity constraints, such that overtime use and/or additional facilities must be instituted, the decision maker must account for these costs as well as the variable costs when estimating the incremental cost of a contemplated decision.

Knowledge of long-run cost functions is important when considering the expansion or contraction of plant size and for confirming that the present plant size is optimal for the output level that is being produced. Recall that the long-run cost function shows the alternate sizes of plant available at the *present* point in time and should not be interpreted as showing the cost levels for various plant sizes that will be available in the future, since both technology and the relative factor prices are likely to change in the future, rendering the present long-run cost function inappropriate. To estimate *future* cost levels we need to forecast changes in the state of technology and changes in the factor price ratios and separate these from the expected effects of inflation in future time periods.

The remainder of this chapter is therefore organized into three main sections: (1) short-run cost estimation, (2) long-run cost estimation, and (3) cost forecasting. Under cost forecasting we examine the "learning curve" phenomenon, whereby per unit costs are seen to decline over time as the cumulative volume of production increases due to the increased productivity of the variable inputs as they better "learn" the production process.

8.2 SHORT-RUN COST ESTIMATION

As implied in the introduction to this chapter, we are concerned here principally with the behavior of variable costs, but we must also be aware of other incremental costs, such as those changes in a fixed-cost category that would be necessitated by a particular decision. We shall discuss short-run cost estimation under four headings: simple extrapolation, gradient analysis, regression analysis, and the engineering technique.

Simple Extrapolation

DEFINITION: *Extrapolation* means to impute values to data outside the extreme points of the data base by projecting the relationship which is apparent within the data base.

The most simple method of cost estimation is probably to ascertain the present level of marginal or average variable costs and to extrapolate this backward or forward to other output levels. Firms often express the belief that their marginal and average variable costs are constant over a range of output levels surrounding the current output level. Note that this implies constant returns to the variable factors, and hence the absence of either increasing or diminishing returns in the short-run production process. If this constant efficiency situation actually exists in the production process, the simple extrapolation method is an adequate method of accurate cost estimation. However, if marginal costs are simply believed to be constant but are in fact increasing with additional output units, the simple extrapolation method may cause poor decisions to be made. It is a common error in business situations to assume that marginal costs are constant, which in effect is assuming the absence of diminishing returns to the variable factors. It should be intuitively obvious that sooner or later diminishing returns will set in and that the decision maker must be constantly aware of this possibility.

When we have only one cost/output observation (that is, the current levels), adjustment for possible diminishing returns must take place on the basis of judgment, experience, or intuition. For example, the decision maker may feel that the most reasonable presumption is that marginal costs are likely to increase by, say, 2 percent for each additional 1-percent change in the output level. Clearly, with only one set of cost/output observations, such an assumption is quite risky since it may easily be significantly inaccurate.

Oppositely, the decision maker may feel that marginal costs are more likely to fall if output is increased, or that there is no reason for marginal costs to either rise or fall, and, hence, the best estimate is that marginal costs are constant. Perhaps the best approach, in the absence of any data to the contrary, is to assume constant marginal costs for extrapolation purposes and then to examine the sensitivity of the decision made to the accuracy of that assumption.

EXAMPLE: The Blissful Underwear Garment Company has an opportunity to sell 500 dozen pairs of panties to a discount store buyer who has made a flat offer of $7.00 per dozen. There has recently been a management shake-up at Blissful Underwear, and the new production manager is appalled that no data have been kept on production or cost levels for these panties and that she, therefore, has no idea what the incremental cost would be. Working quickly, she ascertains that, for the present week, 7,000 dozen pairs were produced at a total variable cost of $42,000. Thus, average variable costs (AVC) are $6 per dozen at this output level, she reasons. Planned output for the next several weeks is also 7,000 dozen pairs, so fulfilling the discount store's order would expand the output rate to 7,500 per week, which is well within the plant's capacity. Without any further information, the production manager has little choice but to extrapolate from the single data point she has observed. In Figure 8-1 we show the TVC, AVC, and MC curves based on an extrapolation of these curves, assuming constant MC, from the output level of 7,000 dozen to 7,500 dozen.

In the absence of any other changes in costs as a result of the decision to fulfill the discount store's order, we estimate that incremental costs will be $3,000 for the additional 500 dozen pairs. The incremental revenue, again in the absence of any other current explicit, opportunity, or future revenues, will be $3,500. Thus, the contribution of this decision is expected to be positive, at $500, and the production manager is inclined to fill the order.

How sensitive is this decision to the underlying assumption of constant

FIGURE 8-1. Extrapolation Based on Constant Marginal Costs of Output

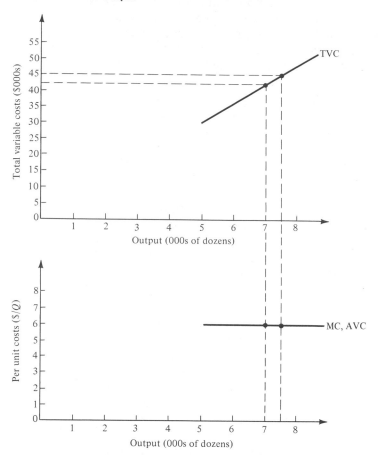

marginal costs? If TVC is not rising at a constant rate but, in fact, rises at an increasing rate over the next 500 dozen units of output, how much could it rise before the decision should be reversed? The answer is $3,500, at which point there would be no contribution from the decision, so it should not be taken. If TVC increased by $3,500 to $45,500 this would represent an increase in AVC to $6.0667, or fractionally more than a 1-percent increase in AVC from the earlier level. Thus, the decision is very sensitive to the assumption of constant marginal costs, and we would probably advise Blissful Underwear not to fill the order unless they were very confident that TVC would, in fact, increase at a constant (or decreasing) rate.

Since output levels typically fluctuate to some degree from period to period, we should be able to find two or more cost/output observations, in which case we can conduct gradient analysis.

Gradient Analysis

DEFINITION: The *gradient* of a total cost curve is defined as the rate of change of those total costs over a particular interval of output levels. Gradient means slope, of course, and the gradient of total costs can be calculated as the change in total costs divided by the change in output levels. That is,

$$\text{Gradient} = \frac{\Delta TC}{\Delta Q} \tag{8-1}$$

NOTE: The gradient of the total cost, or total variable cost, curve is not exactly the same as *marginal costs*, since the latter is defined as the change in total costs for a one-unit change in outputs. In practice, output typically changes by discrete jumps, and we must, therefore, calculate the gradient over intervals greater than one unit. The gradient does provide us with an estimate of the marginal costs over the range of output levels, as we shall see.

EXAMPLE: Suppose that Blissful Underwear accepts the order and produces the extra 500 dozen pants and notes that the total variable cost of producing 7,500 dozen pairs was $48,750. The gradient of total variable costs can, thus, be calculated as:

$$\text{Gradient} = \frac{\Delta TVC}{\Delta Q}$$

$$= \frac{48,750 - 42,000}{7,500 - 7,000}$$

$$= \frac{6,750}{500}$$

$$= 13.50$$

Thus, the rate of change of total variable costs, over the output interval 7,000 to 7,500 dozen, was $13.50 per unit. This is a measure of the marginal cost over that output range. In Figure 8-2 we show our best estimates of the TVC, AVC, and MC curves based on the observation of a second data point.

NOTE: The single MC point shown in Figure 8-2 is plotted in the *middle* of the output interval over which it is calculated, because the gradient is a single-point estimate of the rate of change of total costs over a discrete range of output levels. It is the *average* rate of change over the output interval, or an estimate of the average MC over that range, and is, therefore, plotted in the center of that range.

Gradient Analysis with Several Observations. If we have a few more cost-output observations, we can substantially improve the estimates of the TVC, AVC, and MC curves.

FIGURE 8-2.   Estimated Cost Curves given Only Two Cost-Output
Observations

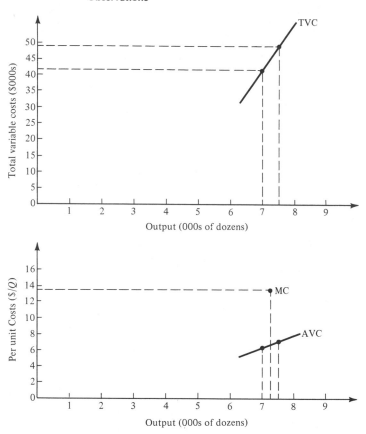

EXAMPLE: The new management of the Blissful Underwear Company, although
planning to produce 7,000 dozen pairs per week in the next several weeks,
finds that it faces a severe absenteeism problem, with weekly absentee rates
ranging between 10 and 25 percent over the next three weeks, such that its
output levels fall below the planned production level in each of these weeks.
Total variable costs also fall, however, since absent labor is not paid for time
missed and purchases of raw materials and the use of electrical energy are
also positively related to the output level. The TVC and output figures
collected over the first five weeks are shown in Table 8-1 and plotted in
Figure 8-3. Note that the output levels have been rearranged in ascending
order, regardless of the chronology of production, in order to facilitate the
calculation of the gradients over each output interval.

The AVC column in Table 8-1 is simply TVC/Q. The last three columns
show the calculation of the gradients (and, hence, the estimated MC at the
midpoint of each interval). When these points are plotted in Figure 8-3, we
can interpolate between each adjacent pair of points and show our best
estimates of the TVC, AVC, and MC curves. Note that the interpolation

TABLE 8-1.   Cost-Output Observations and the Calculation of AVC and MC

Production Period	Output (doz.)	TVC ($)	AVC ($)	ΔTVC ($)	ΔQ (doz.)	MC ($)
Week 4	4,500	27,000	6.00			
				6,600	1,500	4.40
Week 3	6,000	33,600	5.60			
				3,775	500	7.55
Week 5	6,500	37,375	5.75			
				4,625	500	9.25
Week 1	7,000	42,000	6.00			
				6,750	500	13.50
Week 2	7,500	48,750	6.50			

between the gradient values to find the MC curve indicates that the minimum point on the AVC curve must lie somewhere below 6,000 dozen pairs, since the MC curve must cut the AVC curve at the minimum point of the latter.[1]

FIGURE 8-3.   Estimated Cost Curves Given Several Cost-Output Observations

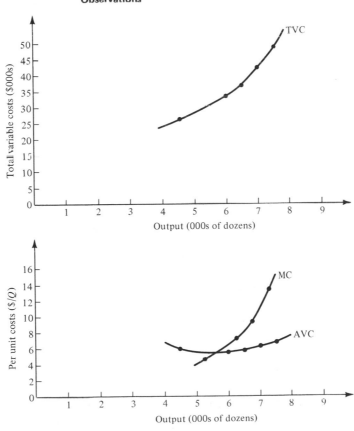

---

[1]A smooth interpolation between the gradient values indicates that AVC is minimized at about 5,500 dozen pairs. This is open to debate, of course, since a straighter MC curve would indicate AVC minimized at a lower volume, for example. Our conclusion that AVC is minimized at 5,500 units is, therefore, sensitive to interpolation error.

Thus, the observation of several pairs of cost-output data allows us to form a more complete estimate of the TVC, AVC, and MC curves. Each additional data point allows the shape of TVC to be seen more clearly, so that more reliable calculations of AVC and MC may be derived.

Regression Analysis Using Time-Series Data

Given a collection of cost/output observations, we can apply regression analysis to estimate the dependence of costs upon the output level and thus obtain an estimate of the marginal cost.[2] Since we wish to estimate the cost function of a particular firm, we must use time-series data from that firm. This raises some of the standard problems with time-series data: If over the period of the observations some factors have changed, the results of regression analysis will be less reliable. For example, factor prices may change because of inflation or market forces in the factor markets, and/or factor productivities may change because of changing technology and worker efficiency. To largely eliminate these problems the cost data should be deflated by an appropriate price index, and time should be inserted as an independent variable in the regression equation. Any trend in the relative prices or productivities will then be included in the coefficient of the time variable.

Regression analysis of time-series cost data is quite susceptible to the problems of measurement error. The cost data should include all costs that are *caused* by a particular output level, whether or not they are yet paid for. Maintenance expense, for example, should be expected to vary with the rate of output, but it may be delayed until it is more convenient to close down certain sections of the plant or facilities for maintenance purposes. Hence the cost that is caused in an earlier period is not recorded until a later period and is thus likely to understate the earlier cost level and to overstate the later cost level. Ideally, our cost/output observations should be the result of considerable fluctuations of output over a short period of time with no cost/output matching problems.

EXAMPLE: Suppose the weekly output and total variable costs of an ice-cream plant have been recorded over a three-month period, as shown in Table 8-2. Output of the product varies from week to week because of the rather volatile nature of the milk supply from dairies and the impossibility of holding inventories of the fresh milk for more than a few days.

It is apparent from the data supplied that total variable costs tend to vary positively with the output level in this ice-cream plant. But what is the *form* of the relationship? The specification of the functional form of the regression equation has resounding implications for the estimate of the

---

[2]The principles of regression analysis and the major problems associated with the use and interpretation of the results of this method were discussed in a self-contained section of Chapter 5. The discussion in this chapter presumes your familiarity with the earlier section.

TABLE 8-2. Record of Output Levels and Total Variable Costs for an Ice-Cream Plant

Week Ending	Output (gallons)	Total Variable Costs ($)
Sept. 7	7,300	5,780
Sept. 14	8,450	7,010
Sept. 21	8,300	6,550
Sept. 28	9,500	7,620
Oct. 5	6,700	5,650
Oct. 12	9,050	7,100
Oct. 19	5,450	5,060
Oct. 26	5,950	5,250
Nov. 2	5,150	4,490
Nov. 9	10,050	7,520
Nov. 16	10,300	8,030
Nov. 23	7,750	6,350

FIGURE 8-4. Linear Variable Cost Function

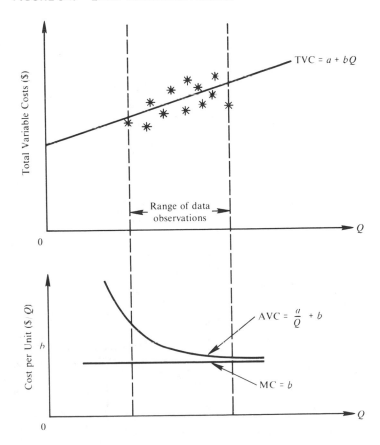

Cost Estimation and Forecasting

marginal cost curve which will be indicated by the regression analysis. If we specify total variable costs as a linear function of output, such as TVC = $a + bQ$, the marginal cost estimation generated by the regression analysis will be the parameter b, since marginal cost is equivalent to the derivative of the total variable cost function with respect to the output level. In Figure 8-4 we show, for a given collection of data observations, the consequent average variable costs and marginal cost curves that would be generated by regression analysis using a linear specification of the relationship. Since average variable costs are total variable cost divided by output level Q, the AVC curve will decline to approach the MC curve asymptotically.

Alternatively, for the same group of data observations, if we specify the functional form as a quadratic such as TVC = $a + bQ + cQ^2$, the marginal cost will not be constant but will rise as a constant function of output. In Figure 8-5 we show the hypothesized quadratic relationship superimposed upon the same data observations, with the consequent average variable cost and marginal cost curves illustrated in the lower half of the figure.

Finally, if we hypothesize that the functional relationship is cubic,

FIGURE 8-5.   Quadratic Variable Cost Function

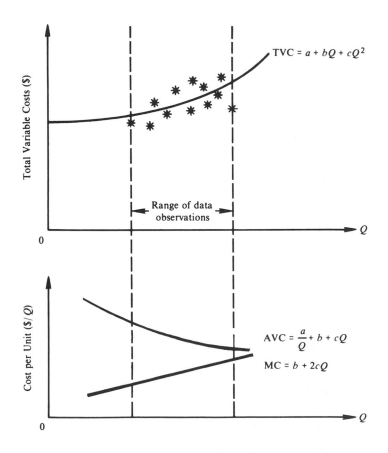

PRODUCTION AND COST ANALYSIS

FIGURE 8-6.   Cubic Variable Cost Function

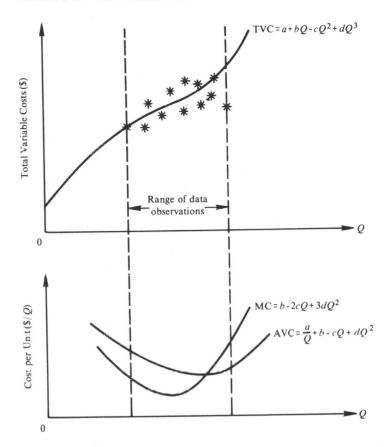

such as TVC $= a + bQ - cQ^2 + dQ^3$, the marginal cost estimate generated by regression analysis will be curvilinear and will increase as the square of the output level. Figure 8-6 illustrates the cost curves consequent upon a cubic expression of the cost/output relationship. Alternatively, a power function or other multiplicative relationship may be appropriate.

Which form of the cost function should we specify? Since the results of the regression analysis will be used for decision-making purposes, we must be assured that the marginal and average cost curves generated are the most accurate representations of the cost/output relationships. By plotting the total variable cost data against output, we may be able to ascertain that one of the above three functional forms best represents the apparent relationship existing between the two variables, and we may thus confidently continue the regression analysis using this particular functional form.

If it is not visually apparent that one particular functional form is the best representation of the apparent relationship, it may be necessary to run the regression analysis first with a linear functional form and later with one or more of the other functional forms in order to find which equation best fits the data base. You will recall from Chapter 5 that the regression equation that generates the highest coefficient of determination (R^2) is the equation that explains the highest proportion of the variability of the dependent variable, and it can thus be taken to be the best indication of the actual functional relationship that exists between the two variables.

EXAMPLE: Fitting a linear regression equation to the cost-output pairs shown in Table 8-2 resulted in the following computer output:

$$TVC = 1395.29 + 0.6351Q \qquad (8\text{-}2)$$

with a standard error of estimate of 182.02 and a standard error of the regression coefficient of 0.0313. The coefficient of determination (R^2) was 0.97614.

Note that this linear regression equation explains 97.614 percent of the variation in TVC as resulting from the variation in the output level.[3]

Suppose we now wish to estimate the total variable costs at output levels of 7,000 and 11,000 units. For 7,000 units

$$TVC = 1395.29 + 0.6351 (7000)$$
$$= 1395.29 + 4445.70$$
$$= 5840.99$$

Using the standard error of estimate we can be confident at the 68-percent level that the actual *TVC* will fall within the interval of $5,840.99 plus or minus $182.02 ($5,658.97 to $6,023.01), and we can be confident at the 95-percent level that the actual TVC will fall within the interval of $5,840.99 plus or minus two standard errors of estimate (viz., $5,476.95 to $6,205.03). Thus, we can be confident at the 95-percent level that TVC will be no higher than $6,205.03, given the production of 7,000 gallons of ice-cream. These confidence limits allow a best-case/worst-case scenario to be developed. Of course, a highly risk-averse decision maker may wish to extend the confidence limits to plus or minus three standard errors of estimate in order to find the TVC below which one can be 99 percent confident that actual TVC will fall.

The estimation of TVC at 11,000 units would proceed in the same way. The result must be viewed with caution, however, because it represents an

---

[3]Adding extra explanatory variables will inevitably explain more of the variation in the independent variable, even if the extra variables are *not* responsible for variation in the independent variable, since the regression analysis tends to capitalize on chance. In this present case, a cubic function of the form $TVC = a + bQ + cQ^2 + dQ^3$ has $R^2 = 0.97642$ and, thus, explains fractionally more of the variation in TVC, although the standard errors of the coefficients are so large that one cannot have confidence in the equation's explanatory value. As a predictive equation, we could use the cubic expression, since the individual coefficients are not given any significance. For simplicity, we proceed with the simple linear specification with insignificant loss of accuracy.

PRODUCTION AND COST ANALYSIS

extrapolation from the data base. The regression equation applies over the range of outputs observed and hence can be applied quite confidently for 7,000 units, a case of *interpolation*. Outside the range of the initial observations the relationship between TVC and *Q* may not continue to be linear but may instead be curvilinear, exhibiting diminishing returns to the variable factors, for example. Extrapolation may be undertaken, however, if we have no good reason to expect that the relationship will *not* hold outside the range of observations, as long as we are fully cognizant that the relationship may not hold.[4]

The Engineering Technique of Cost Estimation

DEFINITION: The *engineering technique* consists of developing the physical production function that exists between the inputs and the output and of attaching cost values to the inputs in order to obtain a total variable cost figure for each output level. For each output level we must therefore calculate, or test for, the amount of each of the variable factors necessary to produce that output level. Attaching costs to these variable inputs we can subsequently calculate the total variable cost for each output level and hence the average variable costs and marginal costs at each output level. Let us demonstrate this in the context of a hypothetical example.

EXAMPLE: Suppose a metal-stamping plant has one large machine that can be operated at five different speeds up to a maximum speed of 100 revolutions per minute (rpm). On each revolution it stamps out one unit of the product, and hence output is proportional to the operating speed of the machine. However, the requirements of materials, labor, electric power, and repairs and maintenance need not be proportional to the operating speed of the machine. In Table 8-3 we show the the relationships that supposedly have been found between the output and the inputs of the variable factors, using this machine at each of its five speeds.[5]

By observing the various input components, you will notice that the ratio of materials used to output per hour increases as the operating speed of the machine is increased. This indicates increased wastage or spoilage as the machine is operated at faster speeds. Labor input, however, increases by different amounts as the operating speed is increased. It apparently requires twenty men to operate the machine at its minimum speed, and the labor requirement increases at an irregular rate as the operating speed is increased, until at maximum speed thirty men are required per hour of operation. Electric power requirements, measured in kilowatt hours, increase

---

[4]Throughout the regression analysis we required *ceteris paribus* to hold. Specifically, the prices of the input factors and the productivities of the factors must reasonably be expected to have remained constant over the period of data collection. The same costs and productivities must be expected to prevail over the prediction period as well.

[5]The figures at any output level should be regarded as the central tendency of the actually observed levels, since we should expect small day-to-day variations in material wastage, labor efficiency, and actual repairs and maintenance requirements.

TABLE 8-3. Physical Requirements of a Metal-Stamping Machine at Various Operating Speeds

Operating Speed (rpm)	Output per Hour (units)	Materials Used (lb)	Labor (man-hours)	Power Requirements (kwh)	R&M Requirements (units)
20	1,200	1,320	20	2,585	10
40	2,400	2,880	25	4,523	20
60	3,600	4,680	27	5,262	30
80	4,800	6,720	28	6,708	35
100	6,000	9,000	30	10,954	60

rapidly at first, then more slowly, and then more rapidly again as maximum operating speed is attained. Repairs and maintenance requirements are indicated by an index of labor and materials necessary to maintain the machine in operating condition, and they evidently increase quite dramatically as the machine attains its maximum operating speed.

Suppose the variable inputs have the following costs per unit: Materials cost $0.15 per pound; labor cost is $8.00 per hour; power cost is $0.0325 per kilowatt hour; and repairs and maintenance cost is $10.00 per unit. With this information we can calculate the total variable cost of the output at various levels, as shown in Table 8-4. Dividing total variable cost at each output level by that output level, we derive the average variable cost for each output level, and the marginal cost figures are derived by the gradient method and are in effect the *average* marginal costs over each 1,200-unit interval. Note that both average and marginal costs decline at first and later rise.

In Figure 8-7 we plot these average variable and marginal cost figures against the output level. Interpolating between these observations we are able to sketch in the average variable and marginal cost curves as indicated by the engineering technique. The production process appears to be most efficient in terms of the variable factors at about 4,600 units, where average variable cost appears to reach a minimum at something like $0.37 per unit. If the speed of the machine were infinitely variable, the firm might wish to operate at this output level by running the machine at approximately 77 rpm. If the firm wishes to maximize profits rather than simply minimize costs, it will seek the output level at which marginal revenues from the sale

TABLE 8-4. Costs Associated with Operating the Metal-Stamping Machine at Various Output Levels

Output Levels (units)	Materials Cost ($)	Labor Cost ($)	Power Cost ($)	R&M Cost ($)	TVC ($)	AVC ($)	MC ($)
1,200	198	160	84	100	542	0.452	
2,400	432	200	147	200	979	0.408	0.364
3,600	702	216	171	300	1,389	0.386	0.342
4,800	1,008	224	218	350	1,800	0.375	0.343
6,000	1,350	240	356	600	2,546	0.424	0.622

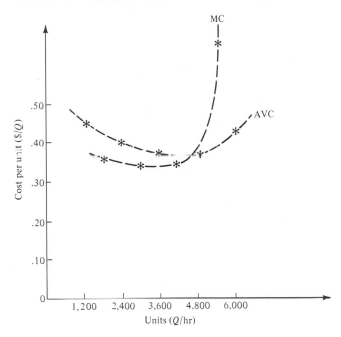

FIGURE 8-7.   Estimated Cost Curves of Metal-Stamping Plant

of these output units equal the marginal cost of producing the last unit of output. Note that by multiplying the scale on the horizontal axis in Figure 8-7 by the appropriate factor, the same cost curves will be applicable for output per day, per week, or for a longer period.

Incremental costs associated with any decision to increase or decrease output levels will be determined on the basis of the variable costs as calculated by one or a combination of the above methods, plus an allowance for any opportunity costs that are involved and any incremental fixed costs that may be necessitated. The incremental fixed costs must be calculated on the basis of the knowledge of the production capacity of the fixed factors involved. This in turn may require an engineering-type investigation of the output capacities of particular fixed facilities. Similarly, increased costs associated with overtime use of facilities must be estimated on the basis of known overtime labor costs.

Studies of Short-Run Cost Behavior

Numerous studies of the short-run cost functions of particular business firms have attempted to ascertain the shape and placement of the cost curves pertaining to those firms. Perhaps the definitive work in this area is the book by Johnston[6], in which the theoretical and conceptual issues

---

[6]J. Johnston, *Statistical Cost Analysis* (New York: McGraw-Hill Book Company, 1960).

of cost estimation by statistical methods are examined in detail before thirty-one separate studies of statistical cost estimation are summarized by the author. With regard to short-run cost estimation, the preponderant conclusion is that marginal cost tends to be constant in the operating range of the firms studied. Hence average variable cost is constant at the same level (or is asymptotically approaching that level), and average total costs are declining because of the influence of declining average fixed costs. That is to say, in most cases a linear total variable cost function provided the best fit to the data observations.

In some cases where a curvilinear total variable cost function was hypothesized, the regression analysis generated a high coefficient of determination, but generally the linear equation provided at least as much explanatory power. Thus, the general conclusion of the statistical cost studies is that marginal and average variable costs tend to be constant over the output range in which firms tend to operate, or they are sufficiently constant over that range that they may be regarded for decision-making purposes as constant. But constant MC and AVC over the range of recent output levels does not mean that we can expect these unit costs to be constant *outside* this range. For decisions that involve output levels beyond the recent range of output levels, the decision maker must consider the possibility that extrapolation of unit-cost levels is an unreliable procedure because of the possible onset of diminishing returns in the production process. The occurrence of diminishing returns in the incremental units of output should always be suspected, and if these are thought likely to occur the incremental cost figure should be adjusted accordingly.

8.3 LONG-RUN COST ESTIMATION

In this section we shall outline methods by which the long-run cost curve, or the alternative short-run cost curves available at a particular point in time, may be ascertained. We shall discuss two methods of long-run cost estimation: cross-section regression analysis and the engineering technique applied to plants of various sizes.[7]

---

[7]G. J. Stigler has suggested a third method of estimating the long-run average cost curve based on the principle that the more efficient firms will survive and expand their market share over time. Plant sizes that allow increased market share over time are inferred to have lower average costs, while plant sizes that are associated with reduced market share over time are inferred to have higher average costs. Stigler's study of the U. S. steel industry inferred an LAC curve that was negatively sloping at first, then more-or-less horizontal for an extended range of outputs, and finally upward sloping at high output rates. This "survivor principle" suffers from several major disadvantages for practical implementation, however. It assumes that all firms have the same objectives, have the same access to labor and materials markets, face constant factor prices over an extended period of time, and that factor productivities are also constant over time. These assumptions are not borne out in the real world. See G. J. Stigler, "The Economies of Scale," *Journal of Law and Economics*, vol. 1, October 1958, reprinted in his *The Organization of Industry* (Homewood, Ill.: Richard D. Irwin, Inc., 1968); see also A. Koutsoyiannis, *Modern Microeconomics*, 2nd ed. (London, Macmillian, Inc. 1979), pp. 146-48.

Regression Analysis Using Cross-Section Data.

Since long-run cost estimation seeks to find the differing scales of plant available at a particular point in time (while technology and factor prices remain constant), it is clear that we cannot use time-series observations to derive estimates of the long-run cost function. Observations from various plants at a particular point in time (cross-section data) may be analyzed, however, using the technique of regression analysis. Thus, we would need to collect pairs of data observations relating the output level to the total cost of obtaining that output level in each plant, for a particular relatively short period of time. Care must be taken to avoid errors of measurement relating either to the actual level or rate of output in that period or to the actual level of costs that should be associated with that level of output in each plant observed.

Specification of the functional form of the equation involves the same problems for long-run cost estimation as it did for short-run cost estimation. We must choose the functional form that best fits a scatter plot of the total cost and output observations. Since we are interested in whether or not there are likely to be economies of plant size, constant returns to plant size, or diseconomies of plant size, we might initially specify the relationship as being cubic, since this is consistent with the presence of increasing, constant, and decreasing returns to plant size. But if, for example, a linear function with a positive intercept value best fits the data, we must conclude that increasing returns to plant size prevail over the range of the data observations. If a power function best fits the data, the size of the exponent to the output variable will indicate whether returns to plant size are increasing (if the exponent is less than one), or constant (if equal to one), or decreasing (if exceeding one).

Two major problems exist with cross-section data for estimation of the long-run average cost curve. The first arises because the observations collected may not be points on the long-run average cost curve at all.

EXAMPLE: Suppose there are five plants observed, and the current output and total cost levels are as shown in Table 8-5. It is clear that economies of plant size exist initially and that diseconomies of plant size prevail for the fourth and fifth largest plants, since the average cost figures decline at first and later rise as we encounter progressively larger plant sizes.

TABLE 8-5. Cross-Section Estimation of the Long-Run Average Cost Curve

Plant	Output (Q)	Total Cost ($)	Average Cost ($/Q)
1	1,500	7,350	4.90
2	3,500	12,600	3.60
3	6,150	18,143	2.95
4	8,750	26,688	3.05
5	11,100	43,290	3.90

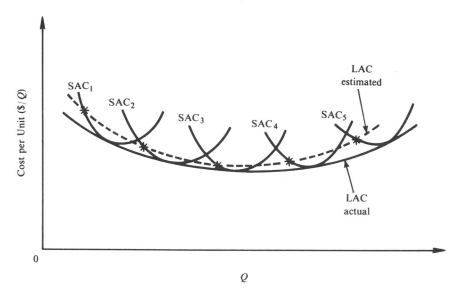

Suppose that the *actual* short-run cost curves for each of the five plants are as shown by the SAC_1, SAC_2, and other short-run cost curves in Figure 8-8. The observed output/average cost values are shown by the point on each short-run cost curve marked by an asterisk. Given this insight, we can see that the above analysis has overestimated the presence of economies and diseconomies of plant size in this instance due to the fact that the observation points for each plant were not the points of tangency with the actual long-run cost curve. This problem is accentuated if smaller plants are operating beyond the point of tangency with the long-run average cost curve and if large plants are operating to the left of the tangency point, but it occurs whichever side of the "actual" tangency point the firms are operating. Since we cannot expect each firm to be operating at precisely the point of tangency of the short-run average cost curve to the long-run average cost curve, the regression analysis of cross-section data is likely to produce a misleading picture of the actual economies and/or diseconomies of plant size that may exist. You will note that this is a case of measurement error—the assumption is that the data points are the points of tangency between the short-run average cost curves and the *LAC*, when in fact the data points are more likely *not* the points of tangency.

The second problem that may arise with cross-section data is that the various plants may not be operating with the benefit of the same factor prices and/or factor productivities. If the plants operate in differing geographical, political, and socioeconomic environments, we may expect both factor prices and productivities of the factors to differ between and among the plants. If this problem exists, regression analysis may indicate economies or diseconomies of plant size where the cost differences are actually due to differences in factor prices and productivities. Alternatively, the differences in these two factors may completely obscure the existence of those economies and diseconomies of plant size that would be seen if the influence of differing factor prices and productivities could be removed from the data. A means of laundering the data to remove these differences is to derive an index for each of the factor price and productivity variables and to deflate each observation by the value of the index. Using one plant observation as the base, we might discover that factor prices at a second plant are 10 percent lower and that factor productivities are 15 percent lower. In order to make this second observation comparable with the first observation, we would thus inflate the cost figure by dividing it by the index of 0.9 and inflate the output level by dividing it by the index of 0.85. Continuing this process with the other observations, we would be able to derive an apparent long-run average cost function that would be tolerably appropriate to the plant that was used as the basis for the adjustment process.

Applying the Engineering Technique to Several Plants

The engineering technique outlined above in the context of short-run cost estimation can be used to find an estimation of the long-run cost function by applying the same analysis to a number of plants of differing sizes at a particular point in time. In the short-run cost estimation section we used the engineering technique to find the cost curves of a particular firm at a particular point in time. If we proceeded in a similar fashion with other plant sizes that are available, we would be able to trace out a series of short-run cost curves that are available to the firm at a particular point in time.

To apply the engineering technique for purposes of long-run cost estimation, we would conduct the analysis as outlined above under short-run cost estimation for each firm. To this we would add the average fixed-cost curve for each plant size, to arrive at the short-run total cost curve for each of the plant sizes. By the shape and placement of the short-run average cost curves, we could infer the presence or absence of economies and diseconomies of plant size. In Figure 8-9 we show a hypothetical case in which five different sizes of plants have been observed, and the short-run average cost curve of each has been derived by the engineering technique. The envelope curve of these short-run curves is the long-run average cost curve. It can be inferred from the figure that there are economies of plant size initially as one moves from the first plant to the second plant, followed by relatively constant returns to plant size as one progresses to the third and fourth plant, and decreasing returns to plant size with the largest plant available.[8]

---

[8]Typically we should expect discrete differences in the plant sizes that are available to the firm, rather than the infinite variability of plant sizes that is implied by a smooth long-run average cost curve.

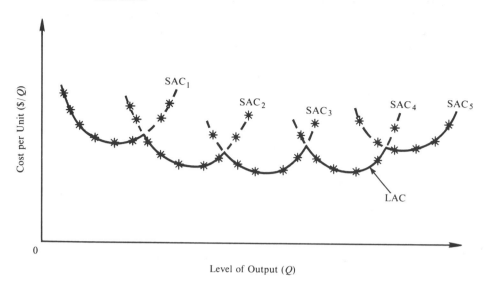

FIGURE 8-9. Engineering Technique of Cost Estimation Used to Derive the Long-Run Average Cost Curve

Note that the construction of the long-run average cost curve by the engineering technique is predicated upon factor productivity and factor prices being at similar levels in each of the available plant sizes. Similarly, the factor prices and productivities depicted by this analysis are applicable only as long as these variables do not change. If they do, a new set of short-run average cost curves must be derived, and a new long-run average cost curve will be found.

Long-Run Cost Estimation Studies

Various studies of the long-run cost function of firms have been undertaken, and a number of these are summarized in the book by Johnston.[9] The most common finding of these studies was that the long-run average cost curve tended to be not so much U-shaped as L-shaped; that is, there were typically significant economies of plant size at relatively low output levels, followed by an extended range of constant returns to plant size with no common tendency for per unit costs to rise at higher output levels. The absence of diseconomies of size in these production processes does not necessarily mean that they would not occur if progressively larger plant sizes were employed. The expectation that per unit costs would increase with a larger plant would presumably cause the firm to operate two smaller plants rather than build one larger plant. Thus, the absence of evidence indicating

---

[9]See Johnston, *Statistical Cost Analysis*, chap. 5.

PRODUCTION AND COST ANALYSIS

diseconomies of plant size does not mean that they would never occur; it simply means that the data base does not include any plant that is experiencing diseconomies (perhaps because of the foresight of the decision makers).

8.4 COST FORECASTING

Cost forecasting is necessary whenever decisions involve cost levels in future periods, such as in bidding for contracts, make-or-buy problems, or in any other decision with cost implications beyond the present period. Forecasting the level of costs for various output levels in future periods requires an assessment of the likely changes in the efficiency of the physical production process, plus changes in the prices of the factors involved in the production process. Changes in the efficiency of factors of production will, as indicated in Chapter 6, change the shape of the production surface and hence the shape of any particular total product curve associated with that production process. If factor prices are expected to change, this will change the relationship between the total product curve and the total variable cost curve which is derived from that total product curve. Hence the change in future costs will be the result of two influences, which we shall consider in turn.

Changes in Factor Productivites

When considering the physical efficiency of the production process in future periods, we should expect the productivities of at least some of the factors of production to change as time passes. Machines and equipment, for example, should be expected to become progressively more efficient in terms of output per hour (or by some other criterion) because of the incorporation of technological advances into those machines. The increasing use of computer-controlled plant and equipment has allowed the productivity of capital equipment to increase substantially in recent years. Similarly, labor productivity may be expected to increase as time progresses because of the workers' higher level of education and increased familiarity with mechanical production processes. On the other hand, changes in the attitude toward work or other sociological factors may lead us to expect reduced labor productivity in the future.

If trends have become apparent in the productivity of the factors of production, we may apply these trends as an estimate of future changes in the efficiency of the physical production process. This extrapolation of productivity trends should be modified by any changes in the productivity of any factor that may be expected to follow foreseen events of an irregular nature.

Labor productivity is typically measured as units of output per labor unit, and hence it takes the credit for increases in the productivity of capital factors such as machines and equipment. Labor productivity figures are therefore an amalgam of labor and capital productivity, and it may be quite difficult to separate the effects of each. Rather than attempt this, we are perhaps better employed searching for trends or patterns in the output per man-hour or some similar index. Data on this measure are frequently available from public sources, and the decision maker may be able to derive estimates of the future productivity of factors based upon these data.

Changes in Factor Prices

If the costs of all inputs increase over time in the *same proportion*, then the factor combination that is initially optimal for a particular output level will remain optimal, although it will cost more dollars. To explain this, let us recall the isoquant-isocost analysis of Chapter 6. In effect, all isocost curves will shift to the left in a parallel fashion, since the factor price ratio is unchanged. Thus a new (higher-valued) isocost curve will now be tangent to any given isoquant curve at the same combination of the input factors. Costs in a future period will therefore be equal to today's costs plus the expected percentage increase in all costs.

If market forces in the factor markets are expected to be such that the price of one factor will rise *relative* to the prices of other factors, we should expect the firm to want to substitute away from this factor and toward other factors that become relatively cheaper as a result of that price change. Thus, if labor costs are expected to increase faster than capital costs in the future, we should expect the firm to want to substitute capital for labor in order to minimize the costs of particular output levels. Historically, we have seen this to be the general case, with the increasing automation of production processes. To the extent that this is expected to continue in future periods, the firm should expect to achieve an increasingly capital-intensive production process in the future. You will recall from the isoquant analysis of Chapter 6 that this represents a cost-minimizing response to changing factor prices.

Forecasting factor price changes—or, more generally, forecasting the rate of inflation—requires techniques similar to those introduced in the appendix to Chapter 5 in the context of demand forecasting. Opinion surveys, trend projections, econometric models, and leading series and other barometric indicators may be used to predict the rate at which costs of production are expected to increase in future periods.[10] Expectations of events likely to influence prices, such as supply shortages or export embargoes, must be incorporated into the cost forecasts. Given a probability distribution associated with future cost levels, we may proceed on the basis of the "expected value" of cost levels in future periods in order to obtain a point forecast of future cost levels for pricing or for other decision problems.[11]

---

[10]See C. A. Dauten and L. M. Valentine, *Business Cycles and Forecasting*, 4th ed. (Cincinnati, Ohio: South-Western Publishing, 1974), chap. 18.

[11]Costs to be incurred in the future have a present value that is less than their future value, of course. Decisions to be made now, but which involve both costs and revenues incurred or received in future periods, should be evaluated in present-value terms.

In a socioeconomic system where inflation has become seemingly endemic and relatively low rates of inflation are welcomed for their beneficial impact on business confidence, we should expect a continuing increase in the nominal prices of all factors in future periods. To the extent that the firm is able to pass inflationary cost increases along to its customers, and maintain the ratio of its prices to costs, the *real* cost of the resources to the firm is unchanged. Thus, a current decision involving future production and costs can be made on the basis of today's cost levels modified only for expected changes in factor price ratios and for any inflationary effects that are not expected to be passed along to the purchaser. We shall see in Chapter 11 that the practice of "markup pricing" ensures that the firm will maintain its *real* contribution margin per unit under inflationary conditions. If the price must be set now but costs will be incurred in future periods, as in competitive bidding and price quotations, the price must include the expected inflation factor in order that the firm's real contribution margin will be preserved.

The Learning Curve

It has been observed in particular production processes that the average costs per unit tend to decline over time as the factors of production learn the production process and become more efficient. K. J. Arrow called this "learning by doing" and empirical studies have shown that costs per unit in many manufacturing processes do exhibit a downward trend (in real terms) over time.[12]

DEFINITION: The *learning curve*, also known as the experience curve, is a curve relating the cost per unit of output to the cumulative volume of output since that production process first started. Empirical studies indicate that unit costs tend to decline by a relatively stable percentage each time the cumulative output is doubled.[13]

EXAMPLE: Suppose that after setting up the assembly process for a new calculator, Texas Instruments finds that assembly time per unit had fallen to 100 minutes for each unit by the time 1,000 units had been assembled. Based on its previous experience that costs decline to 80 percent of their previous level each time output doubles, the company might predict that the 2,000th calculator would require 80 minutes assembly time; the 4,000th would require 64 minutes; the 8,000th 51.2 minutes; and so on. Given constant wages in real terms, the average cost per unit would be expected to decline along the learning curve depicted in Figure 8-10.

---

[12]K. J. Arrow, "The Economic Implications of Learning by Doing," *Review of Economic Studies*, 29, No. 3, 1962. See also J. R. McGuigan and R. C. Moyer, *Managerial Economics*, 2nd ed. (St. Paul, Minn.: West Publishing Co., 1979), pp. 273-77; and "Selling Business a Theory of Economics," *Business Week*, Sept. 8, 1973, pp. 86-88.

[13]See *Perspectives on Experience* (Boston: Boston Consulting Group, 1970).

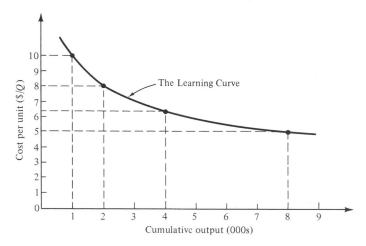

NOTE: The learning curve plots unit costs against *cumulative* output. Cumulative
output grows over time and so the learning curve indicates that unit costs
will decline over time as cumulative volume grows. The impact of this on
the firm's SAC curves, which indicate costs per unit for different *rates* of
output *per period* of time, will be to cause the SAC curve to sink downwards as cumulative volume grows (and time passes). In Figure 8-11 we
show the firm's SAC curves sinking downwards as cumulative volume
(indicated by the subscript to SAC) increases.

The learning curve for a particular firm can be estimated using regression analysis, since the relationship between unit costs and cumulative

FIGURE 8-11.   Impact of the Learning Curve on the Firm's
SAC Curve

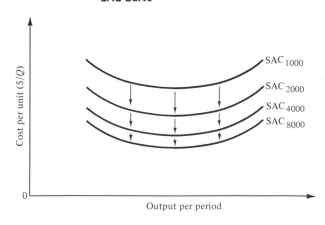

PRODUCTION AND COST ANALYSIS

volume is typically linear in logarithms. That is, the learning curve is typically a power function of the form:

$$SAC = aQ^b \qquad (8\text{-}3)$$

where Q represents cumulative volume levels, a represents the hypothetical cost of the first unit (or batch of units) produced, and b (typically a negative number) indicates the rate at which SAC will decline as output increases over time.

You will recall from Chapter 5 when we introduced regression analysis that a power function can be made linear by logarithmic transformation. Expressing our observed SAC and cumulative output values in logarithms we postulate that[14]

$$\log SAC = \log a + b \log Q \qquad (8\text{-}4)$$

and use regression analysis to estimate the parameters a and b.

EXAMPLE: Suppose that a manufacturing company has observed that the per unit costs of producing a particular product have declined as cumulative output increased, as shown in the first three columns of Table 8-6. The logarithms of SAC and Q are shown in the last two columns. Let us call log SAC the variable Y and log Q the variable X and postulate that $Y = \alpha + \beta X$. The calculations to find the parameters α and β, following the example worked through in Chapter 5, are shown in Table 8-7. Note that $\alpha = 1.7418$ represents log a. To find the parameter a, we must take the antilog of 1.7418, which is found to be 55.18. Thus, the power function expressing the learning curve is estimated to be:

$$SAC = 55.18Q^{-0.3627} \qquad (8\text{-}4)$$

TABLE 8-6.   Cost Per Unit and Cumulative Volume Observations and Their Logarithms

Date of Observation	Cost Per Unit (SAC)	Cumulative Volume (Q)	Log SAC (Y)	Log Q (X)
Sep 30	9.00	150	0.9542	2.1761
Dec 15	7.20	275	0.8573	2.4393
Mar 01	6.50	350	0.8129	2.5441
May 15	5.85	500	0.7672	2.6990

---

[14]Your calculator may be preprogrammed to find the logarithm (and antilog) of any number. If not, find a set of log tables and think about getting a better calculator.

TABLE 8-7. Calculations for Regression Parameters
for Learning Curve

Y	X	XY	X^2
0.9542	2.1761	2.0764	4.7354
0.8573	2.4393	2.0912	5.9502
0.8129	2.5441	2.0681	6.4724
0.7672	2.6990	2.0707	7.2846
3.3916	9.8585	8.3064	24.4426

$$\overline{Y} = \frac{\Sigma Y}{\eta} = \frac{3.3916}{4} = 0.8479$$

$$\overline{X} = \frac{\Sigma X}{\eta} = \frac{9.8585}{4} = 2.4646$$

$$\beta = \frac{\eta \Sigma XY - \Sigma X \Sigma Y}{\eta \Sigma X^2 - (\Sigma X)^2} = \frac{4(8.3064) - (9.8585)(3.3916)}{4(24.4426) - (9.8585)^2}$$

$$= -0.3627$$

$$\alpha = \overline{Y} - \beta \overline{X} = 0.8479 - (-0.3627)2.4646$$

$$= 1.7418$$

To forecast per unit costs at, for example, 1,000 units of cumulative volume, we simply substitute for Q = 1,000 in equation 8-4 as follows:

$$SAC = 55.18 \, (1{,}000^{-0.3627})$$

$$= 55.18 \, (0.0816)$$

$$= 4.50$$

Thus, we expect SAC to decline to $4.50 per unit by the time cumulative volume reaches 1,000 units.[15]

NOTE: Learning curves are often expressed in terms of the *percentage decline* in average costs for each consecutive doubling of cumulative volume. To find this percentage for the example here, we simply choose two output levels (one twice the other) and calculate the percentage by which SAC has declined. For example, estimating the SAC at 200 and 400 units of cumulative output from the learning curve, we have for 200 units:

$$SAC = 55.18 \, (200^{-0.3627}) = 8.076$$

---

[15]To be confident in the prediction, we should calculate the coefficient of determination, the standard error of estimate, and the standard errors of the coefficients. In this example, R^2 = 0.99, and, thus, the standard errors will each be relatively small. The confidence intervals around the estimated SAC will accordingly be quite narrow.

and for 400 units:

$$SAC = 55.18 \, (400^{-0.3627}) = 6.281$$

Thus, SAC at 400 units are:

$$\frac{6.281}{8.076} \cdot \frac{100}{1} = 77.77\%$$

of what they were at 200 units, and we can see that there has been slightly more than a 22-percent decline in average costs as cumulative output doubled. We can predict that SAC will continue to decline by approximately 22 percent for the next and each subsequent doubling of the cumulative output level.

8.5   SUMMARY

Cost estimation is concerned with the levels of cost at various output levels of the firm's plant and with the relative costs of other plant sizes that are currently available to the firm. In the short-run situation we are concerned with the behavior of average variable and marginal costs, plus any other incremental costs that may be required due to the full utilization of some elements of the existing fixed-factor inputs. Long-run cost estimation involves the per unit cost levels of various plant sizes, given the current factor prices and state of technology.

Methods of short-run cost estimation discussed were simple extrapolation, gradient analysis, regression analysis of time-series data, and the engineering technique. Long-run cost possibilities may be estimated using regression analysis of cross-section data or by applying the engineering technique to plants of various sizes. Empirical studies of cost estimation have frequently shown marginal costs to be constant in the short run and the absence of diseconomies of scale in the long run.

Cost forecasting requires the estimation of cost levels in future periods, in which factor productivities and prices may be different from today's levels. Trends in factor productivities that have become apparent over recent years may be used to project future changes in cost levels. Factor price changes that are real rather than simply monetary must also be forecast in order to obtain reliable indications of future cost levels for decision-making purposes.

The *learning curve*, when estimated for a particular production process, allows the cost per unit of future output levels to be predicted, based on the line-of-best-fit to observed average cost data as cumulative volume increases. Production processes tend to become progressively more efficient in the production of an item as the experience in that production process accumulates. Unit costs tend to decline as a decreasing function of the total output, and a firm may use data collected on its past costs per unit to predict, or forecast, future costs per unit.

DISCUSSION QUESTIONS

8-1. Explain the dangers inherent in extrapolation of cost levels beyond the limits of the data base.

8-2. Why are cross-section data likely to be inappropriate for the estimation of short-run cost functions?

8-3. Why is it important to test several specifications of the cost function for their significance and goodness of fit?

8-4. Explain the engineering technique of cost estimation in terms of the production and cost theory of Chapter 6.

8-5. Outline some of the reasons why you might expect raw-material input, labor, and repairs and maintenance not to be simple linear functions of output.

8-6. Discuss the major problems that may arise in regression analysis of cross-section data to estimate the long-run average cost curve.

8-7. Explain why a linear relationship (with positive intercept and slope terms) between total costs (of different plants) and output levels (of different plants) means that the data exhibit economies of plant size.

8-8. Discuss the learning curve and the underlying reasons for its shape. What effect does this have on the firm's SAC curve?

8-9. If the productivities of all factors are expected to improve by the same proportion in the coming years, does this mean that there should be no factor substitution in future periods? Why or why not?

8-10. Summarize the issues involved in the forecasting of cost levels in an inflationary situation.

PROBLEMS AND SHORT CASES

8-1. The Rakita Racquets Company restrings tennis racquets, a business with a highly seasonal demand. The owner-manager, Ian Rakita, has kept a record of the number of racquets restrung and total variable costs for each of the past twelve months, as follows:

Month	Total Variable Cost ($)	Racquets Restrung (units)
June	35,490	9,000
July	42,470	11,150
August	48,980	12,600
September	52,530	13,050
October	37,480	10,650
November	33,510	8,100
December	31,850	5,700
January	27,860	4,900
February	22,160	3,050
March	19,520	1,850
April	25,960	3,850
May	32,980	7,000

Over the past twelve months Mr. Rakita has experienced a constant price level for all variable factor inputs, and he feels that due to the regular turnover of employees, employee productivity and materials wastage are neither better nor worse than they have ever been.

(a) Plot the total variable cost levels against output. Draw a freehand line through those observations that appear to represent the "line of best fit" to the data.

(b) From your freehand TVC cost function, derive the AVC and MC curves for Mr. Rakita's racquet-stringing operation.

(c) Suppose that demand is expected to move from its present level of 7,000 units (May) to 10,000 units next month (June). What is the incremental cost of meeting this additional demand?

(d) Explain how you would set up the data provided in order to use regression analysis to find the line-of-best-fit. What functional form would you use?

(e) Qualify your answers with any implicit or explicit assumptions that are involved in the above analysis.

8-2. The Minical Electronics Company produces pocket calculators which are sold to various retail outlets at a price of $20. Minical feels it can sell all it is able to produce at this price. The following table indicates the physical input requirements for several weekly output levels, as compiled by the production manager, Paula Wald.

Output (units)	500	650	800	950	1,100
Labor hours	1,000	1,200	1,400	1,600	1,800
Component "packages"	750	1,000	1,275	1,575	1,895
Power (kwh)	225	400	500	650	1,000
Maintenance hours	5	15	23	28	42
Machine hours	20	25	29	32	39

The hourly wage rate paid for assembly labor is $5.50. The cost of a "package" of components is $5.00 each. (These packages each contain all the components necessary to produce one calculator. Because of imperfections in some components and breakage due to rough handling, more than one package per calculator is typically required.) Power costs $0.038 per kilowatt hour, machine hours are costed at $10 per hour, and maintenance hours cost $25 each.

(a) Using the engineering technique and gradient analysis, construct the AVC and MC curves implied by the physical input/output relationship and the prices of the inputs.

(b) At what output level are the variable inputs (combined) most efficient?

(c) What output level should the firm produce in order to maximize the contribution from this product?

8-3. The Patches Printing Company has recently expanded its product line to include a set of four-color Christmas and other Seasons Greetings cards. For the past three months it has been building up inventories and keeping records of total costs associated with the output in each month. These are:

August: 1500 dozen cards, Total Cost $8,700
September: 4650 dozen cards, Total Cost $24,645
October: 3300 dozen cards, Total Cost $14,520

In the meantime PPC's market research group have conducted an investigation into the demand side of the year-end greeting card market and have arrived at the following regression equation and associated statistics:

$$Q = 8.41764 - 0.911\,P$$

where Q is quantity demanded in thousands of dozens per month, and P is price per dozen at the wholesale level. The coefficient of determination was 0.8652, the standard error of estimate was 0.6385, and the standard error of the coefficient was 0.3861.

(a) Estimate and plot on a graph the demand and marginal revenue curves PPC might expect to face.

(b) Plot on a graph your estimate of the average and marginal cost curves on which PPC is operating.

(c) What is the profit-maximizing price and output level you would recommend for PPC over the year-end sales period?

(d) What qualifications and assumptions underlie your analysis?

8-4. Every year the Fun in the Sun Vacations company (FSV) places an order with the Brown Bag Company (BBC) for a batch of vinyl flight bags embossed and screen-printed with FSV's logo and current promotional slogan. The size of this order has varied, being 9,000 units in 1979; 4,000 in 1980; and 6000 in 1981. The price quoted by BBC also varies, in each case being equal to average costs plus a 15-percent markup.

Over the past two years there has been considerable inflationary pressure and BBC finds that 1981 input prices are uniformly 12 percent above 1980 input prices and 22 percent above 1979 prices. BBC estimates that the 1981 order will require $7,000 in set-up and other allocated fixed costs, and $23,000 in variable material, labor, and energy costs. The set-up and fixed cost allocation has been the same in constant-dollar terms for the past two years, although in current dollars it was less, of course. The historical cost data for the 1979 and 1980 orders is as follows:

Year	Quantity	Total Cost (Current $)
1979	9,000	36,885.25
1980	4,000	21,428.57

This week two more orders were received, both from affiliated travel agents who want their own names added below the FSV logo and slogan. This will require extra set-up costs of $1000 for each order. Western Europe Travel (WET) wants 2,000 bags and Southern Cross Travel (SCT) wants 1,000 bags. Each firm argues that because most of the set-up and fixed costs will be charged to FSV, they should pay a lower price per unit. Each of these travel firms has made a flat offer of $5 per bag and is adamant that they will buy elsewhere if this price is not given to them. BBC feels that this auxilliary business could grow and augment its profitability in the future, and it is seriously considering these additional offers.

(a) Estimate and plot the MC, AVC, and AC curves associated with the production of this particular line of bags, and comment on these curves.

(b) Advise BBC whether or not they should accept the additional orders, using contribution analysis to support your recommendations.

(c) What qualifications would you add to your recommendations?

8-5. A large new stadium is to be built in your city and contracts are being offered to manufacture certain items. Your company produces molded plastic items and is very interested in obtaining contracts to supply the seats for spectators. You have had substantial experience in making these hard plastic seats, ranging from garden furniture to elegant apartment furniture and including two previous contracts for hinged stadium-type seats. The major contractor for the stadium has determined that it will pay $12.50 per seat in batches of 5,000 seats. Several companies are expected to accept one or more of these contracts for 5,000 seats each. Your problem is to decide how many of these contracts your company should undertake.

Your cost estimating department has produced the following physical production requirements for various output levels.

Output Level (units)	Time to Complete (weeks)	Labor Input (hours)	Materials Required (kg.)
5,000	2	500	11,000
10,000	3	1,053	23,000
15,000	4	1,724	34,500
20,000	5	2,667	54,000
25,000	6	4,167	77,500

Labor costs $10 per hour and materials cost $2.50 per kilogram. Variable overheads are reliably estimated to be very close to 50 percent of labor cost per unit.

Rather than take these contracts, your company could instead devote its attention to making patio chairs for major chain stores and mail-order companies. Your company regularly produces these chairs whenever more lucrative contracts are not forthcoming and adds them to inventory for periodic supply to the chain stores and mail-order firms at a flat rate of $4.50 per chair. In a representative week you can produce 8,000 of these chairs with the following cost structure:

Cost Item	Cost per Week
Labor	$ 5,330
Raw materials	18,000
Variable overheads	2,670
Fixed overhead allocation	7,360

(a) Determine how many contracts (for 5,000 seats each) your company should accept. Explain your answer fully and state explicitly any assumptions or qualifications you feel are necessary.

8-6. The Argus Boat Company manufactures aluminium paddles for use in canoes and small boats. Its demand for this product fluctuates from month to month depending upon orders received. ABC manufactures to order only, and ships the product immediately, since it has very little space for inventory accumulation. Its regular price is $10.00 per unit. Based on past demand, ABC has compiled a probability distribution of demand for next month, as shown on the following page.

Today ABC's top salesman has asked the sales manager to authorize a special deal to a new customer: 2,000 paddles at $9.00 each. The sales manager in turn has asked the production manager for an estimate of costs per unit and has received the production data shown on the next page. This data was derived by a careful analysis of the input requirements for various output levels and is kept in this form because costs of the inputs frequently change. The production manager advises that input costs are currently $12 per hour for labor; $3.25 per kilogram for materials; and $0.035 per kilowatt hour for electric energy. He further advises that they are expected to remain at these levels over the next month, during which time the special batch would be scheduled if the order is accepted.

In addition to the regular production costs, the special batch of 2,000 paddles will require a $3,000 set-up cost for the customer's insignia to be imprinted in the metal and another $3,000 for extraordinary packing and shipping costs. Also, the salesman has just submitted his expense account, which contains $1,000 in expenses associated with a special trip to see this potential new client and to bring negotiations to their present stage. ABC's overhead costs are expected to be $24,000 next month.

(a) Derive the marginal and average cost curves from the data given and show these on a graph.

(b) Advise the sales manager about the appropriate decision, giving full supporting reasoning and calculations.

(c) State any qualifications and/or reservations you have regarding your recommendation.

Demand Data:

Quantity Demanded per Month	Probability
5,000	0.10
6,000	0.15
7,000	0.20
8,000	0.25
9,000	0.20
10,000	0.10

Production Data:

Units of Output	Labor (hours)	Materials (kg)	Energy (kwatt)
1000	477	500	4,885.71
2000	807	1000	7,600.00
3000	1,010	1500	9,857.14
4000	1,140	2000	12,000.00
5000	1,224	2520	13,485.71
6000	1,280	3050	15,071.43
7000	1,337	3600	17,314.29
8000	1,478	4180	19,400.00
9000	1,800	4690	22,214.29
10000	2,407	5320	23,600.00
11000	3,304	5970	25,700.00
12000	4,434	6660	28,200.00

8-7. The Done Brown Cookie Company produces high-nutrition "Brownie" biscuits which it sells to retailers for $22.55 per carton of 24 packets. While demand for Brownies is not seasonal, it nonetheless fluctuates during the year. Over the past nine months of operations demand has varied between 6,000 and 10,000 cartons per months, but there is a general growth trend in sales.

The vice-president of corporate planning, Mr. Black, has put forward the proposal that the firm expand its present plant. Having investigated the financial situation of Done Brown, he suggests that the cash that the directors are considering paying out as an extra dividend would be put to better use if invested in plant expansion and renovation. Mr. Black contends that it would be more economical to run a larger plant at half-capacity than it is to continue running the present plant.

The vice-president of production, Mr. Green, on the other hand, asserts that the plant is running smoothly and that sales forecasts in no way indicate that a larger plant is necessary at this time. Mr. Black, though, seems to have a convincing argument, having procured the cost figures for a competing Brownie manufacturer who has a larger plant than does Done Brown. He suggests that Done Brown should model its plant after that of the competitor.

A task force has been assigned to study the question of expansion. It is to analyze costs for both firms, analyze the sales forecast, as shown below, and submit its findings to the board of directors, along with a recommended plan of action. You are the head of the task force. Is Mr. Black correct? Should Done Brown expand its plant? Support your recommendation with discussion of the issues involved. Defend any assumptions that you feel are necessary.

Sales Forecast: Average Sales per Month over the Next Year

Volume	Probability
8,000	0.05
9,000	0.20
10,000	0.50
11,000	0.20
12,000	0.05

Done Brown's Production Costs: Past Nine Months

Month	Output Level (cartons)	Materials ($)	Direct Labor ($)	Overhead ($)
April	6,000	88,500	21,000	15,200
May	7,500	107,250	24,000	17,450
June	6,500	94,900	22,100	15,950
July	8,000	113,200	24,800	18,200
August	7,000	101,150	23,100	16,700
September	8,500	118,825	28,475	18,950
October	10,000	148,500	45,000	21,200
November	9,000	126,850	32,400	19,700
December	9,500	136,075	37,525	20,450

Competitor's Production Costs: Past Nine Months

Month	Output Level (cartons)	Materials ($)	Direct Labor ($)	Overhead ($)
April	10,000	140,000	30,500	24,350
May	8,500	127,075	27,025	22,175
June	9,000	133,000	28,550	22,900
July	10,500	144,375	32,025	25,075
August	9,500	136,565	29,875	23,625
September	11,000	151,250	33,550	25,800
October	12,500	173,750	47,875	27,975
November	11,500	158,125	36,675	26,525
December	12,000	165,600	41,600	27,250

8-8. The Autoroller Company is situated near Detroit and specializes in producing ball bearings for the automotive industry. Since its inception in 1970 the company has been supplying both the Michigan and the Ohio automobile producers and has had increasing sales each year. in 1982 the company sold 600,000 units in Michigan and 200,000 units in Ohio. In 1983 the Ohio customers contracted for 400,000 units, and Michigan demand was expected to increase by 100,000 units. The Ohio customers indicated that they would need 600,000 units in 1984, and Michigan sales were expected to be 750,000 units in that year. The price per unit was increased to $8, effective January 1, 1983, for the whole of 1983. Since the Ohio customers ship other auto parts to their Michigan plant and return their trucks empty, they purchase at the same price as the Michigan customers at the Detroit plant of Autoroller's.

Autoroller's president, Mr. Blydt-Hansen, was excited about the increasing demand over the years but was concerned about plant capacity and the effect on profitability. The plant's normal capacity was 600,000 units per year, but with a combination of either overtime or a second shift, both at a 50-percent premium on labor cost, demand has been met so far. A third shift was possible and 1984 demand could be satisfied from the existing plant, although costs per unit were expected to increase further. Alternatively, Mr. Blydt-Hansen was considering whether or not to build an identical plant in Ohio. This project could be completed in time for start-up in the beginning of 1984 if a decision was reached immediately. The cost structure of the new plant in Ohio was expected to be identical to that of the existing Michigan plant.

The company accumulated the following data (all figures are thousands):

		1980	1981	1982	1983 (est.)
Sales volume		600	700	800	1,100
Total Revenue		$3,600	$4,620	$5,800	$8,800
Costs:	Direct labor	450	620	818	1,285
	Raw materials	676	983	1,382	2,000
	Variable overhead	900	1,240	1,636	2,400
	Fixed overhead	1,127	1,240	1,364	1,400
Total costs		$3,153	$4,083	$5,200	$7,085
Profit		447	537	600	1,715

The company treasurer advises that hourly wages and all other costs have increased by about 10 percent per year for the last few years, and Autorollers have been able to increase their price each year. These price trends are expected to continue through at least 1984.

Advise Mr. Blydt-Hansen whether or not he should build the new plant in Ohio. Support your recommendation with discussion of all issues involved.

8-9. The Whizbang Electronic Games Company has been producing a particular machine for sale to pinball arcades for about a year. At first its costs per unit were relatively high, but these declined as total production grew, as shown below:

Total Production Since Start-up	Average Cost of Production per Unit
300	$1,000
500	870
1,000	700
1,800	540
2,400	520

(a) Estimate the learning curve for this firm, assuming that the relationship is best represented by unit costs as a power function of total production.

(b) What is the percentage of learning implied by the data?

(c) Forecast the average cost per unit when total production reaches 3,000 units.

(d) What qualifications and/or assumptions underlie your analysis and prediction?

8-10. The DeLorean sports car entered the American market in 1981 after production began in the Northern Ireland plant. Initially, the output rate was low, but it soon picked up as the workers learned their jobs and found ways to save time, materials, and energy in the production process. Suppose that the assembly costs during the first year were as shown below and that the variable factors will continue to become more productive as total output continues to increase.

Total Units Produced	Per Unit Assembly Cost
1,000	$1,582
2,000	1,215
3,000	1,095
4,000	975
5,000	900

(a) Forecast for Mr. DeLorean the per unit assembly cost for each vehicle when total output reaches 10,000 units and 20,000 units.

(b) How well does the learning curve fit the data points? What are the 95-percent confidence limits to your predictions?

(c) What other qualifications should you attach to your predictions?

SUGGESTED REFERENCES AND FURTHER READING

Abernathy, W. J., and K. Wayne. "Limits of the Learning Curve," *Harvard Business Review*, 52 (Sept-Oct. 1974), 109-19.

Dauten, C. A., and L. M. Valentine. *Business Cycles and Forecasting* (4th ed.), chaps. 10 and 18. Cincinnati, Ohio: South-Western Publishing, 1974.

Johnston, J. *Statistical Cost Analysis.* New York: McGraw-Hill Book Company, 1960.

McGuigan, J. R., and R. C. Moyer. *Managerial Economics* (2nd ed.), St. Paul, Minn.: West Publishing Co., 1979, 272-302.

McIntyre, E. B. "Cost-Volume-Profit Analysis Adjusted for Learning," *Management Science*, 24 (Oct. 1977), 149-60.

Nelson, C. R. *Applied Time Series Analysis for Managerial Forecasting.* Holden Day, 1973.

Pegels, C. C. "Start-up or Learning Curves—Some New Approaches," *Decision Sciences*, 7 (Oct. 1976), 705-13.

Simon, J. L. *Applied Managerial Economics*, chap. 13. Englewood Cliffs, N. J.: Prentice-Hall, Inc., 1975.

Spence, A. M. "The Learning Curve and Competition," *Bell Journal of Economics*, 12 (Spring 1981), pp. 49-70.

Stigler, G. J. "The Economies of Scale," *Journal of Law and Economics*, vol. 1 (Oct. 1958).

part

PRICING ANALYSIS and DECISIONS

A Review
of Market
Structures
and Basic
Pricing Models

9

9.1   INTRODUCTION

In this chapter we examine how prices are determined in product markets of various types and how the firm determines the output level it should supply to consumers. The theory of this price and output determination in the product markets is generally known as the *theory of the firm*.

NOTE: The first thing to learn about the theory of the firm is that there is no single theory of the firm. In fact, it is conceivable that one could construct literally hundreds of different theories of the firm simply by including some of the permutations and combinations of the elements that make up a theory of the firm. Any theory of the firm is in fact a model of firm behavior in response to its environment.

In their markets, firms range from the small and virtually insignificant competitors, who are unable to influence market prices, to the large and powerful firms, who are able to dictate the prices consumers pay. It is precisely due to this diversity of business firms that there is no single, universally applicable theory of the firm. A theory that applies to all situations would be too broad and general to be of very much use in explaining or predicting the behavior of a firm in any particular situation. Given the diversity of product market situations and the differences in firm sizes and motivations, it is not surprising to find that there is a proliferation of theories of the firm in the literature of economics. Differences are assumed in the supply-and-demand situations, as well as in the patterns of action and reaction, so that there is a model of the firm to fit each of a wide variety of business situations.

This abundance of theories of the firm can be confusing until one realizes that all can be related to a simple basic structure of the theory of the firm. There are seven major assumptions necessary to generate a theory of the firm, and the multiplicity of models differ from each other only to the extent that one or more of these seven assumptions differ.

The Seven Assumptions of a Theory of the Firm

A theory of the firm requires four structural assumptions to define the supply-and-demand conditions under which the firm operates and three behavioral assumptions to define the manner in which the firm acts or reacts to certain stimuli. With these seven assumptions, we can build a model, or theory, of the firm to suit every imaginable business situation. Let us first look at each of the seven assumptions in some detail.

(1) The Number of Sellers.   The more firms there are in any particular product market, the less power any one supplier has to influence the market price or the total supply of the product in the market. There comes a point, of course, when the number of sellers is large enough that the impact of any one seller on the general price level is insignificant. By this we mean that although a particular firm may adjust its price up or down, this has so little impact on the sales of other firms that they maintain their prices at the same levels. Hence the general price level in the market is effectively unchanged. For our purposes in constructing a theory of the firm, it is only necessary to say whether or not there are enough firms to cause the actions of any one firm to have an insignificant impact on the market price, rather than to specify the exact number of competing sellers. Accordingly, we dichotomize the number of sellers as either many or few.

DEFINITION: *Many firms* is defined as a situation in which there is a sufficiently large number of firms, so that no single firm can directly cause the market price to vary. That is to say, each firm is quite small relative to the market in which it operates. *Few firms* is the converse situation—a sufficiently small number of sellers, so that the firms are necessarily quite large relative to the market and can directly cause the market price to rise or fall as a result of their own pricing or output decisions. This change in market price occurs because competing firms experience a noticeable change in their sales as the result of another firm's action, and they move to correct or modify the impact on their profits by changing their prices, too. Thus in the case of few firms, the initial firm's pricing action leads to a change in the general price level, whereas in the case of many firms, it has no effect on the general price level.

(2) The Cost Conditions. Since firms are typically profit motivated and since profits are the excess of revenues over costs, we must specify the cost conditions in order to compare total costs with total revenues at various output levels. Thus we must specify, either explicitly or implicitly, the production function and the prices of the inputs to the firm's production process. You will recall from Chapter 6 that this specification determines whether there are increasing or diminishing returns to the variable factors in the short run and whether there are economies or diseconomies of plant size in the long run. In effect, we must specify the shape and placement of the cost curves faced by the firm.

The conventional assumption is that the production function is cubic and input prices are constant, which means U-shaped marginal, average variable, and short-run average cost curves. Other assumptions, which in some cases may better represent reality, include constant marginal costs or marginal costs either rising or falling throughout the range of observed output levels. Each of these assumptions has implications for the shape of the average variable and short-run average cost curves and, subsequently, for the price and output decision of the firm.

(3) The Number of Buyers. Buyers, like sellers, have a greater degree of market power the fewer they are in number. The larger the share of market demand that comes from a single buyer, the more pressure that buyer can exert to push the price down. The large buyer can obtain lower prices from a particular seller by threatening to buy from a different seller, who would readily give a slightly lower price for such a large order. As in the supply situation, it is enough to know if there are few or many buyers. With *many* buyers, each one is so insignificant relative to the market, that no one buyer is able to influence the market price directly, whereas with *few* buyers, an individual has the power to reduce the market price.

(4) The Extent of Product Differentiation. Product differentiation varies from zero—when consumers view the different suppliers' products as identical, or perfectly substitutable—to infinite—when consumers regard a particular supplier's product as being unique, or not at all substitutable. In between these extremes there are markets, in which, for example, the suppliers' offerings are perceived as imperfectly substitutable (slight product differentiation) and other markets, in which the products are substantially differentiated. The degree of product differentiation determines the extent to which buyers shift toward a firm's product if its price is reduced, or away from that product if its price is increased. In effect, this assumption helps determine the slope of the firm's demand curve.

We saw in Chapter 4 that a measure of product differentiation is the cross elasticity of demand between two products. Products that are substitutes and that are, therefore, in the same market, exhibit positive cross elasticities with each other. The degree of substitutability is indicated by the size of the cross elasticities. Thus, very good substitutes have relatively high cross elasticities with each other, whereas poor substitutes have relatively low cross elasticities with each other.

(5) The Firm's Objective Function.   In order to predict or explain the actions of a firm, we must know what that firm's objective is. What does it wish to achieve as a result of being in business? The traditional assumption is that the firm wishes to maximize its short-run profits, that is, the excess of revenues over the opportunity costs of all inputs. But note that the traditional theory assumes certainty, or full information with respect to cost and demand conditions, and a planning period no longer than the short run. We saw in Chapters 1 and 2 that in the real world of uncertainty, longer planning periods, and risk aversion, modified objective functions are more appropriate. In this chapter we shall confine our attention to the maximization of short-run profits, but in Chapter 10 we shall examine more realistic extensions.

(6) The Strategic Variable.   In order to model how the firm pursues its objective we must specify the firm's strategic variable or variables. That is, which variables are adjusted to achieve profit maximization, for example? Marketing literature suggests four major contenders: price, promotion, product design, and place of sale, known as the "4 P's." In this textbook we are concerned primarily with *price*, taking the other three strategic variables to be predetermined, although we do examine the use of *promotion* as a strategic variable in Chapter 13. Note that the firm can also adjust its quantity supplied, although this usually follows as a result of a price adjustment.

(7) The Firm's Expectation of Rivals' Reactions.   A firm's action depends upon what it expects rival firms to do in reaction to that action. In the simplest case, the firm expects its rivals to do nothing. This may be due to the insignificant impact the firm's action will have on the sales and profitability of its rivals, or, alternatively, it may be due to the myopia of the firm, which fails to foresee the impact of its actions upon rivals. When a firm expects a reaction from rivals, it should view the outcome of its own action accordingly. For example, since other things will not be equal, it should not expect to face a *ceteris paribus* demand curve. Instead, it envisions a *mutatis mutandis* demand curve, meaning that it should take into account all current and induced effects of its action. Thus, if a price reduction is expected to be matched by rivals, quantity demanded may increase by only 5 percent along the *mutatis mutandis* demand curve (because of an expansion of the overall demand for the product and all firms maintaining their market share) rather than, for instance, a 25-percent increase in quantity demanded (which occurs if no other firms react). In the latter case the *ceteris paribus* demand curve is appropriate.

DEFINITION: The firm's expectation of its rivals' reaction is known as its *conjectural variation.* The firm conjectures that its rivals will vary their own strategic variable(s) to a certain degree. The conjectural variation is calculated as the percentage change in a rival's strategic variable divided by the percentage change in the firm's strategic variable. For a zero conjectural variation, that is, no reaction by rivals, the *ceteris paribus* demand curve applies. For positive conjectural variations, the firm must envision *mutatis mutandis* demand curves that take into account the degree of reaction expected in each case. The most commonly assumed reaction is that rivals will match the extent of the firm's price change, in which case we say conjectural variation is unity.

The above structural and behavioral assumptions form the starting point for any theory of the firm. In the following sections we systematically vary some of the assumptions in order to generate a variety of models of the firm. Each model seeks to show how the firm determines the level of its strategic variable under a particular set of structural and behavioral assumptions.

9.2 THE FOUR BASIC MARKET FORMS AND THE PRICING DECISION

In traditional microeconomic theory of the firm there are four basic market forms: pure competition, monopolistic competition, oligopoly, and monopoly. *Pure competition* is characterized by many sellers producing identical products for many buyers. *Monopolistic competition* differs in only one respect: there are many sellers producing differentiated products for many buyers. *Oligopoly* is fundamentally different from the above, in that there are few sellers producing competing products for many buyers. *Monopoly* is a situation in which there is a single seller producing for many buyers. Its product is necessarily extremely differentiated, since there are no competing sellers producing substitute products.

In terms of the seven assumptions of a theory of the firm, you will note that these four market forms are obtained by varying just two of those assumptions, namely, the number of sellers and the degree of product differentiation. Table 9-1 summarizes the major distinguishing characteristics of these four major market forms.[1]

We shall proceed to examine the theory of the firm pertaining to each of these market forms. For purposes of comparison we shall assume the same behavioral assumptions for the firms in each market situation except for a slight modification under oligopoly. In the latter part of this chapter we shall

TABLE 9-1. The Traditional Spectrum of Market Forms

	Pure Competition	Monopolistic Competition	Oligopoly	Monopoly
Number of sellers:	Many	Many	Few	One
Product differentiation:	None	Slight	Considerable	Complete

[1]Product differentiation in oligopoly could, in theory, range from zero to a relatively high degree. Zero product differentiation is unlikely in the real world, however, when one considers all the attributes involved in the purchase decision.

consider the impact on the price and output decision of different structural conditions, such as a firm having more than one plant and being able to sell in more than one market. The appendix to this chapter will examine the pricing and output consequences of plant size adjustment (and the entry and exit of firms) in the long run. Behavioral assumptions more suited to the uncertainty of the real world will be introduced in Chapter 10, where price leadership and the effect of longer-term objective functions will be examined.

Pure Competition

The price and output decisions of a firm operating under conditions of pure competition can be explained and predicted by a model comprised of the seven assumptions listed in Table 9-2. There are many sellers producing identical products, each adjusting price or quantity when necessary to achieve profit maximization in the short run. Each firm's conjectural variation, or expectation of rivals' reactions to its price or quantity adjustments, is zero, since each firm is small relative to the market.[2]

NOTE: In assumptions 2 and 4 we assume that the firms and the buyers have full information concerning the prices and availability of inputs and products, respectively. Further, sellers all have access to the most efficient technology of production. The assumption of full, or *perfect*, information leads some writers to characterize this market form as *perfect competition* rather than pure competition. For our purposes the terms are equivalent.

Price and Output Determination. In pure competition the equilibrium price is determined by the interaction of the market forces of supply and demand. There are many buyers and many sellers, each too small relative to the market to influence directly the general price level. In aggregate, however, their demand and supply decisions lead to the determination of the

TABLE 9-2. The Seven Assumptions of Pure Competition

Structural Assumptions	(1)	Number of sellers	Many
	(2)	Cost conditions	Cubic production function with constant factor prices. Full information
	(3)	Number of buyers	Many
	(4)	Demand conditions	Homogeneous products. Full information
Behavorial Assumptions	(5)	Objective function	Short-run profit maximization
	(6)	Strategic variables	Price and output levels
	(7)	Conjectural variation	Zero, since there are many firms

---

[2]To follow convention we assume a cubic production function, which means U-shaped average variable and marginal cost curves. Pure competition could exist as long as there were diminishing returns to the variable factors, given the other six conditions.

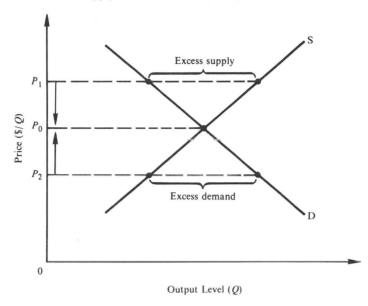

equilibrium market price. The market demand curve is negatively sloping, and the market supply curve is positively-sloping, as shown in Figure 9-1. If, at a particular price level, such as P_1, supply exceeds demand, there will be downward pressure on prices, because of the desire of firms to reduce inventories to preferred levels. Each firm reduces price in order to clear its excess inventories and thus avoid costs associated with holding those excess inventories. Since many firms will be independently reducing their prices, this causes the market price to fall. One firm alone reducing its price would not cause a reduction in the general price level, since it could sell all it wishes at the lower price without any competing firm suffering a significant loss of sales, because of the assumption that firms are small relative to the market. But the combined effect of many firms reducing their prices causes a significant loss of sales to those competitors that have *not* reduced their prices. This in turn causes those firms to suffer excess inventory, and they too will be motivated to reduce price.

Thus excess market supply leads to a reduction in the market price. The lower price causes an increase in the quantity demanded and at the same time causes the firm to be willing to supply a somewhat reduced amount. Prices will continue to fall until finally supply equals demand, as shown at price P_0 in Figure 9-1.

Conversely, if there is excess demand at a particular price level, such as at P_2 in Figure 9-1, there will be upward pressure on prices, because of the willingness of some buyers to pay more than the market price rather than go without the product. Firms will find they can raise their price slightly yet still sell all they wish to produce, since although other firms may be maintaining their price at P_2, those firms are unable to supply the entire comple-ment of buyers willing to purchase at price P_2, and some of those unable to purchase are willing to pay more than P_2 to obtain the product. The firms setting price P_2 then see that they too can ask for a higher price, and the combined effect is for the market price to move upward. As it does, the quantity demanded is reduced as some buyers drop out of the market, and the quantity suppliers are willing to put on sale increases, until finally sup-ply equals demand and no further incentive exists to raise prices. The price P_0 in Figure 9-1 is thus the equilibrium price and is determined not by the actions of any one firm but by the combined effects of individual firms' actions.

Given the market price, the purely competitive firm must decide what output level to produce in order to maximize its profits. Profits are maxi-mized when the difference between total revenues and total costs is greatest. Since the firm is small relative to its market, it can sell all it wants to at the market price, and its total revenue curve is a straight line from the origin, as shown in Figure 9-2, because total revenue is a linear function of output. Following our assumption of a cubic production function, the total cost curve takes the shape shown by TC in Figure 9-2. Profit, the vertical distance between the curves (where TR lies above TC), is maximized at output level Q^*, where a tangent to the TC curve is parallel to the TR curve. A property of parallel lines is that they remain a constant vertical distance apart. The choice of Q^* such that a tangent to the TC curve was parallel to the TR curve ensures that profit is maximized, since output levels to the right or

FIGURE 9-2. Profit-Maximizing Output Determination for a Firm in Pure Competition

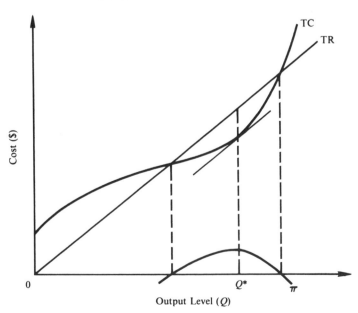

PRICING ANALYSIS AND DECISIONS

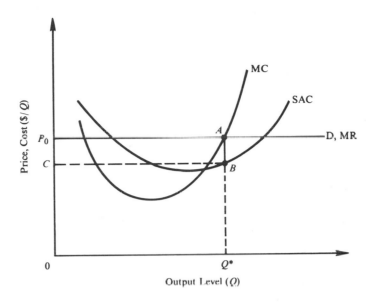

FIGURE 9-3. Output Determination in Pure Competition
Using the Marginal Curves

left of Q^* show the TC level moving toward the TR level and hence away from the tangent that measures the constant vertical distance from the TR curve. The total profit curve can be shown on the same graph, as the curve π.

The profit-maximizing condition, that the slopes of the TR and TC curves should be equal, is the same as saying that profits are maximized where total revenues and costs are increasing at the same rate. The reader will recall from Chapters 4 and 6 that this in turn can be restated as "profits are maximized when marginal revenue equals marginal costs," since *marginal revenue* and *marginal costs* were defined as the rate of change of total revenues and total costs, respectively. Thus we can show the output decision of the firm in terms of the marginal curves, as in Figure 9-3. The marginal revenue curve will be horizontal at the price level P_0, and marginal costs will be U-shaped, as argued in Chapter 6. Note that the MC curve may cut the MR curve twice but that *losses* are maximized where it cuts the MR curve from above, whereas profits are maximized where MC cuts the MR curve from below.

To confirm that profits are maximized at output level Q^* in Figure 9-3, consider an output level slightly to the right of Q^*. Here marginal costs exceed marginal revenues. That is, the units to the right of Q^* add more to costs than they add to revenues, and they therefore must cause profits to be reduced. Accordingly, these output units should not be produced. Alternatively, consider the output units to the left of Q^*. Here marginal revenues exceed marginal costs, and profits are augmented by the production of each of these units. Hence, output should be carried to the level Q^* in order to maximize the firm's profits. Profits can be visualized as the rectangle P_0ABC, which is equal to the average profit per unit, *AB*, times the number of units $0Q*$.

Note that the purely competitive firm has no incentive to either raise or lower its price away from the market price. If it raised its price above P_0 it would sell no units at all, since all its buyers would seek the product from other sellers at the market price. If it lowered price this would also lead to reduced profits, since it would sell fewer units (because a lower MR will cut MC at a smaller output level) at a lower price, without a commensurate reduction in per unit costs. Only when there is excess market demand will the firm have a profit incentive to raise price, and only when there is excess market supply (and there is a cost of holding excess inventories) will the firm wish to reduce its price.

NOTE: Do purely competitive markets exist? Are there any market situations that fulfill the stringent conditions implied by the seven assumptions? In this evolving socioeconomic system there are certainly some markets left that have many buyers and many sellers. The most difficult condition to find is that of identical products. Remember that zero product differentiation requires that all buyers regard all products from the competing suppliers as identical in all respects. Buyers cannot have personal preferences for particular sellers, nor have differing expectations of quality or after-sales service, nor find it more or less convenient to buy from one seller rather than from another. The package of attributes constituting the product must be viewed as identical in all respects.

EXAMPLE: Perhaps the only market in which this condition is fulfilled is the stock exchange, at which hundreds of buyers and sellers meet anonymously (through an agent) to buy and sell a company's stock. Each share in the company has the same rights, benefits, and obligations attached (for each class of shares), and no buyer is likely to care about the identity of the previous owner.

Applications of the purely competitive model as an explanatory or predictive device will be inappropriate to the extent that the seven assumptions involved do not accord with the reality of the situation being explained or predicted. The major value of the purely competitive model is probably as a pedagogical device. It allows the theory of the firm to be introduced in a relatively simple context, free of the complications introduced by product differentiation and fewness of buyers and/or sellers. It thus forms a basis upon which we can build an understanding of more complex theories of the firm.

Monopoly

DEFINITION: *Monopoly* is a market situation in which only one firm faces the entire market demand. In the eyes of consumers, no other firm produces a product that is any more than remotely substitutable for the monopolist's

TABLE 9-3. The Seven Assumptions of Monopoly

Structural Assumptions	(1)	Number of sellers	One
	(2)	Cost conditions	Cubic production function with constant factor prices. Entry of new firms is not possible
	(3)	Number of buyers	Many
	(4)	Demand conditions	Product has no close substitutes
Behavorial Assumptions	(5)	Objective function	Short-run profit maximization
	(6)	Strategic variables	Price and output levels
	(7)	Conjectural variation	Zero, since there are no rivals

product. We can therefore state the seven assumptions of the monopoly model of pricing behavior as shown in Table 9-3.

Monopoly situations may arise and persist for a number of reasons. First, a single firm may control the supply of a necessary input factor. Examples include owning all known reserves of an input (e.g., Alcoa's early monopoly in the aluminum industry), owning the only railroad serving a remote area, or having in your employ the one person who understands a certain phenomenon. As implied above, this type of monopoly tends to become eroded over time as potential entrants overcome these obstacles.

Second, a firm may be given a government mandate to be a monopoly, for reasons of national security, social equity, or economic optimality. The armed forces, post office, and various utilities provide examples of this type of monopoly.

Third, there are so-called natural monopolies. These are firms for which economies of plant size are large relative to the size of the market. This situation is a natural monopoly in the sense that if there were rivals at first, a monopoly would evolve as time passed, due to the profit incentive for firms to merge with or take over rival firms. Per unit costs of production are minimized in such a market situation when only one firm supplies that market. As implied above, the government often bestows monopoly rights on firms thought to be in this type of situation, but to ensure that at least part of these cost savings are passed on to consumers it is frequently necessary for the government to regulate the pricing and/or output of these firms.

Thus, monopolies *exist* whenever there is a single seller of a product in a particular market. They *persist* over time if potential entrants are thwarted by substantial cost disadvantages, lack of a legal right to compete, or if the market is a natural monopoly. The cost disadvantages facing a potential entrant are known as *barriers to entry*. Clearly, if potential entrants cannot gain access to a necessary input or if the price of so doing is prohibitive, the monopoly remains a monopoly until these restrictions are removed. Consumer loyalty for the existing firm's product also operates as a barrier to the entry of new firms. Over time these barriers do tend to crumble, as new sources of raw materials are discovered, alternative materials are invented (for instance, synthetic rubber and plastics), technological breakthroughs are made, and consumers' tastes and preferences change.

NOTE: Monopolists in the real world usually do have some peripheral competition from distant and partial substitutes. The post office experiences competition from the telephone company and from such delivery services as United Parcel Service (UPS), for some of the services it provides. The electricity company competes with the gas company in some households. Bootleggers compete with the liquor control board in some areas. In all these cases, however, the extent of substitution of these products for the monopolist's product is quite small. Thus, the cross elasticity of demand between the monopolist's product and the distant substitutes, over the market as a whole, is quite low.

Price and Output Determination by the Monopolist. The profit-maximizing monopolist will wish to expand output until marginal costs rise to equal marginal revenues. Since this firm faces the entire market demand, the firm's demand curve and the market demand curve are one and the same. Thus the *market* marginal revenue curve is the *firm's* marginal revenue curve. We saw in Chapter 4 that the marginal revenue curve associated with a negatively sloping linear demand curve has the same vertical intercept on the graph and *twice* the slope of the demand curve. In Figure 9-4 we show the market demand curve (D) faced by the monopolist and the corresponding marginal revenue (MR) curve. Superimposed on these are the cost curves of the monopolist—the short-run average cost (SAC) and marginal cost (MC) curves. The profit-maximizing monopolist produces up to the point where marginal costs per unit rise to meet the falling marginal revenues. This occurs at output level Q_m. Notice that every unit to the right of Q_m has a marginal cost greater than its marginal revenue; it therefore *will not* be produced. Con-

FIGURE 9-4. Price and Output Determination for a Monopoly

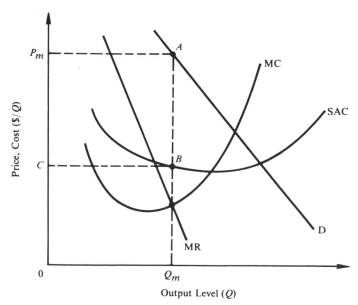

versely, every unit to the left of Q_m costs less than it earns (marginally or incrementally); it therefore *will* be produced and sold. The firm's profits can be visualized as the rectangle P_m *ABC* in Figure 9-4.

Monopolistic Competition

DEFINITION: *Monopolistic competition* is characterized by many firms selling a slightly differentiated product in the same marketplace. It is different from pure competition in only one respect: the products of the competing sellers are differentiated rather than homogeneous. Recall that product differentiation can arise from perceived differences in products themselves or in differences in the various attributes surrounding products, such as a more convenient store location, better customer service and comfort, and better warranties and repair service.

In such market situations the firm must choose price knowing that the consumer has many close substitutes to choose from. If the price is too high, in view of the consumer's perception of the value of the differentiating features of the firm's product, the consumer will purchase a competing firm's product instead. Thus, the monopolistic competitor must expect a relatively elastic demand response to changes in its price level. Yet at the same time, it expects to be able to change price without causing any other firm to retaliate and, consequently, without causing a change in the general price level in the market. This is possible because the firm is one of many firms, and it expects the impact of its actions to be spread imperceptibly over all the other firms, giving no one firm any sufficient reason to react to the initial firm's price change.

The price and output decisions of a monopolistic competitor can be explained and predicted by a model comprised of seven assumptions, as shown in Table 9-4.

Monopolistic competition is so called because it has elements of both monopoly and pure competition. The firm has a significant amount of monopoly power by virtue of the differentiation of its product. It can change price up and down without experiencing the extreme response of pure competition. For price increases it will suffer a loss of sales, but this

TABLE 9-4.   The Seven Assumptions of Monopolistic Competition

Structural Assumptions	(1)	Number of sellers	Many
	(2)	Cost conditions	Cubic production function with constant factor prices. Entry is unrestricted
	(3)	Number of buyers	Many
	(4)	Demand conditions	Products are slightly differentiated
Behavorial Assumptions	(5)	Objective function	Short-run profit maximization
	(6)	Strategic variables	Price and output levels
	(7)	Conjectural variation	Zero, since there are many firms

FIGURE 9-5. Price and Output Determination for a Representative
Firm in Monopolistic Competition

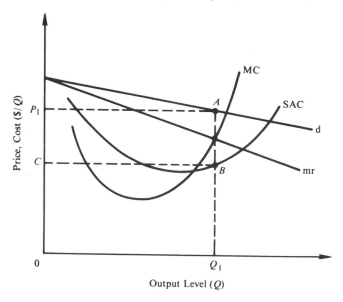

loss is not total, as it would be for the pure competitor. Like a monopoly,
the monopolistic competitor can adjust the price upward or downward to
the level which maximizes its profits. But like the pure competitor, the monopolistic competitor has many rivals in the short run, compounded by the
free entry of new firms in the long run.

EXAMPLE: Monopolistically competitive markets are found where a large number
of vendors gather to sell similar products to a gathering of potential buyers.
The weekly fruit and vegetable market in some communities may be characterized as monopolistic competition. Similarly, the gatherings of artisans selling souvenirs and other goods in tourist resorts act like monopolistic competitors.[3]

---

[3]Be wary about characterizing markets as monopolistically competitive unless there
are many firms in a relatively compact area and consumers could reasonably be expected
to consider purchasing from any one of the firms. This is because seller location (or
convenience of purchase) is a relevant attribute in the purchase decision for most consumers. Several industries have a large number of producers but are not characterized by
monopolistic competition, since the markets for these industries are sparsely dispersed
across the nation. There may be thousands of fast-food outlets in North America, but
each one seldom competes with more than half a dozen other sellers in its local market.
Similarly, there are hundreds of gas stations in and around a large city, but each one is
in competition with the three or four gas stations nearest to it, rather than with every
other gas station in the entire city. One would not expect a consumer to drive across the
city to buy a tankful of gas or a hamburger. Rather, the consumer considers the availability of competing products within a particular geographical market area. This spatial
aspect of some industries means that, rather than being monopolistically competitive, their
markets are characterized by intersecting oligopolies, with each firm competing directly
with only a few nearby rivals.

PRICING ANALYSIS AND DECISIONS

The situation of a representative firm in monopolistic competition is depicted in Figure 9-5. Since the demand curve is negatively sloping, the marginal revenue curve must lie below the demand curve, having twice the slope and the same intercept point. The monopolistically competitive firm maximizes its profits at the price and output level where marginal revenue equals marginal costs. In Figure 9-5 price will be set at P_1; quantity at Q_1; and profits are shown as the area P_1ABC.

The prices set by monopolistic competitors need not be at the same level. In real-world situations we should expect to find slight price differentials between and among monopolistic competitors, with some firms being able to command slightly higher prices and/or larger market shares due to the market's perception of greater value (more attributes per dollar) in the product of some firms as compared with others. Firms with more convenient locations, longer operating hours, and/or quick service, for example, can obtain a premium for what is otherwise the same product (e.g., Brand A bread). Quality differences inherent in the product will also form the basis for price differences.[4]

Oligopoly: The Kinked Demand Curve Model

DEFINITION: *Oligopolies* are markets in which there are only a few sellers. (The word *oligopoly* is derived from the Greek word *oligos*, meaning *few* and the Latin word *polis*, meaning *seller*.) Recall that we use the word *few* to mean a number small enough so that the actions of any one firm have a noticeable impact on the demand for each of the other firms. In oligopolies, a reduction in the price or a change in any other strategic variable by any one firm, causes that firm to gain sales and causes rival firms to suffer a noticeable loss of sales, as consumers switch across to the firm that has made the change in its strategic variable.

EXAMPLE: In the real world the great majority of market situations are oligopolies. Prominent examples are the automobile, steel, aluminium, and chemical industries. These are national and, in some cases, international oligopolies. In your local or regional area, you will notice many more oligopolies. There are probably only half a dozen new car dealerships from which you would consider buying a new automobile (after you graduate and get a high-paying job!). Similarly, there are only a few sellers in a multitude of other lines of business in your area, and these qualify as oligopolies if the actions of any one seller have a significant impact on the sales of any other seller.

---

[4]Price and market share differences arise in the *asymmetric* monopolistic competition model, where both costs and product differentiation are allowed to differ among firms. This is a considerably more complex model that the *symmetric* case outlined above, in which it is implicit that the "representative firm" has the same cost structure and product differentiation advantages as all other firms. The asymmetric model will not be considered here except to note that it allows greater realism, at the expense of greater complexity, by explicitly considering differing cost and product differentiation situations between and among firms.

The essential difference between oligopoly and monopolistic and pure competition is that the sales gain resulting from the actions of one firm is at the expense of *fewer* firms, rather than the effect being spread imperceptibly over numerous rivals. Oligopolists, therefore, should be expected to react to the actions of their rivals, rather than ignore them as in the other two cases. In turn, this implies that a firm contemplating an adjustment in its strategic variable should anticipate the reaction of its rivals when estimating the impact of that adjustment on its sales and profits. Since the actions of any oligopolist have a direct impact on each of its rivals and might be expected to provoke a reaction, we say that the actions of the firms are *interdependent*, or *mutually dependent*.

Recognition of Mutual Dependence in Oligopoly. Models of firm behavior under oligopoly may be dichotomized according to whether or not the firms recognize their mutual dependence. In simple models where the firms do not recognize this fact, the conjectural variation assumption is zero. These models characterize the oligopolist as being incredibly myopic, adjusting prices on the assumption that there will be no reaction from rivals. When rivals do react by adjusting their prices, the oligopolist again adjusts its price, again oblivious to the fact that rivals will react, and so on. These myopic models do not have very strong explanatory or predictive power, since most oligopolists in the real world have long since discovered that imprudent price cuts can lead to damaging price wars, just as ill-considered price increases can lead to substantial losses of market share. Such models are useful, however, for pedagogical purposes, since they illustrate very forcefully the implications of myopia in oligopolistic markets.[5]

When oligopolists *do* recognize their mutual dependence, there are a variety of different conjectural variations they might make. In this chapter we shall examine just one simple model, the *kinked demand curve model*.[6] This model assumes that the firm's conjectural variation will be twofold: for price increases the firm expects no reaction from rivals, since the other firms will be content to sit back and receive extra customers who switch away from the firm raising its price; and for price reductions the firm expects rivals to exactly match the price reduction in order to maintain their shares of the market.

The seven assumptions for the kinked demand curve model of oligopoly

---

[5]In short, failure to recognize mutual dependence leads to the downward progression of prices to a price floor, as in the Cournot model, or to the fluctuation of prices between a price floor and a price ceiling, as in the Edgeworth model. A particularly thorough treatment of these classical models of duopoly (two sellers) under conditions of unrecognized mutual dependence is found in A. Koutsoyiannis, *Modern Microeconomics*, 2nd ed. (London: Macmillan, Inc., 1979), pp. 216-33. Given the space constraints of this textbook, however, I prefer to bypass these models in favor of other models of oligopoly behavior that not only have pedagogic value but also explanatory and predictive value.

[6]This was initially proposed separately by R. L. Hall and C. J. Hitch, "Price Theory and Business Behavior," *Oxford Economic Papers*, May 1939, pp. 12-45; and by P.M. Sweezy, "Demand under Conditions of Oligopoly," *Journal of Political Economy*, (August 1939), pp. 568-73.

TABLE 9-5.   The Seven Assumptions of Oligopoly: The Kinked Demand Curve Model

Structural Assumptions	(1)	Number of sellers	Few
	(2)	Cost conditions	Cubic production function with constant factor prices. Entry of new firms restricted
	(3)	Number of buyers	Many
	(4)	Demand conditions	Product differentiation
Behavorial Assumptions	(5)	Objective function	Maximize short-run profits
	(6)	Strategic variables	Price and quantity
	(7)	Conjectural variation	Zero for price increases, unity for price decreases

are shown in Table 9-5. Since the firm's conjectural variation for price increases is zero, it envisages a *ceteris paribus* demand curve at all prices above the current level, this curve being more or less elastic depending primarily upon the degree of substitutability between its product and rival products. In contemplating price reductions, however, the firm envisages a *mutatis mutandis* demand curve, meaning that it takes into account all reactions induced by, and/or concurrent with, the firm's price adjustment. In this case the *mutatis mutandis* section of the demand curve represents a constant share of the total market for the product in question.[7]

EXAMPLE: In September 1981 Pan American Airways reduced airfares on its major domestic routes by as much as 67 percent. Its major competitors on those routes immediately reduced their prices in order to protect their market share. For example, Pan Am announced their New York-Miami fare of $79 one-way for mid-week flights, which was quickly matched by Eastern Airlines and Delta Airlines, while TWA and Air Florida countered by announcing a $69 fare. Pan Am's intent was presumably to increase cash flow and to avoid financial pressures in times of very high interest rates, and it probably expected to face a *ceteris paribus* demand curve, at least on some routes. If some airlines did not follow suit or reduced price by less, Pan Am could expect to increase both cash flow and market share. For example, on its New York-Los Angeles route, it dropped the fare from $473 to $224. Eastern countered with a $219 day fare and a $195 night fare. But the three largest carriers on that route, United, American, and TWA, maintained their previously announced $300 fares. Thus, Pan Am experienced, and most likely anticipated, a movement down a *mutatis mutandis* demand curve in most of its markets. In some of these markets (routes), the conjectural variation was unity (all rivals would match price cuts), while in other markets, Pan Am doubtless expected its *mutatis mutandis* demand curve to represent an increasing market share, since not all firms would retaliate.[8]

---

[7]Note that while the *ceteris paribus* demand curve is appropriate for "independent action" by a firm not expecting reactions, the *mutatis mutandis* demand curve is appropriate for "joint action" by firms, taking into account rivals' reactions.

[8]See Linda Grant, "Can Pan Am Afford Latest Fare War?" *Los Angeles Times*, September 17, 1981; and "Domestic Fares Reduced by Pan Am," Associated Press, *San Diego Union*, September 8, 1981.

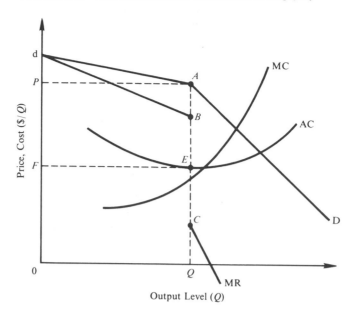

FIGURE 9-6. The Kinked Demand Curve Model of Oligopoly

In Figure 9-6 we show a firm's current price and output levels as P and Q. For prices above P, the firm envisages the relatively elastic *ceteris paribus* demand curve shown by the line dA. For prices below P, it envisages the relatively inelastic *mutatis mutandis* demand curve shown by the line AD. The demand curve facing the firm is therefore dAD, being *kinked* at the current price level. The marginal revenue curve appropriate to this demand curve will have two separate sections. The upper section, shown as dB in Figure 9-6, relates to the *ceteris paribus* section of the demand curve and therefore shares the same intercept and has twice the slope of the line dA. The lower section, CMR, relates to the *mutatis mutandis* section of the demand curve and is positioned such that it has twice the slope of the line AD, and if extended up to the price axis would share its intercept point with the line AD similarly extended.

You will note that there is a vertical discontinuity in the marginal revenue curve, shown as the gap BC in Figure 9-6. Given the foregoing, it is apparent that the length of this gap depends upon the relative slopes of the *ceteris paribus* and *mutatis mutandis* demand curves,[9] which in turn are related to the elasticity of demand under the two conjectural variation situations. If the firm is a profit maximizer, its marginal cost curve will pass through the gap BC. If P and Q are the profit-maximizing price and output levels, this implies that outputs to the left of Q would have marginal rev-

---

[9]See G. J. Stigler, "The Kinky Oligopoly Demand Curve and Rigid Prices," *Journal of Political Economy*, vol. 55 (October 1947).

enues exceeding marginal costs, while outputs to the right of Q would have marginal costs exceeding marginal revenues. This is true only if the MC curve passes through either of the points B or C or through some point in between.[10] The oligopolist's profits are shown by the rectangle $PAEF$ in Figure 9-6.

Price Rigidity in the Kinked-Demand-Curve Model. The KDC model is not a complete theory of price determination, because it is unable to tell us how the firm arrives at the initial price and output levels. Given this starting point, however, the model is able to tell us several things that are important to our understanding of oligopoly markets. First, it offers an explanation of the widely observed rigidity of prices in the face of changing cost and demand conditions. Recall that in each of the models of firm behavior we have examined so far, the firms set price where marginal costs equal marginal revenue. If either costs or demand conditions change, one of these marginal curves shifts, and a new price level is required if the firm is to maximize profits under the new conditions. In the KDC case, however, the marginal cost and marginal revenue curves may shift to a considerable degree without a new price level becoming appropriate, as we shall see. Second, the KDC model tells us when prices *do* change in oligopoly markets. If cost or demand changes are too large to be absorbed at the present price level, the firm adjusts price to the new profit-maximizing level, regardless of what it expects

FIGURE 9-7. **Price Rigidity in Oligopoly despite Changing Cost Levels**

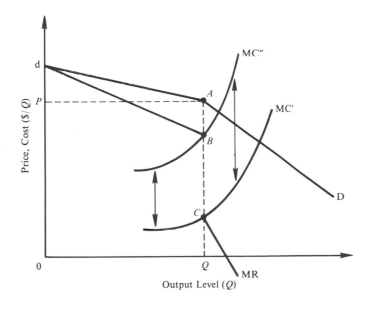

[10]See D. S. Smith and W. C. Neale, "The Geometry of Kinky Oligopoly: Marginal Cost, the Gap, and Price Behavior," *Southern Economic Journal*, 37 (January 1971), 276-82.

rivals to do. Modified versions of the KDC model allow other pricing behavior of oligopolists to be explained and predicted. Let us first examine price rigidity in oligopolies.

In the KDC model the firm does not wish to change price as long as the marginal cost curve passes through the gap in the marginal revenue curve. Thus, costs could increase so that the MC curve moves upward until it passes through point B in Figure 9-7 without the present price becoming inappropriate. Oppositely, if variable costs fall, the MC curve could sink downward until it passes through point C, and price P would remain the profit-maximizing price. As long as marginal revenue exceeds marginal costs for higher prices and is less than marginal costs for lower prices, the present price remains the optimal price. Of course, profits are smaller when costs are higher, but profits are *maximized* when the MC curve passes through the MR gap.

Now consider changes in the demand situation. In most real-world market situations, quantity demanded at the prevailing price level fluctuates up and down over time as the result of seasonal, cyclical, or random influences on the factors determining demand. But as we show in Figure 9-8, demand at price P could fluctuate over the range Q to Q' without causing the MC curve to pass outside the relevant MR gap. At quantity Q, the MR curve is shown by dBCMR, and the MC curve passes through point C. This is the extreme

FIGURE 9-8. Price Rigidity in Oligopoly despite Changing Demand Levels

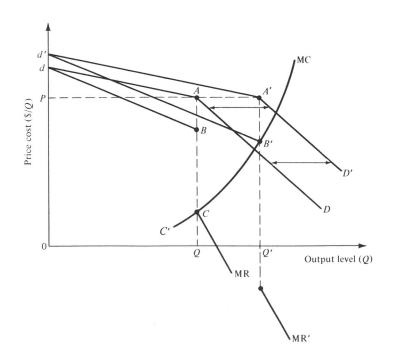

PRICING ANALYSIS AND DECISIONS

leftward point to which the demand curves could shift and yet still allow the MC curve to pass through the gap. The extreme rightward shift of demand, which allows P to remain as the profit-maximizing price, is found when the MC curve passes through point B', as it does at output Q'. Thus, demand could fluctuate over the relatively wide range Q to Q' at price P without the firm wishing to change its price. Profits are lower when demand is lower, but are maximized at price P as long as the demand shift is not so large as to cause the MC curve to miss the gap in the appropriate MR curve.

Price Adjustments in the Kinked-Demand-Curve Model.   Let us look briefly at a cost change that *will* lead to a change in price. As implied above, if the change is such that the new MC curve no longer passes through the MR gap, the firm will want to change price. In Figure 9-9 we show a shift of the marginal cost curve from MC to MC', causing it to intersect the MR curve at point B'. The initial price P is no longer the profit-maximizing price, since marginal cost exceeds marginal revenue for all the output units between Q' and Q. The new profit-maximizing price is thus P', where the MC' curve intersects the MR curve. The firm therefore raises its price to P' and experiences a reduction in its quantity demand from Q to Q'.

Notice that the firm raised its price independently, with the expectation that no other firm would follow its price increase; consequently, it lost part of its market share. Since the firm's price-output coordinate is now point A', it must envisage the new *mutatis mutandis* demand curve, $A'D'$, for any contemplated price reduction. Thus, the firm's share-of-the-market demand curve has effectively shifted to the left as a result of its independent price increase. But the firm, being a profit maximizer by assumption, would rather increase profits than worry about market share, and hence it prefers

FIGURE 9-9.   A Profit-Maximizing Price Change in the Kinked Demand Curve Model

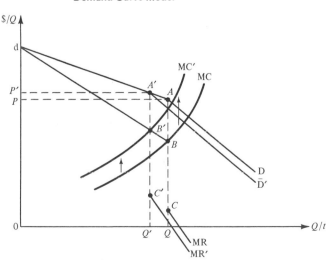

the higher profit situation at price P', given the cost increase that upset the initial equilibrium situation.

Alternatively, we could show the demand curves shifting to the right to such an extent that the firm prefers to raise price (and lose part of its market share) in order to maximize profits. Oppositely, we could show the marginal cost curve falling sufficiently or the demand situation declining sufficiently, causing the MC curve to cut the lower section of the marginal revenue curve.[11] In either of these two cases, the firm would cut its price, notwithstanding its expectation that rivals would immediately follow suit, because cutting price allows profits to be maximized. Since all rivals match the price reduction, all firms maintain their market shares at the lower price level.

Thus, the KDC model predicts that firms will hold price steady, despite the fluctuations of variable costs or demand over a significant range of cost or output levels. Outside the limits set by the requirement that the MC curve pass through the gap in the MR curve, the firm *will* be motivated to change price. It will raise or lower price to the new profit-maximizing level, whether or not it expects rivals to do likewise.

In Chapter 10 we examine "conscious parallelism" and several "price leadership" situations, in which firms jointly raise their prices in the expectation that other firms will also raise their prices. This is typically in response to a common cost increase or demand expansion, whereas the KDC model is particularly appropriate for a cost or demand change which affects only the firm under consideration. Nevertheless, both the conscious-parallelism model and the low-cost firm price-leadership model incorporate a kinked demand curve to explain and predict the pricing behavior of firms.

9.3   SELECTED PRICING MODELS

We now turn to some theories of pricing behavior that rest upon structural assumptions different from those employed in the four basic market forms.

Multiplant Firms

In many cases a firm will have not simply one but two or more plants in which its product may be produced. This may arise as the result of mergers or takeovers or due to expansion at the first site being impossible or uneconomic, for example. In any event, the modification of the structural assumption concerning the cost curves adds an extra decision to the pricing and output decisions of the firm—viz., how should it divide its total output between or among its two or more plants so that profits will be maximized?

---

[11]The lower section of the MR curve may lie completely below the horizontal axis, of course, in which case the MC curve could not intersect it, since MC cannot be negative.

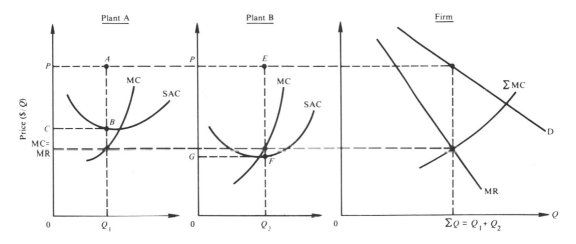

The standard profit-maximizing rule, that marginal costs should equal marginal revenue, remains applicable, but our interpretation of the marginal cost curve must reflect the fact that marginal costs now derive from two or more production sources. The relevant marginal cost curve must show the marginal cost for each incremental unit produced when the firm is free to nominate in which one of its plants that incremental unit should be produced. Clearly, the firm will always nominate the plant that can produce the incremental unit at the lowest additional (or marginal) cost. A simple means of ensuring that this result is achieved is demonstrated in Figure 9-10.

For simplicity, we assume just two plants being operated by a particular firm. In order to make the exercise nontrivial we have assumed differing cost structures for the two plants: Plant A has a higher cost structure than Plant B, due perhaps to its location in a high-land-value area or another factor cost disadvantage or because of the inability of this plant to achieve the same degree of production efficiency as compared with Plant B.

The marginal cost curves of Plants A and B are summed horizontally to find the curve ΣMC shown in the "firm" part of the figure. This curve shows the combined marginal costs of the firm—that is, for a particular output level, some part of the output will have been produced in Plant A and the remainder will have come from Plant B, taking care always to select the incremental unit from the plant that can produce it at lowest marginal cost. From this it follows that at any total output level, the marginal cost from each plant should be approximately equal, since if this were not true the last unit might be taken away from the plant with the higher marginal cost and might be produced instead by the plant with the lower marginal cost, and thus reduce the marginal cost, to the firm as a whole, of the last unit produced. The ΣMC curve thus shows the marginal cost to the firm of each successive output unit, given the ability of the firm to have that unit produced in whichever of its plants can produce it most efficiently.

The firm's profits will be maximized at the output level when the combined marginal cost just equals the marginal revenue. This is shown as output level ΣQ in Figure 9-10, and the demand curve indicates that the firm should set price P. The intersection of the ΣMC and MR curve indicates the *level* at which marginal costs are equal to marginal revenue. If we extend a line at this level across to the cost curves of Plants A and B, this will indicate how the total output, ΣQ, should be divided between the two plants. Marginal costs in Plant A come up to this critical level at output Q_1, and in Plant B marginal costs meet this level at output Q_2. Outputs Q_1 and Q_2 together add up to ΣQ by virtue of the method of construction of the curve ΣMC. Thus, when the output ΣQ is divided among the plants in this way, the marginal cost of Plant A equals the marginal cost of Plant B, and both of these equal the marginal revenue of the final unit sold. The firm's profit is shown as the sum of the two rectangles *PABC* (from Plant A) and *PEFG* (from Plant B), which show the per unit profit margin times the number of units produced, in each of the two plants.

The above analysis of the multiplant firm applies to any market situation where a firm envisages a negatively sloping *ceteris paribus* demand curve. It is thus appropriate for monopoly, monopolistic competition, or oligopoly situations. For oligopolistic markets where mutual dependence is recognized, price may be determined by a price leader or by "conscious parallelism," rather than independently, as suggested in the above, and the demand curve depicted in Figure 9-10 would represent the firm's *mutatis mutandis*, or share-of-the-market, demand curve. But the rule for allocation of output between or among multiple plants remains the same. The firm should ensure that the marginal cost of the last unit produced in each plant is approximately the same and is equal to the marginal revenue obtained for those last units.

Cartel Price and Output Determination

DEFINITION: A *cartel* is a group of firms acting as one, determining their price and/or output levels from within a central administering body. Cartels are illegal in most Western countries, but a couple of major international cartels continue to exist, immune from national legislation.

EXAMPLE: The International Air Transport Association, IATA, determines airfares and many elements of nonprice competition for its members, such as types of meals, beverage prices, and in-flight movie prices. During the 1970s, higher levels of excess capacity due to the advent of jumbo jets, as well as the vigorous competition of third world airlines, reduced IATA's market control to a significant degree. The Organization of Petroleum Exporting Countries, OPEC, undoubtedly the most powerful cartel in the late 1970s, was able to elevate the prices of petroleum products dramatically as its members jointly raised prices to the levels agreed upon. The influence of OPEC waned considerably as the "oil glut" of the early 1980s induced members to offer discounts below the cartel price. As implied by these two examples, the life of cartels tends to be short and stormy. We shall see that cartels are inherently unstable due to the incentives facing each firm to cheat on the cartel agreement.

A cartel may be either profit maximizing or market sharing. The profit-maximizing cartel attempts to maximize the *joint* profits of the firms. The firms then take a share of the total profits as determined by prior agreement or as actually earned. The market-sharing cartel establishes rules that allow each firm to maintain its predetermined or historical share of the market. We examine here each type in turn.

The Profit-Maximizing Cartel. The profit-maximizing cartel has exactly the same price and output decisions to make as does the multiplant firm. The cartel is like the multiplant firm except that it does not own each of the plants; it simply controls their pricing and output decisions. As well as choosing the price and the total output level, the cartel (or multiplant firm) has one additional decision to make, namely, how it should divide its total output among the participating firms or plants in order to maximize total profits.

For simplicity we assume there are two members in the cartel and that the firms have differing cost structures: Firm A has a higher cost structure than firm B, as shown in Figure 9-11.

The marginal cost curves of A and B are summed horizontally to find curve ΣMC shown in the part of the figure labelled *cartel*. This curve shows the combined marginal costs of the cartel; that is, for a particular output level, some part of the output is produced in firm A and the remainder in firm B, taking care always to select the incremental unit from the firm that can produce it at the lower marginal cost. From this it follows that at any particular total output level the marginal cost from each firm should be approximately equal. The ΣMC curve thus shows the marginal cost to the

FIGURE 9-11. **Price and Output Determination by a Joint Profit-Maximizing Cartel**

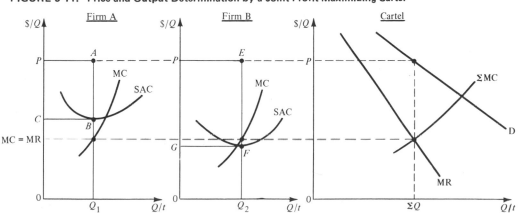

cartel of each successive output unit, given the ability of the cartel to have that unit produced by the firm that can produce it most efficiently.

The cartel's profits are maximized at the output level where the combined marginal cost just equals the marginal revenue. This is shown as output level ΣQ in Figure 9-11. The demand curve indicates that the cartel should set price P. The intersection of the ΣMC and MR curves indicates the level at which marginal costs are equal to marginal revenue. If we extend a line at this level across to the cost curves of firms A and B, we see how total output ΣQ should be divided between the two firms. In firm A marginal costs come up to this critical level at output Q_1, and in firm B they come up to this level at output Q_2. Outputs Q_1 and Q_2 together add up to ΣQ, by virtue of the method of construction of the curve ΣMC. Thus when the output ΣQ is divided among the firms in this way, the marginal cost of firm A equals the marginal cost of firm B. Both of these equal the marginal revenue of the final unit sold. The cartel's profit is shown as the sum of the two rectangles $PABC$ (from firm A) and $PEFG$ (from firm B). These rectangles show the per unit profit margin times the number of units produced, in each of the two firms.

Side Payments and the Incentive to Undercut the Cartel Price. The two member firms may agree to keep the profits they have each earned. Alternatively, there may be a prior agreement that the more-profitable firm B must give some of its profits to the less-profitable firm A. This *side payment* may be thought necessary to help firm A resist the temptation to undercut the cartel price and temporarily, at least, to enjoy an elastic demand response for its product. In fact, both firms face the temptation of large sales gains and higher profits, if they can secretly undercut the cartel price. If either firm can set a price below the cartel price, while the other firm continues to set the cartel price, the price-cutting firm will face a relatively elastic *ceteris paribus* demand curve, on which there will be a lower, more profitable price. Let us illustrate, using firm A as the price cutter in Figure 9-12.

Initially, firm A is setting the cartel price P and producing Q_1 units of output. When contemplating independent price adjustments, the firm envisages the *ceteris paribus* demand curve shown as d. Associated with that curve is the marginal revenue curve, mr, which intersects the firm's marginal cost curve, MC_A, at output level Q'. Profits at the lower price P' are equal to the area $P'A'B'C'$ and are considerably larger than the profits $PABC$ available to the firm as a member of the cartel. Thus there is considerable profit incentive to leave the cartel and price independently. Firm A might require a side payment equal to the difference in these two profit rectangles in order to keep it in the cartel.

But notice that the firm would earn these extra profits only as long as *ceteris paribus* prevailed. As soon as the other firm noticed its loss of sales and ascertained that firm A was "chiseling" the cartel price, it would probably match A's price reduction in order to maintain its share of the market. Alternatively, it might undercut A's price to teach it a lesson, and a price war might ensue. The extra profits are available to firm A only as long as the price

FIGURE 9-12. The Incentive to Undercut the Cartel Price

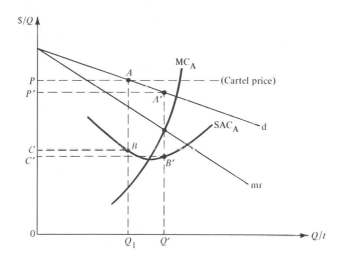

reduction remains unknown to firm B. If A is able to give customers secret discounts, and if sales normally fluctuate considerably in any case, firm B might not discover the duplicity for several weeks or months, during which time A can earn extra profits, which may be worth the risk of setting off a price war or of facing other disciplinary action by the cartel.

The more firms there are in a cartel, the more difficult it is, *ceteris paribus*, for the cartel to control prices or outputs of individual firms. The more firms the more difficult it is for cartel members to find out that they are being undercut, since the "chiseler's" sales gain is comprised of proportionately smaller sales losses for each firm. There is thus a greater inclination for individual firms to undercut the cartel price. In actual business practice the life of cartels has usually been short and stormy, ending with a rapid decline in prices after the discovery that one or more firms were undercutting the cartel price.

The Market-Sharing Cartel. In some instances oligopolists may wish to come to an agreement regarding their share of the market as a primary objective, rather than allow this to be the outcome of their price-fixing agreement, as in the preceding discussion. Firms that are geographically dispersed, for example, may feel that they have a right to sales in their own territory and will want to preclude encroachment by rivals into that territory. In this case the total market would be shared on the basis of the firms' locations and the density of population (and consequent demand) in each territory. Alternatively, firms with large output capacities may feel that they deserve a larger share of the market than would be allocated to them under a joint profit-maximizing cartel agreement. The other firms may be willing to allow these firms to take more than their (joint profit-maximizing) share, rather than risk a breakdown of the cartel's price agreement.

The agreement on market share may be quite an explicit arrangement (firm A gets 15 percent of industry sales) or an implicit, general understanding among the firms concerning each one's annual output levels (firm A has a quota of about 200,000 units annually). We immediately see that problems arise in business situations, since these agreements involve an estimate of annual market demand. Different conceptions of the market, different projections about the coming year's demand, and different perceptions of the same phenomena are likely to lead to disagreements about what constitutes a 15-percent share, for example. Compromises on these issues may leave some firms feeling less happy than others and perhaps more likely to violate the agreement at a later time. Similarly, agreements on the boundaries of each firm's geographical territory may be hard to arrive at and may be quite fragile when finally made.

When business is booming, firms have little time or reason to think about how the market-sharing agreement puts them at a disadvantage. When demand slackens in periods of recession or depression, however, firms may be considerably more inclined to undercut the cartel price or to encroach into another firm's territory and compete for sales. Such price cutting, probably in the form of secret discounts, generous trade-in allowances, or additional goods and services for the same price, soon come to the attention of other firms. The cartel agreement would be expected to break down as other firms begin to take defensive measures to avoid losing any more of their market shares.

Cartel price and market-sharing agreements might be expected to work a lot better if the participant firms have similar cost structures and either identical or symmetrically differentiated products. In such cases a single market price and equal market shares are likely to be relatively palatable solutions to the uncertainty faced by oligopolists.

EXAMPLE: OPEC, the Organization of Petroleum Exporting Countries, is a cartel comprised of thirteen member nations—Algeria, Ecuador, Gabon, Indonesia, Iran, Iraq, Kuwait, Libya, Nigeria, Qatar, Saudi Arabia, the United Arab Emirates, and Venezuela. Representatives of these nations met in Geneva in October 1981 to establish a new world price for oil. They established a new base price of $34 per barrel for Saudi Arabia light crude. Other nation's oils, being of higher and lower qualities, are expected to maintain their traditional price differentials with respect to Saudi light crude. For example, Nigeria's high quality oil usually commands a premium of about $4 per barrel and other heavier crudes are priced as low as $28 per barrel.

The 1981 agreement, intended to prevail through to the end of 1982 at least, represented the end of eighteen months of independent pricing by member nations. The oil shortages that began with the Iranian crisis of 1979 and continued with the Iran-Iraq war, allowed some countries to raise prices to over $40 per barrel. Two previous attempts to unify the price structure had failed during this period, as some members found it preferable to price independently for greater profits. The oil glut of 1981 was enough to induce those nations to agree on the new price structure, however. The reduced consumption of petroleum by most importing nations as they develop alternative energy sources, and the revenue needs of many of the OPEC members, indicates that the world price of oil may, in the future, be reduced further to prevent, or in response to, the price cutting by members. In real terms the price of oil will certainly decline, and the power of the OPEC cartel seems to be diminishing.[12]

Price Discrimination

DEFINITION: *Price discrimination* is the practice of charging different prices to different buyers or groups of buyers for essentially the same product, where these price differences do not simply reflect the cost differences associated with serving different buyers or markets. The monopolist may find it both possible and more profitable to discriminate among buyers on some basis; to charge a higher price to some buyers and a lower price to others, rather than set the same price for all buyers. Price discrimination in the "economic" sense must be distinguished from price discrimination in the "legal" sense. In Chapter 11 we briefly examine the illegal methods of price discrimination. In perhaps most instances, "economic" price discrimination is not illegal.

NOTE: Three major conditions must exist before it is possible and profitable to practice price discrimination. First, the buyers or groups of buyers (markets) must be *separable*. That is, it must be possible to identify and keep separate the two or more buyers or markets, in order to prevent arbitrage selling from the lower-price to the higher-price buyer or market. Second, the two or more buyers (or markets) must exhibit *differing price elasticities of demand* at any particular price level, in order to make price discrimination profitable, as we shall see below. Third, the markets must be characterized by a *lack of price competition* from rival firms, in order to prevent price levels being eroded from the profit-maximizing levels in each market. Clearly, price discrimination is most likely to work well in a monopoly situation, where there are no rivals to worry about, but it is also feasible in oligopoly markets, where the firms coordinate their pricing strategies using conscious parallelism, price leadership, or cartel pricing.

Price discrimination has been categorized into three distinct types. *First-degree price discrimination* occurs when each buyer is forced to pay the maximum that he or she would have been willing to pay for the product. In situations where there is no price discrimination, all but one of the buyers pay *less* than they would have been willing to pay, since there is only one price at which the product is offered, and the last buyer is the one who is

---

[12]See William M. Brown, "Can OPEC Survive the Oil Glut?" *Fortune,* November 30, 1981, pp. 89-96; and Don Cook and Karen Tumulty, "OPEC Sets Unified Oil Price of $34," *Los Angeles Times*, October 30, 1981, pp. 1, 15.

only just willing to pay the price asked. All other buyers (those higher on the demand curve) would have been willing to pay more but were not asked to.[13] First-degree price discrimination involves asking each buyer to pay the maximum he or she would be willing to pay or else go without the product. In practice, of course, this is a difficult pricing decision, since one cannot know the preference structures of all the potential buyers.

EXAMPLE: One means of accomplishing first-degree price discrimination in practice is the so-called Dutch auction in which the price starts at a very high level and the auctioneer calls out prices at slowly reducing price levels. The first person to accept the called price as the purchase price gets the product. This person will have paid the maximum he or she would have been willing to pay, since this buyer did not know what the second-most-eager buyer would have paid and therefore must bid as soon as the price falls to the maximum level he or she would have paid. The more conventional auction, in which price is bid upward, ensures that the successful bidder pays only slightly more than the second-most-eager buyer was willing to pay, rather than the maximum he or she was willing to pay.

Second-degree price discrimination involves discriminating among groups of buyers on a time or urgency basis. Those most eager to purchase the product will pay a higher price than those prepared to wait a little longer, and so on.

EXAMPLE: An amazing example of this was the early sale of ballpoint pens, which reportedly sold for around thirty dollars each, due to their novelty and utility value. Later, as technology advanced and costs fell, and as the market became progressively more saturated, the price fell to the level we know today. Products that have undergone a similar reduction in prices in more recent years are electronic calculators and quartz-crystal wristwatches. One further example is the pricing of tickets for new-movie releases. First runs in city theatres are priced substantially above second runs in suburban theatres, and so on down the line until finally the movie appears on television for virtually no charge at all.

Third-degree price discrimination is a situation whereby the firm can charge different prices in two or more different markets at the same point in time.

EXAMPLE: Examples of this practice are telephone and electricity price differentials between households and business establishments and a firm that charges a higher price for a particular product in a downtown store than in a suburban store. Telephone companies also practice third-degree price discrimination by separating their markets on the basis of the time of day

---

[13]Consumer surplus is the name given to the amount of money the consumer would have been willing to pay over and above the price actually paid. In regular markets all buyers except the last one receive some amount of consumer surplus. With first-degree price discrimination all consumer surplus is expropriated by the seller from every buyer, and it is added to the producer's surplus, which is profit. For more on consumer surplus, see R. A. Bilas, *Microeconomic Theory*, 2nd ed. (New York: McGraw-Hill Book Company, 1971), pp. 97-107.

and the day of the week. Long distance telephone calls during business hours cost more than during early morning hours or on weekends. Business establishments are willing and able to pay the higher prices during the day, since business must be conducted when other businesses are also operating. If the prices were the same twenty-four hours a day, many home users would write letters instead. Recognizing the more elastic nature of home demand, the telephone company offers cheaper calls at less convenient hours in order to increase the use of long distance telephone calls in two ways: first, it attracts buyers who would not otherwise purchase the service; and second, it shifts some of the demand into the offpeak hours, which saves the company from building a larger plant just to handle peak traffic.

To practice third-degree price discrimination the firm must decide what its total output should be, how it should distribute this output between or among the separate markets, and what price it should set in each market, so that profits are maximized. The methodology for solving this problem is similar to that for the multiplant firm's allocation problem. The firm should distribute each successive output unit to the market in which the unit contributes most to total revenues and should continue up to the point where the marginal revenue derived from the sale of the last unit is just equal to the marginal cost of producing that last unit. Figure 9-13 shows two market situations, A and B. Market A has the more inelastic demand situation, perhaps because of fewer competitors, higher incomes of the buyers, or simply because of different taste patterns of the buyers in that market. If the firm were to begin with its first output unit, it would certainly sell this unit in Market A, at a price near P_0, since the marginal revenue of the first unit is higher there than in Market B. As the firm lowers its price to sell successive units, these units too will be best sold in Market A, at least initial-

FIGURE 9-13. Construction of the Marginal Revenue Curve for the Price-Discriminating Firm

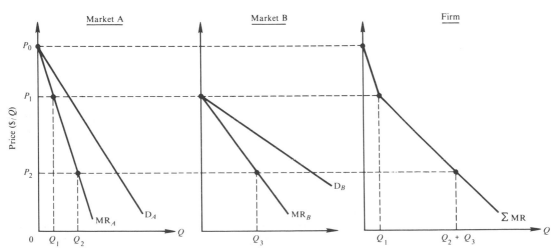

FIGURE 9-14. Prices and Output Determination by the Price-Discriminating Firm

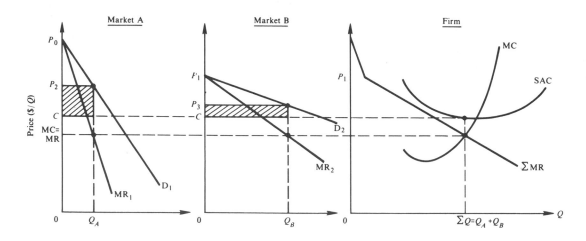

ly. But when price P_1 is reached, buyers in Market B begin to enter the market, and the firm should now allocate successive output units back and forth between Markets A and B, taking care to allocate each incremental unit to the market in which it derives the greatest marginal revenue. The curve ΣMR in the "firm" part of the figure indicates the marginal revenue to the firm when it is free to allocate each successive unit to the market in which marginal revenue is highest. It is found by the horizontal summation of the marginal revenue curves in Markets A and B. Clearly, it must begin at price level P_0 and kink at price level P_1, since below this level it is the horizontal sum of both MR curves rather than just the one.

In Figure 9-14 we superimpose the firm's short-run cost curves upon the ΣMR curve. The output level that maximizes the firm's profits is shown as ΣQ, where its marginal costs rise to equality with its declining marginal revenues. The intersection of the MC and ΣMR curves defines the *level* at which marginal revenues in each market should be equated to the firm's marginal costs. Extending a line at this level across to the graphs for Markets A and B, we see that the firm should allocate Q_A units to Market A and Q_B units to Market B, since marginal revenues in each of these markets at these output levels have fallen to the level to which marginal costs have risen. In Market A, quantity Q_A should be priced at price P_2, and quantity Q_B will be sold at price P_3 in Market B. Note that the more inelastic market is charged the higher price. The firm's total profits may be calculated as the sum of the price-cost margin in each market times the quantity sold in each market. That is, profits in Market A will be the shaded area $P_2 C \times 0Q_A$ and in Market B will be the shaded area $P_3 C \times 0Q_B$.

The output level ΣQ, and the allocation of this output between the markets as shown, is optimal, because if another unit was produced its marginal cost would exceed the marginal revenue in either market, and if the last unit was taken from either market and sold in the other, its marginal revenue would be less than its marginal cost. Thus, any different output level, and/or allocation of output between the markets, would cause the firm's total profits to be reduced.

In summary, price discrimination involves charging different prices to different buyers or groups of buyers when their demand situations differ. If markets or individual buyers can be identified and kept separate, the monopolist can increase its profits by setting different prices for each one.

9.4 SUMMARY

In this chapter we introduced the notion that models of the firm's pricing behavior can be characterized under seven assumptions. The four structural assumptions relate to number of sellers, cost conditions, number of buyers, and degree of product differentiation. The three behavioral assumptions refer to the firm's objective function, its strategic variables, and its conjectural variation. The models of pricing behavior differ from each other only to the extent that one or more of the seven basic assumptions is different. The difference in one or more of the underlying assumptions, however, leads to a different pattern of behavior of the firm. Thus, the price and output levels chosen by a firm depend upon the structural and behavioral conditions under which the firm operates.

The four basic market forms were analyzed for the pricing and output behavior of the firm in each of those market situations. Under conditions of pure competition, monopolistic competition, and monopoly, the pricing and output decision was based on a *ceteris paribus* demand curve because of the expectation that a firm's price or output adjustment would not induce any changes in any other variables. Under oligopoly we introduced the *mutatis mutandis*, or "joint action," demand curve. In the kinked demand curve model of oligopoly the firm envisages no reaction for price increases but expects rivals to match any price reductions. Given these expectations, the oligopolist faces a kinked demand curve, since the *ceteris paribus* section for price increases will be more elastic than the *mutatis mutandis* section for price reductions.

We saw that the pursuit of short-run profit maximization leads the firms in all four market situations to choose the price and output level for which marginal revenue equals marginal cost. (In the kinked demand curve model of oligopoly, MC passes through the vertical discontinuity in the MR curve rather than being strictly equal to the MR curve.) The kinked demand curve offers an explanation for price rigidity despite changes in the cost and demand conditions, within limits. Outside these limits of cost and demand movements the firm will change price and/or output levels, and we shall see in the next chapter that the kinked demand curve is involved in other pricing models as well.

As selected pricing models, we examined the pricing and output decision of the multiplant firm, the multifirm cartel, and the multimarket firm. The multiplant firm and the profit-maximizing cartel have essentially the same decision problem. After determining aggregate output and the profit-maximizing price, they must divide aggregate output among the plants (or firms) such that the marginal cost of each plant/firm rises only up to the level to which marginal revenue has fallen. The multimarket firm can practice price discrimination if it can separate individuals and markets in space and time, charging higher prices to the consumers who expect to derive greater utility, whose demand is more urgent, and whose demand is more inelastic.

DISCUSSION QUESTIONS

9-1. In what single dimension does monopolistic competition differ from pure competition? In what dimension(s) does oligopoly differ from both of the above?

9-2. Pure competitors are assumed to maximize their short-run profits. In this type of market environment is it conceivable that firms might wish to pursue any objective function other than short-run profit maximization? Why or why not?

9-3. The pure competitor's marginal cost curve is, in effect, that firm's supply curve, showing how much it will supply at each price level. Explain this.

9-4. Characterize according to the simple spectrum of market forms the markets in which the following groups of firms operate:

(a) Automobile dealerships in a large city.

(b) College and universities marketing their degrees to potential students.

(c) An art dealer who wants to sell a unique painting, such as the Mona Lisa.

(d) A grain farmer selling wheat to one of forty or fifty flour-milling companies.

9-5. State why you would intuitively expect a monopolistic competitor with a higher-quality product to command both a higher price and a larger market share, as compared with its rivals.

9-6. Given that an oligopolist envisages a kinked demand curve, explain why it is sometimes profit maximizing to raise prices and incur a loss of market share.

9-7. Why would you expect the price rigidity implications of the kinked-demand-curve model more likely to be observed in practice if the cost changes or demand shifts are firm-specific, rather than common to all firms?

9-8. Discuss the operation of cartels and the incentive to undercut the cartel price. Does it make a difference when the products are differentiated and the "cartel price" is in reality a structure of prices around a particular level?

9-9. Outline the principle of profit maximization as applied to a firm that operates three plants within the same market.

9-10. In principle, explain how a firm may increase its profits by discriminating between two distinct markets for its products.

PROBLEMS AND SHORT CASES

9-1. Show graphically the situation in which a purely competitive market suffers a temporary reduction in consumer demand. Summarize what happens to

(a) The price level.

(b) Each firm's output level.

(c) The total number of firms.

9-2. During the 1960s, following the lead of the Beatles and other pop groups, male hairstyles tended toward greater length. Over this decade many barbershops went out of business, and others reduced their size of operation from, say, five or six chairs to one or two chairs.

(a) Characterize this industry in terms of the four basic market forms.

(b) Show graphically the process of adjustment that you think occurred in that industry during the 1960s.

9-3. Suppose the automobile producers are confronted with an increase of 10 percent in the negotiated wage for assembly labor, yet prices of their products remain constant.

(a) Explain with the aid of graphs why the firms might not wish to increase their prices.

(b) Why might you expect these firms to raise prices at the start of the next model year, rather than during the present model year?

9-4. The Prangle Company manufactures and sells several styles of jeans which are branded as the Sizzlers. Several years ago the company introduced the stylized jean look, and Prangle sales increased dramatically. Over the past two years, however, sales have been declining steadily for their stylized jean because of the incursion of several look-alike competing products, even though the total market for stylized jeans is still expanding.

As a result of the increased supply of stylized jeans, the other companies have been selling their competitive jeans at a price below that of Prangle. Prangle's price has not changed from the original price set by the company at the introduction of the jean on the market. Prangle's price at retail was $12, with the retailer paying $9. Other firm's products are retailing for around the same price, with the retailer paying $8.

As a result of the increased supply in the market and Prangle's declining sales volume, Gail Morin, the sales manager, decided to review the cost structure to determine if the margin offered to the retailer could be widened in order to recoup some of the sales share. If she could significantly reduce the price to retailers, Prangle could recapture some of its lost market.

At the present time, variable production costs (including raw materials and labor) are constant at $4 per pair. The sales volume now is 400,000 pairs of jeans. Ms. Morin is wondering what effect a reduction in price would have on sales and on the profitability of the line. The accounting department and the market research department have estimated cost and demand figures applicable for a reduction in Prangle's price to the retailer. If the price were lowered to that of the competition ($8), demand would increase by 150,000 pairs; if the company lowered the retailer's price even further (to $7), demand is estimated to increase to 625,000 pairs. With such an increase in production the firm could more efficiently use its resources and production facilities. The advantages acquired in bulk buying of raw materials and the more efficient use of labor both help to chisel down the variable costs per pair to $3.75 per unit under the latter demand condition.

Ms. Morin has considered all of the information the market research and accounting departments have provided and is about to make a pricing decision. You are asked to advise on the following issues:

(a) Explain why the Prangle Company suffered declining sales in a market that was actually expanding.

(b) Explain the proposed price reductions in terms of the demand curve the Prangle Company is apparently facing, assuming the data are accurate.

(c) Advise Ms. Morin about the contribution-maximizing price level.

9-5. Analyze graphically the case of a two-plant firm that practices price discrimination in two separate markets. Assume two sets of cost conditions and two demand situations, and show the following:

(a) How the firm determines total output.

(b) Allocation of production to each plant.

(c) Allocation of output to each market.

(d) Prices in each of the two markets.

9-6. The Thomas Tent Company has two separate markets for its midsize tent. The domestic market is characterized by the demand curve $P = 100 - 15Q$, and the foreign market is characterized by the demand curve $P = 60 - 2.5Q$, where P represents the price in dollars and Q represents thousands of units demanded. The firm's one plant has a total cost function approximated by TC $= 10800 + 20Q + 0.1Q^2$ in the relevant range of outputs.

(a) What is the profit-maximizing output level of mid-size tents?

(b) How should Thomas divide this output between the two markets?

(c) What price should be set in the domestic market?

(d) What price should be set in the foreign market?

9-7. The Bartram Bitumen Company has two plants producing bituminous tar for its market in which it has a virtual monopoly because of the remote location of other firms producing bituminous tar. The marketing manager has estimated the firm's demand curve as $P = 68.5 - 0.005Q$; and the production manager has estimated the monthly cost functions as TC $= 5,850 + 1.5Q + 0.005Q^2$ for Plant A, and TC $= 6,250 + 1.2Q + 0.003Q^2$ for Plant B, where Q represents pounds of tar in all cases.

(a) Please advise Bartram about the profit-maximizing output level from both plants in total.

(b) How much of this output should come from Plant A?

(c) What price should Bartram set?

(d) Demonstrate that total contribution would decline if the last 100 units to be produced in Plant A could not be produced there because of a breakdown and had to be produced in Plant B instead.

SUGGESTED REFERENCES AND FURTHER READING

Bain, J. S. *Barriers to New Competition.* Cambridge, Mass.: Harvard University Press, 1956.

Baumol, W. J. and R. D. Willig. "Fixed Costs, Sunk Costs, Entry Barriers, and the Sustainability of Monopoly", *Quarterly Journal of Economics*, 96 (Aug. 1981), pp. 405-31.

Chamberlin, E. H. *The Theory of Monopolistic Competiton.* Cambridge, Mass.: Harvard University Press, 1969.

Efroymson, C. W. "The Kinked Oligopoly Curve Reconsidered," *Quarterly Journal of Economics*, 69 (February 1955), 119-36.

Hall, R. L., and C. J. Hitch. "Price Theory and Business Behavior," *Oxford Economic Papers*, (May 1939), 12-45.

Hawkins, C. J. *Theory of the Firm.* London: Macmillan, Inc. 1973.

Hirshleifer, J. *Price Theory and Applications*, (2nd ed.) chaps. 9-13. Englewood Cliffs, N.J.: Prentice-Hall, Inc., 1980.

Kling A. "Imperfect Information and Price Rigidity," *Economic Inquiry*, 20 (Jan. 1982), pp. 145-54.

Loomes, G. "Why Oligopoly Prices Don't Stick," *Journal of Economic Studies*, 8 (No. 1, 1981,) pp. 37-46.

Robinson, J. *The Economics of Imperfect Competition.* London: Macmillan, Inc., 1933.

Smith, D. S., and W. C. Neale. "The Geometry of Kinky Oligopoly: Marginal Cost, the Gap, and Price Behavior," *Southern Economic Journal*, 37 (January 1971), 276-82.

Stigler, G. J. "The Kinky Oligopoly Demand Curve and Rigid Prices," *Journal of Political Economy*, 55 (October 1947), 432-49.

Sweezy, P. M. "Demand under Conditions of Oligopoly," *Journal of Political Economy*, 47 (August 1939), 568-73.

Thompson, A. A., Jr. *Economics of the Firm*, (3rd ed.) chaps. 9-13. Englewood Cliffs, N.J.: Prentice-Hall, Inc., 1981.

APPENDIX 9A: LONG-RUN ADJUSTMENTS TO PLANT SIZE AND THE PRICING CONSEQUENCES

In Chapter 9 the models of the firm were discussed in the context of the short run. That is, the cost structure was given and output was constrained at the upper limit due to the presence of fixed factors of production. A further modification of each of the above models is to relax the structural assumption regarding the firm's cost structure. In the long run the firm is able to adjust its size of plant and thus begin production in the subsequent short-run period with a different cost structure and a different upper limit to its output level.

The long-run adjustments to plant size encompass all degrees of expansion and contraction. The ultimate contraction of plant size is to completely liquidate all fixed factors and leave the industry. At the other extreme is new entry to the industry by establishing a plant (increasing plant size from zero to some finite level). Why are firms motivated to expand or contract plant size or to enter or leave the industry? In a nutshell, firms move in the direction of increased profitability (or reduced losses). The expectation of economic profits (or losses) will induce firms to enter (or leave) an industry, and the expectation of larger profits at a different plant size will induce firms to expand, or reduce, their plant size.

In each of the models of pricing behavior examined above, we presented a situation in which the firms were able to earn economic profits in the short run. Whether or not there will be entry of new firms depends upon the presence or absence of "barriers to entry."

Barriers to the Entry of New Firms

Barriers to entry were absent in the pure competition and monopolistic competition situations and were absolute in the monopoly situation (although we might expect these barriers to break down with the passage of time). In oligopoly, however, barriers to entry will be present to varying degrees, and they may take the form of limited or unavailable factors such as necessary raw materials, technical skills, managerial talent, production and selling locations or, on the demand side, the product differentiation advantage of existing firms. Some of these barriers to entry may be surmountable, given the application of sufficient funds. But the cost of overcoming the barriers and offsetting any continuing cost disadvantages may cause the entrant firm's cost level to be so high that it makes entry and subsequent production insufficiently profitable. On the other hand, a relatively large capital investment required to enter a particular industry, such as automobiles or steel, is not in itself a barrier to entry, since it only precludes those who cannot afford to play the game.[1]

Adjustment of Plant Size in Pure Competition

Since barriers to entry are absent in pure competition, we should expect the entry of new firms as soon as they can establish a new plant and begin production. The advent of new firms will increase the quantity supplied at each price level, and thus the market supply curve will move to the right. This in turn will cause the market price to fall. At the same time, existing firms will see that they can obtain economies of plant size by moving to the plant size that minimizes per unit costs. The net result is as shown in Figure 9A-1.

Let us suppose that in the initial short-run period all firms were producing with the plant size depicted by SAC_1. Each firm was making a profit, since price exceeds average total costs. Given an opportunity to adjust the size of their plants each of these firms will move to the plant size depicted by SAC^*, since this allows the minimum level of per unit costs.[2] New entrants to the industry, attracted by the existence of "pure" profits, also can be expected to establish the plant size depicted by SAC^*. If exactly the right number of new firms enter, the market supply curve will shift across from S to S', and market price will fall from P_1 to P^*. Given the new market price, all firms will produce output level Q^*, price will equal average costs, and all firms can earn only a "normal" profit. You will recall from Chapter 7 that this means that total revenues are equal to the opportunity cost of all inputs, or that inputs are earning as much in this particular usage as they could in their next-best-alternative usage. Hence, no firm will wish to leave the industry, and no new firms will wish to enter the industry, since more entry would depress the price below the normal profit level.

Thus the presence of pure or economic profit in the short run leads to the entry of new firms until profits are reduced to the normal level, given the absence of barriers to entry.

---

[1]See J. S. Bain, *Barriers to New Competition* (Cambridge, Mass.: Harvard University Press, 1956). See also Eaton, B.C. and R.G. Lipsey, "Exit Barriers are Entry Barriers: The Durability of Capital as a Barrier to Entry", *Bell Journal of Economics*, 11 (Autumn 1980), pp. 721-29.

[2]For this reason it is often referred to as the "optimal" size of plant. This is not to say that firms should always choose the SAC curve that is tangent to the LAC curve at the lowest point of the LAC curve, as we shall see in the context of other market situations.

FIGURE 9A-1. Long-Run Plant Size Adjustment in Pure Competition

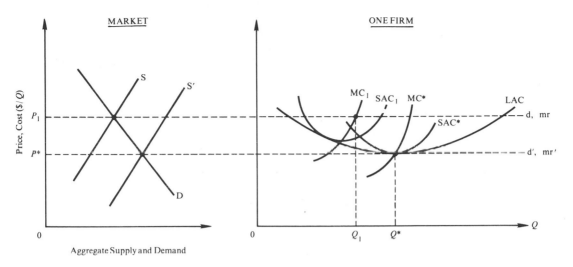

Adjustment of Plant Size in Monopolistic Competition

Long-run plant size adjustment in monopolistic competition proceeds in an essentially similar manner. New firms are motivated to enter by the existence of pure profits, and existing firms are motivated to adjust plant size to that which allows the greatest possible profit.

The entry of new firms, each with a new product slightly differentiated from the other products, causes the total market demand to be shared among more firms. This means that each firm's demand curve shifts to the left, since each firm loses some of its customers to the new entrants. Each firm will be forced to reduce the size of its plant as its share of demand is reduced, until eventually so many firms will have entered that each firm will be earning only a normal profit. This will represent an equilibrium situation, since no more firms will wish to enter and none will wish to leave. The long-run equilibrium situation is shown in Figure 9A-2.

In Figure 9A-2 we show a representative firm facing the demand curve dd in the initial short-run situation. Its plant size is depicted by the SAC_1 curve, it maximizes profits at price P_1, and its output level is Q_1. The entry of new firms causes this firm's demand curve to shift to the left, eventually reaching that shown as d'd'. Given this demand situation, the only way the representative firm can survive is to build the plant represented by SAC*. This is the only plant that allows a normal profit to be made. The firm sets price P* and produces output level Q* in order to maximize profits. Note that these normal profits are sufficient to keep the firm in the industry, since they represent at least as much as the resources could earn elsewhere.

Again we see that in the absence of barriers to entry, the entry of new

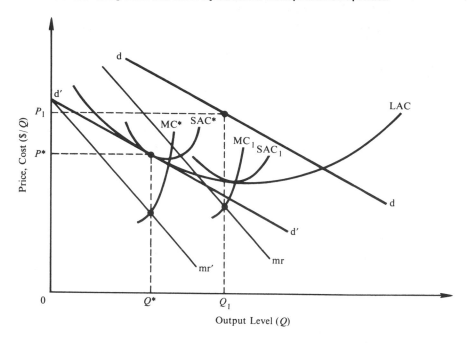

Output Level (Q)

firms tends to reduce the price level to consumers and causes firms to retreat to a position where they are making only normal profits. Let us now examine the case where barriers to entry do exist and prevent the incursion of new competition.

Adjustment of Plant Size in Monopoly

As long as the barriers to entry restrain new competition, the monopolist is faced with the same demand situation (given that market size is neither increasing nor decreasing). The monopolist's problem is to choose the plant size that allows the greatest profits, given the prevailing demand situation. In Figure 9A-3 we show the initial plant size as SAC_1, and we show that the monopolist maximizes short-run profits where MC_1 = MR at price P_1 and quantity Q_1. The plant size that allows the *greatest* short-run profit, given the continuation of this demand situation, is shown as SAC*.

The profit-maximizing plant size is found by equating the long-run marginal cost (LMC) curve with the marginal revenue curve. The LMC curve shows the change in total costs as output changes, when all inputs are free to vary (and the firm follows the economically efficient long-run expansion path). It thus allows us to adjust all inputs to the point where any further input of any factor would cause marginal costs to exceed marginal revenues. The monopolist then builds the plant size (SAC*) that allows the optimal quantity Q^* to be produced at the minimum cost combination shown by the

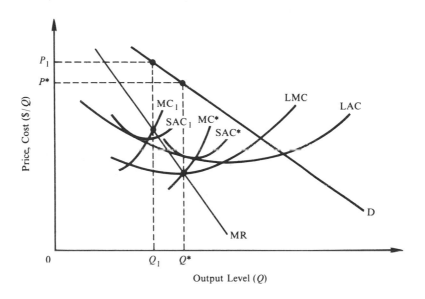

FIGURE 9A-3. Long-Run Plant Size Adjustment in Monopoly

point on the LAC curve. Note that the short-run marginal cost curve associated with the profit-maximizing plant (i.e., MC*) equals marginal revenue at the optimal output level, since short-run and long-run average costs are equal at this output level.

Adjustment of Plant Size in Oligopoly

The oligopoly result is similar to that of monopoly in that the existence of some barriers to entry typically allows the perpetuation of pure profits. In oligopoly situations the barriers are often more accurately described as "hurdles," since they do not necessarily make it impossible to enter an industry—they merely limit the number of firms that are able to enter. Overcoming the hurdles typically involves additional operating costs which means that many potential entrants will *not* enter, since they cannot foresee operating profitably. The firms that now exist in the oligopolistic market may be able to make excess or pure profits in the shelter of these hurdles. This is not to say that either monopolists or oligopolists will always make pure profits. In declining markets, for example, these firms may incur continuing losses, forcing them to eventually leave the industry.

The oligopolist adjusts plant size with an eye to its impact upon rival firms and their likely reactions. Given the split conjectural variation of the kinked-demand-curve model, the oligopolist is likely to adjust to the plant size that produces its current share of the market at minimum cost. In Figure 9A-4 we show such an adjustment.

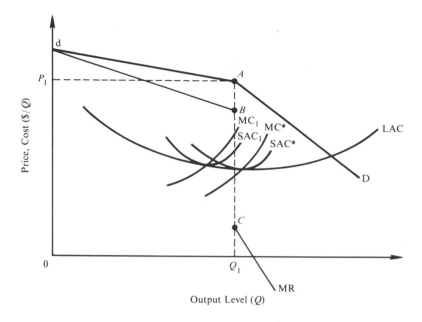

FIGURE 9A-4. Long-Run Plant Size Adjustment in Oligopoly

Suppose the firm is now producing Q_1 units at price P_1 with the plant size depicted by SAC_1. Given an opportunity to adjust plant size, the firm will adjust to the plant depicted by SAC*, since this produces the profit-maximizing output at the lowest per unit cost. Since the new marginal cost curve MC* passes through the vertical discontinuity (BC) of the marginal revenue curve, the present price and output levels remain optimal.[3]

As you will recall from the discussion in Chapter 8, the long-run average cost curve of any firm requires a constant state of factor productivities and factor costs. In the real world, of course, these tend to change over time. The pursuit of long-run equilibrium price and output in any market situation is therefore a lot like shooting at a target that moves just as you pull the trigger. New technology and changed factor prices mean that a new LAC curve (and its associated SAC curves) becomes appropriate, and the firm will select that plant size on the new LAC curve that minimizes the cost of its optimal output level.

The foregoing analysis is nevertheless useful, since it demonstrates the existence of forces that will operate, given time for firms to adjust their plant sizes. They will adjust in the direction of the minimum cost of producing their desired output level. To the extent permitted by restriction to entry, new firms will enter the industry. In all cases (including monopoly,

---

[3]This conclusion depends upon a constant demand situation. If the firm expects the market demand to grow and/or its share of the market to expand, it may wish to build a larger plant.

PRICING ANALYSIS AND DECISIONS

since we expect barriers to entry to break down over time) the passage of time should be expected to cause the reduction of excess or pure profits. Prices, in constant-purchasing-power (or real) terms, are expected to fall as long as the demand situation remains constant. Should market demand increase or decrease over time, prices may rise or fall, depending upon the particular cost and demand situations. These adjustments may be made to the above models without difficulty.

NOTE: In this appendix the plant-size-adjustment decision was approached in the context of certainty, or full information concerning the firm's cost and demand conditions. Moreover, the implication was that the firm's time horizon fell within the confines of the (next) short run period. Hence, the firm adjusts plant size in order to maximize profits in the (next) short-run period. Given the uncertainty surrounding the firm's cost and demand conditions in the real world and since the firm's time horizon often falls some distance into the future, the firm's plant-size-adjustment decision should be viewed in terms of the expected present value (EPV) of profits from the proposed plant vis-a-vis the EPV of the profits from the existing plant. This issue is treated in detail in the context of capital budgeting in Chapter 14.

DISCUSSION QUESTIONS

9A-1.   Explain why the presence of pure profits attracts the entry of new firms and why the absence of normal profits induces the exit of existing firms.

9A-2.   When there are barriers to the entry of new firms, these barriers may be absolute or simply represent cost disadvantages facing the entrant firm. Under what circumstances will entry be effected despite barriers to entry?

9A-3.   What motivates the firm to expand its plant size? How would it know its present plant size was not optimal? Explain how it chooses the new plant size?

9A-4.   What would happen if the oligopolist facing a kinked demand curve ascertained that its long-run marginal cost curve intersected the lower section of its marginal revenue curve?

9A-5.   Suppose the firm expects the market to grow over the next few years. How would you expect this to enter the plant-size-adjustment decision?

PROBLEMS AND SHORT CASES

9A-1.   Suppose the demand for a monopolist, such as the remaining regional producer of horse-drawn buggies, is slowly but inexorably declining.

   (a)   Show graphically how this firm might be expected to react to this situation over a period of years.

   (b)   Does your graph show the price level rising or falling (or both) as the market declines?

   (c)   Under what conditions would market price (in real terms) increase as the market declined over time?

9A-2.   The fishing industry, like small farms, is notorious for the periodic influx of new firms followed later by the exit of firms who are unable to continue taking losses. Explain this in terms of the purely competitive model of the firm, using graphs to illustrate your answer.

9A-3. The market for digital watches has shown remarkable development over the past decade, from a few firms selling digitals at relatively high prices to dozens of manufacturers selling them today at relatively low prices. Over this period the cost of production of these watches fell dramatically and the market's appreciation of these watches increased considerably. Using graphical analysis, explain the entry of new firms and the reduction of prices in terms of the profit-maximizing response of oligopolists facing kinked demand curves.

SUGGESTED REFERENCES AND FURTHER READING

Eaton, B.C. and R.G. Lipsey. "Exit Barriers are Entry Barriers: The Durability of Capital as a Barrier to Entry," *Bell Journal of Economics*, 11 (Autumn 1980), pp. 721-29.

Demsetz, H. "Barriers to Entry," *American Economic Review*, 72 (March 1982), pp. 47-57.

Osborne, D.K. "The Role of Entry in Oligopoly Theory," *Journal of Political Economy*, 72 (August 1964), 396-402.

Pyatt, G. "Profit Maximization and the Threat of New Entry," *Economic Journal*, 81 (June 1971), 242-55.

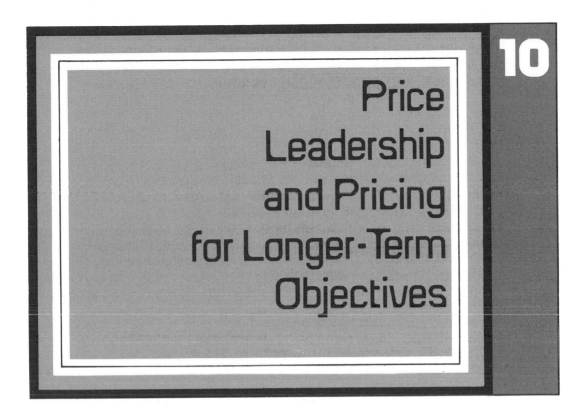

Price Leadership and Pricing for Longer-Term Objectives

10.1 INTRODUCTION

In this chapter we examine several more complex, but at the same time more realistic, pricing models. The models developed here are variants of the basic models introduced in Chapter 9. In that chapter we saw that the basic structure of pricing models consists of seven major assumptions: four structural assumptions and three behavioral assumptions. In the present chapter we shall look at several models that vary on the basis of the behavioral assumptions. We are especially concerned with the pricing behavior of oligopolists. The majority of contemporary business activity takes place in oligopolistic market situations, and it is in this type of market that pricing decisions are most crucial, due to the interdependence of the firms' actions. In fact, it is the interdependence, or mutual dependence, of the firms that causes the behavioral assumptions used in Chapter 9 to be inappropriate in many oligopolistic markets.

The Need for Modified Behavioral Assumptions in Oligopoly

The assumption of short-term profit maximization is appropriate enough for cases of pure competition and monopolistic competition, where entry of new firms is unrestricted, and also for pure monopoly, where entry is typically impossible. In oligopoly, however, while entry is not unrestricted, neither are the barriers to entry insurmountable. Hence if oligopolists set too high a price, this may induce entry of firms that not only expect to make profits at that price level but also will take a share of the market in all future periods. This will in turn dilute future profitability. If the time horizon of oligopolists extends beyond the current time period, we should expect them to wish to prevent this dilution of profits by pricing so as not to attract new competition.

We have considerable reasons *a priori* to expect that oligopolists would be concerned with profitability in future periods. This derives from the form of most oligopolistic firms. By definition, these firms are large relative to their markets, and in most cases this makes them large in absolute terms as well. This in turn favors their taking on corporate form, in order to raise sufficient capital as they expand and to allow individuals to avoid the risk associated with having all their eggs in one basket. The diversity of ownership involved in the firm's being a corporation means that, for operational functionality, the control of the firm will pass to a small group of managers who are responsible only indirectly to the owners. The managers are paid salaries and have a direct interest in profits only to the extent that they are also shareholders and/or that they receive bonuses which depend on profits. But the future of the managers is tied in with the future of the corporation. If the corporation prospers and grows over time, their reputations and salaries would be expected to grow commensurately. If its market share dwindles due to the incursion of new firms, the reputation and tenure of the managers is placed in jeopardy. It is thus reasonable to expect that, especially where there is separation of ownership and control, oligopolistic firms will tend to forego short-term profit maximization in favor of their continued existence and profitability over the longer term.

Next, the use of price as a strategic variable is quite appropriate in short-run pure competition, monopolistic competition, and monopoly situations. Under oligopoly, however, price adjustments are likely to cause retaliatory price adjustments, and this could develop into a price-war situation. Price wars, if not actually causing losses for some or all firms, are typically less profitable than the maintenance of the status quo over the same period would have been. While an individual price cut would be profitable if *ceteris paribus* did prevail as a result of the gain of sales from rival firms, when all firms reduce prices the sales for each firm expand only as a share of the total market's expansion. If the price-war situation is severe and protracted, it could cause the demise of some firms. As a result of this danger and the expected loss of profits associated with price competition, oligopolists would be expected to look elsewhere for their major strategic variable.

Observation suggests that oligopolists use product differentiation as their major strategic variable, along with advertising and other promotional efforts—and product "improvements" (loosely defined!)—as the main means to achieve this. Price is by no means absent as a strategic variable, but price adjustments tend to be used only for temporary sales and/or when the market price is substantially out of line with supply and demand conditions and when price adjustments would be desired by all or most firms, and thus they are not construed as an offensive marketing strategy. The nonprice areas of competition, referred to above, are regarded as more appropriate areas of competition, since a gain in market share is attained by skill and finesse, rather than by the crude and potentially dangerous means of price competition.

The final behavioral assumption is that concerning the firm's conjectural variation. Under pure competition, monopolistic competition, and monopoly it was appropriate to expect no reaction from rivals, since in the first two cases the impact of a firm's action is spread imperceptibly over many rival firms and in the monopoly case there is no rival to worry about. Under oligopoly, the firm's conjectural variation cannot be assumed to be zero without the implication that the managers of each firm are incredibly myopic in their perception of their business environment.

You will recall that in the kinked demand curve model we modified the conjectural variation assumption to recognize that firms might expect rivals to match their price reductions and to ignore their price increases in oligopoly markets. We noted, however, that this model is not a model of price determination but rather explains the frequently observed rigidity of prices in oligopoly. It can be easily modified, however, to incorporate the upward adjustment of prices by all firms acting in unison. In the next section we are concerned with modifications to the conjectural variation assumption. In the following section we examine a number of models that utilize differing assumptions about the objective function of the firms. Models that treat nonprice competition as the strategic variable are deferred until Chapter 13, since this area is quite extensive and in any case is outside the scope of this section on pricing theory and decision making.

10.2 CONSCIOUS PARALLELISM AND PRICE LEADERSHIP

Conscious Parallelism and the Kinked Demand Curve. Under some conditions the firm's conjecture that other firms will ignore its price increase may give way to the expectation that other firms will *follow* a price increase rather than ignore it. Such a situation may arise when a cost increase applies to all firms, such as an increase in the basic wage rate or an increase in the cost of an important raw material. In the case of cost increases that apply to all firms, the individual firm may reasonably expect that all firms would like to maintain profit margins by passing the cost on to consumers, and, especially if there is a history of this practice in the industry, that the firm's conjectural variation for a price increase, up to the extent necessary to pass on the cost increase, will be unity.

DEFINITION: The simultaneous adjustment of prices with the expectation that rivals will do likewise has been called *conscious parallelism*.[1] The firms consciously act in a parallel manner, given their expectation that all other firms are motivated to act in the same way.

EXAMPLE: The American automobile firms have exhibited conscious parallelism in their pricing policies. These firms have traditionally used the new model introductions in the fall of the year as the focal point for their price increases. Each company expects the others to announce price increases to pass on cost increases and subsequently makes its own price changes without expecting any loss of market share. Other focal points for price increases in the automobile industry occur, for example, with the settlement of a new wage contract with the United Auto Workers or with an increase in the cost of a major raw material, such as steel. As this industry moves into the 1980s, the domestic manufacturers have found it increasingly difficult to maintain their market shares and have been raising their new model prices by less than their increases in costs, and they have resorted increasingly to other price incentives, such as rebates and low-interest loans. Furthermore, Chrysler and Ford, in particular, have attempted to keep their price increases to a smaller percentage change, as compared to General Motors and the imports, in an attempt to win back market share.[2]

The relevant demand curve for a consciously parallel price increase is the *mutatis mutandis* demand curve. As indicated in Figure 10-1, the kink in the demand curve moves up the *mutatis mutandis* section to the new price level chosen. It will kink at the level that passes on the cost increase, because the firm expects that any further price increase will not be matched by rivals and therefore expects to experience a more elastic demand response above that price level. The firm's conjectural variation is unity up to the price level that is expected to be agreeable to all firms, and it is zero for price levels above that.[3]

In terms of Figure 10-1, the firm has experienced a shift in its marginal cost curve from MC to MC'. Based on its expectation that rival firms have suffered a similar cost increase and will be raising their prices, the firm raises its price from P to P' in order to pass on the cost increase to consumers. The firm expects its price-quantity coordinate to move from point A to A', along

---

[1] See W. Hamburger, "Conscious Parallelism and the Kinked Oligopoly Demand Curve," *American Economic Review*, 57 (May 1967), pp. 266-68.

[2] See "Why Detroit Still Can't Get Going," *Business Week*, November 9, 1981, pp. 106-110; also, "Chrysler Sets Cash Rebates for Most Models," *Wall Street Journal*, August 4, 1981; and Donald Woutat, "Auto Makers Look Forward to a Bleak Fall, Winter," *Los Angeles Times*, October 21, 1981.

[3] The extent to which price is raised depends on the extent to which the firm expects other firms to raise prices simultaneously; it may be more than, less than, or equal to the cost increase. It would be (joint) profit maximizing to raise price all the way to the point where the MC curve cuts the *mutatis mutandis* MR curve (extended upward). But if some firms are not expected to raise price that far, the demand curve will kink and that MR is thus inappropriate.

PRICING ANALYSIS AND DECISIONS

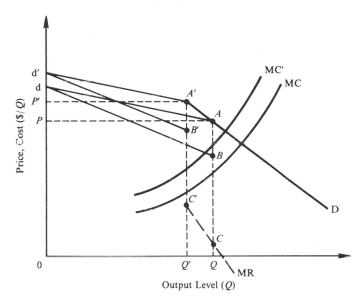

Output Level (Q)

the *mutatis mutandis*, or share-of-the-market, demand curve. If its expectation (that rivals will similarly raise prices) is borne out, it will in fact move to A', its new kinked demand curve will be $d'A'$D, and its new marginal revenue curve will be $d'B'C'$MR.

Since all firms are expected to act jointly, each firm expects to maintain its share of the market at the higher price level, and, by passing on the cost increase to consumers, each firm expects to maintain its profit margin per unit (the difference between price and average costs). In the next chapter we see that the prevalent practice of *markup pricing* allows firms to practice conscious parallelism in the real world, even when they don't know how their demand curves slope away from the present price level.

Price Leadership Models

A number of oligopoly models rely upon the notion of *price leadership* to explain the upward adjustment of prices in oligopoly markets. The major difference between conscious parallelism and price leadership is that in the former situation all firms take the initiative in adjusting prices, confident that their rivals will do likewise, whereas in the latter situation one firm will lead the way and will be followed within a relatively short period by all or most of the other firms adjusting their prices to a similar degree. The price leader is the firm willing to take the risk of being the first to adjust price, but, as we shall see, this firm usually has good reason to expect that the other firms will follow suit. The risk involved here relates especially to price increases, since if the firm raises price and is not followed by other firms, it will experience an elastic demand response and a significant loss of profits before it can readjust its price to the original level.

NOTE: Conjectural variation for the price leader is unity, since this firm expects all rivals to adjust prices up or down to the same degree that it does. For the price followers, conjectural variation is zero for self-initiated price increases, since price followers do not expect to have all firms follow their price increases. For price decreases, the price follower may expect all firms to follow suit to protect their market shares, and so the conjectural variation is unity for price reductions. It should be immediately apparent to the reader that the price follower faces a kinked demand curve.

There are three major types of price leaders: the barometric price leader, the low-cost price leader, and the dominant firm price leader.

The Barometric Price Leader.   As the name implies, the barometric price leader possesses an ability to accurately predict when the climate is right for a price change. Following a generalized increase in labor or materials costs or a period of increased demand, the barometric firm judges that all firms are ready for a price change and takes the risk of sales losses by being the first to adjust its price. If the other firms trust that firm's judgment of market conditions, they too will adjust prices to the extent indicated. If they feel the increase is too much, they may adjust prices to a lesser degree and the price leader may bring its price back to the level seemingly endorsed by the other firms. If the other firms fail to ratify the price change, the price leadership role could shift from firm to firm over time and will rest with the firm that has sound knowledge of market supply and demand conditions, the ability to perceive a consensus among the firms, and the willingness to take the risk of sales losses if its judgment on these issues is faulty.[4]

The Low-Cost Price Leader.   The low-cost price leader is a firm that has a significant cost advantage over its rivals and inherits the role of price leader largely due to the other firms' reluctance to incur the wrath of the lower-cost firm. In the event of a price war the other firms would suffer greater losses and be more prone to the risk of bankruptcy than would the lower-cost firm. Out of respect for this potential power of the lower-cost firm, the other firms tacitly agree to follow that firm's price adjustments.[5] Alternatively, it may be said that the lower-cost firm is the price leader because it has the least to lose if the other firms refuse to follow its lead.

---

[4]Barometric price leadership was first proposed by J. W. Markham, "The Nature and Significance of Price Leadership," *American Economic Review*, (December 1951), pp. 891-905. For a thorough discussion of barometric price leadership, see F. M. Scherer, *Industrial Market Structure and Economic Performance*, (2nd ed.) (Chicago: Rand McNally & Company, 1980), chap. 6.

[5]This agreement is likely to be ruled illegal price fixing if the firms *explicitly* agree on price levels.

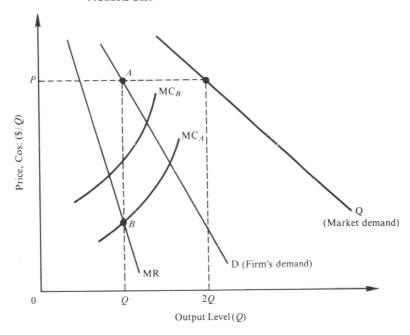

We can show graphically the determination of price in such a situation,
and the most simple situation is the two-firm, identical products case. In
Figure 10-2 we show the demand curve D as the curve faced by either firm
when each firm sets price at the same level. This curve is thus a *mutatis
mutandis* demand curve, predicated upon the simultaneous adjustment of
the other firm's price to the same level. In price leadership situations price
adjustments are more or less concurrent, and the demand curve D in this
case represents a constant (half) share of the total market at each price level.
The marginal cost curves of the two firms are shown as MC_A for Firm A,
the lower-cost firm, and MC_B for Firm B, the higher-cost firm. The lower-
cost firm maximizes its profit from its share of the market by setting price P
and output level Q, and Firm B follows the lead and also sets price P.

Given that it sets price P, what output level should the higher-cost firm
produce? Being a profit-maximizing firm, by assumption, it will simply
choose the output level that maximizes profits, subject to the (self-imposed)
constraint that its price will be the same as the price leader's. The demand
curve facing Firm B, in this simple identical products case, is the kinked line
PAD, since if Firm B sets its price above P, all consumers will purchase from
Firm A at the lower price. If Firm B sets its price below P, the other firm
will match this price reduction to avoid having its sales fall dramatically. The
marginal revenue curve associated with the demand curve PAD is the dis-
jointed line $PABMR$, with a horizontal section relating to the horizontal part

of the demand curve faced by Firm B and section BMR relating to prices below the price P. Firm B should therefore choose output level Q, since below this output level, marginal revenue exceeds marginal costs, and above this level, marginal costs exceed marginal revenue. The firms thus share the market equally at the price level chosen by the lower-cost firm.

The above simple model allowed us to introduce the low-cost price leadership model. Little difficulty is involved in making the model more realistic by changing the assumptions concerning the degree of product differentiation and the number of sellers. The following verbal treatment should be intuitively clear. When products are differentiated, the price followers will face a kinked demand curve in which the upper section is not horizontal but is nevertheless quite elastic, as in Figure 10-1. Where there are more than two firms, the *mutatis mutandis* section of the demand curve will represent the particular firm's share of the total market when all prices are at a similar level. If product differentiation is symmetric among the products of the various firms, the shares of all firms will be equal, as in the identical products case.[6] If we let n represent the number of rival firms, the *mutatis mutandis* demand curve will represent $1/n$ of the total market demand at each price level. If the market divides unequally among the firms when all prices are at a similar level, we say that product differentiation is asymmetric, and the *mutatis mutandis* demand curve will represent a market share that may be greater or less than $1/n$th of the total demand at each price level.

Price Leadership With Price Differentials.   When product differentiation is asymmetric we should expect a range of prices among the rival firms, reflecting the different cost and demand situations facing each firm. Price leadership in this situation requires one slight modification to the above analysis. The price leader may adjust its price by a certain amount, and the price followers will adjust their prices by the *same percentage* as is represented by the price leader's price adjustment. Thus, the relative price differentials that prevailed prior to the price changes are unchanged, and no firm expects to gain or lose sales from or to a rival. The price leader simply initiates an upward (or downward) adjustment in the entire price structure of that particular market.

In Figure 10-3 we show a situation in which three firms produce asymmetrically differentiated products. Firm A is the acknowledged price leader and sets price P_A, selling Q_A units. Firms B and C are price followers, not wishing to initiate price adjustments in case this might precipitate active competition or a price war in which the lower-cost Firm A would have a definite advantage. Firm B's price is above the price leader's price, and Firm C's price is below the other two prices. Firm B's product may be a higher-

---

[6]Essentially, *symmetric product differentiation* means that the products are equally differentiated from each other, and so market shares should be equal when prices are equal.

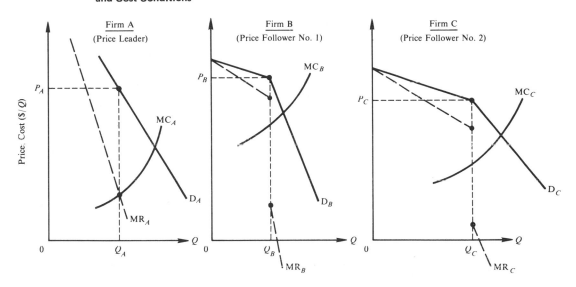

quality item desired by a relatively small segment of the market. This firm's higher cost level may well be the result of higher-quality inputs and more hand finishing of the product, for example. Firm C's product is both lower priced and more expensive to produce, as compared with the price leader's. The lower price may be due to the market's perception of inferior after-sales service, an inferior location, or absence of other attributes, while the higher costs may be the result of more expensive sources of the inputs, inefficiencies in production, or a plant size too small in view of the present output level.

The price followers face the kinked demand curves shown because they expect no reaction from rivals for price increases but expect the price leader and the other price follower to match any price reductions. The price leader's demand curve is simply the *mutatis mutandis* demand curve: The price leader expects the other firms to follow both price increases and price reductions. If, for example, the price leader's costs increase, it will adjust price upward along the D_A curve. The price followers, who have probably incurred a similar cost increase, will follow the lead and adjust prices upward. But for this particular price increase they do not expect *ceteris paribus*; they expect that the other firms will be simultaneously adjusting their prices upward (or have seen them do so). As stated earlier, the firms are likely to adjust price upward by a similar *proportion* in order to maintain their relative prices and, hence, their market shares. In this case, however, the proportion will be decided by the price leader.

We shall see in Chapter 11 that the common business practice of *markup pricing* allows firms to adjust prices to cost increases by a similar proportion. We turn now to the third type of price leader.

The Dominant-Firm Price Leader.   As the name implies, the dominant firm is large relative to its rivals and its market. The smaller firms accept this firm's price leadership perhaps simply because they are unwilling to risk being the first to change prices, or perhaps because they are afraid that the dominant firm could drive them out of business, for example, by forcing raw-material suppliers to boycott a particular small firm on pain of losing the order of the larger firm. In such a situation the smaller firms accept the dominant firm's choice of the price level, and they simply adjust output to maximize their profits. In this respect they are similar to pure competitors who can sell as much as they want to at the market price. Like pure competitors, they will want to sell up to the point where their marginal cost equals the price (equals marginal revenue). The dominant firm recognizes that the smaller firms will behave in this manner and that it must therefore choose price to maximize its profits with the knowledge that the smaller firms will sell as much as they want to at that price.

The first task of the dominant-firm price leader is, therefore, to ascertain how much the smaller firms will want to supply at each price level. Since each of the smaller firms will want to supply up to the point where MC = MR, and since MR = P in a situation where the individual firm is so small that it does not influence market price, each of the smaller firms will regard its MC curve as its supply curve. Note that a supply curve shows the quantity that will be supplied at each price level. At each price level the firms supply the amount for which marginal cost equals price. The MC curve therefore indicates how much the firm will supply at each price level. It follows that a horizontal aggregation of these curves will indicate the total amount that the smaller firms will supply at each price level. In Figure 10-4 we depict this aggregation of the smaller firms' marginal cost curves as the line ΣMC_s.

In Figure 10-4 we show three small firms and the marginal cost curves of each. Suppose the dominant firm sets price P_1. Each of the small firms will expand supply to the point where its MC curve rises to the price level

FIGURE 10-4.   Aggregation of Small Firms' MC Curves to find their Aggregate Supply Curve in the Dominant Firm-Price Leadership Model

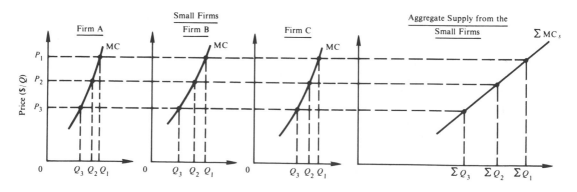

PRICING ANALYSIS AND DECISIONS

FIGURE 10-5. Construction of the Dominant Firm's Residual Demand Curve

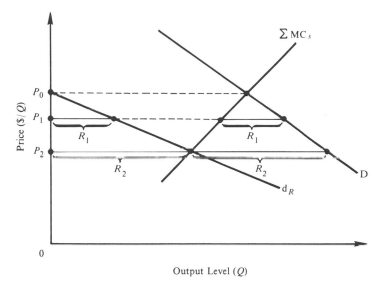

P_1, and will do the same for lower prices such as P_2 and P_3. Adding up the supply of the three firms at each price level, we obtain the ΣMC_s curve in the right-hand part of the figure.

Knowing how much the smaller firms will supply at each price level, the dominant firm can subtract this from the market demand to find how much demand is left over at each price level. This "residual" demand can be measured as the horizontal distance between the ΣMC_s and the market demand curve D at each price level, and is shown as the demand curve d_R in Figure 10-5. Only at prices below P_0 is there any demand left for the dominant firm after the smaller firms have supplied their desired amounts. At price P_1 there is an excess of market demand over the supply of the smaller firms, shown as the horizontal distance R_1 between the ΣMC_s curve and the D curve. Similarly, the residual demand at price P_2 is shown by the distance R_2. Shifting these residual amounts across to the price axis, we find the dominant firm's residual demand curve to be that shown as d_R. This residual demand curve is the amount that the dominant firm can be assured of selling at each price level, since the smaller firms will have sold as much as they wanted to and yet there remain buyers willing to purchase at those price levels.

The dominant firm will choose the price level in order to maximize its own profits from this assured or residual demand. The marginal revenue curve associated with the residual demand curve is shown as the curve mr in Figure 10-6. The dominant firm's marginal cost curve is depicted by MC_D. The dominant firm therefore selects price P_D and output Q_D in order to maximize its profits. Faced with the price P_D, each of the smaller firms produces up to the point where its marginal costs equal that price, and hence the smaller firms in aggregate produce the output level Q_s. Since the residual demand curve was constructed to reflect the horizontal distance between the

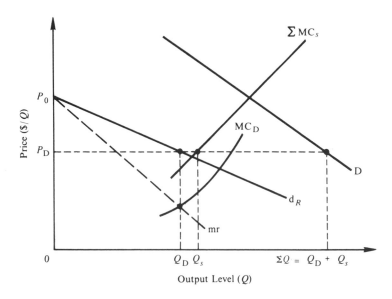

FIGURE 10-6. Price Determination by the Dominant-Firm Price Leader

ΣMC_s and the D curves, the total amount supplied to the market, ΣQ, is equal to the market demand, and an equilibrium situation exists. The dominant firm thus chooses price to maximize its profits under the constraint that the smaller firms will supply the amount at that price level which will maximize their profits.

NOTE: An interesting long-run implication of the dominant-firm-price-leadership model is that if the chosen price allows the smaller firms to earn economic profits, the dominance of the large firm will be eroded over time. The reason for this erosion is that in the long run the small firms will expand their plant sizes in search of even greater profitability, and new firms will enter the industry—if the barriers to entry can be overcome—in search of this profitability. In any case the residual demand remaining for the dominant firm, with market demand static, must be reduced, and the price leader will be forced to set a lower price and accept a reduced market share. Eventually, of course, the dominant firm will no longer be dominant, and the above system of market price determination will give way to some other form of price leadership, conscious parallelism, or independent price setting.

EXAMPLE: Alcoa is said to be an example of a firm that was initially a monopoly, later a dominant-firm price leader, and more recently simply one of several large oligopolists in the aluminum industry.[7] Alcoa was effectively a monopoly at first because it held most of the known reserves of bauxite, from

---

[7]See J.V. Koch, *Industrial Organization and Prices*, 2nd ed. (Englewood Cliffs, N.J.: Prentice-Hall, Inc., 1980), p. 282 and p. 289.

PRICING ANALYSIS AND DECISIONS

which aluminum is derived. As more bauxite was discovered, other firms entered the industry but were small in relation to Alcoa. As time passed and Alcoa's chosen price level allowed the other firms to prosper and grow, Alcoa's dominance in the industry waned to the point where it is no longer clear that Alcoa is the price leader at all.

10.3 PRICING FOR LONGER-TERM OBJECTIVES

The behavioral assumption of short-run profit maximization, which we have used in all the above models of firm behavior, may be criticized for its realism in oligopolistic markets where short-run profit maximization may induce new firms to overcome the barriers to entry and obtain a share of the market and thus dilute future profits of the existing firms. In Chapter 1 and earlier in this chapter it was argued that the time horizon envisaged by oligopolists will extend beyond the short-run period and these firms are likely to forego immediate profits in order not to attract the entry of new firms. This suggests, of course, that a more appropriate objective function for the oligopolist is the maximization of long-term profits.

Long-Term Profit Maximization

DEFINITION: *Long-term profit maximization* may be defined as the maximization of the expected present value of the firm's future profit stream.

In theory, the firm would consider various price levels for each time period up to its time horizon and would form an expectation of demand at each price level for each period. This would need to take into account the loss of sales to new entrants, which may occur at some price levels, and the impact of expected changes in other variables, such as population, incomes, consumer preferences, and prices of competing products, which are expected to influence the sales of the firm's products in future periods. Future profits must be discounted to the present at an appropriate discount rate in order to allow comparability of profit amounts from different time periods. On the cost side the firm would need to form expectations of changes in relative factor prices and in the state of technology, such that it could estimate its marginal cost of production at all output levels in each future period. In practice, of course, the above procedure becomes extremely difficult to calculate due to the problems associated with forming reliable expectations on the matters indicated. Even if such predictions could be made, the search costs of obtaining the information might far outweigh the extra revenue derived, and thus the firm should not undertake the necessary search procedure.

It is more likely that firms that wish to maximize their long-term profits will adopt a "proxy" objective function. That is, they will pursue a policy that gives approximately the same results but is much more simple and inexpensive to administer. In the following sections we shall examine a number of such proxy policies which, it can be argued, are a short-term means of achieving the long-term objective of profit maximization.

Sales Maximization with a Minimum Profit Target

W. J. Baumol has suggested that the appropriate objective function for many firms is the maximization of sales in the short term, subject to the attainment of a certain minimum profit level.[8] First let us consider the minimum profit requirement, which is necessary for two main reasons: (1) a certain minimum profit must be forthcoming to allow payment of dividends sufficient to prevent shareholders from becoming disgruntled and voting for a new board of directors; and (2) the value of the firm's shares on the stock exchange depend, in part, on the current profitability of the firm, since the expectation of dividend payments has a positive influence on the market value of the shares. If, as a result of low current profits, the shares become undervalued in view of the firm's longer-term prospects, the firm may be subject to a takeover bid by another firm, which again involves the risk that managers may lose their jobs. Therefore managers will be motivated to keep profits at a level sufficient to stave off these two possibilities, while at the same time making sure that profits are not so large as to attract the entry of new firms.

Having determined the minimum acceptable, or target, level of profits, the firm will wish to maximize its sales subject to this profit constraint. We can show the sales-maximization decision on the same graph as the one for short-run profit maximization. In Figure 10-7 are displayed the familiar total revenue and total cost curves, with the profit curve indicating the excess of total revenue over total costs at each output level. Suppose the minimum profit constraint is the vertical distance indicated by $0\pi^*$. The profit constraint is satisfied anywhere between output (sales) levels Q_0 and Q_2, but sales are maximized, subject to this constraint, at output level Q_2. It is clear that this output level is larger than the short-run profit-maximizing output level Q_1 and must be offered at a lower price than the short-run profit-maximizing price, since the firm faces a negatively sloped demand curve.

But why is the maximization of sales volume in the short run a proxy for the maximization of longer-term profits? The lower price level, as compared with the short-run profit-maximizing price, has three major implications for future profits. First, it will tend to inhibit the entry of new firms

---

[8]W. J. Baumol, *Business Behavior, Value, and Growth* (New York: Harcourt Brace Jovanovich, Inc., 1967). Note that we mean sales *volume,* not sales *revenue.* Maximizing sales revenue simply means finding the point where MR = 0, and requires no reference to the firm's cost situation. This may be desirable if the firm faces an immediate cash-flow problem, but completely neglects the profit implications since it ignores the cost side. Maximization of sales volume (subject to a profit target) amounts to maximizing the firm's market share, and seems empirically more supportable.

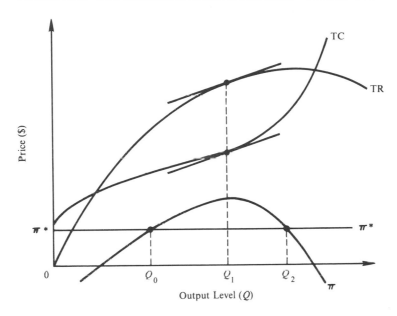

FIGURE 10-7. Sales Maximization Subject to a Minimum Profit Constraint

whose costs may exceed that price level due to the extra expenses associated with overcoming the barriers to entry. Second, it will introduce more customers to the product now and will thus operate to gain more repeat sales in future periods, due to the goodwill and brand loyalty that will develop over time as customers use the product. This cultivation of consumer loyalty and goodwill acts to raise one of the barriers to entry, since a potential entrant firm would need to spend even more on advertising and promotion of its own product in order to induce customers to try that product. Third, the larger market share in the short term provides a larger base for complementary sales in the longer term. This is especially important in the market for some durable consumption goods, such as automobiles and cameras, where apparently quite lucrative markets exist for specialized replacement parts and accessories.

EXAMPLE: The Kodak 110 camera appears to have been priced with a view to maximizing its sales volume in the short run. When it was first introduced, it seemed to offer excellent value and became very popular as a Christmas and birthday gift, particularly for children. As every parent found out, of course, the cost of the camera was simply the start of a series of expenditures benefiting Kodak. Sales of special film cartridges, flash bulbs, developing services, printing and enlarging services, projectors and screens, all served to keep the sales revenue flowing to Kodak. Their strategy appears to have been to get the widest possible penetration of the market with their camera, at a modest profit margin, and to rely on subsequent sales of accessory items to generate continued revenues and profitability. Gillette, who pioneered several advances in shaving equipment during the 1970s, appears to have followed a similar strategy. For both their twin-blade and swivel-head (Atra) blade, they priced the handle at a price that must barely have covered their variable cost per unit and were content to take their profits on the later sales of razor blades.

A policy of sales maximization in the short run thus operates to inhibit the entry of new firms and to generate future sales of the firm's product(s). The resultant profit stream probably comes reasonably close to that which could be attained by the present value calculation for long-term profit maximization, since there are likely to be considerable search costs associated with obtaining the information necessary to make that calculation. Sales maximization is a relatively simple and inexpensive rule-of-thumb procedure which can be applied in each period, and it thus obviates the cost, effort, and uncertainty associated with the continual recalculation of the price that maximizes the expected present value of the firm's profit stream.

Limit Pricing to Deter Entry

DEFINITION: The *limit* price is the price that is not quite high enough to induce the entry of new firms. For the potential entrant whose objective is short-run profit maximization, the limit price is the highest price that can be set without allowing the potential entrant to make normal profits. If the potential entrant takes the longer view and would be prepared to take losses initially if it could foresee profits later, the limit price is the highest price that can be set without allowing the potential entrant's expected present value of profits to be positive.

Limit pricing may also be regarded as a proxy for long-term profit maximization. Preventing the entry of new firms serves to avoid having to share the market with new firms in the future. Thus, the firm expects its future sales and the EPV of profits from the present to its time horizon to be greater if it successfully prevents the entry of new firms.

Deterring Entry of a High-Cost Firm.   In many cases the entrant firm is expected to have higher costs than the existing firms, as a result of its probable smaller scale of operation and the additional product differentiation expense it must incur to offset consumer loyalty to the existing products. Thus the established firms, at the suggestion of a price leader perhaps, choose a price that does not allow the potential entrant to earn even a normal profit at any output level. In Figure 10-8 this price is shown as P_L, which is lower than any point on the potential entrant's short-run average cost curve, SAC_e.

The demand curve D should be interpreted as the *mutatis mutandis*, or share-of-the-market, demand curve of one of the existing firms. Given that the existing firm will not wish to set a price above P_L, it faces, in effect, the kinked demand curve $P_L AD$. Its profit-maximizing output, subject to the self-imposed constraint, is thus Q, where marginal cost and marginal revenue come nearest to being equal.

Since the price set by the existing firms is less than the expected mini-

FIGURE 10-8. Limit Pricing to Deter the Entry of a Higher-Cost Firm

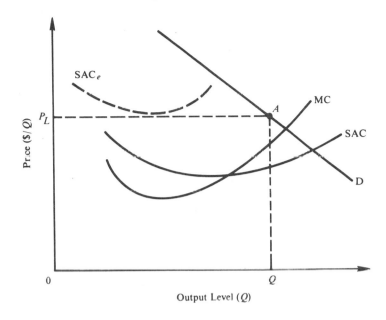

mum per unit cost of potential entrant firms, new firms will not enter, and thus the existing firms' future market shares and profitability are protected from incursions from this quarter at least. Pursuit of a limit-pricing policy is, therefore, like sales maximization, a relatively simple short-run means of approximating a long-term objective. This is not to say that entry will not occur, since there may well be entry of a new firm if the existing firms incorrectly estimate the costs of the potential entrant, if the new firm employs the latest technology while existing firms continue to use older less-efficient plants, or if the entrant firm is prepared to take a loss for a protracted period while gaining a foothold in an expanding market.

Deterring Entry of a Low-Cost Firm. Let us now consider the case in which the potential entrant has access to the same technology and factor markets and hence has the same or lower cost structure, as compared to the existing firms. In this case there is no point in pricing below the new entrant's costs, since all firms would incur losses. Instead, the firms choose price such that the extra quantity supplied by the entry of another firm would cause the market clearing price to be depressed below the level of cost for all firms. The prospect of losses thus prevents the potential entrant from actually entering unless it expects market demand to expand over time or the existing firms to reduce output level such that price is not depressed below cost.[9]

In Figure 10-9 we demonstrate the limit price that deters entry of a

---

[9]F. M. Scherer, *Industrial Market Structure and Economic Performance*, (Chap. 8), 2nd ed. (Chicago: Rand McNally & Company, 1980).

FIGURE 10-9. Limit Pricing to Deter the Entry of a Low-Cost Firm

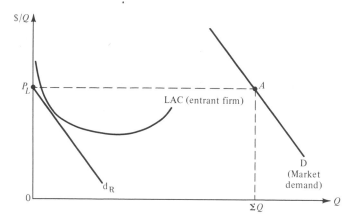

potential entrant that has costs equal to or lower than existing firms. The market demand curve is shown as D, and the potential entrant firm's long-run average cost curve is shown. To simplify the figure the existing firms' *mutatis mutandis* and *ceteris paribus* demand curves are not shown. Suppose that the existing firms follow a price leader and establish the market price shown as P_L. At this price they collectively supply ΣQ units to the market. Note that this means that all buyers willing to pay at least price P_L for the product (that is, those above point A on the demand curve) have been able to obtain the product.

The strategy for deterring entry requires the existing firms to make known the threat that, if a new firm enters, the existing firms will maintain their output levels at the current levels, or ΣQ in aggregate. Thus, the new firm's output would be additional to ΣQ and could only be sold at a lower price. In effect, the new firm would be looking at the market demand curve *below* point A. This is the residual demand left for the new firm after the existing firms have supplied ΣQ units to the market. Shifting this residual section (AD) of the market demand curve over to the vertical axis, we have the demand curve d_R that is faced by the potential entrant firm. Now we see why P_L is the limit price: There is no part of the residual demand curve d_R that lies above the potential entrant firm's LAC curve. Thus, the entrant could not make a profit at any output level.

NOTE: The limit price to deter the entry of a low-cost (or lower cost) firm is, therefore, the price that causes the residual demand curve to lie everywhere below the potential entrant firm's LAC curve. There is then no plant size the entrant can select that would allow normal profits. Notice, however, that the deterrent to entry is simply the threat that existing firms will maintain their output levels, thereby allowing the new firm's output to cause the market price to fall to a lower level until demand equals supply. But at this lower price level, existing firms do not make profits either, since they have no cost advantage over the entrant. It is clear that if the new firm actually does enter the market, the established firms would be better off to reduce their output levels (and market shares) and have the price leader choose a price that would allow all firms to make at least normal profits.

Thus, if a potential entrant firm "calls the bluff" of the existing firms and does enter the market, the firms would be better off to reduce their output levels, despite their earlier threats, and to follow their price leader to a new price level that is acceptable to all. The potential entrant that foresees this and who, in any case, expects to incur losses initially, may not be deterred at all.

Other Objective Functions: Growth, Managerial Utility, Satisficing

More recently several managerial and behavioral models of business firm behavior have been developed, following Baumol's sales-maximization hypothesis which represents a break with the traditional profit-maximizing assumption. Following Baumol's managerial emphasis, it has been postulated that managers of firms wish to maximize the rate of growth of the firm or, alternatively, that they wish to maximize managerial utility. The behavioral model of the firm depicts the firm as simultaneously monitoring several different objectives and being satisfied to attain predetermined targets in each area. Each of these models can in some way be related to the basic objective of maximizing profits over the longer term. Let us look briefly at these models in turn.

Maximization of the Rate of Growth. Considerable attention has been directed to the theory of the firm under the assumption that the firm wishes to maximize the rate of growth of its assets or net worth.[10] In pursuit of this objective, the firm reinvests its profits and/or borrows to expand its facilities, in order to take over or merge with rivals or firms in other industries and, in one way or another, to expand its market share and capital base. Since the major part of a firm's new investment funds will come from internal sources, primarily undistributed profits, growth maximization requires a ready supply of profits. But since growth will be desired over a protracted period, longer-term profits will be preferred over profits that may be short lived. High short-term prices and profits would tend to attract price competition from rivals and the entry of new firms. Since a constant or increasing market share is important to support the growth of the firm, short-term prices and profits would be expected to be kept below the short-term profit-maximizing level, in order to preserve or increase the firm's market share and ensure a continuing stream of profits over the longer term. It can be argued, therefore, that

---

[10]See E. Penrose, *The Theory of the Growth of the Firm* (Oxford: Oxford University Press, 1959); and R. Marris, "A Model of the Managerial Enterprise," *Quarterly Journal of Economics*, 77 (May 1963), pp. 185-209.

pursuit of growth maximization, under some conditions at least, results in an outcome similar to what would be achieved by attempting to maximize long-term profits.

Maximization of Managerial Utility. Another objective function that has been proposed in an oligopoly model is that firms operate to maximize the utility of the managers.[11] Managers may derive utility from a quiet life, high managerial salaries and material comforts, from the goodwill of customers and the public generally, and from other factors. The firm's continuing existence and market standing require continuing public goodwill, and the preference of some managers for the quiet life will inhibit the firm's propensity toward continually seeking higher profits in the short run, a situation which may induce entry. In effect we are saying that firms do what they do in the short term because they expect their actions now to enhance profits some time in the future. A firm that makes a charitable donation, contributes to a political campaign, installs antipollution equipment voluntarily, or refrains from a price rise at the suggestion of government officials is no doubt thinking of the public relations' impact of its actions, which in turn will influence the future profitability of the firm.

Satisficing. Perhaps the most empirically supportable contention is that the objective of the firm is not to maximize any single variable but rather to achieve satisfactory levels of performance, or targets, in a number of variables, which include the production, sales, market share, profits, and inventory levels. This "satisficing" theory of the firm[12] is based on the proposition that firms face considerable uncertainty about costs and demands even in the short run and that they adjust prices, promotional expenditures, and other variables whenever it appears that one of their targets is not going to be attained. Once the profit target is met, for example, managers apply their efforts to satisfying the next constraint that has not yet been met, on the basis of their imperfect information systems and their imperfect expectations of the impact of the adjustments they make. In effect, satisficing managers appear to act according to short-run criteria designed to ensure the continued existence and maintained market standing of the firm they control.

The satisficing model of firm behavior is, in effect, an extension of Baumol's sales-maximization model, if we accept that a minimum-profit target is the firm's first objective. After attaining this minimum-profit level, the firm may pursue a target market share. Having attained this target, it may pursue a target inventory to sales ratio, and so on. In fact, all these targets are simultaneously monitored and attention is directed primarily to whichever of these targets seems to be in jeopardy at any particular time.

---

[11]See H. A. Simon, "Theories of Decision Making in Economics and Behavioral Science," *American Economic Review*, 57 (March 1967), pp. 1-33.

[12]See R. M. Cyert and J. E. March, *A Behavioral Theory of the Firm* (Englewood Cliffs, N.J.: Prentice-Hall, Inc., 1963).

The targets themselves, or aspiration levels, are set by management consensus and usually reflect past achievements plus an additional margin to act as an incentive for improved performance. Thus, the targets, or aspiration levels, may be consistently revised upward, as the firm becomes more and more efficient in its operation. R. H. Day has argued quite plausibly that this continued revision of aspiration levels can mean that a satisficing strategy eventually converges on the long-term, profit-maximizing strategy.[13]

NOTE: The above short-run proxy policies (for the maximization of the expected present value of present and future profits) may not lead to exactly the price and output levels in each period that would allow maximum EPV of profits over the firm's planning period. But these proxies would still be optimal if the amount of revenue lost (by not having the "correct" prices and output levels) is less than the search costs avoided. In such cases the firm would be better off using a relatively simplistic short-run objective function than it would by incurring the search costs and having the "correct" price and output level at all times. Thus, the firm, anticipating high search costs, may actually make more profits by proceeding simplistically than by incurring the search costs and proceeding elegantly, armed with estimates of future cost and demand conditions. Most importantly, the firm should always attempt to evaluate the search costs necessary to obtain the required information, and it should proceed without more information only if it is persuaded that the costs outweigh the benefits which could be derived. We shall pursue this further in Chapter 11.

10.4   SUMMARY

In this chapter we examined several more complex models of pricing behavior in imperfectly competitive markets. These models are both explanatory, in that they explain the pricing behavior observed in some market situations, and normative, in that they indicate the prices that firms should set in different situations in order to pursue their objective function. The models examined were variants of the basic oligopolistic and monopolistic models introduced in Chapter 9, the variations being due to differing behavioral assumptions that were made.

It was argued that the traditional behavioral assumptions—that firms wish to maximize their short-run profits while expecting no reaction from rivals—are inappropriate for oligopolistic markets, in which the firms' actions are highly interdependent. Subsequently we turned to a series of models in which the firm incorporated into its envisaged demand curve an expectation of rivals' reactions to its price or output change. These situations

---

[13]See R. H. Day, "Profits, Learning, and the Convergence of Satisficing to Marginalism," *Quarterly Journal of Economics*, (May 1967).

typically involved a kinked demand curve for some or all firms, with the kink appearing at the price level at which the firm's conjectural variation is no longer zero.

Conscious parallelism is the process by which firms separately but collectively raise prices in response to common cost or demand changes. This allows price adjustments to be coordinated, so that no firm expects to suffer loss of market share because each firm is anticipating the price changes of its rivals. Price leadership, in all cases, is provided by a firm that has a keen awareness of industry cost and market demand conditions, as well as a willingness to risk loss of market share by being the first to adjust price. The price followers accept the leader's judgment and raise prices to the same level (or by a similar proportion). The price followers thus avoid the risk of market share loss, as well as the search costs which might otherwise be spent to ascertain the price change required. Barometric, low-cost, and dominant-firm-price-leadership situations were discussed, and the pricing implications were examined.

When the firm's time horizon falls beyond the present period, a change in the objective function is indicated. We argued in Chapter 1 that the appropriate objective function for the firm facing uncertainty in future periods is the maximization of the expected present value of future profits, also referred to as long-term profit maximization. Given the search costs involved, however, we expect firms to pursue short-run objective functions which are, in effect, proxies for long-term profit maximization. Sales maximization subject to the attainment of a profit target, limit pricing, maximization of the rate of growth or of managerial utility, and satisficing were each argued to be short-run policies which could approximate the maximization of the firm's EPV of future profits over its planning period. Given the search costs avoided, of course, these policies do not need to indicate the actual prices and outputs which would maximize the EPV of future profits; they merely need to get sufficiently close to the optimal price and output levels, so that at least as much profit is earned.

With this grand tour of the theory of the firm behind us, we are now in a position to move to pricing and output decisions in actual business situations. The solution of actual business pricing and output problems is generally facilitated by, and optimized with the aid of, a sound understanding of the normative theory of firm behavior.

DISCUSSION QUESTIONS

10-1. Briefly explain why the behavioral assumptions of monopolistic competition are typically inappropriate for models of oligopolistic price behavior.

10-2. Discuss conscious parallelism in the context of price leadership and followership. Which firms are leaders and which, if any, are followers? Should the firm expect conscious parallelism if a cost change is confined to just that firm?

10-3. Why do firms follow the price leadership of another firm? Is it simply fear of the consequences if they do not? Explain.

10-4. What does it take to be a barometric price leader? Must the barometric price leader be the largest firm in the industry?

10-5. What is the connection between the kinked demand curve model and the low-cost firm price leadership model?

10-6. List the seven assumptions underlying

    (a) The price leader's behavior in the dominant-firm-price-leadership model.

    (b) The price followers' behavior in the dominant-firm-price-leadership model.

10-7. Explain why the objective "sales maximization subject to a minimum profit requirement" may be said to be an operational means of pursuing long-term profit maximization.

10-8. In order for oligopolists to practice limit pricing, what behavioral assumptions must be applicable?

10-9. Why is it that we would not expect maximization of managerial utility to be the actual objective function of a firm in a highly rivalrous market?

10-10. What has the magnitude of search costs got to do with the short-run policy of satisficing and with the adequacy of any one of the proxy policies for long-term profit maximization.

PROBLEMS AND SHORT CASES

10-1. To demonstrate your understanding of the issues involved, draw the graph for and explain the price and output determination in the three-firm, symmetrically differentiated products case of low-cost firm price leadership. Now expand this model to include conscious parallelism when common cost increases are involved, with price leadership remaining in effect when market demand changes. Explain the conjectural variation of the price followers.

10-2. There are two firms in the prefabricated homes industry producing metal-frame houses. The cost structure of Struktatuff Inc. is considerably lower than that of its rival, Steeldeal Inc., although both firms are about the same size in terms of output capacity. The cost functions have been estimated as $TC = 160,000 + 4,850Q$ for Struktatuff, and $TC = 120,000 + 5,250Q$ for Steeldeal. These firms face the market demand curve specified by $P = 36,384 - 1.25Q$.

In past years it has become evident that Struktatuff is the effective price leader. Steeldeal twice tried to set a lower price, but each time Struktatuff undercut this price and forced a return to the price that maximized its own contribution. Product differentiation is such that when prices are equal, Struktatuff always has two-thirds of the market while Steeldeal has the remaining one-third.

    (a) On separate but adjacent graphs, show the *mutatis mutandis* demand curves for both Struktatuff and Steeldeal.

    (b) Show the price level that Struktatuff will prefer.

    (c) Calculate the output level that will be produced by each firm.

10-3. In a dominant-firm oligopoly, the market demand curve has been estimated by the dominant firm to be $P = 100 - 1.25Q$, where Q represents thousands of units. There are twenty very small firms, who each have a cost structure estimated by $TC = 10 + 15Q + 22.5Q^2$.

    (a) Show graphically the derivation of the dominant firm's residual demand curve.

    (b) Suppose the dominant firm's cost structure is represented by $TC = 500 + 10Q + 0.25Q^2$. Show on your graph the profit-maximizing price the dominant firm will choose.

    (c) Calculate the profits earned by the dominant firm and by each of the small firms.

    (d) Comment on what you expect may happen in the long run.

10-4. In the market for introductory economics textbooks there are several competitive textbooks, whose prices range from $15.95 to $22.95. One of the established texts is the major seller and is considered to be the price leader in this field. A new text has recently become available, and its publishing company has priced it at $21.95 and expects to sell 60,000 copies. At this price the company expects to maximize contribution to its overheads and profits. The author of this text receives royalties which are a fixed percentage of total sales receipts. He feels that if the price were reduced to around $16 each, the market would demand 140,000 copies. The publisher feels that the author's perception of the market situation is unrealistic and that a lower price would *reduce* both the contribution and the royalties, as compared with the company's selected price.

(a) Explain the author's side of the argument. What is his objective function and why does he wish to select a lower price than does the publishing company?

(b) Explain the publisher's side of the argument. What is its perception of the market situation? Why does it expect both sales revenue and contribution to fall at lower prices?

(c) What is the major fallacy underlying the author's argument?

(d) What is the major weakness underlying the publisher's argument?

10-5. The cement industry in a particular region is characterized by five firms producing what are highly similar products. Over the years these firms have found that active price competition is to be avoided, since this strategy has led to prolonged periods of low profitability. At the same time, each firm jealously guards its market share and will quickly match any price reduction by a competitor. Whenever costs increase for all firms, the firms act, as if by consensus, to raise prices concurrently to preserve their profit positions.

It has become obvious recently that a cement producer in another region is considering entering the market by building a sixth plant in the vicinity of the plants of the existing five firms. This firm would have higher per unit costs, however, due to the control by the existing five firms of all nearby sources of the basic raw material, limestone.

The existing firms have similar cost structures and find that their marginal costs per ton are virtually constant at $20 per ton. At current output levels of about 200,000 tons each per annum, the firms must cover $5 per ton in overhead costs, and they now price their cement at $32 per ton. The potential entrant's average variable costs are expected to be 20 percent higher and its total fixed costs per annum are expected to be 15 percent lower than those of the five existing firms. If entry takes place next year, the new firm is expected to gain about 10 percent of the market in the first year (pricing at $32 per ton), gradually improving its position to an equal share as a result of the very slight product differentiation involved with this product. The overall market demand for the product is expected to be constant over the next few years, and the market price elasticity of demand is quite low, at 0.2.

(a) Should the existing firms practice limit pricing to forestall the entry of the sixth firm? What price would be necessary to prevent entry?

(b) If the sixth firm does enter the industry, what price level would maximize contribution for each firm after the entrant firm achieves an equal share of the market?

SELECTED REFERENCES AND FURTHER READING

Alchian, A. A.   "Uncertainty, Evolution, and Economic Theory," *Journal of Political Economy*, 58 (June 1950), 211-21.

Amihud, Y. and J. Kamin.   "Revenue vs. Profit Maximization: Differences in Behavior by Type of Control and by Market Power," *Southern Economic Journal*, 45 (Jan. 1979), pp. 838-46.

Bain, J. S. "Price Leaders, Barometers and Kinks," *Journal of Business*, 33 (July 1960), 193-203.

Baumol, W. J. *Business Behavior, Value and Growth* (2nd ed.), esp. chap. 6. New York: Harcourt Brace Jovanovich, Inc. 1967.

Bhagwati, J. "Oligopoly Theory, Entry Prevention and Growth," *Oxford Economic Papers*, 22 (1970), 297-310.

Cohen, K. J. and R. M. Cyert. *Theory of the Firm*, esp. chaps. 15-17. Englewood Cliffs, N.J.: Prentice-Hall Inc., 1965.

Cyert, R. M., and J. E. March. *A Behavioral Theory of the Firm*. Englewood Cliffs, N.J.: Prentice-Hall Inc., 1963).

Dessant, J. W. and R. H. Morgan. "Limit Pricing and the Theory of the Firm," *British Review of Economic Issues*, 2 (Spring 1981), pp. 98-106.

Flaherty, M. T. "Dynamic Limit Pricing, Barriers to Entry, and Rational Firms," *Journal of Economic Theory*, 23 (Oct. 1980), pp. 160-82.

Francis, A. "Company Objectives, Managerial Motivations, and the Behavior of Large Firms: An Empirical Test of the Theory of 'Managerial' Capitalism," *Cambridge Journal of Economics*, 4 (Dec. 1980), pp. 349-61.

Gaskins, D. W., Jr. "Dynamic Limit Pricing: Optimal Pricing under Threat of Entry," *Journal of Economic Theory*, 3 (September 1971), 306-22.

Hamburger, W. "Conscious Parallelism and the Kinked Oligopoly Demand Curve," *American Economic Review*, 57 (May 1967), 266-68.

Hawkins, C. J. *Theory of the Firm*, esp. chaps. 4 and 5. London: Macmillan, Inc., 1973.

Holthausen, D. M. "Kinky Demand, Risk Aversion, and Price Leadership," *International Economic Review*, 20 (June 1979), pp. 341-48.

Leland, H. E. "Theory of the Firm Facing Uncertain Demand," *American Economic Review*, 62 (June 1972), 278-91.

Markham, J. W. "The Nature and Significance of Price Leadership," *American Economic Review*, 41 (December 1951), 891-905.

Sandmo, A. "On the Theory of the Competitive Firm under Price Uncertainty," *American Economic Review*, 61 (March 1971), 65-73.

Scherer, F. M. *Industrial Market Structure and Economic Performance* (2nd ed.), chaps. 5-8. Chicago: Rand McNally & Company, 1980.

Sylos-Labini, P. *Oligopoly and Technical Progress*, esp chap. 2. Cambridge, Mass.: Harvard University Press, 1969.

Thompson, A. A., Jr. *Economics of the Firm: Theory and Practice* (3rd ed.), chaps. 11 and 12. Englewood Cliffs, N.J.: Prentice-Hall, Inc., 1981.

Welch, P. J. "On the Compatibility of Profit Maximization and the Other Goals of the Firm," *Review of Social Economics*, 38 (April 1980), pp. 65-74.

Williamson, J. "Profit, Growth and Sales Maximization," *Economica*, 33, No. 129 (1966), 1-16.

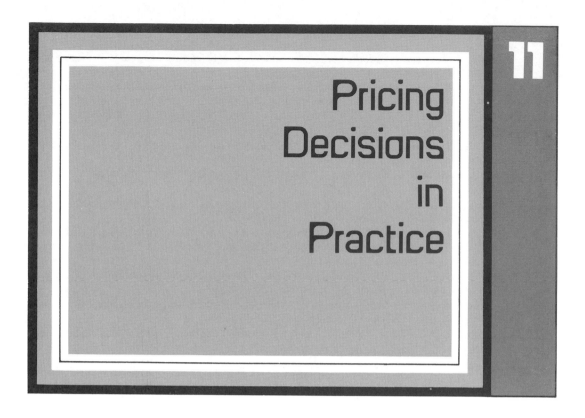

11

Pricing Decisions in Practice

11.1 INTRODUCTION

In the two preceding chapters pricing theory was discussed in the context of *certainty*, whereby firms were assumed to know the shape and location of their cost and demand curves. On the basis of these curves, the firms chose price in order to obtain their desired objective. If their objective was to maximize profit, the firms would equate the marginal cost curve with the appropriate marginal revenue curve.. If the firm's objective function was other than short-run profit maximization, the cost and revenue curves were nevertheless important in the selection of the price that would facilitate the attainment of the particular objective function.

In the real-world business environment, however, firms will not be aware of the exact shape and location of their cost and revenue curves. We have argued in Chapters 5 and 8 that the firm may generate *estimated* demand and cost functions, however. By careful analysis of cost and demand data, the firm may be able to use its best estimate of the MR and MC curves to establish the price that appears to best serve its objectives.

There are three main ways of practicing marginalist pricing under uncertainty, each of which has been outlined in preceding chapters. We shall now summarize the three methods in turn.

Given Estimated Demand and Marginal Cost Curves. Suppose we have estimated the demand curve or have derived the demand curve from an estimate of the demand function, as outlined in Chapter 5. We know that the marginal revenue curve has the same intercept value and twice the slope value as compared with the demand curve, and thus we can quickly derive an estimate of marginal revenue. Suppose also that we find marginal cost to be constant over the relevant range of output, or explained by a linear or other function of output, as outlined in Chapter 8. Setting the expression for marginal revenue equal to that for marginal cost, we can solve for the quantity level that preserves the equality. Inserting the result back into the demand curve gives us the price that, to the best of our knowledge, will maximize contribution and hence profits.

Given Estimated Price Elasticity and Marginal Costs. If we are supplied with an estimate of price elasticity for a product in the vicinity of the current price, we can use the elasticity formula ($\epsilon = dQ/dP \cdot P/Q$) to deduce the slope of the demand curve ($b = dP/dQ$), since we already know the values ϵ, P, and Q. We then deduce the value of the intercept term a in the demand curve expression ($P = a + bQ$), since we would then know the value of P, b, and Q. We then proceed as in the above situation to find the MR expression, and the optimal price and quantity. This method was shown in detail in Chapter 4 in the section entitled "Implications for Optimal Pricing."

Given Estimates of Incremental Costs and Revenues. The incremental or contribution approach is a marginalist approach, since it is concerned with changes in both total revenues and total costs. Unlike the marginal revenue/marginal cost approach, however, the incremental approach does not require the ability to adjust output by one unit at a time. Thus, demand indivisibilities and/or discontinuities can be handled using the incremental approach. Suppose that the following demand situation exists: As price is progressively reduced the quantity demanded will increase by discrete blocks, as a result of gaining particular orders at the lower prices. For example, at a price of $3.80 per unit we may expect to sell 12,000 units, but at $3.79 we expect to sell 14,500 as a result of gaining a particular order at the slightly lower price.

Where demand contains indivisibilities or discontinuities we cannot construct the marginal revenue function, since the total revenue curve is not continuous and therefore is not differentiable. Instead, we must compare the incremental costs and incremental revenues at each price level and choose the price that allows the maximum contribution to be made.

These methods of price determination are only as sound as the under-lying information. To put our faith in the price which is indicated, we should be highly confident that both the demand and the cost estimates do in fact represent the actual situations and that the underlying *ceteris paribus* assumption can reasonably be expected to hold true. If, for example, our calculations indicate a price substantially below the prices of close rivals, we should expect those firms to react in some way and thus violate the *ceteris paribus* assumption. Because the demand and cost data are simply estimates, the actual outcomes may differ substantially from the expected outcomes. This is the nature of decision making under uncertainty, however: We must make decisions on the basis of the best information available, and if new information comes to light at a later point of time, this information forms the basis for a subsequent decision (which may involve the reversal of the initial decision).

Search Costs and Rule-of-Thumb Pricing Practices

In many cases the decision maker may expect that the cost of obtaining the estimates of the MC and MR relationships will exceed the extra revenue that might have been obtained using these estimates. Before attempting to obtain the additional information, the decision maker must expect that the addi-tional revenues to be earned as a result of making the optimal decision (as compared with the revenues expected from the decision to be made on the basis of existing information) will exceed the cost of obtaining that informa-tion. Clearly, in many business situations the decision maker would have no such expectations. Thus it is not surprising that business decision makers, notwithstanding the elegant models of the economists, tend to adopt simple *rule-of-thumb procedures* when setting or changing prices.

Rule-of-thumb pricing procedures should be viewed as shortcut decision-making methods that economize on search costs and on the decision maker's time. These procedures usually result in a suboptimal decision being taken when that decision is compared with one that might be taken if full informa-tion were available. In terms of profits gained by the firm, however, the rule-of-thumb decision-making procedure may be optimal, since although it may never lead to the optimal decision in any specific instance, consistent deci-sion making by rule-of-thumb procedure may approximate the same net profit levels over the longer term. The inefficiency of rule-of-thumb decision procedures arises from the fact that some amount of profitability is lost because the optimal decision in specific instances is not taken. But to know what the optimal decision is requires additional information which in turn has search costs attached, and hence all rule-of-thumb pricing procedures need to do is *lose less* than the information would cost.

The most common rule-of-thumb pricing procedure is known as *mark-up pricing*, and we examine this in the next section. We will see that under a broad range of conditions it may be more profitable for the firm to practice markup pricing rather than to incur the search costs necessary to implement marginalist pricing. Nevertheless, the principles involved in marginalist pricing are indispensible to the optimal use of markup pricing, and the firm should periodically seek cost and demand data to confirm that its prices are at levels which best serve the firm's objectives.

In the remainder of the chapter, we consider the pricing decision as it applies both to established products and to new products, and we look briefly at the legal considerations in the pricing decision.

11.2 MARKUP PRICING

DEFINITION: *Markup pricing*, also known as *cost-plus* pricing, is the practice of determining price by adding a percentage markup to the direct cost (or average variable cost) of the product. Thus:

$$P = AVC + X\%(AVC) \qquad (11\text{-}1)$$

where X is the markup percentage chosen. This markup, in dollar terms, is the per unit contribution to overheads and profits, and hence choosing the size of the markup amounts to choosing the contribution margin. Thus Equation (11-1) may be expressed as follows:

$$P = AVC + CM \qquad (11\text{-}2)$$

Clearly, the markup, or the contribution margin, should be large enough so that, at the attained level of sales volume, the accumulated contributions to overheads and profits actually cover the overheads and allow a profit to be made. The size of the markup is constrained, however, by the willingness of consumers to pay the higher prices associated with higher markups. Even a firm that has a monopoly over a certain product must acknowledge that at higher prices consumers in aggregate will buy fewer units. Firms that compete with other firms in the sale of a similar product must take into account the relative prices of competitors. An individual firm will lose sales to competitors if its price is significantly above the prices of its competitors and consumers do not think the item is worth the extra money.

Markup pricing is often thought to be simply cost based, but it is evident that the amount by which price can be marked up is highly dependent upon the demand conditions facing the firm. When asked what factors determine the size of the markup percentage, business people often respond that they choose the markup with an eye to "what the market will bear" or "in order to meet the competition."[1] These statements carry an implicit message

---

[1] See A. Silberston, "Price Behavior of Firms," *Economic Journal*, 80 (September 1970).

about the demand conditions facing the firm, and hence the size of the mark-up is both cost and demand based, contrary to the naïve view that markup pricing depends upon cost alone.

Since firms tend to use markup pricing in practice, does this mean that they are ignoring the marginalist principles of pricing? Before we are able to answer this question, we must investigate whether markup pricing is necessarily inconsistent with the marginalist principles. In fact, the marginalist-pricing and markup-pricing approaches can be reconciled, which we now demonstrate.

Reconciliation of Markup and Marginalist Pricing

For every price level which is determined by the marginalist procedure of setting MC = MR, there is an *implied* markup percentage. For example, if the profit-maximizing price is $6.00 and the AVC is $4.00, the implied markup is 50 percent, since $6.00 is 150 percent of $4.00. In Figure 11-1 we show this situation. In part (a), we show the marginalist determination of price: MR = MC at output level Q_0 and the profit-maximizing price is found to be P.[2] In part (b), we show the markup approach—without benefit of data on the demand and marginal revenue curves, the firm simply applies a 50-percent markup to AVC and arrives at the *same* price P. At price P, the quantity demanded will be Q_0, and the firm will be setting the profit-maximizing price, even though it did not know where its demand curve was.

FIGURE 11-1. Marginalist vs. Markup Pricing

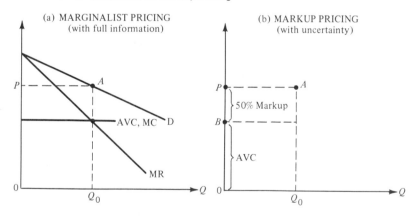

[2]Note that we show a horizontal MC curve, with AVC = MC in keeping with the empirical studies noted in Chapter 8. Constant MC over the relevant range greatly facilitate the analysis of markup pricing. The decision maker should be content that MC are constant in the situation under review before applying the simple markup-pricing rules without the modifications necessary if MC are in fact not constant over the relevant range.

(It now knows one point on its demand curve, namely point A, since consumers demanded Q_0 units at price P.)

In this case we suppose the firm using markup pricing under uncertainty was just lucky—it *happened* to apply the profit-maximizing markup implied by the marginalist approach and, thus, sets the profit-maximizing price without having to spend money on search activity to estimate the shape or placement of its demand curve. How will the firm know whether its markup is profit maximizing or not? By reconciling the two approaches, we can derive a simple rule which will indicate the profit-maximizing level of the markup. To reconcile the markup and the marginalist approach to price determination we must incorporate the MR = MC rule into the markup pricing Equation (11-1). We start by finding an expression for marginal revenue. Recall from Chapter 4 that total revenue is the product of price and quantity:

$$\text{TR} = P \cdot Q \tag{4-11}$$

Marginal revenue is the first derivative of total revenue with respect to output. Using the chain rule, since P also depends on Q, we have

$$\text{MR} = P + Q\frac{dP}{dQ} \tag{11-3}$$

We now perform a manipulation on Equation (11-3) which will allow a substitution. Multiply and divide the last term by P such that we obtain

$$\text{MR} = P + \frac{QP}{P} \cdot \frac{dP}{dQ} \tag{11-4}$$

Factoring out P we obtain

$$\text{MR} = P\left(1 + \frac{Q}{P} \cdot \frac{dP}{dQ}\right) \tag{11-5}$$

Note that the second term in the brackets is in fact the reciprocal of the expression for price elasticity we found in Chapter 4, which is restated here:

$$\epsilon = \frac{dQ}{dP} \cdot \frac{P}{Q} \tag{4-17}$$

Substituting from Equation (4-17) into (11-5) we obtain

$$\text{MR} = P\left(1 + \frac{1}{\epsilon}\right) \tag{11-6}$$

Having derived this expression for the relationship between marginal revenue, price, and elasticity we are now ready to perform the reconciliation. Marginalist pricing requires MC = MR. Setting MC equal to the above expression for MR we have

$$\text{MC} = P\left(1 + \frac{1}{\epsilon}\right) \tag{11-7}$$

Expressed in terms of price, this may be restated as

$$P = \text{MC}\left(\frac{\epsilon}{\epsilon + 1}\right) \tag{11-8}$$

Now, in business situations average variable costs are often constant (or viewed as constant) over the relevant range of outputs. Under such circumstances, marginal cost is equal to average variable cost. Hence we may restate Equation (11-8) as

$$P = \text{AVC}\left(\frac{\epsilon}{\epsilon + 1}\right) \tag{11-9}$$

or

$$P = \text{AVC} + \left(\frac{-1}{\epsilon + 1}\right)\text{AVC} \tag{11-10}$$

Thus the markup rate, X, in Equation (11-1), is equal to the negative reciprocal of one plus the price elasticity.[3]

Let us now substitute into Equation (11-10) an arbitrary value for elasticity, say $\epsilon = -5$. In this case:

$$P = \text{AVC} + \left(\frac{-1}{-5 + 1}\right)\text{AVC}$$

$$\text{or } P = \text{AVC} + \left(\frac{1}{4}\right)\text{AVC}$$

$$\text{or } P = \text{AVC} + 25\%(\text{AVC})$$

Thus a 25-percent markup on average variable cost is the profit-maximizing markup percentage if the elasticity value is equal to 5. Let us repeat this calculation for some other values of elasticity. For $\epsilon = -3$:

---

[3]Note that equation (11-10) is not a formula to find the profit-maximizing price given an estimate of price elasticity at some other price, since P and ϵ vary together. Rather, equation (11-10) is the optimality condition: if the price level and its associated elasticity value are such that the equality of equation (11-10) is preserved, then the markup rate is profit maximizing. If there is an inequality, the optimal markup rate must be found by constructing the firm's demand and marginal cost curves (from the elasticity estimate) and deducing the profit-maximizing markup rate, as in Figure 11-1.

$$P = \text{AVC} + \left(\frac{1}{2}\right)\text{AVC}$$

$$= \text{AVC} + 50\%(\text{AVC})$$

and for $\epsilon = -9$:

$$P = \text{AVC} + \left(\frac{1}{8}\right)\text{AVC}$$

$$= \text{AVC} + 12\tfrac{1}{2}\%(\text{AVC})$$

It is apparent from the above that there is a level of the markup percentage that is profit maximizing, and that this level varies inversely with the value of price elasticity. Products with higher price elasticities of demand should be expected to have relatively lower percentage markups in order to make the maximum total contribution to overheads and profits.[4] From Chapter 4 you will recall that we expect price elasticity to be higher the greater the number of substitutes and the greater the proportion of income that is spent on that particular product. In practice we know that markups on individual items of groceries, for example, tend to be low and that on gift items they tend to be high, in keeping with the above analysis.

Do firms choose their markup with an eye to the value of price elasticity? Certainly most do not. Rather, they find their "best" markup by trial and error or by adopting the same markup that is applied by other firms or by the price leader in their industry. This is not to say, however, that marginal analysis is of limited usefulness to the decision maker. Although firms may not use marginalist analysis in choosing the price levels, they may act as if they do. Marginalist analysis may thus predict the pricing actions of firms, even if in practice they use a markup-pricing procedure. To the extent that they choose the size of the markup with reference to market conditions and to the extent that they wish to maximize the contribution to overheads and profits, the markup price level may closely approximate the price that would be indicated by marginalist procedures.

The Range of Acceptable Markup Levels

Since the markup-pricing procedure avoids the search costs associated with estimating the demand curve, the markup level can vary within certain limits and still be acceptable, in the sense that the firm makes at least as much profit as it would if it incurred the search costs and set the MC = MR price. Consider Figure 11-2, in which we show the total revenue (TR) curve

---

[4]Note that the formula only works for $\epsilon < -1$. But for $\epsilon > -1$, MR < 0 and hence we cannot have MC = MR, since MC must be nonnegative.

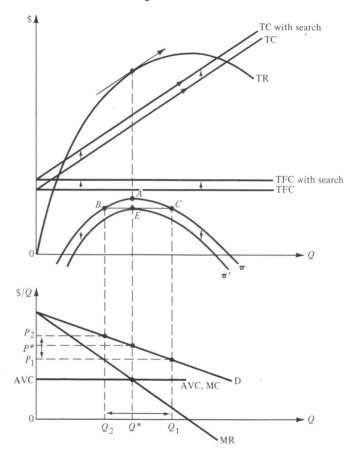

FIGURE 11-2. The Range of Acceptable Markup Levels for the Profit-
Maximizing Firm

associated with the actual demand curve faced by the firm. The total cost
(TC) curve is shown as a straight line, reflecting constant marginal and average variable costs on top of a base comprising the total fixed costs (TFC).
Profits, the vertical distance between TR and TC at each output level, are
represented by the curve π. Now consider search costs. If the firm decides to
spend funds to estimate the demand curve, this expenditure will shift total
fixed costs and, hence, total costs upwards by the amount spent on search
activity (Search costs must be regarded as a fixed cost, since they are not
related to the output level.). Thus, the profit curve must shift down by the
same vertical distance, to that shown as π' in Figure 11-2.

The profit-maximizing price is shown as P^* in the lower part of the
figure and is found where MC = MR or where TC and TR have the same
slope in the upper part of the figure. Note that this price is still the profit-
maximizing price, whether or not search costs are incurred. That is, point A

is the highest point on profit curve π, and point E is the highest point on profit curve π'. But, once the firm incurs the search costs, point E is the *best* it can do. If it does not incur the search costs, it might be lucky enough to set price P^* and maximize profits at point A. But note that any point on the profit curve π between B and C involves *more profit* than does point E. In terms of the demand curve in the lower part of the figure, any price between P_1 and P_2 promises more profit (without search costs) than does price P^* (after search costs have been spent). Sales can vary between Q_2 and Q_1 for prices between P_1 and P_2 and the firm will be at least as well off as (*at* prices P_1 or P_2) or better off than (*between* prices P_1 and P_2) it would be with full information and the "correct" price (where MC = MR).

In terms of the level of the markup, the rate applied to average variable costs could be anywhere between the low rate $(P_1 - \text{AVC})/\text{AVC}$ and the high rate $(P_2 - \text{AVC})/\text{AVC}$, and the firm would make more profits by *not* undertaking search activity to ascertain its demand curve. From Figure 11-2 you will note that in this example any markup between about 50 percent and 100 percent would appear to offer more profits, as compared to the alternative of incurring search costs and setting the "correct" price.

Determinants of the Range of Acceptable Markups. The range of markups which will allow greater profits without search costs will be wider or narrower, depending upon the magnitude of the search costs, the price elasticity of demand, and the firm's cost structure. Let us consider these in turn.

First, the greater the search costs necessary to form a reliable estimate of the demand curve, *ceteris paribus*, the more the profit curve will shift down and the wider the range of outputs and markup levels that will allow the firm to make more profit without undertaking search activity.

Second, the more inelastic is the firm's demand curve in the vicinity of the profit-maximizing price, *ceteris paribus*, the *greater* the range of markups and prices that will keep output within the permitted range, *ceteris paribus*.

Third, the lower the firm's marginal costs, *ceteris paribus*, the *greater* the range of outputs and prices that will allow more profit to be made without search than after search. The second and the third factors considered here interact to determine the kurtosis (or peakedness) of the profit function. The more platykurtic (flatter) the profit curve, the wider the range of outputs permissable for a given level of search costs avoided. You may wish to do some graphical experimentation to confirm the impact of these three factors on the range of optimal markup levels.

The Acceptable Range of Markups for the Sales Maximizer. For the firm that wishes to maximize sales volume in the short run subject to the attainment of a minimum profit target, the analysis proceeds similarly. In Figure 11-3 we show the same cost and demand situation as before, but we now show a minimum profit level, π_{min}, that the firm wishes to attain. If the firm incurs search costs, the relevant profit curve is π', and the sales maximizing output is Q_s, found where π' cuts π_{min} at point A. But, if the firm chooses not to incur search costs, it can achieve greater penetration of the market

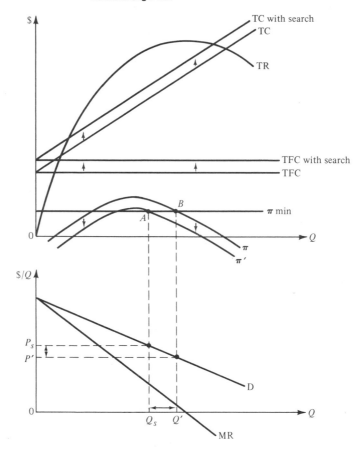

and, hence, market share by letting price fall as low as P'. At this price it will
sell Q' units, the output level where the π curve intersects the π_{min} curve.

NOTE: In a dynamic context the sales maximizer would simply keep price high
enough to attain its profit target and would presumably be unwilling to incur
search costs, since these involve an immediate tradeoff against current sales,
if the profit target is to be attained. Recall that current sales are desired by
the firm wishing to maximize its longer-term profits because of repeat sales
and complementary sales in future periods. Thus, the sales-maximizing firm,
rather than incurring search costs to ascertain the shape and placement of its
demand curve, should prefer, instead, to progressively reduce price until
its profit target is barely achieved. In this way, it would attain a larger share
of the market in the current period than it would if it spent money on de-

mand estimation. We will see later that this will work well enough in established markets but may not be an appropriate strategy for new products.

Periodic Tests to Ensure Acceptability of the Markup. The firm may wish to assure itself from time to time that its markup is in fact within the range of markup levels that allow greater profits (or greater market share in the case of the sales maximizer), as compared with the "correct" price after search costs have been incurred.

A simple test that should involve minimal search costs is the use of the markup rate to infer the value of price elasticity that would be required for the markup level to be profit maximizing.

EXAMPLE: At the beginning of this section, we saw that a markup rate of 50 percent over AVC is profit maximizing if the price elasticity is equal to -3. Thus, a firm using a 50-percent markup and wishing to maximize profits must ponder the question of whether or not its price elasticity of demand is equal to or close to the value -3. (That is, it should ask "would quantity demanded change by 30 percent if price were changed by 10 percent?") If the implied price elasticity seems *too high*, given management's knowledge of the market conditions, the markup percentage is probably *too low*, given the inverse relationship between the price elasticity and the profit-maximizing markup percentage. Thus, the firm might try a higher markup and observe the impact of this on profit (or the contribution to profit generated by this particular product).

NOTE: A simple formula to find what price elasticity *should* be for the current markup rate to be profit maximizing can be derived as follows. We know from Equation (11-10) that the profit-maximizing markup rate is $-1/(\epsilon + 1)$. For example, if $\epsilon = -3$, $-1/(\epsilon + 1) = 1/2$, or 50 percent; or for $\epsilon = -5$, $-1/(\epsilon + 1) = 1/4$, or 25 percent. Thus,

$$\frac{P - \text{AVC}}{\text{AVC}} = \frac{-1}{\epsilon + 1} \tag{11-11}$$

hence,

$$\epsilon + 1 = \frac{-\text{AVC}}{P - \text{AVC}}$$

and,

$$\epsilon = \frac{-\text{AVC}}{P - \text{AVC}} - 1 \tag{11-12}$$

EXAMPLE: Bon Nuit sleeping pills are sold to retailers for $1.15 per packet, representing 30 percent over the manufacturer's average variable cost, which is constant at $0.88 per packet. What must price elasticity be if this contribution margin represents the profit-maximizing markup? Substituting in Equation (11-12), we find:

$$\epsilon = \frac{-0.88}{1.15 - 0.88} - 1$$

$$= \frac{-0.88}{0.27} - 1$$

$$= -3.26 - 1$$

$$= -4.26$$

Thus, price elasticity must be in the vicinity of -4.26 if the 30-percent markup is profit maximizing. The manufacturer must now consider whether or not, for example, a 10-percent price decrease *would* expand sales by 42.6 percent. If even the most optimistic estimate is that sales would increase by only 20 percent, the markup is too low and the firm might cautiously adjust its price upwards to determine the impact on profits.

NOTE: If the firm does adjust its price up or down as a result of its view that the markup and the price elasticity are out of alignment, it will be able to generate information on the slope of its demand curve, as long as *ceteris paribus* holds. Given this estimated slope term, it can quickly solve for the intercept term in the expression for its demand curve and subsequently derive an expression for its marginal revenue curve. Given its knowledge of average variable costs or marginal costs if AVC is not constant, it can solve for the profit-maximizing price, or the sales-maximizing price, or the limit price, and adjust its markup percentage to reflect the ratio $(P - \text{AVC})/\text{AVC}$ given by the optimal price. It can then use that markup percentage in subsequent periods, because, as we shall see below, that markup percentage will remain optimal despite shifts in the demand curve and under conditions of inflation, given certain conditions. In any case, as we saw above, the markup has to stay only within the range of *acceptable* markup rates determined by the magnitude of the search costs and the peakedness of the profit curve.

Rather than change price experimentally, the firm might commission a study to ascertain the price elasticity of demand around its present price. This will generate information which will allow the firm to ascertain the profit-maximizing price, or the sales-maximizing price, or the limit price, as in the above discussion. The firm should undertake search expenditures whenever management expects the value of the information (in terms of the additional contribution generated) to more than cover the search costs of generating the information. It would seem prudent, given human fallibility, to incur these search costs *periodically*, in any case, to ensure that the firm's price does in fact best serve the firm's objective function.

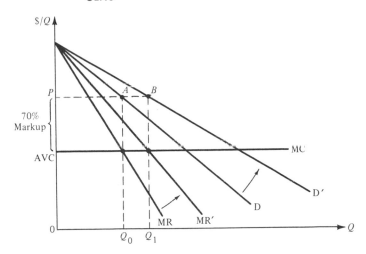

FIGURE 11-4. Constant Markup Given Iso-Elastic Shifts of the Demand Curve

Markup Pricing and Demand Shifts

We can show that if the firm has selected a markup rate which is optimal, it may simply maintain that markup rate despite considerable shifts in its demand curve, and the price will continue to best serve the firm's objective. Consider Figure 11-4, in which we show an initial demand situation represented by the demand curve D and marginal revenue curve MR. Given MC = AVC, the profit-maximizing price is P, implying a markup rate of about 70 percent over AVC, and the profit-maximizing output level is Q_0 units. Now, suppose that the quantity demanded increases by the *same percentage* at every price level—in Figure 11-4 a 40-percent increase in quantity demanded at each price level is indicated by the shift of the demand curve to D'. This is called an *iso-elastic shift* of the demand curve since it maintains the price elasticity of demand at each price level at the same value as it was before the shift. For example, the price elasticity at points A and B is the same; $\epsilon =$ -2.4 at each point.

NOTE: The profit-maximizing price, P, remains the profit-maximizing price despite the shift of the demand curve from D to D'. Thus, the 70-percent markup can be applied to AVC despite shifts in the demand curve, as long as these shifts are iso-elastic and MC remains constant. Iso-elastic shifts in the demand curve are an intuitively appealing notion and may well approximate the actual shifts that firms experience. In any case, we have seen that if the firm starts from, or periodically adjusts price to, the "correct" price (in terms of its objective function and given full information), it can afford to slip away from the "correct" price to a degree before it would be better to undertake search and re-establish the correct price. Thus, even if demand shifts are *not* iso-elastic, the markup can be expected to remain within the optimal range over some range of sales variations at the existing price level.

Markup Pricing under Inflationary Conditions

A markup-pricing policy applied to increasing levels of per unit variable costs will lead to a commensurate increase in the price level. In Table 11-1 we show a situation where average variable costs have increased over a one-year period by 10 percent. The 40-percent markup, when applied to that cost base at the beginning of the year, resulted in a price of $8.40. The 40-percent markup applied to the higher average variable cost figure at the year's end results in a 10-percent increase also in the size of the markup, or the contribution margin. Since both components of price have increased by 10 percent, it is not surprising that price itself has also increased by 10 percent.

Thus, markup pricing under conditions of inflation tends to pass the cost increase along to the consumer of the product. You will notice, however, that the increase in average variable costs was $0.60, while the increase in the price amounted to $0.84. The difference arises, of course, because the absolute amount of the contribution has risen by $0.24. Since this contribution has risen by 10 percent and the cost level has also increased by 10 percent, the contribution at the end of the period of inflation has the same purchasing power as the contribution had at the beginning of the period of inflation: It will now take $2.64 to purchase what was previously purchasable for $2.40. Thus, markup pricing, as well as passing the cost increase along to the consumer of the product, also serves to maintain the purchasing power (or real value) of the firm's contribution to overheads and profits.

NOTE: If during this regime of inflation the consumers' or purchasers' incomes have also gone up by 10 percent, this product will still require the same proportion of their incomes as it did before the inflation. Thus the 10-percent change in the price level is not a *real* price change in the sense that it does not cause consumers' purchasing power to be reduced, but it is a simple monetary price change resulting from the depreciation of the monetary unit. Such a price increase should not be regarded by purchasers as causing the product to become more expensive in terms of their incomes, and hence

TABLE 11-1.   Markup Pricing with Inflation

	Jan. 1 ($)	Dec. 31 ($)	Change (%)
Average variable costs	6.00	6.60	10
40% markup	2.40	2.64	10
Price	8.40	9.24	10

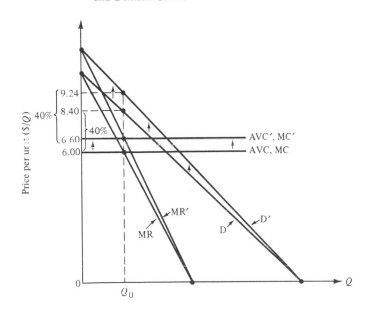

FIGURE 11-5. Constant Markup Given Inflationary Shifts of the Cost and Demand Curves

their quantity demanded should remain constant following the monetary price increase.

This situation is illustrated in Figure 11-5. Note that the demand curve has shifted vertically by a constant percentage, 10 percent in this case. This reflects each consumer's willingness to pay 10 percent more for the *same* quantity demanded as before, given that consumer incomes have gone up by 10 percent. Thus, the vertical intercept of the demand curve shifts up by 10 percent, while the horizontal intercept remains unchanged, so that at each quantity level, price is, therefore, 10 percent higher than before. Note that the new marginal revenue curve, MR', cuts the new marginal cost curve at the *same* output level Q_0. At the new price level, \$9.24, consumers buy the same quantity as before, since both their incomes and the price have risen by the same proportion.

NOTE: The above analysis was conducted entirely in *nominal-dollar* terms. In *real-dollar* terms, or constant purchasing-power terms, neither the cost curve nor the demand curve has shifted. In Figure 11-6 we show two vertical scales on the graph—the inner scale is in constant-dollar terms, showing the initial price at \$8.40 when AVC = \$6.00. The outer scale is in nominal, or monetary, terms, reflecting the nominal cost and price levels after the inflationary period. In effect, the purchasing power of the dollar, for both the firm and its customers, has shrunk by 10 percent; it now takes 10 percent more in nominal dollars to purchase what one could before the inflationary period. Deflating the nominal price and costs by 10 percent, we find that in real terms there has been no change in price or quantity demanded.

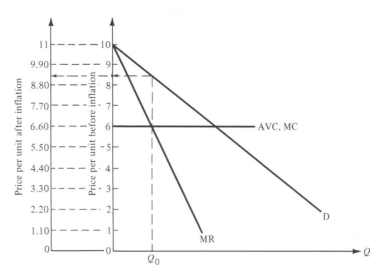

FIGURE 11-6. Constant Purchasing Power Analysis of Price and Cost
Changes under Inflationary Conditions

To the extent that consumers' incomes rise *less rapidly* than the firm's average variable costs in nominal-dollar terms, use of a constant-markup rate will cause the price to rise above the profit-maximizing level. Being cognizant of this danger, the firm should consider whether or not its consumers' incomes have risen by the same proportion as the firm's costs. If not, the firm should *reduce* its markup rate commensurately. Oppositely, if by some chance, its consumers' incomes have risen by a higher proportion than its costs, the firm may *raise* its markup rate commensurately.

Markup Pricing as a Coordinating Device

We know that a crucial element in the oligopolist's decision-making procedure is the decision maker's conjecture whether or not rival firms are likely to adjust prices at the same time and by similar magnitudes. To the extent that price changes are coordinated among firms, the market shares are likely to remain stable. On the other hand, if one firm raises price and rival firms do not, we expect that firm to suffer an elastic demand response and subsequently lose some part of its market share. Similarly, if all firms were to raise prices, yet one firm raised price by a significantly larger amount, that firm would be expected to lose part of its market share.

The existence of an established markup-pricing policy in a particular industry acts as a coordinating device when price changes become necessary. All firms are likely to be faced by similar changes in their cost structure, since they purchase labor and raw materials in the same or in similar markets, and if they each apply the same markup percentage to these average variable costs, their prices will rise by a similar percentage. Hence the *relative* prices of the firms will remain undisturbed at the new general level of prices. Markup-pricing policy and a common markup percentage allow a common and predictable strategy for price increases. Whether under conditions of conscious parallelism, price leadership, or independent action, the firm will expect that other firms will raise their prices to the extent of the familiar markup proportion on the change in unit costs. Thus, when a cost component changes, the firm may confidently adjust its price upward in the expectation that all rival firms will be doing likewise. An established markup-pricing procedure within an industry thus allows the decision maker to predict with a high degree of certainty the responses of rival firms to change in cost conditions.

NOTE: The size of the markup that will maximize profits, or sales subject to a profit constraint, or limit the entry of new firms, will be chosen by the price leader or by the collective consensus of firms operating under conditions of conscious parallelism. Once a level of the markup is found that seems to achieve these objectives, this markup percentage will become institutionalized in the industry and be the standard percentage applied by the firms, as long as the objective functions and general market conditions do not change significantly.

   This is not to imply that competing firms must necessarily mark up their average variable costs by exactly the same percentage figure. We shall see in the following section that the industry standard markup acts as a point of reference which allows the firm to bring its price into the correct "ball park," but in many cases a further price adjustment, or deviation from the standard industry markup percentage, may be necessary to avoid pricing "out on a limb." Let us now turn to an examination of pricing in the context of established market situations.

11.3   PRICING IN ESTABLISHED PRODUCT MARKETS

Price Positioning

In established product markets we can characterize firms as being either price makers or price takers. That is, they are either price leaders or price followers. Price leaders will presumably choose the price that they feel best fulfills their objectives, perhaps subject to the constraint that the chosen price must lie within a range that is acceptable to the price followers. In established product markets the general price level may be regarded as historically determined, in the sense that it has gravitated to a specific level (in real terms) over a prolonged period of time and to the general satisfaction or acquiescence of the firms involved. We might therefore claim, by backward induction, that the general price level prevailing in established markets is the level that serves the objective of the price leaders or of the firms in general. In established markets we would expect the general price level to be revised upward or downward whenever this is deemed desirable by the price leader or by the firms in general, and this may be achieved by a standardized markup policy being applied to the variable costs of each of the firms.

The essence of the pricing decision in established markets is therefore not so much to choose the general level of price as it is to choose the specific level of price relative to the prices of one's competitors. The price ball park is established; the firm must choose its price positioning within that ball park.

The Value of Product Attributes

The price of a product relative to the prices of its competing products should presumably be set higher or lower depending upon the presence or absence of desirable attributes perceived in that product by consumers in general.

EXAMPLE: If Brand A and Brand B typewriters are essentially similar in all mechanical and aesthetic senses except that Brand A typewriter has a self-correcting feature, one would expect that consumers would be willing to pay a slight price premium for the Brand A typewriter, since it offers a total package of attributes greater than that offered by Product B. Rarely are all other things equal, however, and we would typically expect Brand A to offer more of some attributes and less of others when compared with a Brand B typewriter. The price premium, or price discount, that a particular firm may add to or subtract from the general, or average, price level will depend upon the market's appreciation of the value of the total package of attributes involved in that firm's product relative to the offerings and prices of all competitive products.

How might we determine the value of specific product attributes or the value of a total package of attributes embodied in that product? Market research techniques must be applied to find the value placed upon the presence of certain attributes or groups of attributes in a particular product. The desired attributes are likely to be both tangible and intangible. If a large sample of consumers were canvassed, their consensus regarding the extra amount they would be prepared to pay for certain features could be used as a guide for pricing variants or new models of an established product.

EXAMPLE: In the case of a refrigerator, the tangible attributes will include such things as the internal capacity in cubic feet, the number of vegetable and meat trays, the presence or absence of a butter compartment, cheese compartment, butter temperature control, ice trays, ice maker, and various colors, and the availability of left-hand door hinges. Intangible attributes will include the brand name, store name, store location, store type, warranty conditions, and the ambiance presented by the shopping environment in each store.

With the knowledge of which attributes are perceived by consumers in the product under review and the valuation that consumers in general place upon specific attributes, the decision maker should be able to price the product at the level that is appropriate in view of the attributes and prices of competing products. A higher price would cause sales to be reduced, since more buyers would now regard that product as being overpriced in relation to its attributes; whereas a lower price would attract additional buyers, since the product would now represent a bargain for the price. However, if at the lower price, total contribution to overheads and profits is reduced, the price is clearly too low in view of the market's evaluation of the attributes contained in the product.

Product-Line Price Strategy

In perhaps the majority of cases the decision maker is not simply concerned with the price of one product, but with the prices of a line of related substitute and complementary products produced or sold by that firm. Price differentials between and among these products should reflect their place in the overall product line, and the spacing of price levels should be adjusted so that the firm's objective function is maximized.

A frequent procedure is to apply a common markup percentage to the per unit variable costs of each item in the product line. This is not likely to be the optimal pricing strategy, however, since some products must have relatively smaller price elasticities while others have relatively higher price elasticities. The reconciliation of the markup-pricing and marginalist-pricing procedures indicates that those with a lower price elasticity should be expected to contribute a greater relative amount to overheads and profits than those with a higher price elasticity. Keeping in mind that higher price elasticities result from a product's having a variety of substitutes and/or being relatively expensive, we would thus expect the decision maker to consider each product in the light of its absolute cost to consumers and the availability of substitutes both within and outside that decision maker's particular price line before deciding on the appropriate markup over average variable costs. A standard markup percentage applied to all items in a price line is suboptimal when price elasticities differ, since some prices will be lower than the contribution-maximizing level while others will be higher than the contribution-maximizing level. Those that are lower expand unit sales but cause a lower level of total contribution, since in effect the marginal cost exceeds the marginal revenue on the incremental units. Oppositely, for those items on which the price level is too high, there is in effect a situation where the marginal revenue exceeds the marginal cost on the last units produced and sold.[5]

---

[5]If the search costs involved in determining the value of price elasticities are relatively high, it may in fact be contribution maximizing to apply a common markup percentage to all products in a product line, as long as the revenue foregone is less than the search cost not expended.

The maximum total contribution to overheads and profits will be obtained when the contribution from each item in the product line is chosen with respect to its place and function in that product line and the extent of competition it faces on the market. Where products in the line are complementary goods, such as cameras, attachments, films, and projecting equipment, this may mean pricing the basic item (cameras) with a relatively low markup in order to achieve broad penetration of the market. If the complementary products must be purchased from the same manufacturer (for example, special film cartridges), sales of these items in the future will be enhanced by large sales of the basic item now. Thus, total contribution from the product line may be maximized by using the basic item as a "loss leader," or promotional item, pricing it at a level below that which would be indicated by the short-term price elasticity considerations.[6]

Alternatively, where two or more products in the line are substitutes, the price of the "bottom-of-the-line" product must be chosen quite carefully. If potential customers may be attracted to the store by price information and once in the store may be convinced of the virtues of more expensive products in the line, it may enhance total contribution to price the bottom-of-the-line product somewhat lower than would be suggested by price elasticity considerations. Automobile manufacturers might be expected to price their vehicles on this basis, since potential customers are likely to be attracted by relatively low advertised prices on items that are expensive in absolute terms. Once in the showroom the customer may be convinced by a salesperson to purchase a more luxurious version or a larger model (with higher contribution margins) or to "dress up" the basic vehicle with a number of higher-markup options and accessories. For obvious reasons, this type of pricing and personal selling strategy has been called "trading up."

There are three basic decisions to be made in product-line pricing. The first is to choose the price of the basic or bottom-of-the-line item. The "loss leader" or "trading up" considerations must be weighed against the connotations of lower quality that may be attached to lower prices, in order to achieve maximum contribution from the entire product line. The second is to choose the price of the top-of-the-line item with an eye to the impact of that price on sales of the whole line. A high-markup prestige item at the top of the line may confer status and quality connotations on all other items in the line. Alternatively, a price that is too high could give the impression that other items are overpriced as well and could cause total sales and contribution to be reduced. The third, and possibly the most difficult, decision is to choose the price intervals for the remaining items in the line. These price differentials should reflect the presence, absence, or degree of perceived attri-

---

[6]"Loss leader" is generally used to mean pricing one item below full costs in order to attract customers into the store, where they will (or the store hopes they will) also buy other items at the regular prices. It is being used here in the sense of attracting a customer to the product line with (it is hoped) subsequent sales of related items at the regular prices.

butes and should be chosen after observation of rival firms' chosen differentials. In many instances, of course, competitors' prices may constrain or dictate the prices and price intervals in the product line.

Price-Quality Associations

It is often claimed that pricing a product higher will make the consumer perceive it as a higher-quality item and cause sales and profits to be greater than if the product were priced at a lower level. Given our knowledge of consumer behavior theory, we can think of two arguments to support this assertion.

First, if the consumer has no other means of judging quality of the product, price will be the consumer's best indicator of quality, *a priori*. Purchase of the product and subsequent experience with the product should provide other indications of quality which the consumer can use in subsequent purchase decisions. But the absence of *all* other means of estimating quality implies a situation in which the consumer cannot tell by looking, feeling, or shaking the product, or it implies a situation in which there are no consumer reports, comparative tests, word-of-mouth recommendations (or warnings), or any other information available to the consumer. Certainly, there are products for which it is difficult to judge the quality without actually using them.

EXAMPLE: If your car breaks down, you could buy replacement parts made by a different manufacturer rather than by the original equipment manufacturer (OEM). The OEM parts are usually more expensive and the inference is that they are of higher quality. Objective comparative tests may show that there is no difference or even that the OEM parts are inferior to some of the cheaper alternatives. Other examples include electronic air purifiers, burglar alarms, stereo systems, brand-name aspirin, and so on.

Most of the above examples beg the question "why doesn't the consumer do some investigating and find out more information about the quality of the product?" The consumer could shop around, read *Consumer Reports*, ask people who own or use the product, and so on. This brings us to the second argument for using price as an indicator of quality.

Second, if the search costs necessary to ascertain the quality of the product are expected to exceed the consumer's notional value of the information derived, the consumer would rationally use price as an indicator of quality rather than incur those search costs. Note that search costs include time and money; it may take you several hours to find the information, plus the cost of buying magazines, such as *Consumer Reports*, *Road and Track*, *Stereo Review*, or whichever magazine has published a comparative test on the item. Rather than spend the equivalent of $20 searching, the consumer may simply pay the extra few dollars for the more expensive item and hope to get the quality he or she seeks. Notice that it is the price difference between the higher-priced item and the lower-priced item (which are under consideration) that determines the amount of search activity the consumer should conduct. Obviously, one should search for more information when buying an automobile or a stereo system than when buying a smoke detector or barbeque fuel or other relatively low-cost items which are difficult to rank qualitatively.

This leads us to a consideration of the types of products for which the consumer might typically make a price-quality association. Highly technical items are an obvious candidate, since most of us don't understand why they work. Low-cost items that require high search costs to ascertain quality are another contender. Products for which quality is imperative are another.

EXAMPLE: Medicines to correct ailments are often available as brand-name drugs or as generic drugs. Many people choose the higher-priced item, the brand-name drug, over the cheaper but chemically equivalent generic drug, presumably because they feel that their health is imperative and that any doubt they feel about the equivalence of the generics is easily erased by the expenditure of a few more cents or dollars. Cosmetic items to restore facial beauty, to stop the balding process, and to reverse other inevitable consequences of aging are seen as quality-imperative to many of the consumers of these items. When one's self-esteem and ego is at stake, the marketing people do not expect the consumer to respond with caution and cost-consciousness.

New products are ideal candidates for the price-quality association, as long as price is the only real indicator of quality, simply because there will be no prior information for consumers even if they do conduct search. Rather than wait until information accumulates, consumers may prefer to pay the premium price now and avoid the search costs of waiting. We examine new-product pricing in the next section.

Finally, people who pay triple the price for "designer" jeans and sport shirts are doubtless getting superior quality and fit as compared to the mass-market jeans and shirts available at one-third the price. But *three* times the quality? More likely, we are witnessing the Veblen effect, named after the classical economist.[7]

DEFINITION: The *Veblen* effect is defined as the tendency of some consumers to purchase more of an item when its price is higher because of the demonstration effect this has on others (namely, that the purchaser is sufficiently wealthy, exhibits good taste, and so on). This is also known as *conspicuous consumption*, since consumers may want to become conspicuous by their consumption of the more expensive, higher-quality product. It may alternatively be argued that the devotees of designer jeans, shirts, and other designer clothing simply feel that quality is imperative for their self-esteem, image, and lifestyle and that the extra cost is simply an insurance premium to make sure they get it.

---

[7]See H. Leibenstein, "Bandwagon, Snob, and Veblen Effects in the Theory of Consumer Demand," *Quarterly Journal of Economics* (May 1950), pp. 183-207.

11.4 NEW-PRODUCT PRICING

In the marketing sense a product is a new product if it contains a different bundle of attributes as compared with any product that has been offered before. Hence, an annual model change in an established product, or changes in packaging, or some intangible change such as in the image portrayed by the product or the seller of that product, may be interpreted as transforming that product into a new product. Such new products, however, can be treated in the context of pricing in established product markets, since they are essentially products similar to those that have been offered before or that are still being offered, except that there are now some additional product attributes that presumably have a value on the market. Hence, if the new product is an improvement over the earlier model, a price premium may be demanded. However, if all rivals produce their new products at about the same point in time, such as the annual model change in the auto industry, the decision maker must be sure that rivals are likely to raise their prices (perhaps in response to increasing variable per unit costs or by implicit agreement between price makers) before independently raising price, since to raise price independently could lead to a loss in market share.

At the other extreme of the new-product spectrum is the case of a product that contains a bundle of attributes quite unlike anything that has been offered before. In this case the decision maker has no established market from which to draw inferences, no prevailing price level, and no standard markup percentage to use as the basis of the pricing decision. In fact, the decision maker must proceed on the basis of extremely limited information, since both the demand and the cost functions will be subject to considerable uncertainty. Market research techniques may not be able to obtain reliable demand data from consumers who have neither seen nor perhaps even conceived of the proposed new product. On the cost side, since this is a completely new production process, the efficiency in the employment of labor and materials may be subject to considerable uncertainty, and hence it may be difficult to estimate the per unit variable cost. Traditionally, new-product pricing has proceeded on the basis of either skimming or penetration pricing. In effect these are the prices that are expected to maximize short-term and long-term contribution, respectively.

Price Skimming

DEFINITION: *Price skimming* refers to the practice of setting the price of a new product at a relatively high level upon its introduction to the market and, in effect, "skimming the cream" from the market. The product will be purchased only by those consumers who are willing to pay the initial price in order to have the product sooner rather than later. Some time after the product is introduced at this relatively high price, sales will begin to taper off, indicating that the supply of consumers willing to pay that price is diminishing. The decision maker may then decide to lower the price of the product in order that the next-most-eager section of the market will be induced to purchase the product.[8]

In terms of Figure 11-7 we suppose that price was initially set at price P_t and that sales at this level accumulated at Q_t. Supposing the same demand curve to remain appropriate for a later period, if price is then lowered to the level indicated by P_{t+1}, sales in this later period will total Q_{t+1} units. In a later period, perhaps, the price may be lowered to P_{t+2} and sales volume will expand to Q_{t+2}. In Chapter 9 we characterized this type of pricing behavior as second-degree price discrimination. That is, consumers are discriminated among on the basis of their willingness to wait for the product to become available at a lower price. A classic example of this pattern of price adjustment has been provided by ballpoint pens, which now retail for a mere fraction of their introductory price. More recent examples include electronic calculators and quartz digital wristwatches, as noted in Chapter 9.

In the case of virtually all new products, however, the cost per unit falls as the production of the product continues over time. Labor efficiency and the efficiency with which raw materials are used improve as the firm

FIGURE 11-7. Price Skimming over Time

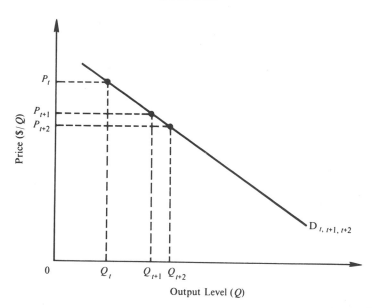

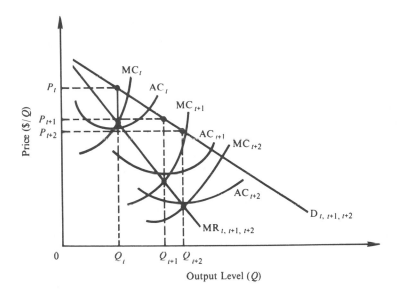

FIGURE 11-8. Profit-Maximizing Price Reductions over Time

obtains more experience in the production of the product. The technology of production is also likely to change as time passes. In other words, there is a "learning curve" in the production of the product. In Figure 11-8 we show this in terms of the marginalist analysis. The initial cost structure at time t is shown as the highest set of cost curves. The profit-maximizing price is thus P_t. During the next time period, however, the cost curves have fallen considerably due to the increased efficiencies achieved in production, and the profit-maximizing (or contribution-maximizing) price is now somewhat lower at P_{t+1}. In period $t + 2$, costs have fallen still further and the contribution-maximizing price is now P_{t+2}. Thus, price skimming, or second-degree price discrimination, may be a profit-maximizing response to the reducing cost level which may be experienced as the efficiency of production of a new product improves over time. In terms of markup pricing, these successively lower prices could result from adding the same markup percentage to progressively declining per unit variable costs.

The price of new products is often reduced over time not simply as the result of an individual firm's wishing to maximize its contribution but also as the result of the increased competition facing that new product as competitive products begin to enter the market. The increased supply of substitutable products for a given market demand situation will cause the general price level to gravitate downward over time, especially if the firm's cost levels are falling over this same time period. We should expect that the percentage markup applied by a particular firm to the average variable costs will decline as the number of substitutes is increased by the entry of the new competition, since this will cause the price elasticity of demand for the product to be increased.

NOTE: Marketers speak of the *product life cycle*, whereby the demand for a new product goes through the stages of introduction, growth, maturity, and decline. Thus, the market demand curve would shift outward for successive periods and eventually begin to shift back as the market declines. Entry of other firms means that the firm must share the market with an increasing number of new firms, at least in the first three stages. The relevant demand curve is, thus, the firm's *mutatis mutandis* demand curve, presuming all firms price similarly via conscious parallelism or price leadership, for example. The firm's demand curve may shift outward at first, or back and forth, depending on the relative rates of growth of the market and of the number of firms. The pattern of prices over time will reflect the shifts in both the firm's cost curves and its demand curves.[9]

Penetration Pricing

DEFINITION: *Penetration pricing* is the practice of pricing at a relatively low level initially in order to achieve a relatively high sales volume and to in effect penetrate the market to a greater degree than could be achieved with a higher price. Such a pricing policy is especially appropriate when the firm's objective is to maximize sales in the short term or to set the price at the limit that will inhibit the entry of new firms. Where the entry of new competition is relatively easy in terms of capital, technology, and manpower required, we would expect penetration-pricing strategies, since they would make the product appear much less profitable, if at all profitable, for new entrant firms. Under easy entry conditions a strategy of price skimming would induce a rush of new competition, with subsequent dilution of longer-term profits.

A second consideration that would influence the choice between penetration pricing and price skimming is the difficulty that potential competitors are likely to have in copying the new product after they achieve entry. If the degree of differentiability is low, the initial firm may wish to use penetration pricing in order to establish a broad market base and build goodwill and consumer loyalty for future sales. On the other hand, if the product is such that there is considerable scope for product differentiation, price skimming may be the appropriate strategy until new firms achieve entry and begin marketing their versions of the product, since at that time the price level will fall and the initial producer will be forced to share the market with

---

[9]For more on the product-life-cycle concept, see P. Kotler, *Principles of Marketing*, chap. 11 (Englewood Cliffs, N.J.: Prentice-Hall, Inc., 1980); also T. Levitt, "Exploit the Product Life Cycle," *Harvard Business Review* (Nov.-Dec. 1976), pp. 81-94; and N.K. Dhalla, and S.Yuspeh, "Forget the Product Life Cycle Concept!" *Harvard Business Review* (Jan.-Feb. 1976), pp. 102-12.

the entrant firms. The initial producer of the product may as well make hay while the sun shines. Finally, penetration pricing is suggested when the nature of the product is such that it will generate a continuing stream of complementary sales. The Kodak 110 camera is an example of a new product that generates a continuing demand for its film, and it appears to have initially been priced at a penetration level.

The Dynamic Price Path for New Products

In the foregoing discussion of price skimming and penetration pricing for new products, it was implied that the price level would change over time in response to the changing cost and demand conditions. As cost per unit falls and/or as the number of competitors and the closeness of competing products increase, we would expect the price per unit to fall. The optimal dynamic price path for new products is that path that fulfills the firm's objectives over the firm's time horizon. Thus, if the firm's objective is to maximize the short-run contribution to overheads and profits, it should choose the markup with reference to the price elasticity of demand faced by the products. On the other hand, if the firm's objective is to maximize long-term profitability by pursuit of a short-run limit-pricing or sales-maximization objective, it should ensure that the price level in each period serves to fulfill that objective.

First-Mover Advantages. The firm which introduces a new product usually expects to earn pure profit by doing so, even if other firms enter the market with their own versions of the product as soon as they are able to. The innovating firm benefits from what are known as first-mover advantages.

DEFINITION: *First-mover advantages* are the benefits accruing to the firm that first introduces a new product that turns out to be successful. These advantages include the monopoly profits it can earn while it is still the only firm in the market, as well as the additional profits it earns from the rapid cost reductions it will experience as a result of the learning curve.

The first firm to introduce the new product is able to start sliding down its learning curve immediately and have significantly lower costs per unit by the time the first competitor's product arrives in the marketplace. It takes time to design and manufacture a competing product, even if it is a relatively close copy of the original. The second and subsequent firms must start at the *top* of their learning curves, giving the first-mover a substantial cost advantage. Now, if prices decline due to the imitator's having to share the market, the first-mover is more likely to be profitable despite declining prices. In Figure 11-9 we show the dynamics of pricing and costs in a hypothetical situation. We suppose that the first-mover sets price $10 and this stays constant until time t_1, when entry of competing products occurs. Prices then decline over time as more firms enter and as the firms engage in price competition initially. Even if price leadership or conscious parallelism follow as the

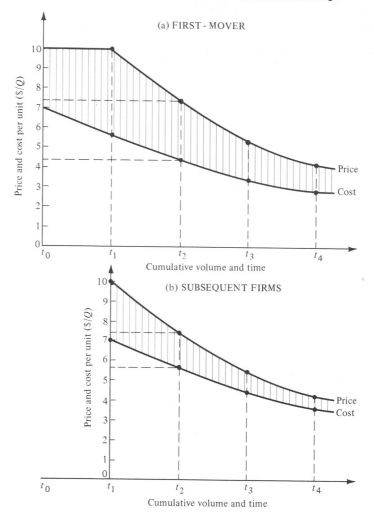

FIGURE 11-9. Dynamic Price Paths and the First-Mover Advantage

market matures, prices are likely to fall in response to falling costs for all firms.

Note that the first-mover maintains its higher profit margin through time despite the falling price level. At time t_2, for example, the price has fallen from its initial level of about $10 to about $7.40. The first-mover's costs have fallen to about $4.40 while the subsequent entrants' costs are about $5.60 per unit. Only if the subsequent entrants learn faster, that is, if they have a higher percentage of learning, or expand output faster, can they catch up with the first-mover firm.

Thus, we see firms striving to discover and launch new products for the first-mover advantages and profits that result. Unfortunately, most new products are *not* major successes and the firm's profits as first-mover with one new product may easily be eroded by its losses with several other new products that did not sell well and were soon discontinued.

New-Product Pricing and Quality Decisions Using Expected Present Value Analysis

Where sufficient information can be generated, the new-product pricing problem may be solved by expected present value analysis. The information that must be generated will include estimates of demand at various outputs and the probabilities of entry by competing firms at each of the various price levels, as well as the time lag before entry is expected to be effected. Where the stream of contributions to overheads and profits is expected to continue beyond the present period, the future earnings must be discounted at an appropriate rate to allow comparability of the income streams associated with each potential price level.

In many cases the price and quality decision is made at the same time. The firm may have several levels of quality it can choose and then be able to set the price according to the level of quality designed and manufactured into the product.

EXAMPLE: Suppose a firm has a new product that can be launched in a luxury design with very high production quality; or a less elaborate design with less attention to detail; or thirdly, in a basic design with relatively low production costs. Let us call these quality modes A, B, and C, respectively. These different quality modes will allow the firm to ask different prices, since consumers are expected to perceive the product differently in the different modes. Market research indicates that the most favorable response to these products would be received at prices $42, $29, and $16 in each of the quality modes, respectively. Cost of production is expected to be $20, $15, and $10, respectively, in the first year, falling to $16, $12, and $8 in the second year, due to the learning curve. Management concedes that there is a probability of entry of competition in the second year, and this varies with the quality mode and price chosen, as shown in Table 11-2. Whether or not there

TABLE 11-2. Prices, Expected Sales, and Entry Probabilities for Each Quality Mode

	A	B	C
Year 1 unit costs	$20	$15	$10
Year 1 price	$42	$29	$16
Year 1 sales volume	6,000	9,000	16,000
Probability of entry	0.9	0.6	0.2
Year 2 unit costs	$16	$12	$8
Year 2 price if no entry	$40	$28	$16
Year 2 sales volume if no entry	8,000	12,000	18,000
Year 2 price if there is entry	$32	$20	$12
Year 2 sales volume if there is entry	2,000	4,000	12,000

TABLE 11-3.   Decision-Tree Analysis of the New-Product Pricing Problem

Quality Mode	FIRST YEAR Price	Volume (units)	Contribution ($)	PV ($)	SECOND YEAR Entry	Prob-ability	Price	Volume (units)	Contribution ($)	EV ($)	PV ($)
A	$42	6,000	132,000	125,902	Yes	0.9	$32	2,000	32,000	28,800	24,972
					No	0.1	$40	8,000	192,000	19,200	16,648
											41,620

Total expected present value for Product A = $125,902 + $41,620 = $167,522

Quality Mode	Price	Volume (units)	Contribution ($)	PV ($)	Entry	Prob-ability	Price	Volume (units)	Contribution ($)	EV ($)	PV ($)
B	$29	9,000	126,000	120,179	Yes	0.6	$20	4,000	32,000	19,200	16,648
					No	0.4	$28	12,000	192,000	76,800	65,593
											82,241

Total expected present value for Product B = $120,179 + $82,241 = $202,420

Quality Mode	Price	Volume (units)	Contribution ($)	PV ($)	Entry	Prob-ability	Price	Volume (units)	Contribution ($)	EV ($)	PV ($)
C	$16	16,000	96,000	91,565	Yes	0.2	$12	12,000	48,000	9,600	8,324
					No	0.8	$16	18,000	144,000	155,200	99,890
											108,214

Total expected present value for Product C = $91,565 + $108,214 = $199,779 is entry, management plans to reduce price in the second year and expects to reduce price much more if there actually is entry, as shown in the table.

You will agree that this looks like a complex problem. Nevertheless, its solution is relatively simple using the decision-tree format. We first calculate the contribution at each price level, given the average variable costs stated above. Since the sales revenue and variable costs are likely to be received and incurred continuously throughout each year, we must choose the discount factor from Table B-2 in Appendix B, where the present value of one dollar received continuously in future periods is shown. Let us assume that the firm's opportunity rate of discount is 10 percent.[10] This implies a discount factor of 0.9538 for the first year's contributions and 0.8671 for the second year's earnings. Table 11-3 presents the decision-tree analysis of the problem. We wish to know which price level promises the greatest expected present value over the two-year period. As you can see from the decision tree, the expected present value of the contribution stream is greatest for the inter-mediate price of $29 per unit in this example, indicating that this is the preferable initial price and quality mode for the product.

You will note that point estimates are shown for the sales volume under each of the various price levels. This implies a probability of unity that these volumes will be attained. More likely, of course, our demand estimates would involve a probability distribution of sales volumes at each price level in each period. This would not change the nature of the problem or its solution; it might simply complicate the solution immensely. Suppose for each price level in each year the probability distribution of sales volumes was distributed around the value shown, with five possible sales volumes shown at each price level. If these values are normally distributed and their mean (or expected value) is equal to the values shown in Table 11-3, there is no need to add extra branches, as the above simplification will give equivalent results. However, if the probability distribution is skewed to one end or the other, I suggest you begin your decision tree on a very large sheet of paper!

11.5 LEGAL CONSIDERATIONS IN PRICING

When making a pricing decision the decision maker must ensure that all legal ramifications of that decision have been taken into account. In most Western economies the law provides substantial penalties for several pricing practices that are considered contrary to the interests of society or of specific groups within that society. *Price fixing*, or collusive agreement about the price levels that will be set by competing firms, is considered as depriving the consumer

---

[10]In practice, of course, we should not simply assume a rate of discount but should attempt to find the firm's opportunity rate of discount. A second oversimplification in this example is the use of the same discount rate for all three pricing strategies. Since the dispersion of outcomes increases as price is reduced, progressively higher discount rates should be used for the lower prices to compensate for the increased risk of these price strategies. Alternatively, the coefficient-of-variation criterion might be used.

of the availability of lower-priced units of the product in question which would presumably be available in a regime of noncollusive competition.

Price discrimination, usually defined legally as the practice of setting differing prices to different customers under essentially the same purchasing conditions, deprives some customers of the lower prices being offered to others in similar geographic areas, time periods, or purchase volumes.

Predatory pricing is the practice of setting a relatively low price with the intent of damaging a competitor. Although consumers may praise these lower prices, we must remember that competitors are people too. As members of society, firms have the right to be protected from the predatory activity of other firms. This is not to say that an efficient, low-cost firm may not price at a level that will damage a competitor's sales and eventually its solvency, since this is an expected part of the Darwinian survival system in a capitalist economy. Price predation involves the (probably temporary) setting of price at an abnormally low level (perhaps even below average variable cost) with the intent of damaging a competitor.

The final legal aspect of pricing we shall mention is *misleading advertising regarding price*. This involves making false or misleading statements concerning the product's current, previous, or future price level and the relationships between these. For example, it is illegal to claim that a product is "on special" or is "ten cents off regular price" if this is not actually true.

In each of the above cases it is no simple matter to establish guilt or innocence. Much depends upon the interpretations of the available facts and the preceding case history. This is not the place for a discourse on the legal complexities of pricing or on any other legal aspects of business behavior, however.[11] There is sufficient material in this area to fill another textbook and to keep you occupied for another semester. Suffice it to say here that litigation can be expensive and that courts do hand down substantial penalties to those found guilty of illegal pricing activities. The decision maker must therefore have considerable knowledge of, or the services of a consultant who can advise on, the legality of particular pricing decision so that the firm's profit-oriented objectives will be achieved.

This is not to insist, however, that every pricing decision will be scrupulously legal, since a firm may at times augment its profitability by breaking the law. If the firm expects to get away with an illegal pricing act or even if caught expects to earn greater profitability than is involved in the legal costs and the fines that may be imposed by the courts, the firm may decide to pursue illegal pricing practices. If the decision maker has no qualms about the immorality of breaking laws established by society for the benefit of members of that society, we may expect him or her to perform an expected value analysis (either explicitly or implicitly) estimating the present value

---

[11]For brief reviews of the legal aspects of pricing, see K. S. Palda, *Pricing Decisions and Marketing Policy*, chap. 7 (Englewood Cliffs, N.J.: Prentice-Hall, Inc., 1971); or M. I. Alpert, *Pricing Decisions*, pp. 16-29 (Glenview, Ill.: Scott, Foresman & Company, 1971); or F. Livesey, *Pricing*, chap. 13 (London: Macmillan, Inc., 1976).

of the probable future contributions under each possible strategy, the probability of being discovered and convicted, and the legal and punitive costs involved.

11.6 SUMMARY

In this chapter we have considered the pricing problem in mature and in newly established product markets. Recognizing that firms may lack the information necessary to price by marginalist principles or that this information may cost more than it is worth, we expect firms to use markup-pricing procedures or to simply follow the price leader(s). We showed, however, that markup pricing can be profit maximizing or contribution maximizing if chosen at the level commensurate with the product's price elasticity of demand. If longer-term profit maximization is desired, the markup percentage is likely to be somewhat lower than for short-run profit maximization, since long-term price elasticities tend to be higher than short-term price elasticities. As well as saving information search costs, markup pricing acts to pass cost increases along to the customer and to maintain the purchasing power, or real value, of the firm's profits, and it assists in coordinating the pricing behavior of firms in oligopolistic markets.

We saw that there will be a range of acceptable markup rates if the firm does not incur search costs and that any one of these rates will allow higher profits and/or greater market share as compared to setting the optimal price *after* incurring search costs. The optimal markup rate remains optimal despite shifts in costs and demand curves, under certain conditions. Periodic search activity is recommended to ensure that the markup rate best serves the firm's objectives.

Choosing the appropriate price level in established product markets requires an evaluation of the attributes perceived to exist in your product vis-à-vis those in competing products. In these markets the general level of prices is established, and the problem is to ensure that each product is positioned in the existing price range such that the firm's objectives are best served. The price chosen should reflect the presence, absence, or degree of desirable attributes in each product, relative to the prices and attributes offered by competing products. Product-line pricing involves essentially the same problem, except that a particular firm produces several of the competing or complementary products and must choose their prices relative to the prices and attributes of products from both its own product line and from its competitors' product lines.

New-product pricing is an area of considerable difficulty largely because of the lack of information regarding probable demand and cost conditions and the number and timing of new entries to this newly established market. To the extent that this information is available with sufficient degrees of accuracy, the decision maker may choose the price that is expected to best serve the relevant objective function. In any case, the cost and demand conditions will be constantly changing and evolving, and considerable price adjustment may be necessary before this market matures and establishes a general price level that is agreeable to all the firms involved.

The decision maker must keep an eye peeled for the legal implications of each pricing strategy. The legal and punitive expenses and customer illwill that may be involved in certain pricing strategies must be considered before each decision is taken.

DISCUSSION QUESTIONS

11-1.   Outline the conditions under which it may be profit maximizing to use a rule-of-thumb price determination procedure rather than to determine price on the basis of estimated marginal revenue curves.

11-2.   In using an estimated demand curve to determine price, there is a risk that the actual price/quantity combination (which eventually occurs) is not a point on the estimated demand curve. Does this mean we should not have used that estimated demand curve?

11-3.   Under what type of cost and/or demand conditions is the contribution approach the only way to implement the marginalist pricing principle?

11-4.   Explain why there is a range of markup rates which make it preferable to avoid search costs. What does this range depend on?

11-5.   Discuss the conditions under which a markup rate, if initially optimal in terms of the firm's objective, will remain optimal despite shifts in the cost and demand curves.

11-6.   Explain why the presence or absence of desirable attributes in your product influences the optimal price positioning of that product in an established market.

11-7.   Summarize the issues involved in product-line pricing strategy.

11-8.   Under what conditions would you expect price skimming to be the profit-maximizing strategy for a new product?

11-9.   Discuss the first-mover advantages for the firm which launches a new product that turns out to be successful.

11-10. Outline the illegal aspects of pricing of which the price maker must be fully aware before determining prices.

PROBLEMS AND SHORT CASES

11-1.   The Ajzenkopf Company has been in operation for almost fifteen years and has enjoyed considerable success in the manufacture and sale of its glass vases.

The Ajzenkopf plant at present has a capacity of 35,000 units per year, and the facilities at the plant are highly specialized. Sales of vases are currently 29,000 units a year. The selling price is $7.00 per unit. Last month the average costs of production were determined to be: average fixed costs, $1.03; average cost of labor, $1.98; and average cost of materials, $1.05. At those present price and cost levels the Ajzenkopf Company received a profit that management believed was quite acceptable.

This agreeable situation came to an abrupt halt, however, when it was learned that the suppliers of raw materials were raising their prices and that there was a labor dispute which forced negotiations to begin. An agreement was reached, and the final settlement had the effect of increasing the average cost per unit of labor by 20 percent. A new contract has been signed with the suppliers of the raw materials, and the new prices of raw materials had the effect of increasing the average materials cost by 30 percent. This contract had been signed after other suppliers were contacted and no less-expensive prices of raw materials could be found.

Faced with this situation, a meeting was called to determine what action should be undertaken to maintain an acceptable level of profit. It was agreed that a profit level of $75,000 was the minimum acceptable point. Two alternative suggestions were made. The first suggestion, made by the marketing manager, was to raise prices to $9.00 a unit, since he was fairly certain that this price level would reduce quantity demanded by only 8,500 units per annum. The marketing manager also offered an estimate of the average variable costs, stating that the average labor cost would be $3.10 and the average materials cost would be $1.39 at this level of output.

The plant manager proposed that the price should be reduced to $6.00. The plant manager was also fairly certain about the demand situation, stating that at this price level 32,500 vases would be demanded. He also offered his estimates of average variable costs, stating that at this level of output the average costs of labor and materials per unit would be $2.85 and $1.24, respectively. The plant manager further supported his proposal by stating that under this alternative, laborers need not be laid off and thus low labor morale would not reduce productivity of the workers.

(a) Using the information given above, derive graphical estimates of the firm's revenue and cost functions.

(b) Assuming that the firm wishes to maximize sales volume subject to obtaining a minimum profit of $75,000, what price do you suggest they charge? Discuss your answer fully. What qualifications do you wish to add to your analysis?

11-2. Regression analysis of the variations in prices and quantity demanded for our major product (conducted under controlled conditions in a consumer clinic by our marketing research department) provides the following results (where P is in dollars and Q represents thousands of units):

Regression equation	$Q = 49.147 - 2.941P$
Coefficient of determination	$(R^2) = 0.96$
Standard error of estimate	$= 0.128$
Standard error of the coefficient	$= 0.086$

Our production department has conducted its own study of the variations of weekly total variable costs and output levels over the past three months. Its results (with TVC in thousands of dollars and Q representing thousands of units) are as follows:

Regression equation	$TVC = 102.35 + 0.025Q^2$
Coefficient of determination	$(R^2) = 0.92$
Standard error of estimate	$= 0.232$
Standard error of the coefficient	$= 0.003$

You are an executive assistant to the marketing manager, Derek Winton. Mr. Winton feels that the present price of $9.95 is fine. He argues that it positions our product in the upper part of the range of our competitors' prices and that the current sales level of approximately 20,000 units a week is fine in view of our full capacity limit of only 25,000 units weekly. While he agrees that a price change of a dollar or so either way would go unchallenged by competitors, he does not think such a price change would improve the contribution made by this product.

(a) What is the contribution-maximizing price? Is the associated output level feasible?

(b) How confident are you that your prediction will in fact generate a greater contribution than the present price level? Explain in detail with supporting calculations.

(c) Are there any reservations you wish to attach to your recommendation?

11-3. The Pittsburgh Plastics Company introduced a new product in January which received strong initial support and has shown a steady growth of sales in subsequent months. The initial price was set somewhat arbitrarily as a 25-percent markup over average costs. The company's objective is to maximize the contribution to overheads and profits, and it is now anxious to know whether the $6.88 price is optimal. In light of the continual growth in sales and changes in certain cost components, it has commissioned a study by Market Researchers Incorporated, who report that the price elasticity of demand is approximately -2.5 at the current (March) price and output level.

The output and cost data for the past three months are as follows:

	January	February	March
Sales (units)	*2,246*	*2,471*	*2,718*
Direct materials	$1,415	$1,557	$1,712
Direct labor	3,369	4,077	4,933
Indirect factory labor	3,000	3,075	3,154
Office and administrative salaries	2,000	2,000	2,000
Light and heat	485	470	320
Other overheads	2,100	2,100	2,100

(a) Supposing that price can be varied each month, estimate the optimal price for the month of April.

(b) What output level could be sold at the optimal price level in April?

(c) What qualifications and other considerations do you wish to add to the above pricing and output decision?

11-4. The Laura Ann Boutique purchases a line of ladies dresses from a wholesaler and pays $30 per dress regardless of quantity purchased. These dresses are marked up 33.33 percent over their invoice cost and sell quite readily. The firm's objective is to maximize contribution to overheads and profits, and management is concerned whether or not 33.33 percent is the profit-maximizing markup rate.

(a) What would price elasticity of demand have to be in order for 33.33 percent to be the optimal markup rate?

(b) Suppose Laura Ann commissions a study that indicates that price elasticity of demand for these dresses is $\epsilon = -3.5$. Given the present price of $40 per dress and weekly sales averaging 300 dresses, was the present markup rate within the range of acceptable markups?

(c) Suppose the study cost Laura Ann $2,000. Was it worth it? Will it pay for itself in the future weeks?

11-5. The Archibald Truck Service (ATS) Company has been successfully servicing and repairing large trucks and tractor trailers for several years, specializing in Kenworth, Peterbilt, and Mack tractor service. Their pricing policy on each job is to charge $25 per hour labor and the "book price" for materials and replacement parts. The labor charge represents the actual cost to ATS plus 25 percent, and the "book prices" represent the invoice cost of the materials and parts plus 25 percent. Thus, ATS effectively sets price by marking up its direct costs by 25 percent. The founder and general manager, Mr. Joseph Archibald, reasons that this relatively low price structure is the best approach, since there is a lot of repeat business in service and repair work. He would rather have more work in the present period and maximize profits over the longer term.

For a typical service and repair job his cost is $600, and he charges $750. He does, on the average, 60 jobs per month. His overhead costs are $8,000 per month. Mr. Archibald is concerned that his monthly profits are too low; he wants at least $2,000 per month and is not presently earning that. He has asked all his customers over the past two months to complete a questionnaire and from this he has been able to estimate that price elasticity for his service and repair job is approximately $\epsilon = -1.1$.

(a) Construct the demand, total revenue, and total cost curves for ATS from the data given.

(b) Advise Mr. Archibald of the price level and the implied markup rate on the average service and repair job which would maximize sales volume subject to the attainment of his profit target.

(c) Explain to Mr. Archibald the conditions under which that markup rate will remain optimal despite shifts in the cost and demand curves.

(d) Give him some guidance on how he should adjust the markup rate if the conditions referred to in part (c) do not hold.

11-6. The Napper Bag and Canvas Co. Ltd. is a specialist manufacturer of down-filled sleeping bags for sale in the camping equipment market. In this market there are several large companies with annual sales between $25 million and $30 million and many smaller companies with sales between $1 million and $5 million. Most of these companies have diversified product lines of camping equipment, including tents, cooking equipment, camping furniture, and sleeping bags with various types of filling. Napper's sales of $1.6 million last year came entirely from down-filled sleeping bags, however. Although more expensive than other materials, down has substantially more insulating value by weight and volume and commands the attention of a loyal segment of serious outdoorspeople. Only a few firms produce quality down-filled bags, but these firms face peripheral competition from other firms producing bags filled with other natural and artificial materials.

Last year Napper sold 21,000 bags directly to large department stores, catalog sales companies, and specialty sporting equipment stores. These clients typically require contracts guaranteeing prices for one year. The cost of manufacturing sleeping bags depends on the size of the bag, the materials used, and the amount of fill. A breakdown of Napper's latest manufacturing costs for a typical style is as follows:

Item	Cost per Unit
Down filling	$30.00
Other raw materials	14.40
Direct labor	8.12
Manufacturing overhead	6.09
Total unit cost	$58.61

To the manufacturing cost is added a markup of 30 percent to provide for selling, administration, financial expenses, and profit.

During the past year the cost of down increased by between 80 to 95 percent, depending on the grade and blend. Napper was able to pass this on to its customers without any apparent loss of sales or share of the market. The suppliers of down are forecasting a minimum increase of 80 percent over the next year. For Napper this will mean that the average price of down will increase from the current $12 per pound to $22 per pound. It is anticipated that the cost of other raw materials will rise by 8 percent and labor by 5 percent over the next year.

George Napper, the marketing manager, is concerned about the prospects for the coming year, and you are called upon to advise him.

(a) What price level do you advise for Napper's typical style bag?

(b) Do you have any other advice for Mr. Napper concerning future marketing strategy?

11-7. The refrigerator market is characterized by a wide diversity of product offerings and a price range from under $400 to over $1,200, depending on the features of the specific refrigerator. Within this range, each manufacturer has a product line extending from the basic no-frills smaller refrigerators to the top-of-the-line luxury units.

A large chain of department stores buys various refrigerators from various manufacturers and sells them under its own brand name "Valhalla." Given the stores' reputation for quality products and after-sales service, this refrigerator line has achieved a substantial market share in the areas where it is sold. The marketing vice-president of the chain has been considering an addition to the Valhalla line. The new refrigerator, designated the Valhalla GE12456A, is made by General Electric and is similar to several sold by other major manufacturers, but it would fill a gap in the product line offered by the chain stores. The details of the Valhalla GE12456A are as follows: It is a 12-cubic feet upright refrigerator/freezer, with two doors, a freezer at the top and freezer capacity of 3.2 cubic feet, and it has four large aluminum trays for fresh meat and/or vegetables (taking up the lower two shelves), fully compartmentalized inner doors, butter and cheese compartments with individual temperature controls, and "easy-glide" wheels underneath. It comes in four colors and with door hinges on either side.

The refrigerators available that would seem most competitive with the Valhalla GE12456A are as follows (apart from the details shown, they are similar in all other respects to the Valhalla GE12456A):

Make/Model	Price ($)	Total Cubic (cu ft)	Freezer Size	Trays	Wheels
General Electric GE12456	525	12.0	3.2	4	Yes
Westinghouse WH11521	505	11.5	2.3	3	No
Store A Housebrand XY-4823	485	12.0	3.0	3	No
Store B Housebrand BK-7742	505	12.5	3.5	4	No
RCA RC-6821	515	11.8	2.8	4	Yes
Kelvinator K-7742	535	12.5	3.5	4	No

You are asked to assist in pricing the new addition to the Valhalla line.

(a) What price level would you recommend?

(b) Explain the basis for your recommendation in detail.

(c) Outline all qualifications you feel should be made to this recommendation.

11-8. The Eastman Paint Company has developed a new paint which is unique in that it allows the user to turn ordinary glass windows and doors into one-way glass. Moreover, it prevents the transmission of ultraviolet rays, a major factor in the fading of furniture fabrics, carpets, and draperies. The production manager, Arthur Eastman, has estimated the following average variable cost levels (per gallon) for the product for this year and for the next two years. Note that costs decline over time as the production process becomes increasingly streamlined.

	OUTPUT LEVEL (gallons/month)				
	2,000	*4,000*	*6,000*	*8,000*	*10,000*
Year 1	$12.61	$11.82	$11.74	$11.84	$12.07
Year 2	10.05	9.76	9.60	9.56	9.82
Year 3	9.22	9.04	8.85	8.80	9.02

The advertising manager, Ms. Lois Eastman, is excited about the prospects of the new paint. She believes that the market has long felt the need for such a product, and she has prepared a large campaign to launch the product. Several television advertisements are being prepared and a brochure is in print, all referring to the extensive test results and benefits of the new paint. The focus of the campaign is on the increased privacy afforded by the new paint, with emphasis given to the protection it provides by filtering out the ultraviolet part of the sun's rays.

The price of the new product is to be determined. Market research suggests that the demand situation will be approximated by $Q = 16 - 0.67P$ in the first year (where Q represents thousands of gallons and P is in dollars); $Q = 20 - 0.77P$ in the second year; and $Q = 17.83 - 0.87P$ in the third year. Indications are that market demand will increase in each of the first three years, but the entry of competitors with substitute paints in year 3 will cause Eastman's demand curve to shift to the left, as implied by the above specifications.

The marketing manager, Ms. Margaret Turriff, is faced with the problem of plotting price strategy over the next three years. While year 2 and year 3 prices can be determined in due time, the president of the company wants to know what type of pricing strategy Ms. Turriff intends to employ, since he is concerned that returns from this product be maximized, given the extensive research and development program that gave rise to the new product.

(a) What is the profit-maximizing price in each of the first three years, as estimated from the data given?

(b) Under what conditions would you advise the Eastman Paint Company to pursue a penetration-pricing strategy?

11-9. Quick New Products, Inc. specializes in launching new products and uses intensive television advertising campaigns to encourage high volume sales before any other firm can enter with a competing product. QNP has a new product ready to launch called the "tender trap," a mousetrap which mice seem to love. Based on its experience, it expects to sell 20,000 units of this product in the first year at the introductory price of $9.95. Its initial cost (for the first 1,000 units) will be $14 per unit, but it expects costs to fall 20 percent for every doubling of output from that point forward. By the time it has sold 20,000 units, it expects two other rivals to be ready to imitate its product, and it expects that it will sell only 5,000 units per year in the following two years, with price gradually falling from $9.95 to $5.95. Total sales (QNP plus rivals') will be 15,000 in each of the second and third years. Its competitors will be subject to the same learning curve when they begin production as was QNP.

(a) Show graphically the dynamic price and average cost path over time for both QNP and one of its rivals (assume the rivals are similar).

(b) Explain the advantages which QNP can expect to derive as the result of being the first-mover in this market.

11-10. The Sharper Shirt Company has recently been formed by an aspiring young designer, Francine Stuart. Her first product will be a man's shirt. At this point, neither the price nor the quality decision have been made. Francine knows that at the retail level shirts typically are sold at certain fairly well defined "price points," notably $10, $13, $17, $23, and $30. Consumers have come to expect these price groupings and the salespeople prefer to deal with shirts that fit neatly into these price groups. Naturally, higher quality shirts are expected at the higher price points.

Francine is trying to decide between going for the $17-shirt market or for the $30-shirt market. She has estimated her average variable costs to be $6.00 for the $17 shirt and $12 for the $30 shirt in the first year and approximately 80 percent of this in the second year. Note that Sharper Shirts would receive the wholesale price of only $12 for the $17 shirt and $20 for the $30 shirt. Market research activity in the form of tentative orders from retailers has resulted in the following probability distributions of demand for each shirt over the first two years:

Sales Level	$17 SHIRT Probability		$30 SHIRT Probability	
	Year 1	Year 2	Year 1	Year 2
10,000	.05	.00	.15	.10
15,000	.20	.10	.25	.30
20,000	.35	.40	.30	.35
25,000	.30	.35	.20	.20
30,000	.10	.15	.10	.05

(a) Using decision-tree analysis and assuming an opportunity discount rate of 15 percent, calculate the expected net present value of each decision.

(b) Is there much difference in the comparative risk associated with each strategy, based on the data provided?

(c) Advise Ms. Stuart about which shirt she should produce and sell.

(d) State any qualifications and assumptions which underlie your answer.

SELECTED REFERENCES AND FURTHER READING

Alpert, M. I. *Pricing Decisions*. Glenview, Ill.: Scott, Foresman & Company, 1971.

Cohen, M. and J. Y. Jaffray. "Rational Behavior under Complete Ignorance," *Econometrica*, 48 (July 1980), pp. 1281-99.

Corr, A. V. "The Role of Cost in Pricing," *Management Accounting* (November 1974), 15-32.

Dhalla, N. K., and S. Yuspeh. "Forget the Product Life Cycle Concept!" *Harvard Business Review* (January-February 1976), 102-12.

Donnelly, J. H., and M. J. Etzel. "Degrees of Product Newness and Early Trial," *Journal of Marketing Research*, 10 (August 1973), 295-300.

Earley, J. S. "Marginal Policies of 'Excellently Managed' Companies," *American Economic Review*, 46 (March 1956), 46-70.

Eichner, A. S. "A Theory of the Determination of the Mark-up under Oligopoly," *Economic Journal*, 83 (December 1973), 1184-1200.

Frankel, M. "Pricing Decisions under Unknown Demand," *Kyklos*, 26, No. 1 (1973), 1-24.

Gabor, A., and C. W. J. Granger. "The Pricing of New Products," *Scientific Business* (August 1965), 141-50.

Kotler, P. *Marketing Management* (4th ed.), chap. 10. Englewood Cliffs, N.J.: Prentice-Hall, Inc., 1980.

PRICING ANALYSIS AND DECISIONS

Lancaster, K.   Competition and Product Variety," *Journal of Business*, 53 (July 1980), pp. S79-103.

Livesey, F.   *Pricing*. London: Macmillan, Inc., 1976.

Palda, K. S.   *Pricing Decisions and Marketing Policy*. Englewood Cliffs, N.J.: Prentice-Hall, Inc., 1971.

Peterson, R. A.   "The Price-Perceived Quality Relationship: Experimental Evidence," *Journal of Marketing Research*, 7 (November 1970), 525-28.

Sabel, H.   "On Pricing New Products," *German Economic Review*, 11, No. 4 (1973), 292-311.

Scherer, F. M.   *Industrial Market Structure and Industrial Performance* (2nd ed.), chaps. 8, 11, and 12. Chicago: Rand McNally & Company, 1980.

Silberston, A.   "Price Behavior of Firms," *Economic Journal*, 80 (September 1970), 511-82.

Simon, J. L.   "Unnecessary, Confusing, and Inadequate: The Marginal Analysis as a Tool for Decision Making," *American Economist*, 25 (Spring 1981), pp. 28-35.

Weston, J. F.   "Pricing Behavior of Large Firms," *Western Economic Journal*, 10 (March 1972), 1-18.

Competitive Bids and Price Quotes

12.1 INTRODUCTION

DEFINITION: *Competitive bidding markets* may be defined as those in which there are a number of sellers who generally cannot or do not communicate with each other and who seek to provide a product or service to a single buyer. The buyer makes it known that he or she wishes to purchase a particular product or service, and the sellers tender their bids or quotes for the supply of that product or service. If the suppliers are quoting to a particular set of specifications, the buyer presumably chooses the lowest bid, whereas if there are quality differences in the products or services offered by the suppliers, the buyer must decide which of the offers represents the "best deal," by considering both the price and the quality differences.

EXAMPLES: Competitive bidding markets are much more common than is generally recognized. As well as the markets for bridges, dams, highways, and buildings, the markets for a wide range of industrial components and household and personal services exhibit essentially the same features. Firms call for bids on everything from office supplies to automobile fleets. Householders call for quotes on repair jobs in the house and on their automobiles. Individuals ask the price when seeking a variety of professional services such as medical, dental, legal, and business consulting. Each supplier should expect the buyer to have obtained price quotes from other suppliers or at least to have a general awareness of the appropriate price level, and the supplier will recognize that if his or her quote is too high the business will go elsewhere. On the other hand, if the quote is too low, the supplier will get the business but it will be less profitable business than it might have been.

The pricing problem in this type of market is essentially that the seller must choose a price high enough to provide a sufficient contribution to overheads and profits, yet low enough to ensure that a sufficient volume of work is actually obtained. In all the above situations, however, the supplier must choose the price in an environment of considerable uncertainty about the behavior of the competitors. When compared with the amount of price information generated by established markets, this type of market situation generates very little information, since each transaction is, in effect, a "one-shot" sale with little relationship to previous sales and with little information value for future sales.

To solve the competitive bidding problem, we consider first the concepts of expected present value and contribution analysis, with which you are by now quite familiar. Thus, we examine the incremental costs and incremental revenues associated with the job, taking care to express these in expected-present-value terms when these cash flows are subject to uncertainty and occur in future periods. We then consider several possible bid price levels as a set of decision alternatives and select the one promising the highest expected present value of the contribution (EPVC) to overheads and profits, subject to allowances for risk, aesthetics, and organizational politics.

When search costs are excessive, the firm will choose to avoid these costs and, instead, to use a simple markup approach to competitive bidding. We can show that this practice can be adjusted to best serve the firm's objectives. In this context we examine the satisficing theory of the firm, in which the firm prices in order to attain predetermined objectives, or targets, relating to the level of capacity utilization and profits.

Finally, we consider the problem of estimating the probability of success. This leads us to a view from the buyer's side—the issue of optimal purchasing practices. The chapter ends with a brief look at collusive bidding and the effects of disclosing bid prices to all interested parties.

12.2 INCREMENTAL COSTS, INCREMENTAL REVENUES, AND THE OPTIMAL BID PRICE

We saw in Chapter 7 that there are three main categories of incremental costs and revenues, namely, present-period explicit costs and revenues, opportunity costs and revenues, and future period costs and revenues. Let us consider these in the context of the competitive bidding problem.

The Incremental Costs of the Contract

DEFINITION: The *incremental costs of the contract* are all those costs, expressed in expected-present-value terms, which are expected to be incurred as a result of winning and completing the terms of the contract. Costs which have been incurred already (sunk costs), plus costs that will be incurred whether this contract is won or lost (committed costs) are not incremental costs for the purpose of the pricing decision to be made.

Present-Period Explicit Costs.   This category of incremental costs consists of the direct and explicit costs associated with undertaking and completing the project. Included are such cost categories as direct materials, direct labor, and variable overhead. For each of these cost categories we must be careful to include only those amounts that are expected to be paid for the purchases of materials, labor and supplies, and services required to complete production and delivery of the specified goods and services. These may be estimated on the basis of requirements for similar projects in the past, given present cost levels, plus a trend factor if one is apparent and the production will take an appreciable period of time.

    In some cases an item of capital equipment must be purchased for a particular job and will have a useful life remaining after the completion of the present job. Incremental reasoning implies that the whole cost is applied to the present job and that the machine will not be part of the incremental cost on any subsequent jobs, if these in fact materialize. If ownership of the item will allow a stream of contributions to be earned in the future, the expected net present value of these contributions should enter the present decision, since they are incremental to this decision.[1]

    Another consideration is the capacity utilization rate of the firm. When the firm is at or near full capacity, it must consider the additional incremental costs that will be incurred if it obtains the contract, such as overtime labor rates, outside contracting, penalty charges associated with existing contracts, and any other additional costs, and hence its minimum bid price must be higher to the extent that these costs are incurred.

Opportunity Costs.   The opportunity cost of undertaking and completing a specific project is the value of the resources employed (that is, their contribution) in their best alternative usage. Hence, if plant, equipment, and personnel are lying idle, the opportunity cost of using them for a particular contract is zero. On the other hand, if these resources are currently employed in a project that will have to be set aside, delayed, or cancelled, the contribution that would have been derived from this alternate project

---

[1]The practice of apportioning the capital cost of an item over the present and future jobs implies a probability of unity that these future contracts will be gained. This may be an overstatement of the probabilities, of course, and may induce the firm to purchase an item, the cost of which may never be recouped. Moreover, the simple allocation of a cost over future jobs ignores the fact that a dollar received now is worth more than a dollar received in the future.

must enter the incremental costs as an opportunity cost. A firm may decide to submit a tender on a specific project, and if successful with that bid may choose to defer completion of another project already in process. To the extent provided by the penalty clause in the earlier contract, this decision to defer completion will cost the firm money that is an incremental cost occasioned by receipt of the latter contract. To the extent that a project in process simply is delayed and is completed later, the opportunity cost is the present value of the contribution when the project is finally completed less the present value of the contribution when it otherwise would have been completed. Alternatively, one might say that the opportunity cost of delaying payment for a job in process is the interest income foregone as a result of the later receipt of payment for that job.

Future Costs. Future incremental costs may include the effects of illwill, deteriorating labor relations and/or supplier relations, and legal recourse by dissatisfied buyers or government prosecutors. Illwill is the EPVC of future contracts *lost* as a result of taking the present contract. There may be longer-term disadvantages, for example, in taking a contract which breaks a strike, or which takes advantage of the misfortune of a competitor or other party. Future labor problems may arise if the present contract would cause the firm to operate at or above full capacity with consequent congestion of work space and facilities. Hard work for employees and good profits for the firm may tip the balance in favor of a labor strike or a slowdown for a wage increase. Supplier relations may be exacerbated by the present contract if it requires very tight deadlines and unusually stringent quality control, leading to the firm's suppliers (or subcontractors) asking for a higher price for materials and supplies needed for future contracts. Finally there is always the possibility of future legal claims for damages associated with the present contract or of prosecution under the provisions of the antitrust laws or of other legislation. To the extent that these costs can be foreseen their EPV should be estimated and included as an incremental cost.

EXAMPLE: Suppose the city's garbage collectors have been on strike for several weeks and the city calls for bids for a one-week contract with an outside firm to move the garbage. Your firm, which is engaged in the construction industry, has the trucks and the personnel necessary, and you consider bidding on the contract. You calculate your incremental present-period explicit costs to be $100,000 for the week, comprised of direct labor, fuel, repairs and maintenance, and so on.

You are currently utilizing your equipment and work force on a day-to-day basis moving landfill to an area which will eventually be a new housing development. The contribution to overheads and profits from this job is $10,000 per week. If you win the contract to move the garbage, you must give up this contribution, and this is, therefore, the opportunity cost of winning the city's contract.

If you win the job, you are afraid that there will be a backlash response from a company with whom you currently hold a contract for the annual removal of debris and waste products. Their labor force is strongly unionized and you feel that there is a fifty-fifty chance the firm may decide not to offer you the renewal of that contract. You reason that they may do this in order to avoid labor strife at their own plant, which they think may result if they renew the contract with the firm that helped break the city garbage workers' strike. Next year's contract with this firm is expected to contribute $20,000 to overheads and profits if it is renewed. Supposing your opportunity discount rate to be 15 percent and the cash flow to be one year away, its present value is $20,000 $\times$ 0.8696 = $17,392. Given your estimate of the probability of losing the contract at 0.5, the EPV of this future cost, or illwill, is $17,392 $\times$ 0.5 = $8,696.

Thus, the incremental cost of the job is estimated to be the sum of the present-period explicit costs, $100,000; plus the opportunity costs, $10,000; plus the EPV of the future costs, $8,696; or $118,696 in total. You would require incremental revenues to be at least this high before you would consider taking the job in order to avoid making an incremental loss on the job.

NOTE: Incremental costs do not include any sunk costs or costs which would have been incurred regardless of this particular pricing decision. As a result, *bid preparation costs* are technically *not* an incremental cost of the job but they are, instead, a cost of preparing to bid on the job. There are two separate decisions to be made: First, will the firm prepare and submit a bid at all; and, second, at what price level will this bid be? Bid preparation costs will include the search costs of generating information about costs, revenues, and probabilities of success at various price levels. On the basis of this information, the firm may decide not to bid at all. If it does decide to bid, the actual pricing decision will be taken after the bid preparation costs have been incurred. They are therefore *sunk* costs as far as the pricing decision is concerned and should not be included as incremental costs.[2]

The Incremental Revenues of the Contract

DEFINITION: *The incremental revenues of the contract* are all those revenues, expressed in expected-present-value terms, which are expected to be received as a result of winning and completing the contract. These revenues may be considered under the same three categories—present period, opportunity, and future revenues.

Present-Period Incremental Revenues.   If the contract will be completed and the bid price received during the present period, the bid price can be included in nominal dollars as an incremental revenue. In cases where pay-

---

[2]At this point it is worth emphasizing that we are calculating incremental costs, not the actual bid price. In order to substantiate its chosen bid price the firm may wish to include various sunk costs and exclude some of its incremental costs. This is effectively a promotional decision, to be taken *after* the pricing decision.

ment will be received during a future period, the bid price should be discounted at the opportunity rate to find the present value of this cash flow. In some cases, the firm will have written into the contract that it will receive some portion of the bid price (for example, one half) when the job is one-half completed. In this case, part of the bid price may be treated in nominal dollars (if it is to be received in the present period) with the balance being discounted to present-value terms.

Opportunity Revenues.   Costs which can be avoided if the contract is won are known as *opportunity revenues*.

EXAMPLE: Opportunity revenues include severance pay and other costs of laying off personnel and the subsequent rehiring and retraining costs which would be incurred if the firm were forced to close down and wait until it won another contract before starting up again. Plant and equipment which will stand idle for a time must be "mothballed" to prevent its deterioration while idle. For example, machinery may need to be sprayed with oil to prevent rusting. Upon start-up, there is an additional cost of cleaning and readying the plant for use again. Another opportunity revenue which is possible is the research and development costs which can be avoided as a result of the present contract. A firm may know it has to develop a particular electronic device, for example, for the improvement of one of its existing products. If the contract currently being considered involves the development of that technology as a by-product, then winning the present contract allows future research and development expenditure to be avoided. For example, Cubic Corporation has found that some of its developments for the aerospace industry have been applicable to its products in other areas, notably elevators and fare-collection systems.

Future Revenues.   The present contract may give rise to future contracts and sales, which represent the *goodwill* to be generated by the present contract. Goodwill should be regarded as the expected present value of the contribution (EPVC) which is expected to be received from subsequent contracts won *as a result* of having won and successfully completed the current contract. Care must be taken to include only *incremental* goodwill; an established firm may foresee contracts which would have been won regardless of the current contract and therefore should not consider the current contract as contributing to goodwill. On the other hand, a firm trying to enter a market may need one or more initial contracts won and successfully completed in order to be considered for future contracts. Counting the EPVC of these future contracts as an incremental revenue of the current contract allows the firm to rationally submit a somewhat lower bid than its established rivals and thus increase the likelihood of its winning the contract.

EXAMPLE: The Universal Lamp Company plans to bid on a contract to manufacture and supply energy-saving fluorescent-incandescent light bulbs for a government building. At present, Universal has no work to do and will have to lay off workers within a few weeks unless it wins this contract.

Universal has never manufactured these new-generation light bulbs before and knows that it must establish its credibility by demonstrating that it can manufacture a high-quality product and that it can meet the delivery schedule proposed. Its proposed bid price is $278,500, which it expects will be at least $100,000 less than the next-lowest bid, given its knowledge of recent contracts awarded and publicized. Universal feels that it must bid this low in order to win the job—any lower price difference may cause the government purchaser to opt for a more expensive, but established, supplier. If it wins the job, it is confident that it will produce a high-quality product and, therefore, make itself eligible for future contracts at higher profit margins.

Suppose that Universal will avoid layoff, mothball, and other costs, of $36,000, associated with closing down and later reopening this plant, if they win this contract. Suppose further that if they win this contract, they expect a 75-percent chance of a follow-up contract, with contribution of $200,000, to be awarded next year. The present value of that contribution (at 15 percent O.D.R., for example) is $173,920. The EPVC is, thus, $173,920 × 0.75 = $130,440.

This contract, therefore, promises incremental revenues of the bid price, $278,500; plus the opportunity revenues, $36,000; plus the EPVC of future sales foreseen, $130,440; or $444,940 in total. Thus, the firm's incremental costs could be anything up to that figure, and it would still be incrementally profitable for Universal to complete the contract with its bid of $278,500.

The Optimal Bid Price

DEFINITION: Given that the firm's objective is to maximize its net present worth, the *optimal bid price* will be the price level which maximizes the expected present value of contribution to overheads and profits.

To find the expected present value of each bid price, we must multiply its EPVC by the probability of winning the contract at that price level. The higher the bid price, the lower the "success probability," or the likelihood that the firm will submit the lowest bid. (For simplicity here, we assume a completely specified contract where there are no design or quality differences between tenders.)

EXAMPLE: Suppose that the firm has obtained a reliable set of success probabilities, after consideration of the past bidding behavior and current capacity utilization of all its rivals. In Table 12-1 we show an assumed incremental cost (in expected-present-value terms and net of any incremental revenues other than the bid price) of $50,000. Several arbitrarily chosen bid prices and the resultant contribution and success probability for each bid price, are shown in columns (2), (3) and (4). The product of columns (3) and (4) is the EPVC for each bid price level. The bid price which appears to maximize EPVC is $70,000. But this price was chosen arbitrarily from a spectrum of possible bid prices. By plotting the EPVC against bid prices and interpolating between

TABLE 12-1. Expected Present Value Analysis of a Bid-Pricing Problem

(1) Net EPV Incre- mental Cost	(2) Bid Price	(3) Contri- bution	(4) Success Prob- ability	(5) EPVC
$	$	$	P	$
50,000	50,000	0	.90	0
50,000	60,000	10,000	.70	7,000
50,000	70,000	20,000	.50	10,000
50,000	80,000	30,000	.30	9,000
50,000	90,000	40,000	.15	6,000
50,000	100,000	50,000	.05	2,500

the points, we would find that the EPVC is maximized when the bid price is approximately $73,500, as indicated in Figure 12-1.

Thus, the firm should bid at $73,500 to pursue the maximization of its net present worth. While it may not win this particular contract, if it bids for a large number of such contracts, the present value of its total contribution to overheads and profits, and hence its net present worth, will be maximized by continually bidding at the price which maximizes EPVC for each particular contract. It wins some and it loses some, but on average comes out ahead, as compared to any other pattern of bidding.

Aesthetic, Political, and Risk Considerations. It is perhaps unreasonable to expect a decision maker to make a choice simply on the basis of quantifiable cost and revenue considerations. In some cases certain aesthetic considerations enter the bidding process. Suppose the project alluded to in Table 12-1 was something other than a straightforward and normal project. On the one hand, it may appeal to the artistic tastes of the decision maker; on the other hand, it may involve considerable amounts of dirty and/or

FIGURE 12-1. The Expected Present Value of Contribution Curve

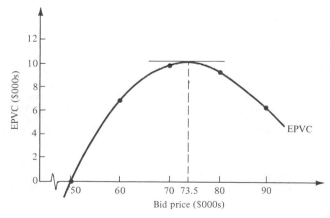

uncomfortable work. In the first case we might expect a decision maker to choose a bid price somewhat below the expected value, since the nonmonetary gratification received by the decision maker would offset some of the monetary compensation involved in the higher bid price. But if the job is expected to be dirty, uncomfortable, or inconvenient in some nonmonetary way, we might expect the decision maker's bid to be somewhat above the $73,500 indicated by the expected-value criterion, since the nonmonetary disutility attached to the job would need to be offset by some additional monetary compensation.

A further consideration that may cause the decision maker to choose a bid price different from the one with the maximum expected contribution is the possibility that the decision maker may see personal gain in bidding at a different price level. Thus, individual decision makers within an organization may practice self-serving, or "political," behavior. This may be "functional" political behavior in that it causes certain actions that at the same time promote the organization's objectives, or it may be "dysfunctional" in that it serves the decision maker's purposes but hinders the attainment of the organization's objectives. Since it is not unlikely that the objectives of the decision maker and the organization will differ on occasion, we should not expect all decisions to reflect single-minded pursuit of company goals. Hence, if the decision maker feels there is some personal gain likely to follow a bid price above or below that indicated by the expected-value criterion, the actual bid price may well deviate from that standard.

The personal gains to the decision maker may include a wide variety of tangible and intangible benefits which the decision maker may expect to receive as the result of a particular decision's being taken. Hence, a relatively low bid price may be chosen when the decision maker feels there is something to gain by winning the contract, and oppositely, a relatively high bid price may be submitted when it is felt that the purchaser owes a favor to the supplier and the supplier expects the purchaser to settle this debt. Simple friendship between the supplier and the purchaser may also cause a lower bid price to be submitted, and the reduction from the expected value bid price can be ascribed to political motivations, namely, to the supplier's recognition of the personal value of the buyer's friendship. Note that these political considerations are separate from the goodwill considerations that we include in the incremental cost calculation.

Risk considerations relate to the risk of not winning the contract.[3] If

---

[3] The risk of cost variability once the contract is won is a separate issue. Costs may exceed expected levels because of unforeseen design problems, labor problems, supplier problems, equipment failure, and so on. The "fixed-price" bid approach discussed in this chapter assigns all the risk of cost variability to the seller. "Cost-plus" bids, whereby the buyer pays the actual cost plus a predetermined percentage, assigns all the risk of cost variability to the buyer. "Incentive" bids share the risk of cost variability between the buyer and the seller, with each paying a predetermined share of the cost overrun. See J.J. McCall, "The Simple Economics of Incentive Contracting," *American Economic Review*, vol. 60 (September 1967), pp. 837-46; and F.M. Scherer, "The Theory of Contractual Incentives for Cost Reduction," *Quarterly Journal of Economics*, vol. 78 (May 1964), pp. 257-80.

the firm bids on many different contracts, it can afford to be risk neutral with respect to any one contract, expecting the law of averages to work in its favor. But, if the firm *must* win this contract for one reason or another, such as impending bankruptcy, or if the firm bids only infrequently, this decision becomes a one-shot deal, and the expected-value criterion is less appropriate. The certainty-equivalent criterion is appropriate for decisions that are made on a "one-shot" basis or, at least, are significantly different from decisions that have been taken in the past and are expected to be taken in the future.[4] That is, where the law of averages is not an appropriate guide, we turn to the decision maker's subjective evaluation of the worth of each gamble, rather than the more objective expected value analysis. A further virtue of the certainty-equivalent approach is that it will include the aesthetic and political considerations influencing the decision, and in addition it incorporates other nonmonetary or nonquantifiable factors influencing the decision. In determining the certainty equivalent of each bid price, the decision maker would use all information at his or her disposal, and using judgment and experience would decide which bid price level to submit.

In the following section we note that, in practice, firms rarely use the theoretical guidelines outlined above. However, the actual decision taken may not diverge significantly from the one that would be indicated by the factors outlined above. Perhaps the greatest value of these guidelines consists of forcing an evaluation of the decision about to be taken; that is, the decision maker may be able to justify the decision or to revise that decision after consideration of the theoretical guidelines. If the proposed bid price level is not the one indicated by the expected-value analysis, or alternatively, if the probabilities (which would need to be attached in order to bring the proposed bid price and the bid price with the highest expected value into agreement) were not reasonable probability values, the decision maker must reevaluate his or her thinking.

12.3 COMPETITIVE BIDDING IN PRACTICE

In practice most firms appear to choose their bid price by applying a markup to some measure of the costs associated with the job. The "cost base" is typically calculated to include all explicit costs, bid preparation costs, and an allocation of other overhead costs. No explicit calculation is usually made to include opportunity costs or other incremental costs, and costs are usually considered only in nominal dollars rather than in present-value terms. The firm will typically choose the markup percentage with an eye to its past pricing practice, modifying this "standard" markup either up or down

---

[4]You will recall that the certainty equivalent of a gamble is the sum of money that the decision maker regards as equivalent to the value of the gamble. Hence, if we were to determine the certainty equivalent of the gamble involved in bidding at each price level, the bid with the highest certainty equivalent would be the one that the decision maker feels is the superior bid price.

depending upon current conditions in the market and the industry and with reference to longer-term considerations in some cases.

Markup Bid Pricing to Maximize EPVC

The firm's decision process described in the above paragraph may be a parallel but effectively equivalent means of arriving at the optimal bid price. Given that search costs are expected to exceed the value of the information derived, firms proceed using the markup pricing rule-of-thumb and keep winning enough jobs to keep them in business and sufficiently profitable. Although they do not typically include all net incremental costs in their cost calculations, they typically allow for these in a crude way by varying the size of the markup applied.

EXAMPLE: Suppose a job is expected to involve future goodwill effects or that getting this job would avoid costly layoffs and subsequent rehiring and retraining expenses, the decision maker would apply a *lower* markup than normally would be applied. Conversely, if lawsuits were likely to follow a particular job or if the firm were near-full capacity and getting the contract might cause labor problems sometime in the future, the markup applied might be *higher* than the standard level. The markup approach incorporates the nonmonetary considerations in the same way: we would expect to see higher markups with consequently higher bid prices to compensate for nonmonetary costs and lower markups to compensate for nonmonetary benefits.

It is clear that the firm could stumble upon the EPVC-maximizing price by using the markup approach. For example, suppose the firm calculates its "cost base" to be $61,250, comprised of direct costs and allocated overheads. A 20-percent markup on that cost base would result in a bid price of $73,500, the same as in the EPVC approach. But this would be sheer good luck, of course. More likely, the firm using the simple (but inexpensive) markup pricing procedure will submit a bid which is either above or below the EPVC-maximizing price level.

How does the firm know if its markup is too high or too low? If it does not win enough contracts to keep its plant and employees operating within the desired range of capacity utilization, it will sooner or later determine that its markup rate (and hence its prices) is probably too high. Lowering the markup rate would be expected to bring improved capacity utilization with consequent larger total contribution to overheads and profits. Conversely if the firm wins too many contracts, so that its capacity is overutilized, with all the attendant costs and problems, it will sooner or later decide to raise its markup in order to reduce demand for its services and consequently increase the profits of the enterprise. In the latter case the firm should also be considering the possibility of expanding its plant size, of course.

NOTE: These capacity-utilization considerations entered the theoretical approach as well, but in the calculation of incremental costs. In the EPVC approach the potential costs of layoffs, rehiring, retraining, and so forth, which were associated with very low capacity utilization, operate to lower the total EPV of incremental costs of the potential job, and, given a structure of success probabilities, subsequently operate to lower the optimal bid price. Oppositely, if the plant were near-full capacity, the expected costs of future labor problems would be incorporated into incremental costs and cause the optimal bid price to be higher than it otherwise would be.

The Reconciliation of Theory and Practice

The first issue is that of information search costs. In practice these are frequently expected to outweigh the benefits of the information derived and the firm takes the completely rational decision to forego the information and proceed using a simple decision rule such as markup pricing. This is rational behavior in that it involves pursuit of the firm's objectives. Although the markup price might be $5,000 less than the maximum EPVC price, if this simple procedure obviates spending more than $5,000 on information search costs, the firm comes out ahead using the simple decision rule.[5]

The second issue follows from the first. Having only an imprecise view of the longer-term incremental costs, opportunity costs, goodwill, and other costs and benefits not immediately calculable but indeed consequent upon this pricing decision, the firm in practice tends to build these into a "cushion" in its markup. If these incalculable costs are larger, so too is the markup, to take into account in a rough way the probability that these incalculable costs will arise. Alternatively, if these incalculable costs are expected to be low and/or the benefits of goodwill are expected to follow, the "cushion" in the firm's profit margin can be reduced by using a lower markup percentage.

Thus, the markup price can be "wrong" to the extent of the information search costs that were avoided, and the markup percentage, and hence the profit margin, must take into account all net incremental costs (in EPV terms) *not* considered and *not* calculated into the cost base for the markup calculation. To the extent that overhead costs, including bid preparation costs, are included in the cost base, the markup percentage will be lower, since the markup will be simply the profit margin, rather than the contribution to overheads and profits. By way of summary, Table 12-2 shows the

---

[5]We have no reason to believe this is the general case, however. In many cases firms would profit by seeking more information, but they abstain from search activity for reasons other than the costs involved, such as ignorance of the information source and the lack of personnel qualified to lead the search.

TABLE 12-2. The EPVC Model and the Markup Model of Competitive Bidding

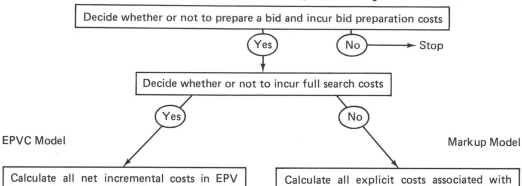

EPVC Model	Markup Model
Calculate all net incremental costs in EPV terms. Include all explicit and implicit costs (including opportunity costs) now and in the future which are expected to be incurred as a result of this contract. Deduct in EPV terms all future revenues and opportunity revenues such as goodwill and costs avoided as a result of obtaining this contract.	Calculate all explicit costs associated with this contract. Add allocated overhead charges and bid preparation costs to arrive at your "standard" cost base.
Estimate the probabilities of success at each of several possible bid prices.	Apply "standard" markup percentage to this cost base to arrive at your "standard" bid price for this contract.
Calculate the EPVC for each of these bid prices and identify the bid price which maximizes EPVC.	(1) Bid at this "standard" price if doing so in the past has kept your capacity utilization and profitability at preferred levels, and if there are no extraordinary incremental costs or benefits associated with this contract. (2) Bid below this "standard" price if capacity utilization and profitability are both lower than desired, and/or if there are extraordinary incremental net benefits expected in the future as a result of this contract. (3) Bid above this "standard" price if capacity utilization is higher and profitability lower than is desired, and/or if there are extraordinary incremental net costs expected in the future as a result of this contract.
(1) Bid at "maximum EPVC" price if this type of decision is taken frequently and if there are no aesthetic, political or other non-monetary considerations involved. (2) Bid below the "maximum EPVC" price if indicated by the certainty-equivalent criterion or by aesthetic or political considerations. (3) Bid above the "maximum EPVC" price if indicated by the certainty-equivalent criterion or by aesthetic or political considerations.	
(1) If successful this time, no change is necessary unless you are successful so often that probabilities appear to be understated. If so, raise success probabilities for your next bid (and investigate plant expansion). (2) If unsuccessful this time, no change is necessary unless you are unsuccessful so often that probabilities appear to be overstated. If so, reduce success probabilities for your next bid (and investigate plant contraction).	(1) If successful this time, no change is necessary, unless you are receiving too many jobs for your limited capacity, in which case raise the standard markup for your next bid (and investigate plant expansion). (2) If unsuccessful this time, no change is necessary, unless you are receiving too few jobs with subsequent underutilization of your plant, in which case reduce the standard markup for your next bid (and investigate plant contraction).

alternate approaches to price determination in competitive bidding situations. Notice that the cost and revenue considerations which are not incorporated in the cost base should be incorporated in the choice of the markup percentage, if the markup is to lead to a price close to (within the search cost differential of) the EPVC-maximizing price.

NOTE: After the firm's bid is submitted, the firm waits to learn the outcome. Suppose it loses this contract. No particular reaction is called for unless it loses "too many" contracts—that is, it finds that its probabilities were too high in the EPVC approach or that its markups were consistently too high in the markup approach. This feedback information calls for a change in the pricing level, as indicated in the bottom part of Table 12-2. Conversely, if the firm is successful "too often," it must revise its estimates of the success probabilities, revise its general price structure upwards, and consider the expansion of its plant size.

Markup Bid Pricing for the Satisficing Firm

Often we notice that the practicing competitive bidder appears to exhibit the four basic features of a satisficing firm, as detailed in the behavioral theory of the firm.[6] First, the firm exhibits *bounded rationality*, calculating only its present costs and declining to search for future costs and probability distributions. Secondly, it practices *selectivity* by not bidding on all contracts offered but confining its attention, instead, to those it is most likely to win and for which it has the technology and capacity. Third, it establishes *decision rules*, like standard cost bases and markup pricing, in order to facilitate and expedite the decision process. Fourth, it establishes *targets* or satisfactory levels for its most important variables, and uses feedback information to adjust these targets and decision rules when it becomes necessary or desirable.

We argued in Chapter 10 that "satisficing," or the pursuit of satisfactory targets, may be considered a proxy policy for the maximization of the firm's net present worth. If the targets are consistently achieved and upgraded, the firm should be expected to approach the bid price level which maximizes its EPVC without having to incur any major search costs.

Observation suggests that the main targets the bidding firm seeks to attain relate to the degree of capacity utilization and the rate of profit-

---

[6]See R.M. Cyert and C.J. March, *A Behavioral Theory of the Firm* (Englewood Cliffs, N.J.: Prentice-Hall, Inc., 1963); and H.A. Simon, "Rational Decision Making in Business Organizations," *American Economic Review*, vol. 69 (September 1979), pp. 493-513.

TABLE 12-3. Decision Sequence for the Satisficing Firm

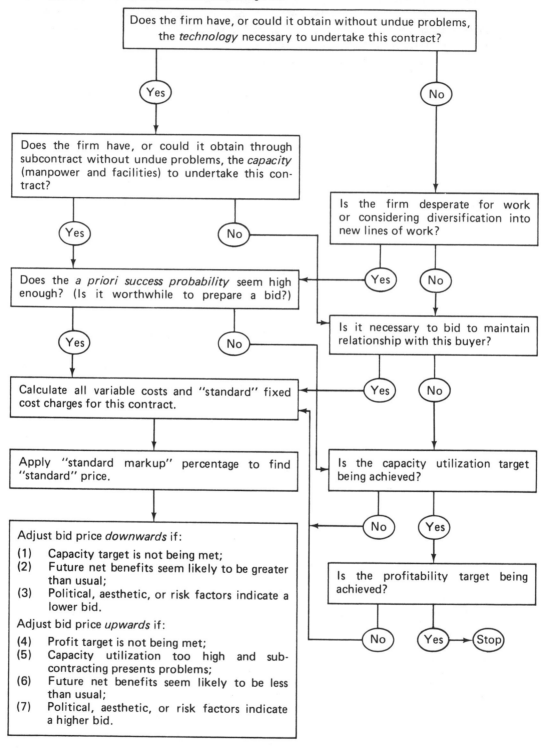

PRICING ANALYSIS AND DECISIONS

ability. The capacity utilization target amounts to the same thing as a sales volume target and has implications for the firm's share of the market. It also has implications for the firm's cash flow and subsequent ability to meet its payroll obligations, interest expense, and other overhead costs. By striving to keep capacity utilization at or above a particular target, the firm expects to avoid the costs of retrenchment, rehiring, and retraining that would follow a plant closure and subsequent reopening. It is often apparent that the capacity utilization target takes priority over the profitability target, since firms seem to sacrifice profitability in order to attain utilization targets, but then they price to obtain their "required rate of return" on contracts when they are at or above their target rate of capacity utilization.

The markup-bid-pricing model shown in Table 12-2 is easily modified to suit the satisficing firm. Table 12-3 shows schematically the decision process for the satisficing firm.

When it first becomes aware of a call for bids on a particular contract, the firm does not immediately decide to prepare a bid. Rather, it first considers several factors of importance to the attainment of the firm's targets. Does it have the necessary technology, or could it obtain this through consultants and/or other subcontract work? Does it have sufficient capacity to handle this job, or could the job be partly or wholly given out to subcontractors without undue problems? Does it seem "worthwhile" to prepare a bid on this job, or alternatively, is there a strong enough chance that the firm will recoup its bid preparation costs by winning the contract?

If the answer is yes to these three basic questions the firm should go ahead and prepare its bid on the contract. If the answer is no to any one question, the firm must consider four subsidiary questions which may induce it to prepare a bid in any case. First, is the firm desperate for work, or is it considering diversification into new lines of work? An affirmative response to this should cause the firm to reconsider preparing a bid despite not having the technology at the present time. Second, is it necessary to submit a bid in order to maintain goodwill with the buyer? If bids are requested privately, rather than being widely advertised, or if the firm feels that it should keep its name in front of the buyer, it may be important to submit a bid even without adequate capacity to do the job. Of course, this bid should be high enough to be profitable if the firm actually wins the contract.

Regarding the prior expectation of winning the contract, two subsidiary questions must be asked if it is not considered "worthwhile" to prepare a bid. Is the firm's capacity utilization target being achieved at present and for the duration of this proposed contract? If not, the firm should prepare a bid anyway, since it will perceive that the maintenance of capacity utilization levels is of primary importance. Even if capacity utilization is satisfactory, the firm should prepare a bid if its profitability target is not being met currently or may not be met in the foreseeable future. Thus, the firm will prepare a bid, despite a low prior expectation of success, if either of its capacity or profitability targets are not met. Of course its final decision on the bid price will reflect the circumstances, being lower, for example, if the capacity target is not met, and higher if the capacity target is met but the profitability target is not.

The firm will prepare its bid on the basis of a standardized "cost-base" which is calculated by the application of several basic decision rules.[7] The bid price obtained by multiplying the standard cost base by the standard markup may be called the firm's standard price for the contract. It will bid at that level if its capacity and profitability targets are being met, and if the contract appears to have no extraordinary features about it. The firm will *lower* its markup percentage and hence its bid price, if capacity utilization is below the target level, or if it foresees abnormal longer-term benefits to be gained by winning this contract, or if political, aesthetic, or risk considerations require a monetary tradeoff to increase the probability of success. Oppositely, the firm will *raise* its markup percentage if the capacity target but not the profitability target is being attained, if future net benefits seem likely to be less than usual, or if political, aesthetic, or risk factors indicate a higher bid price. In addition, the firm would raise its markup if it did not have the capacity needed to complete the contract if won, but it was submitting a bid only to maintain the relationship currently enjoyed with the buyer. In each case the amount by which the bid price is raised or lowered from the "standard" price should be commensurate with the value to the firm of winning or losing the contract, as per the EPVC discussions earlier in this chapter.

The Targets. What are the appropriate levels for the capacity utilization target and the profitability target? The desired rate of capacity utilization should be the same rate at which "standard" overhead charges are calculated and may be chosen, for example, to be 80 percent of full capacity.

DEFINITION: *Full capacity* is defined as the total number of labor-days available per year, using a single shift and the "optimal" complement of manpower. The optimal complement of labor is construed as that quantity which allows average total cost to be minimized. Thus, overfull capacity can be achieved by additional workers during the single shift, overtime operation, multiple-shift operation, or subcontracting. Notwithstanding the fact that average costs are minimized at full capacity, the firm may establish its target capacity utilization at something less than full capacity in order to leave a margin for error in the event of strikes or breakdowns and to avoid the frequent disruption of normal operations associated with overtime and

---

[7]The satisficing firm may have developed a simple "costing sheet" which requires estimates of variable costs, variable overheads, bid preparation costs, and other fixed costs. The decision rules pertaining to variable overheads may be for example, 50 percent of labor costs, and the overhead charges may be the proportion of the firm's work-year devoted to this job times the firm's total fixed costs.

extra-worker operation. Note also that if the target utilization rate is achieved, the firm's overheads are completely covered, and any extra work contributes directly to the firm's profits.

The profitability target, or the firm's required rate of return, will be determined by the firm's opportunity cost of capital. Suppose the firm feels that it could obtain 20 percent before taxes at comparable risk elsewhere: It will set this as its minimum, or target, level. While higher rates of profitability may seem desirable, managers will be inclined to trade off higher profits for reduced risk. They will be content to price somewhat lower than might be possible in order to better ensure the firm's future existence in the market, not to mention the continuation of their tenure as managers.

The Standard Costs, Markup, and Price. The firm's standard cost-base calculations and its standard markup rate may be modified over time as a result of its bidding experience. The model outlined in Table 12-3 allows for adjustment in the markup rate if either of the targets are not met and for other reasons. If the firm wins virtually every contract it bids upon, we would expect it to raise its markup on subsequent bids. Rather than make each bid a special case, the firm in this happy situation may simplify its subsequent pricing decisions by raising its "standard markup" to a higher level. Oppositely, if the firm finds that it is consistently not winning enough contracts to attain its capacity utilization target, it may adjust its markup rate downward to a new, more appropriate, level.

In each case, above, the adjustment is made to cause the firm's bid to be slightly more or less desirable and should have a noticeable effect on the quantity of work obtained. The appropriate level of the markup, and hence the price, is that level which tends to keep the firm at or above its capacity utilization target. At this target level of output, the profitability target will also be attained, except for unforeseen costs associated with jobs-in-process and with unanticipated increases in overhead costs. The feedback to management from past contracts won or lost allows them to judge the most appropriate levels of the standard cost base and markup levels. As before, special circumstances surrounding any particular contract will justify a deviation from the standard price.

If over a prolonged series of contracts it becomes apparent that demand for the firm's services is either too strong or too weak for its present size of plant, the firm must consider adjustment of plant size. A reasonable presumption is that the firm would choose its new plant size such that the new plant's capacity utilization target is equal to the expected value of its annual demand at standard prices. Given the new plant size and potentially different technology, the firm would need to recalculate its standard cost base and may wish to adjust its standard markup percentage in order to bring its new standard price into line with the bid prices of other firms. This it would do in the normal process of winning or losing contracts: if it wins too few it will adjust its standard markup downward, while if it wins too many it will raise the level of its standard markup.

12.4 ESTIMATING THE PROBABILITY OF SUCCESS

In the above sections we skipped over the problem associated with the assignment of probabilities as to the success or failure of the bid at each price level. Let us now examine this problem in some detail. Since the theoretical approaches and the cost-plus approach may be seen as alternative and possibly equivalent ways of determining the optimal price level, the probability of success at each bid price level is an important underlying factor in both approaches. The probability of a successful bid at a given price level depends upon two major factors: the competition for this particular contract and the attributes desired by this particular buyer.

Evaluation of the Competition

We must first ascertain whether or not there are likely to be any other bidders on this particular contract. If not, the probability of attaining the contract must have a value of one, and we could presumably set the price at the highest level that we expect the buyer will accept. More likely there will be other bidders, however. How many other bidders is an important consideration, since the greater the number of bidders in the market, the smaller the probability of success we should expect to exist at each price level. The next piece of information is the identities of the other bidders. If we can identify individual firms, this may add information, since we may know something of their current capacity utilization, their attitude toward this type of project, and their previous behavior patterns in this type of bidding situation.

EXAMPLE: Suppose we have calculated our incremental costs to be $50,000 for a particular contract that is similar to dozens of contracts we have bid for in the last year.[8] Over the past year, four other firms have also been bidding for the same contracts. In Table 12-4 we show the proportion of times that our price level was below each rival's submitted price (or would have been) at each of seven bid prices equal to and above our incremental costs.

If past behavior is expected to be the best indicator of present behavior (given the absence of any significant change in the situation of each of our rivals), we can use the "success ratios" as an estimate of the probability of being successful at each bid price level when any one of the rival firms is expected to bid against us. For example, if we intend to bid $60,000, the probability of success is 0.80 if Firm A is the only other firm bidding; 0.76 if B is the only other bidder; 0.72 if C is the only other bidder; and 0.79 if D is the only other firm bidding on this particular contract.

If we expect two or more firms to submit bids and if we know the identities of those firms, we may estimate the probabilities of success at each

---

[8]This example is loosely based on a similar example in P. Livesey, *Pricing* (London: Macmillan, Inc., 1976), pp. 99-102.

TABLE 12-4. Success Rates Against Rival Firms in Previous Bidding on Similar Contracts

Our Bid ($)	SUCCESS RATE AGAINST RIVAL				Average Success Rate (ASR)
	A	B	C	D	
50,000	1.00	0.98	0.95	0.99	0.9800
55,000	0.92	0.88	0.84	0.94	0.8950
60,000	0.80	0.76	0.72	0.79	0.7675
65,000	0.61	0.55	0.49	0.60	0.5625
70,000	0.43	0.37	0.32	0.41	0.3825
75,000	0.24	0.18	0.15	0.21	0.1950
80,000	0.10	0.03	0.00	0.09	0.0550

price level by finding the *joint* probability of our underbidding those firms on this occasion. For example, if we know that A and B are submitting bids, the probability of our being successful at a price of $60,000 is 0.80 × 0.76 = 0.608. Similarly, if we expect A, B, and C to submit bids, the probability of success with the $60,000 bid is 0.80 × 0.76 × 0.72 = 0.438. And finally, if all four firms are expected to bid, the probability of success for the $60,000 bid is 0.80 × 0.76 × 0.72 × 0.79 = 0.347. Notice the impact upon the probability as the number of bidding firms increases. As more firms enter the bidding, it is increasingly more likely that any one firm will undercut our bid price, at every price level. If the identities of the firms submitting bids are not known, it will be necessary to calculate probabilities on the basis of the average success rate (ASR). If only one rival, identity unknown, is expected to bid, the ASR will be our best estimate as to the probability of success on this occasion. If two or more rivals, identities unknown, are expected to bid, we must find the joint probability of our bid's being the lowest, by finding the square, cubic, or quartic value of the average success rate. These are shown in Table 12-5, which clearly demonstrates the influence that increasing the number of rival firms has upon the probability of success at each bid price level.

TABLE 12-5. Calculated Probabilities of Success with Increasing Number of Competitors, Identities Unknown

Our Bid ($)	NUMBER OF RIVALS			
	1 (ASR)	2 (ASR)^2	3 (ASR)^3	4 (ASR)^4
50,000	0.9800	0.9604	0.9412	0.9224
55,000	0.8950	0.8010	0.7169	0.6416
60,000	0.7675	0.5891	0.4521	0.3470
65,000	0.5625	0.3164	0.1780	0.1001
70,000	0.3825	0.1463	0.0560	0.0214
75,000	0.1950	0.0380	0.0074	0.0014
80,000	0.0550	0.0030	0.0002	0.0000

NOTE: We should be wary of naïve projections. The calculated probabilities are based on past behavior patterns with no input reflecting the present situation. If the present situation is unchanged and we have no other reason to doubt, then these will be our best estimates of the success probabilities. If, on the other hand, we discover that one or more of our rivals are currently experiencing relatively low capacity utilization, we should expect them to bid lower than in the past, and hence we should revise the success probabilities downward. Alternatively, if rivals are at full capacity, we should expect higher bids than usual and accordingly revise the probabilities upward. In fact, all the issues that would cause our own bid price to be higher or lower should be investigated in the context of our rivals in order to discover whether there is any reason to expect their prices to be higher or lower for the current bidding situation. These issues, you will recall, include goodwill considerations, aesthetic and political considerations, and the costs of layoffs, closure, retraining, overtime, and other costs associated with the degree of capacity utilization.

For the firm practicing markup bid pricing, estimation of success probabilities can begin with the firm's past experience. It should calculate the percentage of times it was successful at each markup rate used. For example, suppose it has over the past few years used a 20-percent markup over its standard costs on twenty-three separate contracts for which it bid. Suppose it won fifteen of these and was, therefore, successful 15/23 or 65.2 percent of the time. If all things remain equal, its success probability with a 20-percent markup may be estimated as 0.652. Similarly, it can calculate success probabilities for higher and lower prices based on its previous experience with other markup rates.

Evaluation of the Buyer

Our first consideration when evaluating the buyer is whether or not that buyer will consider any other factor besides the bid price, presuming that all specifications have been met. If so, we must attempt to evaluate the buyer's appreciation of the attributes involved in our supplying the project.

EXAMPLE: We may use higher-quality materials, take more care in finishing, or have some little artistic flair, and we must attempt to set the price in accordance with the value we estimate that the buyer will place on the additional attributes. Other factors such as our meeting the delivery schedule, having sufficient quality control, and having good labor relations and financial stability will be important to the buyer. Clearly, if we think the buyer doubts the verisimilitude of any of these issues, we must adjust the bid price downward to the extent we feel will put the buyer at ease.

Finding out the buyer's exact wants and needs and then tailoring the qualitative aspects of our bid to suit the buyer's particular preferences will improve our chances of winning the contract at any given price level, *ceteris paribus*. To the extent that we feel we have better catered to the buyer's preferences, as compared with rivals' proposals, we should adjust the success probabilities upward at each price level. Alternatively, if we feel we are bidding from a weak position in a particular case—for example, if this buyer had indicated skepticism about our ability to meet the delivery deadlines—we should revise the success probabilities downward. These revisions of the probabilities are likely to shift the maximum expected value to a lower bid level.

To ascertain the value that the buyer is likely to attach to these qualitative and objective considerations, we need to study the buyer's previous purchasing behavior and/or make value judgments based on certain characteristics, such as income, age, and social status. Better still, we could attempt to obtain the information concerning the way in which the buyer chooses among the competing bids. Let us now turn to this issue.

Value Analysis for Optimal Purchasing

The buyer's problem is to choose the bid that not only has an agreeable price attached to it but also includes the most desirable package of attributes in association with that price.

EXAMPLE: Let us consider the purchasing decision of a householder who is contemplating having new windows installed in his somewhat older house. He receives three quotes, as shown in Table 12-6, after inviting representatives from each company to quote on the job. Notice that there is a difference not only in the prices quoted but in the qualitative aspects of the offers.

Which quote should the consumer accept? The answer obviously depends upon a variety of considerations, including the consumer's financial liquidity, his aesthetic feelings and misgivings about the different types of materials and construction, the length of time he expects to own the house, and his attitude toward the risk and uncertainty associated with the different warranties. In the initial discussions with the buyer, the salesperson should attempt to find out exactly what the consumer wants and is prepared to pay for and should then tailor the bid accordingly. The essential consideration is whether the attributes involved in the different bids are worth as much (to the consumer) as the suppliers are asking. Clearly we cannot make the decision for this consumer, but we can say that if he chooses the bid made by Company B, this indicates that he values the attributes provided by Company B for that price more highly than he values the attributes provided by the others, relative to their prices.

TABLE 12-6. Details of Price Quotes on Windows

	Company A	Company B	Company C
Price	$2,200	$1,280	$1,050
Frame	Baked enamel on steel	Baked enamel on aluminum	Anodized aluminum
Glass	Two separate 5-mm panes	Double 5-mm "thermopane"	Double 3-mm "thermopane"
Warranty	10 years, complete	5 years, complete	3 years, complete
Delivery	12 weeks	8 weeks	6 weeks

TABLE 12-7.   Value Analysis in Purchasing

Attribute	Weight	SUPPLIER A		SUPPLIER B		SUPPLIER C	
		Scale	Score	Scale	Score	Scale	Score
Price	7	1	7	5	35	8	56
Quality	4	8	32	7	28	1	4
Delivery	3	1	3	3	9	5	15
Warranty	2	10	20	7	14	4	8
Total score			62		86		83

Industrial purchasers are often required to rationalize their purchasing decisions in some objective manner in order to demonstrate that their purchasing policy is consistent with company objectives. A means of arriving at a purchasing decision (or for *post hoc* rationalization of a purchasing decision) is the technique known as value analysis. Using this approach the decision maker identifies the attributes that are considered desirable and which may be present in each of the bids, applies weights to those attributes in order of importance to the decision maker, ranks and scales each bidder under each attribute, multiplies the weight by the scale, and chooses the bid that has the highest weighted score.

This procedure may be illustrated in terms of the above example. In Table 12-7 we indicate that the attributes of interest to this purchaser are price, quality, delivery lag, and warranty. We presume that the purchaser values these attributes in the proportions shown by the weights. The suppliers are then ranked in terms of their performance on each attribute on a scale of 0 to 10: the better the performance, the higher the scale. Note that for price, Supplier A receives a value of 1, Supplier B is assigned a value of 5, and Supplier C is assigned a value of 8. This reflects the fact that Supplier C has submitted the lowest price, followed by the price of Supplier B, with Supplier A's price a greater distance above. The scale values given to each of the suppliers need not be consecutive numbers if the attributes are different by different amounts.

The buyer then scales and scores each potential supplier on each of the other attributes, as indicated in Table 12-7. Multiplying the scales assigned by the weights for each attribute, we derive each supplier's score on each attribute, and these may be added up to find each supplier's total score over the attributes deemed desirable by the purchaser. Given this system of weighting and scaling the various attributes, it seems that Supplier B has the most desirable bid, since the weighted sum of the scores is greatest.

NOTE: The choice of the weights assigned to each attribute is essentially arbitrary, depending upon the attitudes and judgment of the decision maker. Similarly, the ranking and then the scaling of the suppliers in terms of these attributes are at the discretion of the decision maker. Finally, other attributes may be included in the analysis, such as the previous experience of suppliers with this type of project, financial stability, quality and reputation of personnel, provision of technical or consulting services, inventory charges, and shipping policy. A different decision maker may score the same three bids differently, such that Supplier A or Supplier C becomes the successful bidder.[9]

The importance of value analysis in purchasing is its ability to force the decision maker to rationalize and scrutinize the purchasing decision. The choice of weights, value scales, and desirable attributes must be stated explicitly and is thus subject to argumentation by the decision maker's peers and superiors. Out of the discussion should arise a consensus of those weights, scales, and attributes that are considered consistent with the firm's objectives. Purchasing decisions may thus be justified on this "relatively objective" basis, rather than merely on the basis of unstated preferences and assumptions.[10]

From the supplier's point of view it would be immeasurably valuable to obtain the criteria upon which the purchasing decision is made. With this information the supplier could tailor the bid price and other features such that the bid would score more highly and/or be more desirable to the buyer. In the previous case of the windows, the supplier should attempt to ascertain the likes and dislikes, willingness to pay for certain features, and other information about the prospective customer. In the industrial purchasing situation the potential supplier should attempt to judge which features the buyer regards as more or less important. In both cases the supplier will then be in a better position to supply exactly what is desired by the purchaser and will thus be more likely to be the successful bidder on the contract.

Collusive Bidding and Bid Disclosure

In the foregoing we have presumed that the firms bidding for a particular contract do so without benefit of any interaction or direct information flow between and among the potential suppliers. Where a small group of firms continually find themselves bidding against each other, it is not surprising that they will seek better information concerning each other's intended bids. Since retaliatory action cannot remove the immediate gains of a successful low bid, the firms are likely to try to eliminate the possibility of a rival's submitting an unexpectedly low bid. One means of achieving this is to obtain prior agreement among firms about their bid prices or pricing procedures.

We might expect collusive practices to be more likely to exist in industries in which there is both the ability and the "necessity" to bid

---

[9]The buyer is likely to set some minimum acceptable level or standard for each attribute which must be met in order for the seller's bid to be considered. For example, if the quality or delivery date was unacceptable or was expected to be unacceptable, the seller would be excluded from any further consideration.

[10]Value analysis is implicit in any purchasing decision. It is done explicitly in many companies for the benefits stated above.

collusively. Regarding the ability to collude, where there are relatively few firms we expect firms to be able to communicate with all other firms more easily and effectively. Moreover, the actions of any one firm are more readily visible to the other firms, which assists in the policing of any agreement. Regarding the "necessity" to collude, where contracts are relatively few and far between and are of relatively high value, the incentive will be stronger for each firm to submit a relatively low bid in order to obtain the contract, even if this does not generate a profit above the fully allocated costs of operation. The longer-term result of this could be that all firms are pricing below full costs and that no firm earns a normal profit. As an alternative to some firms' being forced out of the industry, the firms may see collusive bidding as a necessity to avoid a degeneration of prices to unprofitable levels.

Identical Bids. The competing suppliers for a particular contract may agree to submit identical bid prices at a level that ensures that the business will be sufficiently profitable to the successful bidder. The purchaser is then forced to select the successful bidder on some criteria other than price level. This situation is akin to nonprice competition in established market situations. The suppliers will attempt to include those attributes in their bid that are desired by the purchaser, so that at identical prices their bid appears to be the better deal. Suppliers may consider this nonprice competition to be a "more ethical" form of competition, since the successful bidder is rewarded for the expertise and efficiency involved in supplying a particular bundle of attributes at the given price, rather than for the simple ability to cut prices below what rivals are expected to bid.

Bid Rotation. Bid rotation is a method designed to allocate the available business among the competing suppliers in proportions agreeable to all. In effect, the firms take turns in submitting the lowest bid, so that the available business is allocated around the industry. It is not necessarily allocated in equal shares among the competing suppliers, but more likely it will be allocated on the basis of historical market shares or current bargaining power.

As noted in Chapter 11, however, collusive price fixing is illegal, and the firm may face prosecution for engaging in this practice. A second factor militating against the longer-term operation of collusive bidding in any particular industry is the profit incentive that individual firms may have to undercut the agreed price. Firms that are not getting sufficient work to obtain their desired degree of capacity utilization may break out of the agreement when an important contract is at stake. If the available business is not shared among the competing suppliers in a manner that is suitable to all, it is likely that a particular supplier will be motivated to undercut the agreed price in order to obtain the additional business.

While the exchange of information involved in collusive bidding operates to reduce the uncertainty involved in the pricing decision, the risk remains that one or more competing suppliers will operate at variance with their stated intentions. Thus, it is still important to evaluate and form expectations about the probable behavior of competitors. To the extent that rivals are expected not to maintain their previous behavior pattern or are expected not to carry through with their stated intent, the decision maker may wish to adjust the bid price accordingly.[11]

Disclosure of Bids.   After the contract is awarded to the successful bidder, the bid prices of other suppliers may be disclosed to all suppliers or to the public in general. The disclosure of the bid prices generates considerable information which may be valuable to the sellers in their future bidding policies. The unsuccessful bidders will obtain information about the amount they overbid, and the successful bidder will obtain information about the amount that this bid could have been increased without losing the contract. We should expect, therefore, that disclosure of bid prices would lead to a compression of the range of bids over time, since the firms would gain an appreciation of the bid levels that are likely to be submitted by the other firms in the industry. Obviously, disclosure of bids provides information useful for the initiation and the policing of collusive bidding.

From the purchaser's point of view it may be a poor strategy to disclose the bid prices after the contract is awarded, since this may lead to a compression of the bid prices nearer the center of the range of bids and may facilitate collusive bidding. This is likely to lead to an increased level of the lowest bid over time. From the purchaser's point of view it is surely better to keep the suppliers in the dark, since they are more likely to submit lower bids when they are in a greater state of uncertainty about the bids of the other firms. We should thus expect that purchasers would not wish to disclose the bids, and in some industries bid disclosure is considered an unethical procedure. Governments, which frequently purchase goods and services in this type of market, may be required to disclose bid prices, however, in order to show their constituents that the public funds involved have been spent wisely and without corruption.

12.5   SUMMARY

In this chapter we have applied the incremental cost or contribution approach to competitive bids and price quotes. The relevant cost concept is the incremental cost associated with the work involved in undertaking and completing the contract; and as long as the bid price exceeds this incremental cost, some contribution will be made to overheads and profits by obtaining the contract. We considered the optimal bid price from the point of view of

---

[11]Information concerning rival firms' bidding practices and/or intentions may be gleaned in conversation with rival decision makers at business and social gatherings or from industry gossip. Some people even believe in industrial espionage!

expected value analysis, modifying this to the extent that aesthetic, political, and other unquantifiable considerations were involved.

In practice many firms use cost-plus pricing procedures in their competitive bids and price quotes. This can be equivalent to the expected value approach, and it saves time and expense in the decision-making procedure. However, it is important that the decision maker attempt to justify the bid price in terms of the theoretical procedures to ensure that the objectives of the company (or the individual decision maker) are being served. We saw that the satisficing firm may expect to approach the maximization of its EPVC by pursuing capacity utilization and profitability targets.

Both the expected value approach and the markup approach involve an implicit or explicit estimation of the probability of success at each bid price level. The major factors involved in estimating these probabilities are the likelihood of competitors' bidding at various price levels and the appreciation that the buyer will have for price and quality differences. This latter aspect was examined from the buyer's side to show the factors likely to be considered in choosing the successful bid. Potential suppliers would most certainly benefit by an appreciation of the factors considered important by the buyer. The probable bid prices of rivals may be estimated on the basis of information obtained through a collusive exchange of pricing plans, by the disclosure of price levels on previous bid prices, or by knowledge of rival suppliers' capacity utilization levels and other factors.

We should expect a tendency for firms in some industries to bid collusively, either overtly or covertly, but the existence of collusive behavior in past bidding situations does not ensure that all firms will act as anticipated in the next bidding situation.

DISCUSSION QUESTIONS

12-1. Outline three situations in which you have recently been the buyer in a competitive bidding or price quote situation. (Even if you received only one quote in each instance.)

12-2. Make a list of those items that you would expect to enter the incremental cost calculation for a contract to remove the sea gulls from the vicinity of a major coastal airport.

12-3. In calculating the incremental costs of a particular project, how would you treat the possible future cost of a lawsuit that may occur as a result of this project, where the cost of such a lawsuit may range from $10,000 to $500,000 with an associated probability distribution?

12-4. How would you value the goodwill that is expected to be generated as a result of undertaking a particular contract? If there is expected goodwill, does this mean you would be prepared to bid lower than otherwise? Why?

12-5. Explain why the strategy of choosing the bid price with the highest expected value is likely to generate the greatest contribution to overheads and profits over a large number of successful and unsuccessful bids.

12-6. Explain how the strategy of marking up incremental costs by a standard percentage (and subsequently winning some contracts and losing some contracts) may over a period of time give equivalent results as compared with the maximum-expected-value strategy.

12-7. Explain the logic of the declining success probability as more and more rival firms submit bids on a particular contract.

12-8. Outline the factors that would cause you to use a lower markup on incremental costs (as compared with your usual markup) in a particular bidding situation.

12-9. Explain the logic behind value analysis. What is the relationship between value analysis and attribute analysis of consumer choice behavior?

12-10. Why is collusive bidding illegal? Does it hurt the customer? The competing firms? Other firms?

PROBLEMS AND SHORT CASES

12-1. In the text it was shown that the success probabilities decline as the number of firms submitting bids increases. Using the data from Table 12-5, find the optimal bid price level

(a) When there is one other firm bidding.

(b) When there are two other firms bidding.

(c) When there are three other firms bidding.

(d) When there are four other firms bidding.

12-2. Your company is one of several companies manufacturing a special reflecting paint used for traffic signs. Your two major customers are the state and the federal Department of Transport. The federal Department of Transport has recently called for bids for 10,000 gallons of this special paint in a light blue, to be delivered within two months after signing the contract. You can foresee being able to fit in a production run of 10,000 gallons of the blue paint and have decided to bid on the job. This particular contract is absolutely standard, similar in all respects to hundreds of contracts you have bid on in the past two years. Being government departments, the buyers always release the details of the bids received to demonstrate that no patronage is being practiced. You have collected the data on the bid prices of your competitors and have assembled these data for each of the competing firms as a ratio of your own incremental cost on each particular job. You have then calculated the percentage of the total that each firm bid less than 10 percent above your costs, less than 15 percent above, and so on, as shown in the table.

Ratio of Rival's Bid to Your Incremental Cost	PERCENTAGE OF TOTAL CONTRACTS ON WHICH RIVAL'S BID WAS LOWER THAN THE RATIO INDICATED (but higher than the preceding ratio)			
	Rival A	Rival B	Rival C	Rival D
1.00	0.0	1.5	2.6	0.0
1.10	2.5	4.0	5.4	0.0
1.15	6.2	7.1	10.1	0.0
1.20	8.0	10.8	16.8	0.5
1.25	11.1	18.2	27.2	1.5
1.30	17.5	26.1	19.3	8.0
1.35	30.6	17.4	8.5	21.3
1.40	13.4	7.0	5.1	32.2
1.45	7.5	3.2	3.5	20.6
1.50	2.2	2.7	1.5	9.1
1.75	1.0	1.6	0.0	5.8
2.00	0.0	0.4	0.0	1.0
	100.0	100.0	100.0	100.0

Your incremental cost on this project has been calculated to be $76,200.

(a) Use the above information to calculate the success probabilities at markups of 10 percent, 15 percent, and so on, as indicated in the first column of the table, when all four rivals are expected to submit bids.

(b) Which bid price maximizes expected contribution to overheads and profits?

(c) How would your optimal bid price be modified if only one of the firms, identity unknown, is rumored to have submitted a bid?

12-3. The Esna Fabricating Company manufactures valves, faucets, and similar items under contract for various industrial and commercial clients. Whenever the company has no special jobs to do, it uses its labor force and plant to produce a line of faucets which it sells to a distributor for eventual sale in hardware stores. Esna can produce 5,000 of these faucets weekly, on average, and sells them for $1.65 per unit, this representing a 50-percent markup over variable costs. This production is suspended whenever Esna wins a more lucrative contract, however. Esna is currently considering bidding for a contract to manufacture several very large pressure valves for use in the pulp-making industry. It has estimated the costs associated with this job as follows:

Direct labor (300 labor hours @ $20)	$6,000
Direct materials	8,650
Variable overhead expenses	4,270
Allocated overheads (150% of direct labor)	9,000

In addition to the above, Esna has incurred $850 in expenses to acquire the detailed specifications for examination prior to submitting its bid. If the contract is won, Esna expects to incur another $2,500 for design costs before beginning manufacture of the valves, and the manufacturing process is expected to take 300 labor hours, or three weeks of the plant's time. No new direct labor will need to be hired for the job, since the regular labor force (diverted from faucet production) is expected to be sufficient to handle the job.

Esna's bidding policy is to mark up incremental costs of each job such that the expected value of contribution is maximized. An examination of the outcomes of over 300 jobs bid for in the past two years indicates that the probability of winning the contract is related to the ratio of the bid price to incremental cost, for each particular contract, in the following way:

$$P = 2.825 - 0.115R - 1.427R^2$$

where P is the success probability and R is the ratio of the bid price to the incremental costs of each job tendered for.

(a) What are the probabilities of winning the contract at markups of 10 percent, 15 percent, 20 percent 25 percent, and 30 percent, respectively?

(b) What price should Esna submit?

(c) Outline any reservations or qualifications you may have concerning your recommended bid price.

12-4. Bids have been called for the fabrication of a steel watergate, and you are in the process of preparing to bid on this contract. The practice in your company has been to charge each contract with bid preparation costs of $2,000, which is actually about three times the actual value of time and office supplies spent on each bid but is costed this way because the company is the successful bidder only once in every three times it bids, on average. The bidding policy in the past has been to add a 15-percent margin to the incremental and allocated costs, and hence your colleague, a recent M.B.A. graduate from a rival university, insists that the appropriate bid price is $138,230, calculated as follows:

474

Bid preparation costs	$ 2,000
Direct materials	18,600
Direct labor	33,200
Variable overhead	14,400
Fixed overhead	52,000
Profit margin	18,030
Suggested bid price	$138,230

You are a little worried that conditions in the industry have deteriorated recently. You are aware that some of your competitors have been operating below capacity, and you suspect that demand for steel-fabricated products is likely to be depressed for the coming twelve months.

(a) What is the absolute minimum price you would bid on this contract? Explain and defend your answer.

(b) On the basis of the information given, what bid price would you recommend?

(c) What factors would you wish to investigate and evaluate before choosing the actual bid price?

12-5. A large department store has called for bids for the following contracts: A truck plus its driver must be available, given one day's notice, whenever the store's own trucks are fully utilized, to deliver goods to suburban households. The expected number of days for which a truck will be required is 20, and the number of miles is expected to be 4,000, for the coming year.

You are the manager of the Clark Rent-A-Truck Company and have a number of trucks which you rent out on a day-to-day basis. One truck is a little older than the others and is always the last to be rented out because it does less for public relations than the newer trucks. In the absence of a contract with the department store, you expect this older truck to be rented out two-thirds of the 300 "rental days" this coming year. Your normal rental charge is $25.00 per day plus $0.35 per mile.

You estimate the costs of operating the older truck to be as follows, assuming 10,000 miles of rental over the coming year:

Depreciation	$ 800
Interest on investment in truck	360
License fees and taxes	125
Insurance	440
Parking fees (permanently rented space)	300
Gasoline	1,367
Oil, grease, and preventive maintenance	600
Repairs	1,450
Allocated overheads	1,650

You can hire a driver on one day's notice for $50 per day. A one-time cost of $400 will be involved in fitting the truck with a special loading ramp required by the contract. This ramp will not interfere with the normal use of the truck.

(a) On the basis of this information and by making whatever assumptions you feel are necessary and reasonable, calculate the incremental cost that would be involved in accepting this contract.

(b) What price would you bid, assuming that you wish to maximize profits and that you have no knowledge of who else will bid for this job nor of the "going rate" for this type of job? (Outline the considerations involved and choose a bid price that would reflect *your* certainty equivalent for this gamble.)

12-6. Your company has decided to bid on a government contract to build a bridge 50 miles from the city during the coming winter. The bridge is to be of standard government design and hence should contain no unexpected in-process costs. Your present capacity utilization rate allows sufficient scope to undertake the contract if awarded. You calculate your incremental costs to be $268,000 and your fully allocated costs to be $440,000. You expect 3 other companies to bid on this contract, and you have assembled the following information concerning these companies.

Consideration	Rival A	Rival B	Rival C
Capacity utilization	Near full	Sufficient slack	Very low
Goodwill consideration	Very concerned	Moderately concerned	Not concerned
Type of plant	Small and inefficient	Medium-sized and efficient	Large and efficient
Previous bidding pattern	Incremental cost plus 35%-50%	Full cost plus 8%-12%	Full cost plus 10%-15%
Cost structure	Incremental costs exceed yours by about 10%	Similar cost structure to yours	Incremental costs 20% lower but full costs similar to yours
Aesthetic factors	Likes to fully utilize capacity	Doesn't like "dirty" jobs	Likes creative projects
Political factors	Decision maker has friends in government	Decision maker is seeking a new job	None known

Your usual bidding practice is to add between 60 percent and 80 percent to your incremental costs, depending upon capacity utilization rate and other factors. What price will you bid (a) if you *must* win the contract or (b) if you wish to maximize the expected value of the contract? Defend your answers with discussion, making any assumptions you feel are supported by the information given and/or are otherwise reasonable.

12-7. Bids have been called for the construction of a turbine generator for the Caughnawaga Power Station. Your company accountant has examined the specifications and has established the following costs associated with the contract:

Bid preparation costs	$ 750
Direct materials	115,000
Direct labor	252,500
Specialized equipment required*	27,500
Variable overhead	42,000
Allocated overhead	86,750

*This equipment will not be purchased unless the contract is won. It will last for the fabrication of two more generators, should such contracts be forthcoming in the future, although there is no indication at this time that there will be a demand for any more generators like this one.

You are aware of three other companies who are likely to bid on this project. Relevant details are as follows:

Detail	Company A	Company B	Company C
Cost structure	Similar to yours	10% higher	10% lower
Previous bidding pattern	Incremental cost plus 60%	Full cost plus 15%	Full cost plus 40%
Current capacity utilization	Moderate	Very low	Near full

Your current capacity utilization is moderate, leaving sufficient capacity to handle this project. Your previous bidding practice has been to add 25 percent to full costs.

(a) What is the absolute *minimum* price you would bid on this contract?

(b) What is your *actual* bid price, on the basis of the information given?

(c) What other factors would you wish to consider or investigate before making your bid?

12-8. Fact Finders Limited, a marketing research company, has been asked by the marketing director of a large food-processing company to submit a proposal for a small market research project aimed at determining consumers' probable responses to several planned changes in marketing strategy. The proposal should outline the procedures planned and quote a price. The marketing director is not binding himself to accepting the proposal, since he is still formulating his plan of action. It would cost Fact Finders about $200 to prepare the proposal.

Fact Finders' president, Ms. Denise Jutasi, designs each project to fit individual requirements. Furthermore, the nature of the research industry is such that in general the client depends on only one or two research firms, since a certain familiarity with the client's problems is needed in the designing of the project. In addition, although price is important to the client, it is the research house's reputation for doing high-quality work that will largely influence the client's choice of research supplier. This particular client has used Fact Finders' services several times in the past, although it has also adopted other proposals in some cases in preference to the proposals suggested by Fact Finders.

Ms. Jutasi has designed a project which she believes best fulfills the client's needs, and she estimates that the incremental cost of the project could vary between $1,500 and $2,500. The wide variation in cost estimation is due to the many situational difficulties that are part of market research, including snowstorms, respondents not being home, difficulty in obtaining field staff, and unforeseen complications in other projects already in progress which could affect the one in question (for example, cause delays in starting).

The marketing director of the food-processing firm has indicated that he has allocated a budget in the vicinity of $2,500 for this project. At the top of this range, however, and dependent on the type of information the research firm will be able to obtain for him (outlined in the proposal), he may consider other methods of obtaining needed information or go with what information he has.

As a rule of thumb in calculating prices, Fact Finders uses cost plus 10 percent as a regular policy. Following are its best estimates of the probabilities with respect to the cost of the project and its chance of obtaining an acceptance by the client:

Incremental Cost of Project	Probability	Price (cost + 10%)	Probability of Acceptance
$1,500	0.2	$1,650	0.99
2,000	0.5	2,200	0.70
2,500	0.3	2,750	0.10

(a) Find the expected value of the proposal to Fact Finders at each of the three prices stated.

(b) Interpolate between the three prices shown to estimate the probability of acceptance when price is varied by $50 increments above $1,650. Would one of these price quotes be preferable to the initial three prices?

(c) How would you recommend that Ms. Jutasi deal with the risk that costs might exceed the asking price?

12-9. Prentice Plumbing and Pipes Limited specializes in household plumbing installation and repairs. The sales manager received a call this morning to provide a written price quotation for the installation of the entire plumbing system in a new house being built by the owner (with the aid of contractors for the plumbing and electrical work). The owner has called for three or four quotes on each of the plumbing and electrical jobs.

The sales manager, David Katz, sent his estimator to the job site and has since received the following cost estimate:

Materials	$2,422
Direct labor	2,760
Standard charge for detailed quotation	100
Variable overhead (estimated incremental)	650
Allocated overhead	1,380
Estimated total cost	$7,312

Prentice's usual pricing policy is to mark up its estimated (full) costs by 12.5 percent to 25 percent, depending upon (a) how badly it needs the work to avoid employee layoffs, (b) whether or not the buyer is considering one or more other quotations, and (c) whether or not it expects the job to provide an introduction to a client who will have more jobs to be done in the future. The present demand situation for Prentice Plumbing and Pipes is quite pleasing, although Prentice does have sufficient operating capacity to handle the job under consideration. Mr. Katz intends to quote $8,775, which is approximately equal to full cost plus 20-percent markup.

Suppose that you have ascertained that the expected value of the bid price for each of the three other firms also submitting quotes on this job is $8,592, with a standard deviation of $1,032. Assuming the probability distribution of each rival's bid price to be normally distributed around the mean (expected value), find the bid price that maximizes the expected value of the contribution to overheads and profits for Prentice.

(a) Is the sales manager's price quote close enough for maximization of expected profits?

(b) What would you advise Mr. Katz, and why?

SUGGESTED REFERENCES AND FURTHER READING

Alpert, M. I.   *Pricing Decisions*, chap. 3. Glenview, Ill.: Scott, Foresman & Company, 1971.

Edelman, R.   "Art and Science of Competitive Bidding," *Harvard Business Review*, 43 (1965), 53-66.

Ekelund, R.B., Jr. and R.F. Hébert.   "Uncertainty, Contract Costs and Franchise Bidding," *Southern Economic Journal*, 47 (1980), pp. 517-21.

Friedman, L.   "A Competitive Bidding Strategy," *Operations Research*, Vol. 4 (Feb. 1956), 104-112.

Holt, C.A., Jr.   "Competitive Bidding for Contracts under Alternative Auction Procedures," *Journal of Political Economy*, 88 (June 1980), pp. 433-45.

Kottas, J.F. and B.M. Khumawala.   "Contract Bid Development for the Small Businessman," *Sloan Management Review*, vol. 14 (Spring 1973), 31-45.

Livesey, F.   *Pricing*, chap. 10. London: Macmillan, Inc., 1976.

Miller, E.M.   "Oral and Sealed Bidding: Efficiency versus Equity," *Natural Resources Journal*, 12 (July 1972), 330-53.

Oren, M.E., and A.C. Williams.   "On Competitive Bidding," *Operations Research*, 23 (November-December 1975), 1072-79.

Roberge, M.D.   "Pricing for Government Contractors," *Management Accounting* (June 1973), 28-34.

Roering, K.J. and R.J. Paul.   "An Appraisal of Competitive Bidding Models," *Marquette Business Review*, vol. 21 (Summer 1977), 57-66.

Walker, A.W.   "How to Price Industrial Products," *Harvard Business Review*, 45 (1967), 125-32.

TOPICS in MANAGERIAL ECONOMICS

Advertising and Promotional Decisions

13.1 INTRODUCTION

In earlier chapters we confined our attention to *price* as the firm's strategic variable, and we discussed the implications of differing price levels for the attainment of the firm's objectives. In some market situations, however, price competition may be virtually absent because of the nature of the product and/or the market. In some market situations we find that, for the most part, firms leave the price level alone and engage in *non-price* competition through advertising and promotional expenditures, primarily because of the costs associated with price wars. In other market situations we should expect to find firms adjusting both price and advertising expenditures simultaneously to obtain their objectives. Monopolistic competitors and oligopolists gain control over the price level as a result of the differentiation of their product: advertising and promotional expenditures are likely to increase this differentiation and hence increase the control these firms have over their market price, as well as increase the price that might be obtained for any given output level.

In the monopolistically competitive market situation the firm may presume that its actions will have an insignificant effect on each of its competitors and hence may presume that there will be no reaction from competitors to its actions. Thus, we may analyze the monopolistically competitive firm's advertising and promotional decisions under the assumption of *ceteris paribus*. The same applies to the monopolist, since this firm has no existing competition from whom to expect reactions. The oligopolist, however, operating in an environment of strong interdependence of action, must expect its advertising and promotional expenditures to have a noticeable impact on competitors' sales and hence must expect these rivals to react to its advertising and promotional expenditures.

In the following sections we shall first consider the firm's optimal adjustment of its advertising and promotional expenditures under conditions of *ceteris paribus*, (1) given a particular price level and (2) under a situation where both price and advertising may be adjusted simultaneously to their optimal levels. We then turn to the advertising and promotional decision under conditions of oligopoly where the reaction of rivals must be taken into account. Finally, we address the issue of the uncertainty about the impact of advertising upon the level of sales and profits.

NOTE: Throughout this chapter the emphasis will be on the economics of the advertising and promotional decision, and we leave to our confreres in the discipline of marketing the more specialized problems of media selection, message composition, promotional mix, timing, and pattern of promotional campaigns. Throughout this chapter we shall, for simplicity of exposition, use the term *advertising* to include all elements of the promotional mix.

13.2 OPTIMAL ADVERTISING EXPENDITURES UNDER *CETERIS PARIBUS* CONDITIONS

In Chapter 4 we saw that the firm's sales or demand level was a function of several controllable variables and a variety of uncontrollable variables. The controllable variables were later termed the firm's strategic variables and may be familiar to you as the "marketing mix" of price, promotion, product design, and distribution. Since the firm's sales are a function of these variables, it follows that the firm's profits are a function of these variables, and if the firm wishes to maximize profits it should adjust these controllable variables to the point where further adjustment would make no positive contribution to profits.

The Advertising-Sales Relationship

In Chapter 4 we held all other variables in the demand function constant while varying the level of price to find the influence on demand. Analogously, we shall now examine the effect of holding all other variables (including price) constant while varying the level of advertising. Thus, demand will be equal to a constant (which represents the effect of all the other variables), plus some function of advertising expenditures. In the simple linear case:

$$Q = \alpha + \beta A \qquad\qquad\qquad (13\text{-}1)$$

where Q is the quantity demanded, α and β are parameters, and A is the level of advertising expenditure. Note that this implies that the marginal impact on sales for additional units of advertising expenditure (i.e., the parameter β) will be constant regardless of the level of advertising expenditure. More likely we would expect diminishing returns to advertising expenditures at higher advertising levels. Thus, the advertising function may be quadratic in form, such as

$$Q = \alpha + \beta_1 A - \beta_2 A^2 \qquad\qquad\qquad (13\text{-}2)$$

It might be argued that initial levels of advertising may benefit from increasing returns, since certain threshold levels of advertising expenditure must be reached in order to afford certain types of media and to penetrate the buyer's consciousness. However, we would expect that these thresholds would be soon overcome and that diminishing returns would be expected to set in for higher levels of advertising expenditure. Thus, the general form of the advertising function for all levels of advertising might be expected to be cubic, such as

$$Q = \alpha + \beta_1 A + \beta_2 A^2 - \beta_3 A^3 \qquad\qquad\qquad (13\text{-}3)$$

These three types of advertising relationship are shown in Figure 13-1. Note that in all cases quantity demanded has some positive value (viz., the parameter α) when advertising is zero and that the general relationship between advertising and quantity demanded is positive. Clearly, we should not expect the relationship to be linear over a wide range of advertising levels, since this neglects the probable occurrence of diminishing returns to advertising expenditures. Nevertheless, a linear advertising function may be a sufficient approximation of both the quadratic and the cubic functions over a limited range of advertising expenditures.

The appropriate functional form of the advertising sales relationship is of course the one that provides the best statistical fit to the data in a particular case. If a firm could be assured that *ceteris paribus* held for all other significant variables and was able to vary its level of advertising over a period and observe the variations in demand, it could apply regression analysis to the data generated to find which form of the regression equation best fits the observed data.[1]

---

[1]See, for example, V. R. Rao, "Alternative Econometric Models of Sales-Advertising Relationships," *Journal of Marketing Research*, 9 (May 1972), pp. 177-81; and V. K. Verma "A Price Theoretic Approach to the Specification and Estimation of the Sales-Advertising Function," *Journal of Business*, 53 (July 1980), pp. S 115-137; and R. D. Carlson, "Advertising and Sales Relationships for Toothpaste," *Business Economics*, 16 (Sept. 1981).

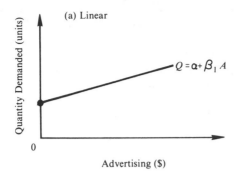

(a) Linear

$Q = \alpha + \beta_1 A$

Quantity Demanded (units)

Advertising ($)

0

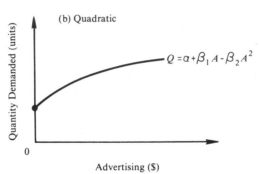

(b) Quadratic

$Q = \alpha + \beta_1 A - \beta_2 A^2$

Quantity Demanded (units)

Advertising ($)

0

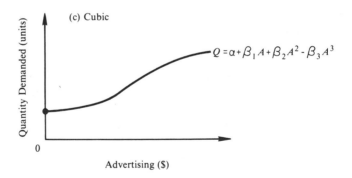

(c) Cubic

$Q = \alpha + \beta_1 A + \beta_2 A^2 - \beta_3 A^3$

Quantity Demanded (units)

Advertising ($)

0

The Optimal Level of Advertising for a Given Price Level

You will recall from Chapter 4 that advertising expenditures are one of the variables that are held constant while a particular demand curve is being discussed. Changes in advertising expenditures cause a *shift* in the demand curve, causing it to move to the right when advertising expenditures are increased or to the left when expenditures are reduced. In Figure 13-2 we

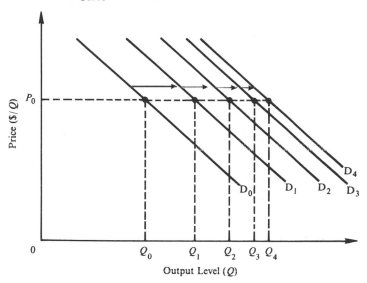

show the initial price and quantity coordinates as P_0 and Q_0 on demand curve D_0. Suppose now that advertising expenditures are increased from their previous level by a given amount and that this causes the demand curve to shift to the right to that shown as D_1. Subsequent increases in advertising expenditures would be expected to shift the demand curve farther to the right, but if there are diminishing returns to advertising expenditures we should expect these subsequent shifts of the demand curve to become progressively smaller as advertising expenditures are increased by equal increments.

As advertising expenses are increased, total revenues derived are also increased, since at the given price level progressively larger quantities are demanded. If total revenues increase by more than the incremental cost of production and the increase in advertising expenditures, we must consider the increased advertising as beneficial if the firm's objective function is concerned with either profits and/or sales levels. That is, increased profits will have been derived by virtue of the increased advertising expenditure, and the sales level will have been increased. Suppose the firm's objective is the maximization of contribution; the decision maker's problem is to increase advertising up to the point where the increase in total revenue just covers the increase in both the production and the selling costs that occasioned that increase in total revenues.

EXAMPLE: To demonstrate this, let us suppose that the advertising function for a particular firm has been estimated as follows:

$$Q = 10{,}000 + 25.2A - 0.8A^2 \qquad (13\text{-}4)$$

where A represents advertising expenditures in thousands of dollars. The optimal level of advertising, using the marginalist approach, will be that level at which the last dollar spent on advertising contributes just one dollar toward overheads and profits. Thus the maximizing condition is

$$\frac{d\pi}{dA} = 1 \qquad (13\text{-}5)$$

where π represents "contribution to overheads and profits" (considering only the variable production costs and not the selling costs). If we consider dA in one-dollar increments, the requirement for profit maximization, that is, $d\pi$, equals one dollar in order to cover the last dollar of advertising expenditure incurred. Note that to find $d\pi/dA$ we must first find how quantity demanded varies with advertising and then how profits vary with quantity demanded. That is, $d\pi/dA$ expands to

$$\frac{d\pi}{dA} = \frac{dQ}{dA} \cdot \frac{d\pi}{dQ} \qquad (13\text{-}6)$$

From Equation (13-4) we can find dQ/dA by taking the first derivative of the estimated advertising function with respect to the level of advertising expenditures. Hence,

$$\frac{dQ}{dA} = 25.2 - 1.6A \qquad (13\text{-}7)$$

The second element on the right-hand side of Equation (13-6), namely, the marginal contribution to overheads and profits, is in fact the contribution on the last unit produced. Supposing a simple case where both market price and per unit variable production costs are constant, we can express Equation (13-6) as follows:

$$\frac{d\pi}{dA} = \frac{dQ}{dA} \cdot CM \qquad (13\text{-}8)$$

Since the maximizing condition is to set $d\pi/dA$ equal to one, we may restate the maximization condition as

$$\frac{dQ}{dA} = \frac{1}{CM} \qquad (13\text{-}9)$$

Supposing the contribution margin to be constant at \$6 per unit, by substitution from (13-7) into (13-9) we can solve for the optimal level of advertising as follows:

TOPICS IN MANAGERIAL ECONOMICS

$$25.2 - 1.6A = \frac{1}{6}$$

$$151.2 - 9.6A = 1$$

$$-9.6A = -150.2$$

$$A = 15.646$$

Thus in the case where the advertising function is represented by Equation (13-4) and the contribution margin is constant at \$6 per unit, the profit-maximizing level of advertising is 15.646 units, or \$15,646.

NOTE: Where there are diminishing returns in production, or a downward-sloping demand curve, we cannot expect contribution margin per unit to remain constant regardless of output level, and hence we must specify the profit function in terms of total revenue and total costs such that we may accurately define the $d\pi/dQ$ term over all values of Q. A second problem arises where the advertising coefficient (dQ/dA) is estimated from a linear multiple-regression equation, in which case it will be the average of the marginal impact of advertising over the range of the data observations. Since we expect the marginal impact of advertising to decline as the level of advertising increases, the coefficient will overstate the effect of additional advertising at the upper end of the observations (where our interest will probably be) and should be used with caution for decision-making purposes.

Simultaneous Adjustment of Price and Advertising Levels

Where the firm is able to adjust both price and advertising, we should not expect the firm to wish to be constrained to a particular price level. The monopolistic competitor, for example, is able to adjust price without expecting retaliation from rival firms, and the monopolist has no rival firm's reactions to consider. Thus, the *ceteris paribus* assumptions are appropriate for these market situations.

NOTE: Advertising expenditures must be regarded as a fixed cost, since they are typically independent of the current level of output and sales. Thus, the average advertising expenditures, or, more broadly, average selling costs, will be graphed as a rectangular hyperbola against the output level. In Figure 13-3 we show the average selling cost curve for a particular level of advertising expenditures, given a particular demand situation.[2] For simpli-

---

[2]This analysis follows N. S. Buchanan, "Advertising Expenditures: A Suggested Treatment," *Journal of Political Economy*, (August 1942), pp. 537-57. An alternate methodology is given by R. Dorfman and P. O. Steiner, "Optimal Advertising and Optimal Quality," *American Economic Review*, 44 (December 1954), pp. 826-36.

FIGURE 13-3. The Average Selling Cost Curve

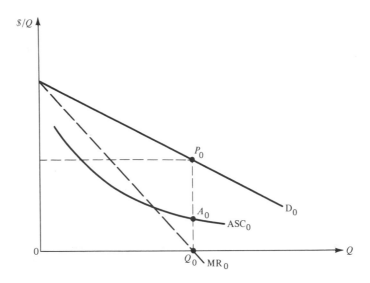

city we shall assume zero marginal costs, initially. The intersection of the marginal revenue curve with the horizontal axis therefore indicates that the profit-maximizing or contribution-maximizing output level is Q_0, to be sold at price P_0. The relevant point on the average selling cost curve (ASC_0) is the point labeled A_0, since this is the average selling cost level at output level Q_0. There is nothing in Figure 13-3 to indicate that ASC_0 is the optimal level of advertising expenditure. Larger advertising budgets will cause the demand curve to shift to the right but will also cause the average selling cost curve to move upward and to the right. To find the optimal level of advertising expenditure and the profit-maximizing price, we must know to what extent additional advertising expenditures will shift the demand curve.

In Figure 13-4 we show the results of increasing the level of advertising expenditure. Starting from the initial advertising level, ASC_0, which gave rise to the optimal quantity and price levels Q_0 and P_0, we suppose that advertising expenditure is increased to the level indicated by the hyperbola ASC_1. This causes the demand curve to shift from D_0 to D_1. The new marginal revenue curve, MR_1, cuts the horizontal axis at the output level Q_1, indicating a new profit-maximizing price level shown by the point P_1. At this output level, A_1 indicates the average selling cost per unit. By continuing this process we could trace a series, or locus, of optimal price points and a similar locus of average selling cost points. The locus of optimal prices for various levels of advertising expenditure is shown as the curve LOP in Figure 13-4, and the locus of the average selling costs for various advertising

TOPICS IN MANAGERIAL ECONOMICS

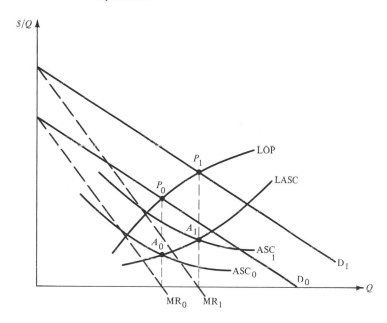

FIGURE 13-4. Optimal Prices for Successive Levels of Advertising Expenditure

and demand levels is shown as the curve LASC. Note that the general shape of these curves reflects the presence of diminishing returns to advertising expenditures.

The LOP curve and the LASC curve in Figure 13-4 are both loci of a variable that represents an average—viz., average revenue (or price) and average selling cost. Each of these average curves will have a curve that is marginal to it. In Figure 13-5 we show the LMR curve (locus of marginal revenue) as the curve that is marginal to the locus of optimal prices curve, and the LMSC curve (locus of marginal selling costs) as the curve that is marginal to the LASC curve. Note that the shape and placement of these marginal curves follow the general principles of the relationships between average and marginal curves. The decision maker's problem is to have the marginal increase in costs just equal to the marginal change in revenues. In this simple case, with zero marginal costs of production, the intersection of the LMSC curve with the LMR curve will indicate the output level at which the increment to revenues will be just equal to the increment to costs. The optimal output level is shown as Q^* in Figure 13-5. The point on the LOP curve at that output level must lie on the optimal demand curve, which we show as D^*, and the optimal price level is thus P^*. The optimal level of advertising can be found from the LASC curve to the ASC*, which represents A^* dollars per unit of output at the optimal output level.

Having introduced this model in the simple context of zero production costs, let us now bring it closer to reality by incorporating positive levels

FIGURE 13-5. Establishing the Optimal Price and Advertising Levels

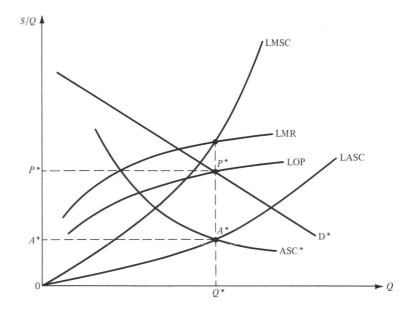

FIGURE 13-6. Optimal Price and Advertising Levels when there are Both Production and Selling Costs

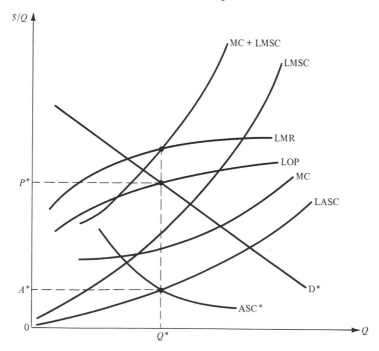

TOPICS IN MANAGERIAL ECONOMICS

of production costs. In Figure 13-6 the MC curve is added to indicate the marginal costs of production. To maximize profits the firm must now expand the total of production and selling costs to the point where the change in these costs just equals the change in total revenues. To show the change in both production and selling costs we add vertically the MC and LMSC curves, and the resulting curve is shown as MC + LMSC in Figure 13-6. This "combined" marginal cost curve crosses the LMR curve at output level $Q*$, indicating that the increment to total revenue is equal to the increment to *all* costs at this point. Thus the profit-maximizing price and advertising levels are $P*$ and $A*$ per unit, respectively.

NOTE: The above approach assumes knowledge of the cost and revenue curves shown in the figures, as well as the underlying production, demand, and advertising functions. In practice, of course, it may be extremely difficult and/or expensive to ascertain the actual shape and placement of these curves. The model is nevertheless useful for its pedagogical and explanatory value, since it incorporates the notions of simultaneous adjustment of price and advertising levels, with the subsequent interaction of the "law" of demand and the "law" of diminishing returns to advertising. Note that in effect this model sets the same optimizing condition as in the earlier simple case where price was held constant—viz., the advertising is carried to the point where the increment to the total advertising cost is just covered by the increment to the total revenue derived from the sale of the marginal unit.

13.3 ADVERTISING AND PROMOTIONAL EXPENDITURES WHEN MUTUAL DEPENDENCE IS RECOGNIZED

Under conditions of oligopoly the firm should be expected to recognize that its advertising and other marketing strategies will have a noticeable impact on the sales and profits of rivals, unless the other firms are simultaneously carrying out new promotional campaigns. Unlike price adjustments, however, promotional campaigns require a significant lead time in which they must be planned and coordinated with the availability of time and space from the various advertising agencies and media channels. This means that if a firm is caught napping by a competitor's new advertising campaign, there will be a significant lag before it can produce its own retaliatory campaign, during which time it may have lost a significant share of its market, which in turn may prove difficult or impossible to retrieve. The existence of this lag thus motivates firms to have an ongoing involvement in promotional activity. If there is always a new campaign in the pipeline, the firm does not expect to be caught napping to the extent that it would be if it waited until a competitor initiated a major new advertising or promotional campaign.

Advertising Interdependence

Given that firms tend to have continual advertising and promotional strategies, changes in market shares should be expected to occur only when the relative advertising and promotional effectiveness of firms is suddenly made different by an increase in the relative size of an individual firm's advertising budget and/or in the relative effectiveness of a firm's advertising expenditures.

EXAMPLE: Suppose two large firms share the major part of a particular market and each budgets approximately $4 million toward promotional expenditures each year. In Table 13-1 we show the payoff matrix for the interaction of the firms' advertising strategies. When both firms spend $4 million, the net profits to each firm are $10 million. By convention, A's payoffs are shown first (followed by B's payoffs) for each combination of promotional expenditure strategies. Suppose now that Firm A contemplates increasing the promotional budget level to $6 million. If Firm B maintains its promotional budget at $4 million, this will cause A's profits to rise to $12 million while B's profits will fall to $6 million. This indicates that the result of A's additional $2 million promotional expenditures will be to cause a substantial proportion of the market to switch from Firm B's products to Firm A's products, with associated changes in the firms' relative profitabilities.

Conversely, if Firm B considered increasing advertising levels to $6 million while Firm A held its advertising constant at $4 million, it would be Firm B that would benefit from the change in market share that resulted. If both firms increased advertising to the new higher advertising levels, the result would be as shown in the lower-right-hand quadrant of the payoff matrix, namely, that profits are reduced compared with the earlier levels of advertising expenditures. This may be rationalized in terms of the market's becoming saturated by the products of the two firms, and/or that the firms' competing messages to consumers tend to offset each other's effectiveness by creating "noise" in the communication process.

Given that the firms are likely to be risk averters and that there will be a significant lag before the firm can retaliate to an increase in advertising expenditures by the other firm, we might expect each firm to wish to avoid the worst possible outcome. Thus we may expect each firm to follow a "maximin" strategy. For each firm the worst outcome associated with the $4 million expenditure is $6 million profit, whereas the worst outcome

TABLE 13-1. Payoff Matrix for Advertising Strategies

		Firm B's Advertising Budget			
		$4 m.		$6 m.	
Firm A's Advertising Budget	$4 m.	10.0,	10.0	6.0,	12.0
	$6 m.	12.0,	6.0	8.7,	8.7

associated with the $6 million promotional budget is $8.7 million profit. The best of these worst situations is the $8.7 million profit associated with the $6 million promotional expenditures. Thus, the maximin strategy for each firm is to increase its promotional budget to the higher level.

In the above example the firms have independently increased their expenditures in pursuit of private gain, but instead they find that the result is inferior to that which was enjoyed at the earlier promotional levels. The firms are subject to what has become known as the "prisoner's dilemma."

The Prisoner's Dilemma

DEFINITION: The *prisoner's dilemma* situation arises when two or more parties are motivated to behave in a self-serving manner, and they assume that their rivals or adversaries will act similarly. The result is that the outcome to all parties is inferior to that which could have been attained if the parties had been able to assume that their rivals would not act in a way detrimental to them.[3]

EXAMPLE: This situation is called the prisoner's dilemma after the supposed situation in which two bank robbers are caught with the proceeds of a robbery, but with no more than circumstantial evidence of their being involved in that robbery. Interrogated in two separate rooms each is told that if he confesses and implicates the other he will go free as a "state's witness" while the accomplice will receive a substantial term in prison. Each prisoner knows that if they both refuse to confess they will receive a short prison term for possession of stolen goods, while if both prisoners confess, neither will be allowed to turn state's witness and both will receive relatively long jail sentences. Given the inability of the prisoners to communicate with each other (and since there is no honor among thieves) and given that each prisoner dislikes time spent in jail, each will be motivated to avoid the worst possible outcome. Since the worst possible outcome is that of not confessing while the other does confess, the maximin strategy for each prisoner is to confess. Since each prisoner confesses, each ends up with a relatively long jail sentence, whereas if they had been able to communicate and coordinate their strategies they would have been sentenced to the relatively short prison term for possession of stolen goods.

The prisoner's dilemma thus applies to firms in situations of advertising rivalry. A lack of communication and coordination between parties with conflicting self-interest can lead to a situation in which both parties are worse off compared with the outcomes that would have been obtained had there been communication and coordination between those firms. Referring back to Table 13-1, had the firms agreed to limit their advertising expendi-

---

[3]See R. D. Luce and H. Raiffa, *Games and Decisions* (New York: John Wiley & Sons, Inc. 1957), pp. 94-102; or F. M. Scherer, *Industrial Market Structure and Economic Performance* (Chicago: Rand McNally & Company, 1970), pp. 142-45 and 335-37.

tures to $4 million each, their net profits would have remained at the $10 million level. In pursuit of independent profit gains, however, and without knowing whether or not the other firm was simultaneously planning an increase in the promotional budget, both firms find themselves at a reduced level of profit.

Note that when both firms have increased their promotional budget to the $6 million level, there is no incentive for either firm to independently reduce the advertising budget, since this would lead to a loss of market share and net profits. Similarly, larger promotional budgets promise increases in net profit levels if they are undertaken independently. When each firm fears that the other may undertake a further increase in promotional expenditures we have the prisoner's dilemma all over again, and both firms will be motivated to spend the additional amount on promotion so that they will not be left standing still when the other's promotional campaign is launched.

Coordination of Advertising Expenditures

Is it reasonable to expect firms to coordinate their advertising and promotional expenditure levels? While firms may achieve an implicit agreement not to escalate advertising budgets beyond present levels, it is unlikely that they will achieve agreement to reduce budget levels to a point that would seem to be more efficient in terms of total profitability. In part this is undoubtedly due to the distrust that a firm may feel about reducing its own advertising expenditures while rivals may not in fact reduce theirs. Given the lead time required to prepare additional promotional campaigns, a firm that double-crosses its rivals could gain a market share advantage that might be impossible to regain.

A second factor militating against the coordination of advertising and promotional competition is that these activities are seen as an appropriate forum for the competitive instincts of rival firms, an avenue for civilized competition that should not be closed to the firms. Promotional competition requires skill and planning and the services of talented people. Price competition, on the other hand, requires little planning and not much skill on the part of the instigator, yet the impact upon the profitabilities of all firms may be significantly adverse. To avoid active competition shifting to the price arena, firms may prefer to compete on a promotional level where gains in market shares and profits are the rewards for exceptional abilities on the promotional side.

13.4 UNCERTAINTY IN ADVERTISING

In the above we have presumed that the firm can foresee the result of a given expenditure on advertising and promotion. In fact, $1,000 spent this month may be very effective in influencing the level of sales, whereas a similar amount spent next month may have virtually no impact. This may be the result of differences in the qualitative aspects of the advertising campaign, a different media mix, autonomous changes in consumer tastes and preferences, or similar changes induced by concurrent advertising campaigns of rival firms. Thus, we must expect a probability distribution of sales increases to exist following an increase in the level of advertising and promotional expenditures.

Predictability and Probabilities

Assigning the probabilities to the possible outcomes represents no small problem. The major issue is to predict the impact of the expenditures on the purchasing behavior of consumers, of course, but underlying this are the twin problems of understanding consumer needs and wants and predicting competitors' simultaneous offerings to satisfy these needs and wants. To increase the probabilities of increased sales levels for a given level of advertising, the firm should have a sound knowledge, through market research, of what tangible and intangible features the buyers want to see involved in the product. The firm's advertising and promotional expenditures should then be directed to informing the buyers of the availability of these attributes in this particular product and to persuading the buyers that the desired attributes can be *best* obtained through purchase of this product.

Modern marketing theory emphasizes that products and promotion should be aimed at segments of the overall market, where each segment is defined in terms of a common set of attributes desired by the buyers in that segment. The attributes that may be perceived and appreciated by consumers may be physically incorporated into the product (tangibles such as strength, durability, and other performance characteristics), or they may be intangibles that the consumer believes to exist (such as style, conferred status, and vicarious enjoyment of an agreeable lifestyle). Different attributes will be stressed (or invented) in the advertising campaigns for different segments, and some part of the persuasive element of advertising may relate to those tangible attributes that cannot immediately be verified by the consumer, as well as to the intangibles.

Once the market research has been conducted to ascertain the attributes desired by consumers and the perception of these attributes in the product vis-à-vis the competitors' products, the choice of message and medium (or media mix) will be selected by specialists in the advertising area and should be confirmed by pretesting and posttesting upon representative potential buyers. In summary, the better able market research is to identify the attributes desired by buyers, and the better the product and the advertising campaign conform to the desires of the target segment(s), the more confident the decision maker can be in assigning probabilities to the various possible outcomes of a given advertising expenditure.

Advertising as an Investment

The impact of an advertising campaign may not be felt simply in the period of that expenditure but should be expected to have a residual impact which gradually attenuates over subsequent periods. Potential buyers may be only partly convinced by a particular campaign, but this may build a necessary base for future persuasion. Alternatively, the campaign may convince consumers to switch to this product, but only after they deplete their personal inventories of rivals' products. Thus, a dollar spent on advertising now may lead to revenues in the same period, plus a stream of revenues in future periods. In this respect advertising can be regarded as an investment project and should compete for funds within the firm on the same basis as other investment projects with multiperiod revenue streams. The following chapter investigates the appropriate decision criteria to be applied when selecting investment projects to be undertaken, and advertising can be treated just like any other investment project.

The conditions for optimal advertising expenditure considered in the earlier sections of this chapter were generated under the implicit assumption that the total impact of the expenditure would be felt in the same period. This analysis remains sufficiently accurate if the residual impact of advertising expenditure is very low or if the time period used for analysis is long enough to include the greater part of the total impact. If there is a significant residual impact of advertising expenditures in subsequent periods, the present value of the future revenues generated must be included in the decision-making process. Current advertising expenditures may exceed the short-run-profit-maximizing level to the extent of the present value of the future revenues generated, before we could say that the firm's longer-term objective of maximizing net worth was not being served.

Advertising to Raise Barriers to Entry

It is widely supposed that advertising and promotional efforts operate to raise and/or maintain barriers to the entry of potential competition.[4] Repeated messages concerning existing firms and their products are said to increase consumer loyalty to existing products and cause consumers to be reluctant to switch to the products of new entrant firms.[5] To convince consumers that their products have comparable quality, reliability, and other

---

[4]Following J. S. Bain, *Barriers to New Competition* (Cambridge: Harvard University Press, 1956), many economists have argued along these lines. For a recent view and a comprehensive bibliography, see D. Needham, "Entry Barriers and Non-Price Aspects of Firms' Behavior," *Journal of Industrial Economics*, 25 (September 1976), pp. 29-43.

[5]Notice that this argument involves the residual effects of past advertising and promotional efforts. It is the sum of these residual effects that operates to enhance consumer loyalty to existing firms' products.

desirable features, the entrant firms may need to spend more on advertising and promotion at least over the first few years, as compared with the existing firms. It has been argued that the prospect of these additional expenses in an uncertain market for their products causes potential entrants to decide against entry because of the low or negative level of expected profits.

Thus, high levels of advertising by existing firms in a particular industry might be expected to allow those firms to continue to earn higher than "normal" profits, since entry is not attempted (or successfully accomplished) due to the expectations (or actuality) of significantly higher cost structures for entrant firms. Various studies have been reported in which tests were made for the empirical relationship between levels of advertising and levels of profitability. The results of these tests tend to be ambiguous.[6] A more recent and probably much more fruitful avenue of inquiry concerns advertising's function of imparting price and quality information which can be expected to increase competition rather than inhibit competition.[7]

13.5 SUMMARY

Advertising and promotional decisions within the firm are an important adjunct to the firm's pricing decision, and in some cases they become the firm's primary strategic variable. Advertising and promotional expenditures are expected to shift the demand curve outward and cause the price elasticity of demand to be reduced at any given price level. The advertising function should be expected to exhibit diminishing returns to additional expenditures as the marginal consumer becomes increasingly more difficult to convince and the market approaches saturation.

The optimal level of advertising expenditures is that level at which the incremental cost of advertising is just equal to the incremental net revenues associated with that expenditure. If these revenues extend beyond the current time period, they must be evaluated in present-value terms for comparability with the current advertising expenditures. The general (marginalist) rule for optimality expressed above applies both to situations where price is held constant and to situations where price is adjusted simultaneously.

In practice, several problems inhibit the application of the marginalist rule for optimal advertising. First, *ceteris paribus* is not likely to hold in many market situations as rival firms simultaneously adjust their pricing and/ or advertising strategies. Second, the impact of advertising expenditures cannot easily be predicted with any great degree of accuracy. This in turn is

---

[6]See the papers by Comanor and Wilson, Schmalensee, Peles, and Ayanian, which are listed at the end of this chapter.

[7]See "A New View of Advertising's Economic Impact," *Business Week*, December 22, 1975, pp. 49 and 54.

due to the uncertainty as to what it is that potential buyers want and whether or not the selected message and media will effectively inform and persuade the buyers that this particular product best provides the desired attributes.

In oligopoly situations the level of advertising and promotional expenditures may be taken to excess due to the uncertainty facing the decision maker concerning the simultaneous actions of rivals. Even when the future impact of advertising expenditures is taken into account, oligopolists unable or unwilling to coordinate their advertising strategies may be expected to spend beyond the point where profits (short- or long-term) are maximized. They must continue to run in order to stay in the same place, since any unilateral reduction in advertising expenditures would cause them to lose some part of their market share and would reduce the present value of their future profit stream.

Advertising and promotional expenditures tend to generate a stream of future revenues as new customers finally purchase the product and current customers return to purchase more units in the future. Advertising and promotional expenditures may therefore be considered as an investment in future revenues, and they should therefore compete with other investment projects for the funds available. This is the subject matter of the following chapter.

DISCUSSION QUESTIONS

13.1. Under what conditions may a firm expect *ceteris paribus* conditions to hold for changes in its advertising and promotional expenditures?

13.2. Discuss the idea of a minimum threshold of advertising and promotional effectiveness. Is it reasonable to argue the existence of such a threshold?

13.3. Why should we expect diminishing returns to (eventually) apply to advertising and promotional efforts? Outline several reasons.

13.4. What is the rule for optimal advertising expenditure in the short run, given price and average variable cost levels? Explain.

13-5. Outline the process underlying the simultaneous selection of the optimal level of advertising and the optimal price.

13-6. Why do oligopolists face a "prisoner's dilemma" problem when it comes to deciding on the level of advertising expenditures?

13-7. If firms decided to limit their advertising expenditures to a given amount, would this mean that market shares would then remain stable at the present levels? Why or why not?

13-8. Outline the issues involved in attempting to predict the impact of an advertising or promotional campaign.

13-9. If there are residual impacts in future periods from this period's advertising expenditure, is it necessarily excessive to spend beyond the point where short-run incremental cost of advertising exceeds short-run incremental revenue from advertising?

13-10. Outline the issues involved in the argument that advertising and promotional expenditures raise the product differentiation barriers to entry. Would these barriers exist without advertising? Why?

PROBLEMS AND SHORT CASES

13-1. The Thompson Textile Company has asked you for advice as to the optimality of its advertising policy with respect to one of its products, Product X. The following data are supplied:

Sales (units)	282,500
Advertising elasticity of demand	2.50
Price per unit	$ 2.00
Marginal cost per unit is constant at	$ 1.00
Advertising budget for Product X	$ 56,000

(a) Is Thompson's advertising budget for Product X at the profit-maximizing level?

(b) If not, can you say how much more or less it should spend on advertising? Discuss all relevant issues and/or qualifications you think are important.

13-2. The McWilliams Bottling Company bottles and markets under license a major brand-name soft drink. Prices of soft drinks are virtually dictated by the market and the preponderance of dispensing machines that require a time-consuming adjustment in order to allow price changes to be effected. In the regional market that it serves, McWilliams has noticed that quantity demanded responds to variations in the level of advertising and promotional expenditures. The firm has kept the following records of sales (units) and advertising and promotional expenditures over the past two years:

Last Year	Sales (units)	Advertising/ Promotion ($)
1st quarter	96,000	3,400
2nd quarter	103,000	4,350
3rd quarter	93,000	3,750
4th quarter	111,000	5,900
Preceding Year		
1st quarter	90,000	2,600
2nd quarter	76,000	1,850
3rd quarter	104,000	5,200
4th quarter	120,000	7,300

McWilliams's present advertising and sales (units) levels are $4,000 and 99,500 units. Contribution margin (per unit) is considered to be constant at $0.22. The marketing department at McWilliams feels that there were no significant changes in any factors that would prevent the above data from being used to reliably estimate the firm's sales/advertising function.

(a) Plot the sales data against the advertising expenditures and sketch in what appears to be the line of best fit to the data.

(b) Please advise McWilliams as to the estimated optimal level of its advertising and promotional expenditures. Explain and defend your recommendation.

13-3. Flintrock Fixtures is a small partnership that produces and markets a variety of kitchen and bathroom fixtures in ceramics, metal, and marble. The market for these products in

Flintrock's area is not highly competitive, since the rival firms tend to compete in separate market segments of the fixtures market. Over the past year, one of the major partners, Charles Flint, has been experimenting with advertising and promotional levels in order to ascertain the impact of this variable on sales. Regressing monthly sales revenue against monthly advertising and promotional expenditures, Mr. Flint has obtained the following regression equation: $TR = 110{,}482.5 + 2318.6A - 103.2A^2$, where TR represents sales revenue in dollars and A represents advertising and promotional expenditures in thousands of dollars. This equation was derived from data ranging from $1,000 to $8,500 spent per month on advertising and promotion. ($R^2 = 0.99$, significant at the 1-percent level.) The present level of advertising and promotional expenditure is $6,000 per month, and Mr. Flint, who wishes to maximize sales revenue, wishes to increase this to $7,500 per month, which is the maximum that Rocky Spinelli, the other major partner, will agree to.

A minor partner in the enterprise, Peter Pebble, is concerned with the short-term profits of the enterprise. He argues that given the firm's pricing policy of marking up average variable costs by 100 percent, monthly profits would be increased significantly by reducing advertising and promotional expenditures. Mr. Pebble argues that a reduction of at least $2,000 per month would augment profits considerably.

Another minor partner, John Stone, argues that the longer-term profitability of the enterprise is the appropriate objective to pursue and that he supports Mr. Flint.

(a) What level of expenditure on advertising and promotion would maximize monthly sales revenue, given no limit on this level? How confident are you about the accuracy of this prediction? Explain.

(b) What level of expenditure on advertising and promotion would maximize monthly profits? Explain.

(c) Make an argument to support Mr. Stone's position.

(d) Presuming Mr. Stone to be correct in his reasoning and Mr. Pebble to be outvoted, what do you suggest Flintrock do?

13-4. Record Breakers is a downtown store selling phonograph records and tapes. Its nearest competitor is about six blocks away, and its clientele is almost entirely composed of downtown office workers and other personnel from nearby buildings. Record Breakers has found that the sales of phonograph records vary with the number of records it places on special at $3.99 (compared with the regular price of $6.99) and with the space purchased in the city's morning newspaper for advertising these specials. The specials are intended to attract customers into the store where they will (it is hoped) also purchase one or more other records at the regular price. The greater the number of specials offered, the lower the total revenue per record, or average price of the records sold. Given any specific number of records on special, the store finds that record sales vary positively, but with diminishing returns, with the area devoted to advertising these particular records in the newspaper. Regression analysis indicates that

$$Q = 624.3 - 216.52P + 481.8S - 35.85S^2$$

where Q represents the weekly sales (units) of albums; P is average price in dollars; and S is space units (100 square inches daily for five days) in the morning newspaper. This regression equation is highly significant and explains virtually all the variation in weekly record sales.

The average variable cost per record is constant at $3 and space units in the newspaper cost $300, and this space is available in continuously variable fractions of a unit. The "average" situation is that Record Breakers will place six records on special and buy 2.5 units of advertising space each week. This causes the average price to be $5.75 over all records sold. The relationship between average price and number of records on special has been estimated as $Av.P = 6.93 - 0.19\ NS$ (with $R^2 = 0.97$, significant at the 5-percent level) over the range of one to fifteen records on special. This relationship holds independently of the units of advertising space purchased, although the latter does influence volume, as indicated by the earlier regression equation.

   (a)   Using graphical analysis, find the level of average price and the level of advertising space purchased that allow short-run profit contribution to be maximized.

   (b)   How many records should be put on special each week? Explain.

13-5.   Vincenzo Pizzeria Limited operates the only pizza place in town, although there are several other fast-food outlets in peripheral competition with Vincenzo. The manager, Vincenzo Fiorelli, feels that he has a virtual monopoly, since his clientele is largely comprised of fervent pizza lovers, and that selling more pizzas is just a matter of inducing people to "eat out" more often. Consequently Mr. Fiorelli holds prices constant and advertises in local newspapers and on a local television. His pizzas come in three sizes and with a variety of toppings, from "plain" (tomato paste and cheese) all the way up to "deluxe" (mushrooms, peppers, olives, ground beef, pepperoni, and heaps of mozzarella cheese).

   Mr. Firorelli's son Paolo has recently obtained his business degree and has joined the family business as marketing manager. Paolo is interested in maximizing profits of the enterprise, since his father has promised him half of any extra profits generated as a bonus. Paolo decides to conduct an analysis of the cost and demand conditions facing the firm. First he examines the cost structure. Given the three different sizes of pizza and the various combinations of toppings, the firm is in effect offering a very broad product line. Paolo's first task is to convert all the product offerings into the terms of a common denominator, which he calls a medium-pizza equivalent (MPE). The weights attached to each product reflect the relative variable costs of that product. Thus a medium-deluxe pizza is equal to 1 MPE, a small-deluxe pizza is equal to 0.75 MPEs and a large-deluxe is equal to 1.5 MPEs, with lower weights given in each size category where the pizza is less than deluxe. The average variable cost of an MPE is $2.65, and Paolo finds this to be constant in the relevant output range. The first major decision Paolo makes is to standardize prices on all pizzas by marking up the average variable cost by 50 percent.

   The marketing manager then undertakes a study of demand conditions. After examining past records and interviewing a random sample of five hundred customers and potential customers, Paolo generates the following demand function for Vincenzo's pizzas:

$$Q = 28105.1 - 5842.2P + 1061.6A - 22.5A^2$$

where Q is the number of MPEs demanded per month; P is the price of an MPE in dollars; and A is the advertising and promotional expenditures per month in thousands of dollars.

   At present, prices are as indicated by the above markup-pricing policy, and advertising and promotional expenditures are running at the rate of $8,000 per month.

   (a)   Using graphical analysis (with algebraic confirmation of results), find the optimal price and advertising/promotional levels.

   (b)   How much will Paolo's monthly bonus be? (State all qualifications and assumptions, if any, underlying your answers.)

13-6.   The Silk Purse Cosmetics Company operates in close competition with several other major suppliers of cosmetics and toiletries. In this market, consumers do not seem to be very price conscious: If they believe a product will help them, they tend to buy that product as long as its price lies below a limit that the consumer considers intolerable. Consequently, Silk Purse and its rivals tend to compete via their advertising and promotional expenditures, which are typically aimed at informing consumers of the virtues of their new and established products. Silk Purse's advertising and promotion budget is $25 million for this year, and it estimates that its rivals will collectively spend about $100 million this year. Silk Purse's net profits are projected to be $2.8 million this year.

   The vice-president of finance is worried that the expected profits this year will not be high enough to support the continuation of Silk Purse's research and development program, given that dividends, taxes, and managerial bonuses must be paid out of profits.

He suggests that a reduction of advertising to around $20 million would cause the profit situation to improve.

The vice-president of marketing argues that a reduction in the advertising budget to $20 million would cause sales to drop by $10 million, meaning a $1.7 million dollar reduction in net profits. On the contrary, she says, Silk Purse should increase advertising and promotional expenditures to $30 million. This will increase sales by $8.5 million and net profits by $1.2 million.

The president of Silk Purse, M.C. Hogg, fears that an increase in advertising and promotional expenditures of this magnitude will very likely cause a competitive reaction from the major rivals. You are called in to advise Mr. Hogg.

(a) With the aid of a payoff matrix, explain the vice-president of marketing's argument to Mr. Hogg.

(b) How does Mr. Hogg's assessment of the situation differ from that of the marketing vice-president?

(c) What information would you encourage Mr. Hogg to obtain before making his decision?

13-7. The automobile-manufacturing industry has three major domestic producers, one minor and several miniscule domestic producers, and several major foreign producers, each supplying vehicles to the North American market. Advertising and promotional expenditures constitute a large part of the competitive effort in this industry, once the product design and price levels have been determined for each model year. With a major purchase like an automobile, the potential purchaser must feel confident about the quality of the vehicle, the efficacy of after-sales service, and the future value of the automobile at trade-in time. Advertising campaigns typically stress these factors and are also aimed at reducing postpurchase dissonance and building brand loyalty.

Suppose you are the advertising manager of one of the very small domestic auto producers. Your company's sales have been hovering perilously around one-fortieth of one percent of the entire market. Your advertising budget is $1.5 million, and your projected net profits before taxes are less than $5 million. Your advertising budget represents 10 percent of sales revenue, compared with an industry average of 7.5 percent. Net profits are low, largely because of your relatively short production runs, which do not allow overheads to be amortized over large output levels.

(a) Prepare an argument to convince the marketing vice-president that your advertising budget should be increased. Include counterarguments to his probable objections in your proposal.

(b) Outline the information you would want the marketing research department to obtain before planning your major campaigns for this year.

SUGGESTED REFERENCES AND FURTHER READING

Ayanian, R.   "Advertising and Rate of Return," *Journal of Law and Economics*, 18 (October 1975), 479-506.

Brush, B.C.   "The Influence of Market Structure on Industry Advertising Intensity," *Journal of Industrial Economics*, 25 (September 1976), 55-67.

Clarke, D.G.   "Sales-Advertising Cross-Elasticities and Advertising Competition," *Journal of Marketing Research*, 10 (August 1973), 250-61.

Comanor, W.S. and T.A. Wilson.   "The Effect of Advertising on Competition: A Survey," *Journal of Economic Literature* , 17 (June 1979), pp. 453-76.

Cubbin, J.S.   "Advertising and the Theory of Entry Barriers," *Economica*, 48 (Aug. 1981), pp. 289-98.

Dorfman, R., and P.O. Steiner.   "Optimal Advertising and Optimal Quality," *American Economic Review*, 44 (December 1954), 826-36.

Kotler, P.   *Marketing Management* (4th ed.), chaps. 7, 15, and 16. Englewood Cliffs, N.J.: Prentice-Hall, Inc., 1980.

Leffler, K.B.   "Persuasion or Information? The Economics of Prescription Drug Advertising," *Journal of Law and Economics*, 24 (April 1981), pp. 45-74.

Needham, D.   "Entry Barriers and Non-Price Aspects of Firms' Behavior," *Journal of Industrial Economics*, 25 (September 1976), 29-43.

Nerlove, M., and K.J. Arrow.   "Optimal Advertising Policy under Dynamic Conditions," *Economica* (May 1962), 129-42.

Peles, Y.   "Rates of Amortization of Advertising Expenditures," *Journal of Political Economy*, 79 (September-October 1971), 1032-58.

Primeaux, W.J., Jr.   "An Assessment of the Effect of Competition on Advertising Intensity," *Economic Inquiry*, 19 (Oct. 1981), pp. 613-25.

Rao, V.R.   "Alternative Econometric Models of Sales-Advertising Relationships," *Journal of Marketing Research*, 9 (May 1972), 177-81.

Scherer, F.M.   *Industrial Market Structure and Economic Performance* (2nd ed.), chap. 14. Chicago: Rand McNally & Company, 1980.

Schmalensee, R.   "Advertising and Profitability: Further Implications of the Null Hypothesis," *Journal of Industrial Economics*, 25 (September 1976), 45-54.

———, *The Economics of Advertising*. Amsterdam: North-Holland Publishing, 1972.

Simon, J.L.   *Applied Managerial Economics*, chap. 7. Englewood Cliffs, N.J.: Prentice-Hall, Inc., 1975.

Spence, A.M.   "Notes on Advertising, Economies of Scale, and Entry Barriers," *Quarterly Journal of Economics*, 95 (Nov. 1980), pp. 493-507.

Telser, L.   "Advertising and Competition," *Journal of Political Economy* (December 1964), 537.

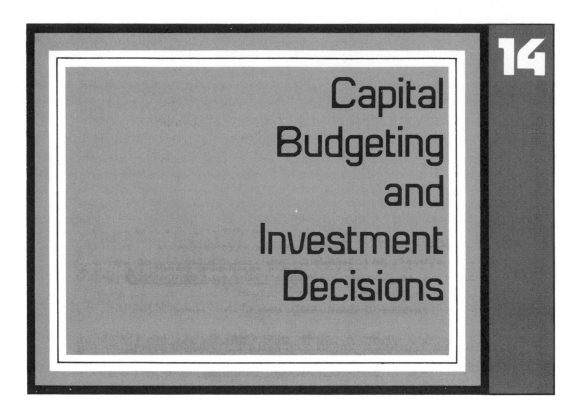

14.1 INTRODUCTION

DEFINITION: *Capital budgeting* is defined as the decision-making process concerned with the firm's decision (1) whether or not to invest financial resources and (2) how to choose between and among the available investment projects. These projects may be to replace or expand existing plant and equipment, to diversify the firm's activities, to take over another firm, to mount an advertising campaign, to put funds into bonds, or simply to hold the funds in liquid form for future investment projects. In general, the available investment projects will involve cost reduction, or revenue generation, or some combination of the two. Pure cost reduction investments include replacement of existing assets that are now relatively inefficient due to physical depreciation and technological obsolescence. Pure revenue-generating projects may be the investment in new-product development or advertising campaigns where these are treated as an investment that leads to a future revenue stream. Expansion projects typically involve both cost reduction and revenue generation, since newer plant and equipment is typically technologically superior to that being replaced.

Where there are no limits on the availability of capital, the capital-budgeting decision is simply to accept or reject each particular project. The following section establishes a number of criteria that allow the accept/reject decision to be made. Where some investments are mutually exclusive, in that they are alternative ways of achieving the same end or are alternative uses of available space or other resources, the available investment projects must be ranked in order of preference. The third section of this chapter establishes the criterion for ranking mutually exclusive projects. When there are limits to the availability of capital, a criterion must be established which ensures that the available capital is efficiently allocated between and among the possible projects so that the firm's objectives are achieved. Capital budgeting as an allocation problem is examined in the final section of this chapter.

You are already familiar with the basic structure of capital budgeting since it is essentially the same as the decision-making structure introduced in Chapters 1 and 2. In this chapter, we reconsider the expected-present-value decision criterion in the context of the investment decision and discuss new and related investment decision criteria. For ease of presentation, the analysis will be presented, for the most part, in terms of the firm's having full information about future costs and revenues associated with each investment decision. Thus, we speak of the net-present-value (NPV) criterion, for example, rather than the *expected*-net-present-value criterion. The analysis is easily modified for uncertainty—the single point estimates of future costs and revenues can be designated to represent the expected values of the probability distributions surrounding each expected future cost and revenue. Rather than repeat all the analysis of Chapter 1 dealing with decision making under uncertainty, this chapter introduces new material and presumes that you will have little difficulty implementing this in the context of uncertainty.

14.2 CAPITAL BUDGETING WITH UNLIMITED AVAILABILITY OF FUNDS

As stated above, when funds are unlimited the capital budgeting decision is whether to accept or reject each available investment project. This decision must be based upon whether or not each project contributes to the attainment of the firm's objectives. In the following paragraphs we shall take the standard view that the firm's objective is to maximize its long-term profitability, or its net worth in present-value terms. In some cases, of course, the firm's time horizon may be somewhat shorter due to cash-flow or accounting profit considerations. In such cases a less profitable project may be undertaken if it promises a very short payback period or relatively large immediate gains, in preference to a more profitable project that generates its income over a longer period of time.

We shall consider five separate criteria for the accept/reject decision. We shall examine the relationships between these criteria and show why some of these criteria are superior to others.

The Net-Present-Value Criterion

You will recall from Chapter 1 that *net present value* refers to the sum of the discounted value of the future stream of costs and revenues associated with a particular project. If the net present value of a project is positive, this indicates that the project adds more to revenues in present-value terms than it adds to cost in present-value terms and should therefore be accepted. Symbolically, we can express the net present value as follows:

$$\text{NPV} = \sum_{t=1}^{n} \frac{R_t}{(1+r)^t} - C_0 \tag{14-1}$$

where R_t signifies the contribution to overheads and profits in each future period; C_0 represents the initial cost of the project, including installation charges and any other expenses such as increases in working capital required by the investment; r is the opportunity rate of interest; and $t = 1,2,3, \ldots, n$ is the number of periods over which the revenue stream is expected. Thus, the revenue stream is discounted at the rate of interest that the firm could obtain in its next-best-alternative use of these investment funds at a similar level of risk. The revenue stream referred to in Equation (14-1) by R_t should be regarded as the net cash flow after taxes.

DEFINITION: *Net cash flow after taxes* can be defined as incremental revenues minus incremental costs, plus tax savings that result from depreciation charges that are deductible from taxable income, plus tax credits (if any) allowed against tax liability in connection with the particular investment project. If a tax credit (for example, 15 percent of the initial cost) is available for net investment, this will be deducted directly from the tax liability, and it thus avoids an outflow of a certain amount. Although this is not an actual inflow of cash, it is an opportunity revenue; the avoidance of what would otherwise be an outflow of cash in effect amounts to a cash inflow. Depreciation charges against revenues enter the cash-flow picture only indirectly and as a result of the tax saving that can be obtained by subtracting the depreciation charges from the income of the firm.

EXAMPLE: To demonstrate this, suppose an investment project involves an initial cash outlay of $10,000 and will generate revenues for three years, after which time it has a salvage value of $1,000. The value of the investment project to be depreciated over the three-year life of the project is thus $9,000, and for simplicity we use the straight-line method of depreciation to allocate $3,000 to each of the three years of the project's life. In Table 14-1 we show the calculation of the cash flow after taxes, given the contribution stream indicated.

We assume that the firm is subject to the tax rate of 48 percent: the tax saving shown as $1,440 in each of the three years represents 48 percent of the depreciation figure. The cash-flow-after-taxes column shows the sum of the contribution and tax saving for each year. The next column shows the

TABLE 14-1.   Calculation of NPV of Cash Flow after Taxes

Year	Contri- bution	Depre- ciation	Tax Saving	Cash Flow After Taxes	Discount Factors	Net Present Value
0	$−10,000	−	−	$−10,000	1.000	$−10,000.00
1	5,000	$3,000	$1,440	6,440	0.909	5,853.96
2	3,000	3,000	1,440	4,440	0.826	3,667.44
3	2,000	3,000	1,440	3,440	0.751	2,583.44
						$ 2,104.84

discount factors at an assumed opportunity rate of 10 percent, and the final column shows the net present value of the cash flow after taxes in each year and in total.

Note that the sum of the net present value of the cash flow after taxes is positive, and hence this investment project adds to the net present value, or net worth, of the firm. It should therefore be accepted and the firm should continue accepting projects for implementation until it is left with only those projects that have zero or negative net present value at the appropriate opportunity rate of discount.

Different Depreciation Methods.   The method of depreciation employed has important implications for the NPV of the investment project. In the above example we used the *straight-line* method of depreciation, in which the difference between the initial cost of the asset and its salvage value is allocated equally to each year of the asset's life. Alternatively, we might have used a method of depreciation that accelerates the recovery of the difference between the initial cost and the salvage value, so that the depreciation expense is largest in the first year and declines each year until the asset is fully depreciated. Two such methods are the sum-of-years-digits method and the double-declining-balance method.

The *sum-of-years-digits* method, as implied by its name, adds up the digits of the years that the asset will last and each year depreciates a proportion of the amount to be recovered equal to the ratio of the number of years remaining to the sum of the digits. In the above example the asset is expected to last for three years, so the sum of the years' digits is $1 + 2 + 3 = 6$. Thus three-sixths, or one-half of the total depreciation expense, will be deducted in the first year; two-sixths, or one-third, will be deducted in the second year; and one-sixth will be deducted in the final year.

The *double-declining-balance* method takes twice the depreciation rate implied by the straight-line method but applies it to the undepreciated balance remaining in each year. Thus, using this method we would recover two-thirds of $9,000 (that is, $6,000) in the first year; two-thirds of the remaining $3,000 (that is, $2,000) in the second year; and the remainder ($1,000) in the third year. Notice that both of these "accelerated" depreciation methods shift forward in time part of the net cash flow after taxes and thus increase the NPV of these dollars, since they will be multiplied by a larger discount factor when received earlier.

TABLE 14-2.　Impact of Depreciation Method upon Net Present Value

Year	Contri- bution	Depre- ciation	Tax Saving	Cash Flow After Taxes	Discount Factors	Net Present Value
0	$-10,000	—	—	$-10,000	1.000	$-10,000.00
1	5,000	$4,500	$2,160	7,160	0.909	6,508.44
2	3,000	3,000	1,440	4,440	0.826	3,667.44
3	2,000	1,500	720	2,720	0.751	2,042.72
						$　2,218.60

EXAMPLE:　To demonstrate this effect, let us rework the above example using the sum-of-years-digits depreciation method. In Table 14-2 we show half of the depreciation (that is, $4,500) being deducted in the first year; one-third being deducted in the second year; and one-sixth being deducted in the third year. The tax saving is now weighted toward the earlier years, which in turn have larger discount factors. Hence, the net present value of the same project with an accelerated depreciation method can be shown to be significantly higher than it was as calculated using straight-line depreciation. In fact, the accelerated depreciation provisions of the tax laws exist primarily to encourage firms to invest in new plant and facilities for the employment multiplier impact of such investment upon the economy. [1]

The Internal-Rate-of-Return Criterion

DEFINITION:　The *internal rate of return* (IRR) is that rate of discount that reduces the present value of the income stream to equality with the initial cost. It can be shown symbolically as

$$C_0 = \sum_{t=1}^{n} \frac{R_t}{(1 + i)^t} \qquad (14\text{-}2)$$

where the only symbol different from Equation (14-1) is i, which represents the internal rate of return.

　　Note that the internal rate of return will be that rate of discount that reduces the net present value of the income stream to zero. In the previous example we know that the internal rate of return exceeds 10 percent, since the net present value is positive at 10 percent. It will take a larger rate of discount to reduce the net present value to zero. We can calculate the internal rate of return for a given project by a process of trial and error. (This beats attempting to solve a polynomial function of degree n.)

EXAMPLE:　In Table 14-3 we show the process of iteratively calculating the net present value at various discount rates, zeroing in on the rate of discount

---

[1]See R. E. Hall and D. W. Jorgenson, "Tax Policy and Investment Behavior," *American Economic Review*, 57 (June 1967), pp. 391-414.

TABLE 14-3. Calculation of the Internal Rate of Return

Year	CFAT	NPV @ 20%	NPV @ 25%	NPV @ 23%	NPV @ 23.2%
0	$-10,000	$-10,000.00	$-10,000.00	$-10,000.00	$-10,000.00
1	6,440	5,364.52	5,152.00	5,235.72	5,227.27
2	4,440	3,081.36	2,841.60	2,934.84	2,925.24
3	3,440	1,991.76	1,761.28	1,847.28	1,839.61
		$ 437.64	$ -245.12	$ 17.84	$ -7.88

that reduces the net present value to zero. We start by testing for the value of net present value at the discount rate of 20 percent. This leaves a net present value of $437.64, indicating that it requires a larger discount rate to reduce net present value to zero. We then try a discount rate of 25 percent and find that the net present value at that discount rate is negative. Thus, the internal rate of return lies between 20 percent and 25 percent. We try 23 percent and find that the net present value is $17.84. Clearly, a slightly larger internal rate of return is indicated, and we try 23.2 percent in the last column of the table to find a net present value of a mere − $7.88. Further iterations would show the internal rate of return to be precisely 23.1415873 percent.[2]

RULE: The IRR *decision rule* is that projects with an internal rate of return greater than the opportunity rate of interest should be accepted and implemented by the firm. Given the availability of investment funds, investment in various projects should be taken to the point where the internal rate of return on the last project accepted just exceeds the cost of capital (the opportunity rate of interest for that project). Note that this decision rule is equivalent to the NPV rule that says to accept any project for which the NPV (when discounted at the opportunity rate) is above zero.

EXAMPLE: In Figure 14-1 we show a series of investment projects as the blocks A, B, C, D, E, and F. These investment projects are ranked in order of their internal rate of return, which represents the height of each block, and the width of each block represents the amount of capital required for the implementation of each project. The top of these blocks, shown as the heavy stepped line, is the curve relating the IRR to the level of investment expenditure.

The cost of capital to the firm is also likely to be a step function. Initially the firm will be able to utilize internal funds (undistributed profits), and the cost of these funds is their opportunity cost. That is, these could be invested elsewhere at a level of risk similar to that involved in holding the

---

[2]In case you are wondering how many iterations it took to find that answer, I must confess that my calculator is preprogrammed for the IRR calculation. Such calculators are becoming increasingly available at moderate cost and are, I think, an essential part of the business student's tool kit.

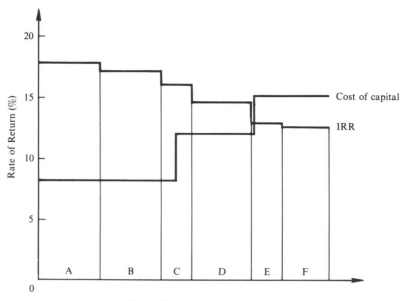

FIGURE 14-1. Determining the Level of Investment Expenditure

Level of Investment Expenditure

funds as undistributed profits, and the firm would wish to receive at least that rate by utilizing these funds in the proposed investment projects. After a point, however, the internal funds will be exhausted and the firm will need to borrow on the financial markets. We must expect the rate for such borrowing to exceed the opportunity cost of using internal funds, since the market will view the firm as involving at least some degree of risk. In Figure 14-1 we indicate that the firm's opportunity rate on internal funds is about 8 percent and that the firm can then borrow from the market (up to a point) at around 12 percent.

As the firm continues its borrowing in the financial market, however, the market will recognize the change in the financial structure of the firm and will at some point wish to impose a higher interest rate on loans to the firm. The greater debt-equity ratio (leverage) of the company as it continues to borrow in the market causes the firm to be a more risky proposition in the eyes of lenders. There is now a greater risk of default on the loans, and hence subsequent borrowing by the firm will take place only at a higher rate of interest. In Figure 14-1 we show the higher rate of interest demanded by borrowers to be in the vicinity of 15 percent. The top line of the blocks, which represents the availability of funds, may thus be regarded as the cost-of-capital line. It can be seen that Projects A, B, C, and D promise an internal rate of return greater than the cost of capital, while Projects E and F promise lower rates of return which do not compensate for the cost of capital. Thus,

TOPICS IN MANAGERIAL ECONOMICS

the firm in this particular situation would be advised to undertake Projects A to D only.

Relationship between NPV and IRR

It should be firmly understood that if the internal rate of return exceeds the opportunity rate of interest, the net present value of the proposed investment project will be positive. Using the example discussed earlier, we can plot the net present value of a project against all values that may be assigned to the rate of discount, as in Figure 14-2. To construct the net present value curve we have three points that are known to us. Point A in Figure 14-2 represents the net present value at a discount rate of zero. That is, when the future stream of profits is undiscounted (or discounted at zero percent), the project will have a net present value of $4,320, which we know from Table 14-1. The second point that is known to us, also from Table 14-1, is point B, which indicates the net present value of the project when discounted at an opportunity rate of 10 percent. The third point known to us is point C, which indicates the discount rate that reduces the net present value to zero. This is of course the internal rate of return, and we plot C at a discount rate of 23.14 percent.

DEFINITION: Thus the *NPV curve* is a locus of the points representing the NPV of a project and the rate at which it was discounted, for all rates of discount between zero and the *IRR*. Note that the *NPV* curve is not a straight line but is slightly convex toward the origin. We shall return to the net present value curve later in the chapter.

FIGURE 14-2. Net Present Value Curve

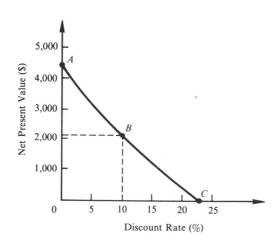

The Profitability-Index Criterion

DEFINITION: The *profitability index* is defined as the ratio of the present value of the future stream of net cash flows to the initial cost of the investment project. Symbolically, it may be represented as

$$PI = \frac{\sum\limits_{t=1}^{n} \dfrac{R_t}{(1+r)^t}}{C_0} \qquad (14\text{-}3)$$

Note the relationship of this criterion to the earlier formulas for the net present value and the internal rate of return. The profitability index is also called the *benefit/cost ratio* of an investment project or the *present value per dollar of outlay*. In the previous example with $r = 0.10$, the profitability index may be calculated as

$$PI = \frac{12{,}104.84}{10{,}000}$$

$$= 1.210484$$

RULE: The decision rule using the profitability criterion is to implement any investment project that promises a profitability index exceeding unity. Any such project will thus add more to the present value of revenues than it will cost. It will therefore add to the present value, or the net worth, of the firm.

There is no conflict between the net present value, internal rate of return, or profitability index for accept-reject decisions. If a project is acceptable under one criterion, it will be acceptable under all three. Thus, any one of these criteria could be employed alone for accepting or rejecting investment projects when capital availability is unlimited. We now consider two investment criteria which are commonly used in practice.[3]

The Payback Period Criterion

DEFINITION: The *payback period* is defined as the period of time which elapses before an investment earns sufficient revenue to cover its initial cost.

EXAMPLE: In Figure 14-3 we show graphically the determination of the payback period relating to the investment project we have been discussing. The initial cost of the project is shown at the $10,000 level and remains at that level over time. The undiscounted revenue stream reaches $6,440 at the end of the first year; $10,880 at the end of the second year; and $13,320 at the end

---

[3]For empirical evidence of the capital-budgeting techniques and criteria actually used in business practice, you are referred to the papers by Fremgen, Klammer, Mao, and others which are listed at the end of this chapter.

FIGURE 14-3. The Payback-Period-Investment Criterion

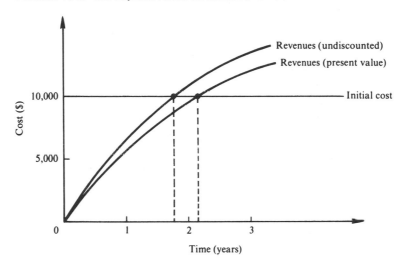

of the third year. Interpolating between these points we are able to generate a curve showing the nominal dollar inflow as a function of time. This curve crosses the initial cost line at approximately 1.8 years, which is therefore the payback period.

Note that the payback-period criterion in this form ignores the time value of money. To avoid this fundamental shortcoming we could plot the present value of the revenue stream over time, and we have done so in Figure 14-3. In present-value terms, revenues amount to $5,853 in the first year; $9,521 in the second year; and $12,105 in the third year. The curve representing the present value of the revenue stream intersects the initial cost curve at approximately 2.18 years, and this is the payback period when determined by present values of the revenue stream. In either case the firm's decision rule will be to accept projects that have a payback period less than or equal to a specified period required by the firm.

A second problem is that the payback-period criterion ignores the revenues that occur after the payback period of that investment. A decision is made based simply upon whether or not the investment pays back the initial cost before the elapse of a certain period. It would thus be unable to discriminate between two investment projects that had a payback period of, say, three years, but differed in that the net present value of one was substantially higher than the other due to a different or longer revenue stream.

NOTE: The payback criterion may be appropriate for decision makers or firms with short time horizons, in which case managers are more concerned with short-term profitability. Projects that promise an early return of the outlay and hence will contribute well to accounting net income in the shorter term would be favored by decision makers under such an objective function. In a crude way the payback-period criterion also acts as a screen against risky projects. Since uncertainty increases with the length of time into the future that cash flows must be estimated, the payback period selects the less risky projects at the expense of those that have longer gestation periods and longer revenue streams.

Reconciliation of Payback-Period and IRR Criteria. It can be shown that the payback-period criterion may approximate the internal rate of return criterion under certain conditions.[4] If the original cost is the total cost, if projects are long lived, and if the revenue stream is uniform, we can show that the internal rate of return and the payback criteria would rank projects identically. Where the revenue stream is expected to be uniform in nominal dollars, we can express the sum of this revenue stream as

$$\sum_{t=1}^{n} R_t = \frac{U}{1+i} + \frac{U}{(1+i)^2} + \dots + \frac{U}{(1+i)^n} \tag{14-4}$$

where U is the uniform annual net cash flow after taxes. The sum of the geometric progression represented by Equation (14-4) is

$$\sum_{t=1}^{n} R_t = \frac{U/1+i\,[1-(1/1+i)^n]}{1-(1/1+i)} \tag{14-5}$$

which simplifies to:

$$\sum_{t=1}^{n} R_t = \frac{U}{i} - \frac{U}{i}\left(\frac{1}{1+i}\right)^n \tag{14-6}$$

Or, in terms of the internal rate of return:

$$i = \frac{U}{\Sigma R_t} - \frac{U}{\Sigma R_t}\left(\frac{1}{1+i}\right)^n \tag{14-7}$$

The first term in the above expression is in fact the reciprocal of the payback period, since it is the uniform annual revenue stream divided by the total revenue stream. Where the project is long lived the second term will approach zero, since the exponent n will be large. Hence, the internal rate of return will approach the reciprocal of the payback period when projects are long lived and the revenue stream is uniform and when there are no other capital costs during the life of the investment project. Thus, decision makers using the simple payback criterion may not be too far wrong in some cases.

---

[4]See M. H. Spencer, K. K. Seo, and M . G. Simkin, *Managerial Economics*, 4th ed. (Homewood, Ill.: Richard D. Irwin, Inc., 1975), p. 449-56.

The Average-Rate-of-Return Criterion

DEFINITION: The *average rate of return* is defined as the average annual revenues (undiscounted) divided by the initial cost. Symbolically:

$$\text{ARR} = \frac{\left(\sum_{t=1}^{n} R_t\right)/n}{C_0} \tag{14-8}$$

EXAMPLE: In the example we have been using, the total (undiscounted) revenues from the project are $14,320: the average annual revenues are, therefore, $4,773. Hence,

$$\text{ARR} = \frac{4,773}{10,000}$$

$$= .4773$$

Note that this criterion ignores the time value of money and would therefore be unable to discriminate between two projects with the same initial cost and revenue totals, but with differing patterns of the receipts. If we modify the ARR criterion to include the discounted present value of the revenue stream, we have

$$\text{ARR} = \frac{(12,104.84)/3}{10,000}$$

$$= \frac{4,035}{10,000}$$

$$= .4035$$

Note that this result is exactly the profitability index divided by three, that is:

$$\frac{\text{PI}}{3} = \frac{1.210484}{3} = .4035$$

This should be no surprise, for the only difference between the PI formula and the ARR formula (using the present value of the revenue stream) is that the latter is divided by the number of years of the project's life. The additional step of averaging the income stream may obscure important cash-flow information, however. Thus the ARR criterion is seriously deficient in undiscounted form and can be regarded as inferior (or at least redundant) to the PI criterion even when the former is calculated using the present value of the revenue stream.[5]

14.3 MUTUALLY EXCLUSIVE INVESTMENTS

In many cases a firm will be considering investment projects that are mutually exclusive. For example, two or more projects may be able to perform the same function or will utilize the same space or other constrained resource, such as skilled labor within the firm. We defer discussion of investment projects that utilize the same funds to the next section, where limited availability of capital is discussed. Where investment projects are mutually exclusive, it is necessary for the firm to rank the investment projects in order of their desirability. It will then choose the project that contributes the most toward the firm's objective function.

EXAMPLE: Suppose a firm is planning to introduce a new product and has called for bids for the construction of the plant and physical facilities to manufacture that product. Let us consider two bids, which we will call Plant A and Plant B. Plant A is more expensive but also more efficient in terms of cost per unit and maintenance requirements, as compared with Plant B. The relevant cash flows and net present values are shown in Table 14-4.

It can be seen that Plant A offers the greater net present value when discounted at 15 percent. If the firm's objective is to maximize the present value of its longer-term profitability, it should thus choose Plant A, since this contributes more in present-value terms than does Plant B.

TABLE 14-4. Comparison of Costs and Revenues from Two Alternative Investment Projects

	PLANT A		PLANT B	
Cash Flow	($)	NPV at 15% ($)	($)	NPV at 15% ($)
Initial cost	−100,000	−100,000	−60,000	−60,000
Year 1	45,000	39,150	30,000	26,100
Year 2	55,000	41,580	37,000	27,972
Year 3	50,000	32,900	28,000	18,424
Net cash flow	50,000	13,630	35,000	12,496

[5]A variation of the ARR criterion is the accounting return on investment (AROI) criterion. The latter is calculated as the ratio of accounting net income (undiscounted) to the initial cost of the project. This criterion is clearly inferior to those discussed above, since it ignores the time value of money, is subject to ambiguity resulting from the several acceptable accounting methods of calculating net income (for example, treatment of depreciation and allocation of overheads), and moreover allows sunk costs to enter the decision-making process.

TABLE 14-5.   Calculation of Internal Rate of Return: Plant A

Year	CFAT	NPV @ 25%	NPV @ 20%	NPV @ 23%	NPV @ 22.8%
0	$−100,000	$−100,000	$−100,000	$−100,000	$−100,000
1	45,000	36,000	37,485	36,585	36,644
2	55,000	35,200	38,170	36,355	36,471
3	50,000	25,600	28,950	26,850	27,000
		$ −3,200	$ 4,605	$ −210	$ 114

The Superiority of NPV over IRR for Mutually Exclusive Investments

Let us now consider the relative internal rates of return of the two plants. Once again we need to find the internal rate of return by a trial-and-error procedure of zeroing in on the discount rate that reduces the net present value to zero. In Table 14-5 we perform this exercise for Plant A and see that the internal rate of return is slightly more than 22.8 percent.

In Table 14-6 we perform the search procedure for the internal rate of return to Plant B and find that the rate of discount that reduces the net present value to zero is slightly more than 27.2 percent. Thus, the internal-rate-of-return criterion would suggest that Plant B is preferable to Plant A, and it evidently conflicts with the judgment of the net-present-value criterion.

To see why this conflict arises, let us plot the net present value curves of both Plant A and Plant B, as shown in Figure 14-4. To plot the net present value curve for Plant A, we know that at a zero rate of discount the net present value will be equal to the net cash inflow (in nominal dollars) of $50,000. From Table 14-4 we know that at a discount rate of 15 percent, the net present value of Plant A is $13,630. Finally, we know that the rate of discount that reduces the net present value to zero is approximately 22.8 percent. Similarly, for Plant B we can plot its present value curve, beginning at $35,000 when the discount rate is zero, passing through $12,496 when the discount rate is 15 percent, and terminating at 27.2 percent on the horizontal axis.

It is clear that the net present value curves for the two projects intersect at approximately the 18-percent rate of discount. For discount rates below

TABLE 14-6.   Calculation of Internal Rate of Return: Plant B

Year	CFAT	NPV @ 25%	NPV @ 28%	NPV @ 27%	NPV @27.2%
0	$−60,000	$−60,000	$−60,000	$−60,000	$−60,000
1	30,000	24,000	23,430	23,622	23,580
2	37,000	23,680	22,570	22,940	22,866
3	28,000	14,336	13,356	13,670	13,608
		$ 2,016	$ −644	$ 232	$ 54

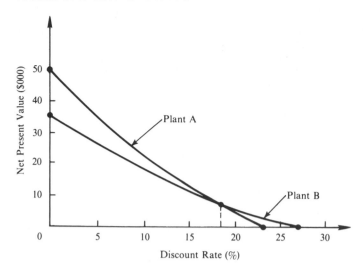

FIGURE 14-4. Net Present Value Curves

18 percent, the net-present-value criterion would suggest Project A, but above 18 percent the net-present-value criterion would suggest Project B. The internal-rate-of-return criterion, since it looks at only one point on the net present value curve, would suggest Project B under all opportunity rates of discount up to 27.2 percent. However, for actual opportunity rates of discount less than about 18 percent, the internal-rate-of-return criterion would suggest the investment project with the lower net present value and would thus lead decision makers to a suboptimal decision in terms of the addition to the firm's net worth, since Plant A clearly has the greater net present value at these lower opportunity rates of discount.

NOTE: Why does this conflict arise between the net-present-value and the internal-rate-of-return criteria? It arises because of the implicit assumption that the profit stream of each project could be reinvested at the internal rate of return. To see this, note that discounting a future stream of profits is the reverse of compounding a presently held sum over the same period of time at the same rate. At higher interest rates (namely, greater than 18 percent), the net present value of Plant B would compound to a greater value over the three years than would the net present value of Plant A at the same interest rates. The conflict with net present value arises because the calculation of net present value implicitly assumes the reinvestment of the profit stream at the opportunity discount rate rather than at the internal rate of return.

    As a decision criterion, we need the criterion that will always indicate the project that adds the most toward the attainment of the firm's objective function. Hence, the net-present-value criterion is superior to the internal-rate-of-return criterion for situations where mutually exclusive projects must be evaluated.

TABLE 14-7. Calculation of Profitability Index

	Plant A	Plant B
PV of revenues	113,363	72,496
Initial costs	100,000	60,000
Profitability Index	1.13363	1.20826

The Superiority of NPV over the Profitability Index

Let us now calculate the profitability indices for each of the projects under consideration. According to the profitability-index criterion, the plant with the higher profitability index should be chosen for implementation. The calculations are as shown in Table 14-7.

Note that the profitability index supports the judgment of the internal-rate-of-return criterion, by indicating that Project B is superior to Project A in this situation. However, it is inferior to the net-present-value criterion for the same reason that the IRR criterion is: namely, it would indicate acceptance of the project that contributes the lesser amount to the net worth of the firm in at least some cases and would therefore result in decisions that do not accord with the objectives of the firm.

NOTE: The conflict between the profitability-index criterion and the net-present-value criterion arises due to what is known as the "size disparity" problem. Where there is a difference in the size of the initial cost or in the magnitude and time pattern of the revenue streams, the profitability-index criterion and the net-present-value criterion may rank projects differently. If the firm's objective is to maximize its net worth, the net-present-value criterion must be used, since although the profitability index indicates which project is the most efficient at generating net present value, this is a "relative" consideration rather than the "absolute" consideration of maximizing the firm's net worth.

Thus, in general, it is preferable to use the net-present-value criterion for ranking mutually exclusive projects under situations of unlimited availability of capital. Both the internal rate of return and the profitability index may indicate the acceptance of projects that are not in the best interest of the firm's objective to maximize the present value of its longer-term earnings.

Capital Budgeting Given Limited Availability of Capital

The availability of investment funds should not, in theory, ever impose a constraint upon the level of investments. We saw in Figure 14-1 that although the cost of capital may increase as the level of investment is increased, the level of investment will be carried to the point where the marginal investment project has an internal rate of return at least equal to the cost of capital. Thus, if the internal rate of return exceeds the cost of capital, or the net present value at the opportunity rate is positive, or if the profitability index exceeds unity, the project should be implemented, since it will contribute to the enlargement of the firm's net present value. Where investment projects are mutually exclusive, the problem was to choose the one project of those available that would best serve the firm's objective function. The implicit assumption was that once this choice for this particular purpose was made, the firm would continue to consider other investment projects and/or groups of mutually exclusive investment projects and would implement those that met the acceptability criterion. In theory, the funds are always available, although at progressively higher rates of interest perhaps, and if the net present value is positive at this higher cost of capital, the investment project under consideration should be undertaken.

In practice, however, we often find the situation of a decision maker facing a constraint upon investment funds. It is common business practice to set investment budgets for departments or divisions within the firm, such that the decision-making unit faces a constraint upon investment funds. Setting investment budgets for individual departments or decision-making units, and/or for the firm as a whole, may reflect the reluctance of top management to take on additional debt, with its subsequent impact upon the leverage position and the market value of the firm's shares.

In such situations the decision maker faces an allocation problem, and should proceed to select the investment projects which maximize the return from that limited supply of investment funds. The projects should be ranked in order of their NPV, and implemented up to the point where the next project cannot be afforded. If any remaining projects (with positive NPV) further down the list can be afforded, by virtue of their lower initial cost levels, the decision maker should skip over the unaffordable projects and implement the remaining projects which can be afforded before the capital budget is depleted. The remaining funds, if any, should then be invested at the opportunity rate of interest.

Some Qualifications

The estimation of the future cash flows associated with investment projects involves techniques discussed in Chapters 5 and 8. Initial costs should cause few estimation problems, since they are to be incurred in the very near future and thus should be determined with relative accuracy. Future costs and revenue streams, however, are subject to uncertainty and thus may be accompanied by a probability distribution. The above analysis would need to be modified by insertion of the expected values of the net cash flow after taxes for each project rather than the point estimates used in the above examples.

Use of probability distributions and the resultant expected value of net cash flows after taxes for each year in the future involves the law of averages and could therefore cause the net-present-value criterion to be an unsuitable decision criterion for some investment decisions. "One-shot" investment decisions may expose the investor to the risk of a very low outcome, which cannot be averaged upward by other similar projects having outcomes above their expected values. Thus, we might expect the firm with a one-shot decision involving capital budgeting to apply the certainty-equivalent criterion, which allows the decision maker to place his or her own evaluation upon the risk and other nonquantifiable aspects of the investment decision, as explained in Chapter 2.

Differing risks of differing investment projects are adjusted for by the use of differing opportunity rates of discount. Recall that the opportunity rate of discount for any project is what the investment funds involved in that project could earn elsewhere at a comparable degree of risk. Thus, a firm considering a series of investment projects may discount these projects at differing opportunity discount rates if the degree of risk perceived to be associated with each project differs.[6]

14.4 SUMMARY

In this chapter we have considered the capital-budgeting decision, which is the decision to invest in plant, equipment, and other projects expected to generate a future stream of net cash flows. Given unlimited availability of capital, but typically with an increasing cost of capital, the firm should invest up to the point where the marginal investment project implemented has an internal rate of return at least equal to the cost of capital. This will mean that the project has a net present value that is nonnegative, or a profitability index of at least unity. When investment projects are mutually exclusive the three investment criteria mentioned above may give conflicting results, and we found the net-present-value criterion to be the only reliable guide if the firm wishes to maximize its net worth. Where the investment funds available are constrained, the firm would implement the projects in order of their NPV ranking, up to the point where the next project cannot be afforded. It would then implement any other affordable projects, and invest the remaining funds at the opportunity rate of interest.

The techniques introduced in Chapter 2 regarding the decision-making process under conditions of risk and uncertainty must be applied to the capital-budgeting decision, since there will be a probability distribution surrounding the expected values of future cost and revenue streams. Similarly, the techniques outlined in Chapters 5 and 8 for demand and cost estimation

---

[6]An alternate means of adjusting for differing risks is to reduce the period over which you will recognize the revenues from the more risky projects. See J. C. Van Horne, "Variation of Project Life as a Means of Adjusting for Risk," *Engineering Economist*, 21 (Spring 1976), pp. 151-58.

and forecasting must be used to establish the future stream of net cash flow after taxes for each project under consideration. Finally, it should be noted that the appropriate decision criterion in any particular firm is the one that best pursues the firm's objective function. If the firm has a long time horizon and wishes to maximize the net present value of the firm, the net-present-value criterion is appropriate under most circumstances. On the other hand, if the firm's time horizon is relatively short and management is concerned with accounting profitability, market value of outstanding shares, and other considerations involving immediate or short-term cash flow, the payback criterion or the average-rate-of-return criterion may be the appropriate investment criterion in these cases.

DISCUSSION QUESTIONS

14-1. Explain in three sentences why the NPV criterion and the IRR criterion must always agree on the accept/reject investment decision, given the availability of sufficient funds.

14-2. In calculating the expected net revenue stream associated with an investment project, what factors enter the calculation?

14-3. When comparing possible investment projects, why is it important to ensure that all projects have been evaluated using the same depreciation method?

14-4. Why is the cost of capital to the firm likely to be a step-function of the amount of funds demanded for investment purposes?

14-5. Under what circumstances is the use of the payback-period investment criterion appropriate?

14-6. Why is the average rate-of-return criterion inferior to the other investment criteria discussed?

14-7. Where projects are mutually exclusive, the IRR criterion may rank projects in conflict with their ranking by the NPV criterion. Why? Does this invalidate the IRR criterion?

14-8. Under what circumstances might the profitability index disagree with the NPV criterion in the ranking of mutually exclusive projects? Explain.

14-9. Suppose investment projects are divisible, in the sense that any part of each project can be undertaken, with the return being proportionate to the investment. Does this change the analysis?

14-10. Why can the payback criteria be regarded as appropriate, in a crude way, for a risk-averse investor?

PROBLEMS AND SHORT CASES

14-1. The Omega Investment Corporation has over half a million dollars to invest as the result of a recent windfall gain from the revaluation of a foreign currency it was holding. Failing all else, these funds can be invested in government bonds, which are considered to be risk free, at 8 percent per annum. Omega is evaluating four other investment projects as well. These projects seem to be equally risky and Omega feels they should return at least 10 percent per annum in order to be considered an equivalent proposition to placing the funds in the risk-free bonds. The initial outlays and net cash flows after taxes (NCFAT) for each year of each project's life are as follows:

Project	A ($)	B ($)	C ($)	D ($)
Initial outlay	100,000	135,000	85,000	122,000
NCFAT—Yr. 1	−12,200	26,300	56,000	−25,000
NCFAT—Yr. 2	−8,500	34,400	32,000	10,600
NCFAT—Yr. 3	76,600	48,600	18,600	48,200
NCFAT—Yr. 4	62,400	56,500	12,400	96,500
NCFAT—Yr. 5	23,500	22,000	5,500	34,000
NCFAT—Yr. 6	9,500	10,000	0	18,700

You are asked to advise Omega about which of these projects, if any, it should undertake. Explain your reasoning.

14-2. The Anderson Electronics Company is considering investing $1 million in a major advertising campaign. This expenditure will be tax deductible at the end of the year in which it is incurred, and Anderson's tax rate is 48 percent. It will take a year to produce the campaign after the million dollars is spent, and the impact of the campaign on sales is expected to be felt over the following three years. The precise outcomes are uncertain, however. The marketing research department has generated the following estimates (and associated probabilities) of incremental net cash flows after taxes that will result from this campaign for each of the three years.

Incremental NCFAT ($)	PROBABILITIES Year 2	Year 3	Year 4
50,000	0.05	0.10	0.25
150,000	0.10	0.20	0.35
250,000	0.15	0.40	0.25
350,000	0.35	0.15	0.10
450,000	0.25	0.10	0.05
650,000	0.10	0.05	0.00

The probability distributions should be treated as being independent from year to year (hence no conditional probabilities), and the NCFAT figures should be regarded as arriving at the end of each year. Anderson considers this project to be about as risky as investing the funds in the bonds of a large trust company which would currently pay 12 percent per annum. Assume that Anderson's tax assessment will be finalized one year after the million is spent.

(a) What is the net present value of this investment project?

(b) What is the internal rate of return of the project?

(c) Sketch the NPV curve against various opportunity discount rates and estimate from this the NPV if the appropriate discount rate is 10 percent.

14-3. Custy Canoe and Kayak Inc. is considering investing in a facility that would allow it to manufacture lightweight fiberglass sports kayaks. The proposed plant would involve an initial investment of $212,500 and would have an expected life of four years, after which time its expected scrap value would be $12,500. The marketing manager, Maureen Custy, expects these kayaks to become increasingly popular in future years, although other firms are likely to begin supplying competitive canoes within two or three years. Extensive market research and cost estimation studies have established the following (independent) probability distributions of the level of contribution to overheads and profits in each of the four years.

Contri- butions ($)	PROBABILITIES			
	Year 1	Year 2	Year 3	Year 4
10,000	0.05	0.05	0.10	0.20
25,000	0.20	0.15	0.20	0.30
50,000	0.40	0.20	0.35	0.25
75,000	0.25	0.35	0.20	0.15
100,000	0.10	0.15	0.10	0.10
125,000	0.00	0.10	0.05	0.00

Note that the contribution figures do not include consideration of the tax savings due to depreciation. For tax purposes, depreciation is calculated using the sum-of-years-digits method. The finance manager, Michael Gable, advises that the applicable tax rate is 48 percent, and that this project should be evaluated in terms of the alternative use of these funds to establish a camping resort area for canoe enthusiasts, which he considers to be of equal risk. The resort project has an expected internal rate of return of 15 percent.

Assume that the kayak plant can be purchased and installed at the start of this year, that tax payments or refunds are due at the end of each year, that the profit contributions are received continuously throughout each year, and that the expected scrap value is realized at the end of the fourth year.

(a) Calculate the expected net present value of the kayak project, taking care to use the appropriate discount factors.

(b) Using the same discount factors, find the approximate internal rate of return of the kayak project.

(c) Recalculate the expected net present value of the kayak project, assuming this time that all cash flows take place in lump sum at the start or end of each year.

(d) Explain why there is a difference between your answers to (a) and (c).

(e) In which project (kayak or resort) should Custy Canoe and Kayak invest the funds? Explain.

14-4. Marilyn Monibaggs is considering investing in a small shop in the downtown area of a large city. Ms. Monibaggs has not been lax in her investigations but has found that only two locations are feasible. Ms. Monibaggs is considering establishing either a sportswear boutique or a sporting equipment store, and she could put either type of store at either location. Location A is initially more suitable for the sportswear boutique, but the profitability of this venture will decline in the future due to the planned establishment of a major department store and other shops nearby. After this event the sporting equipment shop would be more profitable than the sportswear shop at this location. Location B, on the other hand, is close to several competitors in both types of merchandise but is frequented by a larger number of potential customers. The initial cash outlay will be $50,000 for the sportswear store versus $60,000 for the equipment store, and Ms. Monibaggs will pay a monthly lease on the location chosen. The net cash flows after taxes for each of the four alternatives have been carefully estimated as follows:

Year	LOCATION A		LOCATION B	
	Sportswear	Equipment	Sportswear	Equipment
1	$−18,000	$−24,000	$−24,000	$−30,000
2	37,400	26,000	32,000	28,600
3	26,200	28,400	33,500	30,800
4	22,400	29,800	34,300	36,400
5	20,800	30,200	35,000	38,900

These figures include the initial cash outlay for inventories which was incurred at the start of the first year. Treat the other net cash flows as arriving in a continuous stream throughout each year. Ms. Monibaggs is only interested in a time horizon of five years and considers the opportunity discount rates to be 14 percent and 15 percent for the sportswear and equipment stores, respectively, at location A; and 17 percent and 20 percent for the sportswear and equipment stores, respectively, at location B.

(a) What is the net present value of each of the four projects?

(b) Estimate the payback period for each of the four projects.

(c) Supposing Ms. Monibaggs is interested in maximizing her net worth but at the same time wants to get her (undiscounted) money back quickly in order to be ready to invest elsewhere if an opportunity arises, which alternative should she choose? Explain.

14-5. A consortium of business professors at a city university are thinking of investing in the takeout food industry. A location has been found which is considered to be highly suitable due to its proximity to thousands of downtown offices and stores, a major stadium, and two very large high schools. The professors are in the process of deciding whether they should go with hamburgers, chicken, or tacos as their product line. Extensive studies have provided the following estimated probabilities for various levels of net cash flow after taxes in each of the first three years for each of the three projects.

NCFAT	PROBABILITIES		
($)	Hamburgers	Chicken	Tacos
Year 1			
$−10,000	0.05	0.10	0.15
0	0.10	0.15	0.20
10,000	0.25	0.30	0.35
20,000	0.35	0.25	0.15
30,000	0.15	0.15	0.10
40,000	0.10	0.05	0.05
Year 2			
$−10,000	0.00	0.05	0.05
0	0.05	0.05	0.10
10,000	0.15	0.10	0.15
20,000	0.20	0.25	0.20
30,000	0.30	0.35	0.30
40,000	0.20	0.15	0.15
50,000	0.10	0.05	0.05
Year 3			
$ 0	0.00	0.05	0.00
10,000	0.15	0.10	0.05
20,000	0.20	0.30	0.10
30,000	0.30	0.35	0.40
40,000	0.20	0.15	0.25
50,000	0.10	0.05	0.15
60,000	0.05	0.00	0.05

The above net cash flows after taxes do not include the initial franchise fee of $50,000 for "Hamburgers"; $40,000 for "Chicken"; and $35,000 for "Tacos." They do allow for depreciation, however. The professors' time horizon is only three years, since they are all on three-year contracts at the university and expect their research and teaching efforts to suffer so badly that their contracts will not be renewed and they will have to go elsewhere for a job. Their collective judgment is that the opportunity discount rate is 15 percent for "Hamburgers"; 13 percent for "Chicken"; and 16 percent for "Tacos." Treat the expected net cash flows after taxes as arriving continuously throughout each year and the probability distributions as being independent of each other.

(a) Calculate the expected net present value of each alternative, assuming that the franchise fee cannot be recovered at the end of the period.

(b) Estimate the payback period for each project, using the undiscounted net cash flows after taxes.

(c) Advise the professors as to which project, if any, to undertake. Support your recommendation.

14-6. You have recently been hired as an assistant investment analyst in a small corporation which promotes new products and inventions. Your boss has asked you to evaluate and rank four potential investment projects. He tells you that the capital budget for the year is $105,000 and that anything left over can be invested in government bonds at 8.5 percent per annum. The details of the four projects are as follows:

	PROJECT			
	A	B	C	D
Initial cost	$35,000	$28,000	$16,000	$40,000
Expected NCFAT				
Year 1	12,681	9,650	8,480	22,680
Year 2	28,323	25,462	12,624	51,070
Year 3	36,084	31,836	28,970	28,218
Year 4	20,880	42,420	14,381	8,440
Salvage value	$10,000	$ 8,000	$ 2,000	$12,000
Opportunity discount rate	12%	10%	14%	15%

Your boss tells you that it is "company policy" to consider the expected net cash flow stream up to and including the fourth year only. He says to treat flows as if they were to arrive in lump sum on the last day of each year.

(a) Calculate the expected net present value of each project, and rank the projects in descending order.

(b) Calculate the profitability index for each project and rank them in descending order.

(c) Which projects do you recommend should be implemented if your boss wishes to maximize the expected net present value of the capital budget?

(d) What is the maximum expected net present value of the capital budget? Explain.

14-7. A large real estate firm has half a million dollars which it wishes to invest in urban-housing development projects. The available opportunities have been carefully evaluated and the four most promising projects have been thoroughly examined, with cost and demand estimates being supplied by a reliable group of consultants at a cost of $10,000. The projects are known as North, South, East, and West due to their locations, relative to the firm's main office. The relevant details are as follows:

	PROJECT			
	North	*South*	*East*	*West*
Initial cost	$120,000	$180,000	$250,000	$285,000
Expected NCFAT				
Year 1	$ 40,000	$ 62,000	$ 90,000	$115,000
Year 2	42,000	75,000	88,000	140,000
Year 3	45,000	81,000	84,000	132,000
Year 4	48,000	84,000	82,000	90,000
Year 5	51,000	80,000	80,000	75,000
Salvage value	$ 30,000	$ 20,000	$ 50,000	$ 70,000
Opportunity discount rate	10%	15%	12%	18%

Each project would be developed in five yearly stages, with all accounts being paid and all revenues being received from sales on the last day of each year. The initial costs shown refer to the cost of purchasing each tract of land, and this must be paid before any activity can begin.

(a) Calculate the expected net present value of each project and rank the projects in descending order.

(b) Calculate the profitability index for each project and rank them in descending order.

(c) Which projects should be undertaken in order to maximize the net present value of the funds available?

(d) What is the maximum net present value of the funds available? Explain.

SUGGESTED REFERENCES AND FURTHER READING

Ahmed, S.B. "Optimal Equipment Replacement Policy," *Journal of Transport Economics and Policy*, 7 (January 1973), 71-79.

Baumol, W.J. *Economic Theory and Operations Analysis* (4th ed.), chap. 25. Englewood Cliffs, N.J.: Prentice-Hall, Inc., 1977.

Clark, J.J., T.J. Hindelang, and R.E. Pritchard. *Capital Budgeting*. Englewood Cliffs, N.J.: Prentice-Hall, Inc., 1979.

Eisner, R. "Components of Capital Expenditures: Replacement and Modernization versus Expansion," *Review of Economics and Statistics*, 54 (August 1972), 297-305.

Feldstein, M.S., and D.K. Foot. "The Other Half of Gross Investment: Replacement and Modernization Expenditures," *Review of Economics and Statistics*, 53 (February 1971), 49-58.

Fremgen, J.M. "Capital Budgeting Practices: A Survey," *Management Accounting* (May 1973), 19-25.

Hall, R.E., and D.W. Jorgenson. "Tax Policy and Investment Behavior," *American Economic Review*, 57 (June 1967), 391-414.

Hirshleifer, J. "Investment Decision under Uncertainty: Choice-Theoretic Approaches," *Quarterly Journal of Economics*, 79 (November 1965), 509-36.

Jorgenson, D.W. "Econometric Studies of Investment Behavior: A Survey," *Journal of Economic Literature*, 9 (December 1971), 1111-47.

Klammer, T.   "Empirical Evidence of the Adoption of Sophisticated Capital Budgeting Techniques," *Journal of Business* (July 1972), 387-97.

Lorie, J.H., and L.J. Savage.   "Three Problems in Rationing Capital," *Journal of Business*, 28 (October 1955), 229-39.

Mao, J.C.T.   "Survey of Capital Budgeting: Theory and Practice," *Journal of Finance* (May 1970), 349-60.

Petty, J.W., D.F. Scott, Jr., and M.M. Bird.   "The Capital Expenditure Decision-Making Process of Large Corporations," *Engineering Economist*, 20 (Spring 1975), 159-72.

Van Horne, J.C.   "Capital Budgeting under Conditions of Uncertainty as to Project Life," *Engineering Economist*, 17 (Spring 1972), 189-99.

_____. *Financial Management and Policy* (6th ed.), chaps. 4-8. Englewood Cliffs, N.J.: Prentice-Hall, Inc., 1983.

_____. "Variation of Project Life as a Means of Adjusting for Risk," *Engineering Economist*, 21 (Spring 1976), 151-58.

Weingartner, H.M. *Mathematical Programming and Analysis of Capital Budgeting Problems.* Englewood Cliffs, N.J.: Prentice-Hall, Inc., 1963.

Appendix: A

A Review of Analytic Geometry and Calculus: Functions, Graphs, and Derivatives

Functions and Graphs

A *function* is an expression of the dependence of one variable upon one or more other variables. In *general* form we may write

$$Y = f(X) \qquad \text{(A-1)}$$

to read the value of Y is a function of, or depends upon, the value of X. Note that Y is known as the dependent variable, while X is the independent variable. The value of Y may depend on more than one independent variable, of course, such that we might express in general form the functional relationship as

$$Y = f(X_1, X_2, X_3, \ldots, X_n) \qquad \text{(A-2)}$$

In this multivariable function the value of Y is seen to depend upon the value of several independent variables, where n is the number of these independent variables. For example, the sales of umbrellas may be a function of the price of umbrellas, the income of consumers, the rainfall levels, the advertising expenditures of umbrella manufacturers, and the price of taxi fares.

The form of the functional dependence of Y upon the independent variables X_i, $(i = 1, 2, \ldots, n)$, remains unspecified in the above expressions. To find the exact nature of the dependence we must examine the specific form of the function. This may take a variety of mathematical forms: for example, Y may be a linear, quadratic, cubic, quartic, or higher-order function of X (or the X's) or it may be a power function, an exponential function, a hyperbolic function, or take some other form. Let us examine these in turn.

Linear Functions. The general form of a linear function is

$$Y = a + bX \qquad \text{(A-3)}$$

EXAMPLE: Suppose $Y = 4 + 0.5X$. In this example, $a = 4$ and $b = 0.5$. We can array the values for Y given the values for X, as shown in Table A-1. These values indicate the specific dependence of the variable Y upon the variable X. When X is zero, the second term in Equation (A-3) drops out and Y is simply equal to the parameter a. Each time the variable X is increased by one unit, the value of Y increases to the extent of the parameter b.

Let us plot the above values on a graph that has X on the horizontal axis and Y on the vertical axis. Using the pairs of observations for X and Y as coordinates, we are able to plot the equation $Y = 4 + 0.5X$ as shown in Figure A-1. Strictly, the graph of this equation would extend into three of the four quadrants, but we show only the northeastern quadrant where both variables have positive values, since for most economic applications these are the only meaningful values of the function.

NOTE: Notice that the graph intercepts the Y axis at the value of 4: Hence the parameter a is known as the *intercept* parameter. Similarly, the graph slopes upward and to the right at the rate of half of one unit of Y for each one-unit increase in X. The slope of the line (the vertical rise over the horizontal run) is thus equal to 0.5, precisely the value of the b parameter. Accordingly, b is often called the *slope* parameter. Thus, by observing the values of the a and b terms in a simple linear function, we are able to envisage the graphical form of that function.

For multivariable linear functions we simply extend the above analysis for the case of additional explanatory variables, such as

$$Y = a + b_1 X_1 + b_2 X_2 + b_3 X_3 + \ldots + b_n X_n \qquad \text{(A-4)}$$

TABLE A-1. Values of *Y* for Various Values of *X*

Values of X	0.0	1.0	2.0	3.0	4.0	5.0	6.0
Values of Y	4.0	4.5	5.0	5.5	6.0	6.5	7.0

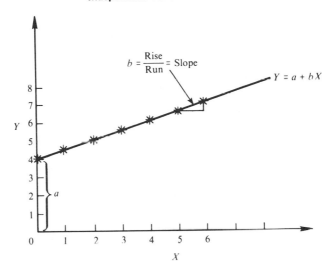

where the X_i, ($i = 1, 2, 3, \ldots, n$), represent several independent variables, and the b_i coefficients represent the influence that a one-unit change in the value of each independent variable would have on the value of Y.

EXAMPLE: A simple example of a multivariable linear equation is $Y = 2 - 0.4X_1 + 0.3X_2$. Substituting values for X_1 and X_2 into this expression allows us to obtain the values for Y, as shown in Table A-2. The values in the body of the table represent the value of Y for the values of X_1 and X_2 given by the coordinates of that value. Graphing the values of Y against the values of X_1 and X_2 we obtain Figure A-2, in which it can be seen that the above equation is that of a plane. Note that the parameter a is again an intercept value, or the value of Y when the values of the independent variables are zero, and that the b coefficients represent the slope of the function as we move one unit in the direction of a particular independent variable. Note too that the sign of b_1 is negative, indicating that the value of Y declines as additional units of X_1 are added.

TABLE A-2. Values of Y for Various Values of X_1 and X_2

		VALUES OF X_1					
		0	1	2	3	4	5
	0	2.0	1.6	1.2	0.8	0.4	0.0
	1	2.3	1.9	1.5	1.1	0.7	0.3
	2	2.6	2.2	1.8	1.4	1.1	0.7
Values of X_2	3	2.9	2.5	2.1	1.7	1.4	1.0
	4	3.2	2.8	1.4	1.0	1.7	1.3
	5	3.5	3.1	2.7	2.3	2.0	1.6

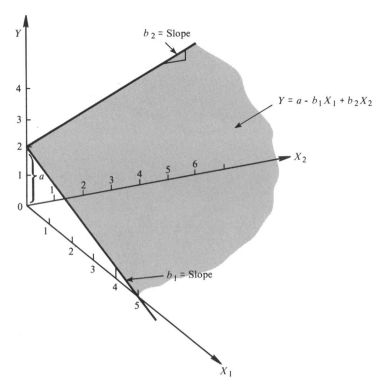

FIGURE A-2. Graph of a Linear Function with Two Independent Variables

b_2 = Slope

$Y = a - b_1X_1 + b_2X_2$

X_2

a

b_1 = Slope

X_1

Quadratic Functions. The above linear relationships represent what are known as first-degree functions, since each of the independent variables was raised to the first power only. We move now to quadratic, or second-degree, functions, in which one or more of the independent variables will be squared, or raised to the second power, such as

$$Y = a + bX + cX^2 \qquad (A-5)$$

Hence Y is a function of the constant a plus the constant b times the independent variable X, plus the constant c times the square of that independent variable.

EXAMPLE: Suppose we let a = 5; b = 3; and c = 2. We may calculate the values of Y for various values of X, as shown in Table A-3. Plotting these values as a graph, we obtain Figure A-3, in which it can be seen that the graphical repre-

TABLE A-3. Values of Y for Various Values of X

Values of X	0	1	2	3	4	5
Values of Y	5	10	19	32	59	70

FIGURE A-3. Graph of Quadratic Functions with Only One Independent Variable

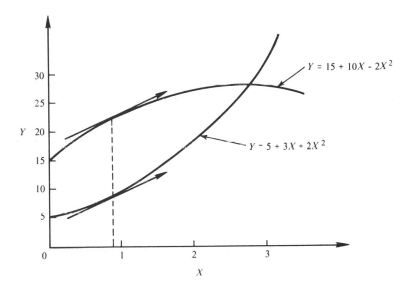

$Y = 15 + 10X - 2X^2$

$Y - 5 + 3X + 2X^2$

sentation of a quadratic function is curvilinear, whereas linear functions are rectilinear. Notice that the parameter a remains the intercept term, but the slope depends not only upon the value of X but also upon the square of the value of X. In Figure A-3 we show a second quadratic function, $Y = 15 + 10X - 2X^2$, and it can be seen that the curvature of this function is concave from below, whereas the curvature of the first function was concave from above. This results from the negative sign in front of the second-degree term in the latter expression.

When there are multiple independent variables and the relationship between these variables and the independent variable is quadratic, we may express the function as follows:

$$Y = a + bX_1 - cX_1^2 + dX_2 - eX_2^2 \qquad \text{(A-6)}$$

for the simple case in which there are only two independent variables, X_1 and X_2. This relationship is graphed in Figure A-4, where it can be seen that the negative signs preceding the second-degree terms indicate that the surface representing the function will be convex from above. Once again the parameter a is the intercept on the Y axis and takes a positive value. In other cases, of course, the parameter a may be zero or negative, just as the other coefficients may take values positive, zero, or negative.

Cubic Functions. We turn now to the third-degree terms in the functional relationship. Cubic functions may have first-degree, second-degree, and third-degree terms such as the following:

$$Y = a + bX + cX^2 + dX^3 \qquad \text{(A-7)}$$

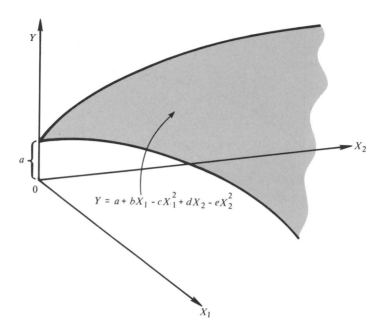

$$Y = a + bX_1 - cX_1^2 + dX_2 - eX_2^2$$

When all the coefficients have positive signs, it is clear that the values of Y will increase by progressively larger increments as the value of X increases. When the signs of the coefficients differ, the graph of Y may display both convex and concave sections, may have hills and valleys, or may simply exhibit a monotonically increasing or decreasing shape, depending upon the values of the coefficients.

EXAMPLE: Consider the function $Y = 25 + 10X - 5X^2 + 2X^3$. In Table A-4 we calculate the values of Y for several values of X. Plotting the values of Y against the value of X as in Figure A-5, we see that the above function is monotonically increasing yet exhibits convexity from above at first, changing at the inflection point to concavity from above. In the same figure we show the graph of the equation $Y = 100 + 5X - 10X^2 + 2X^3$ and note that it has sections of both positive and negative slope. This indicates that the values of the

TABLE A-4. Values of Y for Various Values of X

Values of X			0	1	2	3	4	5
Calculations	25	=	25	25	25	25	25	25
	$10X$	=	0	10	20	30	40	50
	$-5X^2$	=	0	-5	-20	-45	-80	-125
	$2X^3$	=	0	2	16	54	128	250
Values of Y			25	32	41	64	113	200

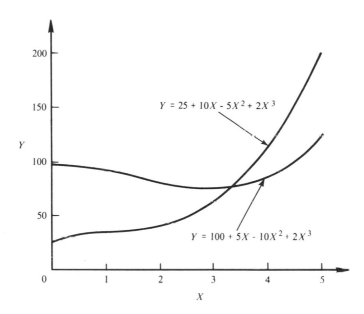

parameters are instrumental in determining the shape of the graphical relationship. The distinguishing feature of a cubic function as compared with a
quadratic function is that the former may have an inflection point (where
slope changes from convexity in one direction to concavity in that direction, or vice versa), whereas the latter does not.

Cubic functions in two independent variables will produce a three-
dimensional surface when graphed, as in Figure A-6. Again, the value of the
parameters and the signs of these parameters and coefficients operate to
determine the shape and placement of the surface depicting the functional
relationship.

We could continue the examination of functional relationships with
fourth-degree and higher-degree terms influencing the value of the variable
Y, but these are not necessary for an understanding of the material in this
textbook. Instead we shall turn to some other types of functions that are
useful to us.

Other Functional Forms. *Exponential functions* take the form:

$$Y = a + b^X \tag{A-8}$$

As you look at this specific form of the functional relationship, you should
appreciate that the value of Y will increase monotonically as X increases,
since the second term in the function assumes progressively higher degrees.
An exponential function is shown in Figure A-7.

FIGURE A-6.   Graph of a Cubic Function with Two Independent Variables

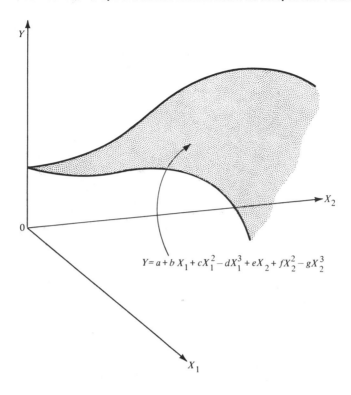

$$Y = a + b\,X_1 + cX_1^2 - dX_1^3 + eX_2 + fX_2^2 - gX_2^3$$

FIGURE A-7.   Graph of Other Functional Relationships between Y and X

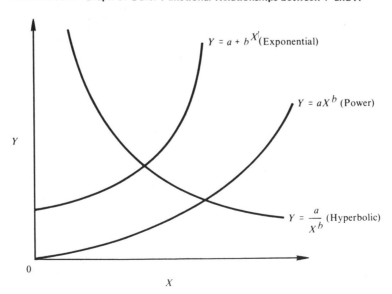

$Y = a + b^X$ (Exponential)

$Y = aX^b$ (Power)

$Y = \dfrac{a}{X^b}$ (Hyperbolic)

Power functions take the form:

$$Y = aX^b \qquad \text{(A-9)}$$

and can be seen from Figure A-7 to exhibit the general parabolic shape, as did the exponential and quadratic functions.

Hyperbolic functions take the general form:

$$Y = \frac{a}{X^b} \qquad \text{(A-10)}$$

In this case, as X grows larger the value of Y diminishes and approaches zero asymptotically, as shown in Figure A-7. You will note that hyperbolic functions are in fact power functions where the parameter b has a negative sign. That is, $Y = a/X^b = aX^{-b}$.

NOTE: A special case of the hyperbolic function is the rectangular hyperbola $Y = a/X$, where the parameter b takes the value unity. Hence $YX = a$ at all points on the curve. In verbal terms the product of the two variables is a constant at all levels of the two variables indicated by points on the curve. The rectangular hyperbola has applications in managerial economics such as the representation of the average-fixed-costs curve, since total fixed costs are a constant equal to the product of the number of output units and the average fixed costs at each output level.

Derivatives and Slopes

The size of the coefficient to the independent variable indicates the extent to which a marginal change in that variable influences the dependent variable. Examination of the marginal impact of one variable upon another is commonly referred to as *marginal analysis*. Economists make extensive use of marginal analysis when establishing normative rules for decision making. If Y is to be maximized, for example, the impact on the value of Y for a marginal change in the value of X is sought in order that we may decide to increase, decrease, or hold constant the value of the independent variable X. In general terms we would wish to know whether it was worthwhile in terms of the increment to Y to increase or decrease X. In terms of the graphical representations above, we are therefore interested in the slopes of the functions.

A mathematical technique that generates a slope of functions is one in which we take the first derivative (or differential) of the function. The derivative of a function shows the change in the value of the dependent variable Y given an infinitesimal change in the variable X, and is written as dY/dX, where d connotes the increment (or decrement) to each variable. For marginal analysis it is imperative that we consider small increases in the independent variable, since larger increases may incorrectly indicate the extent of change in the dependent variable. In Figure A-8 we depict a changing mar-

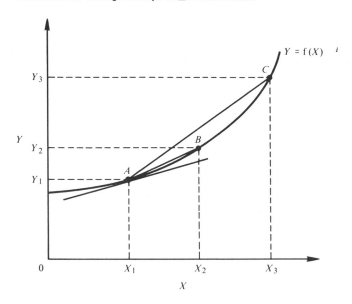

FIGURE A-8. Change in Slope as $\triangle X$ is Increased

ginal relationship between Y and X. Suppose that the values of X and Y are as indicated by point A in that figure. The marginal relationship (or the slope of the function) is given by the slope of a tangent to the curve at point A. But this is only a correct representation of the slope of the function for an infinitesimal change in the variable X. For larger changes such as to X_2 or X_3, the slopes of the arcs AB and AC are not accurate representations of the slopes of the function over those values of X and Y. They are in fact approximations or averages over the wider range of X and Y values. For decision-making purposes we are typically concerned with the incremental units of output (or some other variable) and hence require the more accurate marginal relationship between variables. It is therefore important that we understand the rules of derivation for use in optimization procedures.[1]

Rules of Derivation

Constants. Since the derivative shows the amount by which the dependent variable changes for a change in an independent variable and since a constant by definition does not change, it is clear that the derivative of a constant must be zero. Therefore,

$$\text{If } Y = a, \text{ then } \frac{dY}{dX} = 0$$

---

[1]These rules are stated without proof. See Baumol, *Economic Theory, and Operations Analysis*, chap. 4, 4th ed. (Englewood Cliffs, N.J.: Prentice-Hall, Inc., 1976) or any good introductory calculus textbook, for formal proofs.

The Power Rule. When the function includes a term that is raised to the first or higher degree, we use the power rule, which may be stated as follows:

$$\text{If } Y = aX^b, \text{ then } \frac{dY}{dX} = baX^{b-1}$$

EXAMPLES: To illustrate this, let us begin with a first-degree function such as $Y = aX$. Since X is implicitly equal to X^1, it is clear that the application of the power rule reduces the X term to X^0. Since X^0 equals 1, the derivative of $Y = aX$ is simply the coefficient of the X term. Thus, if $Y = aX$, then

$$\frac{dY}{dX} = 1 \cdot a \cdot X^{1-1}$$

$$= 1 \cdot a \cdot X^0$$

$$= 1 \cdot a \cdot 1$$

$$= a$$

For higher-degree terms the power function is applied similarly. Suppose $Y = a + bX^2$, then

$$\frac{dY}{dX} = 2bX^{2-1}$$

$$= 2bX^1$$

$$= 2bX$$

To demonstrate the power rule in the context of terms of various degrees, consider the function $Y = 5 + 3X + 2X^2 + 5X^3$. Treating one term at a time, $dY/dX = 3 + 4X + 15X^2$. (Is that correct? Confirm it for yourself, using the above steps.)

The Function of a Function Rule. In the case where Y and X are related through an intermediate variable Z, to find the change in Y caused by a variation in X we need first to ascertain the impact on Z of the change in X, and then multiply this by the impact of a variation in Z upon Y. Thus:

$$\text{If } Y = f(Z) \text{ and } Z = f(X),$$
$$\text{then } \frac{dY}{dX} = \frac{dY}{dZ} \cdot \frac{dZ}{dX}$$

EXAMPLE: If $Y = 4 + 6Z^2$ and $Z = 8 + 3X^3$, then

$$\frac{dY}{dX} = 12Z \cdot 9X^2$$

$$= 108Z(X^2)$$

A Review of Analytic Geometry and Calculus: Functions, Graphs, and Derivatives

The Chain Rule. Where Y is the product of two variables X and Z which are themselves related, and we wish to find the derivative of Y with respect to X, we must consider both the "direct" influence on Y of a change in X and the "indirect" influence on Y of the change in Z that the change in X provokes. Thus:

$$\text{If } Y = ZX \text{ where } X = f(Z),$$

$$\text{then } \frac{dY}{dX} = Z + X\frac{dZ}{dX}$$

Partial Derivatives

When a function has multiple independent variables and, consequently, each independent variable is only one of a number of variables that affect the value of the dependent variable Y, we take what is known as the partial derivative of the function for each independent variable. This is equivalent to the *ceteris paribus* assumption in economics; that is, we examine the influence of one of the independent variables upon the dependent variable while holding all other variables constant. The partial derivative thus shows the impact upon Y of an infinitesimal change in one of the independent variables while all other independent variables are held constant. By convention, and to distinguish it from the derivative of functions with only one independent variable, we depict the partial derivatives by the lowercase delta (δ), rather than the lowercase d as used above. Thus if Y is a function of several variables such as

$$Y = a + bX + cX^2 + dZ + eZ^2 + fQ^3$$

$$\text{then } \frac{\delta Y}{\delta X} = b + 2cX$$

$$\text{and } \frac{\delta Y}{\delta Z} = d + 2eZ$$

$$\text{and } \frac{\delta Y}{\delta Q} = 3fQ^2$$

Each partial derivative shows the marginal impact of one of the independent variables upon the dependent variable while holding constant the impact of the other independent variables.

Maximum and Minimum Values of Functions

In the above we have been concerned with "first" derivatives, which show the slope of the function as the independent variable (or *one* of the independent variables) is varied by a small amount. The first derivative thus shows the rate of change of the dependent variable relative to the specified

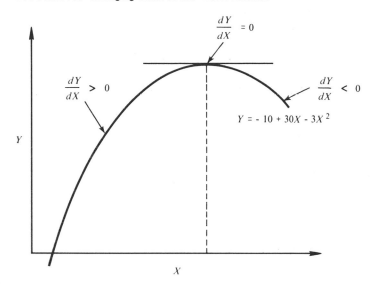

independent variable. With curvilinear functions that rate of change will vary for different starting points in the value of X. In Figure A-9 the quadratic function $Y = -10 + 30X - 3X^2$ is graphed, and it should be appreciated that the derivative of the function is positive initially where the graph is sloping upward and to the right, but it is negative later where the value of Y decreases as additional increments of X are made. It is clear that the derivative is taking progressively declining values, being positive at first, falling to zero, and thereafter becoming increasingly negative. You may confirm this by taking the derivative of the above-mentioned function—viz., $dY/dX = 30 - 6X$—and substituting values for X into this expression. Clearly for values of X less than 5 the derivative is positive, but where X is equal to 5 the derivative is zero, and for values of X greater than 5 the derivative is negative.

RULE: The above discussion allows us to establish a simple rule for finding the maximum of a function. To find the value of X for which Y is maximized, we simply set the derivative of the function equal to zero and solve for the value of X. Thus where we have

$$\frac{dY}{dX} = 30 - 6X = 0$$

Solving for X,

$$6X = 30$$

$$X = 5$$

Thus Y is at a maximum when X takes the value of 5.

NOTE: A zero first derivative may indicate a *minimum* of a function rather than a maximum if the function is concave from above rather than concave from below. Suppose

$$Y = 100 - 16X + 2X^2$$

The first derivative of this function is

$$\frac{dY}{dX} = -16 + 4X$$

and is equal to zero when

$$X = 4.$$

Inspection of the function should indicate to you that it is a parabola that is concave from above, since for small values of X it will be falling, reaching a minimum when X equals 4, and it will rise progressively more steeply for higher values of X. In more complex functions, however, the shape of the function may not be obvious from inspection, and thus we must check whether the zero first derivative implies a maximum or a minimum by means of taking the *second* derivative of the function.

Second Derivatives

DEFINITION: The *second derivative* of a function is simply the derivative of the first derivative of that function. Since the first derivative indicated the rate of change of the function, the second derivative indicates the rate of change of the rate of change of the function. If the second derivative is negative, this indicates that the rate of change is falling. Referring to Figure A-9 we can see that the negative second derivative indicates that the curve is concave from below (or convex from above), since the first derivative at low values of X starts at a relatively high number and progressively falls to zero and then to negative values. Alternatively, if the curve was concave from above, the first derivative would be negative at first, rising to progressively smaller negative values, passing through zero and taking on progressively increasing positive values as X is increased. Thus we can say that the sign of the second derivative will be negative when the first derivative is set equal to zero if the function is concave from below and that the sign of the second derivative will be positive when the first derivative is set equal to zero when the function is concave from above.

RULE: Thus, the "second-order" condition for a maximum is that the second derivative must be negative, and the second-order condition for a minimum is that the second derivative must be positive.

Referring back to the function graphed in Figure A-9, where the first derivative was $dY/dX = 30 - 6X$, we may confirm that the sign of the second derivative is negative. The second derivative is equal to the derivative of the first derivative and is expressed as follows:

$$\frac{d^2Y}{dX^2} = -6$$

where the squared terms indicate that the value shown is the second derivative of the function. For the other function mentioned above, the first derivative was $dY/dX = -16 + 4X$. The second derivative of this derivative is equal to

$$\frac{d^2Y}{dX^2} = 4$$

The signs of these second derivatives confirm that the function of Y reaches a *maximum* in the first case when $dY/dX = 0$ and that it reaches a *minimum* in the second case when the first derivative is set equal to zero.

Use of Derivatives in Managerial Economics

Since one of the central aims of managerial economics is to establish rules and principles for achieving objectives, it is not surprising that derivatives may be helpful, since in many cases we are interested in maximizing profits, or minimizing costs, or optimizing some other variable.

EXAMPLE: Suppose that a particular firm's cost and revenue functions are of quadratic form as follows:

$$TC = 1500 + 50Q + 2Q^2 \tag{A-11}$$

$$TR = 250Q - 3Q^2 \tag{A-12}$$

where TC represents total costs; TR represents total revenues; and Q represents the output or sales level. Profits, represented by π, are the surplus of revenues over costs. Hence,

$$\pi = TR - TC$$
$$= 250Q - 3Q^2 - (1500 + 50Q + 2Q^2)$$
$$= 250Q - 3Q^2 - 1500 - 50Q - 2Q^2$$
$$\therefore \pi = -1500 + 200Q - 5Q^2 \tag{A-13}$$

represents the profit function. Assuming that the firm wishes to choose the output level that maximizes profits, we may find that output level by setting the first derivative of the profit function equal to zero and solving for Q. Thus,

$$\frac{d\pi}{dQ} = 200 - 10Q = 0$$

$$10Q = 200$$

$$Q = 20$$

The output level that appears to maximize profits is thus 20 units (where the "units" may represent single units, thousands, or millions, depending upon the initial specification of those units). To ensure that this output level represents the maximum profit rather than the minimum profit, we check the second-order condition. The second derivative of the profit function,

$$\frac{d^2\pi}{d^2Q} = -10$$

is negative, indicating that profits are indeed maximized at the output level of 20 units.

An alternative approach to finding the profit-maximizing output level using derivatives is as follows. We know that profits will be maximized when the difference between revenues and costs is greatest. In terms of Figure A-10, where the cost and revenue functions are depicted, we wish to find the output level for which the vertical separation of the two curves is greatest.

Observe that the slope (or derivative) of the cost function takes increasingly larger values as output is increased, while the slope of the revenue function takes increasingly reduced values. At some point the slopes of the two functions will be equal, and hence tangents to the two functions at that output level must be parallel lines, as shown in Figure A-10. Since a property of parallel lines is that they maintain a constant vertical separation, it must be true that as the slope of the cost function continues to increase and as the slope of the revenue function continues to decrease for larger output levels, the vertical distance between the two functions must be decreasing. Thus, profits are maximized when the slopes (or first derivatives) of the functions are equal.

To solve for the output level where the slopes (first derivatives) are equal, let us restate the cost and revenue functions:

$$TC = 1500 + 50Q + 2Q^2 \tag{A-11}$$

$$TR = 250Q - 3Q^2 \tag{A-12}$$

Finding the first derivatives of these functions, equating them, and solving for Q, we have

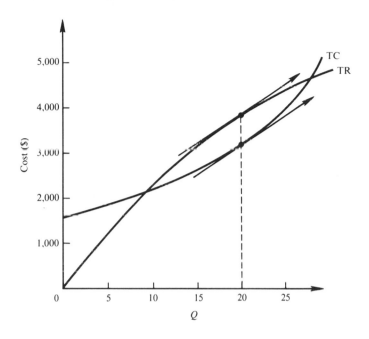

$$\frac{d\text{TC}}{dQ} = 50 + 4Q$$

$$\frac{d\text{TR}}{dQ} = 250 - 6Q$$

Set

$$\frac{d\text{TC}}{dQ} = \frac{d\text{TR}}{dQ}$$

$$50 + 4Q = 250 - 6Q$$

$$10Q = 200$$

$$Q = 20$$

Not surprisingly this alternate approach gives the same profit-maximizing output level as did the initial approach. The latter approach has received some fame (or notoriety) in economics as the "marginalist principle," whereby marginal cost (the increment to total cost for a one-unit change in output level) is set equal to marginal revenue (the increment to total revenue for a one-unit increase in output or sales level). We discuss this in the context of different market situations in Chapters 9 and 10.

DISCUSSION QUESTIONS

A-1. Define the following terms:
   (a) function
   (b) independent variable
   (c) dependent variable
   (d) slope parameter
   (e) constant
   (f) intercept
   (g) quadratic function
   (h) exponent.

A-2. Explain the logic of using the derivatives of a function to find the maximum or minimum of that function.

A-3. Explain the power rule of differentiation.

A-4. Explain the function-of-a-function rule of differentiation.

A-5. Explain the chain rule of differentiation.

PROBLEMS AND SHORT CASES

A-1. Rewrite $Y = f(X)$ in symbolic form as a function that is
   (a) linear
   (b) quadratic
   (c) cubic
   (d) exponential
   (e) power
   (f) hyperbolic

A-2. Find the first derivative, with respect to X, of the following functions:
   (a) $Y = 36 + 4.5X^3$
   (b) $Y = 8 - 3Z^2$, where $Z = 4 + 3X^3$
   (c) $Y = 7KX$, where $X = 3 - 2K^2$
   (d) $Y = -16 + 4J^2 - 6K^3$, where $J = 8 - 6X^2$ and $K = -3 + 4X^3$
   (e) $Y = 3M\,(4N^2)$, where $M = -6 + 2X$ and $N = 4 - 2X^2$
   (f) $Y = 4e^{2X}$

A-3. Solve for the maximum or minimum value of the following functions, using the second-order condition to specify whether it is a maximum or a minimum:
   (a) $Y = -32 + 6X - 2X^2$
   (b) $Y = 28 - 8X + X^2$
   (c) $A = 4285 - 625B + 5B^2$
   (d) $K = 178 + 40J - 6J^2$

A-4. Suppose the monthly cost of maintaining a certain machine in operating order is a function of the time elapsed between shutdowns for servicing and maintenance as follows: $C = 1400 - 30T + 0.7T^2$ where C represents cost in dollars and T represents time between services in hours. What is the optimal period between services?

SUGGESTED REFERENCES AND FURTHER READING

Baumol, W. J. *Economic Theory and Operations Analysis* (4th ed.), chaps. 2, 3, and 4. Englewood Cliffs, N.J.: Prentice-Hall, Inc., 1976.

Childress, R. L. *Calculus for Business and Economics* (2nd Ed.), Englewood Cliffs, N.J.: Prentice-Hall, Inc., 1978.

Khoury, S. J., and T. D. Parsons. *Mathematical Methods in Finance and Economics*, New York: Elsevier-North Holland, Inc., 1981.

Kooros, A. *Elements of Mathematical Economics*, chaps. 1, 2, 5, 6, and 7. Boston: Houghton Mifflin, 1965.

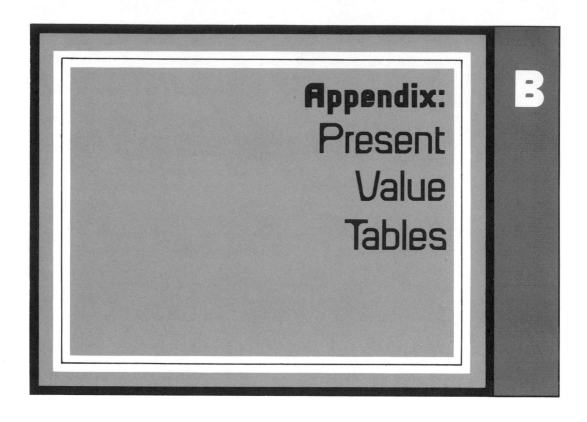

I wish to express my thanks to Deena Eliosoff and Brian Chernoff for their assistance with the mathematics, the programming, and the generation of the following tables.

TABLE B-1. Present Value of $1 Received at the End of N Years

DISCOUNT RATE

Years Hence	1%	2%	3%	4%	5%	6%	7%	8%	9%	10%	11%	12%	13%	14%
1	.9901	.9804	.9709	.9615	.9524	.9434	.9346	.9259	.9174	.9091	.9009	.8929	.8850	.8772
2	.9803	.9612	.9426	.9246	.9070	.8900	.8734	.8573	.8417	.8264	.8116	.7972	.7831	.7695
3	.9706	.9423	.9151	.8890	.8638	.8396	.8163	.7938	.7722	.7513	.7312	.7118	.6931	.6750
4	.9610	.9238	.8885	.8548	.8227	.7921	.7629	.7350	.7084	.6830	.6587	.6355	.6133	.5921
5	.9515	.9057	.8626	.8219	.7835	.7473	.7130	.6806	.6499	.6209	.5935	.5674	.5428	.5194
6	.9420	.8880	.8375	.7903	.7462	.7050	.6663	.6302	.5963	.5645	.5346	.5066	.4803	.4556
7	.9327	.8706	.8131	.7599	.7107	.6651	.6227	.5835	.5470	.5132	.4817	.4523	.4251	.3996
8	.9235	.8535	.7894	.7307	.6768	.6274	.5820	.5403	.5019	.4665	.4339	.4039	.3762	.3506
9	.9143	.8368	.7664	.7026	.6446	.5919	.5439	.5002	.4604	.4241	.3909	.3606	.3329	.3075
10	.9053	.8203	.7441	.6756	.6139	.5584	.5083	.4632	.4224	.3855	.3522	.3220	.2946	.2697
11	.8963	.8043	.7224	.6496	.5847	.5268	.4751	.4289	.3875	.3505	.3173	.2875	.2607	.2366
12	.8874	.7885	.7014	.6246	.5568	.4970	.4440	.3971	.3555	.3186	.2858	.2567	.2307	.2076
13	.8787	.7730	.6810	.6006	.5303	.4688	.4150	.3677	.3262	.2897	.2575	.2292	.2042	.1821
14	.8700	.7579	.6611	.5775	.5051	.4423	.3878	.3405	.2992	.2633	.2320	.2046	.1807	.1597
15	.8613	.7430	.6419	.5553	.4810	.4173	.3624	.3152	.2745	.2394	.2090	.1827	.1599	.1401
16	.8528	.7284	.6232	.5339	.4581	.3936	.3387	.2919	.2519	.2176	.1883	.1631	.1415	.1229
17	.8444	.7142	.6050	.5134	.4363	.3714	.3166	.2703	.2311	.1978	.1696	.1456	.1252	.1078
18	.8360	.7002	.5874	.4936	.4155	.3503	.2959	.2502	.2120	.1799	.1528	.1300	.1108	.0946
19	.8277	.6864	.5703	.4746	.3957	.3305	.2765	.2317	.1945	.1635	.1377	.1161	.0981	.0829
20	.8195	.6730	.5537	.4564	.3769	.3118	.2584	.2145	.1784	.1486	.1240	.1037	.0868	.0728
21	.8114	.6598	.5375	.4388	.3589	.2942	.2415	.1987	.1637	.1351	.1117	.0926	.0768	.0638
22	.8034	.6468	.5219	.4220	.3418	.2775	.2257	.1839	.1502	.1228	.1007	.0826	.0680	.0560
23	.7954	.6342	.5067	.4057	.3256	.2618	.2109	.1703	.1378	.1117	.0907	.0738	.0601	.0491
24	.7876	.6217	.4919	.3901	.3101	.2470	.1971	.1577	.1264	.1015	.0817	.0659	.0532	.0431
25	.7798	.6095	.4776	.3751	.2953	.2330	.1842	.1460	.1160	.0923	.0736	.0588	.0471	.0378

TABLE B-1.—Continued

							DISCOUNT RATE							
Years Hence	15%	16%	17%	18%	19%	20%	21%	22%	23%	24%	25%	26%	27%	28%
1	.8696	.8621	.8547	.8475	.8403	.8333	.8264	.8197	.8130	.8065	.8000	.7937	.7874	.7813
2	.7561	.7432	.7305	.7182	.7062	.6944	.6830	.6719	.6610	.6504	.6400	.6299	.6200	.6104
3	.6575	.6407	.6244	.6086	.5934	.5787	.5645	.5507	.5374	.5245	.5120	.4999	.4882	.4768
4	.5718	.5523	.5337	.5158	.4987	.4823	.4665	.4514	.4369	.4230	.4096	.3968	.3844	.3725
5	.4972	.4761	.4561	.4371	.4190	.4019	.3855	.3700	.3552	.3411	.3277	.3149	.3027	.2910
6	.4323	.4104	.3898	.3704	.3521	.3349	.3186	.3033	.2888	.2751	.2621	.2499	.2383	.2274
7	.3759	.3538	.3332	.3139	.2959	.2791	.2633	.2486	.2348	.2218	.2097	.1983	.1877	.1776
8	.3269	.3050	.2848	.2660	.2487	.2326	.2176	.2038	.1909	.1789	.1678	.1574	.1478	.1388
9	.2843	.2630	.2434	.2255	.2090	.1938	.1799	.1670	.1552	.1443	.1342	.1249	.1164	.1084
10	.2472	.2267	.2080	.1911	.1756	.1615	.1486	.1369	.1262	.1164	.1074	.0992	.0916	.0847
11	.2149	.1954	.1778	.1619	.1476	.1346	.1228	.1122	.1026	.0938	.0859	.0787	.0721	.0662
12	.1869	.1685	.1520	.1372	.1240	.1122	.1015	.0920	.0834	.0757	.0687	.0625	.0568	.0517
13	.1625	.1452	.1299	.1163	.1042	.0935	.0839	.0754	.0678	.0610	.0550	.0496	.0447	.0404
14	.1413	.1252	.1110	.0985	.0876	.0779	.0693	.0618	.0551	.0492	.0440	.0393	.0352	.0316
15	.1229	.1079	.0949	.0835	.0736	.0649	.0573	.0507	.0448	.0397	.0352	.0312	.0277	.0247
16	.1069	.0930	.0811	.0708	.0618	.0541	.0474	.0415	.0364	.0320	.0281	.0248	.0218	.0193
17	.0929	.0802	.0693	.0600	.0520	.0451	.0391	.0340	.0296	.0258	.0225	.0197	.0172	.0150
18	.0808	.0691	.0592	.0508	.0437	.0376	.0323	.0279	.0241	.0208	.0180	.0156	.0135	.0118
19	.0703	.0596	.0506	.0431	.0367	.0313	.0267	.0229	.0196	.0168	.0144	.0124	.0107	.0092
20	.0611	.0514	.0433	.0365	.0308	.0261	.0221	.0187	.0159	.0135	.0115	.0098	.0084	.0072
21	.0531	.0443	.0370	.0309	.0259	.0217	.0183	.0154	.0129	.0109	.0092	.0078	.0066	.0056
22	.0462	.0382	.0316	.0262	.0218	.0181	.0151	.0126	.0105	.0088	.0074	.0062	.0052	.0044
23	.0402	.0329	.0270	.0222	.0183	.0151	.0125	.0103	.0086	.0071	.0059	.0049	.0041	.0034
24	.0349	.0284	.0231	.0188	.0154	.0126	.0103	.0085	.0070	.0057	.0047	.0039	.0032	.0027
25	.0304	.0245	.0197	.0160	.0129	.0105	.0085	.0069	.0057	.0046	.0038	.0031	.0025	.0021

TABLE B-1.—Continued

Years Hence	DISCOUNT RATE											
	29%	30%	31%	32%	33%	34%	35%	36%	37%	38%	39%	40%
1	.7752	.7692	.7634	.7576	.7519	.7463	.7407	.7353	.7299	.7246	.7194	.7143
2	.6009	.5917	.5827	.5739	.5653	.5569	.5487	.5407	.5328	.5251	.5176	.5102
3	.4658	.4552	.4448	.4348	.4251	.4156	.4064	.3975	.3889	.3305	.3724	.3644
4	.3611	.3501	.3396	.3294	.3196	.3102	.3011	.2923	.2839	.2757	.2679	.2603
5	.2799	.2693	.2592	.2495	.2403	.2315	.2230	.2149	.2072	.1398	.1927	.1859
6	.2170	.2072	.1979	.1890	.1807	.1727	.1652	.1580	.1512	.1448	.1386	.1328
7	.1682	.1594	.1510	.1432	.1358	.1289	.1224	.1162	.1104	.1049	.0997	.0949
8	.1304	.1226	.1153	.1085	.1021	.0962	.0906	.0854	.0806	.0760	.0718	.0678
9	.1011	.0943	.0880	.0822	.0768	.0718	.0671	.0628	.0588	.0551	.0516	.0484
10	.0784	.0725	.0672	.0623	.0577	.0536	.0497	.0462	.0429	.0399	.0371	.0346
11	.0607	.0558	.0513	.0472	.0434	.0400	.0368	.0340	.0313	.0289	.0267	.0247
12	.0471	.0429	.0392	.0357	.0326	.0298	.0273	.0250	.0229	.0210	.0192	.0176
13	.0365	.0330	.0299	.0271	.0245	.0223	.0202	.0184	.0167	.0152	.0138	.0126
14	.0283	.0254	.0228	.0205	.0185	.0166	.0150	.0135	.0122	.0110	.0099	.0090
15	.0219	.0195	.0174	.0155	.0139	.0124	.0111	.0099	.0089	.0080	.0072	.0064
16	.0170	.0150	.0133	.0118	.0104	.0093	.0082	.0073	.0065	.0058	.0051	.0046
17	.0132	.0116	.0101	.0089	.0078	.0069	.0061	.0054	.0047	.0042	.0037	.0033
18	.0102	.0089	.0077	.0068	.0059	.0052	.0045	.0039	.0035	.0030	.0027	.0023
19	.0079	.0068	.0059	.0051	.0044	.0038	.0033	.0029	.0025	.0022	.0019	.0017
20	.0061	.0053	.0045	.0039	.0033	.0029	.0025	.0021	.0018	.0016	.0014	.0012
21	.0048	.0040	.0034	.0029	.0025	.0021	.0018	.0016	.0013	.0012	.0010	.0009
22	.0037	.0031	.0026	.0022	.0019	.0016	.0014	.0012	.0010	.0008	.0007	.0006
23	.0029	.0024	.0020	.0017	.0014	.0012	.0010	.0008	.0007	.0006	.0005	.0004
24	.0022	.0018	.0015	.0013	.0011	.0009	.0007	.0006	.0005	.0004	.0004	.0003
25	.0017	.0014	.0012	.0010	.0008	.0007	.0006	.0005	.0004	.0003	.0003	.0002

TABLE B-2. Present Value of $1 Received Continuously during the Nth Year

Years Hence	DISCOUNT RATE													
	1%	2%	3%	4%	5%	6%	7%	8%	9%	10%	11%	12%	13%	14%
1	.9950	.9902	.9854	.9806	.9760	.9714	.9669	.9625	.9581	.9538	.9496	.9454	.9413	.9373
2	.9852	.9707	.9567	.9429	.9295	.9164	.9037	.8912	.8790	.8671	.8555	.8441	.8330	.8222
3	.9754	.9517	.9288	.9067	.8853	.8646	.8445	.8252	.8064	.7883	.7707	.7537	.7372	.7212
4	.9658	.9331	.9017	.8718	.8431	.8156	.7893	.7641	.7398	.7166	.6943	.6729	.6524	.6326
5	.9562	.9148	.8755	.8383	.8030	.7695	.7377	.7075	.6788	.6515	.6255	.6008	.5773	.5549
6	.9467	.8968	.8500	.8060	.7647	.7259	.6894	.6551	.6227	.5922	.5635	.5365	.5109	.4868
7	.9374	.8792	.8252	.7750	.7283	.6848	.6443	.6065	.5713	.5384	.5077	.4790	.4521	.4270
8	.9281	.8620	.8012	.7452	.6936	.6461	.6021	.5616	.5241	.4895	.4574	.4277	.4001	.3746
9	.9189	.8451	.7779	.7165	.6606	.6095	.5628	.5200	.4808	.4450	.4121	.3818	.3541	.3286
10	.9098	.8285	.7552	.6890	.6291	.5750	.5259	.4815	.4411	.4045	.3712	.3409	.3133	.2882
11	.9008	.8123	.7332	.6625	.5992	.5424	.4915	.4458	.4047	.3677	.3344	.3044	.2773	.2528
12	.8919	.7964	.7118	.6370	.5706	.5117	.4594	.4128	.3713	.3343	.3013	.2718	.2454	.2218
13	.8830	.7807	.6911	.6125	.5435	.4828	.4293	.3822	.3406	.3039	.2714	.2427	.2172	.1945
14	.8743	.7654	.6710	.5889	.5176	.4554	.4012	.3539	.3125	.2763	.2445	.2167	.1922	.1706
15	.8656	.7504	.6514	.5663	.4929	.4297	.3750	.3277	.2867	.2512	.2203	.1935	.1701	.1497
16	.8571	.7357	.6325	.5445	.4695	.4053	.3505	.3034	.2630	.2283	.1985	.1727	.1505	.1313
17	.8486	.7213	.6140	.5236	.4471	.3824	.3275	.2809	.2413	.2076	.1788	.1542	.1332	.1152
18	.8402	.7071	.5962	.5034	.4258	.3608	.3061	.2601	.2214	.1887	.1611	.1377	.1179	.1010
19	.8319	.6933	.5788	.4841	.4055	.3403	.2861	.2409	.2031	.1716	.1451	.1229	.1043	.0886
20	.8236	.6797	.5619	.4655	.3862	.3211	.2674	.2230	.1863	.1560	.1307	.1098	.0923	.0777
21	.8155	.6664	.5456	.4476	.3678	.3029	.2499	.2065	.1710	.1418	.1178	.0980	.0817	.0682
22	.8074	.6533	.5297	.4303	.3503	.2857	.2335	.1912	.1568	.1289	.1061	.0875	.0723	.0598
23	.7994	.6405	.5143	.4138	.3336	.2696	.2182	.1770	.1439	.1172	.0956	.0781	.0640	.0525
24	.7915	.6279	.4993	.3979	.3178	.2543	.2040	.1639	.1320	.1065	.0861	.0698	.0566	.0460
25	.7837	.6156	.4847	.3826	.3026	.2399	.1906	.1518	.1211	.0968	.0776	.0623	.0501	.0404

TABLE B-2.—*Continued*

DISCOUNT RATE

Years Hence	15%	16%	17%	18%	19%	20%	21%	22%	23%	24%	25%	26%	27%	28%
1	.9333	.9293	.9255	.9216	.9179	.9141	.9105	.9068	.9033	.8998	.8963	.8929	.8895	.8861
2	.8115	.8011	.7910	.7810	.7713	.7618	.7525	.7433	.7344	.7256	.7170	.7086	.7004	.6923
3	.7057	.6906	.6761	.6619	.6482	.6348	.6219	.6093	.5971	.5852	.5736	.5624	.5515	.5409
4	.6136	.5954	.5778	.5609	.5447	.5290	.5139	.4994	.4854	.4719	.4589	.4463	.4342	.4225
5	.5336	.5133	.4939	.4754	.4577	.4408	.4247	.4094	.3946	.3806	.3671	.3542	.3419	.3301
6	.4640	.4425	.4221	.4029	.3846	.3674	.3510	.3355	.3208	.3069	.2937	.2811	.2692	.2579
7	.4035	.3814	.3608	.3414	.3232	.3061	.2901	.2750	.2609	.2475	.2350	.2231	.2120	.2015
8	.3508	.3288	.3084	.2893	.2716	.2551	.2398	.2254	.2121	.1996	.1880	.1771	.1669	.1574
9	.3051	.2835	.2636	.2452	.2282	.2126	.1981	.1848	.1724	.1610	.1504	.1405	.1314	.1230
10	.2653	.2444	.2253	.2078	.1918	.1772	.1638	.1515	.1402	.1298	.1203	.1115	.1035	.0961
11	.2307	.2107	.1925	.1761	.1612	.1476	.1353	.1241	.1140	.1047	.0962	.0885	.0815	.0751
12	.2006	.1816	.1646	.1492	.1354	.1230	.1118	.1018	.0927	.0844	.0770	.0703	.0642	.0586
13	.1744	.1566	.1406	.1265	.1138	.1025	.0924	.0834	.0753	.0681	.0616	.0558	.0505	.0458
14	.1517	.1350	.1202	.1072	.0956	.0854	.0764	.0684	.0612	.0549	.0493	.0443	.0398	.0358
15	.1319	.1163	.1027	.0908	.0804	.0712	.0631	.0560	.0498	.0443	.0394	.0351	.0313	.0280
16	.1147	.1003	.0878	.0770	.0675	.0593	.0522	.0459	.0405	.0357	.0315	.0279	.0247	.0218
17	.0997	.0865	.0751	.0652	.0568	.0494	.0431	.0377	.0329	.0288	.0252	.0221	.0194	.0171
18	.0867	.0745	.0641	.0553	.0477	.0412	.0356	.0309	.0268	.0232	.0202	.0176	.0153	.0133
19	.0754	.0643	.0548	.0468	.0401	.0343	.0295	.0253	.0218	.0187	.0161	.0139	.0120	.0104
20	.0656	.0554	.0469	.0397	.0337	.0286	.0243	.0207	.0177	.0151	.0129	.0111	.0095	.0081
21	.0570	.0478	.0401	.0336	.0283	.0238	.0201	.0170	.0144	.0122	.0103	.0088	.0075	.0064
22	.0496	.0412	.0342	.0285	.0238	.0199	.0166	.0139	.0117	.0098	.0083	.0070	.0059	.0050
23	.0431	.0355	.0293	.0242	.0200	.0166	.0137	.0114	.0095	.0079	.0066	.0055	.0046	.0039
24	.0375	.0306	.0250	.0205	.0168	.0138	.0114	.0094	.0077	.0064	.0053	.0044	.0036	.0030
25	.0326	.0264	.0214	.0174	.0141	.0115	.0094	.0077	.0063	.0052	.0042	.0035	.0029	.0024

TABLE B-2.—*Continued*

	DISCOUNT RATE											
Years Hence	29%	30%	31%	32%	33%	34%	35%	36%	37%	38%	39%	40%
1	.8828	.8796	.8764	.8732	.8701	.8670	.8639	.8609	.8579	.8549	.8520	.8491
2	.6844	.6766	.6690	.6615	.6542	.6470	.6399	.6330	.6262	.6195	.6130	.6065
3	.5305	.5205	.5107	.5011	.4919	.4828	.4740	.4654	.4571	.4489	.4410	.4332
4	.4113	.4004	.3898	.3797	.3698	.3603	.3511	.3422	.3336	.3253	.3173	.3095
5	.3188	.3080	.2976	.2876	.2781	.2689	.2601	.2516	.2435	.2357	.2282	.2210
6	.2471	.2369	.2272	.2179	.2091	.2007	.1927	.1850	.1778	.1708	.1642	.1579
7	.1916	.1822	.1734	.1651	.1572	.1498	.1427	.1361	.1298	.1238	.1181	.1128
8	.1485	.1402	.1324	.1251	.1182	.1118	.1057	.1000	.0947	.0897	.0850	.0806
9	.1151	.1078	.1010	.0947	.0889	.0834	.0783	.0736	.0691	.0650	.0611	.0575
10	.0892	.0829	.0771	.0718	.0668	.0622	.0580	.0541	.0505	.0471	.0440	.0411
11	.0692	.0638	.0589	.0544	.0502	.0464	.0430	.0398	.0368	.0341	.0316	.0294
12	.0536	.0491	.0449	.0412	.0378	.0347	.0318	.0292	.0269	.0247	.0228	.0210
13	.0416	.0378	.0343	.0312	.0284	.0259	.0236	.0215	.0196	.0179	.0164	.0150
14	.0322	.0290	.0262	.0236	.0214	.0193	.0175	.0158	.0143	.0130	.0118	.0107
15	.0250	.0223	.0200	.0179	.0161	.0144	.0129	.0116	.0105	.0094	.0085	.0076
16	.0194	.0172	.0153	.0136	.0121	.0108	.0096	.0085	.0076	.0068	.0061	.0055
17	.0150	.0132	.0117	.0103	.0091	.0080	.0071	.0063	.0056	.0049	.0044	.0039
18	.0116	.0102	.0089	.0078	.0068	.0060	.0053	.0046	.0041	.0036	.0032	.0028
19	.0090	.0078	.0068	.0059	.0051	.0045	.0039	.0034	.0030	.0026	.0023	.0020
20	.0070	.0060	.0052	.0045	.0039	.0033	.0029	.0025	.0022	.0019	.0016	.0014
21	.0054	.0046	.0040	.0034	.0029	.0025	.0021	.0018	.0016	.0014	.0012	.0010
22	.0042	.0036	.0030	.0026	.0022	.0019	.0016	.0014	.0012	.0010	.0008	.0007
23	.0033	.0027	.0023	.0019	.0016	.0014	.0012	.0010	.0008	.0007	.0006	.0005
24	.0025	.0021	.0018	.0015	.0012	.0010	.0009	.0007	.0006	.0005	.0004	.0004
25	.0020	.0016	.0013	.0011	.0009	.0008	.0006	.0005	.0004	.0004	.0003	.0003

TABLE B-3. Present Value of an Annuity of $1

DISCOUNT RATE

Years Hence	1%	2%	3%	4%	5%	6%	7%	8%	9%	10%	11%	12%	13%	14%
1	0.9901	0.9804	0.9709	0.9615	0.9524	0.9434	0.9346	0.9259	0.9174	0.9091	0.9009	0.8929	0.8850	0.8772
2	1.9704	1.9416	1.9135	1.8861	1.8594	1.8334	1.8080	1.7833	1.7591	1.7355	1.7125	1.6901	1.6681	1.6467
3	2.9410	2.8839	2.8286	2.7751	2.7232	2.6730	2.6243	2.5771	2.5313	2.4869	2.4437	2.4018	2.3612	2.3216
4	3.9020	3.8077	3.7171	3.6299	3.5460	3.4651	3.3872	3.3121	3.2397	3.1699	3.1024	3.0373	2.9745	2.9137
5	4.8534	4.7135	4.5797	4.4518	4.3295	4.2124	4.1002	3.9927	3.8897	3.7908	3.6959	3.6048	3.5172	3.4331
6	5.7955	5.6014	5.4172	5.2421	5.0757	4.9173	4.7665	4.6229	4.4859	4.3553	4.2305	4.1114	3.9976	3.8887
7	6.7282	6.4720	6.2303	6.0021	5.7864	5.5824	5.3893	5.2064	5.0330	4.8684	4.7122	4.5638	4.4226	4.2883
8	7.6517	7.3255	7.0197	6.7327	6.4632	6.2098	5.9713	5.7466	5.5348	5.3349	5.1461	4.9676	4.7988	4.6389
9	8.5660	8.1622	7.7861	7.4353	7.1078	6.8017	6.5152	6.2469	5.9952	5.7590	5.5370	5.3282	5.1317	4.9464
10	9.4713	8.9826	8.5302	8.1109	7.7217	7.3601	7.0236	6.7101	6.4177	6.1446	5.8892	5.6502	5.4262	5.2161
11	10.3676	9.7869	9.2526	8.7605	8.3064	7.8869	7.4987	7.1390	6.8052	6.4951	6.2065	5.9377	5.6869	5.4527
12	11.2551	10.5753	9.9540	9.3851	8.8633	8.3838	7.9427	7.5361	7.1607	6.8137	6.4924	6.1944	5.9176	5.6603
13	12.1337	11.3484	10.6350	9.9856	9.3936	8.8527	8.3577	7.9038	7.4869	7.1034	6.7499	6.4235	6.1218	5.8424
14	13.0037	12.1063	11.2961	10.5631	9.8986	9.2950	8.7455	8.2442	7.7862	7.3667	6.9319	6.6282	6.3025	6.0021
15	13.8651	12.8493	11.9379	11.1184	10.3797	9.7122	9.1079	8.5595	8.0607	7.6061	7.1909	6.8109	6.4624	6.1422
16	14.7179	13.5777	12.5611	11.6523	10.8378	10.1059	9.4466	8.8514	8.3126	7.8237	7.3792	6.9740	6.6039	6.2651
17	15.5623	14.2919	13.1661	12.1657	11.2741	10.4773	9.7632	9.1216	8.5436	8.0216	7.5488	7.1196	6.7291	6.3729
18	16.3983	14.9920	13.7535	12.6593	11.6896	10.8276	10.0591	9.3719	8.7556	8.2014	7.7016	7.2497	6.8399	6.4674
19	17.2260	15.6785	14.3238	13.1339	12.0853	11.1581	10.3356	9.6036	8.9501	8.3649	7.8393	7.3658	6.9380	6.5504
20	18.0456	16.3514	14.8775	13.5903	12.4622	11.4699	10.5940	9.8181	9.1285	8.5136	7.9633	7.4694	7.0248	6.6231
21	18.8570	17.0112	15.4150	14.0292	12.8212	11.7641	10.8355	10.0168	9.2922	8.6487	8.0751	7.5620	7.1016	6.6870
22	19.6604	17.6581	15.9369	14.4511	13.1630	12.0416	11.0612	10.2007	9.4424	8.7715	8.1757	7.6446	7.1695	6.7429
23	20.4558	18.2922	16.4436	14.8568	13.4886	12.3034	11.2722	10.3711	9.5802	8.8832	8.2664	7.7184	7.2297	6.7921
24	21.2434	18.9139	16.9355	15.2470	13.7986	12.5504	11.4693	10.5288	9.7066	8.9847	8.3481	7.7843	7.2829	6.8351
25	22.0232	19.5235	17.4131	15.6221	14.0939	12.7834	11.6536	10.6748	9.8226	9.0770	8.4217	7.8431	7.3300	6.8729

TABLE B-3.—*Continued*

							DISCOUNT RATE							
Years Hence	15%	16%	17%	18%	19%	20%	21%	22%	23%	24%	25%	26%	27%	28%
1	0.8696	0.8621	0.8547	0.8475	0.8403	0.8333	0.8264	0.8197	0.8130	0.8065	0.8000	0.7937	0.7874	0.7813
2	1.6257	1.6052	1.5852	1.5656	1.5465	1.5278	1.5095	1.4915	1.4740	1.4568	1.4400	1.4235	1.4074	1.3916
3	2.2832	2.2459	2.2096	2.1743	2.1399	2.1065	2.0739	2.0422	2.0114	1.9813	1.9520	1.9234	1.8956	1.8684
4	2.8550	2.7982	2.7432	2.6901	2.6386	2.5887	2.5404	2.4936	2.4483	2.4043	2.3616	2.3202	2.2800	2.2410
5	3.3522	3.2743	3.1993	3.1272	3.0576	2.9906	2.9260	2.8636	2.8035	2.7454	2.6893	2.6351	2.5827	2.5320
6	3.7845	3.6847	3.5892	3.4976	3.4098	3.3255	3.2446	3.1669	3.0923	3.0205	2.9514	2.8850	2.8210	2.7594
7	4.1604	4.0386	3.9224	3.8115	3.7057	3.6046	3.5079	3.4155	3.3270	3.2423	3.1611	3.0833	3.0087	2.9370
8	4.4873	4.3436	4.2072	4.0776	3.9544	3.8372	3.7256	3.6193	3.5179	3.4212	3.3289	3.2407	3.1564	3.0758
9	4.7716	4.6065	4.4506	4.3030	4.1633	4.0310	3.9054	3.7863	3.6731	3.5655	3.4631	3.3657	3.2728	3.1842
10	5.0188	4.8332	4.6586	4.4941	4.3389	4.1925	4.0541	3.9232	3.7993	3.6819	3.5705	3.4648	3.3644	3.2689
11	5.2337	5.0286	4.8364	4.6560	4.4865	4.3271	4.1769	4.0354	3.9018	3.7757	3.6564	3.5435	3.4365	3.3351
12	5.4206	5.1971	4.9884	4.7932	4.6105	4.4392	4.2784	4.1274	3.9852	3.8514	3.7251	3.6059	3.4933	3.3868
13	5.5831	5.3423	5.1183	4.9095	4.7147	4.5327	4.3624	4.2028	4.0530	3.9124	3.7801	3.6555	3.5381	3.4272
14	5.7245	5.4675	5.2293	5.0081	4.8023	4.6106	4.4317	4.2646	4.1082	3.9616	3.8241	3.6949	3.5733	3.4587
15	5.8474	5.5755	5.3242	5.0916	4.8759	4.6755	4.4890	4.3152	4.1530	4.0013	3.8593	3.7261	3.6010	3.4834
16	5.9542	5.6685	5.4053	5.1624	4.9377	4.7296	4.5364	4.3567	4.1894	4.0333	3.8874	3.7509	3.6228	3.5026
17	6.0472	5.7487	5.4746	5.2223	4.9897	4.7746	4.5755	4.3908	4.2190	4.0591	3.9099	3.7705	3.6400	3.5177
18	6.1280	5.8178	5.5339	5.2732	5.0333	4.8122	4.6079	4.4187	4.2431	4.0799	3.9279	3.7861	3.6536	3.5294
19	6.1982	5.8775	5.5845	5.3162	5.0700	4.8435	4.6346	4.4415	4.2627	4.0967	3.9424	3.7985	3.6642	3.5386
20	6.2593	5.9288	5.6278	5.3527	5.1009	4.8696	4.6567	4.4603	4.2786	4.1103	3.9539	3.8083	3.6726	3.5458
21	6.3125	5.9731	5.6648	5.3837	5.1268	4.8913	4.6750	4.4756	4.2916	4.1212	3.9631	3.8161	3.6792	3.5514
22	6.3587	6.0113	5.6964	5.4099	5.1486	4.9094	4.6900	4.4882	4.3021	4.1300	3.9705	3.8223	3.6844	3.5558
23	6.3988	6.0442	5.7234	5.4321	5.1668	4.9245	4.7025	4.4985	4.3106	4.1371	3.9764	3.8273	3.6885	3.5592
24	6.4338	6.0726	5.7465	5.4509	5.1822	4.9371	4.7128	4.5070	4.3176	4.1428	3.9811	3.8312	3.6918	3.5619
25	6.4641	6.0971	5.7662	5.4669	5.1951	4.9476	4.7213	4.5139	4.3232	4.1474	3.9849	3.8342	3.6943	3.5640

TABLE B-3.—*Continued*

DISCOUNT RATE

Years Hence	29%	30%	31%	32%	33%	34%	35%	36%	37%	38%	39%	40%
1	0.7752	0.7692	0.7634	0.7576	0.7519	0.7463	0.7407	0.7353	0.7299	0.7246	0.7194	0.7143
2	1.3761	1.3609	1.3461	1.3315	1.3172	1.3032	1.2894	1.2760	1.2627	1.2497	1.2370	1.2245
3	1.8420	1.8161	1.7909	1.7663	1.7423	1.7188	1.6959	1.6735	1.6516	1.6302	1.6093	1.5889
4	2.2031	2.1662	2.1305	2.0957	2.0618	2.0290	1.9969	1.9658	1.9355	1.9060	1.8772	1.8492
5	2.4830	2.4356	2.3897	2.3452	2.3021	2.2604	2.2200	2.1807	2.1427	2.1058	2.0699	2.0352
6	2.7000	2.6427	2.5875	2.5342	2.4828	2.4331	2.3852	2.3388	2.2939	2.2506	2.2086	2.1680
7	2.8682	2.8021	2.7386	2.6775	2.6187	2.5620	2.5075	2.4550	2.4043	2.3555	2.3083	2.2628
8	2.9986	2.9247	2.8539	2.7860	2.7208	2.6582	2.5982	2.5404	2.4849	2.4315	2.3801	2.3306
9	3.0997	3.0190	2.9419	2.8681	2.7976	2.7300	2.6653	2.6033	2.5437	2.4866	2.4317	2.3790
10	3.1781	3.0915	3.0091	2.9304	2.8553	2.7836	2.7150	2.6495	2.5867	2.5265	2.4689	2.4136
11	3.2388	3.1473	3.0604	2.9776	2.8987	2.8236	2.7519	2.6834	2.6180	2.5555	2.4956	2.4383
12	3.2859	3.1903	3.0995	3.0133	2.9314	2.8534	2.7792	2.7084	2.6409	2.5764	2.5148	2.4559
13	3.3224	3.2233	3.1294	3.0404	2.9559	2.8757	2.7994	2.7268	2.6576	2.5916	2.5286	2.4685
14	3.3507	3.2487	3.1522	3.0609	2.9744	2.8923	2.8144	2.7403	2.6698	2.6026	2.5386	2.4775
15	3.3726	3.2682	3.1696	3.0764	2.9883	2.9047	2.8255	2.7502	2.6787	2.6106	2.5457	2.4839
16	3.3896	3.2832	3.1829	3.0882	2.9987	2.9140	2.8337	2.7575	2.6852	2.6164	2.5509	2.4885
17	3.4028	3.2948	3.1931	3.0971	3.0065	2.9209	2.8398	2.7629	2.6899	2.6206	2.5546	2.4918
18	3.4130	3.3037	3.2008	3.1039	3.0124	2.9260	2.8443	2.7668	2.6934	2.6236	2.5573	2.4941
19	3.4210	3.3105	3.2067	3.1090	3.0169	2.9299	2.8476	2.7697	2.6959	2.6258	2.5592	2.4958
20	3.4271	3.3158	3.2112	3.1129	3.0202	2.9327	2.8501	2.7718	2.6977	2.6274	2.5606	2.4970
21	3.4319	3.3198	3.2147	3.1158	3.0227	2.9349	2.8519	2.7734	2.6991	2.6285	2.5616	2.4979
22	3.4356	3.3230	3.2173	3.1180	3.0246	2.9365	2.8533	2.7746	2.7000	2.6294	2.5623	2.4985
23	3.4384	3.3254	3.2193	3.1197	3.0260	2.9377	2.8543	2.7754	2.7008	2.6300	2.5628	2.4989
24	3.4406	3.3272	3.2209	3.1210	3.0271	2.9386	2.8550	2.7760	2.7013	2.6304	2.5632	2.4992
25	3.4423	3.3286	3.2220	3.1220	3.0279	2.9392	2.8556	2.7765	2.7017	2.6307	2.5634	2.4994

Appendix: Short Answers to Odd-Numbered Problems

C

1-1. (a) $9,856,300.

(b) You should explain the present value concept, and why $10 million outright grant is preferable in PV terms.

(c) At 12% the $11.5 million has PV of $10,057,600, making it preferable. At 16% ODR, its PV is $9,664,400 making it even less attractive.

1-3. (a) $273,114.81.

(b) Because it is guaranteed and thus has zero risk, exactly like the contract which obligates the firm to pay for the pollution control system.

1-5. (a) $3,518.

(b) The restaurant management opportunity should be chosen since it promises $3,518 more than the next-best alternative, as well as managerial experience and the establishment of contacts in the industry.

1-7. (a) Project A NPV is $70,424; Project B NPV is $78,626 when the appropriate (year end or continuous) discount factors are used.

(b) Machine B is preferable due to greater NPV and more desirable cash flow pattern.

1-9. (a) Using the midpoints assumes that all outcomes within each range are equally likely. Point estimates for extreme ranges are essentially arbitrary. $850 and $1,200 can be rationalized as maintaining the $50 interval. Probabilities are obtained by converting the percentage chances to fractions of unity (divide each by 100).

(b) $1,049.50 based on the above point estimates.

(c) $625.78 compounded annually at 9% will grow to $1,049.50 in 6 years, and is thus the real value in 1981 dollars.

2-1. (a) Minor Face Lift: Expected Value $34,000, Standard Deviation 24.58 (thousand dollars), and Coefficient of Variation 0.723. New Model: Expected Value $34,000, Standard Deviation 60.53 (thousand dollars), and Coefficient of Variation 1.780.

(b) EV criterion is unable to discriminate between the two alternatives; Coefficient-of-variation criterion favors the Minor Face Lift; and the Maximin criterion favors the Minor Face Lift ($10,000 worst outcome as compared to the New Model's worst outcome—$20,000).

(c) Minor Face Lift must have the greater CE for a risk-averse decision maker, since it has less risk for the same return. Its indifference curve in risk-return space must have a higher intercept on the return axis, and hence, a higher certainty equivalent.

2-3. (a) Medium-price strategy has EPV = $3,806.30 followed by high-price strategy ($1,505.00) and low-price strategy ($—291.88).

(b) No, the bonds would earn $5,843.75 over the two years but this is future value. The present value of the bond alternative at 12.5% is zero.

(c) In terms of absolute risk, high price has outcome dispersion of $16,791 and standard deviation of $4,290.53; medium price has outcome dispersion of $12,444 and standard deviation of $3,385.40; low price has outcome dispersion of $12,013 and standard deviation of $3,405.71. Thus, in terms of absolute risk, the ranking is high, medium, and low.

(d) In terms of relative risk, or risk per dollar of return, the ranking is low, high, medium. The coefficients of variation are —11.67, 2.85, and 0.89 respectively.

(e) No, the coefficient-of-variation criterion and the certainty equivalent criterion both rank the alternatives the same: medium, high, low. Plotting the EV and SD coordinates in risk-return space you will find that a risk-averse person's indifference curves will rank them in the same order, and hence the CE (intercept on the return axis) will rank them in the same order.

2-5. (a) EV_a = $31,412 (treat $10,000 as sunk cost)
EV_b = $50,247
EV_c = $57,272, therefore maximum EPV strategy.

Minimum A = $10,413.00
Minimum B = $17,355.00
Minimum C = $24,297.00, therefore maximin strategy.

Coefficient of Variation:
Necktie A = 0.237, therefore least risk per dollar.
Necktie B = 0.280
Necktie C = 0.331

(b) Necktie C has the greatest EV, the maximin outcome, and its risk per dollar is only slightly higher. But if you plot the EV's against the standard deviations you will see that either A, B, or C could be on the highest indifference curve, and hence have the highest certainty equivalent, depending on your (or the firm's) degree of risk aversion. So its your choice, but you should rationalize your answer.

2-7. (a) Lease ENPV $12,400.55; Buy ENPV $16,521.13.

(b) Lease Standard Deviation $7,184.65; Buy Standard Deviation $5,005.13.

(c) Advise management to buy the truck, since all criteria (EV, Coefficient-of-Variation, Maximin, and Certainty Equivalent) favor that option.

(d) Estimates of future cash flows are assumed to be accurate; the probability distribution is assumed to accurately represent the *a priori* probabilities; and we assume *ceteris paribus*.

2-9. (a) ENPV is $6,188,567.40 for Strategy 1 and $5,526,570 for Strategy 2, using the discount factors of 0.8565 (first year) and 0.7336 (second year).

(b) Standard deviation is 1,339,359 for Strategy 1 and 1,524,498 for Strategy 2.

(c) EV criterion favors Strategy 1; Maximin favors Strategy 1 ($2,323,700 c/f $1,590,100); Coefficient-of-Variation criterion favors Strategy 1 (0.209 c/f 0.275); Certainty Equivalent criterion favors Strategy 1, since it has both higher ENPV and lower SD. Thus there is unanimous support of these criteria for Strategy 1.

(d) Assume that management is risk averse (risk preferers may prefer Strategy 2); that estimates of profits are accurate; that probability distributions are accurate; and that *ceteris paribus*.

Chapter 3

3-1. Check your graph against the following: Call the original tangency of the budget line (B-line) with the indifference curve (I-curve), point A. The increased price causes the original B-line to pivot on its vertical intercept to cut the horizontal axis closer to the origin. The new B-line will be tangent to a new I-curve; call this point B. Move the new B-line out until it is tangent to the original I-curve, at point C. Now, A to C (in terms of the product on the horizontal axis) is the substitution effect and C to B (in terms of the horizontal axis) is the income effect.

To do this for the product on the vertical axis, follow the same steps as above, switching the words "horizontal" for "vertical," and vice-versa.

3-3. The marketing manager wants to increase consumers' perceptions of the attributes in product X, and perhaps also wants to influence consumers' tastes toward attributes contained in X. Changed perceptions would shift the product ray for X and relocate the efficiency frontier, while changed tastes would shift indifference curves. Both would operate to cause greater quantity demanded for X as consumers maximize their incomes, *ceteris paribus*. Raising price after advertising would still cause sales to fall, but they should not fall as far as they would have fallen for the same price increase without the advertising campaign. This should be shown graphically.

3-5. You should show three sets of indifference curves with differing MRS between power and economy through any particular combination of these attributes. Where at least three automobiles are offered at competitive prices (on the efficiency frontier) with different attribute ratios being perceived, each consumer attains his or her highest I-curve by selecting a different automobile. (If the consumers regard automobiles as indivisible goods and can afford no more than one, the efficiency frontier will be a series of points.)

3-7. This is a consumer's decision-making problem for which you can use the analysis from Chapters 1 and 2. To weight the ratings of the attributes, give "reliability" the weight of one, and weight the others accordingly:

(a) For "summer use only" the EV of utility is 51 utils, 52.5 utils, and 48 utils, for cars A, B, and C respectively. Thus, sportscar B is expected to maximize his utility.

(b) For "year-round use" the EV of utility is 51, 49, and 46.7 utils, respectively. Thus, sportscar A should be purchased, using the EV criterion, if he is not to be transferred.

(c) Sportscar B has the greatest expected utility, $E(U) = 52.5(0.7) + 49(0.3) = 51.5$, compared to 51 for A and 46.7 for C. But note that the maximin strategy favors sportscar A; the coefficient-of-variation criterion favors A (since its standard deviation is zero); and the certainty equivalent criterion also favors A, unless Mr. Poirier has an extremely low degree of risk aversion, is risk neutral, or is a risk preferer. Thus, if he is risk averse he should probably buy sportscar A.

Chapter 4

4-1. (a) Set up a table with four columns headed P, Q, TR, and MR. TR is P · Q, and MR is $\Delta TR/\Delta Q$ between each price level. Plotting these requires a careful choice of scale, since the relevant range is relatively narrow.

(b) Calculate *arc* elasticity, since the changes in price are discrete rather than continuous. From the highest price down, the values are 3.03, 2.53, 2.16, 2.00, 1.24, 0.87, 0.85, 0.75, and 0.65.

(c) Demand passes from elastic to inelastic somewhere close to the $4.75 price. It is thus elastic above $4.75, unitary around $4.75, and inelastic below $4.75. (More precise calculations will be introduced in Chapter 5.)

4-3. **(a)** Price elasticity for Reinhart beer is -0.437.

(b) Advertising elasticity for Reinhart beer is 1.422.

(c) Profit-maximizing price is $8.39, *ceteris paribus*.

(d) Sales-revenue maximizing price is $7.39, *ceteris paribus*. (Note that although these prices are substantially above the present price of $4.50, the price elasticity of demand is very low and the cross elasticity with the rival beer is also very low ($n = 0.06$). *Ceteris paribus* might hold, since the rival would be barely affected by Reinhart's price adjustment. However, we might expect the rival to also raise price, whether affected or not, following Reinhart's example.)

4-5. **(a)** The profit-maximizing price is $1.81.

(b) The sales-revenue-maximizing price is $1.31.

(c) Assumptions are that *ceteris paribus* (particularly that the demand curve does not shift in the next period, and that marginal costs stay constant at the same level despite the higher output levels), and that the estimates of price elasticity and marginal costs were accurate. If changes do occur, by how much can they change before the current price is best left alone? Do some experimenting on this.

4-7. **(a)** From the demand function, obtain the demand curve $P = 1,500 - 0.00125Q$, and hence $MR = 1,500 - 0.0025Q$. For sales-revenue maximization set $MR = 0$ to find $Q = 600,000$, and find $P - 750$ from demand curve.

(b) From the demand function, deduce first, second, and third quarter sales as 565,000, 415,000, and 815,000 units respectively. Thus 205,000 units are required to meet the objective. Substituting for Q and solving for A in the demand function we find $A = \$10,800,000$.

Chapter 5

5-1. **(a)** The intercept on the price axis is approximately 12.84 and the slope (dP/dQ) is -0.2063.

(b) Since the market is 10,000 times the sample, for every dP there will be 10,000 times dQ. Hence the slope of the market demand curve for Hermanos Tequila is -0.00002063.

(c) $6.42.

(d) Price elasticity is -1.00, indicating that TR will not change for a small price increase, or decrease, *ceteris paribus*.

Cross elasticity is 0.561, indicating that the tequilas are indeed substitutes, and that increased prices of Hermanos will benefit sales of the others. (Hint: Plot Q_y against P_x (Hermanos) and estimate $Q_y = a + bP_x$.)

5-3. **(b)** Line of best fit is (exactly) $S = 5,283.74 + 4.15H$ where S = thousands of units sold and H = thousands of households. Your estimate should be reasonably close to this.

(c) 11,488 units.

(d) Line of best fit seems to fit data points reasonably well, but extrapolation to 1,495 households is risky due to apparent trend in last few observations. Projection of this relationship depends on *ceteris paribus*.

5-5. **(a)** $P = 40 - 0.5Q$ approximately.

(b) $P = 39.859 - 0.4825Q$ with $R^2 = 0.95$.

(c)   34.938, or 35 hours, approximately. Since the R^2 is quite high, we can be fairly confident, but we really need to calculate the standard error of estimate and the standard error of the coefficient before making any predictions.

(d) $24.93. In practice, however, it is unlikely that such a small price reduction would be noticed and cause quantity demanded to increase (due to "price-awareness thresholds" of consumers).

5-7. (a)   Price elasticity is −3.83, indicating that demand is quite "elastic," and for example, that a 10% price reduction would increase sales volume by 38.3%, *ceteris paribus*.

Cross elasticity is 2.59, indicating relatively strong substitutes, and for example, that a 1% price reduction by the rival would cause AA's sales volume to decline by 2.59%.

Income elasticity is 0.475, indicating that the product is regarded as a "normal" (or superior) good and within that class of goods is a "necessity." For a 1% change in income, sales volume would change in the same direction by a little less than half of one percent.

(b) $P_x = 239.55 - 0.000537Q_x$ and MR $= 239.55 - 0.001074Q_x$.

(c)   Profit-maximizing price is $186.01.

(d)   86,808.6 and 112,539.6 units.

(e)   *Ceteris paribus*, from estimation period to current period; data accuracy; absence of the six major pitfalls in regression analysis; and that rival firm will not react to AA's price reduction. (Is it likely to?)

APPENDIX 5A

5A-1. (a)   Sales = 0.06976 + 3.8398 (Index) where both sales and the index are expressed in thousands of units.

(b)   Coefficient of determination (R^2) is 0.9992 indicating very high (virtually total) explanatory power of the regression equation. The standard error of estimate is only 0.05324 and the standard error of the coefficient is 0.03617. These are both relatively small, and hence the 95% confidence limits are very narrow. The 99.7% limits are only a little less narrow. For example, the 99.7% confidence limits for the coefficient are 3.8398 ± 3(0.03617), and are therefore 3.7313 and 3.9483. Thus the composite index appears to be very reliable as an explanatory variable.

Chapter 6

6-1. (a)   Increasing returns up to 5 divers employed; constant returns from 6 to 12 employees; and diminishing returns for the thirteenth and subsequent employees.

(b)   5 (average product is at its maximum).

(c)   14 (total product is maximized).

6-3. (a)

	UNITS OF LABOR					
	1	*2*	*3*	*4*	*5*	*6*
Total Product	66.2	85.0	99.1	103.6	93.2	63.0
Marginal product	66.2	18.8	14.1	4.5	−10.4	−30.2

(b)   Since MP falls after the first unit of labor, diminishing returns are evident throughout. (There may be increasing returns to fractions of the first labor unit, however.)

(c)   385 labor hours, because TP is maximized at this input level.

6-5. (a)   To find average cost per unit of output, find total cost at each output level by multiplying capital and labor units by the cost per unit and summing these capital and labor costs, before dividing by the output level. For example, for plant size 1, average cost is $1,000 at 30 units of output, $769.24 at 52 units, and so on.

(b) Economies of scale up to and including the third plant size, with diseconomies beyond that.

(c) (1) Plant 1. (2) Plant 3. (3) Plant 3 has lower costs over most of this range. Assuming a normal probability distribution over this range, the extremes (where either plant 2 or 4 would be preferable) will have low probabilities of occurring. The expected value of cost per unit is therefore likely to be lower with plant 3.

Chapter 7

7-1. **(a)**

"Make" option:

Foregone revenue	$5,640
less Costs saved	−460
plus Costs incurred	775
Incremental costs	$5,955

"Buy" option:

Foregone revenue	$1,880
plus Costs incurred	3,050
Incremental costs	$4,930

Therefore buy the chassis units from Fenton.

(b) We have assumed constant materials cost per unit for both the fork and chassis assemblies. Second, we assume that the quality of Fenton's units is at least as high as Muscle-Man's. We assume no problems with the delivery schedule resulting in no bottlenecks in M-M's production process.

7-3. Take the order, for a contribution to overheads and profits of $4,910. Assumptions involved are: labor is a variable factor, not fixed from 8,000 to 10,000 units of production; March output will otherwise be the same as current output; data provided is accurate; special sale will not supplement regular sales; and buyer relations will not be disturbed by this deal.

7-5.

Expected cost of driver	$1,000.00
Incremental running expenses	1,366.80
Cost of installing loading ramp	400.00
Expected opportunity costs	338.87
Incremental costs	$3,105.67

7-7. **(a)** Incremental costs, $8,745 weekly.

(b) *Ceteris paribus* with respect to input costs and factor productivities underlying the estimated TVC curve; data accuracy, particularly the absence of measurement error in the cost-output pairs; that the TVC equation is a good fit to the data, with high R^2 and low standard errors of estimate and of the coefficients; absence of specification errors, heteroscedasticity, autocorrelation and the identification problem. (Note multicollinearity must be present but is tolerable for a predictive equation.)

APPENDIX 7A

7A-1. Breakeven volume 3,692.31 units. Demand study indicates TR is curvilinear not rectilinear, and that B/E volume will not be attained at price $45 per 1000 units. Set MC = MR to find loss-minimizing price $46.25 and output 3,375 units. Should reconsider design and quality, or consider promotional campaign.

8-1. (b)

Output units	Estimated TVC	AVC $	MC $
2,000	20,000	10.00	
			3.00
4,000	26,000	6.50	
			2.75
6,000	31,500	5.25	
			1.25
8,000	34,000	4.25	
			1.50
10,000	37,000	3.70	
			4.50
12,000	46,000	3.83	

(c) $4,000 (TVC rises from $33,000 to $37,000).

(d) Line of best fit appears to be a cubic function, so hypothesized relationship is $TVC = a + bQ + cQ^2 + dQ^3$. To set up data you would need to add two columns ie: Q^2 and Q^3.

(e) *Ceteris paribus* is assumed to prevail over the observation period, and over the projection period; we assume data accuracy, particularly the absence of measurement error in the cost-output pairs; and the freehand line of best fit is assumed to be the true relationship between TVC and Q (i.e., deviations from this line are due to random influences).

8-3. (a) $P = 9.24 - 1.0977\,Q$ and $MR = 9.24 - 2.195Q$.

(b) AC = $5.80 at 1500 units, $4.40 at 3,300 units, and $5.30 at 4,650 units. Marginal costs are $3.23 at 2,400 units, and $7.50 at 3,975 units.

(c) Approximately $6.50 per dozen, and 2,500 dozen cards per month.

(d) That cost estimates are accurate, and that there is no learning curve effect—if so, per unit costs would be lower; that the regression analysis avoided the six major pitfalls; and that *ceteris paribus* will prevail. Note that R^2 is only 0.8652 leaving 13½% of the variance in Q unexplained, and that the standard error of estimate is relatively large, meaning wide confidence intervals (e.g., 95% confidence interval is $2.5 \pm 2(0.6385)$ thousand boxes, or 1,223 boxes to 3,777 boxes). We therefore have little confidence in our expected volume of 2,500 boxes at price $6.50.

8-5. (a) Incremental costs are labor, materials, variable overheads, and opportunity costs, totalling $55,000 for 5,000 seats; $103,295 for 10,000 seats, and so on. Incremental revenues are $62,500 for 5,000 seats; $125,000 for 10,000 seats, and so on. Your company should accept 3 contracts for 15,000 seats in total.

8-7. For each plant, arrange observations in order of output levels, calculate average and marginal costs (using gradients), and plot the AC and MC curves. It is evident that the competitor's plant benefits from economies of plant size and is better suited to the expected demand situation. You could calculate the expected values of costs in each plant, given the cost and demand estimates, and then apply the various decision criteria. Assumptions include *ceteris paribus* (in particular, the same factor prices and productivities in both plants); and that the probability distribution of demand is accurate (since actual demand of 8,000 or 9,000 units would cause the present plant size to be preferable).

8-9. (a) Learning curve is $SAC = 6,669.68Q^{-0.3299}$

(b) 20.45 per cent

(c) $475.03 per unit

(d) Factor prices remain the same; absence of measurement errors and the other major pitfalls of regression analysis.

9-1. (a) Due to the leftward shift of the market demand curve, the price falls until supply and demand are equal at the market price.

(b) Each firm will decrease its output level until MC = MR = *P*. If price falls below AVC for any firm, that firm will cease production.

(c) If the temporary fall in demand lasts longer than it takes to liquidate plant, some firms will leave the industry.

9-3. (a) These firms probably envision a kinked demand curve and each does not wish to be the only firm raising prices with subsequent loss of market share.

(b) The auto firms traditionally set prices at the start of the new model year. They expect to raise prices together and therefore do not expect to encounter a kinked demand curve.

9-5. (a) The firm determines its profit-maximizing output level by finding the intersection of its ΣMC and ΣMR curves.

(b) ΣMC = ΣMR defines a level of MC which should be made equal in each plant. Thus, each plant is utilized until its MC rises to that level.

(c) ΣMC = ΣMR defines a level of MR which should be equal in each market. Thus, each market is supplied until its MR falls to that level.

(d) Price in each market is the clearing price for the quantities determined in part (c) above. That is, read it from the appropriate demand curve.

9-7. (a) From the graph, the profit-maximizing total output is approximately 4,886 pounds of tar per period.

(b) Approximately 1,813 pounds.

(c) Approximately $44.07 per pound.

(d) For 1,813 pounds and 3,073 pounds the total cost is $63,280.27. For 1,713 pounds and 3,173 pounds the total cost is $63,359.07. The difference is $78.80.

APPENDIX 9A

9A-1. (a) Your graph should show the demand curve shifting to the left over time, with the firm choosing successively smaller plant sizes. Since several years are involved, factor prices and productivities probably changed, so the SAC curves are probably from different LAC curves.

(b) Price would decline in real terms if the leftward shifts of the demand curve were roughly parallel.

(c) If the demand curve becomes progressively more steep as it moves to the left, and demand becomes progressively more inelastic, price would increase over time. Similarly if there were substantial economies of plant size initially, this would contribute to increasing prices as demand falls.

9A-3. Entry of new firms arose in response to the economic profits being made by the innovating firms. For these firms, the learning curve caused the reduction in per unit costs, which in turn caused the new MC curve to intersect the lower section of the MR curve, indicating that a price reduction would be profit maximizing. To protect their market shares other firms followed these price reductions whether they wanted to or not.

Chapter 10

10-1. Your graph should show the firms' *mutatis mutandis* demand curve one-third of the distance between the price axis and the market demand curve. Three different MC curves should be shown with the intersection of the lowest one and the MR curve determining each firm's price and output levels.

With conscious parallelism for common cost increases, all firms would independently raise price to cover the cost increase. For changes in market demand the price followers await the price adjustment by the price leader. The conjectural variation of the price followers is zero for price increases, except when there are common cost increases, and unity for all price reductions.

10-3. (a) Plot the market demand curve and one of the small firm's MC curve. For each level of MC multiply the quantity supplied by 20 to find the ΣMC_s curve. The dominant firm's residual demand is the horizontal difference between the market demand and the ΣMC_s curves.

(b) Profit-maximizing price, approximately $39.25.

(c) Dominant firm's profits, approximately $108.21; small firms each make approximately $3.18 profits.

(d) Small firms may be expected to expand, new small firms may be expected to enter the industry, with the result that the dominant firm's market share, and price, may be expected to fall.

10-5. (a) The limit price is somewhere between $32.49 and $29.09 per ton, depending on the entrant's time horizon, opportunity discount rate, and how quickly it attains an equal share. It is higher, the shorter the entrant's time horizon, the higher the ODR, and the longer it takes to attain an equal share. Simulate several scenarios and you will find that a $30 price seems reasonable.

(b) $106 per ton, although we don't expect the firms to set this price unless they want to attract more entry very quickly. (To find this answer, find the market demand curve using P, Q, and the elasticity expression. Then each firm's *mutatis mutandis* demand curve has six times the slope. Assume a low-cost price leader.)

Chapter 11

11-1. (a) Plot the points for the firm's demand curve, and sketch in the line of best fit. From this derive the marginal revenue and total revenue curves. Plot in the total cost curve, and derive two points for the MC using gradients. Average cost curves could be plotted in although these are not necessary for the analysis.

(b) The $75,000 profit is impossible, given the new cost situation. Maximum profits are approximately $70,000 at price $7.95 and volume 24,600 (approximately). Hence firm should set price at $7.95. Assumptions include accuracy of cost and demand data, *ceteris paribus*, and absence of the morale problems envisioned by the plant manager.

11-3. (a) $7.15. (Method: Given price elasticity, solve for the demand curve expression for March. Note that April demand will be 2,990 units at price $6.88. Solve for the new (April) intercept. Thus $P = 9.907 - 0.0010125Q$ for April. Extrapolating from the two gradients we find MC = MR at price $7.15.)

(b) 2,720 units.

(c) Data accuracy, continuation of trends in demand, the extrapolation of marginal costs, the parallel shift of the demand curve, the absence of competitors' reactions, and so on.

11-5. (a) Use the elasticity formula to find the slope of the demand curve. $P = 1431.8182 - 11.3636Q$. Plot TR and TC curves from calculated points.

(b) Price $772.73 on 58 jobs per month will give $2,018.30 profits per month. A few cents less would squeeze the profits down to the $2,000 target. ($772.31 would mean 58.0369 jobs and $2,000.34 profits per month.) Implied markup rate is 28.78%.

(c) Demand shifts must be iso-elastic, and customers' discretionary incomes must increase by the same proportion as repair costs.

(d)   If demand shifts cause demand to become more elastic, lower the markup rate. If less elastic, raise it. If costs increase in real terms for customers, lower the markups. If costs decrease in real terms, raise the markup.

11-7. (a)   The price should be selected with reference to the value of the attributes involved in the Valhalla unit (including its brand name, Valhalla), vis-à-vis the attributes of the other six units available. Somewhere in the range $495 to $505 seems reasonable. I like $499.95.

(b)   Support your answer.

(c)   Qualifications relate to the assumptions you have made, including the assumption of *ceteris paribus.*

11-9. (a)   Plot QNP's learning curve and one of the rival's learning curves (starting at 21,000 units and $14 per unit). Plot the price path, horizontal from 0 to 20,000 units at $9.95, then falling smoothly to $5.95 at 50,000 units.

(b)   Average costs fall below price at about 3,500 units, and QNP will have broken even (TR = TC) by about 8,000 units. Profit per unit is highest at 20,000 units (about $4.50) but remains positive even as the new firms enter, falling to about $2 per unit. (The new firms get average costs below price after about 5,500 units and then make smaller profits per unit, assuming the same rate of learning.)

Chapter 12

12-1. (a) $65,000.

(b) $61,500.

(c) $58,750.

(d) $56,500.
These figures are found by plotting the EPVC curve for each case and estimating the maximum EPVC from each curve.

12-3. (a)   0.9718; 0.8055; 0.6321; 0.4516; and 0.2639.

(b) $35,200, or close to this level.

(c)   Are other things equal for this bid vis-à-vis the bids of the past two years? Are the cost estimates accurate? Is any part of the allocated overheads variable?

12-5. (a)   Incremental cost is $3,105.67, being comprised of the expected cost of the driver, the incremental running expenses, the cost of the ramps, and the opportunity costs. (See answer for problem 7-5.)

(b)   You should argue for any price above $3,105.67. Note that Clark's truck is older, and may have higher operating costs than rivals' trucks; that the older truck may be undesirable from the store's point of view; and that Clark will receive beneficial exposure by being associated with the store. All of these indicate a lower bid rather than a higher bid. A bid of $3,450, for example, represents only a little more than 10% over incremental costs, but would probably win the contract and give Clark greater contribution to overheads and profits than the next best alternative.

12-7. (a)   The minimum bid price under any circumstances would be the incremental costs of $437,000.

(b)   A bid of $630,000, representing a 20% markup on full costs, would probably win the contract. This lower than normal bid is indicated by Firm B being likely to bid abnormally low because of its very low capacity utilization. Your answer may be higher or lower than the above figure. The point of this question is to get you to discuss the issues involved.

(c)   Will deviating from your usual pattern start a price war on subsequent contracts? Is the quality comparable between the different bidders? Is overtime production possible for Firm C? Do the other firms also have to purchase the specialized equipment, or will their incremental costs be lower? Are there other factors influencing rivals' bids about which we are not familiar?

12-9. **(a)** The sales manager's quote is probably too high; the expected value of contribution is maximized with a bid price around $8,150. (Find this by deriving the success probability distribution. Note that 68.26% of competitors' bids are expected to be within plus or minus two standard deviations of the expected value, and so on.)

Chapter 13

13-1. **(a)** No, because the last dollar spent on advertising increases quantity demanded by 12.61 units (and hence increases profits by $12.61).

(b) We can't say, since the advertising elasticity allows only a point estimate of the slope of the sales-advertising function. We expect diminishing returns to advertising, so Thompson should not increase advertising expenditures indefinitely. It could, however, make a series of increments and note the impact each time, to better approach the profit-maximizing level of advertising expenditures. This would require *ceteris paribus*, of course.

13-3. **(a)** $11,233.53 per month. The regression equation explains nearly all the variance and is highly significant, but the above answer represents a considerable extrapolation beyond the data base. Thus we can be highly confident as long as the extrapolation is valid, depending on *ceteris paribus* in particular.

(b) About $1,625 per month. (Interpolate from a total profit function $\pi = \text{TR} - \text{TVC} - A$.)

(c) The impact of advertising expenditure is unlikely to accrue totally in the current period. Given a lagged impact of advertising, the current level of expenditure may not be too high.

(d) Maintain advertising at $6,000 per month; investigate the residual impact of advertising; and have the partners come to an agreement regarding the firm's objective function and advertising policy.

13-5. **(a)** Approximately $11,000 advertising expenditure and $4.50 price for medium pizza, $3.38 for the small pizza, and $6.75 for the large pizza. (Method: For several levels of advertising, condense the demand function into a demand curve and find the profit-maximizing price for each advertising level.)

(b) $563.26 per month. These results depend upon the accuracy of the demand estimates, the constancy of variable costs, no change in consumers' tastes or incomes, no change in the marketing strategies of competing firms, and the validity of the extrapolations involved.

13-7. **(a)** The argument is essentially that your company can increase its promotional expenditures without causing any reaction from the other firms. Since your firm is very small relative to the market, this seems a reasonable assumption. The additional advertising should improve your product image and brand loyalty.

(b) You should start with an investigation into the attributes which consumers desire, and the extent of their willingness to pay for these features. Promotional campaigns should be designed to stress these features and to make favorable comparisons with rivals' products. Possible reactions of rivals should be considered.

Chapter 14

14-1. Undertake projects A, B, and C only, since the NPV of these projects is positive. ($2,007.26, $11,744.97, and $18,212.75, respectively, with 10% discount factors. Project D has NPV of −$2,178.75.)

14-3. **(a)** NPV is $49,416.53.

(b) Fractionally below 30%.

(c) NPV is $37,031.18.

(d) The year-end method underestimates the present value of funds arriving during the year, since these funds can be reinvested at the opportunity rate and earn interest until the end of the year.

(e) The Kayak project is preferable, since its NPV is positive when discounted at the ODR of the Resort project. Alternatively, the IRR of the Kayak project is almost double that of the Resort project.

14-5. (a) Hamburger NPV is \$10,172.85; Chicken NPV is \$12,283.25; and Taco NPV is \$16,488.75.

(b) Approximately 2 years and 60 days for Hamburgers; 2 years and 28 days for Chicken; and 2 years and 26 days for Tacos, assuming a uniform rate of cash flow during the third year.

(c) The Taco project, since it has both the shorter payback and the larger NPV. Both of these criteria are risk adjusted (the payback in a crude way).

14-7. (a) West (NPV \$103,144.46); East (NPV \$86,177.72); South (NPV \$81,627.58); and North (NPV \$67,962.82).

(b) North (PI = 1.5664); South (PI = 1.4535); West (PI = 1.3619); and East (PI = 1.3447).

(c) Projects West and South, with the balance of funds invested at the appropriate opportunity rate (i.e., 12%).

(d) \$103,144.56 plus \$81,627.58 = \$184,772.14. (The NPV of the remaining funds, invested at 12%, then discounted at 12%, is zero.)

APPENDIX A

(All answers given.)

A-1. (a) $Y = a + bX$

(b) $Y = a + bX^2$ or $Y = a + bX + cX^2$

(c) $Y = a + bX^3$ and so forth.

(d) $Y = ae^{bX}$

(e) $Y = aX^b$

(f) $Y = a/X^b$ or $Y = aX^{-b}$

A-2. (a) $13.5X^2$

(b) $-54X^2 (4 + 3X^3)$

(c) $21 - 42X^2$

(d) $24 (-32X + 27X^2 + 24X^3 - 36X^5)$

(e) $24 (4 - 2X^2) (4 + 24X - 10X^2)$

(f) $8e^{2X}$

A-3. (a) Y is maximized when $X = 1.5$

(b) Y is minimized when $X = 4$

(c) A is minimized when $B = 62.5$

(d) K is maximized when $J = 3.333$

A-4. Cost is minimized when the period between services is 21.42357 hours, or 21 hours, 25 minutes approximately.

Author Index

Edelman, R., 478
Edgeworth, F.Y., 350n
Efroymson, C.W., 370
Eichner, A.S., 444
Eisner, R., 529
Ekelund, R.B., Jr., 478
Eliosoff, D., 550
Etzel, M.J., 444

Fama, E.F., 37
Feldstein, M.S., 529
Ferguson, C.E., 169
Flaherty, M.T., 403
Foot, D.K., 529
Francis, A., 403
Frankel, M., 444
Fremgen, J.M., 514n, 529
Friedman, D., 78
Friedman, L., 479
Friedman, M., 8, 8n, 78

Gabor, A., 444
Gadon, H., 66n
Gaskins, D.W., Jr., 403
Gold, B., 258
Goldberger, A.S., 198n, 206
Gordon, G., 37, 78
Granger, C.W.J., 217, 444
Grant, L., 351
Green, P.E., 121n, 128, 173n, 206
Greenebaum, M., 237n
Greer, H.C., 287
Grossack, I.M., 6n, 37

Hall, R.E., 510n, 529
Hall, R.L., 350n, 370
Halter, A., 78
Hamburger, W., 382n, 403
Hanke, J.E., 217
Hawkins, C.J., 370, 403
Haynes, W.W., 287
Hébert, R.F., 478
Henderson, W., 37
Hendler, R., 112n, 128
Henry, W.R., 287
Hindelang, T.J., 529
Hirshleifer, J., 78, 128, 169, 370, 529
Hitch, C.J., 350n, 370
Holt, C.A., Jr., 479
Holthausen, D.M., 403
Horngren, C.T., 206n, 262n, 287, 296
Horowitz, I., 78
Huber, G.P., 37, 78

Jaffray, J.Y., 444
Jensen, M.C., 37
Johnson, A.C., Jr., 169
Johnston, J., 185n, 189n, 200n, 206,
    311, 311n, 316, 316n, 331
Jones, L., 180n
Jorgenson, D.W., 510n, 529

Kamin, J., 402
Kavesh, R.A., 217
Khoury, S.J., 19n, 21n, 37, 549
Khumawala, B.M., 479
Klammer, T., 514n, 530

Kling, A., 370
Knight, F.H., 25n
Koch, J.V., 390n
Kooros, A., 549
Kotler, P., 132, 173n, 206, 430n, 440,
    505
Kottas, J.F., 497
Koutsoyiannis, A., 312n, 350n

Lancaster, K., 106, 106n, 111n, 112, 445
Leffler, K.B., 505
Leftwich, R.H., 169, 258
Leibenstein, H., 123n, 128, 426n
Leland, H.E., 403
Lempert, L.M., 213
Levin, R.I., 185n, 191n, 192n, 193n,
    198n, 206
Levitt, K., 430n
Lipsey, R.G., 372n, 378
Livesey, F., 436n, 445, 464n, 479
Loomes, G., 370
Lorie, J.H., 530
Lublin, J.S., 234n
Luce, R.D., 495n
Luck, D.J., 173n, 206

Madansky, A., 121n
Mansfield, E., 169
Mao, J.C.T., 514n, 530
March, J.E., 398n, 403, 459n
Markham, J.W., 384n, 403
Marris, R., 397n
Martin, D.D., 6n, 37
Martin, R.L., 169
Maurice, S.C., 169
McCall, J.J., 454n
McGuigan, J.R., 319n, 331
McIntyre, E.B., 331
Meckling, W.H., 37
Miaoulis, G., 66n
Miller, E.M., 479
Miller, R.L., 169
Morgan, R.H., 403
Moyer, R.C., 319n, 331

Neale, W.C., 353n, 370
Needham, D., 498n, 505
Nelson, C.R., 217, 331
Nerlove, M., 505
Nicholson, W., 169

Oren, M.E., 479
Osborne, D.K., 378

Palda, K.S., 436n, 445
Pappas, J.L., 287
Papps, I., 37
Parsons, T.D., 19n, 21n, 37, 549
Paul, R.J., 479
Pegels, C.C., 331
Peles, Y., 499n, 505
Penrose, E., 397n
Pessemier, E.A., 207
Peterson, R.A., 445
Petty, J.W., 530
Platt, R.B., 217
Pressman, I., 37, 78

Subject Index

Horizontal summation: (*cont.*)
    of marginal revenue curves, 366-67
Hyperbolic functions, 539

Identical bids, 470
Identical products, 337, 339
    in oligopoly, 339n
    in pure competition, 340
Identification problem, the, 102, 121,
        196-97
Indivisibility of products, in the attribute
        approach, 112-13
Illwill, 272, 449-50
Impact effect of a price change, 180-81,
        189
Implicit costs, 261-63
Incentive bids, 454n
Income (budget) constraint, 88-93, 96-97
    defined, 89
    in attribute space, 108-109
Income-consumption curve, the:
    defined, 96-97
Income effect, the, 95-98
    defined, 95-96
    impact on price elasticity, 152-53
    separating the income effect from the
        substitution effect, 99-103
Income elasticity of demand, 154-58
    business implications of, 158
    defined, 154
    formula, 154
    point vs. arc, 155
Increasing marginal disutility, of risk, 51,
        60
Increasing returns, in production, 226-28
Incremental cost analysis, 266-82
    defined, 266
    for competitive bidding, 447-50
    for pricing decisions, 405
    future costs, 269-70
    opportunity costs, 269, 277-78
    present period explicit costs, 268-69
    using gradient analysis, 310-11
Incremental revenues 271-72, 275n,
        277-78
    defined, 271
    for competitive bidding, 450-52
Independent probability distributions,
        44-50
Indifference:
    curves, 83-88
    defined, 83
Indifference curve analysis, 50-53, 58-62,
        82-121
    assumptions underlying, 85
    between risk and return, 50-53
    defined, 50, 82
    in attribute space, 109-21
    of certainty equivalent, 58-62
    properties of indifference curves,
        86-87
Indirect demand estimation, 172,
        182-200
Indirect, or overhead, costs, 260-61
Inelastic demand, 146
    defined, 146
Inferior goods, 96, 97, 155-58

Inferior goods (*cont.*)
    defined, 157
    income and substitution effects for,
        100-102
    indifference curves for, 100n
Inflation, 105
    forecasting the rate of, 318-19
    impact on real prices, 105
    impact on opportunity costs, 262
    markup pricing under, 418-20
Inflection, point of, 228, 241
    defined, 537
Information search activity, 66-70
    See also Search costs
Inputs, in production, 222-29
Insurance, 25-26, 63-65
Intention surveys, 207-208
Intercept term, 532
    for demand curve expression, 136
    for isocost line, 231
    for regression equation, 184-88
Interest rate, 11-13, 14
    opportunity interest rate, 13, 14, 15
Internal rate of return, 510-13
    decision rule, 511
    defined, 510
    reconciliation with payback criterion,
        516
    relationship with NPV, 513
    superiority of NPV for mutually
        exclusive investments, 519-20
Interpolation, 15n, 224, 303n, 309
Interviewer bias, 172
Interviews and surveys, 172-73
Irrationality, in decision making, 65-66
Irrelevant costs, 267-68
Isocost:
    analysis, 231-38
    defined, 231
Iso-elastic shifts, of demand curve,
        417-18
Isoquant:
    analysis, 229-38
    defined, 229

Jargon, verbal models, 6, 10
Joint probabilities, 44-50

Kinked demand curve:
    conscious parallelism and the, 381-83
    model of oligopoly, 349-56
    price adjustments, 355-56
    price followers and the, 384, 385-87
    price rigidity, 353-56
    seven assumptions, 351
Kurtosis, of profit function, 413

Labor:
    costs, 234-36
    defined, 222
    intensive, 235
    productivity, 317-18
    relations, 275-76, 449
    unions, 222n, 234
Lagging indicators, 213
Law of averages, 31, 62, 63

Monopolistic competition (*cont.*)
    profit maximization, 347-49
    seven assumptions of, 347
Monopoly, 339
    advertising decisions, 483-93
    defined, 344-45
    examples, 345-46
    plant-size adjustment, 374-75
    profit maximization, 344-47
    seven assumptions of, 345
Movements along demand curves, 137-40
Multicollinearity, 197-98
Multiperiod contribution analysis, 279-81
Multiplant firms, 356-58
Multivariate regression analysis, 193
Mutatis mutandis, 339, 351, 351n, 352
    demand curve, 351-52, 358, 382, 394
Mutual dependence recognized:
    advertising, 493-500
    in oligopoly, 350
Myopic models of oligopoly, 350, 350n

Natural monopolies, 345
Necessities, 155-56
    defined, 155
Neoclassical microeconomics, 4, 5, 106
Net cash flow after taxes:
    defined, 508
Net present value criterion, 508-10
    relationship with IRR, 513
    superiority over IRR for mutually
      exclusive investments, 519-20
    superiority over profitability index,
      521
    See also Present-Value Analysis
Net Worth, 29-32
    defined, 29
New products, 119-20
    pricing, 427-35
Nominal costs, dollars, income, 16, 98, 99
Nominal price changes, 105, 418-20
Nonbusiness organizations, 4
Noneconomic factors in decision making,
    65-66
Nonmonetary goals, 66
Nonprice competition, 483-500
    See also Advertising
Nonsatiation, 85, 86-87
Normal distribution, 190, 192
Normal goods, 96, 97
Normal profits, 265-66
    and risk considerations, 266
Normative economics, 5

Objectives of the firm, 29-32, 60, 65-66,
    338, 379-80
    de facto objectives, 66
    growth maximization, 29n, 397-98
    in oligopoly, 351, 379-80
    managerial utility, 29n, 60, 398
    maximize net worth, 29, 60
    maximize profits, 29, 30, 338
    maximize sales, 29n, 392-94
    satisficing, 29n, 398-99
Oligopoly, 339
    advertising decisions, 483-84, 493-500
    defined, 349

Oligopoly (*cont.*)
    examples, 348n, 349
    kinked demand curve model, 349-56
    modified behavioral assumptions,
      378-79
    myopic models, 350, 350n
    plant-size adjustment, 375-76
    seven assumptions of, 351
One-shot deal, 62, 523
Opportunity costs, 262-63
    as incremental costs, 269
    in competitive bidding, 448-49
    normal profits, risks, and, 266
    See also Alternative costs
Opportunity Discount Rate, 13, 17
    compared to cost of capital, 57n
    defined, 13
    examples, 15, 17, 45, 55-57
Opportunity revenues:
    defined, 271
    in capital budgeting, 508
    in competitive bidding, 451
Optimal level:
    of advertising and price, 489-93
    of advertising, given price, 486-89
    of the bid price, 452-55
    of the markup, 5, 408-16
Optimum size of plant, 252, 372n
Ordinary least squares method, 184-88
Organizational politics, 65-66
    defined, 65
    functional vs. dysfunctional, 65
Output:
    hill, production surface, 225-26,
      229-30
    of the production process, 223
Owners' equity, 29, 30

Partial derivatives, 542
Payback period:
    decision criterion, 515
    defined, 514
    reconciliation with IRR criterion, 516
Pecuniary economics, 252-53
Pedagogical function of models, 7, 105,
    344, 350
Penetration pricing, 393-94, 430-31
    defined, 430
Perceptions, consumer, 116-19, 131,
    422-23
Perfect competition, 340
    See also Pure Competition
Place of sale, 131
Planning period, and time horizon, 22-23
    defined, 22
    examples, 280
Plant size adjustment, 229-33, 371-77
    diseconomies, 251-52
    economies of plant size, 251-52
Point elasticity, 147
    point cross elasticity, 159
    point income elasticity, 155
    point price elasticity, 147, 179n, 188
Politics, organizational, 65-66, 453-54
Positive Economics, 5
    vs. Normative, 5
Power function, 183, 194, 224, 234,
    321-23